HTML 4 Bible

HTML 4 Bible

Bryan Pfaffenberger and Alexis D. Gutzman

IDG Books Worldwide, Inc.
An International Data Group Company

Foster City, CA ✦ Chicago, IL ✦ Indianapolis, IN ✦ New York, NY

HTML 4 Bible

Published by
IDG Books Worldwide, Inc.
An International Data Group Company
919 E. Hillsdale Blvd., Suite 400
Foster City, CA 94404
www.idgbooks.com (IDG Books Worldwide Web site)

Library of Congress Catalog Card No.: 98-71150

ISBN: 0-7645-3220-0

Printed in the United States of America

10 9 8 7 6 5 4 3 2 1

1B/RV/QX/ZY/FC

Distributed in the United States by IDG Books Worldwide, Inc.

Distributed by Macmillan Canada for Canada; by Transworld Publishers Limited in the United Kingdom; by IDG Norge Books for Norway; by IDG Sweden Books for Sweden; by Woodslane Pty. Ltd. for Australia; by Woodslane (NZ) Ltd. for New Zealand; by Addison Wesley Longman Singapore Pte Ltd. for Singapore, Malaysia, Thailand, Indonesia, and Korea; by Norma Comunicaciones S.A. for Colombia; by Intersoft for South Africa; by International Thomson Publishing for Germany, Austria, and Switzerland; by Toppan Company Ltd. for Japan; by Distribuidora Cuspide for Argentina; by Livraria Cultura for Brazil; by Ediciencia S.A. for Ecuador; by Ediciones ZETA S.C.R. Ltda. for Peru; by WS Computer Publishing Corporation, Inc., for the Philippines; by Unalis Corporation for Taiwan; by Contemporanea de Ediciones for Venezuela; by Computer Book & Magazine Store for Puerto Rico; by Express Computer Distributors for the Caribbean and West Indies. Authorized Sales Agent: Anthony Rudkin Associates for the Middle East and North Africa.

For general information on IDG Books Worldwide's books in the U.S., please call our Consumer Customer Service department at 800-762-2974. For reseller information, including discounts and premium sales, please call our Reseller Customer Service department at 800-434-3422.

For information on where to purchase IDG Books Worldwide's books outside the U.S., please contact our International Sales department at 650-655-3200 or fax 650-655-3297.

For information on foreign language translations, please contact our Foreign & Subsidiary Rights department at 650-655-3021 or fax 650-655-3281.

For sales inquiries and special prices for bulk quantities, please contact our Sales department at 650-655-3200 or write to the address above.

For information on using IDG Books Worldwide's books in the classroom or for ordering examination copies, please contact our Educational Sales department at 800-434-2086 or fax 317-596-5499.

For press review copies, author interviews, or other publicity information, please contact our Public Relations department at 650-655-3000 or fax 650-655-3299.

For authorization to photocopy items for corporate, personal, or educational use, please contact Copyright Clearance Center, 222 Rosewood Drive, Danvers, MA 01923, or fax 978-750-4470.

The IDG Books Worldwide logo is a trademark under exclusive license to IDG Books Worldwide, Inc., from International Data Group, Inc. Leading the Knowledge Revolution is a registered trademark of IDG Books Worldwide, Inc.

ABOUT IDG BOOKS WORLDWIDE

Welcome to the world of IDG Books Worldwide.

IDG Books Worldwide, Inc., is a subsidiary of International Data Group, the world's largest publisher of computer-related information and the leading global provider of information services on information technology. IDG was founded more than 25 years ago and now employs more than 8,500 people worldwide. IDG publishes more than 275 computer publications in over 75 countries (see listing below). More than 90 million people read one or more IDG publications each month.

Launched in 1990, IDG Books Worldwide is today the #1 publisher of best-selling computer books in the United States. We are proud to have received eight awards from the Computer Press Association in recognition of editorial excellence and three from *Computer Currents'* First Annual Readers' Choice Awards. Our best-selling *...For Dummies®* series has more than 50 million copies in print with translations in 38 languages. IDG Books Worldwide, through a joint venture with IDG's Hi-Tech Beijing, became the first U.S. publisher to publish a computer book in the People's Republic of China. In record time, IDG Books Worldwide has become the first choice for millions of readers around the world who want to learn how to better manage their businesses.

Our mission is simple: Every one of our books is designed to bring extra value and skill-building instructions to the reader. Our books are written by experts who understand and care about our readers. The knowledge base of our editorial staff comes from years of experience in publishing, education, and journalism — experience we use to produce books for the '90s. In short, we care about books, so we attract the best people. We devote special attention to details such as audience, interior design, use of icons, and illustrations. And because we use an efficient process of authoring, editing, and desktop publishing our books electronically, we can spend more time ensuring superior content and spend less time on the technicalities of making books.

You can count on our commitment to deliver high-quality books at competitive prices on topics you want to read about. At IDG Books Worldwide, we continue in the IDG tradition of delivering quality for more than 25 years. You'll find no better book on a subject than one from IDG Books Worldwide.

John Kilcullen
CEO
IDG Books Worldwide, Inc.

Steven Berkowitz
President and Publisher
IDG Books Worldwide, Inc.

Eighth Annual
Computer Press
Awards ≥1992

Ninth Annual
Computer Press
Awards ≥1993

Tenth Annual
Computer Press
Awards ≥1994

Eleventh Annual
Computer Press
Awards ≥1995

Credits

Acquisitions Editor
Greg Croy

Development Editor
Barbra Guerra

Technical Editors
Tamra Heathershaw-Hart
Ken Cox

Copy Editors
Marcia Baker
Barry Childs-Helton
Eric Hahn

Project Coordinator
Susan Parini

Cover Design
Murder By Design

Graphics and Production Specialists
Mario Amador
Jude Levinson
Linda Marousek
Hector Mendoza
Mark Yim

Quality Control Specialists
Mick Arellano
Mark Schumann

Illustrator
Donna Reynolds

Proofreader
Jennifer K. Overmyer

Indexer
James Minkin

About the Author

Bryan Pfaffenberger is the author of more than 75 books on computers and the Internet, including the best-selling *Discover the Internet,* from IDG Books Worldwide. He teaches advanced professional communication and the sociology of computing in the University of Virginia's Division of Technology, Culture, and Communication. Bryan lives in Charlottesville, Virginia, with his family and an extremely spoiled cat.

Alexis D. Gutzman is a computer systems engineer at the University of Virginia, where she plays on the Web and administers NT servers. She has 12 years of systems experience on a variety of platforms and a master's degree in public affairs from the LBJ School at the University of Texas, which she hopes to use some day. Alexis lives in Charlottesville, Virginia, with her husband and soon-to-be-two children, one of which was percolating while this book was being written.

For Suzanne
—B. P.

For Constantine, ο πιο λεβεντης
—A.G.

Preface

Remember all that late-1980s talk about the Information Superhighway? You learned you'd get 500 cable channels, not just 50 (or, as comedians put it, 500 terrible channels instead of 50 terrible channels). Like most predictions involving technology, this one was way off the mark. (Add this one to the growing catalog of predictions gone awry, such as the famed remark by a 1950s IBM executive that the world would need, at most, a dozen or so computers.) The Information Superhighway didn't happen at the TV; instead, it happened at the personal computer, connected to the Internet and the World Wide Web.

Far more important, though, the Information Superhighway that has developed isn't like TV at all. TV is a broadcast medium, in which corporate content providers determine what you're going to see. The Web, from the beginning, was designed to transform couch potatoes into content producers. You can do nothing but consume Web content, to be sure, and millions of Web surfers are out there who are happy to flit from site to site without making their own contribution. And WebTV, of course, brings the Web-as-TV to the TV — and in so doing, robs the Web of part of its power.

What makes the Web such a powerful medium is, unlike all other mass media, it's inherently a two-way street, content-wise. Anyone who can consume content on the Web can also produce it, using HTML, the easy-to-learn page definition language that underlies the Web's appearance. It's as if you got a morning paper, but by afternoon, you could publish your own take on the news — and make it available, potentially, to millions of people.

The implications of this startlingly novel, two-way mass medium are only now starting to come into focus.

The Web is probably the most important development in support of free speech since the invention of the printing press, in that it enables virtually anyone to originate content cheaply and make this content available to a potentially massive audience.

Unquestionably, the Web is good for the environment: millions of tree-killing publications are moving to the Web. Within corporations, for example, voluminous publications — directories, employee manuals, procedure manuals, agendas, reports, and meeting minutes — appear in Web-based internal networks called *intranets*; the environmental plusses, coupled with significant cost savings, make this innovation a no-brainer.

For even the smallest business, the Web provides a way to get your message out, stay in touch with customers, and provide needed information, but without running up a huge bill at the printer. And the best part of all is no one can tell how big or small you are. No reason exists for them ever to know only one little scientist is behind the curtain in the Emerald City.

The list of Web impacts could go on for dozens of pages, but the pattern's clear: the Web is fast becoming an indispensable new way to make information available to others. This doesn't mean the Web is going to replace other media anytime soon. If you're running a retail business, you'd be wise to advertise in the local newspaper as well as set up a Web page, but it *does* mean the Web is no longer something you can prudently ignore. No matter what your message might be, you want to get it out on the Web.

Who Should Read This Book?

What all this means for you is simple: Whatever your walk of life—whether you're a businessperson, a manager, a student at any level, a retired person, a homemaker, or the vice president of the United States (a confessed Web junkie)—you owe it to yourself to learn how to originate Web content. And this means learning HTML. To do this, you need a book—a comprehensive book, and what's more, a book that teaches you how to take full advantage of this exciting new version of HTML, Version 4. Whether you're a complete beginner or someone who's already delved into previous versions of HTML, you'll find this book is absolutely the right one for learning and mastering HTML 4—and in so doing, assure your place in the Web's future.

What's So Special About This Book?

The *HTML 4 Bible* is your ticket to mastery of the newest version of HTML, Version 4. As you learn in the next section, HTML 4 is the most significant revision of the Web's publishing language to appear since the language's invention. You need a book that recognizes these novel features and takes a novel approach.

For the first time, HTML provides Web publishers with the power and flexibility to create page layouts rivaling those found in professionally designed magazines and newsletters. HTML 4 requires a new approach to HTML, however. If you've learned previous versions of HTML, you need to unlearn some old habits—a lot of old habits. If you're learning HTML for the first time, you need to learn it the *right* way, by reading a book that's not just a quickie rehash of a book on some previous version of HTML.

From the first sentence to the last item in the final appendix, this book was written from scratch to emphasize the HTML 4 Way, the radically new approach to Web publishing made possible by this exciting new version of HTML. Not a single word of this book appeared in any previous edition that focused on an earlier, flawed version of HTML. This book teaches a new approach to learning and using HTML 4, one that fully enables you to realize HTML 4's incredible layout potential. Once you learn what HTML is and understand the important implications of HTML Version 4, you'll understand why you need a book that's been written from the ground up to emphasize HTML 4's incredible new capabilities.

How This Book Is Organized

This book has nine parts. All of them adhere strictly to the HTML 4 Way.

Part I focuses on getting you up to speed on Web publishing: what's in it for you, what's involved, and what the future holds.

Part II teaches the basics of HTML — you create your own first page and you learn how to publish to your Web server.

Part III helps you turn your idea of a Web site into specific pages in support of your message. Part III also includes a review of the latest HTML-editing software on the market with special attention to whether it supports the HTML 4 Way (and all of it is included on the CD-ROM in the back of the book).

Part IV teaches strict HTML structure.

Part V helps you design the look of your site with graphics and cascading style sheets.

Part VI teaches advanced cascading style sheets — something not covered in any other book of this type about HTML 4.

Part VII explains how to add bells and whistles to your site with multimedia and interactivity.

Part VIII explains what has become known as *dynamic HTML*, which is the new Document Object Model animated with JavaScript (do you wonder why the marketing department found something more interesting to call it?).

Part IX discusses stray Web publishing issues such as standardization of the Web, intellectual property, pornography and indecency, privacy, and defamation and libel.

Using This Book's Special Features

Because this book can't make use of hypertext, it implements several special conventions to draw your attention to things you might want to know or need to know outside the text.

Vocabulary. To help you become familiar with new terms, we introduce new terms and acronyms (and, boy, are a lot of acronyms associated with HTML!) in special vocabulary boxes. You'll know them when you come across them by looking for this Vocabulary icon.

In Depth. This book addresses the needs of a number of audiences, each of which desires a different level of technical detail. To accommodate all levels, the main text covers what you *need to know* to publish your pages successfully. When there is more you might *want to know,* the topic is covered in-depth because we set it apart from the text with this icon.

Tip. If we suggest a particularly useful way to achieve something, a marvelous short-cut, or a clever alternative, we identify it with this icon to save you both time and frustration . . . at no extra charge!

Warning. Many of you are already familiar with HTML 3.2 and earlier versions. For you, knowing both how HTML 4 does it and when doing it the pre-HTML 4 Way might get you into trouble with subsequent versions of browsers is important. The W3C calls certain uses of elements and attributes *deprecated.* Rather than ignoring deprecated elements and attributes, in which case you might go ahead and use them, this book flags them with an icon, along with any other special information you should know.

CD-ROM. Content you find included on this book's CD-ROM is flagged with a CD icon for your convenience.

Cross-Reference. Sometimes you are directed to other sections of the chapter or other chapters in the book for more information on a topic. In addition, each chapter ends with a section telling you where you go next in the book — a particularly useful feature if you're not following the book sequentially.

Hot Stuff. Because of the incredible growth of Windows NT server, this book has special sections dedicated to working in a Windows NT server environment. If your Web server runs on Windows NT, this book, like no other, takes you through all the steps you need. Occasionally, you can also find other particularly interesting information highlighted by this icon.

Where Should You Start?

This book is designed to meet the needs of several audiences:

Veteran Web developers. If you have experience with HTML and already manage Web sites, you probably want to review the section in Chapter 16 that covers the new HTML 4 elements, the deprecated HTML 3.2 and earlier elements, and the obsolete elements. Chapter 14, where we review the latest versions of all the HTML-editing tools, may be of interest; you can see how the version you are using now measures up. Then you want to skim through Part IV and see how HTML 4 changes things. You definitely want to pay attention to Parts V and VI, where we give intensive instruction in the finepoints of even the most sophisticated techniques using CSS. Part VIII covers the Document Object Model (DOM) and how you can use JavaScript to create much-touted dynamic HTML.

Webmasters with large sites to maintain. Look at Chapters 8 and 9, especially the bonus section about maintaining a large Web site. Chapter 15 gives you an introduction to middleware, something you may consider using. Part IV has excellent material to help you educate your Web development team in HTML 4 structure. Part V, where we give you a thorough grounding in style sheets, can help you enforce consistency across your site.

Small business and home business owners who want to develop a presence on the Web. We understand you wear many hats and you don't have much time to devote to your site — either to get it up and running or to maintain it. This book can best serve you if you pay special attention to Chapter 5, where you create your first page, Parts IV and V, where you learn the basics of HTML and CSS, and Part IX, where you can read about legal and ethical issues about which you, as a business owner, might have concerns.

Web enthusiasts. If you are already maintaining a site, find out what you're missing with cascading style sheets in Part V. Discover how to add sensory excitement, multimedia, and interactivity in Part VII. Learn how to use JavaScript to create dynamic HTML in Part VIII. Also glance at Chapter 13 to read about browser compatibility issues. Finally, see how your HTML editor stacks up against the latest crop in Chapter 14.

Aspiring Web developers. For you, this book is your oyster. We didn't include anything unimportant. If you read a chapter every night, you can be as knowledgeable as the pros in less than two months! In what other career could you know what the experts know this quickly? What are you waiting for? Begin!

Acknowledgments

Writing this book has been a real adventure. So many, many people have helped us along the way. With the breadth of material this book covers, we occasionally turned to specialists to make sure everything we said was up-to-the-moment correct. Many thanks to Peter Dalianis for his professional and thoughtful comments on defining the message. Thanks also to Rick Provine for his invaluable assistance with digital audio. Michael Tuite provided thoughtful assistance with digital video and a host of other issues, for which we are grateful. We are indebted to Chuck Moran and Debra Weiss, who generously assisted with professional design advice for the section on site design. Thanks also to Tim O'Brien for his help with Java rapid development environments.

Thank you to Carole McClendon at Waterside Publications for pulling this opportunity together and making it happen.

Thanks to *everyone* at IDG Books Worldwide; a more professional group has never been assembled. Thanks to development editor Barbra Guerra, acquisitions editor Greg Croy, technical editors Tamra Heathershaw-Hart and Ken Cox, senior copy editor Marcia Baker, and production coordinator Susan Parini.

Finally, Alexis would like to thank Constantine, her wonderfully patient and supportive husband, Trianna, her daughter who spent a lot of time watching mama type, and her parents, who entertained their granddaughter while she wrote.

Contents at a Glance

Contents

Part II: HTML Quick Start   59

Part IV: Developing Document Structure with HTML 4 285

Chapter 21 Adding Tables 345

Chapter 22 Testing and Validating Your HTML 361

Part V: Enhancing Presentation with Style Sheets   367

Chapter 23 Introducing Cascading Style Sheets 369

Chapter 37 Producing and Adding Sounds 517

Chapter 38 Producing and Adding Video............................527

Chapter 39 Incorporating Plug-Ins 535

Chapter 43 Creating Subscriptions with the Channel Definition Format

Chapter 44 Accessing External Databases

Part VIII: Building Dynamic Pages with Javascript   623

Introduction

What Is HTML?

Short for HyperText Markup Language, *HTML* is one of many markup languages that have appeared in recent years. In brief, a *markup language* provides guidelines for adding markup — in the form of special symbols — to text documents. These symbols describe the parts of the document. For example, you can use a markup language to identify a portion of the text as an *abstract*, a brief summary of the document's contents. HTML is a markup language designed for Internet documents.

Introducing markup languages

Markup is needed because computers are quite stupid when it comes to understanding text. A computer can't really tell whether a certain portion of a text is an abstract, a title, a heading, or a paragraph. Without some kind of additional coding, the computer doesn't know how to display the text so it looks like an actual document.

Word processing programs provide the necessary coding by means of proprietary formatting codes, but these have a gigantic downside: they work only if you're looking at the document using the same word processing program and type of computer that created it. If you ever tried to exchange a WordPerfect file with a Macintosh MS Word user, you can understand the difficulties involved.

Markup languages solve the file-compatibility problem by using nothing but *ASCII* (plain text) characters and, what's more, by breaking the connection between structural markup and presentation.

In structural markup, you identify the parts of a document — in effect, you say, "This is a title," or "this is a heading" — but you say nothing about how this part of the document should be presented using specific formatting (fonts, alignment, and so on). You mark up the document's structure by identifying the document's parts (title, abstract, headings, paragraphs, lists, and so on).

But there's more. *Presentation* — how the document is formatted for display or printing — is left entirely up to a *browser,* a program designed to read the marked-up document for display on a specific type of computer hardware.

The distinction between structure and presentation is important, for in it lies the key to a markup language's capability to work smoothly in a cross-platform environment (a computer network in which people are using many different types of computers). With a markup language, you can create just one version of a document. People can run browsers designed to function on Macintoshes, UNIX computers, and all the various versions of Windows (3.1, 95, 98, and NT), and they can display your document with absolutely no trouble. For each of these computers, a browser knows how to display the marked-up document on a given system.

Does a downside exist to markup languages? Yes. If you do pure structural markup, with no presentation at all, you give up control over how your document appears. On one system, it may appear with black Times Roman text — but, on another, some crazy user may have set up his or her browser to display your text in 28 point Demented Bold. And there's nothing you can do to stop this user.

HTML — a HyperText Markup Language

HTML is a markup language with all the advantages of other markup languages when it comes to separating structure from presentation. But HTML has something more: HTML is a hypertext markup language.

What's hypertext? In brief, *hypertext* is a way of organizing information so readers can choose their own path through the material. Instead of clicking through sequentially organized pages, a hypertext user clicks specially highlighted text, called a *hyperlink* (or just a *link* for short), to go directly to information of interest. There's more to say about hypertext but, for now, the important point is this: HTML is the first markup language to incorporate markup for hyperlinks. When you mark up a document with HTML, you can define some of the text as a link, within which you embed the computer address of another resource on the Internet. This could be a document, a movie, a sound, an animation, or a file to download.

Eroding the structure/presentation distinction

As you just learned, the whole purpose of a markup language lies in separating structure from presentation and, in so doing, enabling content developers to create documents that can be displayed faultlessly on any type of computer. But this distinction hasn't fared well. By the time HTML got to Version 3.2, it had been seriously eroded.

Why did this erosion occur? The reason lies in the Web's rapid commercialization. If you write "pure" HTML, emphasizing structure and ignoring presentation, you get a document like the one shown in the first figure. Pretty boring, huh? Actually, HTML was initially designed to enable physics researchers to make their preliminary papers available to other physics researchers and the humdrum appearance of plain-vanilla HTML wasn't an issue. As the Web migrated to the private sector and became an important way for giant corporations to get their message out, Web developers couldn't ignore presentation anymore. They needed to emulate the page layout designs worked out by professional newsletter and magazine designers. They didn't like the idea of a pure markup language, which would let someone display America, Inc.'s pages using 28-point Demented Bold (see Figure I-1).

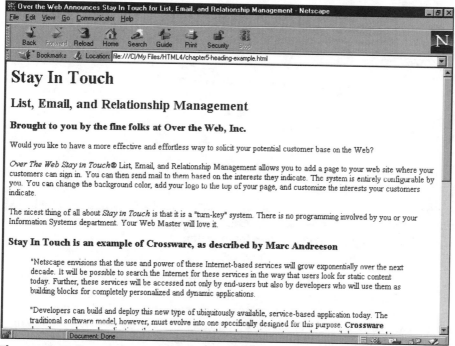

Figure I-1: Web page that has only structural tags

So what did Web developers do? They learned a whole series of tricks to fake layout. For example, they used tables — initially designed to group data in tabular form — to emulate newspaper columns and magazine layouts (see Figure I-2). Browser publishers, including both Netscape Communications and Microsoft, tried to expand their market share by creating browsers that support *extensions*, nonstandard additions to HTML that provide presentation capabilities. (The most egregious of these is probably Netscape's notorious blink extension, which enables Web authors to create text that blinks away annoyingly while you're trying to read the page.)

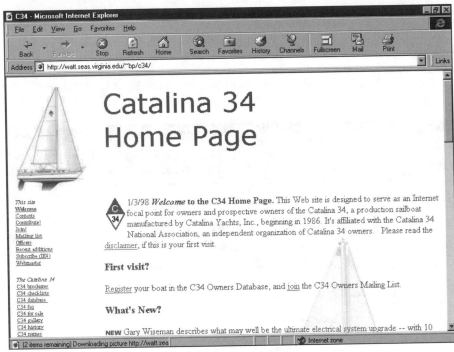

Figure I-2: Web page that uses tables for formatting

What's the result of HTML's commercialization? In brief, a mess. You can use the tricks and extensions to fake presentation with a Web page, but how it's going to look on a given computer and monitor is anyone's guess. HTML pages are crammed with HTML code that's been elaborated to a ridiculous extent to emulate magazine layouts, but editing and maintaining these pages is a costly nightmare. To correct errors in the text, you have to pick through reams of messy code. And suppose you create a whole series of pages, but later find they look terrible when displayed on a Macintosh. You'd have to go back into each page and change the offending code.

In short, the erosion of the structure versus presentation distinction has seriously damaged HTML's underlying purpose. What's worse, it's slowing down the Web's development. To be sure, creating a simple page is easier. But the cost of creating and maintaining HTML that generates professional-looking results is so prohibitive, many would-be content providers are shying away. Bad scene!

HTML 4 and the HTML 4 Way

Realizing that something drastic had to be done to rescue HTML, the *World Wide Web Consortium* (W3C) — the nonprofit, standards-setting body responsible for HTML — has published a specification for a new version of HTML, Version 4. Although HTML 4 is downwardly compatible with previous versions of HTML, the new version is designed to restore the lost balance between structure and presentation. What's more, it does so in a way that gives Web content developers precisely what they want: total control over document layout. The secret? Cascading style sheets (CSS).

Introducing cascading style sheets

The W3C-originated cascading style sheets (CSS) specification is a dream come true for Web content developers. To understand why it's such a big deal, think about word processing.

The earliest word processors gave you formatting commands, but made you use them over and over. For example, suppose you wanted to format a paragraph with a first-line indent, double line spacing, and Times Roman text. With early programs, you had to apply three different formatting commands to every paragraph you typed. What a hassle! Then along came Microsoft Word. Word enabled you to define a named style. You could create a style called "Body Text," and then define this style with all the formats you want. You then apply this style to any paragraph you type. When you apply the style, Bingo! You get all the formats you assigned to the style. Once you've tried this, you can never go back — and that's one reason Microsoft Word has an overwhelming market share in the word processing world.

Styles have another huge benefit. Suppose you've created dozens of documents that all have the same style. If you've created a separate *style sheet* (a list of styles and their format definitions), you can make one little change to the style in the style sheet and, lo and behold! All the documents are *automatically* altered.

Harnessing the power of styles

Cascading style sheets bring the power of styles to HTML and the Web. Using CSS, you define styles, which tell Web browsers how to display the text you marked up with HTML. Suppose, for example, you marked up some of the text as a heading. With CSS, you can define the heading so it appears with the following formats: centered, 12 points above and below, 14-point Helvetica, and bold. The marked-up text is clean, structure-only HTML — no gobbledygook designed to hassle HTML into a presentation language. And what's more, you get all the benefits of styles. Make one change to the underlying style definition and you change every instance of text to which the style is assigned. Even more powerfully, you can use external style sheets, which define the styles appearing in dozens or even thousands of documents. One little change to the underlying style and all the linked documents are changed, too.

CSS is easy to learn, easy to use, and — once you grasp what CSS can do — totally indispensable. And the benefits are amazing. By removing the presentation from HTML, you let HTML do what it does best — namely, define structure. Your HTML will be cleaner, much more readable, and much easier to edit. What's more, CSS does a far better job of presentation than HTML ever could. For example, the latest version of CSS enables *absolute positioning*, in which you can nail down the precise location of text or graphics on the page. You can create newspaper column effects, and even superimpose text on graphics.

What about the structure versus presentation distinction?

Wait a minute! Doesn't CSS violate the structure versus presentation distinction? In some ways, yes. Admittedly, it's a compromise, but an elegant compromise. The CSS authors recognized Web developers wanted and needed to control their documents' presentation aspects. But they wanted to give authors presentation control without harming the basic benefit of a markup language, namely, the ability to create documents that function well in a cross-platform environment.

CSS does enable you to define presentation — in fact, that's its point. With CSS, you can, indeed, define presentation aspects such as fonts, and a CSS-compatible browser respects your choice. The guy who wants to look at your page with 28-point Demented Bold sees your Times Roman instead. Unlike a word processor's formatting codes, though, CSS doesn't lock users into a rigid straightjacket. If Times Roman isn't available, the browser looks for fonts you listed as likely alternates. And, if these aren't available, the browser defaults to a fallback font. All this is totally automatic, so no one is prevented from reading your page. In short, CSS pulls off something word processing programs can't: CSS creates richly formatted documents that are easily exchanged and used in a cross-platform environment.

What's more, CSS enables you to move the presentation out of HTML. To be sure, you can include CSS style specifications within your HTML, but this book doesn't recommend this practice. It's much better to move the style specifications out of the HTML entirely, either in a grouped style specification within the document's header or (better yet) in a separate file. With the presentation code out of the way, you can write pure, structure-only HTML. And this is precisely the controlling theme of the HTML 4 revision.

Back to pure structure with HTML 4

Although HTML 4 supports the various presentation features and extensions shoehorned into previous versions of HTML, this new version's real significance lies in its reassertion of pure structure. By moving the presentation to CSS, your HTML goes back to what it should be: Clean, easy to read, inexpensive to maintain, quick to process and display, and—most of all—ideal for a cross-platform environment.

The HTML 4 Way

This book teaches an entirely new approach to HTML, one you won't find in competing books that explore HTML as extensively as this one. It's called the HTML 4 Way.

The *HTML 4 Way* takes full advantage of the exciting new possibilities of HTML and CSS, and calls for learning both, from the beginning. That's why this book's approach is unique. Almost all HTML books begin with HTML, teach all those horrible presentation tricks that have accumulated over the years, and then throw in a chapter on CSS as an afterthought. Not so with this book. As you'll see, you begin by writing pure structural HTML, with absolutely no presentation included. You then learn how to weave CSS into your documents to obtain total, impressive control over every aspect of your documents' presentation. You produce code that's beautifully simple and clear, easy and inexpensive to maintain, and absolutely stunning onscreen.

Introducing Web Publishing with HTML

Understanding Web Publishing Opportunities

The world's biggest carnival is on your desktop computer. It has everything from animal acts to funnel cake (recipes). You can gawk at the exhibits; you can buy things; you can sell things. We call the ringmasters by slightly (and only very slightly) different names: Webmasters.

With the Web, you gain the opportunity to create a community of people with common interests and to communicate your message to others with similar interests, as well as career opportunities of unparalleled potential.

This chapter explains the genesis of the Web, the future of the Web, and the bright future that exists for those who know how to publish on the Web and, therefore, capitalize on the vast and growing audience of Web surfers.

What Is the World Wide Web?

The World Wide Web — the *Web* for short — is a network of computers able to talk to each other. On these computers reside Web pages and Web sites. By sitting at a computer that is attached to the Web, via either a phone line or a direct connection, you can visit Web pages or Web sites that actually reside on other computers, next door, or halfway around the world.

How does this work?

The computers attached to each other that have all these Web pages on them are called *Web Servers*. They all speak a common language — communicate with a common protocol — called *HyperText Transfer Protocol* (HTTP). Regardless of where these computers reside — China, Norway, or Austin, Texas — they can talk to each other through HTTP.

HTTP. HyperText Transfer Protocol. This is a set of rules that enables Web browsers to communicate with Web servers.

When you send a request to find a Web page, say the IDG Books Worldwide Web site, you type the following into your browser: `http://www.idgbooks.com`. With newer browsers, you only need to type `idgbooks` and they add the rest.

So how does this network of computers know which computer has the IDG Books Web site on it? Through a Web address phone book, called domain name system (DNS). When you type `www.idgbooks.com`, your browser actually contacts this giant phone book asking where `www.idgbooks.com` is physically located. The physical address is a string of numbers, such as 206.80.51.140! Your browser now knows to send this request to this string of numbers.

DNS. Domain Name System. This is actually a great big table of every domain (such as `idgbooks.com` or `virginia.edu` or `w3c.org`) and its physical IP address (such as 206.80.51.140 or 128.143.208.39). This table is replicated all over the Internet and enables browsers to find Web servers. It would be much more difficult to find the IDG Books site if you had to remember to type 206.80.51.140, instead of `www.idgbooks.com`. DNS makes Web addresses memorable.

Who Makes the Rules?

Every organization has its own rule-making body. In the case of the Web, the rule-making body is the World Wide Web Consortium (W3C). The W3C is composed of representatives from a number of high-tech companies who want to have a say in the standards. The W3C tries to balance the interests of the academy, the companies producing the Web browsers (notably Netscape and Microsoft), and the technology. The W3C pulls together committees with representatives from interested members and puts the specifications in writing for HTML, CSS, XML, and other essential technologies. If the W3C weren't maintaining a standard, all browsers might eventually be unable to talk to all Web servers. You can visit their Web site at `http://www.w3c.org`.

The other half of the question is: how does the network of computers know where 206.80.51.140 resides? The network asks for directions. The browser on your computer asks other computers to direct it toward the physical address of the Web site you seek.

Fortunately, you needn't know any of this to use your browser — neither does anyone else. This is part of the reason the Web has grown so fast. Just type a URL into your browser and off you go, surfing the World Wide Web.

Vocabulary

URL. Uniform Resource Locator. The Web acronym for someone's Web page address. A URL can point to a Web page/HTML file, an image, a movie, a sound file, or an animation.

Why is this so special?

In case you are too young to remember the way things used to be, let's reminisce. Figure 1-1 recalls the olden days, when, if you had a computer on your desk and it was set up properly, your computer could talk to your printer. That was it. If you wanted to add software, you got in your car, went to the office supply store or the computer store at the mall, and bought software. Software producers, on the other hand, had to write different software for each platform: Mac, PC, UNIX. If you wanted to send a document you wrote to someone else, you saved it to a floppy disk, sent it to that person, and hoped that person was running exactly the same platform and word-processing software you were running, so the file could be opened and read.

The Web solves all these problems because it is distributed, cross-platform, and interactive:

> **Distributed** across millions of desktops. Processing takes place on many different Web servers, so no single mainframe (the old-fashioned way) has to do all the processing or control all the traffic geographically around the world.

> **Cross-platform.** Regardless of what platform you have before you, if it runs a browser, you can get to the Web and it looks pretty much the same. This means a lot of software no longer must be written for individual platforms. Instead, the software can be (and is being) written for the browser as the platform.

> **Interactive.** You can use the Web to download software, saving you a trip to the mall or the office supply store.

Additionally, the Web is based on a hypertext model. If this book used hypertext, the word *hypertext* in the previous sentence would have a link to a definition of the word. This way, someone who knew what *hypertext* meant could continue to read this chapter and someone who wanted to know could click the word, see a definition, and then return to the sentence just where he left off. This is powerful for many reasons. In fact, it makes the network of computers a Web. Any page on the Web can contain a link to any other. So you can bounce around the world across the Web without ever typing a URL.

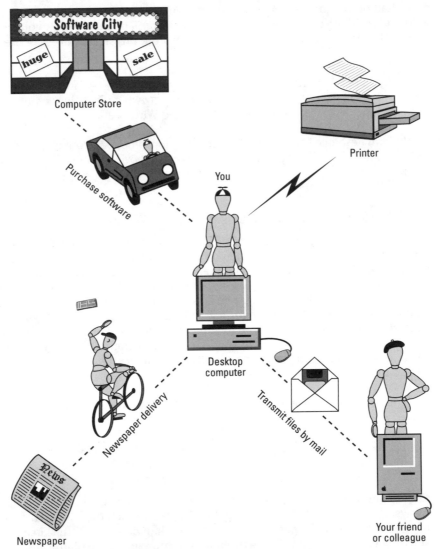

Figure 1-1: Computer communications before the Web

Vocabulary   **Hypertext .** Clickable, usually highlighted and underlined, text or image, which, when clicked, takes you to a new place either in the page you are viewing or on another page altogether. Hypertext is also sometimes called a *link*.

How is it interactive? What you see depends on the way in which you interact with the Web. With a book, you can turn the page to change what you see, but pretty much everyone who reads the book sees the same things in the same sequence. With the Web, in addition to reading a page from top to bottom, you can send mail from some pages, fill out forms to enter contests, search catalogs, and download and order software.

This new model for computing, shown in Figure 1-2, completely changes our picture.

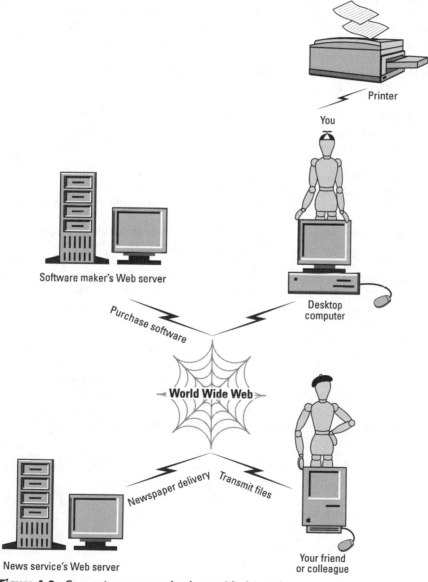

Figure 1-2: Computer communications with the Web

Where the Web Came From

The Web is based on the Internet, which was created by the federal government to ensure communications within the Department of Defense, should phone lines be cut. The Web — the idea of linking documents or images in multiple locations to each other — was the brainchild of Tim Berners-Lee in 1980, who wrote a paper proposing the idea be implemented in 1989. In September 1993, the first Web browser that allowed the inclusion of graphics — before this, the Web was all text — Mosaic was developed at the National Center for Supercomputing Applications (NCSA) at the University of Illinois, Champaign-Urbana. One of the graduate students involved in the creation of Mosaic was Marc Andreesen, who later went on to found Netscape.

With the advent of Web browsers that could show graphics, the use of the Web skyrocketed. No longer was interest in the Web limited to academics sharing technical research papers. A new commercial outlet suddenly existed: the Web.

The interesting thing about the origin of the Web is, once you read an article about it, you could (if you had a connection to the Internet) go to the site where Mosaic resided, using the File Transfer Protocol (FTP), and download the Mosaic browser.

In Depth

Protocols. Protocols are a convention all computer programs use to communicate something with each other. The common ones are: HyperText Transfer Protocol (HTTP), File Transfer Protocol (FTP), Simple Mail Transfer Protocol (SMTP), Transmission Control Protocol (TCP), Internet Protocol (IP), and Post Office Protocol (POP). How they do this and what they send doesn't matter to you as the user. All you need to know is what they expect from you. For the HTTP protocol, the computer expects a URL, otherwise known as a Web address. For the FTP protocol, the computer expects a URL, an ID, and a password. For sending mail, your mail package, whether it be Eudora, Netscape Messenger, or Outlook, will know what to send.

The advent of common protocols, universal standards for computers to communicate with each other, has facilitated the growth of the Web. That your computer can communicate with any other computer that communicates with the same protocols, increases the value of your computer immeasurably and makes the Web possible.

By December 1993, articles started to appear in mainstream publications about Mosaic and the World Wide Web. At first, the only type of commerce that took place on the Web was advertising. Today, thousands of sites offer everything from spices to cars for sale over the Web.

Why the Web Grew So Fast

In real estate, the three reasons a piece of property is valuable—so the saying goes—are location, location, location. For the Web, those three reasons might be: price, information, and location.

Price

From a Web developer's perspective, in the early days of the Web, there weren't too many interesting things you could put on your Web page, so it was fairly easy to put up a nice-looking (by those standards) Web page without spending a lot of money. Consequently, people began putting up Web pages with things of interest to them—pictures of their cat, favorite recipes, lists of speed traps on interstate highways—just for the fun of it.

From the Web surfer's perspective, once the user had a connection to the Internet, everything else was free. If the user wanted to see the Meteora Monasteries, as in Figure 1-3, which perch on high rock formations in Northern Greece, it was only a click away. After a while, subscription-only sites began to appear, one of the more popular of which is the ESPN sports site, shown in Figure 1-4, but, by then, millions of people were hooked on the idea of valuable information being only a click away.

Figure 1-3: The Web page for the Meteora Monasteries in Greece

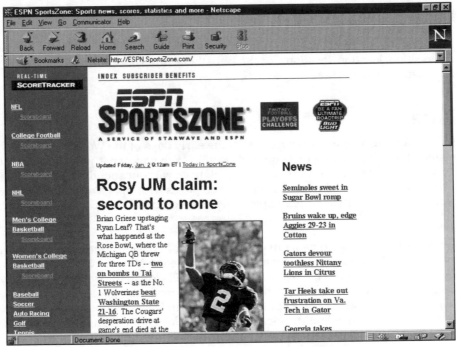

Figure 1-4: ESPN was an early comer to subscription Web sites.

Information

We all are overloaded with information every day. From news broadcasts, to the little headline ticker at the bottom of sports broadcasts, to the national news updates on the hour on the radio. In some cities, you can even get the traffic report every ten minutes! Why do we need more information?

Most people recycle their body weight in junk mail every week, so they don't necessarily need *more* information. What they need is the right filtered information. The Web can help you find just what you want, if you know how to use it.

In fact, some places, such as *search engines* — the places where people go to find the information they want — became so popular, they began showing ads at the top of the pages. This was the first commercial use of the Web. Because these places were otherwise free, people continued to use them to find the information they wanted. And where were these search engines and other useful things located? Right on your desktop.

Location

What could be better than free access to information you want anyway, right on your desktop? Whether or not the Web page you want to see is in your own home town, the Web is always right on your desktop. You have no lines to wait in, no annoying Muzak while you wait on hold, and no crowds to push through. You don't even have to worry about your car getting a ding in the parking lot.

Part of the phenomenal growth of the Web — in this age of microwave popcorn, frozen dinners, and convenience stores — is the convenience. If you know what you are doing, you can find a recipe for Bok Choy on the Web in less than five minutes. This recipe is free, it represents only the information you want (as opposed to an entire cookbook of vegetables), and it is right on your desktop.

This kind of demand for specialized information has forced companies to spend millions of dollars to put up elaborate Web sites. Most of them hope to recover this money through savings in printed materials and increasing sales through exposure to new audiences. At the very least, they don't want to lose market shares to their competitors, who are putting up their own Web sites.

Where the Web's Going

The Web is moving in some definite directions. You can see these directions in the headlines on some of the trade publications that serve the Web. They can be summarized as: narrowcasting, the Web as a marketplace, and integrating existing databases into the Web. HTML 4 addresses them all. Learn HTML 4 and you can be one of the problem solvers.

Narrowcasting

Information is king on the Web. But is there too much information out there? How can you sift out only what you want? How about search engines? The major problem with the Web and, thus, with the search engines, is not everything on the Web is fresh. Much of the content on the Web is out-of-date. What constitutes out-of-date varies by industry. Stock quotes from last week are out-of-date. Computer configurations from 1996 are out-of-date. AIDS drug-treatment guidelines from 1993 are out-of-date.

Narrowcasting solves this problem. *Narrowcasting* is defined as delivering precisely targeted information to a small group. Narrowcasting has many names on the Web: customized content delivery, channels, server push. Narrowcasting is implemented on the Web with software like PointCast, Castanet, and InBox Direct. The other model of narrowcasting is channeling — which has nothing to do with talking to Eleanor Roosevelt.

In narrowcasting, you tell the software what you care about, which stock quotes you want to see, what countries' coups you want to follow, whether you want health news or sports news or both, and then the software delivers only what you requested. The ultimate news filter! This is better than the remote on your television because there is always something good to watch and it is always on your desktop!

The way these technologies work depends on whether they are client-based or server-based. Chapter 15 discusses client and server issues in depth but, for now, just realize the client is on your desktop and the server is off in the abyss of the Web. Client-based narrowcasting requires you to install software on your desktop — the most popular client-based software is already built into the major browsers. Your news is delivered to you over a channel. Server-based narrowcasting only requires you to go to a Web site with your browser. Figure 1-5 shows server-based narrowcasting at the Excite Web Search Engine. In any case, you tell the software what you want to know about and it filters through all the news of the day, as it becomes available, and updates your screen.

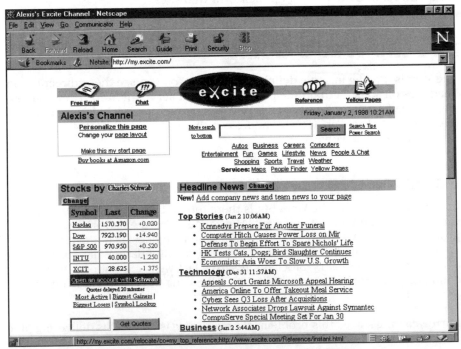

Figure 1-5: This customizable Web site is known as *narrowcasting*.

HTML 4 recognizes the Channel Definition Format: the standard way to set up your Web site as a channel so it works with any HTML 4-compliant browser.

The Web as a marketplace

The future of the Web depends on commerce. Effective Web sites are essential to successful commerce on the Web. Consumers expect the Web interface to be as compelling as the graphics on their television screen.

For the first time—in HTML 4—you can actually meet that expectation.

One of the criteria of a successful marketplace is that it is dynamic. Information on products and services must be constantly updated. HTML 4's dichotomy between content and design helps you keep your content constantly updated. If you are familiar with HTML 3.2 and previous versions of HTML, you know your content and your design were inextricably interwoven. If you wanted to add a new paragraph of text to your page, you had to encode it with all the same HTML you had already applied to every other paragraph in your document. HTML 4 changes all that. Define your styles for your paragraphs in a style sheet and your Web page becomes strictly content. HTML 4 just made it fast and easy for you to update your site.

For really serious dynamic content, let your Web page update itself from a database!

Integrating existing databases into the Web

You may already have databases full of information that you'd like to get to your Web visitors, your business partners, or even just to everyone in your organization over an Intranet.

Intranet. A computer network, typically within a company or limited in some way, that takes advantage of all the protocols used on the Web. To keep people who shouldn't have access to an intranet from getting to it, a firewall is built around it. The *firewall* is a computer-based security system. Usually the people on the inside of the firewall can get to things outside the firewall, such as the Internet, but people outside can't get in.

HTML 4 and the XML standard make this easier. You have many options for delivering your database content to your Web pages. After you choose the best one for you (see Chapter 44), you can take advantage of the HTML 4 style/content dichotomy to deliver beautiful content to your Web site, by placing a minimum of HTML in your document, and all your formatting codes in your style sheet. You can even use dynamic HTML so visitors to your site can sort and filter the data from the database on their own computers. This can relieve the burden on your Web server.

Increasingly, It's Indispensable

Try calling Microsoft on the telephone. You'll be surprised. You won't have to wait on hold at all because no hold exists and no operators are on duty. Microsoft's message directs you to its Web site, where everything you could want to know about Microsoft products can be found. How many other companies will move in this bold direction is difficult to say. But Microsoft has always been a trendsetter.

If you own a Dell computer and you want to upgrade the memory, where do you go to find a list of the memory modules that work with your machine? To the Web, of course! How about if you are a member of Columbia House Record Club and you want to tell them not to send this month's selection? Or you threw out *Bon Appétit* from April and lost that great Mochaccino Cheesecake recipe. No need to worry; just go to the *Bon Appétit* recipe archives and pull it up. Need airline tickets? The origin of the word *concomitant*? A custom CD-ROM cut with all your favorite songs from different artists? Thomas Jefferson's opinions on the appropriate use of nose piercing?

It's all on the Web! Once you get used to the convenience of the Web to find answers and buy products and services, you'll wonder how you ever got by without it.

The need for talented Web developers and compelling Web sites has never been greater. HTML 4 makes it easy to create gripping designs and to populate your Web site with winning content.

How Intranets and Extranets Are Spreading Web Technology

You have information. You have people with whom you want to share this information. Perhaps they have something they can add to your information to make it more valuable to you. You want to keep this information from the rest of the world. What is the solution? Intranets and Extranets.

Intranets are a network within an organization. While using the same technology as the Internet, all the Web pages are accessible only to those in your organization (usually inside the firewall). Extranets are intranets that also give access to your data and your private pages to your business partners.

Vocabulary

Extranet. A computer network that takes advantage of the Web to connect intranets from companies working together in some way.

An example: Your company sells aircraft parts. You keep your inventory in a database. You decide everyone in your sales department should be able to read the database to find out what parts are in stock so they can answer questions for your customers. You implement an intranet, giving everyone in your company (or at least in sales) read-access to your database over the intranet.

Someone in sales tells you half the calls taken by sales are from your biggest client. This client is always calling to ask about inventory and to order parts. You talk to this client and implement an Extranet to enable the purchasing department at your client's office to have read-access to your database. Eventually, you let your client's purchasing department purchase parts from you online and their purchases immediately affect your database. This means the next person looking at the inventory will have an accurate picture of what is still available.

The Rise of HTML-Savvy E-Mail and Usenet Articles

E-mail has been on the Internet longer than the World Wide Web. Simply put, *e-mail* is a way to send unformatted, plain text to anyone around the world who has an e-mail account. Until now!

E-mail was . . .

. . . pretty boring. Remember that laser printer your office had in 1989? It had one font: Courier. `Everything looked like this.` At least e-mail was fast. That printer took forever! Chances are most of the e-mail you receive today is still boring, black-on-white text. Sure you can probably change the way you see the messages, but, still, they will all look the same, much like Figure 1-6. If you are using an HTML-aware e-mail package, such as Netscape Messenger or Microsoft Outlook, it doesn't have to be this way.

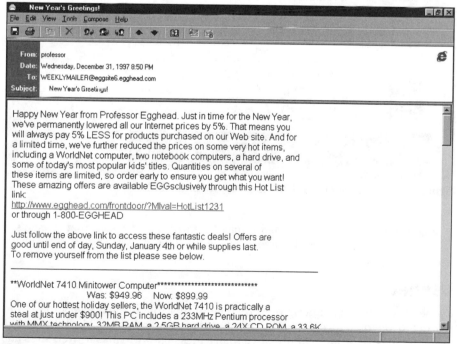

Figure 1-6: This e-mail certainly doesn't grab you.

E-mail can be . . .

. . . just as compelling as the most interesting Web page. Why not include HTML in your e-mail messages? Why not include links to your Web pages, rather than just the URL of your site, as in Figure 1-7? If the link is there, the reader is only one click away from being captivated by your site. If the URL is there, you go onto the To Do list of the e-mail recipient, who may or may not ever get around to pasting the URL into the browser.

If you want your e-mail to be noticed and get results, put it into HTML format. HTML 4 has several new features to spur your audience into action.

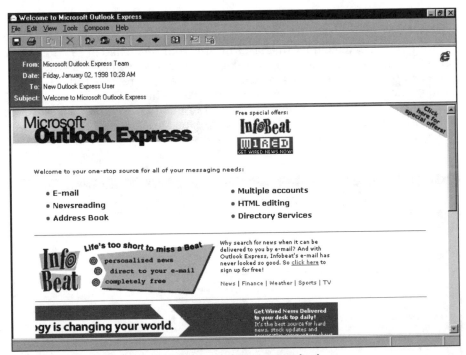

Figure 1-7: This e-mail uses HTML to grab your attention!

Note   Before you send HTML-enriched e-mail to anyone, make sure that person's mail reader can handle the HTML; otherwise, the result will be almost completely illegible.

Usenet

Usenet, the network of newsgroups on the Internet that discuss everything from child rearing to *Melrose Place*, is another great place to implement HTML. What could be more persuasive or more informative than a message with links to Web sites and an attractive design? Add animation and layers and you'll have them captivated!

The Web: Taking over the Desktop, too?

The Justice Department has a bone to pick with Microsoft. Internet Explorer 4 (IE 4) implements desktop integration. This means when you install IE 4 (unless you specifically tell it not to), your entire desktop becomes part of your browser or vice versa. In any case, you can no longer tell them apart. Is this the future of the Web?

Larry Ellison, president of Sun Microsystems, says the network is the computer. Is this true?

An undeniable move is toward the integration of the desktop with the Web. Intranets, Extranets, and Crossware (see sidebar) all point in this direction. And why not? Bandwidth is growing: Through the use of more intelligent communications strategies, the available bandwidth over the same amount of fiber cable is increasing. On top of this, the amount of fiber cable hooked up to the Internet is growing.

Crossware

Now here is something about which everyone can get excited. This term — *crossware* — introduced by Marc Andreesen in a Netscape white paper in the summer of 1997, refers to software that runs over the Web. A small component of crossware sits on your desktop (say, in a browser); the rest of the crossware sits on a server. How does this differ from the traditional client-server model of distributed computing? Unlike the traditional model, with crossware, the client component is the browser. No technician needs to come to your desk, make you feel stupid, and type long strings of indecipherable code while mumbling. What does this mean to businesses? Cost savings. Any upgrades to crossware take place on the server. This means everyone running the crossware on their browsers automatically gets the latest version of the software. Also, those technicians who used to visit your desktop can stay at their own desks and improve the crossware.

What does this mean to consumers? Cheaper and more available software, and less demand on your desktop computer. If you want to know the hexadecimal code for the color red, you can go to a Web site (http://www.digits.com/chart.html) and ask it to convert the code for you (the answer is FF0000). What if you need to calculate your taxes? Wouldn't it be nice if you could do it from your desktop without actually installing tax software on your desktop? Why not? As it turns out, you can, in fact, do your taxes over the Web using crossware. Even if you have to pay for the services you use on the Web, which you do in the taxes example, you have saved the time and hassle of purchasing and installing the software on your desktop. You have also avoided the gnawing fear of installing new software (will it break something else?) so many computer owners have.

What does this mean to businesses? Labor and hardware savings. Businesses save money if they don't have to send technicians around to desktops to install software. They also save money if they effectively implement an Extranet and have their partners doing the work that used to be done by their own staff. Finally, if only a minimum of computing needs to take place on the desktop and little needs to be stored on the desktop, then businesses can implement *thin clients* (meaning inexpensive desktop computers) and still get the same results from their employees.

The Range of Web Publishing

You can do so much on the Web today to inform, persuade, and sell your visitors, you may be intimidated about getting started. Don't be. No one was born knowing HTML. If you are already using HTML, great. If you aren't, better. You won't have any trouble getting used to the HTML 4 way of separating content from design.

You needn't think in terms of putting up an entire Web site right away. Perhaps all you'll ever need is a simple home page. Even if you do need an entire site, this book helps you organize your content, your design, and your resources so you have a plan for action. Whether you want to put up a simple list of links to services for children in the greater Nashville area or a completely searchable site of back issues of the *Daily Texan*, this book will help you get where you want to go.

Regardless of the scope of your projected Web site, you will find nearly everything you need to produce the most compelling content, without any traditional programming, right here in HTML 4.

From Here

If you are getting started with HTML for the first time, it's time to read Surveying the Web Publishing Process (Chapter 2).

If you are tired of looking at your Web pages and seeing more HTML than content, learn about Introducing The HTML 4 Way (Chapter 3).

If you already know a thing or two about HTML and you want to see how to separate style from content, jump to Chapter 23, Introducing Cascading Style Sheets.

Summary

On the Web, information is king. Detailed, targeted information is what we all want. Your mission, should you choose to accept it, is to help develop and deliver this information to the people who are looking for it. Through the use of HTML 4, you can:

✦ **Develop channels,** allowing server-push of your content to desktops

✦ **Separate content from design completely,** allowing faster update of Web pages

✦ **Grab your audience** by sending compelling e-mail and Usenet messages

By taking advantage of the newest Web technologies, you can have your Web pages update themselves from a database, increase your exposure to your audience, and become one of the most highly sought professionals in the world: a first-class Web developer.

✦   ✦   ✦

Surveying the Web Publishing Process

So you want to publish a Web site? Why? Unless you have a clear purpose, you won't be able to create a compelling site. Who is your audience? Surely you must have some idea of who will care about what you have to say (other than your mother and she's just being polite). What do you want to tell people? Your message must be crystal clear. No fancy design will compensate for a murky message. What do you suppose your audience wants to know? Don't assume what you want to tell them and what they want to know are the same thing. Because you probably can't influence what they want to know, you may have to modify what you want to tell them to answer *their* needs.

What tools do you need? This book is an excellent start, but you need some basic software on your desktop (some that is probably there already) to get started. You do have a desktop computer, don't you? Where is your Web site located (both physically and in Cyberspace)? If you are fortunate enough to have your own server, that's great. You may even know how to get your pages onto your server. If not, we have to get some basic questions answered before we can talk about publishing your pages to your server. After all, your site is just the combination of carefully planned pages, so if you can upload your pages, you can upload your site.

Finally, how do you plan to attract your audience? Don't assume they just show up. Perhaps you want to create a community. It worked for Gund (the teddy bear people). We also must do some work to find appropriate alliances for you on the Web. After all, isn't that how you find other sites of interest? Don't think only in terms of search engines. You must create alliances where you link to their pages and they link to yours.

What's Your Purpose?

Think of the last time you saw a presidential press conference or speech. Do you suppose the speech writer planned ahead which of the president's quotes would make it onto the evening news? You bet the writer did! Did you notice after the speech how all the high mucky-mucks in the president's party had exactly the same thing to say? Sure, they used different words, but they all had the same message. Of course, this is no accident.

You have to plan your own Web site with the same single-mindedness. What is the purpose of putting up your Web site? First, will your site be a transit point or a destination?

Transit point

A *transit point*, like a train station, is a place people pass through to get where they really want to go. A search engine is a transit point. A list of places to find 100-percent cotton, organic baby clothes is a transit point. Lots of people put up pages full of pointers to other pages. Whether they realize it or not, these are transit points. Figure 2-1 shows a Web site with various transit points.

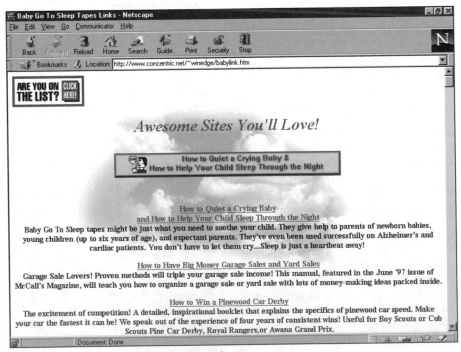

Figure 2-1: The classic transit point Web page

Want to put up a commercial Web site? You can make money from advertising banners, if you can attract a crowd to your transit point Web site.

How long will you stay at a page that does nothing more than point you to other pages? What if you want people to stay in your site and look around, read all the pages, perhaps contribute their opinions, or purchase something? Then you don't want to put up a transit point site; you want to put up a destination site.

Destination

A destination Web site is the site through which you were looking. You normally won't leave a destination Web site until you have found it or you've given up trying. Then you may take one of the links off one of the pages and see what you can find there.

Five types of destination Web sites exist:

- ✦ **Educational:** Teach your visitors about something.
- ✦ **Motivational:** Motivate your visitors to take some action.
- ✦ **Informational:** Tell your visitors something.
- ✦ **Persuasive:** Convince your visitors of something.
- ✦ **Sales:** Sell your visitors a product or service.

Frequently, elements of more than one of these exist in a site.

Educational

Once upon a time, the Web was primarily populated with educational sites. Because the Web's first inhabitants were primarily academics and researchers, this only made sense. Although times have changed, you can still find excellent educational resources on the Web. One of the earliest top-notch educational Web sites was published by the Curry School of Education at the University of Virginia, as shown in Figure 2-2.

While you may not aspire to supplement classroom materials with your educational Web site, you want to conform to the vocabulary of education if you expect your site to be used by educators. If you simply want to educate your lay visitors about the ethnic cleansing of Armenians from Turkey between 1913 and 1922, you needn't worry as much about the jargon of academe. Figure 2-3 shows a Web site with educational content that appeals to a general interest audience.

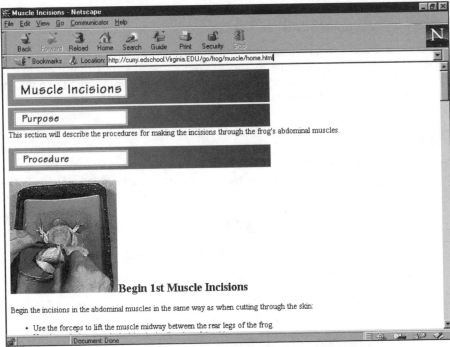

Figure 2-2: Frog Dissection Web Site — a top-quality educational site

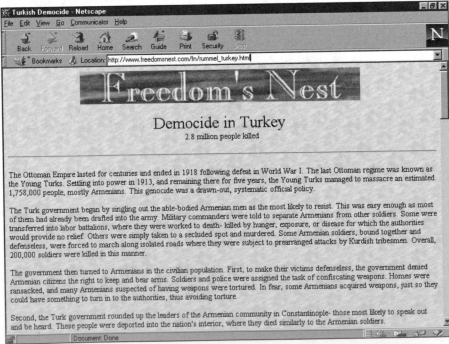

Figure 2-3: Educational site about ethnic cleansing of Armenians from Turkey

Motivational sites

Perhaps you are putting up a Web site to get people to take action: Give money to their favorite charity, volunteer their time with their local library, call their member of Congress to demand stricter enforcement of immigration laws, or start exercising regularly. You may or may not be able to assume your visitors already believe in the value of your cause. You may have to do some persuading, as well.

Motivational sites are what you probably have in mind if your message is related to improving your community, the society, or the environment. Giving people information (education) is not enough. You will probably also want them to take action: join the PTA, drop off food at the soup kitchen, or recycle.

The Natural Resources Defense Council maintains a constantly changing site with the intent of motivating you to take action (see Figure 2-4). The actions they want you to take range from contacting elected officials about legislation to delaying having children to reduce population growth. This type of site is a lot of work to create and maintain, but can be effective. Elements of education, information, and persuasion are on this site, as you would expect.

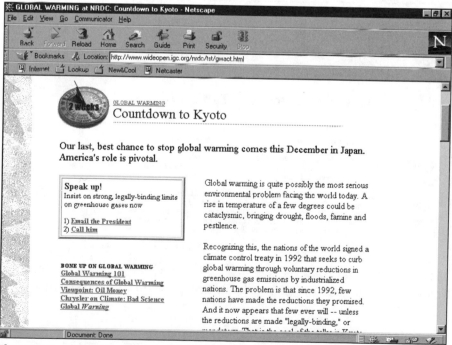

Figure 2-4: The National Resources Defense Council urges visitors to write to the president about the Global Warming Summit.

You may not need to get your visitors to call the president, but you may want to assist them in managing their time so they can find time to exercise. Or, you may list local public health clinics in your state where they can get their children vaccinated. If you are going to motivate your visitors to do something, you must give them all the information they currently need to take action.

Informational

In an informational site, you simply want to tell your visitor something. It could be your family history, the cute things your cat does, or the services provided by the local United Way. If your page is strictly informational—such as design tips for quilting (see Figure 2-5)—then you are under less pressure to conform to standards. You will, however, still want to have a clear message, good content, and a clean design, as this page has.

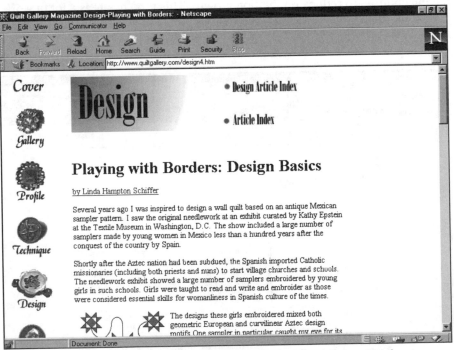

Figure 2-5: Quilting design basics—a lovely example of an informational page

Persuasive

With a persuasive site or page, you have a clear message. You want your visitor to agree with you about something. Your job is to explain your cause and then support it with enough evidence to win your visitor over to your way of thinking.

If you don't have a clear idea of what you want your visitors to take away from your site—what you want them to remember—then they won't either. On the Confederate States of America Home Page (shown in Figure 2-6), the message is clear.

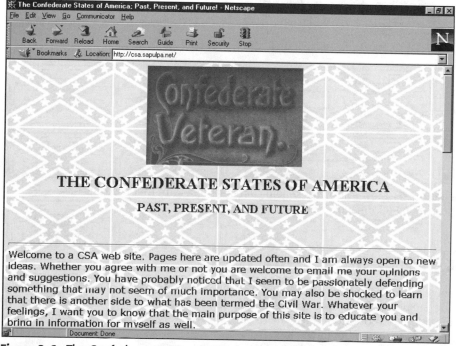

Figure 2-6: The Confederate States of America Home Page

Sales

This is perhaps the most straight-forward purpose of a Web page: selling. In other words, you want your visitor to buy a product or service. What does it take to convince your visitor to make a purchase? You have to educate, inform, persuade, motivate, and, finally, sell! On a sales site, you probably want to have some sort of server processor to handle payments and security to insure that information for payments is safe. Figure 2-7 shows a form used to capture a prospective buyer's information.

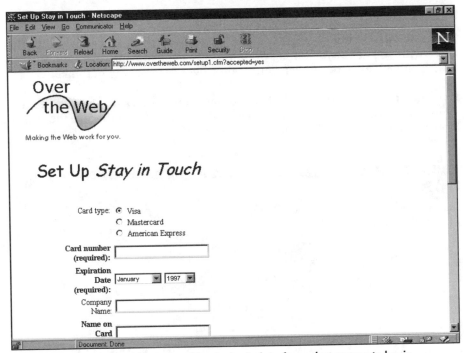

Figure 2-7: Most sales sites should culminate in a form that requests basic purchasing information.

Understanding Your Tools

Have you clarified your message at all since the beginning of this chapter? What is the purpose of your site or page? What kind of site or page will it be? Will it have elements of more than one type of site? Fortunately, you have a few more topics to cover before you begin writing.

As you probably guessed from the title of this book, the primary tool you use to create your Web site is HTML 4. So what is HTML anyway?

Simply put, *HyperText Markup Language* is a set of rules for marking up text so a browser knows what to do with that text. Do you want to see some HTML right now? While browsing any page on the Web, select View Source or View Document Source from the View menu at the top of your screen. Just in case you're not currently online, here is some HTML from the IDG Books Worldwide Web site.

```
<!-- Item One -->
<P><font size="4"><b><tt>Hot and Happening</tt></b></font><BR>
Master the art of creating good-looking, fast-loading graphics
with <a href="/cgi-bin/db/fill_out_template.pl?idgbook:0 7645-
3055 0:book-idg::uidg250" >Web Graphics Bible</A>. Learn
Windows 98 hands on with <a href="/cgi-
bin/db/fill_out_template.pl?idgbook:0-7645-3191-3:book-idg:
:uidg250" >Presenting Windows&reg; 98 One Step at a Time</A>, a
<a href="/cgi-
bin/gatekeeper.pl?uidg250:%2Frc%2Fwindows%2Fforum%2Fwin98.html"
><NOBR>book+<WBR>software</NOBR></a> tutorial
featuring a simulated Windows 98 environment. Get a <a
href="/cgi-
bin/gatekeeper.pl?uidg250:%2Frc%2Fwindows%2Fforum%2Fwin98.html"
>sneak peek</a>.
<!--
Get a handle on Adobe's top drawing program with <a href="/cgi-
bin/db/fill_out_template.pl?idgbook:0-7645-4027-0:book-idg::uid
g250" >Macworld&reg; Illustrator 7 Bible</A>.
Going <a href="/cgi-
bin/gatekeeper.pl?uidg250:%2Fbookstore%2Fbacktoschool.html"
>back to school</A>? Our titles put you at the head of the
class. </P>
-->
```

As you can see, HTML looks like text with other things inserted between less than (<) and greater than (>) signs. If you try to read the previous HTML, you should be able to extract the following text from it: "Hot and Happening Master the art of creating good-looking, fast-loading graphics with Web Graphics Bible. Learn Windows 98 hands on with Presenting Windows 98 One Step at a Time. . . ."

Your browser makes sense of the tags within the < and > (often referred to collectively as *angle brackets*) so the text between the codes looks exactly as the designer wants it to look. What a great idea! You write the content, then you mark-up the text to look the way you want using HTML.

SGML

Standard Generalized Markup Language (SGML) is the basis for HTML. SGML became standard in 1988, when it was approved by the International Standards Organization (ISO). Why should you care? You will better understand where HTML is going if you understand where it came from. Briefly then, SGML is a standard for electronic document exchange. It was, in fact, used in the publication of this book!

How does SGML work? When you read a book manuscript, each element on the page (paragraph, section heading, block quote) has its own typographical convention. For example, in this book, anything representing HTML code appears in courier font, such as the previous HTML code. The publisher communicates to the printer that the code sample should be typeset a certain way by marking up the text with special codes and then telling the printer that whenever he sees those codes, he should change the font to the appropriate font for that element (the publisher gets to define this).

If you've ever tried to write your own Web page, you've noticed you can't always get things to look precisely the way you want. Why is that? You are like the publisher: you mark up your text and tell the printer how you want it to look. The browser is like an arrogant printer, who reads what you have to say and, sometimes, does it his own way despite your instructions.

As a Web page designer, you are at the mercy of the browser. If the publisher doesn't like the way the printer follows directions, he can take his business elsewhere. If you don't like the way a particular browser handles your Web page, you can't do much about it. Fortunately, this is changing with HTML 4.

HTML

When the first graphics-capable browser (Mosaic 1.0) was released in 1993, it handled only a small subset of all the SGML tags. Essentially, as a designer, you could center text, chose from one of four font sizes, separate paragraphs with a blank white line, and do a few other things to make your text look nice.

We've come a long way since then. Today, you have extensive control over white space and formatting. However, HTML is still only a small subset of SGML. HTML is definitely growing in the direction of SGML.

Enough about the history of HTML.

HTML editors

Where do you write your HTML? One of the nice things about HTML is it is just text. The content is text and the tags are text. As a result, you can write your HTML in any text editor. If you are running any flavor of Windows, you can use Notepad, which comes installed with Windows. If you have a Mac on your desk, you can use SimpleText, as shown in Figure 2-8. If you work in UNIX, you can use emacs, vi, jove, pico, or whatever you normally use to edit text.

For your first page, we use your regular text editor. Later in the book, an entire chapter is dedicated to HTML-editing programs that increase your productivity over a plain old text editor. But for now, we focus on the fundamentals: HTML elements and content.

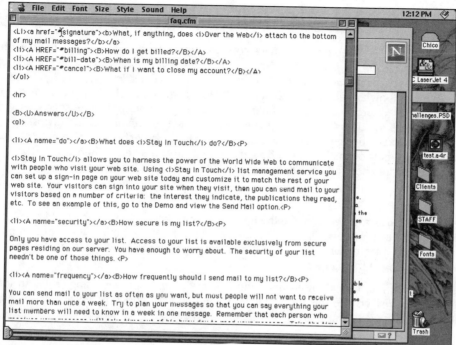

Figure 2-8: SimpleText editor

Writing HTML

What else do you need to know to write your HTML? Presumably, by now, you know:

✦ What your purpose is (at least generally)

✦ You need to write your content from your focused message

✦ You mark up your content with HTML tags

✦ You can write your page with a text editor that is already installed on your computer

Obviously, you need to know the elements. But before discussing those, here are a few guidelines about how you should and shouldn't use HTML.

HTML shouldn't be used to format your text: it should be used to structure your document.

Desperate men (and women)

The lengths to which Web designers have gone to format their pages the way they wanted was quite absurd. HTML had a limited tag set, meaning everything you may want to do to your text wasn't necessarily possible. Yet visitors' expectations for graphically appealing pages were still high. Web designers, before HTML 4 came along, had to get creative. One devious device to force indentation of paragraphs or a set amount of white space between paragraphs was the clear GIF. A *GIF* is an image file (called *somename.GIF*). It is possible (in a software package designed for image creation, such as Photoshop) to create a 1x1 pixel image. A *pixel* is the smallest unit of measurement on the screen. Then with HTML, the image can be stretched to fill the desired space. The evil tag would look something like this:

```
<img src="clear.GIF" width="18" height="1">
```

Then the Web designer would write the text for the paragraph. The result would be 18 pixels of white space (or about $1/4$ inch on most monitors) before the first word of that paragraph. You can imagine what this did to the readability of the HTML when all that junk went at the beginning of the paragraph!

The other common formatting tactic of the desperate designer was using tables to force white space. We'll go into this trick — and why you needn't operate this way anymore with HTML 4 — in Chapter 3.

Format your text

If you are already writing HTML pages, you may need to be broken of your bad habits. You probably already think in terms of getting the browser to make your page look the right way. And you use HTML to make it do this. If you are really underhanded, you may even use goofy conventions like 1-pixel-wide clear image files (usually GIFs) and stretch them to indent your paragraphs.

Fortunately, with HTML 4, you needn't out-maneuver the browser. Browsers that support the HTML 4 standards display your pages as you define them; no more of that arrogant printer stuff! And, fortunately, with HTML 4, you can define the way you want your pages to look outside of the content, so your HTML won't be all cluttered with tags.

Structure your document

So, if you are not supposed to use HTML to format your pages using HTML, how *should* you use HTML? Glad you asked.

HTML defines the structure of your document. Then, outside the main body of the document (or even in a separate file, if you prefer), you define the appearance of each element of the structure. Just like the publisher and the printer in the previous example.

With few exceptions, you will want all your paragraphs to be formatted the same—uniform margins, indents, fonts, spacing between lines, and color.

So, within the main body of your document, you type your text for each paragraph and mark up your document to indicate where each paragraph begins and ends. Then, in a separate location and *only once,* you define how you want all your paragraphs to look. Ways exist to override this universal definition, but we discuss them later.

The most important thing to remember—and this is a big change for you if you've already been writing HTML 3.2 or earlier versions—is the HTML only defines the *structure* of your document. The *formatting* of your document is handled separately.

What is so great about this? First, your text doesn't get all cluttered up with tags. And second, you can define the look for your whole site in one place. You simply have every page in the site (even if some pages in your site are being written by people you have never met) point to the style sheet (the place where you put all those style definitions).

Including Multimedia

Throughout this explanation, we have been talking about text. What if you want to include images? Sound? Video? Animations? 3D models? HTML 4 supports the use of multimedia in your pages.

Two ways exist to include multimedia features in your page: inline and out-of-line, and uses exist for both. The only way to insure your visitor sees or hears your multimedia, however, is to put it inline. For example, advertising banners wouldn't get seen much if they weren't inline!

Inline

Visitors to your page can see or hear an inline element without taking any additional action. Inline elements are supported by HTML directly. Examples of inline elements are images, sound, and animated images (called *animated GIFs,* because this is the only type of image that supports animation). Figure 2-9 is an example of an inline image.

Inline Images

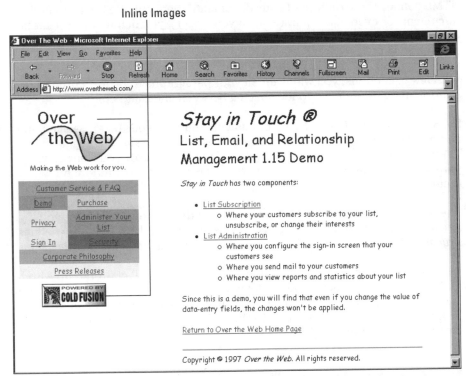

Figure 2-9: The Over the Web logo in the upper left-hand corner is an inline image.

Unless an image is huge (and justifiably so), meaning greater than the size of your screen, you probably want to keep your images inline. Exceptions always exist. Say you want to show a map of Chicago. You may allow your visitors to click a neighborhood and see a more detailed map of only that neighborhood. In this case, you need both inline and out-of-line images. A really large image may, indeed, be justified — as in a map — where detail matters. If you are only showing a photo of Monticello (Thomas Jefferson's home), that level of detail probably isn't necessary. You would be better off, in this case, to show the entire house in one photo and then show separate smaller images of the details you want to discuss.

Out-of-line

When your visitors have to take additional action, such as click an image or agree to initiate a plug-in to see or hear your element, then it is an out-of-line element. Examples of out-of-line elements are images, sound, video, 3D models to be navigated, and animations. Figure 2-10 shows an example of a still image linking to a QuickTime VR movie.

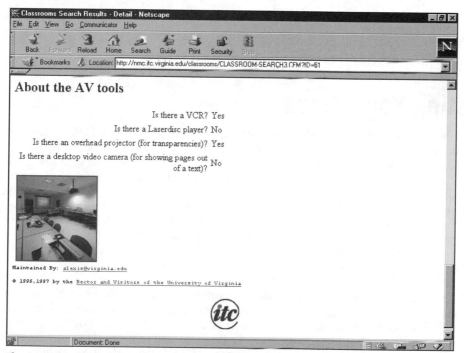

Figure 2-10: The photo of a room on this page links to a QuickTime VR movie of the room in 3D.

Your visitors may get annoyed if they must take action too often to see or hear your multimedia. A good use of out-of-line sound is a music store that lets you click an icon to hear a music clip from an album. This enables the store to list many album titles on one page—obviously, there wouldn't be any way for you to hear the music clips from every album concurrently. Then the detail page from each album may have inline sound, with a clip from the most popular song on the album.

Objects

Because the number of types of multimedia you can add to your page—many of them proprietary (meaning the technology is owned by only one company)—is growing faster than anyone can count, the WC3 isn't trying to keep up. Instead, it has defined a type of element, called an *object,* which you define when you want to refer to any of these proprietary multimedia types (RealAudio, Worlds, and Shockwave come immediately to mind).

Chapter 39 explains how to incorporate proprietary multimedia technologies into your page. It also introduces some of the more common "plug-ins" that Web sites use.

Testing Your Pages

Once you have what you think is a nice approximation of the HTML you need to have on your page, you'll want to test it. You want to do two types of testing. Obviously, you want to look at your page in one or more browsers, to see if it looks the way you had planned. The reason to look at it in more than one browser is they all implement HTML in slightly different ways. For example, in Netscape Navigator 3 or 4, if any tag was missing from within your table, the entire table wouldn't appear on your page! Internet Explorer 3 (IE 3) and 4 (IE 4) does its best to show the table, even with the tag missing. If you created a page and only tested it in IE 3 or IE 4, you may not know you had left off a tag. You also might not know that everyone looking at your page with Netscape 3 or 4 couldn't see your table.

The second type of testing you want to perform is HTML validation. You want to run your HTML through an *HTML validator* (a program that checks syntax to make sure no tags are missing, none of your tags are misspelled, and you haven't used any tags or attributes that aren't valid). Because you're using HTML 4, you must be certain the validator you select supports the HTML 4 specification. Otherwise, you'll be frustrated when all the new HTML 4 elements you just learned are marked as errors.

Chapter 22 covers HTML validation in detail.

Publishing Your Pages

When you like what you see when you test your page or pages, then it's time to publish them. This is actually less climactic than it sounds. Publishing your page simply means copying it from wherever you have been saving it to your Web server.

A number of software packages are available to make this copying pretty straightforward. However, you will need answers to some questions before you can do this:

✦ What is the address of my Web server?

✦ Is it an NT or a UNIX server?

✦ How am I supposed to sign on?

✦ What is my user ID and password?

✦ Do I need to know about any directory information?

Chapter 6 takes you through enough to feel comfortable talking to your server administrator. We've even included a worksheet so you can record the information your server administrator gives you in a place where you can use it.

Publicizing Your Pages

What do you think about when you think of publicizing your pages? Don't think in terms of calling a press conference. It would take a pretty slow news day to get the press interested in this.

Several ways exist to publicize your site, though. You should try to take advantage of as many of these as apply to your situation. Don't just fill out the forms at the big search engines and think you've done all you can. Fifty million Web pages are out there right now. They can't all come up Number 1 on a search.

Some of the ways you should consider publicizing your site include:

Search engines. You didn't expect us to leave this out. It simply isn't the *only* way to publicize your site. Most search engines have a form, or a series of forms, you must fill out to get listed with them. Many search engines give preference to organizations that advertise on their sites — meaning, unless you advertise, you probably won't come up on the first page on any given search. Some search engines let you type in your *URL* (the address of your site) and then send an *agent* (a computer program that reads through your material) to index your pages. At least one search engine is reminiscent of high school popularity contests: You apply to be considered and then, if the committee of cool thinks you're cool enough, your page gets listed.

Newsgroups. If one or more newsgroups discusses the message of your site, you'll want to post a message with that newsgroup announcing your site. An example: a new Stroller Safety Web site would want to post an announcement to misc.kids and misc.kids.pregnancy. You obviously must be careful not to violate the rules of the group. Some newsgroups frown on anything they consider ads. It is usually considered better netiquette if you are already a regular contributor to the group before you post such an announcement. At the least, read through a few days' postings on the group to gauge the tone, so your message doesn't read like a bull in a china shop.

Mailing Lists. Mailing lists are more private than newsgroups. The cautions previously voiced go double for mailing lists. But don't be scared away from posting here. If your site may help solve a problem of the newsgroup's readers or mailing list, then post one (not 22) carefully worded announcement and expect some people to flame you (some people would flame their own mothers). For *moderated* newsgroups — newsgroups that have a person read and approve each message before it goes to the list — you'll be best off to contact the moderator directly and find out what the standards are.

Makers of the software you used. You'll have the best luck, generally, with small software manufacturers. If you created your site with, say, iWrite, then perhaps the makers of iWrite have a page where they link to any pages created with their tools. These software makers often have a small image (usually based on their logo) they want you to put on your page with a link back to them. Figure 2-11 shows a Web page making use of such a logo.

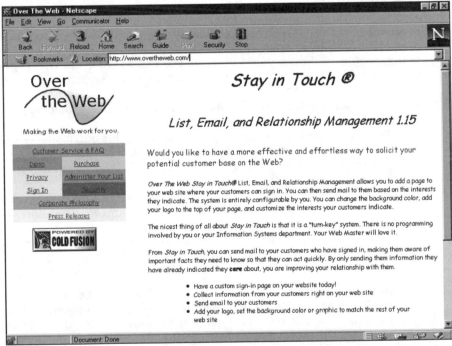

Figure 2-11: An example of a logo from the software you used in the creation of your site — in this case, Cold Fusion.

Makers of the browser that best displays your site. You may find you want to use features of HTML that are really well-supported in only one browser. You take a chance some people visiting your site won't be able to see it the way you want when you do this, but this is certainly your decision. Under these circumstances, you may find the maker of the browser you prefer people to use has a place in its site for links to sites like yours. Even Netscape — hardly a small company — has benefits for sites that display the "Best viewed with Netscape" image on their sites. Figure 2-12 shows this type of indication on a Web page.

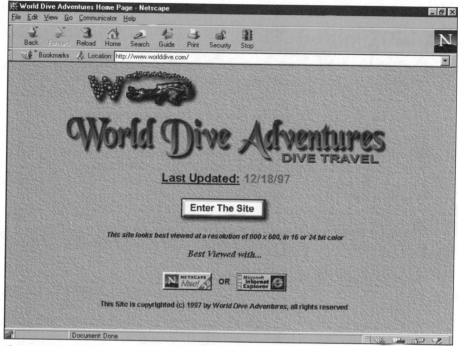

Figure 2-12: This page tells you it is best viewed with Internet Explorer or Netscape (not too picky, is it?).

Your ISP. Many Internet service providers (ISPs) have pages that list all the sites of their clients. Contact your ISP and make sure you get listed.

Your Chamber of Commerce or other local business group. If you are a member of your local chamber, you can find out how to get listed with it. Frequently, members of these business groups look to do business with other members before they look outside the circle.

Community organizations. Is there a community Web site? Get a link from there.

Professional Associations, Alumni Associations, or Social Clubs. Why have you been paying dues all these years? Contact any organization to which you or your company belongs and see about getting a link from there.

Sites with similar missions. If you were going to put up a Stroller Safety site, you would want to consider contacting other sites that discuss safety and are of interest to parents. Chances are a large audience crossover would occur between your site and any of those other sites. You may also be able to form an alliance with any of them.

Forming Alliances

The Web is a Web because there are links between pages. If all pages only connected to each other through search engines, then it would be the World Wide Hub. It is your job to find appropriate alliances on the Web — people who may be interested in your site.

Generally, you don't need anything in writing (although legal documents are available for this and they can be found on the Web). You'll find the people who have put up these other sites are only to happy to exchange a link from their page to yours for a link from your page to theirs. Usually, they'll wish *they* thought of it! Go ahead: create your own Web with your site right in the middle of it.

Maintaining Your Pages

Your site should always read like it was written this morning. Schedule face lifts and reviews of contents occasionally. Don't just assume your site is being kept up. Also, be wary of only adding more pages. Sometimes you have to remove pages, as well. And when you remove pages, make sure you tell the search engines with which your site is listed to have them remove those pages, too.

Cross-Reference

In Chapter 14, we discuss tools that can help you manage the links in your site. Some of these even repair the links for you, if they can. Other software is available that tells you which links in your site lead to dead ends.

Creating a Community

One rather spiffy feature you may want to consider adding to your site is some sort of online chat or threaded discussion group. People will return to your site over and over if they can get their questions answered there, even if their questions are directly about what your site does.

Two examples of this use of Web sites can be found at the online homes of Allaire and Gund.

Allaire, the makers of Cold Fusion, has moved all its customer support over to a threaded discussion group on its Web site. If you want your questions answered free, you have to post there. Consequently, people return again and again to read other people's questions, ask their own, and answer others' questions. At the top of that page is an ad for Allaire's latest product, as shown in Figure 2-13.

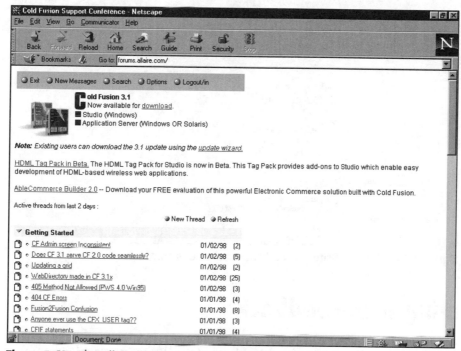

Figure 2-13: The Allaire forum — a community discussing Allaire products

The Gund site has a threaded discussion group that appeals to collectors of teddy bears. Not surprisingly, Gund sells teddy bears. But Gund doesn't sell teddy bears on that discussion group. Collectors get others excited about Gund's products. (See Figure 2-14.)

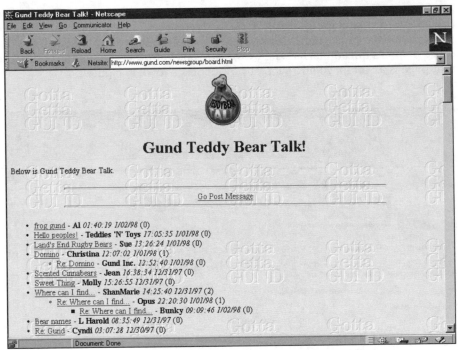

Figure 2-14: The Gund site — a teddy bear collector's community

Dealing with Feedback

At the bottom of all your pages, you'll want to put a way for your visitors to get in touch with you. Usually, the e-mail address of the Webmaster is adequate. You may also want to put up a feedback or comments form on your site. People like to be asked for their opinions.

Another way to collect feedback is through an online survey. If you want a lot of feedback, offer some prize to a randomly selected participant. To be effective, a survey will require some server-side scripting.

Cross-Reference You can read more about scripting in Chapters 15, 42, and 44.

However you collect feedback, you will want to have some polite, friendly answer ready to mail back to anyone who bothers to tell you what you could improve — whether or not you want to hear it. Finally, you will want to consider implementing changes that visitors suggest to you — if you think the changes may improve your site. It isn't necessary for you to respond to every suggestion, but you should always listen with open ears.

From Here

Cross-Reference Read more about what makes HTML 4 so special in Chapter 3, Introducing the HTML 4 Way.

Jump right into Chapter 5, Creating Your First Web Page.

Begin the serious work of Chapter 8, Defining Your Message and Your Goals.

Summary

Sure you have a lot to do to get that award-winning site up and running, but at least now you know what's involved.

✦ Define your purpose and your message

✦ Identify the editor you want to use

✦ Write the HTML, separating structure from formatting

✦ Consider including multimedia

✦ Test your pages for both appearance and syntax

✦ Publish your pages

✦ Publicize your page

✦ Form alliances to increase visibility

✦ Make a plan to maintain your pages

✦ Create a community to keep visitors coming back

✦ Welcome feedback and respond to it

✦   ✦   ✦

Introducing the HTML 4 Way

Let's talk for a moment about history. Not ancient history but, say, mid-1997 Web-publishing history. What were people's biggest concerns about publishing a page back then?

✦ **Compatibility across browsers.** Would a page that looked awesome in Internet Explorer 4 look right in Netscape Navigator 4? Would JavaScript, which animated a figure perfectly in Navigator 4, work in Internet Explorer 4? And what if a visitor to your site was using Netscape Navigator 2? Did you really have to maintain a nonframes-compatible version of every single page?

✦ **Keeping content fresh.** People expect to come to your Web site to get accurate, up-to-date answers to their questions. Can you afford to be constantly updating your content when it is buried in a bunch of HTML? You practically need a Web developer just to correct a misspelling, when the content and the design are so closely interwoven.

✦ **Keeping a current look.** The standards for gorgeous Web page design are climbing every week. Keeping your site looking HOT is both costly and time-consuming.

HTML 4 can't completely solve all these problems, but it can reduce the magnitude of these problems. This chapter explains how.

The Extension Problem

In America, we value innovation. We celebrate people who make a lot of money by being the first to implement great ideas. This culture of reverence for mavericks creates a lot of problems for Web developers when the mavericks are producing the browsers that have the lion's share of the market.

Both Netscape and Microsoft are to blame (don't try to pin it all on Bill Gates, president of Microsoft and the subject of an entire genre of humor); both these companies have introduced proprietary *extensions* (ways of marking up HTML) that only work on their own browsers. Of course, they aren't doing anything car manufacturers don't do every year. When the first minivan manufacturer added cupholders, did anyone complain? This feature may have made you purchase that minivan instead of the competitor's. Today, every minivan has cupholders — so it goes with great innovations!

So what do cupholders and mavericks have to do with your Web site? Everything. The people who make browsers are trying to get more people to purchase and use their own browsers — rather than the competitors — by adding more new features. Of course, you are thinking, isn't this contrary to the idea of the Web, that everything would be standard so everything could be seen on every computer, regardless of platform or software installed? You've obviously been paying attention. It is, indeed, antithetical to the very basis of the Web. In fact, if these motivations had been in place when the Web got off the ground, we'd probably have two or three different Webs and nothing from one could be viewed on either of the others!

Let's look at the specific problems browser manufacturers introduce when they add new features no one else has.

Compatibility across browsers

When Netscape introduced frames with Version 3 of Navigator, designers had a problem: Did they start using a feature that not only couldn't be seen by a visitor who came to their sites from any other browser, but couldn't even be seen by a visitor who came to their sites from all previous versions of Netscape Navigator? The answer is many of them started to use frames, but maintained two separate sites: one for people coming to the site with Netscape Navigator 3 and one for everyone else. They also put little icons (provided by Netscape at no charge) on their pages saying: This site looks best when viewed with Netscape Navigator. What could be more of a pain for designers? Figures 3-1 and 3-2 show the same page viewed in Netscape Navigator and Internet Explorer.

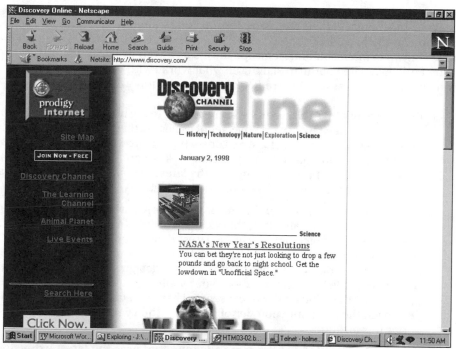

Figure 3-1: A page in Netscape Navigator

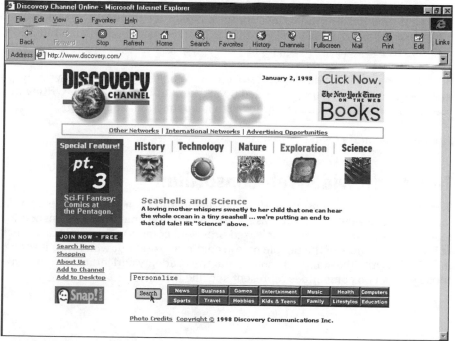

Figure 3-2: The same page in Microsoft Internet Explorer

What could be better for Netscape? As it turned out, Microsoft ended up adding support for frames to their own browsers, making frames a standard. So, didn't it all end happily ever after? Not exactly. This constant battle for market share that rages between Microsoft and Netscape means as a Web designer, you will constantly evaluate your material to see what works with which browser. You will always have to assess the trade-off between the following three positions:

1. **Don't use any tags that aren't widely supported.** The result of this decision is you will only have to support one set of pages (rather than one for the latest set of extensions and one for everyone who has browsers that don't support those). But — and this is the major drawback — your site will never look as cool as the sites of those who do use the latest extensions. You won't be able to implement the latest and greatest design features.

2. **Use the proprietary tags and to heck with people who haven't upgraded.** Arrogant but, for certain sites, this works. If your site is about design, you don't have any choice but to use the latest design tools. (No one attends fashion shows of last year's clothes.) If, however, you are trying to sell something on your site (other than your own design services), then you'd better be a little less cavalier about your visitors' experiences. If your site appeals to education or social causes — where you can do the most good if you reach the maximum number of people — then you should probably not adopt this attitude.

3. **Support two versions of the same site: one that uses the latest extensions and one that doesn't.** Later in this book, you learn how to use JavaScript to find out which browser your visitors are using when they come to your page and then to show them the appropriate page for their browsers. Of course, this approach is the most expensive, because you have to maintain the site in two versions — what a pain!

How did it happen that on this cross-platform Web, where everything was supposed to work on every computer, we ended up in a situation where we are writing browser-specific pages? Isn't someone supposed to keep this from happening?

Indeed, someone is trying.

The World Wide Web Consortium

The *World Wide Web Consortium* (W3C) is the organization created to set standards for the Web. However, the W3C has no means of enforcement (and no inspection teams to make sure soon-to-be-released browsers comply). The W3C has a small staff of its own, but most of the people on the committees (about which you'll soon hear more) who write the standards come from the academy and industry. Sometimes those who sit on committees represent specific interests.

While the theory goes that the W3C sets a standard and the industry follows, the reality is, the W3C is usually following the actions taken by the largest browser manufacturers: Netscape and Microsoft. Because Microsoft and Netscape continue to add their own proprietary extensions, the W3C is often in the position of simply compiling a list of the features already in use on either browser and deciding which ones will be declared standard. The W3C also does a lot of interesting work in developing standards for ancillary Web technologies. At publication, a new standard for encoding a page with HTML, so it would print in a predictable manner, was under development by the W3C. This isn't currently supported by either Netscape or Microsoft.

The Ideal: Separating Structure from Presentation

The most expensive thing about publishing a Web site isn't the cost of your account with an ISP. It isn't the cost of any tool you may purchase to increase your productivity when writing HTML. It isn't the time spent learning HTML. What is it? It's the time spent maintaining your site.

HTML 4 tackles this problem head-on by storing all the information about the way things should look in a separate location (either in a separate place in the same document or, better yet, in a separate file altogether) from the content. You simply indicate what type of element (paragraph, title, list, heading) each block of text is, using HTML, and then, in a style sheet, you describe how you want each element to look.

Cluttered HTML (the pre-HTML 4 universe)

Unless you are content to let your content get stale and your style become dated, you need to put time into updating both your design and your content. In the pre-HTML 4 world, you needed to hire a Web developer to do both of these, which became expensive. Why did you need a Web developer simply to update your content? Consider the following HTML:

```
<li><FONT SIZE="+1" FACE="comic sans ms" FAMILY="sans-serif"
COLOR="#0000FF"><P><A name="do"></a><B>What does <i>Stay In
Touch</i> do?</B></P></FONT>

<FONT SIZE="-1" FACE="comic sans ms" FAMILY="sans-serif"
COLOR="#000000"><P><i>Stay In Touch</i> allows you to harness
the power of the World Wide Web to communicate with people who
visit your web site. Using <i>Stay In Touch</i> list management
service you can set up a sign-in page on your web site today
```

and customize it to match the rest of your web site. Your visitors can sign into your site when they visit, then you can send mail to your visitors based on a number of criteria: the interest they indicate, the publications they read, etc. To see an example of this, go to the Demo and view the Send Mail option.</P></FONT>

<li><FONT SIZE="+1" FACE="comic sans ms" FAMILY="sans-serif" COLOR="#0000FF"><P><A name="security"></a><B>How secure is my list?</B></P></FONT>

<FONT SIZE="-1" FACE="comic sans ms" FAMILY="Sans Serif" COLOR="#000000"><P>Only you have access to your list. Access to your list is available exclusively from secure pages residing on our server. You have enough to worry about. The security of your list needn't be one of those things.</P></FONT>

Figures 3-3 and 3-4 are what it looks like in your browser on a PC and then on a Mac (notice the font is slightly different).

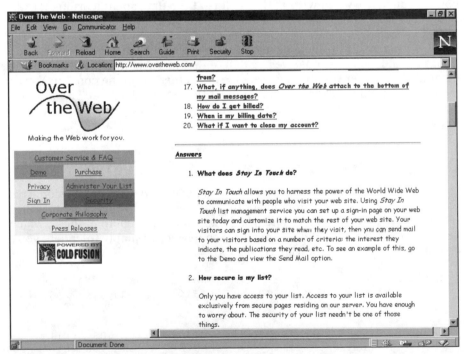

Figure 3-3: The previous text displayed in a browser on a PC.

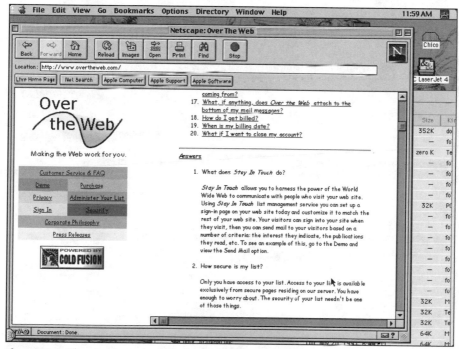

Figure 3-4: The previous text displayed in a browser on a Mac.

The maintenance nightmare

From looking at the HTML and then seeing the HTML interpreted by the browser, you can pretty much tell what part of the text is instructions to the browser and what part is the content. But would you feel comfortable making changes to the content — say, adding another bulleted set of questions and answers? Probably not. And you probably wouldn't want someone else who didn't know what all those codes meant doing it either.

HTML 4 almost eliminates this problem of site maintenance having to be done by an HTML expert. This means HTML 4 helps reduce the cost of maintaining your Web site! When was the last time you heard anything about reducing costs being associated with the Web?

Consider the site map in Figure 3-5. Every screen should have the same formatting: same font, same heading sizes, same alignment, same text color, same background color. Wouldn't it be nice if you could put all this information in one place and have every page look to that page for formatting instructions?

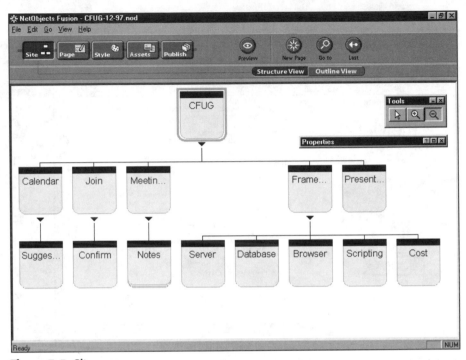

Figure 3-5: Site map

HTML 4 defines structure

Let's return to the SGML analogy presented in the previous chapter. The book publisher marks up a text using SGML and then tells the printer to print it by providing a list of how each element of SGML should appear.

> **Title:** Make this blue, 18pt. Times New Roman. Also center it.
>
> **Section headings:** Make them black (the rest of the book should all be black, by the way) and 18pt. The font should be Times Roman. They should be left-justified and triple-spaced.
>
> **Paragraphs:** Each paragraph should be indented $3/4$ inch. Font should be 12pt. And Times Roman.
>
> **Examples of code:** These should be in Courier 12pt. They should be indented from each margin by $3/4$ inch.

The publisher uses SGML to indicate where titles, section headings, paragraphs, and code examples (referred to collectively as *elements*) begin and end. When HTML was first created, this was how it was supposed to work. But designers weren't happy with the lack of control over formatting, so they started to use it in a way that never had been intended.

HTML 4 enables us to return to the ideal of HTML. What does this mean to you and your ability to maintain a site? If the only codes that appear in your HTML are structure codes (with the presentation codes appearing elsewhere), then no reason exists why you can't use less expensive talent to maintain your content.

Consider the following code. It produces the same results as the previous example in the browser. Notice there is no formatting. All the HTML you see is related to the structure. We discuss the formatting code in the next section. For now, just remember we put the information related to presentation into a style sheet.

```
<LI>What does <i>Stay In Touch</i> do?

<P><i>Stay In Touch</i> allows you to harness the power of the
World Wide Web to communicate with people who visit your web
site. Using <i>Stay In Touch</i> list management service you
can set up a sign-in page on your web site today and customize
it to match the rest of your web site. Your visitors can sign
into your site when they visit, then you can send mail to your
visitors based on a number of criteria: the interest they
indicate, the publications they read, etc. To see an example
of this, go to the Demo and view the Send Mail option.</P>

<LI>How secure is my list?

<P>Only you have access to your list. Access to your list is
available exclusively from secure pages residing on our server.
You have enough to worry about. The security of your list
needn't be one of those things.</P>
```

How comfortable would you be updating the previous HTML? How about if you needed to add another set of questions and answers? Already, you can see using HTML 4 makes a world of difference. The information the browser must know to format the previous text is stored separately, in a style sheet.

Introducing Cascading Style Sheets

A *style sheet* contains information about how you want your page to look. The idea and the name come from the publishing industry, where style sheets are still used today. But why *cascading* style sheets (CSS)? Good question. Most of the time, when you create a site, you want a uniform look across the site. You probably don't want each different section of a site to use a different font or a different background color. You probably also don't want one section to have all the text left-justified (like this book) and have another section right-justified, just for the heck of it. If you are creating the site yourself, this kind of uniformity is easier to maintain, but even you may sometimes forget how you did it on another page.

The answer to uniformity is a style sheet. Define your style sheet outside any of your pages (give it a name like `MyStyleSheet.css`) and link all your pages to it. Now, any element you have described in your style sheet will look the way you want it to (and the same) in every page where that element is used.

But what if you want the color of some text to be different on one page? Say, to indicate this is a new addition to your site or a limited time offer? Easy. Just define the style for this element right there, in that tag. Isn't this the way pre-HTML 4 worked? Exactly. Except you will use style definitions within elements only as the exception, not as the rule.

The browser knows to look in the external (global) style sheet for style definitions about each element it encounters (see Figure 3-6). It uses those unless it finds locally defined styles and then those locally defined styles override the globally defined styles. Finally, you can define styles for an entire page. Element-level styles override page-specific styles, which override global styles.

As confusing as this sounds, most often you only have a globally defined style sheet. Still, it's nice to know you can override the global style sheet if you like.

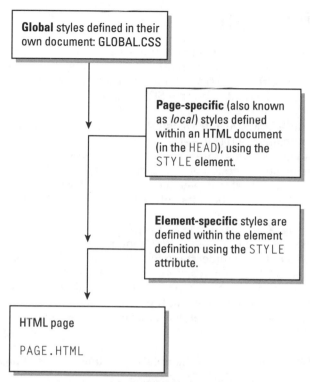

Figure 3-6: The cascading model of style definitions

The HTML 4 Way

So what is the HTML 4 Way? The *HTML 4 Way* is using HTML within your document only to define structure and putting all information your browser needs about presentation into a style sheet.

The rest of this book focuses on the HTML 4 Way. If you are already a veteran Web developer, then you may have to break some bad habits. If you are new to Web development, then you have it easier; you can learn it right — right from the beginning.

The Future (Maybe): XML

Let's go back to SGML—standard generalized markup language—again. HTML came from SGML, but those folks who live and breathe SGML in publishing and the academy were not satisfied with what HTML could do. They kept complaining to the W3C about the things HTML couldn't do that SGML could.

The W3C tried to appease these SGML-zealots (using the term advisedly) who complained about the shortcomings of HTML—now remember the reason HTML became so popular so quickly was it was simple—by expanding the HTML specification. Each time a new version of HTML came out, the SGML fanatics complained at greater length (if you ever see SGML, you'll see it is not known for its brevity, unlike HTML) about its failure to perform like SGML.

You can see where this is going: XML. Extensible Markup Language (XML) was approved in January 1998, by the members of the W3C, and recommended by the W3C shortly thereafter. To help you understand why the W3C had delayed supporting the demand of the SGML advocates, note, at the time XML was approved, neither of the major browsers supported it (please recall that every feature of HTML 4 was already supported in one of the two major browsers— and had been for almost a year—by the time it was approved). So why would you want to know or use XML? Two reasons:

✦ **Flexibility.** Unlike HTML, XML gives you the ability to define your own tags.

✦ **Power.** Unlike HTML, XML enables the use of variables you can define externally to your page. This makes XML more like a programming language. Before XML, you had to use server-side scripting, JavaScript, or Java to include variables in your documents. Because XML isn't implemented (at time of publication), you still must use one of these.

And why wouldn't you want to use XML?

✦ **Flexibility.** With flexibility comes responsibility. You have to properly define each of your tag definitions in a document type definition (DTD).

✦ **Complexity.** XML is a lot like a programming language. None of the programming languages have taken off the way HTML has. The average Web developer isn't ready for this kind of complexity. Figure 3-7 shows a snippet from the XML specification.

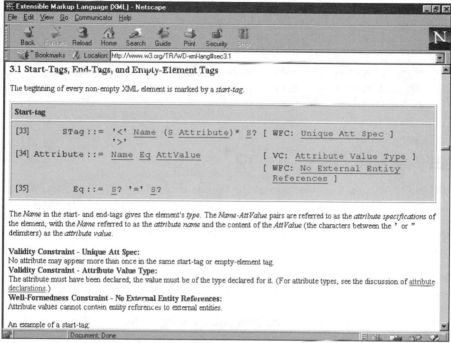

Figure 3-7: W3C publishes XML specification — not for the faint-hearted

Whether you think XML is the best thing since a two-button mouse or hope it never catches on, for now, it is not widely supported, so you won't have to make any decisions (or look for the *XML Bible* just yet).

The Ideal versus the Reality

While HTML 4 addresses all three of the major concerns of Web developers outlined as we began this chapter — compatibility across browsers, keeping content fresh, and keeping a current look — as a designer, you are still somewhat trapped by the dilemma that has frustrated all previous Web designers contending with new versions. Until all browsers support all features of HTML 4 and you can be sure all visitors to your site are using HTML 4-compatible browsers, you are left with decisions to make:

> **Don't use any HTML 4-specific tags or methodology.** Just keep doing things the way you have been. Clutter up your document with formatting and structural HTML and take a new job when the mess becomes too unmanageable.

Use HTML 4 and to heck with people who haven't upgraded to HTML 4-compatible browsers. Use HTML for structure only within your documents. If people are viewing your site with a browser that doesn't support HTML 4, then they will see minimalist formatting, but this is basically their problem.

Support two versions of the same site: one that uses HTML 4 and one that doesn't. Keep the content up-to-date in your current site. Apply any face-lifts to the HTML 4 version of your site.

Where's All This Going?

Without question, the direction of the Web is toward the HTML 4 Way. Whether it is with HTML 4 this year or XML next year, you can count on the need for the separation of structure from design. As HTML becomes more sophisticated and more and more formatting features are added, the need for separation will become even clearer.

Web designers want to make their pages more visually compelling, taking the best practices from print and the best practices from television. Management wants the ever-spiraling cost of maintaining a Web site to level off or drop—why should they have to pay high-priced Web designers just to update the text on a page? HTML 4 meets both these needs in a concrete way.

Unlike previous versions of HTML, HTML 4 is pretty well-implemented in both Navigator and Internet Explorer. With HTML 4, you'll find you can do things you only dreamt of before now. Indenting a paragraph? No problem. Indenting every paragraph? No problem. Change the text color of every heading? No problem.

The die is cast, and even though you may have to change the way you think about creating and maintaining a Web site, it is for the better. Never before have you had the kind of control over formatting you have now. Never before have you had the flexibility to make your text do whatever you want, including moving!

What Should You Do Now?

Get excited! The face of the Web will never look the same. You are going to be part of the story whether you are an example in the next version of this book of the bad, old way people used to write HTML or an award-winning Web designer, implementing HTML 4 to bring traffic and recognition to your Web site.

Don't necessarily look to the Web for the future of design. Few places exist where you can see the power of HTML 4 in action. Look to print—where few formatting constraints exist (they, unlike we, are constrained by two dimensions). Look to television where animated text is something we take for granted.

The Web is not completely devoid of people using HTML 4 with style. Take a look at Nadja Vol Ochs' column in the Microsoft DevEdge site (see Figure 3-8). Of course, Microsoft calls it *dynamic HTML*, which is its marketing name for HTML 4, but it is pretty much the same thing. Microsoft did a better job than Netscape in implementing the features that eventually became HTML 4 in their Version 4 browsers.

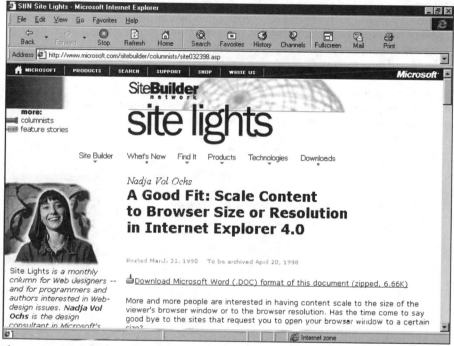

Figure 3-8: A stylish place to find information about designing with HTML 4

From Here

Cross-Reference

If you are an old hand at HTML and you have been bearing with us to see what this HTML 4 Way is all about, you can jump right into Part V: "Enhancing Presentation with Style Sheets."

If you are just getting started with HTML, proceed to Part II: "HTML Quick Start."

Summary

The HTML 4 Way is, indeed, the future of Web publishing. It reduces the cost of maintaining a Web site, increases the speed of giving your site a periodic face-lift, and completely changes the paradigm of Web development by separating presentation from structure.

XML may or may not take over as the king of the Web for reasons, principally, of complexity. In any case, the design choices available to you as a Web designer continue to increase. Even if the W3C didn't have this as a goal, Netscape and Microsoft continue to try to sell their own browsers, which necessitates the inclusion of new features.

While it is true you can't assume every visitor to your site has the most recent browser supporting HTML 4, you can still provide adequate content to your foot-dragging visitors and stunning design to your visitors who are keeping up.

✦   ✦   ✦

HTML
Quick Start

Introducing HTML Basics

When you learn a language, you need to learn rules, called *syntax*. Unless you follow these rules, your statements don't have any meaning. Consider this statement, for instance: "Extra! Pizza, with a bring pepperoni me; cheese." The word order is out of whack and so is the punctuation. You can say this to a waiter, but good luck getting your pizza! Like any language, HTML has syntax rules. Fortunately, they're simple and easy to learn. Before you start trying to write HTML, you'll be wise to spend a little time learning these rules. It doesn't take long and there's a huge payoff: You'll avoid confusion and find it much easier to track down your errors.

This chapter introduces the basic building blocks of HTML, including elements, attributes, and entities. (Don't worry about defining these terms right now; that's done in this chapter.) You also learn the basics of nesting tags and about the basic, underlying structure of every HTML document. Once you learn these concepts, you're ready to starting writing HTML!

Introducing the Basic Building Blocks: Elements

When you write your HTML, you use *elements* to define the structure of the document, to define the presentation of your document, to define links to other documents, and to specify desired behavior. Examples of elements are: HEAD, BODY, P, BLOCKQUOTE, and UL. When you actually go to insert these elements into your text, you surround them with < (less than) and > (greater than) symbols, which are collectively referred to as *angle brackets*. Once you have done this, you have <HEAD>, <BODY>, <P>, <BLOCKQUOTE>, and <UL>. These are no longer called elements; they are now called *tags*.

Elements versus tags

The W3C uses the word *elements* in two ways, which is rather confusing. You may have noticed this book does the same thing. In this chapter, we discuss elements in the *tag* sense of the word. The other kind of element is the *element of structure* of a document (for example, title, paragraph, blockquote).

Even elements have parts

Unlike the elements in the Periodic Table, elements in HTML usually have three parts: start tags, content, and end tags. Most elements have start tags and end tags. The *start tag* is the element name surrounded by angle brackets: <HEAD>, <BODY>, <P>, <BLOCKQUOTE>, and <UL>. The *end tag* is the element name, preceded by a / (called a *slash*), surrounded by angle brackets: </HEAD>, </BODY>, </P>, </BLOCKQUOTE>, and </UL>.

When the browser sees a start tag, it knows the text to come will all be of the type defined by the start tag. Not until the browser sees an end tag does it stop expecting the text to be of that type. Because elements can often be nested — not all elements can be nested within all other elements, but there are valid element nestings — it doesn't automatically assume a different start tag indicates the previous element type has ended. In fact, the browser assumes nothing. Forget about the benefit of the doubt. The browser takes everything you send it absolutely literally.

Vocabulary

Nesting. Placing elements within other elements. For example, in a table, the rows are nested within the table element, and the cells are nested within the row elements.

Between the start tag and the end tag, you place the *content*. In reality, you usually write the content first and put the start tag before your content, and then put your end tag after your content. A major cause of errors in HTML documents is forgetting the slash in the end tag. Be careful when you type your HTML and be sure you spell your tag names correctly, include both angle brackets, and include your backslash. Three examples of syntactically correct HTML follow:

```
<H1>This is the <B>bolded title</B> of the page</H1>
<B>This statement will be in bold.</B>
<I>This statement will be in italics.</I>
```

Recap: This stuff is really important!

Every element has a *name*.

The *start tag* is the element name surrounded by angle brackets.

The *end tag* always starts with a slash, has the element name, and is surrounded by angle brackets.

Most elements have content, which occurs between the start and the end tags.

Some elements have no content.

Some elements have no end tags.

Some elements don't take any content, such as `BR`, which forces a line break. Some elements have optional end tags, such as `LI` and `P`, which are list item and paragraph elements. When we explain an element, we tell you whether it has any content and whether it has a required end tag. Elements are case-insensitive: `<TITLE>`, `<Title>`, and `<title>` are all the same to the browser. To make reading your mark-up easier, though, we recommend your element names be written in all caps. This is the convention this book uses.

Understanding Your Options: Attributes

Elements have attributes that give you flexibility in writing your HTML. Each element has its own unique attributes. You see patterns, but you can't just apply any old attribute to any old element.

Couples only: Fox Trot

Attributes have values. In fact, they come in pairs. If you are going to include an attribute, you have to include the value for that attribute. The value for the attribute is always enclosed in double quotes. Examples of attribute-value pairs are:

```
align="center"
width="33%"
size="12"
name="first_name"
```

Always shop from a list

The values for some attributes come from a list of acceptable values that the W3C creates, when it sets the standards. In the case of *valign* (an attribute frequently used to tell the browser where on the page you want an image or a table to appear, relative to text) your choices are: top, middle, bottom, and baseline. In the next chapter, you learn the shorthand for the element rules.

Please take a number

Some attributes take numbers as their values. In some cases, the numbers can be either a set number (usually of pixels, which are just the dots on your screen — comparable to DPI, the measurement for dots on your printer) or a percentage. For example, when you define a table, you may want the first column to be 25 percent of the screen width, the second column to be 50 percent of the screen width, and the third column to be 25 percent of the screen width. Regardless of how the screen is sized, it changes size to fit in proportionately. If you were to assume the screen was 636 pixels and divide it yourself, the last column of the table may not be visible if the visitor to your page didn't have the browser open in full-screen mode. For a form, however, when you indicate the *size* (one of the attributes for text fields) of a field, you are indicating the number of characters. For an image, when you indicate the *width* (one of the attributes for object elements), you are indicating the number of pixels.

The colors of the world

In both the HTML document itself and in the style sheet, some attributes take a color for a value. As you may have noticed, colors don't appear the same from one monitor to the next. You can, however, say a lot with colors. For example, take a page where everything is in seafoam green or watermelon; this page says: beach.

Cross-Reference

Not only don't colors look the same from one monitor to the next, Macs and PCs actually use different system palettes. Chapter 34 covers this topic in detail.

Just as with everything else, an HTML way exists to convey information about colors. HTML gives you two choices: the name of the color (from their approved list) and the hex (hexadecimal) representation of the color. Only 16 named colors exist, so if you are picky about the color you use, then you'll want to find the hex representation of that color.

Another thing you should know about colors on the computer is that colors are composed of red, green, and blue, thus the *RGB scale*. In hex, the first two digits are the amount of red, the next two are green, and the next two are blue. So FF0000 would be pure red. Did we mention the highest any digit can go is *F*? We discuss this next. One more thing: 000000 is black; FFFFFF is white. That's not very intuitive, so you just have to remember when you add color to the screen, it gets lighter. Unlike paper, which is white when blank, the screen is black when blank.

When you indicate the value of an attribute is a color and you use hex representation, you need to precede the hex value with a # (pound sign). The 16 named colors are listed in Table 4-1 with their hex names. If you know you want a color between two of the colors in the chart, try selecting the value between the two hex values. First, you must know how to count in hex. *Hex* counts from 1 to 9, then A, B, C, D, E, and F. If you need to add 1 to F, you go to 10 (that's one-zero, not *ten*). Try this math problem along with us: 5 plus 6 is B. Plus 5 is 10. Plus 7 is 17. Minus 9 is E. That's not too hard, is it? Fortunately, we don't need to multiply or divide in hex!

Table 4-1
Color Codes in Hex

Color Name	Hex Representation
Black	#000000
Green	#008000
Silver	#C0C0C0
Lime	#00FF00
Gray	#808080
Olive	#808000"
White	#FFFFFF
Yellow	#FFFF00
Maroon	#800000
Navy	#000080
Red	#FF0000
Blue	#0000FF
Purple	#800080
Teal	#008080
Fuchsia	#FF00FF
Aqua	#00FFFF

A few cool resources for selection are on the Web. Visit this hIdaho Designs Web site (see Figure 4-1) at `http://www.hidaho.com/colorcenter/cc.html`

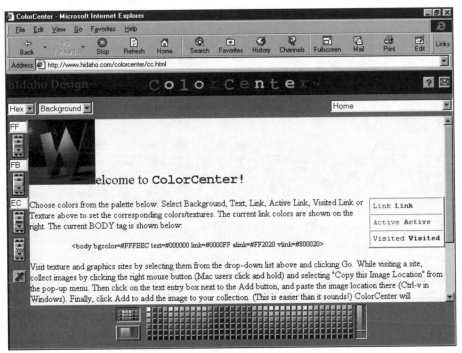

Figure 4-1: hIdaho Designs' very intuitive color selection tool

Or, this one (see Figure 4-2), published by Rafael Garrido: `http://www.ctv.es/USERS/rafa/lab/lab-uk.htm`

Either Web site will convince you that you needn't do math in hex to find the color of your dreams.

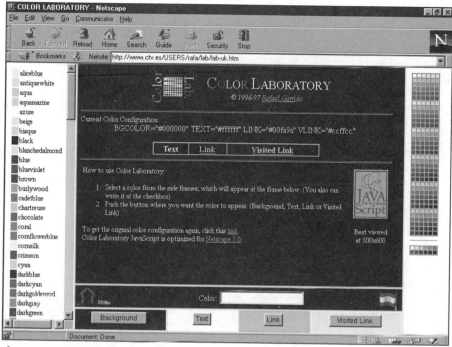

Figure 4-2: Rafael Garrido's excellent color selection tool

Creativity counts

For some elements, the attribute value is something you make up yourself. For example, if you want to create a form and you want people to enter their first names, you assign the value of the attribute *name* to be "first_name." Normally, when you are working with fields, some server-side scripting is going on. Your field names should match the names you expect in your script.

Recap: More important stuff!

Attributes are specific to the elements they modify.

Attributes always have values.

Attribute values must be enclosed in double quotes.

Attribute values can be one from a list, a number, a percentage, or a name of your creation.

Using Special Characters: Entities

Another example of the W3C's penchant for academic vocabulary, *entities* are simply characters you may want to display that don't appear on your keyboard or are characters with special significance to HTML (notably <,>,&,"). The most common of these are © (copyright) and ™ (trademark). Three ways exist to write a code for an entity in your HTML. Whichever way you choose, you will find all entities begin with an ampersand (&) and end with a semicolon (;):

✦ **Using character notation.** While this is the easiest way to show an entity, there isn't a character notation for every single entity. For the most common ones, there are character representations. For example, © is the entity for the copyright symbol. Character notation to indicate entities is one of the rare parts of HTML that is case-sensitive.

✦ **Using decimal notation.** The decimal representation of a copyright symbol is ©. Sure, you knew that!

✦ **Using hex notation.** Programmers dig this method. Instead of © to indicate the copyright symbol, they get to type ©, which is, obviously, way cooler. For the rest of the population, knowing A9 in hex (hexadecimal notation) equals 169 in the decimal system is useful. All hex numbers are preceded by a lowercase *x*.

Entities exist for many foreign languages, mathematical symbols, and English symbols that either can't be produced on a normal keyboard or are special to HTML. For example, if you wanted to write "Good idea" in Greek, but the bulk of your document was English, you'd write:

```
&Kappa;&alpha;&lambda;&eta;&eta;&delta;&epsilon;&alpha;
```

which would render as: Καληιδεα.

Table 4-2 has the entities you will need most often, if you aren't planning to include foreign languages in your pages to any great extent. A complete list of entities can be found in Appendix F.

Table 4-2
Common Entities

Character notation	Hex notation	Entity created
		nonbreak space
&iexcl;	&#161;	inverted exclamation mark
&cent;	&#162;	cent sign
&pound;	&#163;	pound sign
&curren;	&#164;	currency sign
&yen;	&#165;	yen sign
&brvbar;	&#166;	broken bar
&sect;	&#167;	section sign
&uml;	&#168;	diaeresis
&copy;	&#169;	copyright sign
&ordf;	&#170;	feminine ordinal indicator
&laquo;	&#171;	left-pointing double-angle quotation mark
&not;	&#172;	not sign
&shy;	&#173;	discretionary hyphen
&reg;	&#174;	registered trademark sign
&macr;	&#175;	macron
&deg;	&#176;	degree sign
&plusmn;	&#177;	plus or minus sign
&sup2;	&#178;	superscript two
&sup3;	&#179;	superscript three
&acute;	&#180;	acute accent
&micro;	&#181;	micro sign
&para;	&#182;	paragraph sign
&sup1;	&#185;	superscript one
&ordm;	&#186;	masculine ordinal indicator
&raquo;	&#187;	right-pointing double-angle quotation mark
&frac14;	&#188;	fraction one quarter
&frac12;	&#189;	fraction one half
&frac34;	&#190;	fraction three quarters
&iquest;	&#191;	inverted question mark

Adding Comments to Your HTML

You have spent so much time with your HTML, no way could you ever forget what you were thinking when you wrote it, right? Maybe, maybe not. Most people can't remember where they put the bank statement they meant to balance from last month. How can you expect to remember what you were thinking if you have to modify your HTML in six months?

Realistically, you want to use comments in your HTML to tell yourself — and anyone who inherits your files — basic information about what you are doing in there. For example, putting a comment line near the top of your document telling who created the file and on what date is pretty standard. If you expect your HTML to be a teaching tool at all, with people viewing the source to see how you did things, then you want to have especially helpful comments.

Begin your comment with <!--. Any text you put after the two dashes is comment. The browser will not even try to read it. Even if you use special characters, such as ampersands and slashes and quotes and angle brackets; your browser ignores everything it comes across until it sees -->. Your comments can span multiple lines. The browser doesn't care. It is only looking for -->.

Later, in Chapter 14, we discuss the use of special programs that increase your productivity when you write your HTML.

One of the nice features of most of these programs is colored tags. If your editor changes the color of the tags, then you can see visually whether you have remembered to close your comments — or whether the rest of your document will be processed as a comment (usually not what you want).

Making Your HTML Readable

Most of the mark up of your HTML document (that is, the actual HTML elements that mark up your content) is case-insensitive. This means you can pretty much type your HTML as you please. You don't want to work this way, though, because you want your HTML to be readable both to you and to others. Consider the following HTML:

```
<html><head><title>Over the Web, Inc.</title></head><body>
<object type="img/gif" src="logo-f.gif" height="155" width
="90"><h1>List, Email, and Relationship Management 1.15</h1>
<p>Would you like to have a more effective and effortless
way to solicit your potential customer base on the Web?</p>
<p><i>Over The Web Stay in Touch&reg;</i> List, Email, and
Relationship Management allows you to add a page to your
```

```
Web site where your customers can sign in. You can then send
mail to them based on the interests they indicate. The system
is entirely configurable by you. You can change the background
color, add your logo to the top of your page, and customize the
interests your customers indicate.</p>
```

What a mess! Even if you know what all the tags mean, you won't want to dive into that! Now consider:

```
<HTML>
<HEAD>
<TITLE>Over the Web, Inc.</TITLE>
</HEAD>
<BODY>
<OBJECT type="img/gif" src="logo-f.gif" height="155"
width="90">
<H1>List, Email, and Relationship Management 1.15</H1>
<P>Would you like to have a more effective and effortless
way to solicit your potential customer base on the Web?</P>
<P><I>Over The Web Stay in Touch&reg;</I> List, Email, and
Relationship Management allows you to add a page to your Web
site where your customers can sign in. You can then send mail
to them based on the interests they indicate. The system is
entirely configurable by you. You can change the background
color, add your logo to the top of your page, and customize
the interests your customers indicate.</P>
```

This is much friendlier on the eyes. We encourage you to make use of white space in your file (as well as in your pages, which we discuss later). The file won't be any larger (each line of blank space is only sent as one or two bytes of data).

Another convention you may have noticed is the use of all caps for element names and lowercase for attribute-value pairs. You needn't be fanatical about this. If the editor you use does something else, don't worry. Being consistent and leaving lots of white space when you write your markup, though, makes maintenance easier.

Avoiding Common Syntax Errors

Syntax isn't a tax on cigarettes and beer. *Syntax* is the rules of a language. In English, you don't even think about syntax. You know most sentences have a syntax of subject-verb-object. You know not to say (poets excluded): "Wrote the book me."

HTML has syntax, too. When you break the rules, it is politely referred to as a syntax error. When you sit down to start writing HTML, you may find one of the following in your page:

Everything from the first italicized word on is italicized.

You can see one of your tags in your browser.

A form field does not appear, even though you know you created it in HTML.

Figure 4-3 shows these syntax errors appearing on a Web page.

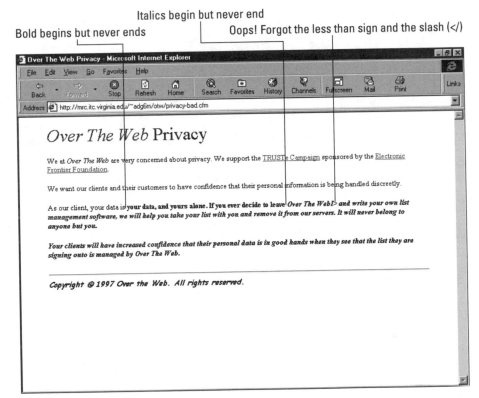

Figure 4-3: Common syntax errors

Checklist for avoiding common errors when writing HTML

√ Do you have angle brackets surrounding the start and end tags?

√ Do you have a slash at the beginning of your end tag?

√ Do you have quotes around the values of your attributes?

√ Are all the attributes for your tags valid?

Understanding Nesting

As we discussed, sometimes you want to nest elements within other elements. For example, you may want to italicize something that occurs in a paragraph. You've seen the paragraph element, P, in all our examples. The italics element is I. In the previous code example (see "Making Your HTML Readable"), the words "Over the Web Stay in Touch" are italicized within a paragraph.

Many valid types of nesting exist. For example, nearly any element you put within the BODY element is valid, except for the HEAD element. Some things you can't nest, such as a link inside a link.

What is important to remember about nesting is you must close the inner element before you close the outer element. Consider this example of *invalid* HTML:

```
<H1>Over the Web Presents <I>Stay In Touch</H1></I>
```

The *valid* equivalent of this would be:

```
<H1>Over the Web Presents <I>Stay In Touch</I></H1>
```

Because the I element was the last one opened, it must be the first one closed. Be careful to close the inner element before you close the outer element. Most browsers know what to do with the previous invalid HTML but, as more and more elements become available, browsers will enforce rules more strictly. A day may come when the previous invalid HTML does not render properly.

The Basic Structure of an HTML Document: HEAD and BODY

A valid HTML 4 document has three parts:

1. **Version information.** This is also called the document type declaration used by this document. Earlier, we discussed that HTML is a document type declaration (DTD) of SGML. Three HTML DTDs exist; the version information should include which DTD you are using. If you are using an HTML editor, it takes care of this for you. If not, you will be safe using `<!DOCTYPE HTML PUBLIC "-//W3C//DTD HTML 4-0 Frameset//EN" "http://www.w3.org/TR/PR-html40/frameset.dtd">`, which is the most permissive of the three.

2. **The HEAD.** The HEAD, in addition to being part of the HTML element, is an element of its own. The HEAD element can contain the title and meta data.

3. **The BODY.** Everything else you want to put into an HTML document belongs in the BODY. The BODY, like the HEAD, is also an element.

What we haven't mentioned yet is HTML itself is an element. The HTML element has both a start tag and an end tag. The start tag should be placed after the version information and before the start tag of the HEAD element. The end tag goes at the very end of your document, after the end tag of the BODY element.

```
<!DOCTYPE HTML PUBLIC "-//W3C//DTD HTML 4-0 Frameset//EN"
"http://www.w3.org/TR/PR-html40/frameset.dtd">
<HTML>
<HEAD>
<TITLE>My Valid HTML document</TITLE>
</HEAD>
<BODY>
If this had been an actual HTML document, this is where I would
have put the content.

</BODY>
</HTML>
```

The previous code example shows how a valid HTML document is structured. Notice how the BODY element is closed before the HTML element is closed.

From Here

Cross-Reference

For the more practical-minded, proceed to Chapter 5 to begin creating a Web page.

For the more theoretical-minded, jump to Chapter 7 to read about the potential of hypertext, but realize, eventually, you need to take the plunge and actually *write* some HTML.

Summary

HTML syntax is straightforward. If you follow a few simple rules, you won't find your HTML document full of syntax errors and, more important, your pages will look right in a browser. The basic building block of HTML is an element. Elements have attributes that enable you to customize them. Attributes require values. Values should be enclosed in double quotes.

Most elements have both start tags and end tags. These tags surround the content. Both the start tags and end tags consist of the element name surrounded by angle brackets. The end tag has a slash before the element name, within the angle brackets.

An HTML document should have version information at the top. After that comes the HTML element, which consists of a HEAD and a BODY. To ensure you have nested elements properly, always close the inner element before you close the outer element.

✦   ✦   ✦

Creating Your First Web Page

Now that you understand a bit about how the Web works, how links work and why they matter, what's involved in publishing a site, and the basics of HTML syntax, it's time to get your hands dirty (figuratively speaking, of course). By the end of this chapter, you'll have a working Web page. We won't make it do tricks yet, but it will have all the basics. Later, we can add the bells and whistles.

Fire Up Your Editor

For this first Web page, you use the plain text editor that came built into your computer. If you are on a PC running Windows 95 or Windows NT, from the Start Menu, select Program and then select Accessories and then select Notepad. You will see something similar to Figure 5-1. If you are on a Mac, open SimpleText and you will see something similar to Figure 5-2. If you are in a UNIX environment, open your text editor of choice (vi, pico, jove, or emacs).

Even if you have some fancy tool that was bundled with your computer when you purchased it, or you downloaded from the Web, or you purchased yourself, don't use it yet. There's time for productivity-enhancing tools later. Right now, you need to learn some basic HTML and, depending on the HTML-development program you have, it may get in your way.

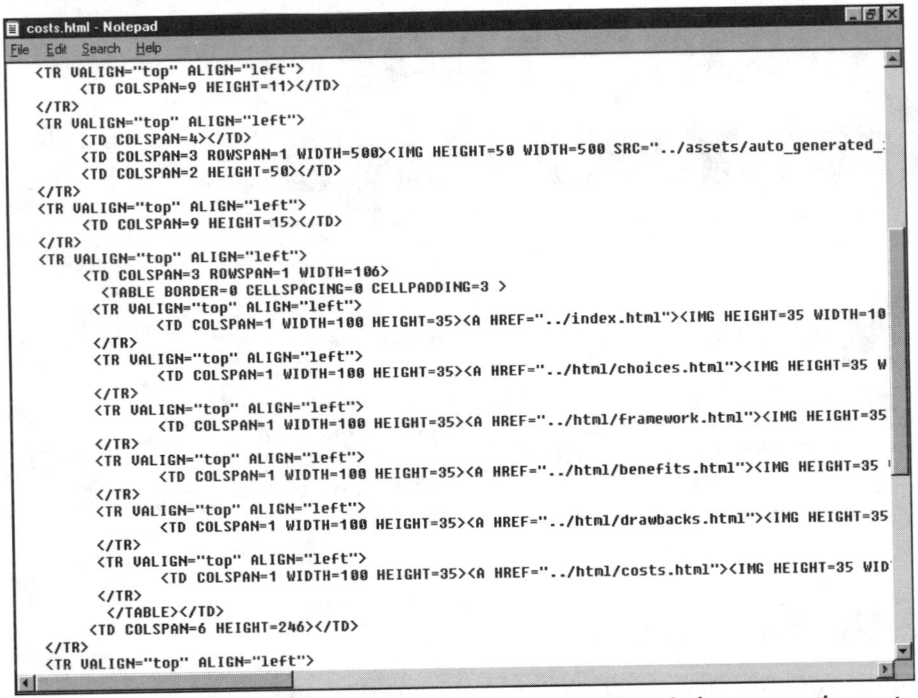

Figure 5-1: NotePad is the text editor that comes with the Windows operating systems.

Titling Your Page

Have you ever tried to set a bookmark for a page, only to find the bookmark had a meaningless name? This was a particular problem in earlier browsers, which didn't permit you to edit bookmark properties. Why didn't a meaningful name — or, sometimes, any name at all — show up in your bookmark list? The inconsiderate or careless Web developer hadn't bothered to put a title into the page.

The TITLE element is among the simplest elements. It takes no attributes. In previous versions of HTML, a title was not required. Under HTML 4, absence of a title is a syntax violation. Both a start tag and an end tag are required.

Using as descriptive a title as possible is always a good idea. In addition to showing up in the bookmark folder, the title also displays across the top of your browser. Some Web developers have been in the habit of titling all their pages with the same title — usually the name of the company. This isn't a useful practice because the title should impart useful information. Unlike book titles, where publishers may be imposing limits, with Web page titles, you can take all the words you need to convey your message — within limits, of course. The two major browsers support title length between 96 and 100 characters. Because search engines frequently use the title of your page as the heading for the entry to your page, it is triply important for you to use a good, descriptive title.

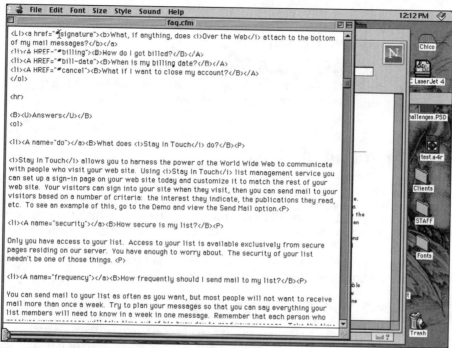

Figure 5-2: SimpleText comes with the Mac OS.

First things first

As you learned in the last chapter, the TITLE element goes in the HEAD element. But where does the HEAD element go? That's right — in the HTML element. So, before you can really put a title on your page, you want to write the following into your empty document:

✦ Version information

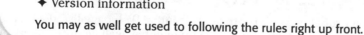

You may as well get used to following the rules right up front.

✦ The HTML element start tag

✦ The HEAD element start tag

Consider this your first quiz. We give you the answer to the requirement for version information, so you don't have to flip back a few pages, but you must remember what the HTML and HEAD start tags look like.

```
<!DOCTYPE HTML PUBLIC "-//W3C//DTD HTML 4.0 Strict//EN"
"http://www.w3.org/TR/PR-html40/Strict.dtd">
```

Go ahead and add the HTML element start tag and the HEAD element start tag next. Be sure to put each of these on a separate line. If you want, you can leave blank lines between these tags, as well.

Next, we add the title, which requires the TITLE element start tag: <TITLE>. The content for the TITLE element should be your actual page title, so put that next. At the end of your content, put the TITLE element end tag: </TITLE>.

Identifying the Author

If you recall, we said one other thing went into the HEAD of an HTML document which was meta data. *Meta data* is information about the information on your page. This would include the name of the author, the software in which the page was written, the company name — if there is any — contact information, and so forth.

We won't go into the syntax of the META element right now. You want to indicate you are the author and there is a META element perfect for this:

```
<META name="Author" content="put your name here">
```

As you can see, the META element has at least two attributes. We have two in the previous example. The META element is unique because, instead of having content between a start tag and an end tag, the META element has a CONTENT attribute. And there is no end tag. You will see a variety of uses for the META element.

In general, you won't see anything from META elements displayed in your browser. The W3C leaves the implementation of the META element to the discretion of the browser. In the future, it is conceivable some of this data could be viewed from within your browser — yet another reason to include it.

Defining key words for better retrieval

While we realize you probably won't try to get this initial Web page listed with a search engine — although you certainly can — you might as well get into using good habits. A good habit to be in when creating a Web page is adding a META element for keywords.

Add the following tag to your document:

```
<META name="keywords" content="list of keywords">
```

where *list of keywords* is a comma-delimited list such as "list management, email, crossware, relationship management, guestbook, sign-in page." With some search engines, capitalization matters, so it is to your advantage to include "guestbook," "Guestbook," and "Guest Book" as three different keywords. Unfortunately, other search engines might interpret this as "spamming" — trying to fool them into listing you higher for a more relevant match.

A note about search engines

Most of the search engines use the META data you provide about keywords to help index your page. Rules exist about these things, but they change from search engine to search engine. Extensive resources are also on the Web for finding the techniques to get your page listed higher in the search engines. For example, one search engine automatically ignores any word listed more than seven times in the keyword string—even if it is listed in different ways. Knowing the rules when you submit with search engines is important. They are getting harder and harder to fool.

An interesting tool, which can help you identify what ranking your page is, on a variety of search engines is WebPosition Analyzer. At publication date, this was the only commercial software that could go out to a variety of search engines and find what number your site is, based on the keywords you provide. Many services will do this for you, but WebPosition Analyzer enables you to do it yourself on a scheduled basis, if you wish, from your own desktop. A trial version of WebPosition Analyzer is available as a free download at `http://www.webposition.com/cgi-local/index.pl?DS1=RP&DS2=7A9-55A6`. Figure 5-3 shows a screen from WebPosition Analyzer.

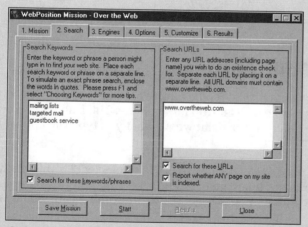

Figure 5-3: WebPosition Analyzer finds your site in all the search engines and reports back to you.

A variety of newsletters can tell you about tips and tricks to get your site listed higher. WebPosition Analyzer publishes its own newsletter. Another excellent one is Danny Sullivan's *Search Engine Report,* which you can subscribe to from the Search Engine Watch page (`http://www.searchenginewatch.com`).

Beginning the BODY

What do you have to do before you can begin the BODY element? Close the HEAD element. Go ahead and add the end tag for the HEAD element. Then add the start tag for the BODY element.

The BODY element has several attributes that you can use to customize the look of your document. In previous versions of HTML, this is where you set the background image, if there was one. This image would tile across the screen, which could look nice or it could look horrid. This is also where you would set the background color, the text color, the link color, the visited link color, and the active link color. In the HTML 4 Way, these presentational qualities are all set in the style sheet. This keeps down the amount of markup in your document and it keeps the visual clutter to a minimum when you are editing your document. The W3C refers to those BODY attributes as *deprecated.*. A deprecated element or attribute is one the W3C would rather you not use. In future versions of HTML, that element or attribute might not work in browsers or might do something unexpected. For now, all the major browsers support deprecated elements. This means you won't have any problems with them, but it is a good idea to try to steer clear of them as you develop new pages.

Adding an Apparent Title

Going along with these instructions and typing junk everytime we instruct you to type content would be easy. Instead, let's stop for a minute. Think about what you want on your page. We are finally at the point where what you type will appear in your browser window.

What did you entitle your page, using the previous TITLE element? Is this really what you want to call your page? If not, go back and change it. Later on in the book, we focus at length on the content of your page, but that doesn't mean you want to publish junk until then.

To add a title to your page, we use the heading elements. In the HTML 4 Way, all we do is tell the browser this is a heading, along with the importance of this heading (number 1 being the most important and number 6 being the least important). As far as presentation goes, we can either let the browser have its way with our headings or we can use style sheets to define the presentation.

Note   Don't be confused by the terms used here. When we discuss the TITLE element, you see the term as uppercase code font. In this discussion of using heading elements on pages, we use title in lowercase.

The heading elements are: H1, H2, H3, H4, H5, and H6. Don't try to make them look the way you want your page to look. We can do this later with style sheets. For now, just assign them to headings in order of importance. If you have been in the habit of adding an align attribute, you want to stop doing that. W3C deprecates the use of align as an attribute of heading elements (that's why style sheets are used).

Figure 5-4 shows how you may use elements H1, H2, and H3 to indicate varying degrees of importance in your page. The HTML follows:

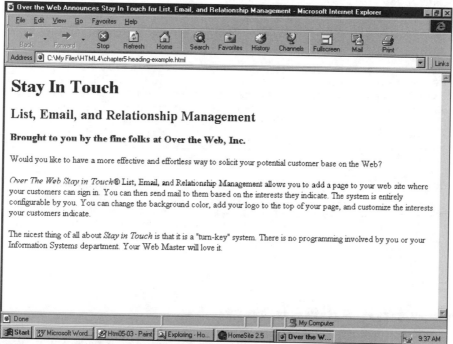

Figure 5-4: Example of using heading elements on your page

This is also a good time to check your own HTML. If the following markup doesn't match your own, you'll want to review your own and see what you missed. Of course, the content won't match.

```
<!DOCTYPE HTML PUBLIC "-//W3C//DTD HTML 4.0 Strict//EN"
"http://www.w3.org/TR/PR-html40/Strict.dtd">

<HTML>
<HEAD>
```

```
<TITLE>Over the Web Announces Stay In Touch for List, Email,
and Relationship Management</TITLE>
<META name="author" content="Alexis D. Gutzman">
<META name="keywords" content="list management, relationship
management, email, mailing lists, turn-key">
</HEAD>

<BODY>
<h1>Stay In Touch</h1>
<h2>List, Email, and Relationship Management</h2>
<h3>Brought to you by the fine folks at Over the Web, Inc.</h3>

<P>Would you like to have a more effective and effortless way
to solicit your potential customer base on the Web?</P>

<P><I>Over The Web Stay in Touch&reg;</I> List, Email, and
Relationship Management allows you to add a page to your web
site where your customers can sign in. You can then send mail
to them based on the interests they indicate. The system is
entirely configurable by you. You can change the background
color, add your logo to the top of your page, and customize the
interests your customers indicate.</P>

<P>The nicest thing of all about <I>Stay in Touch</I> is that
it is a "turn-key" system. There is no programming involved by
you or your Information Systems department. Your Web Master
will love it.</P>
</BODY>

</HTML>
```

Typing and Editing Text

Now you want to enter your text—the main content of your page. You may want to use two types of text: paragraphs and blockquotes.

Paragraphs

Most prose is divided into paragraphs. HTML provides the P element to identify paragraphs. The P element has a start tag and an end tag. You put your content between the two. For our purposes in this section, we won't include any attributes. The one you may have seen or used in the past was the align attribute, but as we noted, that is deprecated by the W3C.

Blockquotes

The other kind of prose you may want to include is a quote from someone else. If this quote extends beyond a line or two, you will want to set it off in its own block. This is the way we often see reviews of software or reviews of pages. The following figure shows two quoted paragraphs from Marc Andreesen in a Netscape White Paper:

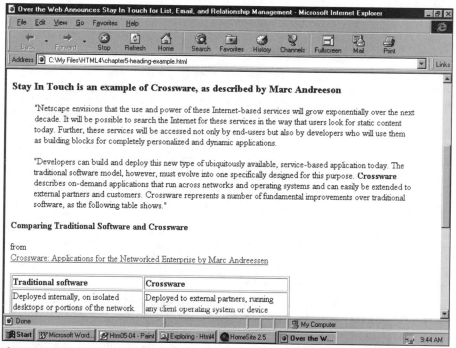

Figure 5-5: A blockquote

Breaking Lines and Starting New Paragraphs

Sometimes you want to add extra blank space. Perhaps you have text that doesn't belong in a paragraph. In the previous example, after the table heading, we have the word *from* on its own line. To achieve this, we inserted the BR element after the table heading. We wouldn't have wanted this word to be a paragraph by itself, in part, because, structurally, it is not. Had we made this word a paragraph, and in a style sheet indicated that paragraphs should have a half-inch indentation on the first line, then this word would have been indented a half inch. Wouldn't that look strange?

The BR element takes no attributes. It only has a start tag. There is no content and no end tag. This is the easiest element to get right.

```
<H4>Comparing Traditional Software and Crossware</H4>
<p>from <BR>
<A HREF=
"http://developer.netscape.com/library/wpapers/crossware/index.
html">Crossware: Applications for the Networked Enterprise by
Marc Andreessen</a>
```

Preventing line breaks

The opposite of creating a line break is preventing a line break. Sometimes you want a string of words to appear all on the same line. For example: March 1788. For a variety of reasons, you may always want March and 1788 to appear on the same line. You can prevent automatic wrapping of lines resulting in March appearing at the end of one line and 1788 appearing at the beginning of the next line by inserting a nonbreaking space between *March* and *1788*. The nonbreaking space is an entity (remember, in entities — unlike the rest of HTML — capitalization *does* matter), as described in Chapter 4, but it is not a printable character. To insert a nonbreaking space, you can use either the character representation of   or the decimal representation of . Thus, March 1788 would look like:

```
March 1788
```

Adding horizontal lines

Your page may benefit from horizontal lines. For example, it is not unusual to see a horizontal line between the page and footer text. *Footer text* is text that appears on every page and is not specifically related to the content of the page. For example, at the bottom of this page of the book, there may be a page number or a section name. You almost always see footers on magazine pages.

On a Web page, a footer usually includes copyright information, perhaps the date of publication of the page, and how to contact the Webmaster. Particularly pathetic pages still include *hit counts* which in no way represent the actual number of visitors, even if they say they do. We discuss the meaning (lessness) of Web site statistics, particularly hit counts, later in this book. Figure 5-6 is an example of a page footer with the perfunctory horizontal line.

The horizontal rule HR element is almost as foolproof as the BR element. It requires a start tag, forbids an end tag, and has no content. If you have any memories of using attributes with the HR element, forget them. Any formatting attributes are deprecated by the W3C.

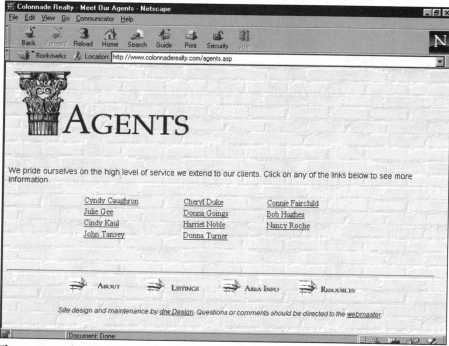

Figure 5-6: The horizontal rule element is right at home in the footer of a page.

Creating a List

You may want to include a list for many reasons:

✦ You think in lists

✦ You are trying to persuade people and you want to make your evidence clear

✦ You use lists as shorthand

✦ You want people to know the sequence of events in instructions

✦ You know people more often remember material set apart from the main text

✦ You just want an example of a list

Whatever your reasons, HTML accommodates your wish for a list. Three types of lists actually exist in HTML:

✦ Bulleted lists (called *unordered lists*)

✦ Numbered lists (called *ordered lists*)

✦ Definition lists

We discuss them all in further detail, later in the book, but for now, we plan to discuss only bulleted lists and numbered lists.

Bulleted lists

You and I call them bulleted lists, or simply bullet lists, but HTML calls them *unordered lists*. An unordered list is created with the UL element. For each item in the list, you need the LI element.

The UL element requires a start tag and an end tag. Between those go each item on your list. You can, of course, include other text between the start and end tags, but unless that other text is part of the LI element, it won't appear with a bullet in front of it.

The LI element requires a start tag. The end tag is optional. Following the start tag, you put whatever you want in the list. Each item in your list gets its own LI element. Witness:

```
<UL>

<LI> Have a custom sign-in page on your Website today!
<LI> Collect information from your customers right on your Web
site
<LI> Send email to your customers
<!--LI> Export customer information to spreadsheet, database,
or word processing software for paper mailings-->
<LI> Add your logo, set the background color or graphic to
match the rest of your Web site

</UL>
```

Cross-Reference   You can do other interesting tricks with unordered lists such as nesting them, but we save this for Chapter 17, where we cover lists in depth.

Numbered lists

A numbered list uses the OL element (ordered list). The OL element requires a start tag and an end tag. Each item in the list is part of its own LI element. You use the exact same LI element as in the ordered list. Look at the following code:

```
<H2>Setting up your list is as Easy as 1-2-3</H2>

<OL>
<LI> Get a Stay in Touch Account
<LI> Click through our easy set-up wizard to customize your
pages
<LI> Link to your list from your Web site
</OL>
```

Figure 5-7 shows what the browser does with your lists.

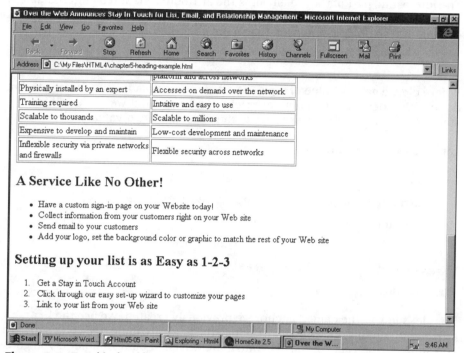

Figure 5-7: Two kinds of lists

Adding a Link

How can you create a hypertext page without a link—*at least one* link? The syntax for linking is quite simple. You use the A (anchor) element to create a link. Just for fun, let's put one link in your document to something else in your document. The other link, we'll put to the IDG Books Web site. For now, we'll use text to link to the IDG Books Web site but, before you know it, we'll use an image from the CD-ROM in the back of the book. You wondered what was on the CD, didn't you?

Simply, here is the syntax for the A element. Both a start tag and an end tag are required. For the *hot text* (that is, the text that can be clicked to jump elsewhere), content is required. For the destination of the link, content is optional, but we recommend you do include content because some browsers won't find a *named anchor* (the W3C term for destination) that does not have content.

Adding an internal link

The interesting part of the A element is the attributes. To add an internal link, you use the A element to create both the link and the destination. First, we create the destination. To do this, you need to use the name attribute of the A element, thus:

```
<A name="Features">Features of this product include:</A>
```

Where did we get the value of the name attribute? We made it up. What good does it do to have a destination in our page right now? None. But we can use it in conjunction with hot text elsewhere in the page to make it valuable.

Let's dissect the previous A element, just for review:

Start tag:	`<A name="Features">`
Attribute-value pair:	`name="Features"`
Attribute:	`name`
Value:	`Features`
Content:	`Features of this product include:`
End tag:	`</A>`

Now, let's link to the named anchor we previously created. We use the href attribute to do this. As with all attributes, the href attribute needs a value. What do you suppose the value of the href attribute will be in our example? If you guess *features*, you are getting good at this. We just need to add one little twist. We need to add a # (pound sign) in front of the value, inside the double-quotes.

```
Stay in Touch is loaded with <A href="#Features">
features</A> that no other product has.
```

When you look at this code in a browser, you can't see the named anchor, but if you click the highlighted (underlined in Figure 5-8) word *features*, you can jump to the features list. The browser knows where the named anchors are, but it doesn't show them to you.

You've done the harder version; now let's do the easy version.

Adding an external link

When you link to someplace outside your page, whether this is within your site or on some distant server, you use the A element with the href attribute, such as in the immediately preceding example. Pointing to a page somewhere else requires a little more than is required when pointing to a place within your document. The value of the href attribute will be a bit longer.

Link from   Link to

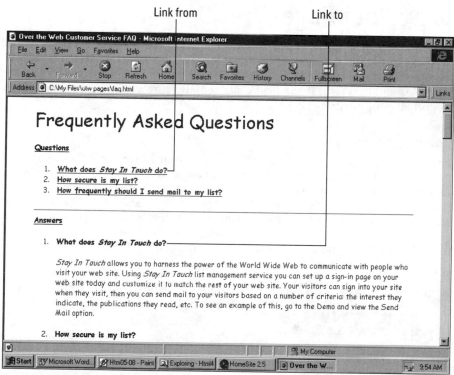

Figure 5-8: An internal link

For this example, you are going to point to the IDG Books Worldwide page. You decided, somewhere on your page, you want to mention your page uses The HTML 4 Way. This should look familiar to you, with one twist. The value of the href attribute is a URL: the home page of IDG Books.

```
<A href="http://www.idgbooks.com">This page was created The
HTML 4 Way</A>
```

That's not the sexiest text, but later we'll replace it with an image, anyway. For now, you have a working link to a distant server. Isn't that the point of this whole hypertext thing, anyway?

Caution

STOP: Save your file now! Call it **MyFirst.html** unless you are working in Windows 3.1, in which case, you need to call it **MyFirst.htm.** If you are working in Windows 3.1, you'll want to remember that everytime we talk about your files as *something*.html, your files will actually be *something*.htm, okay? That's the last time we'll mention it.

Preview Your Page

Now that you've saved your page, you can open it in a browser and look at it. If anything doesn't look the way you expected, you'll want to review the *Checklist for avoiding common errors when writing HTML* that appeared at the end of Chapter 4. Check for end tags (and those pesky slashes). Be sure you have double quotes around all your attributes.

Opening a local file

You are probably used to opening Web pages in your browser by clicking on the *location* line and typing a URL. The page you have created isn't sitting on a Web browser, so there isn't a URL for it yet. But you can still see your page in your browser. How? On the File Menu of your browser, you'll see either Open Page or Open (depending on the browser maker and version). Select whichever one you have.

You will get a dialog box, like the one shown in Figure 5-9.

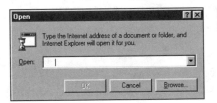

Figure 5-9: File open dialog box from Internet Explorer 4

Select either Choose File or Browse, depending upon which you have on your screen. Using the standard file management dialog box that opens up, find your HTML file, called MyFirst.html. Select it. Then click Open.

For the remainder of this session, when you make changes to your HTML file, you can just click the Reload or Refresh button at the top of your browser to see your changes.

Finishing Touches

Break out that CD-ROM!

Because you've been good and followed the HTML 4 Way, you're about to be rewarded. We have created four different style sheets to make your page look truly marvelous, darling! This last section tells you where to find the style sheets files, where to copy the style sheets files, and how to link to them.

Loading your style sheets

You could certainly link to style sheets on your CD-ROM without ever copying them, but, because we assume someday you may want to use your CD drive for something else, we'll tell you how to get them loaded onto your computer.

On the CD-ROM

Copy the four files located in the **Chap5** folder on your CD to the same directory where you stored your HTML file called MyFirst.html.

The files are called:

```
prof.css
wild.css
retro.css
earthy.css
```

If you want to, you can open them in your text editor and look at them. We tell you what this all means later. If you do open them to read, don't modify them yet. There's time for that later.

Linking to style sheets

Linking to a style sheet requires the use of the LINK element. This is a completely different type of link than linking to another page. The LINK element takes a start tag, no end tag, no content, and three attributes (when we use it to link to an external style sheet).

The first attribute is the href attribute. You should recognize the href attribute from the previous A element; it does exactly the same thing here. In this case, the value of the href attribute is the name of your style sheet. Because all four style sheets are in the same directory where your HTML file is located, you needn't add any directory information in the href attribute. We discuss later how you do this when your style sheets are stored elsewhere.

The next attribute is the rel (relationship) attribute. This attribute specifies the relationship of this link to your page. The two most common relationship values are *stylesheet*, which means this is the default style sheet for this page and *alternate stylesheet*, which means this is the alternate style sheet for this page. Because this page only has one style sheet (be patient—we get to the fancy stuff later), you use *stylesheet* as the value of the rel attribute.

The final attribute should tell you the LINK element has more than one use. In this case, we use the LINK element to link to a style sheet, so the value of the type attribute is *text/css* (meaning the file is only text and the extension of the file is *css*, which happens to be the extension of the files you copied from the CD-ROM).

This give us the completed tag:

```
<LINK href="prof.css" rel="stylesheet" type="text/css">
```

You want to put this tag into your HEAD element. It can go anywhere in the HEAD, but we suggest you put it after your META elements. Then you want to save your file and pull it up in your browser. Don't feel you must close out your text editor to see your file or close your browser to edit your file. This will only slow you down. The text editor hardly takes up any resources, anyway.

Note

In case you aren't used to having more than one software program open at a time, you'll find it useful to know, first, that you can have more than one program open and, second, how to switch between them. If you are using any flavor of the Windows operating system, you can switch between open software packages by holding down your Alt key and pressing Tab. You will cycle through all the open software packages (including the Program Manager in Windows 3.1). When you see the icon of the package you want to use, let go of the Alt key. The software you left is still there; it is just in the background.

For a Mac, click the icon in the upper right-hand corner of the screen. You will see the icons of all open software. Click the one you want to use.

Change your style

Now, flip back to your text editor and change the value of the href attribute. Use one of the other style sheets. Save your file and look at it. Try them all out and see which one you like best.

Remember, you must first save your HTML file in your editor; then Reload or Refresh your page *before* you can see the changes you made.

The sequence is:

1. Edit your file in your text editor; save your changes.
2. Reload or Refresh your page in your browser.
3. View your changes.

HTML Elements in Shorthand

We intended this chapter to get you up to speed on the basics of marking up your text with elements. If all elements in the book and their attributes were explained in such length as those in this chapter, this book would be three times as thick as it is. This book uses shorthand to give you the basics of each element. This shorthand includes whether there is a start tag, whether there is any content, whether there is an end tag, and whether any of those are forbidden or optional. This shorthand also includes a list of attributes along with information about which, if any, are required, optional, deprecated, or obsoleted. For attributes, new attributes will be explained at length. Attributes you have seen before won't be explained.

Here are two examples:

List Item (LI)

Start Tag:	required
Content:	optional
End Tag:	optional
Attributes:	none

Blockquote (BLOCKQUOTE)

Start Tag:	required
Content:	required
End Tag:	required
Attributes:	`cite`: URL
	`id,class`: document-wide identifiers
	`lang`: language information
	`dir`: text direction
	`title`: element title
	`style`: inline style information

From Here

Cross-Reference

Proceed to Chapter 6 and learn about publishing your page. After all, everyone won't get to see your masterwork until it resides on a Web server.

Jump to Chapter 8 and define your special purpose. Remember, unless you have a carefully honed message, you won't effectively communicate it to your site visitors.

Already tired of typing all those tags? Jump to Chapter 14 and find the HTML-development software program that's right for you, from a comparison of nine.

Summary

Once you understand the structure of HTML, actually assembling your page is a snap. You want a title, some meta data about your page — those go into the HEAD of your document. Most pages have some headings in the BODY of the page. Add some text, perhaps a blockquote, some lists, and, of course, some links, and you have a solid foundation. You understand the structure of HTML, so actually assembling your page is a snap.

It really gets sexy when you add the style sheets. In one line of code, you can completely change the look of your page. Later, you learn to write your own style sheets, but you can always find some on the Web and link to those (why not?).

✦   ✦   ✦

Going Public!

Now that you have something to publish, you need to know how to get it to your Web server. Do you have a Web server? Do you have your own domain? What is your platform? In this chapter, we have a worksheet to help you get answers to the right questions.

Once you get your files up to your server, you want to organize them effectively so you always know how to link between files. We discuss the various approaches to organizing your files and weigh in with our opinion on the best way (as if we could resist). Finally, we discuss the methodology of testing your files. When you finish this chapter, you'll be ready to publish your files correctly, manage the directory structure, and test your site thoroughly.

Getting Your Facts Straight

To publish your page in a way visitors to your site can view it properly, you should know a few things. This section helps you ask the right questions of your system administrator, or ISP, if you have one, or to make the right decisions about deploying your own Web server, if you are thinking about this.

We start with the worksheet. If you already have this information at your fingertips, you can skip the definitions of each item and go directly to the detailed instructions about publishing.

Information on the Web site publishing worksheet

This worksheet is for you to fill out. Having this information in writing should be helpful, especially if you are doing something other than publishing for a month or so. You may well have forgotten how you did everything. You obviously don't need to write down your password. Many times a systems administrator creates a standard password for you and then you're expected to change it to something no one can guess. This would be the place to write the password the administrator gives you.

Web Site Publishing Worksheet

My Web server is:
____ on my desktop
____ not on my desktop

My Web server administrator is:
____ me
____ someone within my organization
____ someone outside my organization

My Web server platform is:
____ UNIX
____ Windows NT
____ Mac

My desktop platform is:
____ Windows 95
____ Windows NT
____ Mac
____ UNIX

My Web server name is:
DNS: _____
IP address: _____
NT domain: _____
NT name: _____
NT share name: _____

Contact information:
Name: _____
E-mail: _____
Phone: _____

My account information is:
Account ID: _____
Password: _____

Desktop Web Servers

Do you have your own Web server? If you hunt around on your computer, you may find you do have Web server software on your computer. The most common Web server software for your desktop is Personal Web Server by Microsoft, which is free from the Microsoft Web site, but others exist. You are most likely to have acquired one of these packages when downloading some Web-related software from a Web page.

You can install a desktop Web server, if you wish. Should you? Probably not. The disadvantages of using your desktop machine for a server outweigh the advantages. Consider the following pros and cons:

Pros

No charge for disk space usage. Most ISPs charge you by the megabyte you use, after some small initial amount included with your monthly fee. Many organizations have disk quotas enforced on their servers and getting more space is difficult or impossible. If you have a 2 GB hard drive and you want to have 1GB of images on your Web site, you can do it free on your desktop. (We discuss why you don't really want 1GB of images in your Web site later.)

You have control over the directory structure. Many of these pros are autonomy issues. This is certainly one. You may be working within an organization or with an ISP that has strict rules about where you can put HTML files, where you can put images, where you must put anything you want to execute (scripts), and where style sheets must be stored. If you can't live with those constraints, then you may need your own Web server.

You can create as many mappings as you like. Consider the URL http://www.overtheweb.com/purchase. You know there is a server called www.overtheweb.com, but is there really a directory called *purchase?* It doesn't matter. Your Web server can create virtual directories, called *mappings,* that point visitors to some remote location on the Web server with one easy-to-remember virtual directory name. Some ISPs charge you for creating mappings. They are convenient for you as a developer — creating links between documents — and for visitors, too.

Cons

You can't ever turn off your machine. You have to think twice when you want to install new software and it wants you to restart your computer to take effect. This is doubly true if you have any downloads from your site. Having a Web site going up and down all the time doesn't look professional.

You have to solve all your server problems yourself. Are you ready to start worrying about registry entries in Windows 95 or NT? The alternative is to turn your whole server administration over to someone else. Don't think of this as some big loss of autonomy. You don't learn how to dry-clean just so you can dry-clean a few suits and sweaters, do you? No. You are willing to depend on the dry cleaner to do it right because doing it yourself for the little you do simply isn't worth the trouble.

You must have a direct connection to the Internet with a permanent IP address. A dial-in connection to the Internet is inadequate. See the sidebar for more information about IP addresses and domain names.

(continued)

Pros

You can associate as many server-side applications with your Web site as you like. If you want to run any server-side processes, such as forms processing or database interaction, you may want to use something that isn't built into your desktop Web server. Most ISPs charge for the software and again for setup. Some ISPs charge by the month for using specialized server-side applications. Some organizations won't install server-side applications on their Web servers for maintenance reasons. On your own computer, you can install whatever you want.

Cons

Ease of publishing a page. This one applies to everyone. Publishing a page is as simple as saving it to the right directory on your hard drive.

Enterprise Web Servers

The alternative to a desktop Web server is an enterprise Web server. Many varieties of these exist: O'Reilly Web Site Pro, Netscape ONE, Microsoft Internet Information Server, Apache, and many others. Generally, they run on UNIX or Windows NT, although they can also run on Macs.

An enterprise Web server can be within your own organization or with your Internet service provider. In either case, there is a systems administrator who should be able to answer all your questions.

An enterprise Web server is usually a robust, turnkey environment for your Web site. It is directly connected to the Internet (as opposed to being connected by a modem). Usually there are backup procedures and an uninterruptable power supply (UPS) to prevent downtime due to power outages.

When you are the systems administrator

For some lucky few, you will have your own Web server and it will reside on a dedicated server—then you are a systems administrator. You are the person everyone else must come to for answers to these questions. You are the top dog.

As the systems administrator, you can have all the hard drive space you want, all the mappings you want, and, as long as it doesn't conflict with other vital services your server provides, you can install all the additional applications you want.

Publishing on Your Own Server

If you have your own server, you should know just where to save your files. If your server is an enterprise server, you may have to transport them using FTP, but you probably know about all this. When you are publishing to your own server, it's easy not to follow good practices of file organization. Heck, no one enforces any rules on you. For this reason, deciding on a directory structure and being disciplined about following your own rules is even more important. If you don't impose discipline on yourself, you can have a big mess on your hands in no time.

Cross-Reference   Skip down to the section called "Developing Directories to Store Your Pages and Graphics" to learn more about the choices of philosophies you have. Make some rules for yourself and follow them.

Publishing on Your Service Provider's Server

Mere mortals must consign themselves to publishing their pages on someone else's server. The major disadvantage is loss of autonomy: you have to play by someone else's rules. However constraining this sounds, its advantages are overwhelming.

✦ **A functioning, reliable server provides a turnkey environment for your site.** You needn't pull anything out of a box, install any software, or find answers to difficult technical questions. You just sit at your desk, develop your site, and then when the time comes, you publish to your site and everything works (from the server side, anyway).

✦ **Someone else already has answers to your questions.** Even though your systems administrator may be hard to find, he or she does have answers to your questions. Heck, at one time, your systems administrator didn't know the answers and had to find them out by doing research. It is so much easier for you.

✦ **More time to create Web sites.** What do systems administrators do? They install software. They answer questions from their users. They create new accounts. They answer questions from their users. They perform backups and restores. They answer questions from their users. They create Web sites. Oh, yeah, and they answer questions from their users. Your time can be spent developing great Web sites instead of all these other fun things.

As an industry, ISPs have grown out of nowhere. This isn't the place to discuss everything you need to consider before selecting an ISP, but know both great ones and awful ones exist. Ask for referrals. Let someone else keep an account at the awful one. If your ISP isn't great, switch. Even though they can't guarantee the network will always be up, your ISP should take great pains to keep you informed. This is the minimum you should demand.

Figure 6-1 shows an ISP network status page.

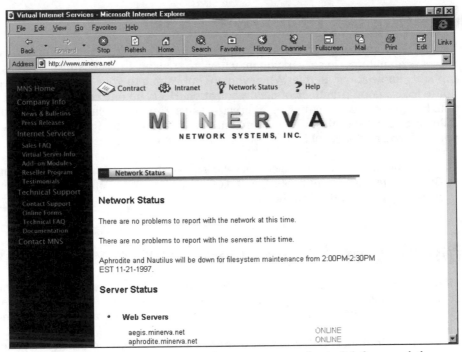

Figure 6-1: This Web site does more than attract new clients; it informs existing clients. Demand this from your own ISP.

Platform Issues

Now that you have found out who your systems administrator is, you can find out on what platform your Web server runs. How you move files between your desktop and your server depends on three things:

1. **Your desktop platform.** Are you sitting at a Mac, a PC, or a UNIX workstation, or at a terminal running x-window? Even if you are at a PC or a Mac, if you operate within the UNIX environment, for example, from a telnet session, UNIX is your platform.

2. **Your server platform.** Ask that elusive systems administrator.

3. **The HTML editor you use.** We discuss this in-depth in Chapter 14. The good HTML editors have built-in publishing capabilities. You can even save your file directly to a UNIX server from a PC or a Mac.

Because we don't yet know which HTML editor you'll like the best or even whether you want to fork out the dough to get one, and because your plain old text editor did such a nice job in the last chapter, we proceed assuming you don't have any fancy tools to get your pages to your server.

Extra: Publishing to an NT server

You lucky dog! Publishing to an NT server is easier than publishing to a UNIX server. Unlike UNIX, an NT server can be mapped as a hard drive on your PC or on your Mac. This means, instead of using FTP, which we discuss next, you can copy your files as if you were just copying them from one directory (or folder) to another. This won't work if you are running Windows 3.1 on your desktop (but why would anyone still be running Windows 3.1?).

From Windows 95

You can connect your Windows 95 desktop computer to an NT server in two ways: the easy way and the other way. The easy way isn't available to everyone, but everyone can use the other way.

First, the easy way:

1. **Make sure you have Client for Microsoft Networks and NetBEUI running.**
   You can do this by:

   a. From the Start Menu, Select Settings, and then Control Panel.

   b. Select the Network Control Panel.

   c. On the Configuration tab, make sure you have both Client for Microsoft Networks and NetBEUI listed, as shown in Figure 6-2.

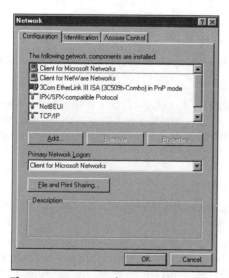

Figure 6-2: Network Control Panel in Windows 95

2. **If you don't, you must add them and then restart your computer.** Client for Microsoft Networks is a *Client* and NetBEUI is a *protocol*. Chances are, if these weren't already running, you won't be able to use the easy way.

3. **Open your Network Neighborhood.** If you see your NT server on the list of available machines, you're in luck. Try checking under Entire Network. Otherwise, skip down to the other way. You still need to have accomplished Step 1.

4. **Double-click the NT server that is your Web server.** This opens a window with all the share names on the NT server. These are directories or disks available to be shared, if you have permissions.

5. **Right-mouse click the share name you were instructed to use.** This brings up a list of the things you can do with the share.

6. **Select Map Network Drive.** This brings up a dialog box in which you can select which drive letter you want to associate with the server, as shown in Figure 6-3. You can actually map more than one drive from a single NT server; each would get a drive letter.

Figure 6-3: Mapping a network drive in Windows 95 is easy when your NT server is in your Network Neighborhood.

7. **Select the drive letter you want to associate with the NT server.**

8. **Check the Reconnect at Login box**, if you want to map to this drive each time you log in. If you don't check this box, you must repeat Steps 2–6 each time you want to copy or save files to your NT server.

Now, you can either save your HTML files directly to your Web server directory or save them to your local hard drive, wherever you want to put them, and then copy them to your Web server directory when you are ready to publish. Graphics files, which can sometimes be tricky, move over correctly if you just copy them this way.

Now, the other way:

1. **Make sure you have Client for Microsoft Networks and NetBEUI running.** See Step 1 under the easy way for instructions.

2. **Edit your HOSTS and LMHOSTS files.** These can be found in your Windows directory. If you don't have either one, create them. There may also be HOSTS.SAM and LMHOSTS.SAM files, but those are different files. Don't touch those! You need both the name, the domain name, and the IP address of your server. Your systems administrator can provide these for you. Here is what they need to have:

LMHOSTS file:

```
206.55.47.87 nautilus  #pre #dom:minerva
```

You can get the IP address from your systems administrator or, if he or she gives you the domain name—in this case, `nautilus.minerva.net`—you can go to a DOS prompt on any computer hooked up to the Internet and type **ping your.domain.name** and the system will return the IP address of `your.domain.name`. The domain name sometimes has four parts, as in `nmc.itc.virginia.edu`. The next item in the LMHOSTS file is the NT name of the server. You have to get this from your systems administrator. The `#pre` tells your system to preload this network connection. The `#dom:` tells the system it should find the `minerva domain`. Again, you need to get the domain name from your systems administrator.

HOSTS file:

```
206.55.47.87 nautilus.minerva.net
```

The item after the IP address is the domain name of the server. Both these files have no extensions. If you create them using Notepad, it adds `.txt` to the end of the file name. You must find them in your Windows directory and rename them *not* to have an extension.

3. **Restart your computer.**

4. **Sign into the Microsoft Networking dialog box with the ID and password provided by your systems administrator** (even if this isn't what you normally do). You may get weird errors from your regular servers, if you normally sign into a server other than the NT Web server (such as a different NT server or a Netware server), but just click through them.

5. **Right-mouse click Network Neighborhood.** You get a list of the things you can do with networking.

6. **Select Map Network Drive.** This brings up the dialog box, shown in Figure 6-4, where you can indicate what you want to map (your NT server) to which drive letter.

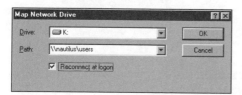

Figure 6-4: Mapping a network drive to a remote host in Windows 95

7. **Enter the NT server name, followed by the share name in the first blank as follows:**

```
\\nautillus\users
```

Again, you don't actually type nautillus\users; you type your machine name, followed by the share name given to you by your systems administrator. Be sure to type back slashes (\), not forward slashes (/), or it won't work.

8. **Enter the drive letter to which you want to map in the second blank.** This will default to the next available letter of the alphabet.

9. **Check the Reconnect at Login box**, if you want to map to this drive every time you log in. If you don't check this box, you must repeat Steps 4–8 every time you want to copy or save files to your NT server.

From Windows NT

You can attach a Windows NT workstation to a Windows NT server in three ways. For all these methods, you must have Client for Microsoft Networks and NetBEUI running. You can do this by checking the Network Control Panel, under the Services tab. If these are already running, try the easy way explained in the previous section on Windows 95. If these aren't already running, you need administrator privileges on your NT workstation to install these services. If you can't use the easy way, use this other method:

1. **Right-mouse click Network Neighborhood.** This brings up a list of system options.

2. **Select Map Network Drive.** A dialog box like the one in Figure 6-5 pops up.

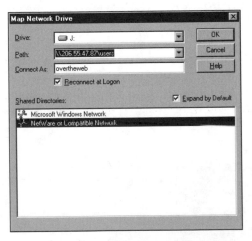

Figure 6-5: Mapping a network drive using an IP address in Windows NT

3. **Enter the following in the first blank:**

```
\\206.55.47.87\users
```

The first part is your IP address and the second part is your share name. Make sure you use back slashes (\) or it definitely won't work.

4. **Enter your login ID in the second blank.**

5. **Indicate the drive letter you want to assign.**

6. **Check the Reconnect at Login box.**

Now you can save or copy files to the drive letter you indicated. If you click My Computer (or whatever you have renamed your computer), you see a list of all your drives, including the one you just mapped to your NT server.

From a Mac

The only way to map an NT server as a local drive on a Mac is if you are sharing a network and the NT server has Services for Macintoshes turned on. If this is the case and you can find the NT server in the right zone in the Chooser, then you can sign on to the NT server, using the share name the systems administrator gave you. Then you can save or copy files directly to your NT server directory.

If you save or copy HTML or CSS files from your Mac to the NT server and then you try to open them from a PC, they will look strange, but they will still work properly. Figure 6-6 shows a file with a line-length problem.

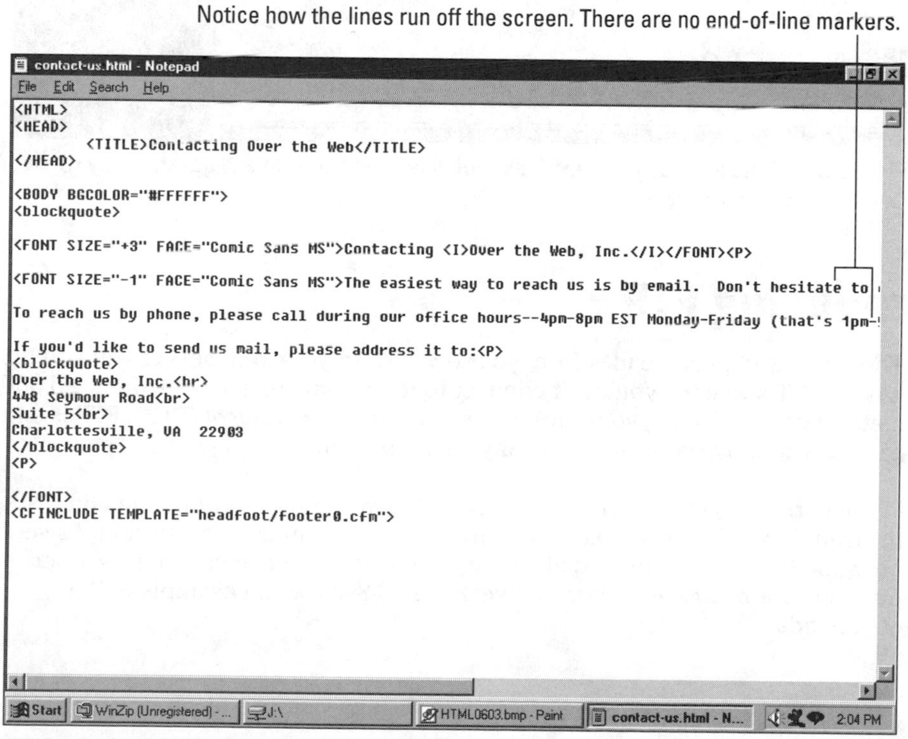

Notice how the lines run off the screen. There are no end-of-line markers.

Figure 6-6: This is what your HTML or CSS file looks like if saved or copied from a Mac and then opened on a PC.

If you save or copy from a PC and then open on a Mac that has a mapping to the NT server, then your file will look like the one in Figure 6-7.

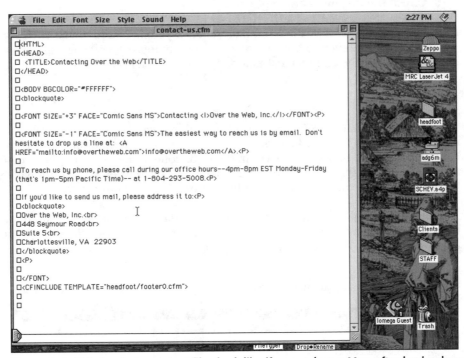

Figure 6-7: This is what your text files look like if opened on a Mac, after having been saved or copied from a PC.

Introducing FTP

The other way to move files from your desktop to your Web server — if you don't have an NT server or you can't connect to it for some reason — is the tried and true method of transferring your files, called *File Transfer Protocol* (FTP). FTP is a fast, easy way to move your files from any desktop to any server.

In the early days of FTP and still today in non-x-window environments on UNIX, all file transfers relied on a text-based interface. Commands were short and sweet, but only one file could be moved at a time. This was the entire vocabulary: open, get, put, bini (for *binary file transfer*), bye. Figure 6-8 shows an example of FTP commands.

FTP predates the Web

Before there was a World Wide Web, there was an Internet. The World Wide Web relies on the HyperText Transfer Protocol (HTTP). The Internet relied on the File Transfer Protocol (FTP). FTP is a simple concept. One computer establishes a connection with another computer using TCP/IP (more on this follows). Then the first computer tells the second computer whether the data about to be passed will be text or binary data (*binary data* is any file that looks like gobbledygook when opened in a plain text editor; this would include word processing documents, spreadsheets, and image files). Then the first computer either puts one file onto the second computer or gets one file off the second computer. All this assumes the first computer has the necessary permissions to read or write files on the second computer. That's all: so simple, so elegant.

FTP takes advantage, as does HTTP, of TCP/IP. This is a double-decker protocol. The Transmission Control Protocol (TCP) part packages the data a certain way so when the packages get to the other side, the computer over there knows how to unpackage them and reassemble the data into the right file. When the receiving computer gets data, it needs to know whether it is putting together an e-mail message (plain text) or an image. The Internet Protocol (IP) part handles getting those packets to the correct address. TCP is like the mailroom and IP is like the post office.

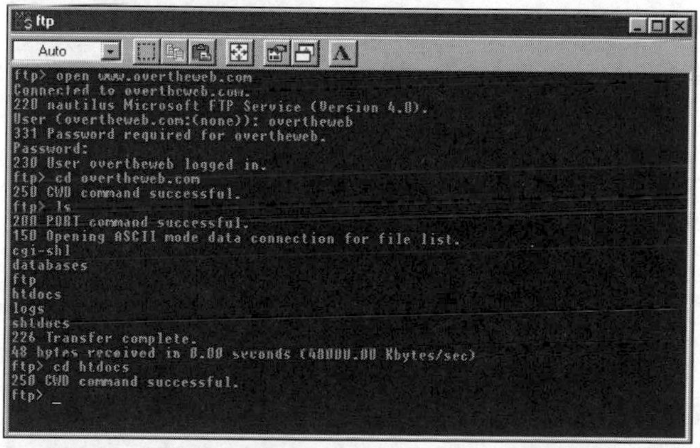

Figure 6-8: Text-based FTP client

File types

You will upload two kinds of files: binary and text. When you think about it, everything on your computer is binary, even your text files. *Binary* just refers to the way the data is stored: as ones and zeros. With a *text file*, every set of 8 ones and zeros translates neatly into a letter, a number, or a special character on your keyboard. With a binary file, all the ones and zeros translate into something bigger, such as an image. If you open a text file with a plain text editor, you see text. If you open a binary file in a plain text editor, you see junk. The plain text editor has tried to turn every set of 8 ones and zeros into a number or letter.

Introducing FTP clients: CuteFTP, WS_FTP, Fetch

Once every computer had a mouse, drag-and-drop FTP software was not long in coming. Today, several visual FTP clients are available. For the Mac, it is easy: Fetch. Fetch even guesses whether your file is text or binary (what it calls *raw data*). You can drag a file right out of the folder on your desk into the Fetch client and watch the dog run. Figure 6-9 shows Fetch capabilities on the Mac.

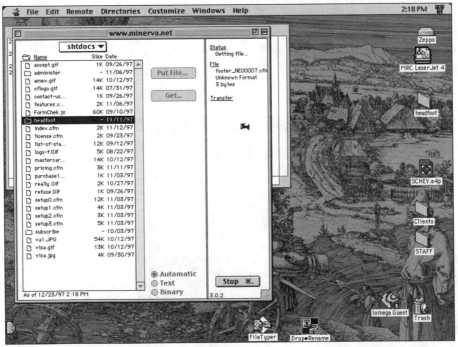

Figure 6-9: Fetch makes FTPing easy on the Mac.

For the Windows environments, the most common are WS_FTP, for which a lite version is available, and CuteFTP (shown in Figure 6-10), which is shareware. In both of these packages, you can set up a list of the most common places to which you connect, including your login ID, your password, and the directory on the remote machine. Then you can drag-and-drop files or directories full of files from your desktop machine (by pointing the software to the right directory) to the Web server (or any remote machine that has a IP address). This software makes a reasonably accurate guess as to whether your file is binary or text.

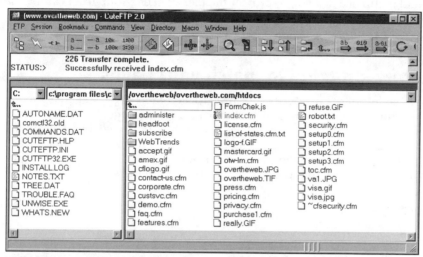

Figure 6-10: CuteFTP makes light work of FTPing files and folders.

Developing Directories to Store Your Pages and Graphics

Before you start uploading those pages, you should decide how you want to structure your directories. You have three choices: put everything into one directory, put your files into a directory structure that mirrors your site (for example, one directory per page), or put your files into directories by type. Making this decision early and enforcing discipline on yourself to keep your structure clean is important. The alternative is to recode all your links when you rearrange your files.

Some of the tools to make this easier are found in Chapter 14 — but it is still not much fun.

Unless your site is small (one page with a photo of your cat and your grandmother's baklava recipe), you don't want to put all your files into one directory. This leaves two choices: having your directory structure match your pages, which we tell you in the next section heading is generally a bad idea, or structuring your directories by file type, which is, generally, a better way.

The reason we include an explanation of both theories is, for some organizations, having your directory structure come closer to matching your pages than to being by file type does make sense. This is the case in a large organization when dozens of people publish pages to one site. You probably don't want everyone to have permission to overlay everyone else's files. Breaking up the directory structure by functional group enables you to protect the files of each group from carelessness by anyone in any of the other groups (say, two people naming their files the same thing).

Directory structure to match your pages

The idea behind this is pretty straightforward. For each page, you create a directory. You call it something related to what's on the page. You can either use a flat directory structure, where every page is on the same level, or a hierarchical directory structure, where a page that serves as a pointer to four other pages is actually closer to the root than those four pages, which will be under it. Figure 6-11 shows a directory structure that matches the pages in the site.

Flat directory structure

```
www.overtheweb.com
```

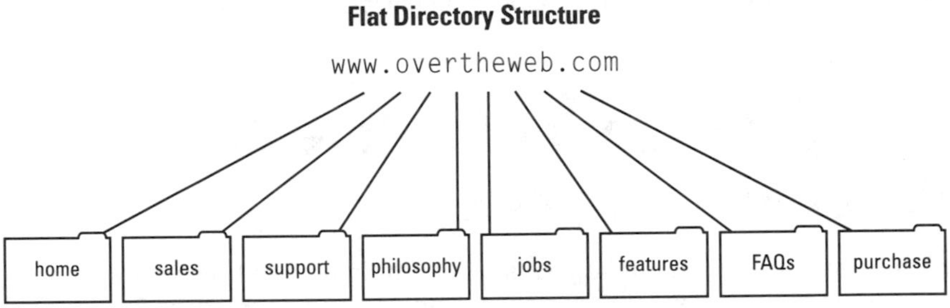

Figure 6-11: Flat directory structure with one directory per page

Having one directory per page doesn't make sense, but it may make sense to have one directory per functional unit involved in creating your site. You could modify the previous diagram by removing the directories for features (a subset of sales), FAQ (a subset of support), and purchase (a subset of sales), and lumping those three in with the pages they modify. If you have a handful of people working on each unit, you can protect your site better by restricting the permissions of the people in each group only to the folder where all their files go. Figure 6-12 shows an even more convoluted directory tree with one page per directory using hierarchical structure.

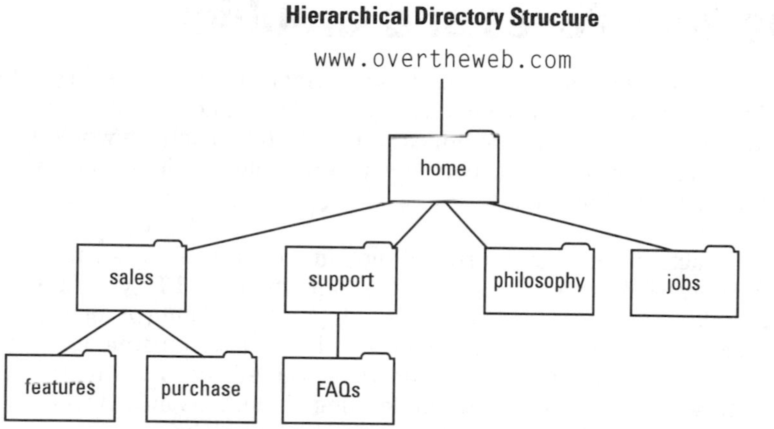

Hierarchical Directory Structure

Figure 6-12: Hierarchical directory structure with one directory per page

It's hard to imagine where this model makes sense because it just doesn't scale. If you rearrange your site, you may as well start over.

Directory structure by file type (generally a better idea)

HTML files go into the root directory for your site. Style-sheets files go into a style-sheets directory (as shown in Figure 6-13). All media go into subdirectories of a media directory based on media type (if you think you'll have more than just images — be realistic). If you think you'll have only images, skip the media directory and have a directory in your root directory named images.

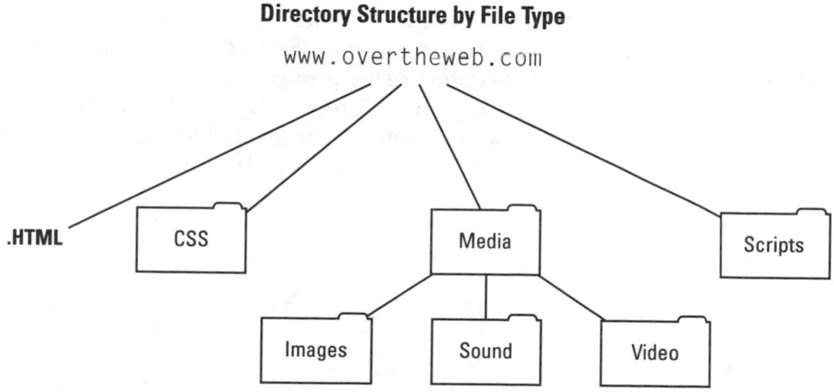

Directory Structure by File Type

Figure 6-13: Nice and simple. Directory structure by file type. Especially good for small sites.

Uploading Your Pages and Graphics

Earlier in this chapter, we mentioned text files are binary files where every set of 8 ones and zeros neatly convert into one character. This is almost perfectly true. Text files are more than what you see. If text files were only text, each file would be one long line of text. In fact, at the end of each line in a text file is at least one character indicating this is where a line ends.

PCs use two characters: carriage return (CR) and line feed (LF). Macs use only CR and UNIX uses only LF. What a pain! Indeed it is, but when you FTP your files, your FTP client can take care of this for you. If you tell your FTP client (or let it guess) your file is a text file, then it automatically makes the proper adjustments to the end of the lines to correct for the file's new platform. If you tell your FTP client your text file is actually binary, then it leaves the whole thing alone. This means when you open your file on the new platform, the line ends won't be right.

What if you upload your binary file as text? Disaster. The FTP client has conveniently gone through your file and changed every string of 8 ones and zeros that translate into an LF or CR and tried to convert them as if they were text. You won't recognize your file and neither will a browser.

If you are working on either a Mac or a PC and your Web server is UNIX or, if you are working on UNIX or a Mac and your Web server is Windows NT, then try this experiment: upload a text file (any old HTML file will do) to your Web server as text and then download it as binary. Your end of file characters will be wrong because you didn't let the FTP client fix it on the way back down.

DNS

What will you call your site? Do you have a domain name (like `ibm.com`)? You can do this from the official organization that registers domain names, called `Internic`: `http://www.internic.net`. You can also get your ISP to do it for you, but they usually charge something extra. One enterprising group on the Web chose to call itself `www.internic.com`. Guess what it does? It registers your domain name with the official group and charges you twice as much! The group has easy online forms, but usually your ISP will do it for less than twice the registration amount.

Before you can get a domain name, you must have the technical information from your ISP, such as the IP address of your ISP. This is yet another good reason to let your ISP do it for you.

Permissions

In addition to needing an account on your Web server, you also need permissions to perform basic file management tasks. You must be able to create new directories within your root directory, unless your systems administrator is a real dictator and creates them for you according to a prescribed system. You need permissions to write to your directory to upload files.

When visitors come to your site with their browsers, they either read or execute files on your Web server. The permissions for the directories must be set to permit this. Your systems administrator will probably want all your executable files (scripts and programs) in one directory so just that directory can be marked as executable.

Testing Your Work

You have to test your work. Because of the informal system of creating pages and publishing them, which most of us work in, this is easy to forget. Don't wait until you receive mail from someone who visited your site telling you links don't work to learn this. Your visitors shouldn't be your beta testers.

Where should you test? On your server. While this sounds dangerous, you can ask your systems administrator to create an obscure mapping name, so if a browser comes to www.overtheweb.com, it returns a 404 not found error, while you are testing it. You will know the only way to see the site is to go to www.overtheweb.com/blahblah. When you are done testing, you ask your systems administrator to delete the blahblah mapping and reinstate www.overtheweb.com to point to your home page.

What about testing on a desktop server? Good reasons exist not to do it this way. The following chart discusses the pros and cons of testing on a desktop Web server, if this is not where you ultimately plan to publish.

Pros

No special file manipulation is required. Just save your pages to your Web server's home directory, which is right on your local hard drive.

Permissions are not an issue because you should have God-like permissions on your own workstation. The exception to this is if you are running Windows NT Workstation on your computer. If you are running NT and you don't have administrator privileges, then you may not even be able to install a desktop Web server.

Testing is instant. Just save your HTML file, as we did in the last chapter, and reload your page.

Cons

Permissions may be different on your production Web server. If your permissions aren't the same on your desktop server as they are on your production Web server, then you need to make changes. How will you know they're different? You have to test. This means you will test your page twice.

Unless you are doing server-side scripting, you get the same results as if you just opened the file locally. Let me explain. In Chapter 5, we taught you how to open a local file from your browser. If you install a desktop Web server, you can pull up the file using the IP address of your computer, if you know it, or `http://127.0.0.1/yourpage.html`, if you put your page into your desktop Web server's root directory. Instead of opening the file locally, it opens the file as if it were coming from somewhere on the Internet. Your page looks exactly the same as it did by opening it locally. The only time this kind of round-about page loading is necessary is if you are doing some kind of server processing of your page. In this case, you would also have some other software on your desktop computer (such as Cold Fusion, Tango, FileMaker Pro, and so on).

Testing is less thorough. Why? Because you know you have to test again anyway. You'll be better off using the mapping suggestion we made previously and doing your testing once on your production server.

How do you test?

The most important points to remember when you test are as follows:

✦ Look at your site, clicking through all the links from a variety of browsers (both Netscape and Internet Explorer in their most recently released versions and one or two versions earlier). Looking at your site from a few versions of AOL's browser is also not a bad idea because they have such a large installed base.

✦ Look at your site from both Macs and PCs.

✦ Look at your site after setting your screen resolution to 640×480, 800×600, and 1024×768.

✦ Look at your site with the browser sized to the full screen and with the browser taking up only part of the screen.

✦ Look at your site from within your domain and then from outside your domain. Permissions may be different if you are coming to your site from outside your domain.

✦ Look at your site from the desk of someone who doesn't have privileges on your server.

Note

Both Windows NT and Windows 95 send your Login data to an NT Web server (pretty tricky, huh?), so if you are authorized to see a certain page because of your ID and password, the Web server already knows this and doesn't even bother to ask you to sign in. If you are not authorized, you get a sign-in screen. Of course, as the Webmaster, you never see this screen—thus, you never know everyone else can't get to your site—unless you try this from someone's computer who doesn't have the permissions you have. In fact, if you didn't know this, you'd never be able to duplicate this permissions problem from your own desk and you'd assume everyone coming to your page was doing something wrong, because it worked for you!

Complete a testing worksheet, something like the one shown in the accompanying sidebar, and you won't go wrong.

From Here

Cross-Reference

Proceed to Chapter 7 and start exploring the potential of hypertext.

Find servers fascinating? Wish you could be a systems administrator and have your own enterprise Web server? Then jump to Chapter 15, Understanding Server Options.

Testing worksheet

Web Site Publishing Worksheet

My Web server is:
___ on my desktop
✔ not on my desktop

My Web server administrator is:
___ me
___ someone within my organization
✔ someone outside my organization

My Web server platform is:
___ UNIX
✔ Windows NT
___ Mac

My desktop platform is:
___ Windows 95
✔ Windows NT
___ Mac
___ UNIX

My Web server name is:
DNS: minerva.net
IP address:
NT domain: minerva
NT name: nautilus
NT share name: users

Contact information:
Name: Alex Subacz
E-mail: support@minerva.net
Phone:

My account information is:
Account ID: overtheweb
Password:

Summary

You now have everything you need to begin publishing your pages. You have a completed worksheet with all the information you need about your server. You understand file types. You have made some decisions about how you want to structure your directories. You know how to get your files to your server using an FTP client. Or, if you have an NT Web server, you know how to map a drive to your NT server.

You're ready to publish your files correctly, manage the directory structure, and test your site thoroughly.

✦   ✦   ✦

Fundamentals of
Web Publishing

✦   ✦   ✦   ✦

✦   ✦   ✦   ✦

Exploring the Potential of Hypertext

We all throw around the word *hypertext* as if it were a common parlance. Where did it come from? Who had this great idea in the first place? This chapter answers those questions along with a spate of more immediately useful ones. This chapter includes explanations of sequential and nonsequential writing, chunking (which has nothing to do with gaining weight), Xanadu and other futuristic ideas about hypertext, and a discussion of the limits of hypertext.

Origins of Hypertext

The essence of *hypertext* — that a term or an idea can be further described outside the main body of a text — is as old as fourth-century writings of the church in Greece and Asia Minor. In these writings, the authors made notes referring to passages in other texts — such as *The Bible* — and to other passages within the same text. This isn't exactly what we think of when we hear hypertext, but the concept is the same.

More recently and more relevantly, hypertext is used in recipes. A quiche recipe includes hypertext:

> **Ingredients:**
>
> 1 partially prebaked pie shell (see recipe on previous page)
>
> 1 cup whole milk

1 cup cream

2 eggs

2 egg yolks

Salt and pepper to taste

How does this differ from hypertext? Not at all. You didn't realize your grandmother was ahead of her time!

In 1945, Dr. Vannevar Bush, science advisor to President Roosevelt, proposed a desktop device in an *Atlantic Monthly* article entitled "As We May Think" that sounds a lot like a personal computer hooked up to the World Wide Web. Dr. Bush's device didn't have a network connection or a computer (since there weren't any yet), but it allowed for searches of linked text using microfilm and a microfilm reader. He was trying to replicate the way the brain works, with associated ideas being associated in the text. A visionary, wouldn't you say?

The word *hypertext* was first used by Ted Nelson in 1965, in a paper presented to ACM. Nelson defined it as "nonsequential writing — text that branches and allows choice to the reader," and goes on to say that it is best read at an interactive screen. This sounds more like what we think of today.

In 1967, Dr. Andries van Dam and a group of researchers at Brown University created (and IBM funded) the first implementation of hypertext. In 1972, the first multiuser hypertext system, based on a large database called *ZOG*, was implemented at Carnegie-Mellon University.

Defining Hypertext

Hypertext is expanding on a text outside of the text. That's how we carry on conversations, isn't it? Few truly interesting conversations have no tangents. Hypertext enables authors to write what they set out to write and still have a place to put all that tangential material about grandfather's restaurant that charged 22¢ for lunch with coffee and dessert during the depression.

What's in it for readers? Hypertext is hugely emancipating for readers. Readers get to decide what to read, in what order, skipping what they choose, and seeing all the details of what they want. Arguments have been made that any book with an index or a table of contents is a hypertext, but we won't expound on those, because they were lame arguments in the first place.

Sequential versus Nonsequential Writing

How does writing for hypertext (nonsequential writing) differ from writing for beginning-to-end reading (sequential writing)? In several ways:

Organization. Nonsequential writing does not require the same kind of organization sequential writing requires.

Completeness of thoughts. Nonsequential enables you to complete your thoughts more thoroughly than does sequential writing, where only those thoughts directly relevant to the main argument can be fully developed.

Less well-suited to persuasive writing. Nonsequential writing is not particularly well-suited to persuading readers because you can't be sure they have read all your arguments (unless you include them all in the same place, in which case, you are still writing sequentially). With sequential writing, readers can be assumed to have made it through all your material.

Never concluded. Sequential writing ends; nonsequential writing never ends. As long as you can make another link, your book has another chapter.

Organization

When you write sequential text, you must do a lot of organizing before you can even put pen to paper (or fingers to keyboard, as the case may be). You need to organize the thoughts into a main topic—what is the point of your writing?—and subtopics that you will explain along the way. You also must plan your thoughts and make sure that when one thought ends, you have a smooth transition into the next thought.

In nonsequential writing, each thought can stand alone. In fact, it's ideal if each thought does stand alone. You can link from any thought to any related thought, and others can link to any of your thoughts. Transitions aren't necessary. In fact, organization isn't really necessary. Just complete the thought before moving onto the next thought.

The article by Dr. Vannevar Bush, previously mentioned, did a good job of spelling out how hypertext ought to work. Dr. Bush said the system he was describing, which he called *Memex,* should work like the brain. No transitions exist between pieces of information in your brain. You make sense of that information in your own way. The connections in your brain are unique to you. In nonsequential writing, you can share your thoughts and your connections between thoughts. Readers can choose the order in which they read your thoughts.

Completeness of thoughts

With nonsequential writing, you are not bound by the dictates of good breeding to keep your thoughts on any topic brief. When you write a sequential text, you don't want every subpoint leading up to your main point to overtake the work, so you keep them brief, so they support, rather than distract from, your point.

Sequential writing can be compared to talking at a cocktail party. You aren't sure how interested the people with whom you are talking are in your topic. You must make sure you don't lose their interest. You don't want to carry on a monologue, so you keep your comments brief, limiting them to others' responses. You have to be polite.

Nonsequential writing is much more flexible for the writer, as well as for the reader. Imagine you are asked to give a lecture about a single thought and everyone there is fascinated with your topic. While you go on and on, they hang on every word. Each thought is given that much flexibility. People only show up to read what you've written if they are interested in the thought. Every time you would have gone off on a tangent, you can link to a separate, completely developed thought about that. People who want to join you on your tangents are free to do so. People who want to follow your thought to the end can do that. You aren't constrained by the bounds of politeness!

Less well-suited to persuasive writing

Imagine the State-of-the-Union Address being presented as a hypertext. We could skip all the blather about all the great accomplishments of the president, skip every reference to the children and all the pandering to the elderly, and read the three sentences that comprise the fully developed thought at the core of the speech. That would be great for the reader, but rather a problem for the author or speaker.

Persuasive writing simply isn't well-suited to nonsequential text. How can you bring your readers to your conclusions if you aren't even sure they have read all your arguments? Simply put: you can't.

Never concluded

Remember that childhood song about John Jacob Jingleheimer Schmidt? It never ended. While not exactly an example of nonsequential writing, it is roughly analogous to how nonsequential writing works. That is both a plus and a minus. Nonsequential writing links to other nonsequential writing, both of your own and of others. Consequently, there are no consequentlies. In sequential writing, you are expected to wrap up your point and leave your reader with a sense of completeness. In nonsequential writing, you complete your thought, link to other thoughts, and the reader can leave with the satisfaction of having heard you out on that thought, or the reader can read about related thoughts.

Introducing Chunking

Chunking is how we describe the process of breaking a text into what we have heretofore been calling *thoughts*. You need to know a thing or two about some guidelines for chunking an existing text, if this is what you have to do. If you are fortunate enough to get to write original material for nonsequential reading, then you need a slightly different set of guidelines.

The basic rule for chunking a text is to keep thoughts intact. More specifically, let's discuss how to do this and how not to do this for both existing writings and new writings.

Chunking an existing text

First, let's cover when *not* to chunk:

Persuasive texts. If your text is persuasive, don't chunk it. Just leave it alone, even if it is long.

Printed materials. If your text is something that is likely to be printed by a large percentage of the people who come across it, don't chunk it.

Long texts. Length alone is no reason to chunk a text. The instructions for installing memory in a particular model of a computer may be long — what with removing the screws, removing the case, removing some boards to expose the memory (stupid design, no?), holding the memory properly, inserting the memory in parallel, and putting the whole thing back together — but that is no reason to cut it up. It is one related thought and a reader is unlikely to want to read only Step 7!

Complete thoughts. Most important of all of these, keep a thought together.

So, when *should* you chunk a text?

At section breaks. Headings are a big clue the author is beginning a new thought. If you chunked this chapter by dividing it at the section headings, you'd have done well.

At new thoughts. For texts that don't have "cut along the dotted line at the headings" written on them, you'll have to read through the material and find where one thought ends and another begins. Keep complete thoughts together. When you see a new thought getting up a head of steam, back up and find the end of the previous thought. Chunk it there.

At structural transitions. Most decent authors are kind enough to provide clues that they are moving from one thought to another. Structural transitions usually begin paragraphs, rather than one of the other sentences in a paragraph. Rarely do you have to divide paragraphs to chunk a text.

Chunking as you go

If you are writing for nonsequential use, then you need to think in terms of telling your audience what they need to know about that topic. Consider the quiche recipe presented previously in this chapter. The crust recipe could be found elsewhere. It wasn't repeated in the quiche recipe itself. The origin of the eggs was also omitted, as was the butterfat content of the cream. Say what you need to say to complete your thought, but don't belabor it; move tangents to other chunks.

Lost in Hyperspace?

How do you keep your reader from getting lost navigating between your chunks of prose? This is a question about site architecture and navigational tools. The short answer is you provide links to related topics and usually to one additional place all the pieces of your text have in common. We call this place a *Welcome page* or a *list of links*.

The long answer involves a discussion of hierarchical, linear, and anarchical site architectures, an explanation of the various tools you can put on your page to facilitate navigation by the visitor, and good site organization. Fortunately, we cover this at length later.

Cross-Reference See Chapter 9 for a more in-depth discussion of these various tools.

A World Hypertext System: Xanadu

In 1981, Ted Nelson, the man who coined the term *hypertext,* who never really went away as a visionary, was back on the scene with the idea of Xanadu, which he described in brief as:

✦ Xanadu is a system for the network sale of documents with automatic royalties on every byte.

✦ The transclusion feature allows quotation of fragments of any size with royalty to the original publisher.

✦ This is an implementation of a connected literature.

✦ It is a system for a point-and-click universe.

✦ This is a completely interactive docuverse.

Xanadu, which has yet to materialize, has been the source of a lot of digital debate ever since. Many of the ideas were transformed into what the Web is today. The part that is notably (and gratefully) absent is the part about royalties going to the original publisher for every byte. Figure 7-1 shows the Xanadu home page (`http://www.xanadu.net/xanadu`).

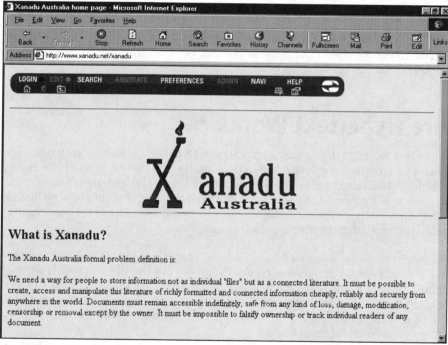

Figure 7-1: Xanadu

Xanadu versus the Web

Xanadu has some attractive features associated with it. First of all, using a sophisticated algorithm, it keeps a history of all revisions of a document. Documents never die. It actually keeps only the most recent version and then uses historical information stored in a file to re-create previous versions from the current one. The benefit of this is visitors never receive a "404 not found" error because no link can ever be broken. The drawback to this is every stupid thing you've ever published is there for all eternity. This sure would make being a college student a lot less fun, wouldn't it?

Another nice feature is the transclusion feature mentioned previously. Not the royalty part, but the part about text being included by reference (which is what *transclusion* means). It actually goes one step beyond the Web's idea of linking to other text. With Xanadu, you can include text from another location in the middle of your document without actually putting it there. Using a more sophisticated linking system, Xanadu creates a page from multiple locations. The Web does this with images (which you can include in the middle of your page without having them reside where your text resides), but not with text.

The only real problem with Xanadu is it doesn't exist. This is one disadvantage that is hard to get past. Still, the Web owes much of its interactivity to the visionary genius of Ted Nelson.

Where Hypertext Works

Hypertext lends itself to many applications. Hypertext is ideally suited to recipes, as you've already seen, and other sets of instructions where part of the instructions could be considered a chunk of its own using the guidelines previously given. Hypertext is excellent for lists of items, where the reader wants to see the complete list, then see the specifics about only one or two items. The list is one chunk; the detail for each item on the list another, as illustrated in Figure 7-2.

Hypertext is also wonderful for definitions. Throughout this book, we use one of two conventions to define new terms. Either we put the word in italics with a brief definition next to the word itself, or we define the word in a note with an icon to set it aside completely. This note more closely resembles hypertext, except it disrupts the flow of the main document. With hypertext, you can link from new terms you introduce to definitions of them.

Hypertext does a good job anywhere various levels of detail are needed. Marketing information is a good example of this. The first chunk may be a list of products. For each product, a list of features exists. From the chunk about features, there is a list of system requirements, details about implementation, and disclaimers.

Finally, hypertext serves the short text well. Poetry, while not always short, has thrived in hypertext form (see Figure 7-3). Annotations can be hyperlinks, the referent of the poem can be a hyperlink, and other poems by the same poet can be hyperlinks.

Click INFO button to see details

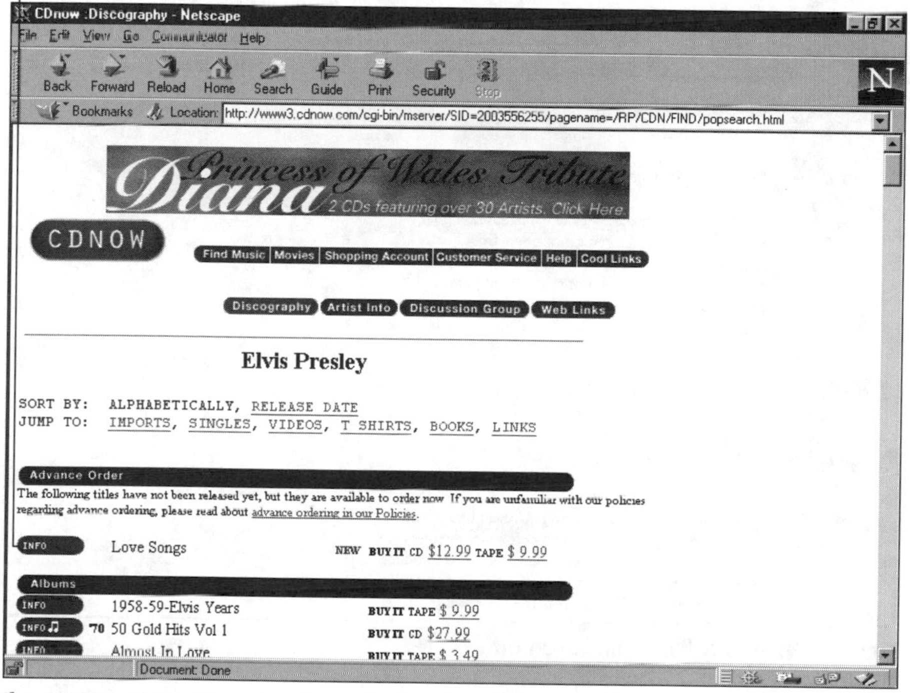

Figure 7-2: Using Hypertext for selecting details from a list is ideal.

Where Hypertext Doesn't Work

If you can't chunk your document using the previous guidelines, you probably don't want to use hypertext. Hypertext works poorly in persuasive documents, fluff-filled documents (colloquially referred to as *blather*), and for novels. We've already discussed the reasons why persuasion doesn't carry over well to hypertext.

Documents with little substance don't work well in a hypertext environment because readers will leave them as soon as they arrive. Emanations of the penumbra don't fit into the "information now" model of the Web. Figure 7-4 illustrates just such an example (`http://www.teleport.com/~cdeemer/novel.html`).

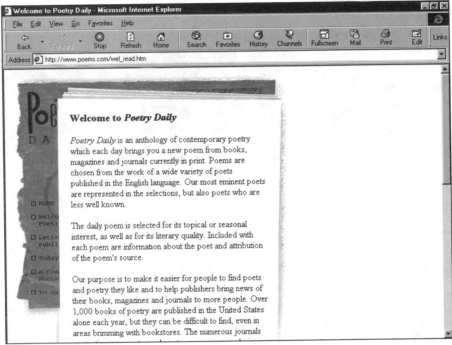

Figure 7-3: Poetry has really taken off.

Despite a few success stories of interactive hypertext novels, novels as a rule haven't translated well to the world of hypertext. Poetry, on the other hand, has taken off. Good reasons exist why novels don't seem to work in hypertext. First, it is far more work to create a novel with various directions for the reader to go next. Second, the reader is supposed to come to the climax of the novel having collected certain information in a certain order. Finally, a novel is usually associated with relaxing. How relaxing is it to sit at a computer with your hands on the keyboard?

From Here

Cross-
Reference

Proceed to Chapter 8 and learn about defining your message.

Jump to Chapter 9 and learn about site architecture and navigational tools you can use to prevent the lost in Hyperspace experience we discussed previously.

Jump to Chapter 11, Writing for the Web.

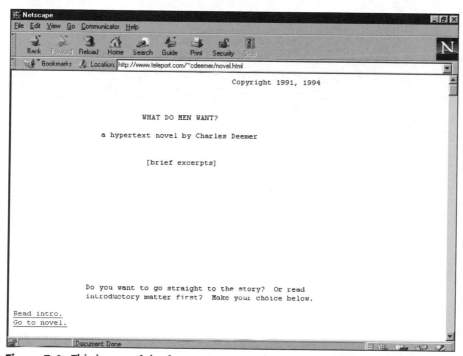

Figure 7-4: This is one of the few attempts at a hypertext novel on the Web.

Summary

You can do much with hypertext. As an author, hypertext frees you from many constraints of sequential writing. Hypertext has worked effectively, albeit in different media, for over a thousand years. The interesting and colorful history of hypertext is inextricably linked with that of the Web (no pun intended).

Some types of documents exist for which hypertext isn't as effective as regular, sequential text. But for most types of documents, you can chunk your document to make it work with hypertext. In Chapter 11, we discuss writing for the Web, where you learn more about turning your prose into hypertext-ready prose.

✦   ✦   ✦

Defining Your Message and Your Goals

Why are you publishing a Web page? It's okay if you still don't have a razor-sharp message. This chapter helps you gain focus. We discuss why you should know what your message is. After all, how can you communicate your message if you don't know what it is. Some examples help make the point. Then we discuss the purposes that underlie various kinds of Web sites.

When you think about the purpose of publishing your page, you also need to think about the audience: why are they *reading* your page? Who is your audience? Who's on the Web, anyway? How big is your potential audience?

Knowing Your Message

You're armed with a nice-looking Web page from Chapter 5; you selected your style sheet — maybe you even plan to make some improvements on it when you get to Chapter 23 — and now that you've read Chapter 6, you know how to publish your Web page to your Web site. You are champing at the bit to get all those beautiful, HTML-4-compliant pages up for the world to see.

Wait! If you can't explain the purpose of your pages and your site in clear, concise language (where language is used broadly to include text, graphics, and colors), none of it matters.

Knowing Your Audience

You should have some great ideas to get your message across at this point. But again, before you run off and start writing your material, remember your audience. Who is your audience? With the Web, knowing your audience is often hard to tell. Literally anyone from a seven-year-old kid to a 70-year-old retiree might come across your page.

You want to answer four questions about your audience:

1. **Who is likely to be interested in your message?** You probably have a mental picture of who would be interested in your message. Put it in writing. Would anyone else be interested? Make a list of all the types of people or companies who might be interested in your message. You want to make sure something is in your site for each of them. Some sites are so bold as to ask you who you are when you arrive (Web master, novice, programmer) and then direct you to the right area based on your answer. Dell takes this approach, as shown in Figure 8-1.

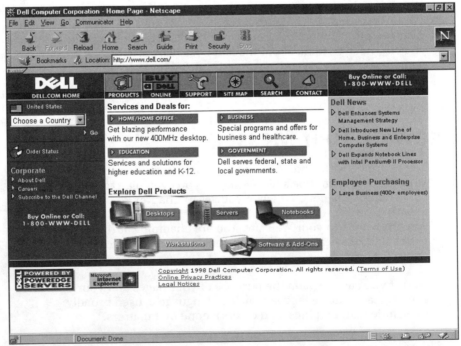

Figure 8-1: Dell Computers arranges their site by visitor types. How's that for thinking about what the visitor wants?

2. **Who is likely to be able to find your message?** What kind of people use the Web? Are the people who are interested in what you have to say even on the

Web? Don't get all fired up to put up a Web site for a group of people who don't have Web access. The Graphics, Visualization, and Usability Center at Georgia Tech conducts an annual survey to determine who is on the Web. Take a look at the results at `http://www.cc.gatech.edu/gvu/user_surveys/User_Survey_Home.html`.

3. **How can you find out more about your audience so you can further tailor your message to them?** Only one way exists to find out about your audience right now on the Web: ask them. You can use a variety of Web statistics packages to find out about your visitors' usage of your site, but they won't tell you anything about your visitors — either in the aggregate or individually. One way is by using forms and asking your visitors. Another rather clever way of finding out things about your visitors — not necessarily accurate things, but *something* about your visitors — is to read their history files using JavaScript. Each of these topics deserves its own section, later in this chapter.

Forms are discussed in detail in Chapter 42. JavaScript is discussed in Chapter 48.

4. **How else can you communicate with your audience?** Push, Channels, E-mail, and Spam. Again, these each deserve their own sections, so we cover them later.

Knowing Your Goals

Putting up a Web site requires many goals. Before you can know the strategy you should use to achieve your goals, you have to identify your goals.

Individual goals

In the beginning, the Web was populated almost entirely with personal Web pages. In fact, we used to joke that more links were on the Web than pages because everyone who put up a page linked to the same several hundred places. A lot of promise, but little substance, existed then. Today, when you make a personal Web page, you have many choices about the kinds of things you want to put up. Figure 8-2 shows a creative individual page.

Many, many individual pages are still on the Web. What might the goals be of someone who puts up an individual Web page? No list can be comprehensive, but any list might include:

✦ To share a favorite recipe

✦ To share a favorite quote

✦ To show the world what your new daughter looks like

✦ To explain your love for boats and sailing

✦ To provide a list of the places you like best on the Web

✦ To provide resources for other people who share the same hobby

✦ To showcase your work

✦ To publicize your resume

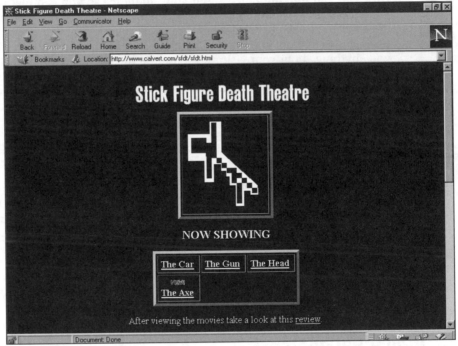

Figure 8-2: Stick-art murders make for one unique individual page.

If your goal is personal, then the action you want visitors to take might include:

✦ Returning

✦ Linking to your page because it is cool or useful

✦ Telling others about your page

✦ Finding a job or selling your work

You can do some things to increase the chances of any of the previous happening. You want to make sure your strategy includes some tactics to make these things more likely.

Vocabulary

Tactics. *Tactics* are the specific tasks you perform or actions you take to achieve your strategy. For example, if your strategy includes collecting data from your visitors in a form, your tactics will include the questions you want to ask.

Business goals

Like it or not, most of the Web exists for commercial reasons. If you're clever, you can find a way to put the Web to work for your business. If your goal is to do business, then you probably already realize you have a lot of competition out there. Many businesses are on the Web. To attract people away from your competitors' dazzling Web sites to yours, you must put a lot of energy into cultivating just the right message so people will

✦ Find what they want.

✦ Find what they need to determine they want to purchase your product or service.

✦ Develop a sense of urgency to take that action.

✦ Buy your product or service.

Remember, people don't come to your site because of what you *have*; they come because of what they *want*. If you are able to convince them a large overlap exists between the two and you can make them see they need it *now*, then they will buy what you have to offer.

Even though your Web site will probably cost a lot less than a television ad campaign would, you need to spend just as much time cultivating your message. Read books and talk to experts. If your company has a marketing department, let them create the message for you to implement.

Social goals

Is your Web site dedicated to making sure people tear their rolls before buttering them (rather than cutting their rolls, of course), then your Web site has a social goal. This is not the limit of social goals, as worthy a goal as this is. *Social goals* include protecting the environment (although this could certainly be a community site if it is a local environmental organization), improving society, affecting politics, educating about health, and explaining foreign affairs. Figure 8-3 shows a site for helping kids have healthy diets.

If you are putting up a Web site with a social goal, then chances are you don't want people to fork out dough (except maybe for a fundraising campaign), but to take a certain action. It might be a free action, but it still requires some energy from your visitors. Your strategy must include the wherewithal for your visitors to take this action. If you want them to reduce their overall fat intake to 35 grams per day, then you have to persuade them this is good for them and their children. You also have to tell them what a gram of fat is, what the fat content in various food are, and how to cook without using a lot of fat. A site with such a worthy goal might include:

✦ Health information about the benefits of a low-fat diet

✦ Charts of fat content in food that can be printed and carried around in a purse or pocket

✦ Cooking tips for low-fat cooking

✦ Recipes for delicious low-fat meals the entire family will love.

✦ A chart for recording your daily fat intake or a food diary — maybe this is something you want them to print and take home or maybe it is something you want them to fill out on your site, where they now feel like a member.

✦ A mailing list or threaded news group for people who have chosen to stick to a low-fat eating regimen. This approach creates a sense of community, which is something we talk about at length in Chapter 45. It also works like nothing else to bring people back again and again.

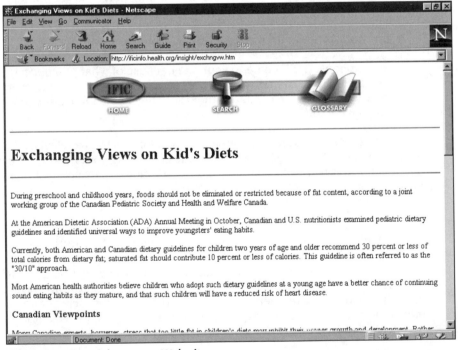

Figure 8-3: A social purpose Web site

Community goals

This is a subset of social goals and can include social organizations, churches, schools, and others. These groups often have a goal of bringing a community closer together, improving a community, improving the situation for some members of the community, safeguarding the environment, or educating the children. These would all fall into the category of community purposes.

The Web is a fabulous way for these community-minded organizations to reach their audiences and motivate them to action. It is also a fabulous place to form a network of like-minded organizations. After all, other groups that want the same results your group wants are only a link away. And even these cash-strapped organizations can afford links, because links are free! Some basic information about a Greek Orthodox Church is in the Web page in Figure 8-4.

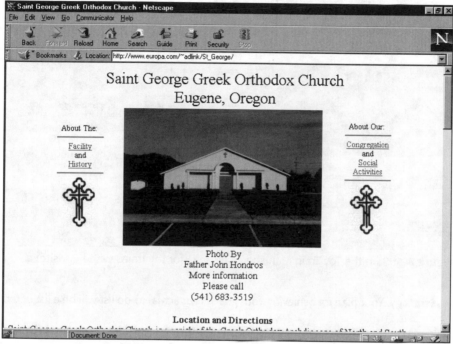

Figure 8-4: Getting people to attend church is a fine example of a community purpose.

Converting Your Goals into a Strategy

Now that you know, broadly, the goals of your site, you can begin to think about the strategies you will use to achieve the goals for your site. Your purpose includes goals. A community purpose has goals related to the community. A business purpose has goals related to making money. Your strategy will be the means to achieve those goals.

Defining a Web Site Strategy

Are you catching on to how this purpose thing works? Your purpose isn't necessarily exactly what you put on your page. Your purpose is to get a certain response from your visitors. If you are philanthropic, your purpose might just be to share information about your hobby. Sharing interests, as shown in Figure 8-5, is a perfectly legitimate purpose for putting up a Web site. In this case, your purpose is to have them stay a while and find useful information.

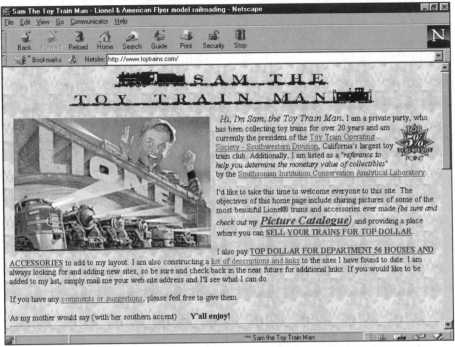

Figure 8-5: Sam the Toy Train Man shares his love for toy trains with his visitors.

Vocabulary
a b c

Strategy. Your plan for achieving your goals. Your actual to-do list will be a list of tactics.

Before you start to create content for your site, you need to know the following things about your site:

- ✦ What result do I want from my visitors?
- ✦ What do I need to tell them to get this result?

Getting results

The results you want may vary. Most Webmasters want people to return to their sites. This is a pretty basic result, but not one you should overlook. If you are selling things, you want people to buy them. If you are trying to motivate people to take action, say, e-mail their Congressperson, then you want to have some way to know they did it.

When you state your purpose, at least to yourself, you should be aware of what results you want. If you think about it, there *is* a result; you might not have included it in your purpose, though. Even if you put up a Web page with links to ethnic recipe archives, you want your visitors to think well of you and to come back often. These desired results need to be included in your strategy.

Direct support

Some pages will directly support your strategy. These pages might include a features list, a comparison of your product to the competition, or a page that includes an independent party endorsing your product (say a page of awards from *PC Week, Mac Week,* and so forth with quotes from the reviews, as shown in Figure 8-6). You need to make sure you have these pages prominently located within your site.

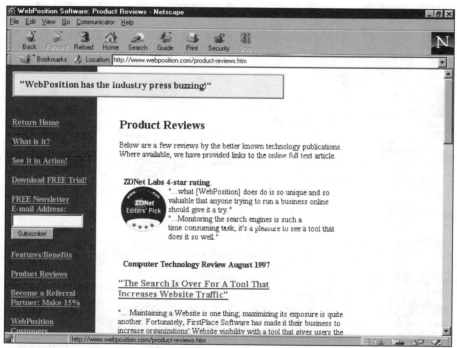

Figure 8-6: Do these awards and quotes contribute to their strategy of selling you software? You bet!

Make a list of the kinds of things that could persuade your visitors to take the action you'd like them to take (remember, this must be *their* decision). Then make sure each of those things is somewhere in your site they can find easily. You can't necessarily fit all these things in one place, so break it out by area onto different pages or even groups of pages. Just make sure everything your visitors need to know is somewhere they can find easily.

Indirect support

Of course, information you need to give your visitors, which is not directly related to your purpose, should also be on your Web site. You'll have to put this somewhere, too. When you design your site, you can make this information a little further from the place where most people enter your site. What kind of information might fall into the category of indirect support for your mission? Well, if you sell something from your page, you want to have a page where you explain your policy about returns. This probably won't make anyone buy at that moment, but it could reassure your visitors that you are a reputable business and your customers' satisfaction is important to you. Egghead Software has an FAQ of shipping-related information on its Web page, shown in Figure 8-7.

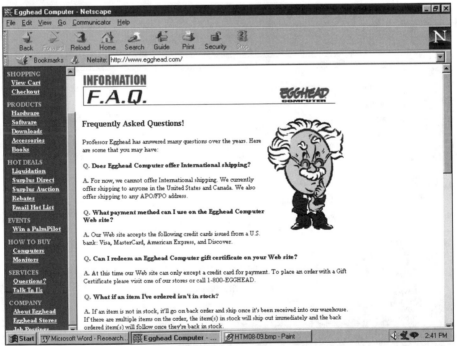

Figure 8-7: If people want to know information about you, include it as indirect support for your purpose.

Other things that fall into indirect support might be technical support topics: how to assemble the bicycle you sold them; a list of replacement cartridges for the printers you manufacture; how to contact your organization by e-mail, phone, fax, and U.S. mail. These kinds of things should all be there somewhere. Just because they don't directly contribute to your purpose, don't leave them out. Just don't place them as prominently in your site.

Your strategy is to get a certain result by having your visitors take a certain action. You need to motivate them to take this action. What kind of actions might you have in mind? The most common action is *returning*.

Another result Webmasters want is information about their visitors. How do you get information about your visitors? Ask. Have a form on your site your visitors can fill in. Does this work? Not without a hook. If you want your visitors to sign into some sort of a guest book, you need to give them something in return. The most common thing to give them is a chance to win something, as shown in Figure 8-8.

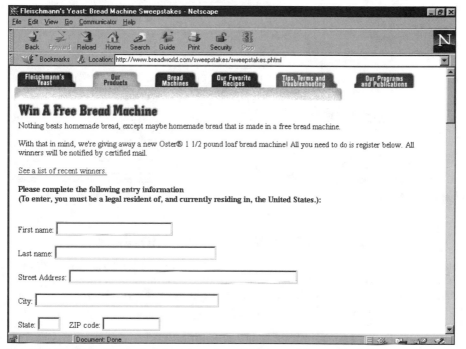

Figure 8-8: For a chance to win a bread machine, would you sign in?

One way to get people to return is to promise them something. Lately, that something is a custom experience. If your page is configurable by visitors, then they may feel they are saving time by going back to your page, where they find just what they need in their custom experience, as shown in Figure 8-9.

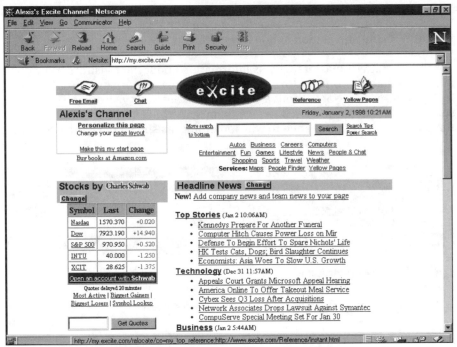

Figure 8-9: If you can customize what you see, you might be more likely to return.

Telling them what they need to know

Up until now, you've probably thought in terms of what you want your visitors to know about you, your company, your product, or your cause. Now turn that coin on its head. Think in terms of what *they want* to know, first, and then in terms of what they need to know.

Obviously, if you want visitors to come to your site (or even more importantly, to return to your site), you need to tell them what they want to know. If you want them to take a particular action, you must include the information they need to make that decision.

What should you do with all the other great stuff you want to tell them? Nothing. If you clutter up your clear message with other things you think they want to know — just because you want them to know it — your message will get muddy. Your visitors won't find what they *want* and they won't find what they *need*.

How to Achieve Your Goals

Start looking at Web pages with a more critical eye. Can you tell the purpose of each page you visit? For transit pages, such as search engines, they generally want you to stay long enough to see their ads (and perhaps even to click their ads and get distracted from what you set out to find). For destination pages, which make up the bulk of pages on the Web, they may want to inform you, to educate you, to persuade you, to motivate you to take action, or to convince you that you can't live without something.

Can't live without it

Check out the page in Figure 8-10. Even if you don't know what they are selling, the idea of a no-risk, 30-day free trial can be very compelling.

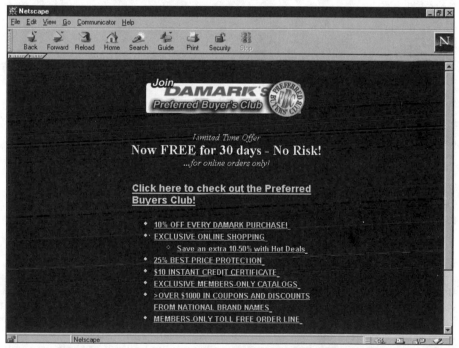

Figure 8-10: This page makes you want to join, even if you don't know exactly what you're joining.

So now, suddenly, you have a problem you didn't necessarily have when you arrived at this page. Should you join or click away and never know what you're missing?

Clear as a bell

What can you do to make your purpose even clearer? That depends. Sometimes a picture *is* worth a thousand words. What is the purpose of the page shown in Figure 8-11? What can you tell just from looking at their page?

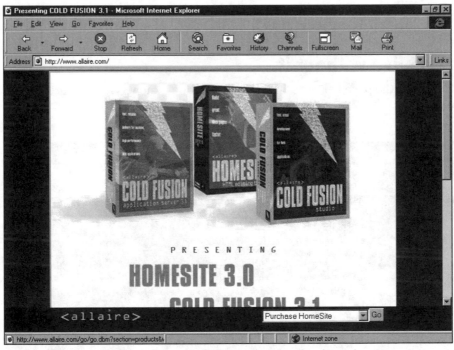

Figure 8-11: Sometimes a picture really *is* worth a thousand words.

First of all, they probably make, or at least sell, computer software. Those graphics in the middle of the screen look distinctively like computer software boxes. The products are named *Cold Fusion 3.1* and *HomeSite 3.0*. The use of the word *presenting* makes you think this may be a new release. It's true you don't know what the products do, but you have a pretty clear idea what the company does. That's something. Maybe they only expect visitors who already know a thing or two about their products. Maybe they talk about what their products do elsewhere.

Sure, they don't necessarily motivate you to take action on this page. Most motivation to take action takes place further into a site. The first page where your visitor arrives, the front door to your site, is referred to as your *Welcome page.*

How Not To Achieve Your Goals

Consider the following Web page, as shown in Figure 8-12. What is the purpose of this page? It looks like they are selling something. Can you figure it out? If you take the time to read through the text, you might have some idea. Are you inspired to take action? Do you want to pull out your credit card and buy it right now? Probably not.

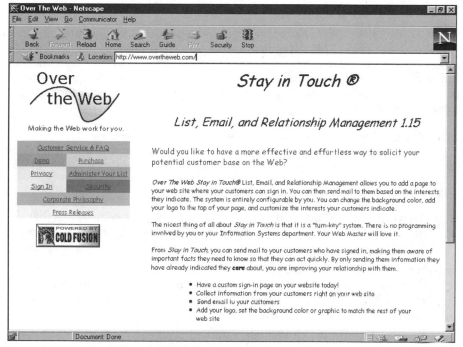

Figure 8-12: What is the purpose of this page?

This is not an unusual Web page. Most Web pages are published by people with strong technical skills, but not necessarily the strongest writing or marketing skills. When you learn writing, and especially marketing, you learn about making your point in a clear, concise manner. Does this page do this? Definitely not. The bullet lists help, but they are too little too late to save the page from the generally murky impression with which the visitor leaves. Not only isn't this the kind of impression you want your visitor to have, it isn't the kind of action you want your visitor to take: *leaving*.

Acquiring Information about Your Visitors

Exactly who is coming to your Web page and exactly what they want to know is difficult to know. Obviously, if you have this information, you have a leg up when it comes to achieving your goals. Fortunately, you can take actions to collect this type of information so, as your site evolves, it comes closer to meeting the specific needs of the visitors.

Web sign-in pages

Guest books, like the one shown in Figure 8-13, sign-in pages, whatever you call them, do they work? This depends on what you want them to do. Most sign-in pages ask for far too much personal information. Does anybody really need a home phone number, work phone number, and fax number? And why is race, sex, or age anybody's business? Bad guest book pages also fail to ask for the *right* information, namely:

Which of our products or services are you interested in?
If you plan to use this information later, which is something we talk about at the end of this chapter, then you want to make sure you can target your promotions to the right people.

How did you find out about us?
Are your ads working? Did a favorable article appear somewhere that you didn't know about? Is one of your strategic partners doing a great job of referring people to you? Your visitor is one click away from telling you!

What type of visitor are you?
Customer, member of the press, programmer, medical professional? This list should reflect the types of visitors you expect. You learn more about why you want to know this in Chapter 9.

What publications and Web sites do you read regularly?
You might as well ask them how you should advertise to reach other people like them. A smart site provides them with a list and lets them check all the boxes that apply. Most people won't consider this too personal.

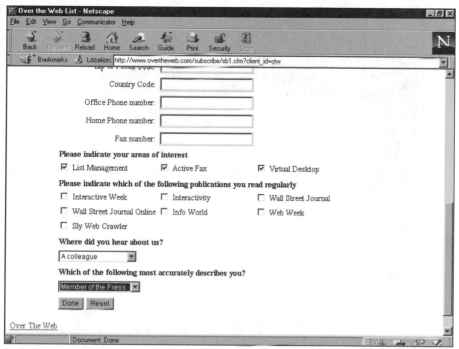

Figure 8-13: Over the Web sign-in page; look at the types of questions they ask!

Many people like the anonymity of the Web. In theory, you can go anywhere without anyone knowing who you are or where you've been.

In general, Web sign-in pages work when there is something in it for the person signing in, as in Figure 8-14. What can you give them?

✦ **A chance to win a prize.** Many people will sign in to win anything. Even a T-shirt. Give it a try.

✦ **Something free.** 3D glasses were being given away for signing into the Insight Direct Web site.

✦ **An enrollment in a mailing list the visitor would presumably care about.** NT server administrators, the audience for the products carried by Sunbelt Software, can sign in to receive wonderful mail about software that helps NT servers and NT server administrators.

✦ **A regular mailing about special deals.** American Airlines mails out lists of super deals on travel weekly to people who sign in to their site.

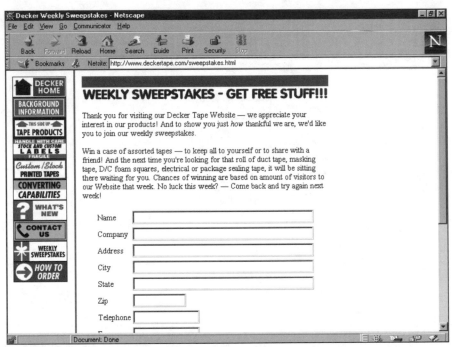

Figure 8-14: Would you sign in for a chance to win a case of assorted tape?

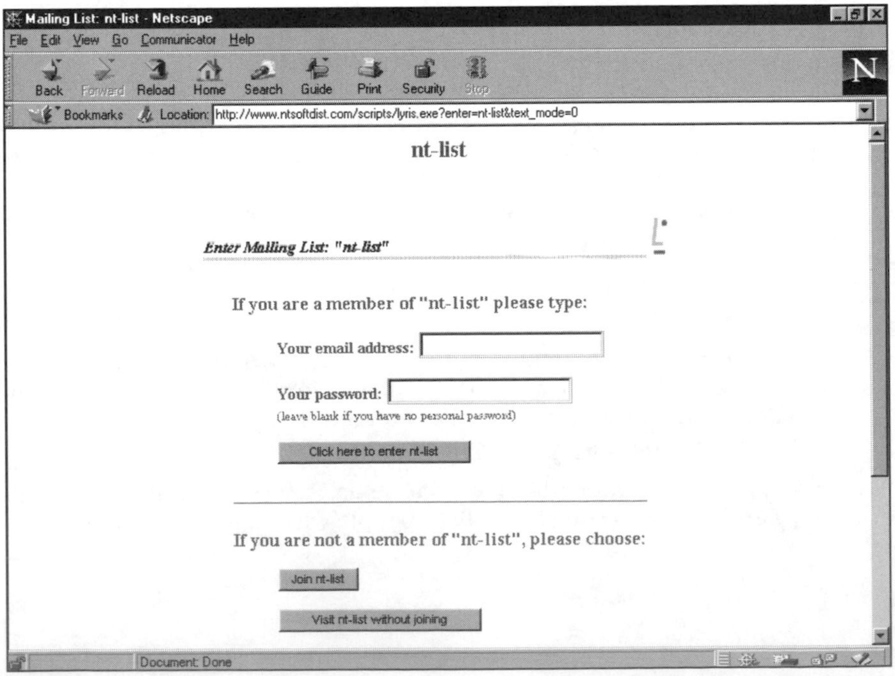

Figure 8-15: If you can give people mail they care about, they will want to sign in.

Open Profiling Standard

Imagine a system where every citizen of the Web could create files with information about themselves that would sit on their own computers. When users came to a site asking for personal information, they could choose to give none or it, some of it, or all of it, and they could also give or deny permission to share this information with others. This would mean visitors to Web sites would never again have to complete another sign-in page. Sound too good to be true?

The Open Profiling Standard, which would do just this, has been proposed by Netscape Communications, Firefly Network, VeriSign, and more than 60 leading companies and organizations.

As a Web developer, this frees you from the hassles of creating a sign-in page for your site. You simply find out the specifications for requesting the file (undoubtedly, a new protocol will be created for this) and program your site to make use of the data. Very, very cool, indeed.

What is the downside to a sign-in page? People can lie. However, they won't lie if they won't get what you are offering without valid information. For example, those 3D glasses won't arrive if they lie about their address; their valued newsletter won't arrive if they lie about their e-mail address.

Now what happens with this data once your visitors have clicked the submit button? You can have the results of each submission mailed to you, but this won't give you any kind of aggregate picture of who your audience is — unless you want someone to rekey all the information into a spreadsheet for some sort of statistical analysis or into a database for direct marketing. Another option is to have server-side scripting populate a database or spreadsheet automatically. This is a good option if you have a programming staff on hand or you want to become a programmer. The third option is to contract with an Internet service provider who does this for you. Some of the more sophisticated ISPs do this, as does Over the Web (http://www.overtheweb.com).

Forcing compliance with a sign-in page

Another clever way exists to get people to sign in: deny them access to the good stuff until they have! Some sites use this approach. When you visit these sites, you get a sample of valuable information. If you are willing to join their site, by signing in and giving them your personal information, then you get to see the rest of the information you came to see. Implementation of this approach requires *cookies* (small files left on the visitors' computers) to store the sign-in information so, on subsequent visits, the visitor automatically enters the members-only site.

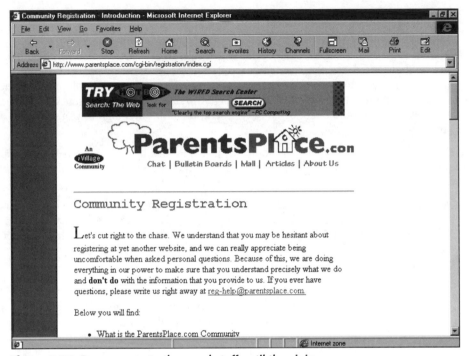

Figure 8-16: Deny access to the good stuff until they join.

Using a sign-in page like this requires server-side scripting, which goes beyond what this book covers. Additionally, server-side scripting only really works when you have a lot of information that might be unavailable elsewhere. People will not return, even if they have joined, if what they find at the members-only site is junk.

Reading a history file

A trick you can perform with JavaScript is to read the history file of the visitor to your page to find out what sites have been visited before coming to your page (only since opening the browser on the current day, however). Have you ever clicked the back button on your browser ten times? Your browser keeps a list of all the places you have visited since you opened it. What you probably didn't know is when you visit a Web site, that information is also available to the Web site. Without knowing too much JavaScript, you can find out where your visitors have been since today.

Cross-Reference   Chapters 48–51 discuss JavaScript and how you can use JavaScript methods to accomplish this.

Is this useful? Marginally. Your visitor may have spent an hour at a certain URL (this is all that is stored in the history file); arrival to the site may have been an accident, or the visitor may have hated it. If a URL appears in the list ten times, then you can be reasonably confident the visitor was at least looking around the site for something, whether or not it was found.

What can you do with this information? Probably not much. By implementing this trick to find out where your visitors have been, you can end up with more information than you know how to handle. It takes careful planning to make use of this information. *And* you probably don't want to use it on an individual level, but on an aggregate level. Again, you need some server-side scripting, in addition to client-side JavaScript, to get this working.

Is it worth it? It might be. It might be useful, at the least, to see where people were right before they came to your page. We are not endorsing this approach, but you should be aware of it.

The Value of Web Site Statistics

What about all the hullabaloo about Web site statistics and hit counts? That really doesn't tell you anything about who your audience is. Bad statistics packages — those that count how many times the URL was requested — don't tell you anything and they include the number of times Web agents come to your page (where no human eye will see it) as "hits." How legitimate is that? Considering the increase in push technology, that could account for half the hits your page receives. It's pretty discouraging to know half your hits were not hits at all, but computer programs searching for the occurrence of certain words.

Good statistics packages keep track of the IP addresses of the calling agents, be they browsers or computer programs. They can tell you about return visitors, to some degree. They also tell you about *when* people are coming to your site, which is important to know if you manage your own server. Not only does how many people are coming matter, but also what the load is on the server, in that case.

Defining a Page-by-Page Strategy

How does your Web site strategy manifest itself? One page at a time. For each page you create (or plan to create), you need to answer the following questions:

1. Where will my visitors want to go after visiting this page?
2. Where will my visitors have come from when they arrive at this page?
3. In what way will this page contribute to the results I want?

Other Ways to Communicate Your Message

Your site should be about your message, not vice versa. Sometimes other ways exist to get your message across. You can use push technology, channels, e-mail, and even spam to get your message across. The rest of this chapter discusses these other options.

Push

Push technology enables your users to define what things they care about and to use some sort of an agent to search the Web looking for it. Then, the things the agent finds come right to their desktops.

Cross-Reference

Push technology is discussed in detail in Chapter 43.

Channels

You can define your page as a channel that gets delivered to the desks of people who subscribe.

Cross-Reference

Chapter 43 tells you how to define channels.

Communicate with your visitors via e-mail

In a book about the Web, we suggest you communicate via e-mail? Yes. Sometimes you can communicate best with your intended audience by e-mail. Be careful not to send too much or they will get annoyed. Be sure to tell them when they sign in to your page that they may receive e-mail and give them a way not to receive the mail — both when they sign in and after they have received the e-mail.

Vocabulary

E-mail. *Electronic mail*, a relatively old technology, is a way of sending a message without paper using the Internet. Two essential components exist in sending e-mail: the first is an outgoing mail server. This is a computer capable of sending mail. Normally, when you configure your e-mail software, it asks you for the name of your mail server. The second component is a valid e-mail address for the recipient.

Also, be sure to ask visitors whether they want HTML-enhanced e-mail or non-HTML-enhanced e-mail. This is just one more piece of data about each of your visitors who sign in to your guest book you want to store in your database for easy processing. If the recipient's e-mail system can't handle HTML, then it will look like junk, as shown in Figure 8-17. Your messages will be much more compelling if you include HTML, as shown in Figure 8-18.

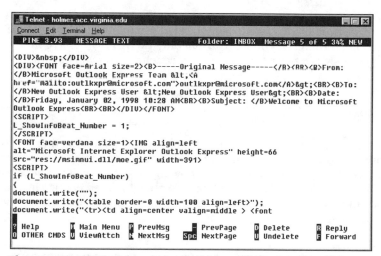

Figure 8-17: HTML-enhanced e-mail in a plain-text mail reader: incomprehensible and ugly

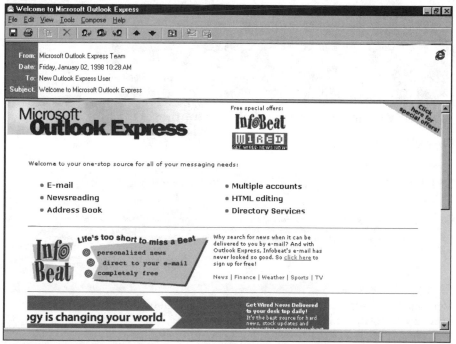

Figure 8-18: The same message in a mail reader that can handle it: lovely and compelling

Why use e-mail? New product announcements. Special promotions. News about legal things. Your visitors might have forgotten how valuable your site is. This is your chance to remind them. Of course, you can only do this if you have their addresses from your sign-in page stored some place where you can use them for e-mail.

Spam

Spam is another word for unsolicited bulk e-mail. We are not endorsing this approach, but this list wouldn't be complete without it. Services exist you can use to send mail to millions of people (so they say; who's to say how much of this mail bounces?) with your message. You might just find some people who are interested enough in your message to visit your site. Spam is not targeted. Figure 8-19 shows an organization that exists to combat spam.

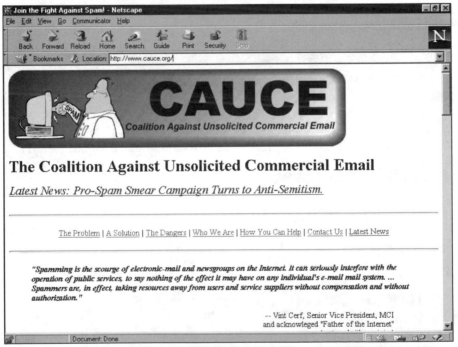

Figure 8-19: Direct marketers will argue spam is a legitimate tool, but antispam activists are organized.

Spam is highly controversial for several reasons:

People feel their mailboxes are *private* and they get annoyed when something appears they didn't request with a return address they don't recognize (and that is often false). Do you suppose these same people get as upset when they receive a bulk mailing in their postal mailboxes?

Internet service providers don't want to have to store this unsolicited mail. And many are threatening to bounce all mail from domains known to be involved in spam. Some have already begun bouncing (that is returning undelivered) spam.

Most spam is for something a majority of recipients don't care about. The majority of spam is for get-rich-quick schemes, credit-improvement services, pornography, or diet plans.

No way exists to get off these lists. True spam doesn't give you a way to remove yourself from the list.

If you are going to use this highly controversial technique, you are going to make some enemies, but you might just reach your audience. You can do things to reach your audience, however, without annoying a vast number of users who don't care about your product or service.

Spam light

What if there were a way to reach a large group of people who might actually be interested in your message, but never have heard of you? Consider buying targeted lists from companies that also deal with your audience. Contact companies who have nice Web sites with sign-in pages to see if they sell their information. Even though people who sign in don't like it, many companies do this. At least when you send mail to this group, you will know you have reason to believe they care.

A final word about using spam: Always give people a way to get off your list. If they do request never to hear from you again, respect their wishes. A difference does exist between being assertive and being a pain.

From Here

Cross-Reference

If you are ready to create your site, proceed to Chapter 10: Essentials of Web Page Design.

If you want to learn more about the server-side scripting mentioned in this chapter, jump to Chapter 15.

Summary

Without a clear purpose for your Web site, your visitors won't find what you want them to, they won't stay, and they won't return. Treat the development of your site's purpose and message as carefully as you would your company's marketing strategy. Your Web site is an extension of your company's marketing strategy.

Know your audience as well as you can. Several good ways exist to collect information about them; consider which ones result in you having the information you need. Finally, select a message that is compatible with the purpose of your page.

✦   ✦   ✦

Creating Multipage Sites

Now it's time to move from defining the message of your site to the delivery of that message on pages. In this chapter, we discuss the variety of choices you have to implement a multipage site with the pros and cons of each. We talk about the pitfalls to avoid when creating multipage sites. This chapter discusses the types of organization and the architectures available to you when you build a multipage site. Navigation also figures prominently in this chapter. If you are going to have more than one page in your site, you need to have a logical, intuitive, consistent way for your visitors to get around it. Finally, we discuss maintaining your site.

Possibilities and Problems of Multipage Sites

Most Web sites are implemented across multiple pages. Isn't that the great thing about the Web? You can break up your content by type and group it together, so if visitors to your site only want to know how to order spare parts for the exercise equipment you manufacture, they needn't read through all your marketing literature and the entire service manual.

Good and bad things exist about breaking your content into multiple pages: both for you, as the Webmaster, and for your visitors. First, let's look at the pros and cons for your visitors (because those should receive greater weight in your calculus).

Pros

Your visitors can (theoretically) find what they want without having to read through everything on your site. It is a great feeling to go to a site with a clear idea of what you want and to find it within two or three clicks, even when you have never been to that site before. Visitors will return to such a site often.

A site is richer. There is more content to choose from. A well-done multipage site gives visitors the choice of knowing a little or a lot about the topic in which they are interested.

All the information visitors need is there. While visitors certainly don't want all the information at once, they may eventually want all the information. One of the nice things about the Web is supposed to be you don't have to wait on hold to get answers.

Cons

Navigation can be confusing. Especially for first-time visitors, what are obviously clear directions to you may not even be noticed by visitors. Sometimes subtle imagemaps (graphics with hot spots, which, when clicked, take you somewhere else, just like hypertext), which may be obvious to the designer, and may not be at all obvious to visitors. This is something you can avoid with good design, which we discuss later in this chapter. Figures 9-1 and 9-2 show two subtle and very clear navigational tools.

Loading time. If visitors have to wait for big, cumbersome graphics to load for each page, they may well get impatient. Fortunately, technical and design solutions exist to this problem, which we discuss later.

Printing. If the content you have split into multiple pages is something you imagine people may want to print, and they may have to go to both pages to print the entire thing, then dividing it into two pages is a hassle for your visitors.

Imagemap. An *imagemap* is an image with clickable regions. Each clickable region acts as a hyperlink. Plenty of free or cheap software exists to help you convert an image into an imagemap. Many HTML editors have this tool built-in.

For an in-depth examination of imagemaps, including instructions for creating one, see Chapter 36.

Of less import, but certainly worth mentioning, are the pros and cons of developing a multipage Web site to you, the Webmaster.

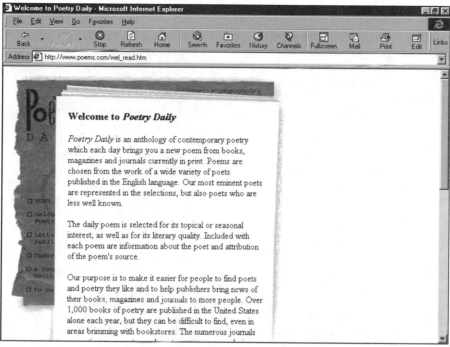

Figure 9-1: Can you find the navigational tools on this site? Perhaps too subtle.

Figure 9-2: How about on this site? Much more obvious, don't you think?

Pros

You can break up your content into manageable pieces. For most sites, this is going to be necessary. The question you must answer through the rest of this chapter and in the next is: how to break up the content? Being able to break up your content is a great thing for you if your site is being developed by a team. Each Web page is stored in a separate file, so if you had several people writing to the same file, you'd have a mess. Dividing the team work among the team members is much easier when the site is also divided.

Updating your content is easier. Different pages require different frequencies of update. Much of the site you should be able to leave alone for months at a time (the "Contacting Us" page, for example), which leaves you more time to update the pages that do need work.

Cons

If you aren't focused on your message and your visitors' needs, you could end up breaking content unnecessarily. This is a major inconvenience for your visitors, who won't know intuitively where to go to find what they need.

Maintenance requires more organization. You are going to have more files to monitor. Especially if you are working with a team, you need to have good organizational skills and even tools to facilitate organization to make sure nothing falls between the cracks and you don't have two people overlaying each other's work.

 Cross-Reference   Chapter 14 has detailed information about team and site management tools.

Dividing the Site

How do you divide your content? How you break up your content and how you indicate to your visitors that the content you have available *is* available, is the tricky part. This is one of the two main questions you want to have answered by the end of this chapter. Included in this question is *how much* do you divide your content? The other main question is: how do you provide navigation around your site? First, we address dividing your content.

You can divide your content in three ways, assuming it needs to be divided at all. These are:

✦ By origination of content

✦ By type of content

✦ By visitor type

By origination of content

If your organization is large enough to have multiple departments, then you may be thinking of dividing your content by where the content comes from or the functional group that owns that content. In this approach, your Web site organization reflects your organizational chart to some degree. Figure 9-3 shows an example of an organizational chart.

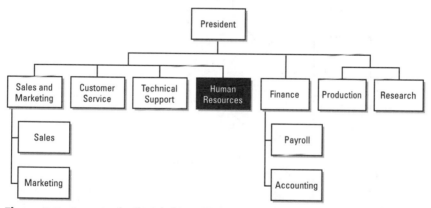

Figure 9-3: An organizational chart

It may make sense to divide the site by functional unit. In the case of Over the Web, the Web site would be organized, as shown in Figure 9-4. Just because only one box exists for an item (say, product listings) doesn't mean there is only one page; it's just easier to represent it that way for this example.

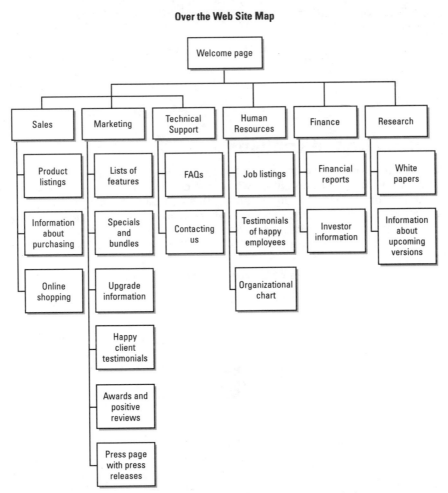

Figure 9-4: A site map based on the preceding organizational chart

Obviously, links, which simply aren't apparent in this type of site map, would be across the chart. For example, "Contacting Us" may merit its own link on the highest level; indisputably, you'd want to link to it from at least the Online Shopping Page (in case visitors have questions before they order), the Press Page, and Job Listings Page. This is also true with Information about Upcoming Versions, which is listed under Research; certainly, marketing would want to link to that.

Dividing your site by where the content originates is not a bad way to go, but read through the other two systems before you commit to it. For large organizations, this may be the only way to manage your content reasonably. If you use links effectively, this type of organization can appear intuitive and seamless. If you use links poorly or, if communication between departments (or Web builders in different departments) is poor, it can look like the right hand doesn't know what the left hand is doing.

By type of content

Another way to organize your site is by type of content. This organizational scheme often results in a similar site map to the previous system of site organization, by functional unit of your organization. The difference in this method of breaking up your content is, by using this approach, you are less interested in where the information for the content comes from than in what type of information it is. For example (from the preceding example), the finance department is the place where strategic alliances are brokered. They are the ones who make these arrangements, but who would think to look there? Figure 9-5 reflects this new information.

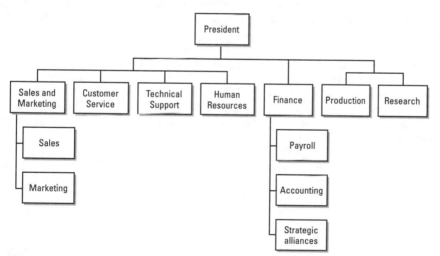

Figure 9-5: This organizational chart reflects that the finance department negotiates strategic alliances.

Even if the marketing department has a link to the Finance Page or the Strategic Alliances Page, you have to wonder if that is adequate prominence for this information. If the marketing department isn't involved in arranging these alliances, then they probably won't be enthusiastic about promoting them; heck, they may not even be aware of them!

Another obvious place to question the logic of the site organization, shown in Figure 9-5, is in the separation of sales from marketing. Wouldn't it make sense that a features list would be something you'd want to see on the way from Product Listings to Online Shopping?

If this site were now to be organized by type of information, instead of origin of information, then Figure 9-6 reflects what the site map would look like.

By visitor type

Another way to organize your site is by your visitors' interests. Remember them? We always come back to them eventually and so will you. Can you break your visitors into groups? Say, members and nonmembers? That's too easy. Here are some other examples: end users, programmers, and other interested parties; doctors and patients; activists and citizens; clients, potential clients, and others. Whatever division you come up with, others will always be the last item in the list. This is simply the nature of the Web. You can't predict who is going to show up on your site.

To continue with this example, Over the Web has decided to consider breaking up their site by visitor type. They have broken their visitors into the following groups: customers (or people who are interested in becoming customers), the press, job hunters, investors, programmers, and others. Because knowing what *others* want to see is impossible, they won't have their own pages. Figure 9-7 shows an attempt at reorganizing their site along these lines.

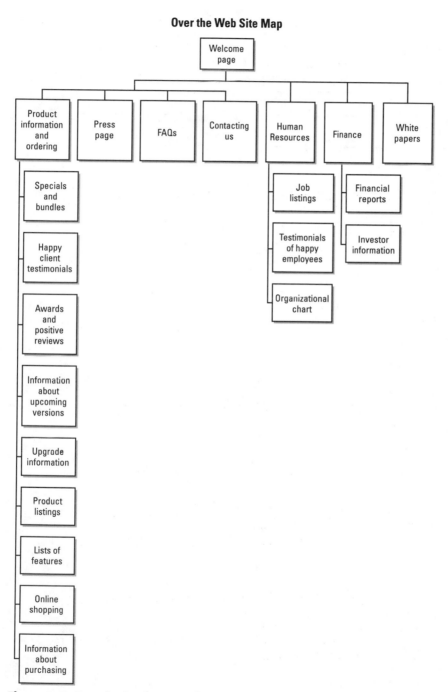

Figure 9-6: Organization by type of content

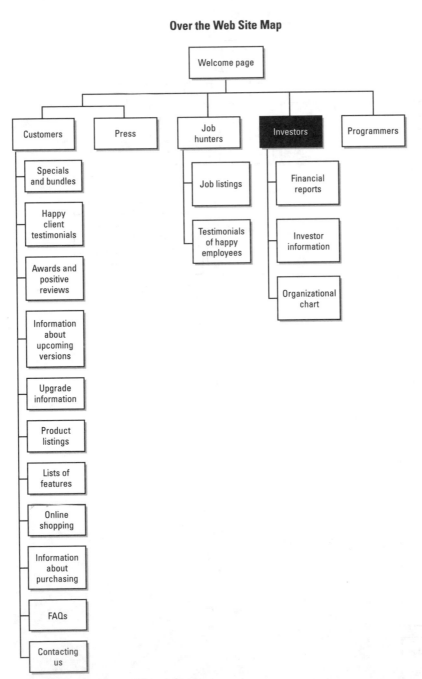

Figure 9-7: A site map by visitor type

Dividing Content

How much information goes on a page? Even if you have determined which of the previous models suits your site best, you must break up content within each section, as well. Within what we represented as the previous Press Page, will everything go on one page or will there be multiple pages? How do you decide?

Some of the factors you need to consider are:

What information do visitors need to see at once? Don't think in terms of the length of the material; think in terms of the use of the material. How do you anticipate the information being used? Most of the time, these decisions are between having one longish page or breaking the same material into multiple pages. If you think most of the people who come to the first part of your material will proceed in a linear manner through the material, then save them the trouble and put all the material on one page.

Will visitors be printing this information? If you want your visitors to be happy with their experience of visiting your site, don't annoy them by dividing information they may want to print. Sure, some people print everything and you can't plan around them, but some pages just lend themselves to printing. One example of this is a review of a book or a software package. Another is instructions. Who would want to print only half a set of instructions?

As you provide the information visitors need, are there points where visitors may want to go more than one place? If yes, then stop the page and give the visitor choices of places to go. If no, then continue the page.

What about the notion your visitors should never have to scroll? This is a crazy idea. Sure, you want the screen visitors see to look *complete*, but this doesn't mean everytime you have enough text to fill a screen, you should force the visitor to click and wait to link to what is really only a continuation of the same material. UI Engineering (`http://world.std.com/~uieweb`) did a study that showed visitors don't mind scrolling to get to the information they are seeking.

Site Architecture

We've already touched on this previous topic, but it deserves more attention. What is the architecture of your site going to be? Because we are confined to a two-dimensional space, the previous site maps all look hierarchical. That is simply the easiest way to represent a site. In fact, a site map may look more like the one represented in Figure 9-8.

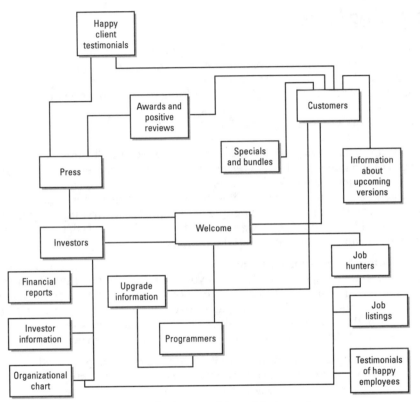

Figure 9-8: Mapping your site in a nonhierarchical way is messy.

Site architecture has to do with the way that pages link to each other. On one extreme, there is a linear site architecture, where you torture your visitors by forcing them to click a link to get to another page, where there still are no choices. On the other extreme, there is the completely anarchical architecture, where pages link to each other without any structure behind the links — call it *stream-of-consciousness* architecture. In the middle, you have hierarchical sites. We discuss all three of these in the following.

Linear architecture: The forced march

Hypertext is supposed to give readers the control to decide what they want to learn about next and when they want to know more. Only a control freak would work in this freedom-loving medium and then try to deny visitors their rights as Web surfers. People don't especially like to sit through presentations. When you arrange your site with linear architecture, this is what you do.

Linear architecture assumes pretty much everyone wants to see pretty much everything. There are times when linear architecture may be appropriate for a portion of your site. Suppose you have a site that, among other things, has a virtual museum exhibit. In most museum exhibits, the material is arranged in a particular order for a particular reason. How might the site map look for this kind of architecture? (Hint: See Figure 9-9.)

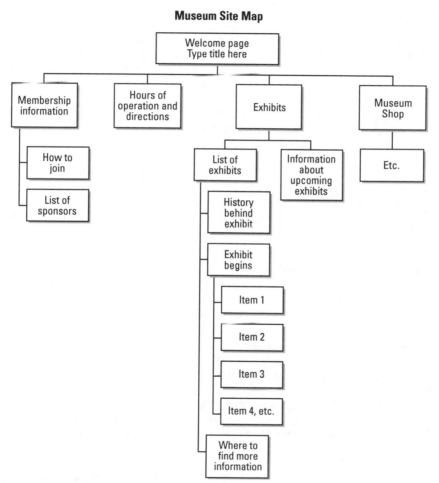

Figure 9-9: Site map including linear section

The key to using linear architecture is not to apply it to the entire site. Certain areas of a site may lend themselves to a linear approach, but it is inconceivable the entire site should be a forced march. Other times you may need to use a linear architecture are when giving quizzes (a quiz to determine whether you are left-brained or right-brained) and when giving a virtual tour (of the Blue Ridge Mountains on Scenic Drive in Virginia).

Hierarchical architecture

Hierarchical architecture depends on the idea of grouping content by some criteria, then providing a list of the members of the group. Each item in a group can also be a group, but you can get carried away with this if you are not careful. Eventually, your visitors want to come to something other than a list of items. They want to come to real content. Real content is something more substantive than a list of places to go (unless your site is a transit site and then this doesn't apply). Most sites use a hierarchical architecture for the framework. All the previous examples use a hierarchical architecture.

Hierarchical architecture is a useful way to organize your site. It is relatively easy to map and to divide a hierarchical site for team development and maintenance. Best of all, visitors understand the idea of a hierarchical site, where each subsequent page has a greater level of detail until, eventually, they find the material they were seeking.

Slavish devotion to hierarchy: Bad

Slavish adherence to hierarchical architecture can be a problem. Visitors should not have to click more than two or three times to get to a page where it is clear to *them* they are at least in the neighborhood of the material they need.

What makes you have a positive experience on a site? Your perception. If you *feel* like you can find it — based on the navigational controls visible to you on the Welcome Page or your previous visits to this site — and within two or three clicks you get to the neighborhood where you believe it should be and then two clicks later, you find it, you have a positive experience with that site. You don't feel like you wasted your time (or worse yet, that *they* wasted your time). If you keep coming to lists that either don't have the level of detail you need or a vocabulary you recognize, then you get frustrated and leave.

Visitors shouldn't have to click four or five times to feel they are finally in the right area. Isn't this why site searches are so popular? When you go to a site where you don't know if they have what you want, you click Search on the Welcome Page. On the Search Page, you type your keywords and click Find. Then you see the list of pages. That was two clicks. Your keywords may have been overly broad and your search may not have been effective but, within two clicks, you feel you can find what you came to find or you learn the site doesn't have what you were looking for and you go elsewhere.

Visitors failing to find what they want on a site, by the way, is not a disaster. Your visitors can have a positive experience on your site even if they don't find what they want, as long as they quickly realize they aren't going to find it, and they are confident they aren't missing it only because of the site's organization. When your visitors begin to think, "It must be here somewhere, I just can't find it," click around your site for 20 minutes looking for it, and then finally leave, this has not been a positive experience!

Anarchy

Sound emancipating? Forget it. Anarchy only works for really small sites. An *anarchical hierarchy* (a contradiction in terms?) is based on the idea that organization isn't necessary and visitors only want to wander through the site not looking for anything in particular. They can click any link they find, but no guarantee exists they can ever get back to a page they visited, unless they click the back button the correct number of times.

This feeling of groundlessness that anarchy creates is not positive for visitors. They aren't familiar with this feeling and it assumes visitors have nothing better to do than wander aimlessly around your site. It may work if your audience consists of college students with free Internet access and a need to avoid studying but, unless you are really clever with this approach, it will fail and so will your site.

A seamless web

How, then, do you create the feeling your site is a seamless web of related content, the page visitors want is only a click or two away, and visitors will be able to find this content again? You need to find the right combination of the various architectures for your content and you need good, consistent navigational tools.

The following rules will help:

Have a search option on your site. This will require that your site be indexed. Software that indexes sites is included with many Web servers (especially NT Web servers). Unfortunately, installing indexing software on UNIX servers is a bit of a trial. If you have an internal server, ask your systems administrator about this option. If you have an ISP, ask them. Especially as your site grows, your visitors will benefit greatly from the ability to search your site. Being able to search if you keep archival information on your site is also useful. Often archival information is only available by search (it is not linked into the current material on your site).

Have navigational controls in the same place on every page. We discuss this further in the next section. It is that important.

Don't be afraid to link across divisions. Linking from a page full of highly technical information about your product to a page of job listings in your company makes perfect sense if your company needs people who are highly technical. Information about contacting your company (including the mailing address) should be available from lots of places; don't expect visitors to remember they can get to it from your Welcome Page. Remember: links are free; your visitors' time is not. Because of all these links across groups, having your files organized according to some formal system (as discussed in Chapter 6) is especially important. Otherwise, your team members may rearrange their own files, not realizing they just broke all your links.

Select an architecture and be consistent. Visitors want to know what to expect. Whichever architecture you select, be consistent and make it obvious to visitors. They don't want to learn different site navigation on each page.

Providing Navigational Aids

Now it's time to think about visitors again. We won't let you forget them for a while. Whichever architecture you select, your job is to make getting around your site easy for them. Visitors need to know how to get to what they seek, how to get back to the Welcome Page, and how to find what they seek on subsequent visits.

You can use several tools to make the process of navigating around your site as painless as possible for your visitor. Let's start with the ideal: In the ideal world, your site would be able to read visitors' minds (or read some sort of configuration file their browsers provide) to give them a Welcome Page that showed exactly what they were seeking. You can't do this today, but no technical reason exists why you couldn't do it (if not the mind-reading part, at least the configuration file part) in a few years.

More realistically, you can provide some or all of the following devices to make navigation intuitive and easy for your visitors:

Table of contents. Easy enough, right? Using client-side scripting techniques (you learn about these later and they are only available in HTML 4), you can even make your table of contents *expand and retract* (see Figure 9-10). This means if visitors click a section heading, they see a listing of the contents of that section, right onscreen, without going elsewhere. If they click a different section heading, the details of the first section they clicked retracts and the new section expands. What a great way to give your visitors the information they need, not take up a lot of screen real estate (more on this later), and not make users bounce all over the place!

Search function. We talked about this previously. It isn't much extra work to index your site and provide for searching (for an example, see Figure 9-11). You can find plenty of free or inexpensive tools to do this if your Web server doesn't include site indexing. You want to make certain the search is available from every page. Remember: links are free.

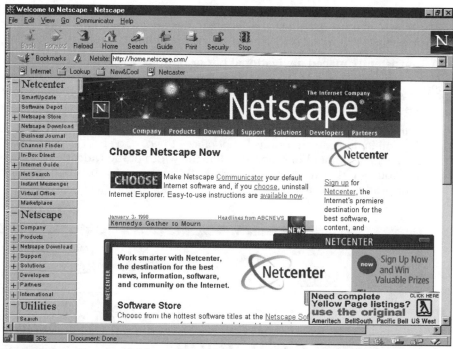

Figure 9-10: An expandable and retractable table of contents on the Netscape site

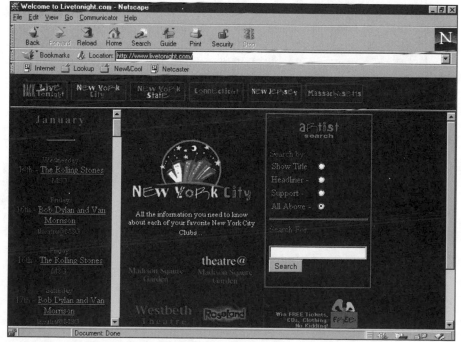

Figure 9-11: Search functions are a staple of easily navigated sites

Site Map. This one is a little bit trickier to implement. You need to think about a way to show — graphically — where things are on your site. This is done most elegantly with JavaScript, but it can be difficult.

Consistently placed navigational bar or buttons. (See Figures 9-12 and 9-13 for examples.) Of all of these, this is the easiest to implement. Nearly every decent site has navigational buttons or bars. Visitors expect them to stay in the same place from one screen to another. Don't surprise them.

Drop-down list of places to go. This is a great way to save page real estate. You can include an enormous list of places to go, or a short one, and it takes up the same amount of space: one line the width of the widest entry in your list. You can use this approach for links to sections of your site or for links to your product information.

Figure 9-12: Navigational buttons consistently placed

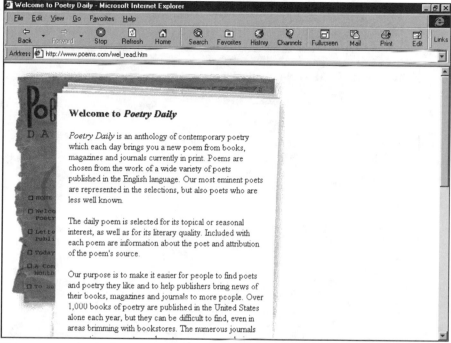

Figure 9-13: Navigational buttons should stay put.

Maintaining a Multipage Site

You need to start thinking about many maintenance issues. A reasonably comprehensive list follows:

Scheduling face-lifts to the site. While we haven't talked about the look of your site yet, you need to make certain you update your look periodically. You don't want to change it just because you discovered a new font you like, but you may want to change it when your organization makes changes to other marketing literature. You'll also want to change your site to take advantage of the latest technologies and looks being used by other cool people on the Web.

Running link-checking software on a regular schedule. If your site has more than a dozen pages, you'll want to take advantage of link-checking software (see Figure 9-14). This product tests out every link in your site (Remember what we said in the last chapter about false hit counts? Well, every time this software checks a link, it gets counted as a hit!) and reports back with a list of broken links. Acquiring this software, learning it, and running it on a regular schedule is worth your peace of mind.

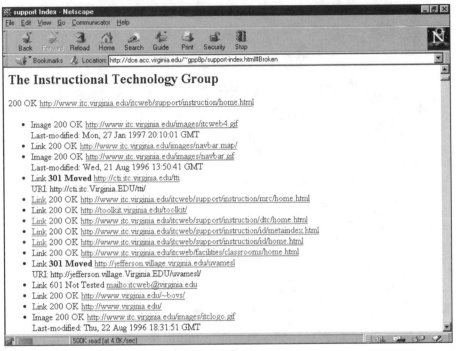

Figure 9-14: Report from link-checking software

Testing your site daily or finding an agent to do it and to notify you if it is down. If your site is hosted elsewhere and you don't have reason to visit your site daily, how will you know whether you are up and running or dead in the water? A number of ways exist to check your site and to make sure it is up. The easiest, but least reliable, is to go to it yourself. Remember, every time an agent checks to see whether your site is up, it counts as a hit! (Are you convinced yet how stupid hit counts are?)

Keeping your index up-to-date so the search is always accurate. If you are going to index your site to provide a search function, then you must be sure you have the index function running at some regular interval so your search function is always up-to-date. The index for a site with constant changes shouldn't be maintained manually because it's a hassle. Figure 9-15 shows Cold Fusions' Verity Indexing, an automatic way to index a dynamic site.

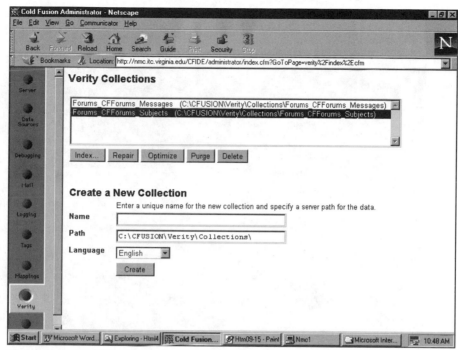

Figure 9-15: Cold Fusion's Verity Indexing

Reviewing and revising your content on a scheduled basis so it always sounds fresh. Don't take this for granted. Lots of Webmasters publish content and forget about it. Even a month after you have published a page, you may have forgotten the details of what it says. Set aside time to review all your content on a regular basis. Is it any wonder maintaining a Web site is so expensive?

Keeping your competitors' or alliances' information up-to-date. Providing a comparison chart with features of your product and your competitors' products is not generally frowned upon, but it is bad form for your information about your competitors' products to be out-of-date. People will wonder what other information is incorrect. If you are going to include information about your competitors' products, keep it up! Figure 9-16 shows an example of making comparisons with the competition.

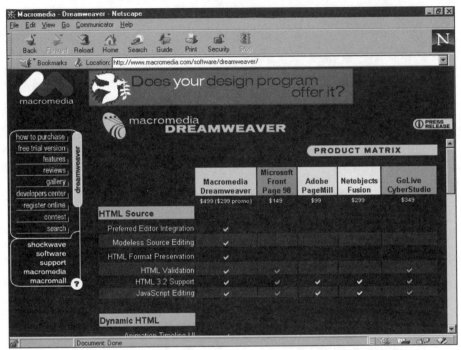

Figure 9-16: Macromedia compares its own Dreamweaver to the competition.

Bonus: Maintaining a Really Large Web Site

You may be getting in really deep. If you are or you think you may eventually be responsible for maintaining a thousand-page Web site, then you need to start thinking about how to manage two things: how will you manage the information and how will you manage the people who do the work? Some practices you may want to implement are:

1. **Create a Central Web Team.** This team will be working on the Web site full-time.

2. **Have all design decisions, all procedural changes, and all organizational decisions originate with the Central Web Team.** You need to set a precedent right away that every page can't be unique. HTML 4 supports your decision to control the look of the site by providing you with style sheets. Create your style sheets at this level.

3. **Have content originate with distributed Web developers who are closer to the content.** These are basically loaners to the Central Web team. We'll call them the *Distributed Web team.*

4. **Have meetings of both groups together.** You need to keep the Distributed Web team informed about new policies you institute, any changes to servers or accounts, and procedures you implement. You also want to be respectful of

their time because you aren't their real boss and you want them to *want* to do the work for you.

5. **Use e-mail to notify the Distributed Web Team of changes to the look and to procedures.** Create a mailing list to notify the Distributed Web team of changes. Consider having a mailing list where they can ask each other questions and help each other.

6. **Have written procedures and standards for publishing a page for the Distributed Web Team.** Tell them enough, but don't tell them more than they need to know. These are people who have other responsibilities. If you make the Web maintenance part of their jobs too big of a pain (with too much mail and too many meetings), then they will put it off and avoid you. Include information about linking to style sheets, in your written instructions, with an example — or better yet, give them a copy of this book.

7. **Organize accounts and permissions on your Web server so people can't accidentally delete or overlay each other's files.** What files are called, where they go, and how they get there must be part of your written procedures. Publish your written procedures to a page on your Intranet so people can check on things without bothering you and so new members of the Distributed Web team can get up-to-speed quickly.

8. **Follow the procedures yourself that you impose on the Distributed Web Team.** No cheating. You won't exactly inspire the trust and enthusiasm of the Distributed Web team if you don't have to follow the rules yourself.

From Here

Proceed to Chapter 10. Learn the essentials of Web page design.

Jump to Chapter 14 and find the HTML editor that's right for you.

Summary

We covered a lot of ground in this chapter. You learned the pros and cons of developing a multipage site, effective ways to organize your site for easy navigation, and intelligent ways to break up your content into pages. You also learned about site architecture: good and bad ways to use hierarchy, as well as times when you may want to mix in linear or siblings-based architecture into your hierarchy.

You learned about the basics of navigational aids to make the journey through your Web site easy and intuitive for your visitors. We also covered the basics of site maintenance for most sites and, as a bonus, for really big sites.

✦   ✦   ✦

Essentials of Web Page Design

A re you ready to design a page? The preceding chapters took you through your message, your site strategy, and your page strategy; this chapter talks about *tactics*. How you design your page is a *tactical* decision.

Your page design must be focused to contribute the feelings you want your visitors to have about your site. It needs to incorporate consistency, predictability, navigability, and a clear purpose with visual appeal and interactivity. When you finish this chapter, you'll be ready to start designing your content.

What's in a Page?

The first thing you must do is decide what you want to communicate in each page. Chapter 9 talked about mapping your site. The site maps showed a single box for what will actually be a set of pages. In fact, you need to apply the chunking guidelines from Chapter 7 to the material you think should go into one of these groups. The result will be a number of pages. Each page will contribute in some way to the overall goal of your site, either directly or indirectly.

Figure 10-1 shows a diagram of a listing page.

Figure 10-1: A detail from the fully developed Over the Web site map

What needs to be in a page?

Generally, you want all your pages to have certain items. These include:

✦ The name of the organization or person publishing the page. Remember, with search engines indexing your site, someone can jump into the middle of your site. If you don't say who you are on every page, visitors may not know.

✦ A way to get to your Welcome page. This follows from the previous one. Don't assume everyone coming to your site is coming through the front door.

Other optional elements include:

✦ Your logo

✦ How to contact you

✦ A navigation bar or navigation buttons

✦ A link to a table of contents

✦ A link to a site search page

✦ A link to a site map

✦ A drop-down list of places to go

✦ Content, if a terminal page

✦ Links to a group of pages, if a links page

Focusing on Your Message

Now that you have a page-size morsel of information, you should have an idea of what the message of that page is. If you don't know, consider how it fits into the site. If you don't think it contributes to the overall goals of the site in some way, drop it.

Everything you put on your page should contribute in some way to communicating your message. One of the secrets of creating consistent, easily navigated, visually appealing, compelling sites is to limit the amount of content on each page.

Keeping it to the point (your left brain)

Your message needs to be short and sweet. Remember the section on chunking in Chapter 7? If you find you have too many different things to communicate in your page, take one of three actions:

1. **Unless your page is a** *terminal page*, **you can group related material and link to it.** Be careful about adding too many layers of linking pages, though. Whenever possible, group your links so even though the list of links might be long, your visitors can still find what they want relatively easily. The nicest way to do this is by using dynamic HTML, which is discussed in Part VIII. The next best thing is to give a list of the groups of links on your page at the top of your page and then use internal links (remember learning about them in Chapter 5?) to jump within your page to the group of links associated with the short list.

2. **Decide what is important and forget about the rest.** You keep reading this, don't you? Simply too much information is on most sites. Unnecessary information does not help your visitor understand your message. Unnecessary information just clutters.

3. **Break your material into more than one page.** We put this last because if you've already applied the chunking guidelines in Chapter 7 to your material and you still think you have too much to put into one page, then you probably have material that isn't well-suited to hypertext. Or, you have material that will be printed, your visitors will appreciate you *not* breaking up your material if they plan to print it.

 Vocabulary

Terminal Page. A terminal page is a page whose primary function is to provide content, rather than to provide links. This is what your visitors came for: content. Your site is composed of a Welcome page, linking pages, and terminal pages. You can visualize the Welcome page as the root of a tree, the linking pages as the trunk and branches, and the terminal page as the leaves.

Go with the feeling (your right brain)

What kinds of thoughts and feelings do you want to convey with your page? What adjectives do you want people to use when they describe your site? Your page design will evoke certain feelings in your visitor, even if you don't want it to do this. What kinds of feelings do you get from each of the following?

✦ White background with black text, Helvetica font

✦ Cream background with brown text, brush script font

✦ Cool gray background with burgundy and black lines breaking up the black text, font that looks like printing

✦ Tan background, forest green text, mustard-colored lines and accents

Take a look at the Web page shown in Figure 10-2 and consider the impression you get.

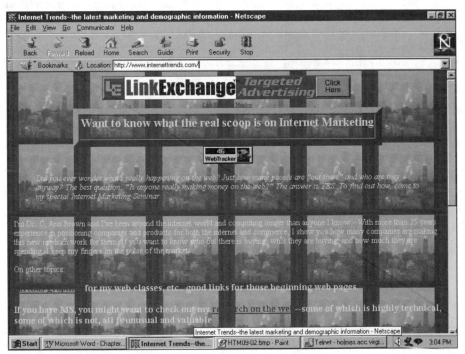

Figure 10-2: What were the designers of this page thinking?

Your colors, accents, graphics, and text style and size can all contribute to your message. They make an impression on your visitors whether or not you intend them to do so. Don't take shortcuts here.

When to ask for help

If, after reading through this chapter, you decide you are simply not a *designer*, and many of us are not, then hire someone to provide just the *look* of the page. You can do everything else with the HTML; your designer can just create the style sheet and the graphics. This is too important to take shortcuts.

How do you find a good designer? Surf the Web. If you find a site that rings your bell, write to the Webmaster and find out who designed it. Designers each have their own looks. Find a designer who has the look you want. Professional designers often leave their signatures on the site, as an artist signs a painting. Look for this. Explain that you will create the site and all you are looking for is the design work. It won't cost that much. The labor-intensive part is creating and maintaining the HTML.

Notice the link at the bottom of the Web page in Figure 10-3. This is a good way to find a designer whose work you've already seen.

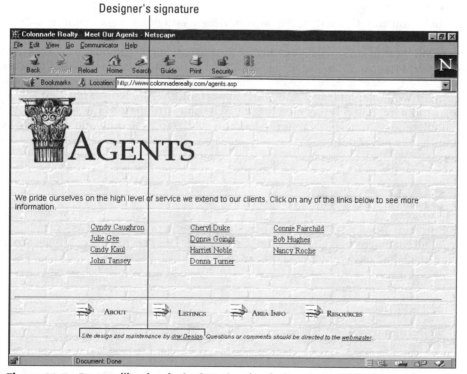

Figure 10-3: Do you like the design? Notice the designer's identification at the bottom of the page.

Note
One respected professional Web designer, Tamra Heathershaw-Hart, had this to say about the costs of creating versus maintaining a Web site, "I've found that for most 20-page sites, graphic design (and the management of getting the design) takes 50 percent of the cost. Another 30 percent is HTML and production, and 20 percent is for content creation. Because graphics are so subjective (unlike a typo), there's a lot of overhead in the graphics production process. It also usually takes 4–6 weeks to get a design from first meeting to HTML comps—producing the pages is quick once that's all done."

Lead me not into temptation

It's easy to get distracted from the message of your page, when you start thinking about graphics, fonts, colors, animations, and so forth. You need to balance these competing interests. The HTML 4 Way helps relieve you of this temptation. You can actually separate your right-brain work—design—from your left-brain work—content and structure—by using style sheets.

To help you stay focused, settle on your design and *move on*. Commit to a design and don't go back and fiddle with it. You can easily change the style sheet later, but you will have more work if you change the basic design. The best way to avoid the constant temptation to add nice-looking things to your site is to divide the work of your site between two people or teams. This way the person responsible for the content won't get off track. And, most important, the site will be finished—at least for a moment! Later in this chapter, we give some attention to the myth of Web site completeness. You will be relieved to know you aren't the only one who feels like your site is never done.

The Shell Game

Is there any good way to assure consistence, predictability, and easy navigation from all the pages of a site? You bet! Use a shell. The previous vocabulary box says your page has basically three types of pages:

1. A Welcome page
2. Links pages
3. Terminal pages

Each of these three types of pages requires a slightly different design. Page shells — or templates — provide the consistency you need.

The word *shell* is more accurate than the word *template* because templates traditionally have formatting information in them. Because The HTML 4 Way pulls all this formatting out, what is left is a shell of a page. Look at the three screen captures, shown in Figures 10-4, 10-5, and 10-6. They show the page design for each of the three types of page for this site. Wouldn't it be easy to create a great-looking site if you had shells that looked like this into which to insert your content?

Figure 10-4: This Welcome page isn't really a shell, because there will only be one, but it is consistent with the design of the rest of the site.

Consistency

You want to make sure your entire site has the same look. Not just in the big picture, but in the details. Fortunately, style sheets can help you here. You can assure all your paragraphs have the same level of indentation and the same amount of white space above and below them.

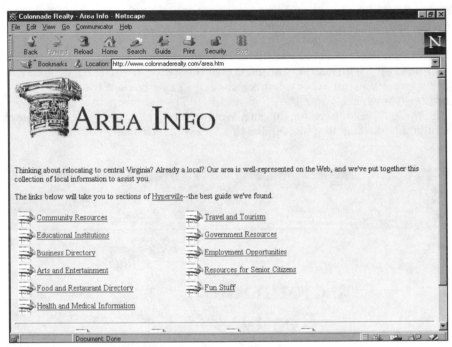

Figure 10-5: Links pages share the look of the Welcome page.

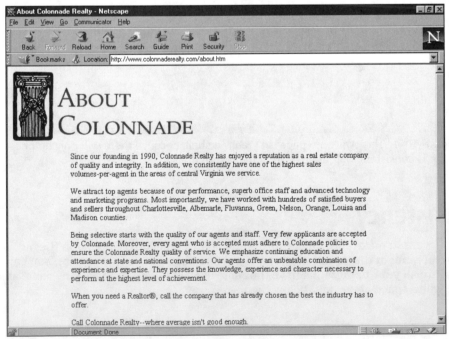

Figure 10-6: Terminal pages carry out the same design theme.

As a Webmaster, you do have to make sure everyone developing content for your site understands when to use the paragraph element and when to use the blockquote element. Veteran Web developers have had to use a lot of tricks in the past to get paragraphs to look nice; one of these tricks was using the blockquote element to format paragraphs. This is a habit you should help them break.

Figure 10-7 illustrates the problem of distinguishing one from the other.

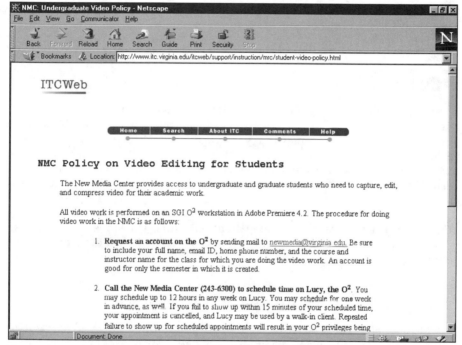

Figure 10-7: Are these paragraphs or blockquotes? You'd have to view the source to find out.

Applying a style sheet to a page with paragraphs formatted with the blockquote element can have unpredictable and unattractive results.

Predictability

No one really likes surprises. Elements of your page should behave the way visitors expect. Don't format text in blue with an underline because it will look the way visitors expect links to look, but won't link. Don't create button-looking designs with text in your graphic unless your graphic is also an imagemap. On the other side of the coin, don't format your links to be the same color as your other text or visitors won't know to click it. Also, while subtlety is nice, don't make the buttons on your imagemaps so subtle, no one would think to click them.

The Web is a fabulous platform and is unique among platforms because your visitors don't have to learn to use a new interface to view your material. In the olden days, before the Web, every software program had its own interface. This meant users of the software had to learn new interfaces every time they wanted to use new software. With the Web, if you give users what they expect, the interface is a nonissue for you. Take advantage of it.

Navigability

The previous chapter talked about site architecture and navigational controls. Because this is the tactics chapter, this is where you need to think about how you are going to implement them within your page design. In the previous chapter and earlier in this chapter, some attention was devoted to navigational controls. Which ones should you use? How much screen real estate should you devote to them? You certainly need to use *some* navigational controls. Figure 10-8 shows a page with a clear course for navigation.

You certainly need to use *some* navigational controls. The simplest kind to use is a navigation bar or navigation buttons. Other options include a table of contents, site searching, and site maps.

Navigation bar or navigation buttons

The simplest kind of navigational tool to use is the navigation bar. A *navigation bar* can be either text, text in a table, or an imagemap. The navigation bar should appear on every page in the same place or places. Many sites use frames to keep the navigation bar or buttons stationery while the content and links move into and out of a different frame. The navigation bar with text in a table, shown in Figure 10-9, is in a different frame from the content on the right. Figure 10-10 shows a navigational bar used with an image map.

Cross-Reference

Pros and cons to using frames exist; Chapter 30 discusses them at length.

Vocabulary

Frames. Frames are a way to have two different HTML files open at the same time in the browser. You can divide your browser page either vertically, horizontally, or both. Frames keep your visitor grounded because only part of the browser gets updated most of the time, which leads to faster page-loading.

Figure 10-8: This page uses a shell to convey a feeling and provide navigation.

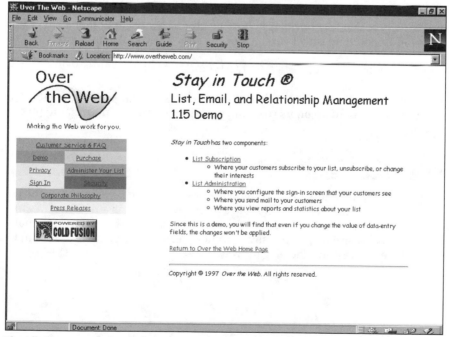

Figure 10-9: Over the Web uses a navigation bar with text in a table.

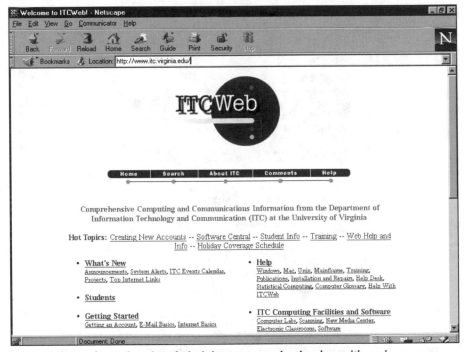

Figure 10-10: The University of Virginia uses a navigation bar with an imagemap.

You are likely to see text navigation bars on the *text-only* version of a site, but you can certainly put them on all versions of the site. They look like this:

```
[Home][Support][Service][Sales][Contact Us][Feedback]
```

Each item within the square brackets is a hyperlink to that area of the site. A text navigation bar should go on its own line and should appear in the same place on every page.

Table of contents

Having a table of contents (TOC) only one click away can be a life saver for your visitor. This can also save you valuable screen real estate as a designer. A site map and a TOC should contain basically the same information, but a TOC is usually text-based, whereas a site map is usually graphical. You can implement a TOC in two ways — the easy way and the elegant way.

Text-only sites

Should you create a text-only version of your site? Yes. Every site should have a text-only version to allow maximum access even to people whose Internet connections involve cups and a string. Is that realistic? No.

If you have the resources to maintain a text-only site, great. But for most Webmasters, who are struggling just to keep the primary Web site up-to-date and keep up with emerging technologies, it is simply not realistic.

Why maintain a text-only site? Faster access for people with slow Internet connections who have never heard of turning off the graphics, and for people using Lynx browsers, who can't see graphics.

Why not maintain a text-only site? Time, energy, and expense.

What alternative do you have to providing a text-only site? You can do several things to increase downloading speed and they are all discussed later in this chapter. In addition, there are things that will make a page heavily dependent on graphics useful to a visitor who arrives with image-loading turned off. Watch for the `alt` attribute to elements throughout this book (See Figure 10-11.)

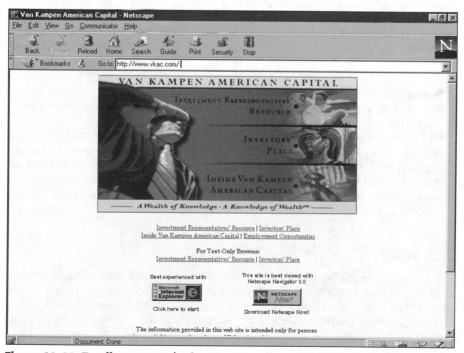

Figure 10-11: To offer a text-only site or not to offer a text-only site: that is the question.

The easy way

Even if you choose to implement the TOC the elegant way, you still need to implement it the easy way for people who have old browsers. In the easy way, every page in your site has a button or part of the navigation bar that links to a separate page where the TOC resides.

If the TOC is large, then you want to have all the major headings near the top of the page with links to the details later in the same page. If you can, try to keep the short list at the top of the page only one screen long.

If the TOC is not that long, just list all the pages. You probably want to have the names of the pages in the TOC correspond with the titles of the pages. You certainly want every page name in the TOC to link to the corresponding page in your site.

If the page names, or if only a few page names, aren't adequately descriptive, include a brief description under those page names. Use the brief description only if it increases clarity; you needn't do it for every single page.

The elegant way

Using JavaScript and the document-object model, collectively known as *dynamic HTML,* you can create an incredibly rich, interactive table of contents that can make your site look like a million dollars. Of course, this only works on browsers that support HTML 4, but you can use another line or two of JavaScript to check to see what browser your visitor is running and implement the Easy Way for those who can't see your work of art in dynamic HTML.

Vocabulary

Document-object model (DOM). A set of rules that when implemented by browsers, give you, the designer, incredible access to the elements on your Web page. Formerly, if you wanted to have JavaScript change the color of your text, you had to reload your page; with the DOM the change to text color can happen when the user clicks a radio button or a check box. You can create dynamic forms, where the next field on the screen appears in response to the information entered in the previous field. The DOM empowers the designer enormously and saves the visitor page reloads and multiple screens. This is so exciting and important, Part VIII is devoted to it.

Site map

Site maps can be useful. Consider including one like the ones in Chapter 9. You want to be careful how much detail you include in your site map, which should be an imagemap, as well. If you include too much detail either it will take a long time to load, because the graphics file will be enormous, or the text will be tiny and difficult to read, or both.

Site mapping tools

There are site mapping tools and there are site mapping tools. Most often when one hears about site mapping, it is about mapping the site from a Webmaster's perspective: Do all the links work? Where are the files physically located? This is not the kind of site map a visitor to a site needs. In addition, tools that map sites for purposes of site management rarely produce Web-quality digital images that make sense to the visitor. Two different approaches you can take to creating a site map for the Web visitor are demonstrated by Microsoft Organization Chart and Dynamic Diagrams' MAPA Service.

On the low end is Microsoft Organization Chart. This is an easy tool to use to create attractive site maps, but you have to do all the work yourself. If you have PowerPoint installed on your computer, then you already have it. Whenever you change your site, you must remember to update your site map published with the new version. This product only works for small sites. The amount of energy required to maintain the site map for sites developed by the team would soon outstrip the economy of the initial software price.

On the high end is Dynamic Diagrams' MAPA Service. This is written in Java and lets your Web site map itself. Because it is a service, there is no software to purchase, upgrade, or install. You always get the most recent version of the product. MAPA creates a 3D animated map, a Java applet, that runs on the Java-enabled browsers of your visitors. The MAPA service is priced based on the size of your site. You pay a monthly fee for either daily or weekly mappings. The price is so low that if your site is over 100 pages, you shouldn't even consider creating and maintaining the site map yourself. The applet it creates is so smooth and well-designed, it solves all your navigation problems. Definitely look at it at `http://www.dynamicdiagrams.com`. (See Figure 10-12 for an example of a 3D animated site.)

Site search

Some sites include a search field on every page; some link to a search page. If your audience is sophisticated enough to know how to use the search field *and* you can spare the space on your page, then go ahead and put the search field on every page. If your audience is likely not to be too technically sophisticated or you want to give them more information about searching, then link to a separate page for entering search terms. In either case, you need either a separate page or a separate frame for search results. On the back-end, you need to be sure your server has a search and index program running or your visitor's search will never return any results.

Site drop-down list

This is a clever item to add to your arsenal of navigational tools. Using a drop-down list, you can give your visitors the power to link anywhere on your list with just one click. The list can be as long as you want. The drop-down list (called a *select list* in HTML) takes up little screen real estate, so it is a double value.

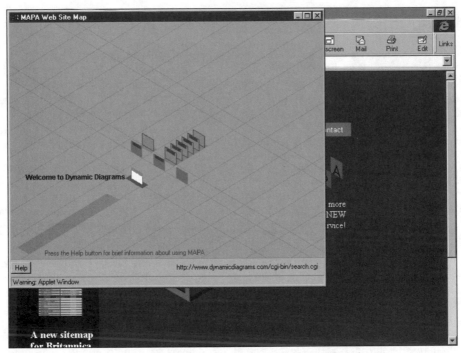

Figure 10-12: The 3D animated site map of the Digital Designs' site

Tip   Make sure your visitors understand the drop-down list is another navigational tool. Otherwise, the value is wasted. Visitors to your site — especially inexperienced users — may need a little direction.

Visual Appeal

Beautiful pages are not that plentiful on the Web. What do people find beautiful on a page? The same things that are beautiful on a brochure: clean lines, smooth shapes, complementary colors. In 1765, Edmund Burke, the English political philosopher, wrote *A philosophical enquiry into the origin of our ideas of the sublime and beautiful*. This short book — less than 200 pages — about what we find beautiful is as accurate today as any book you can find on creating graphics for electronic delivery. Nothing has changed. Beauty is timeless.

You are receiving a lot of design suggestions in this chapter. You might be wondering how you can fit all these things into just one page and *still* have room for the content or the links. Try to incorporate as many guidelines as possible into your page. The page shown in Figure 10-13 meets every test of good design in this chapter and it looks like it isn't even trying. Good design is like that. Great athletes make their feats look effortless; good design works the same way. At the end of this chapter is a checklist you can use to make sure your pages have the essentials of good design for the Web.

Figure 10-13: A beautiful page doesn't sacrifice anything to be beautiful.

Interactivity

Your visitors expects almost every page to have some level of interactivity. For links pages and the Welcome page, this is easy. That is really all they do. For content pages, however, they also expect to be able to interact with your site. You can include interactivity by using hyperlinks and imagemaps to link both within and outside of the site. You can use dynamic HTML to have interactivity within your page. Forms are another way to provide interactivity.

The facts about Internet connections

T1, T3, dial-up, 56K, cable modem: what does it all mean in plain English? T1 and T3 are types of Internet connections used by those users willing to pay more for the faster connection—typically businesses, universities, and probably by your ISP, if you have one. The backbone of the Internet is T3. T1 transfers data at 1.5Mbps. T3 communicates at between 3Mbps and 45Mbps (something you want to ask your ISP about if it claims to have a T3 line). When you have a dial-up connection to the Internet, your modem communicates with your ISP's modem at the speed of the slower modem. So even if you have a 56K modem, if your ISP has 28.8 lines, you communicate at 28.8. Some technologies, such as 56K modems and cable modems, use asymmetrical communication, which means download *from the Internet* is at one speed and upload *to the Internet* is at another speed. Download may approach the promised speed, but upload won't. This chart should help. It assumes the other end of the connection is at least as fast.

Type of connection	Download	Upload
28.8K modem	28.8K	28.8K
56K modem	53K	28.8K
cable modem	4500K	14.4K
T1	1500K	1500K
T3	3000K–45000K	1500K–45000K

Of course, there is no guarantee you will ever communicate at the ceiling speed, which is what the table shows, but for purposes of calculation, you must assume something. An overloaded Web server could cut download speed by a factor of ten or more. The chart doesn't define *K*, which is 1,000 bytes per second or 1,000 characters per second, but what really matters is you see the relationship between the different connection speeds. If a page takes a moment to download for you when you are connected via a T1, imagine it will take a long while to load for your visitors.

Speed

How much should you worry about speed? Worry may be too strong a word. Even though bandwidth is getting cheaper and more available, don't make the mistake of believing everyone accessing your page is on a T1 line (with fast access). You still should be considerate about the amount of data you expect them to download to see your page. Even though this book talks about *visitors to your site*, in fact, your site is *delivered to* the desktops of the people who request it in their browsers.

When you design your pages with huge graphics — background images that fill the screen, large image maps, graphical representations of text rather than text — you are telling your visitors you don't respect their time. Is this the message you want to send?

Design Guidelines

Good page design is a skill. If you know absolutely nothing about page layout and design, it'll show. If you are attempting to design a site for commercial use, it's probably best to hire a professional. You can learn it yourself, but you must expend some intensive time and effort. For those of you insistent upon doing page layout yourselves, here are ten things to remember:

1. **Think of the underlying design as a "hanger."** Once you figure out what the basic design is, everything else "hangs" off it. If you don't have the hanger, you're going to be struggling with each element and it's going to drive you insane.

   Look at Figure 10-13 again. The designer, Debra Weiss of drw Design (`http://www.cstone.net/~debra/drwdesign`), had this to say about it:

   "I was struggling over the look and feel of this site for quite some time. I wanted it to look elegant, but I didn't want the design to get in the way of the functionality. Then, it struck me. When I was visiting the Colonnade offices, I remembered noticing several framed prints of Greek architectural drawings of temples and columns and admiring them. I was able to locate some wonderful digital artwork of this type — floorplans, pillars, columns, and colonnades. This concept became the hanger. Each section of the site has a different column that represents it. One of the page backgrounds is a screened-back floor plan. The headline font is Palatino, a classical font. The navigational icons are teeny column tops. The design just snapped into place."

2. **Decide on an underlying grid structure and don't deviate.** Look at any magazine or publication. Analyze how the text and graphics are aligned. Is it a one-, two-, three-, or four-column grid? For consistency, use the same number of pixels for horizontal spacing between text and images — at least 5 pixels.

3. **Use real typographical marks.** This is a subtlety, but it makes a subconscious impression on the reader. Most Web browsers display quotation marks like this: "hello." You want this: "hello." While not all browsers support these entities yet, ideally you can insert real typographical quotes using entities as follows :

   ```
   " = &ldquo;
   " = &rdquo;

   ' = &lsaquo;
   ' = &rsaquo;
   ```

4. **Decide on your color palette, and stick with it.** If your colors are navy, burgundy, and cream, don't make your links in green.

5. **Anti-alias your display fonts.** The mark of a professional site can sometimes be as simple as the look of the fonts.

This font is not anti-aliased

This font is anti-aliased and the edges are smooth. See the difference? You need software that does this, such as Adobe Photoshop.

6. **Be target-aware.** Many sites make the mistake of providing hundreds of links to other sites. It's hard enough to get people to come to your site—why send them away? If you link to other sites, use the `target =_blank` attribute-value pair to open the link in a new window. This way, visitors can return to your site easily. Opening links in a separate window also solves anomalies that occur when your site has frames and you link to a site that also has frames.

7. **People read from left to right and from top to bottom.** This seems obvious, but inexperienced designers seem to have trouble remembering this. Put your most important elements at the top left of the page. If you don't grab the reader's attention there, you're never going to get them to read more.

8. **Think carefully about bells and whistles.** Animations, marquees, DHTML, and so forth are all great, *when used in moderation*. Don't pull all your tricks out of the bag and plop them all on one page. If your content isn't good enough to stand alone, rethink it.

9. **Use different font styles sparingly.** A good rule of thumb is to pick two font families *at the most*. Use one for your headlines and subheads. Use the other for body copy.

10. **Look at your site using the worst conditions possible.** Get a copy of Netscape 2.0. Set your display to 600×480, 256 colors. Set your modem down to 14.4 or 28.8 and look at your site. Every page. If you can't stand it, redesign until it's acceptable. If your page looks great under the worst conditions, it'll shine under the best ones.

Speed versus design

Does this mean you have to sacrifice design to keep pages loading quickly? Not necessarily. The important thing is you don't add gratuitous graphics if you can avoid it. If you need slow-to-load features on your site—as an example, Java applets can be very slow to load—then you want to do what you can to have them load without making the visitor wait for them. Just ignore this whole section if you are designing for an intranet where every visitor to your pages will have a reliably fast connection. There are environments where you don't have to worry about these things. For the rest of us: things can be done to speed the delivery time of your pages. But first you need to understand what slows the loading of your page.

Slow modems and large graphics are the biggest offenders. Because you can't control the modem speed of your visitor, you have to do what you can on your end to make sure your page won't take an unreasonably long time to download. The only control you have is to control the size of graphics on your page. By using intelligent compression on your images and by using multiple small images with white space around them (rather than one large image), you can reduce the size of the files your visitor has to download, thus reducing the download time.

Cross-Reference   Chapter 34 explains all these concepts and more.

Without getting a Ph.D. in Digital Art, the following guidelines can help you make intelligent decisions about how to show you respect the time of your visitors:

1. **Reduce the number of graphics files on your pages.** Simple enough. Decide what you need (element-wise) on your page and see how you can convey the information you want to convey without using graphics. Two no-brainers are: Don't use custom bullets in a bulleted (unnumbered list) or if you feel you absolutely *must* use custom bullets, use only one bullet graphic for every bullet in your site; and don't create custom "Go" or "Submit" buttons.

2. **Reduce the size of graphics files.** You can do this two ways: reduce the dimensions of the file (height and width) before you publish it; or, reduce the bit depth of the images (the amount of color information the file carries). You can also use a trick under certain circumstances to load a tiny file and show a full-sized file. If what you want to do is show some pattern of colors, create the file as a tiny version of the image you want and use the height and width attributes of the object element or the image element (whichever you prefer) to *stretch* the file to the dimensions you want.

Tip   Check out GIF Wizard at http://www.gifwizard.com. This is a Web-based utility that analyzes and shrinks your GIFs and JPGs.

GIF or JPG? For additional information, check out the collection of excellent articles on the Microsoft Site Builder site at http://www.microsoft.com/workshop/design/color/default.asp.

3. **Don't use a background image.** Or, if you absolutely must, then use a tiny background image that tiles well. See Figures 10-14 and 10-15.

Cross-Reference   Chapter 26 discusses the use of background images at length.

Figure 10-14: The background image on this page is a 6×6 pixel file.

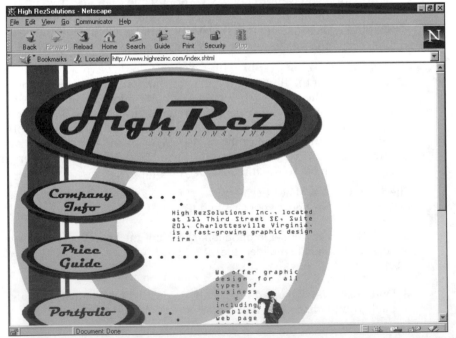

Figure 10-15: This page boasts a full-screen background image and a full-screen image map! They must know their visitors are all using high-speed connections.

4. Use text when you can use text. What a concept! Next time you have your word processor open, if you use either Windows 95 or Windows NT, click the list of fonts available to you. Unless you installed some fancy fonts package, you have the base install of fonts. These same fonts are available to everyone else on the Web who is browsing from either Windows 95 or Windows NT (your results will vary on a Mac or on UNIX). Is this huge list so limiting, you have to recreate text in a graphics package and load it as an image? Get real!

Tip

You can create nice bullets using symbol fonts, such as Wingdings. To figure out what keystrokes to use to insert into your file, use the Windows Character Map, found under Accessories. If you don't have this installed, you should. Don't do this if you expect a significant number of visitors to come to your page from Macs. Macs don't have Wingdings as an installed font and what they see will be unpredictable.

Effective Use of White Space

White space has the most remarkable effect on a page's design. It improves it immeasurably. When you are designing, make sure you allow plenty of it. When you have a lot of white space, you can include the same information (sure the page will be longer) without creating the feeling of frenzy and chaos that permeates the Web. White space is relaxing. White space doesn't have to be white. If your background is pale powder blue, then your *white space* is really *blue space.*

Vocabulary

White space.   Uncluttered space on the page. Margins around text and images is white space.

You can use white space to draw attention to a title, a heading, or even a list. Why do you suppose your eye is drawn to a bulleted list? White space contributes to the effect. When in doubt, use white space to break up your design.

Optimum Page Length

Forget about the idea that your entire page needs to fit into one screen without scrolling. What you really must do is to make sure what you do see looks complete. How can you tell how much will fit into a screen? Don't assume all your visitors are running their browsers the way you are. The following section on testing walks you through all the ways you need to test your design to make sure visitors see what looks like a complete page.

More important than the page length is the page content. You don't want to break up your content into annoyingly small bites just to have everything fit into one screen. Frames can help you maintain the sense of completeness so even if visitors have to scroll, they won't lose their grounding.

What you want to avoid at all costs is horizontal scrolling. Do not make your visitors pan across your page to see your content. If you design your pages with a width of 550–600 pixels, you avoid this.

Tip   If you want to see how your pages look at different resolutions, check out Windows Power Toys at `http://www.microsoft.com/windows/windows95/info/powertoys.htm` and get the Quick Res utility. This enables you to switch screen resolutions without rebooting.

Future Expandability

You mean there'll be more? Definitely. Assume your site will never go away. It will continue to grow. Paying close attention to the site architecture and site organization, as described in Chapter 9, and to navigational controls as previously described, takes you 80 percent of the way toward having an infinitely expandable site. Creating effective page shells and applying them with discipline takes you the rest of the way.

Designing an Effective Welcome Page

However you decide to organize your site and the content on the pages within your site, you need a Welcome page. The *Welcome page* is the first place visitors see when they come through the front door of your site. As discussed, some visitors will come to your site through other doors.

What should you have on a Welcome page? Just enough. Look again at Figure 10-13, because a picture really is worth a thousand words. Just enough to convey a sense about who put up the site. Just enough to get you heading in the direction of the content.

Splash Screens

What about splash screens? *Splash screens* are pages that appear before the Welcome page, as shown in Figure 10-16. They can also be called *Entry Tunnels*. Usually all they do is enable you to pass through to the Welcome page. There is just one link on a splash screen and it takes you to the Welcome page.

The theory behind the splash screen is you have the visitors' complete attention and you can use this moment to create one strong impression (whether this impression is that you have a great logo or graphic artist or you are wasting their time with slow-loading graphics is hard to say). If you are going to use a splash screen, which is of arguable value—how much attention is the loss of good will worth?—then at least look around the Web and find some nice ones. Make sure your splash screen fits into one screen on all browsers at all screen resolutions; this is no time to scroll.

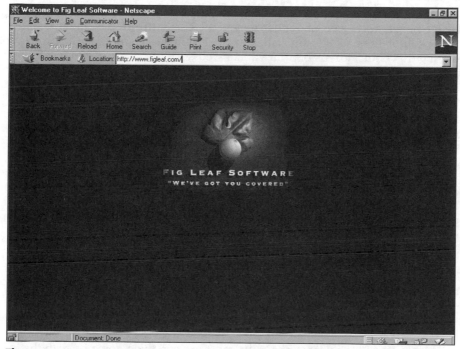

Figure 10-16: An example of a really top-notch splash screen

Testing

The importance of testing your page design cannot be emphasized enough. Look at it in all browsers on all platforms at all screen resolutions you can possibly conceive of your visitors using. Subtle differences exist between browsers and you can't assume things will look the same. If you are one who spends weeks at the paint store trying to find just the right shade of paint for your room, then you will waste a lot of time playing with colors in your design only to learn that what looks like a beautiful, rich burgundy on one screen is brown on another and purple on yet another.

Tip   Looking for information about the Web-safe palette? An excellent article is at
http://www.microsoft.com/workshop/design/color/safety.asp.

The Myth of Completeness

Never, never, never say "under construction". The entire Web is under construction. If it is complete enough to publish, publish it; otherwise, don't. In the process of writing this book, dozens of professional Web developers were contacted for permission to use their materials in the figures throughout these pages. Probably half of them said something about how the screen captures shouldn't be taken until they had fixed just one more thing they didn't like. You will never be entirely satisfied with your page. You will always want to do more. If it is so embarrassing you have to tell people it is under construction, then it probably shouldn't be published yet.

Along the same lines, don't be afraid to retire pages. Don't leave old junk up there if it is no longer attractive or accurate. Run link-checking software right away to make sure all your links still work. Because others will retire their own pages occasionally, you'll want to run link-checking software regularly to be sure your external links aren't broken either.

From Here

Cross-Reference   Proceed to Chapter 11, Writing for the Web.

Jump to Part VIII and learn about the most exciting thing going on with the Web: Dynamic HTML.

Jump to Chapter 34 and get an intensive course in graphics.

Summary

Page design requires balancing visual appeal against speed, consistency, predictability, easy navigation, and a host of other things. Getting distracted is easy when you are involved in the design process. Remember, this is just a step on the way to publishing your site. If you continually change your design, you'll never get your site published. The HTML 4 Way supports the separation of content from presentation that can help keep you focused. Finally, test, test, test your design to make sure all visitors, no matter where they come from, have a positive experience on your site.

✦   ✦   ✦

Writing for the Web

If you are not in the habit of writing, you may be a little intimidated by the idea of putting your thoughts into writing. Remember high school composition classes? Probably not, but that's okay. This chapter takes you through what you should know to communicate well in writing for digital, nonsequential reading.

If you are in the habit of writing, you may still need some guidance. Business, academic, or government writing doesn't always carry over to the Web with its passive voice—for example, *mistakes were made*. This chapter gives you guidelines you can apply to your writing style to make it more readable on your Web pages.

Designing for Quick Scanning

Most visitors who come to your page won't actually read all the text. You should expect this. Don't let it hurt your feelings. If you know people won't actually read much of your prose, then you can write with this in mind. So, if visitors don't read your pages, what do they do there? They scan them, looking for specific information.

Can you make your pages easier to scan? Yes. Some of the design ideas discussed in Chapter 10 can help. What follows is a set of guidelines that overlaps with the design ideas from Chapter 10. Most of the design ideas of Chapter 10 relate to designing the shell pages. This chapter addresses what you actually put into your terminal pages, your Welcome Page, and, to some degree, your links pages (when they have prose).

Cross-Reference

If you're scanning this book, like most of us do a Web site, you may want to take a minute to read the design ideas in Chapter 10!

Here are some basic guidelines to consider:

✦ **White space.** You've heard it before, you'll hear it again. White space draws the eye. Chapter 10 recommended white space play prominently into your design. White space should also play prominently in your page layout. Separate paragraphs of text adequately with white space. Leave plenty of white space around headings and images.

✦ **Use lots of headings.** Headings are valuable to visitors because they give visitors the first clue they have found the right page and the information they need is contained on it.

✦ **Wrap text to create a visual flow.** You can do interesting things with text flow both around images and around white space (or what looks to be white space) that help make your point. When you add an image to your page, whether or not the text wraps around the image makes a difference in how people perceive it. Try it both ways (text wrapped around image and text not wrapped around image) and see which seems more effective for your application.

✦ **Keep paragraphs short.** This means several things. You have to limit the amount you say about any one thing and organize the material you include and then you have room for more white space. All these things are good for your visitors.

✦ **Use bulleted lists.** Bulleted lists are often the first place the eye goes. People remember items displayed in lists better than the same items comma-delimited in a paragraph. Why do you suppose this book uses so many bulleted lists?

✦ **Use numbered lists.** Especially when you are informing your reader of things that happen in a particular sequence, numbered lists are effective in drawing the eye. Try using the technique used in this book. Begin each list item with the short version in bold and then explain it further as part of the same list item. This makes for especially easy scanning.

✦ **Include graphics when appropriate.** Chapter 10 tried to make it clear you should consider removing unnecessary graphics from your design to make download times shorter. Graphics as part of your *content* (as opposed to part of your *design*) are another story. If a diagram is more effective at communicating your message than words, include it. Remember, different people learn differently. Some people would rather see the picture than read the text. Include both so you don't exclude anyone.

✦ **Use hypertext to define terms.** Take advantage of the power of hypertext. Define your terms either elsewhere in your same page or on another page. That a hypertext link is underlined and a different color than the rest of the text also draws the eye to the term. This helps readers by keeping the text shorter and making scanning easier.

Writing Concisely

You've done everything you can to make your site easy to scan. Visitors can find what they want. And what they want is in a short paragraph. But you can do more. Consider the following two paragraphs (underlined text represents hyperlinks):

> "All Over the Web services make use of the latest security technologies, including Secure-sockets layer (SSL), which allows all transactions to be encrypted so that only you and the server know what you're sending, which should give you peace of mind to know that no one lurking on the Web can read your private information. Additionally, your own site visitors, who are just as concerned about the privacy and security of their own personal information, will feel more comfortable entering their own personal information into your guestbook when they see that your guestbook is administered by Over the Web."

Or

> "Over the Web employs SSL, the latest security technology available, to guarantee all transactions with our secure server are indecipherable to hackers lurking on the Web. Your private information stays private."

> "Visitors to your site, wisely concerned about their own privacy, will have confidence their personal data is in good hands when they see Over the Web administers your guestbook. And this gives them confidence in *you*."

Active verbs

Active verbs make your writing more interesting to read. Between "extensive customization is supported by Stay In Touch" and "Stay in Touch supports extensive customization," which reads better? The second example makes use of an active verb. The first example uses the passive voice, where the subject of the verb is either missing or an inanimate object. Take responsibility for the action. People don't speak in the passive voice—unless they're in politics and they've done something wrong—and you shouldn't write in it.

Active verbs also give you more of a sense of action. Consider the following examples:

"Pollution endangers the native wildlife."	"The native wildlife is endangered by pollution."
"Our product performs calculations like nothing else on the market."	"Calculations are performed by our product like nothing else on the market."
"Your donation can save the life of a hungry child."	"The life of a hungry child can be saved by your donation."

Active verbs are simply more compelling.

Subordination

Your sentence usually has a main point and then there may be some relevant, ancillary data, which is outside the main point. Without resorting to diagramming sentences (remember that from the 7th grade?), you should be able to find the main point by finding the verb, the subject of the verb, and the object of the verb. An example helps:

> "A bomb, the third in as many years, damaged the Church of St. George in the Greek Orthodox Patriarchate in Istanbul and seriously injured one priest (he's still recovering)."

What is the verb? What is the subject? What is the object of the verb? All the other words are part of the ancillary information. The verbs are (trick question) *damaged* and *injured*. The subject of both verbs is *a bomb*. The objects of the verbs are *the Church* and *one priest*. Everything else in the sentence is either part of a prepositional phrase, an appositive, or a parenthetical.

Subordination is the process of deciding what the main point is and moving the rest of the sentence either into another sentence or into a subordinate clause. Subordinate clauses often begin with *that*, *which*, or *who*.

Parentheticals

You've seen a lot of these in this book. In fact, one occurs in the last paragraph. A *parenthetical* is something you insert in parentheses. At least three good reasons exist to use parentheticals:

1. To give your opinion in a sentence that is otherwise fact.

2. To interject tangentially related information.

3. To include details about the preceding word.

Appositives

People use appositives when they talk:

> "I ran into Chuck, that designer I told you about from the Neon Guild, today at the mall. He said he did have Windows NT server experience."

That designer . . . is the appositive. *Appositives* directly follow the noun they modify; an appositive is preceded and followed by a comma.

Expletives

Even though writing for the Web can be quasi-conversational, expletives may be out of place, depending on your audience. Instead, use exclamations and italics to make a point:

"This particular beta software is nowhere ready for production. After installing my operating system for the *third* time, all I could say was: 'what a *complete waste of time!*'"

Expletives may work in conversations in the movies, but they may bring down the quality of your Web pages immeasurably.

Sentence length

Given a choice, shorter sentences are better than longer ones. As much as possible, break up your sentences. If you must use long sentences at times, make sure the preceding and following sentences are short. See if you can break up your long sentence with lists or with subordination. Shorter sentences require less concentration to be understood. What you really want to avoid is sentences that are so long that they span several lines.

Write Vividly

Writing vividly involves selecting the most appropriate and powerful words and omitting any unnecessary words. If you think your vocabulary isn't that strong, get a thesaurus. Consider the following sentence. What can you do to clean it up, given the suggestions in this chapter?

"This product manufactured by ABC is unlike any others on the market in that it removes spots from wool, cotton, and other natural fibers, melts ice even on the coldest days, protects your bathroom enamel from hard water marks caused by calcium and iron, and can be delivered directly to your door in one-gallon jugs overnight."

First, the comma-delimited list goes into a bullet list. Notice the last item isn't really a feature of the product, but information about distribution; that'll go into its own sentence. Also, *This product* isn't very vivid; use the product's name. *Unlike any others on the market* translates to *unique*. What does *in that it* add? Finally, *manufactured by ABC* should be moved into an appositive or into the sentence about distribution. So, we have:

"Toxic-toner, manufactured by ABC,

removes spots from cotton, wool, and other natural fibers

melts ice even on the coldest days

protects your bathroom enamel from hard water marks cause by calcium and iron.

This unique product can be delivered overnight to your door; it is available in convenient one-gallon jugs."

Check Spelling and Proofreading

It seems so obvious, but you do need to edit your page. Just as you put your HTML through a validator, you need to put your text through a spelling checker and then have it carefully reviewed by someone with a good command of the language to make sure all your verbs agree with your nouns, your references make sense, and that generally it is readable.

The editor you have been using up to this point, either SimpleText or NotePad, doesn't have a spelling checker. All the HTML-editors reviewed in Chapter 14 do have one. If you are serious about developing Web pages, you'll want to find an editor with a spelling checker. Start looking around the Web. Many pages have misspelled words. We wouldn't mention this problem if it didn't happen a lot!

From Here

Cross-Reference

Proceed to Chapter 12 and learn about HTML versions.

Jump to Chapter 14 and select your HTML editor.

Jump to Part IV: "Developing Document Structure with HTML 4."

Summary

Writing for the Web is different from most of the writing you do in other professions. You need to make sure the page can be easily scanned because most people looking at your pages are looking for something in particular. You can use white space, short paragraphs, lists, lots of headings, hypertext, and graphics to make your page more easily scanned. You also want to make sure your sentences are vividly written, using just the right, but not too many, words. Finally, you want to take that extra minute or two after you think you are done writing your page to edit it carefully and run it through a spelling checker. Embarrassing typos are completely avoidable.

✦   ✦   ✦

Examining HTML Versions

This book teaches HTML 4, but, as mentioned earlier, not everyone who comes to your Web page will be running a browser that supports HTML 4 features. In the next chapter, you see how the browser your visitors use affects how they see your site. In this chapter, you get a brief overview of the process involved in getting a version of HTML recommended by the World Wide Web Consortium (W3C). You also see what the document type definitions looks like that SGML uses to specify HTML. Finally, this chapter takes you through the evolution of HTML from Version 1.0, which was never even published by the W3C, to Version 4.0, which is the current version.

The HTML Standardization Process

The standards-setting body for the World Wide Web is the W3C. Its membership is derived from companies involved in technology, researchers, governments, and others. The W3C has a process for recommending versions of HTML and other Web-related technologies. Currently in the hopper are CSS level 2, XML, PICS, and the Web Accessibility Initiative (WAI).

Buzz and scrambling

How does the W3C decide when a new technology must be standardized or a new version of an existing technology must be developed? Newsgroups and mailing lists exist where leading figures in the relevant field talk about the shortcomings of an existing version or the idea of a new technology (that's the *buzz*). If a ground swell of support seems to exist for a new technology or a new version, the W3C begins the process of specifying it. Figure 12-1 illustrates one such initiative.

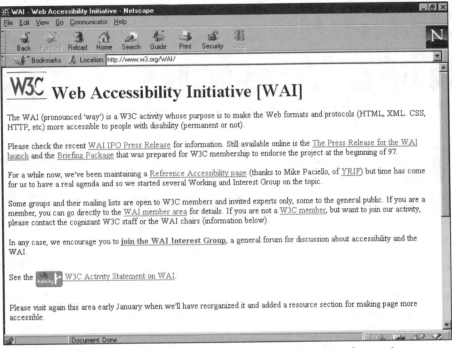

Figure 12-1: The Web Accessibility Initiative, a W3C undertaking, has an interest group that is open to the public.

Something else, however, carries more weight and more urgency than discussion by agitators and activists. This is ongoing development by software developers (that's the *scrambling*). Nothing gets the W3C activated quite so quickly. In reality, the W3C is mostly involved in trying to standardize the proprietary extensions developed by software developers, such as Netscape and Microsoft. If the W3C didn't do this, within two versions of their browsers, HTML might not run the same (or at all) on both systems. The W3C reigns them in to some degree. Neither one wants to produce a browser that lacks support for recommended HTML elements so, even if Netscape introduced it, in the subsequent version of their own browser — after an official recommendation by the W3C — Microsoft will incorporate the element (and vice versa).

Committees and working drafts

When a new technology or a new version of an existing technology is required, the W3C convenes a committee of interested parties to write the specification. The committee publishes its work on an ongoing basis as a *working draft*. The point of publishing these working drafts is this: Software developers, who want to implement the new technology or the new features of the new version, can get a jump on things and build their new product to incorporate the new features. When the specification is finalized and developers are ready to use it, products are on the market that implement it. Figure 12-2 shows the CSS2 specification—a work in progress.

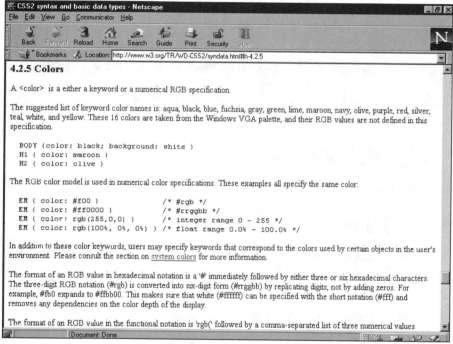

Figure 12-2: A working draft of CSS level 2

There is also the issue of books. You want books on new technologies to be in the bookstores the day the recommendation is finalized. For this to happen, authors must write the books using the working drafts—a moving target—as the reference materials. The CSS2 working draft has changed during the writing of this book. Sometimes this works and sometimes it doesn't. If the specification changes radically from the working draft to the final version, then the book will be inaccurate. Most of the time, working drafts only get thicker as they approach approval time.

Voting process

Democracy: you just can't get away from it. When a working draft reaches a point where the committee is pleased and believes it is complete, the working draft is released to the public as a *proposed recommendation*. Members of the W3C have up to six weeks to vote on it — votes can take the form of any one of three choices: yes; yes if certain changes are made; or no. At the conclusion of the voting process, the W3C can either recommend the specification officially, make the requested changes and recommend the specification with the changes, or discard the proposal. Figure 12-3 shows the way the process works.

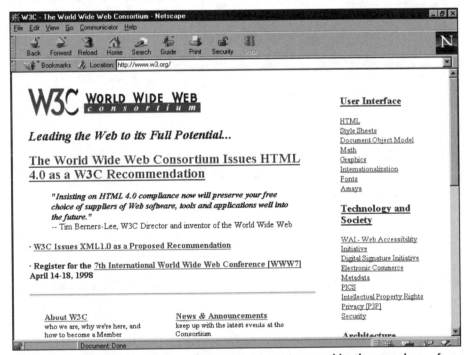

Figure 12-3: The announcement that HTML 4 was approved by the members of the W3C

SGML and the HTML DTD

You've read that HTML is a subset of SGML. What you probably didn't realize is HTML is actually specified in SGML. In other words, SGML is used to define HTML. SGML uses document type definitions (DTDs) to specify itself, the elements of HTML, and XML. How does this work?

Actually, it's rather frightening to look at this. In Figure 12-4, you can see part of the DTD for HTML 4. You can see why this book chose to create its own convention for telling you about new elements.

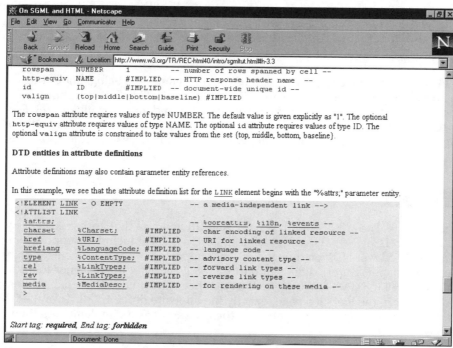

Figure 12-4: This is an excerpt from the DTD for HTML 4.

HTML 1.0

HTML 1.0 was never formally specified by the W3C because the W3C came along too late. HTML 1.0 was the original specification Mosaic 1.0 used and it supported few elements. What you couldn't do on a page is more interesting than what you could do.

You couldn't set the background color or background image of the page. There were no tables or frames. You couldn't dictate the font. All inline images had to be GIFs; JPEGs were used for out-of-line images. And there were no forms.

Every page looked pretty much the same: gray background, Times Roman font. Links were indicated in blue until you'd visited them and then they were red. Because scanners and image-manipulation software weren't as available then as they are today, the image limitation wasn't a huge problem. HTML 1.0 was only implemented in Mosaic and Lynx (a text-only browser that runs under UNIX).

HTML 2.0

Huge strides forward were made between HTML 1.0 and HTML 2.0. An HTML 1.1 actually did exist, created by Netscape to support what its first browser could do. Because only Netscape and Mosaic were available at the time (both written under the leadership of Marc Andreesen), browser makers were in the habit of adding their own new features and creating names for HTML elements to use those features.

Between HTML 1.0 and HTML 2.0, the W3C also came into being, under the leadership of Tim Berners-Lee, founder of the Web. HTML 2.0 was a huge improvement over HTML 1.0. Background colors and images could be set. Forms became available with a limited set of fields but, nevertheless, for the first time, visitors to a Web page could submit information. Tables also became possible.

HTML 3.2

Why no 3.0? The W3C couldn't get a specification out in time for agreement by the members. HTML 3.2 was vastly richer than HTML 2.0. It included support for style sheets (CSS level 1). Even though CSS was supported in the 3.2 specification, the browser manufacturers didn't support CSS well enough for a designer to make much use of it. HTML 3.2 expanded the number of attributes that enabled designers to customize the look of a page (exactly the opposite of the HTML 4 Way). HTML 3.2 didn't include support for frames, but the browser makers implemented them anyway.

Note   **Frames.** A page with two frames is actually processed like three separate pages within your browser. The outer page is the *frameset*. The frameset indicates to the browser which pages go where in the browser window. Implementing frames can be tricky, but frames can also be an effective way to implement a Web site. Most sites that use frames use one frame for advertising and another for page content.

HTML 4.0

What does HTML 4.0 add? Not so much new elements — although those do exist — as a rethinking of the direction HTML is taking. Up until now, HTML has encouraged interjecting presentation information into the page. HTML 4.0 now clearly deprecates any uses of HTML that relate to forcing a browser to format an element a certain way. All formatting has been moved into the style sheets. With formatting information strewn throughout the pages, HTML 3.2 had reached a point where maintenance was expensive and difficult. This movement of presentation out of the document, once and for all, should facilitate the continued rapid growth of the Web.

Use the Web Page Purifier, available at `http://www.delorie.com/web/purify.html`, to check your HTML against most of the versions mentioned in this chapter.

Document Object Model

One major improvement to HTML 3.2 that empowers the creative Web designer is *the Document Object Model* (DOM). The DOM enables you to script any part of your page. What does this mean? So much!

✦ **Dynamic updating of your page.** Before the DOM, you could use JavaScript to script forms, but if you wanted anything visible to happen in the open browser window, you had to reload the page (or, if you were clever, you could reload the frame and keep most of the page the same). With the DOM, you can change something on the page and it updates right before your eyes without reloading. Why is reloading bad? Any form fields filled out by visitors are cleared on the reload.

✦ **Animate your page.** This is the easy kind of animation that doesn't require visitors to your page to download any huge files or have any special plug-ins. You already have cool things on your page, right? Well, with the DOM, you can move them around! You don't need any special, expensive animation tools, either. All you need is a little knowledge of JavaScript and the DOM.

✦ **Dynamic form creation.** You've always thought another way should exist, right? You fill out a form that asks for your state and ZIP code, and then for your country, if it's not the U.S. Shouldn't the form know because you entered a state in the U.S. that you live in the U.S. or, if you entered a province of Canada, shouldn't the form know you live in Canada? Now it can. With some pretty simple JavaScript, you can create dynamic forms. Based on the way visitors to your site complete the form, you add additional fields to the bottom of the page *dynamically*. You won't have to see anymore of this: "If No, skip to Question 8."

✦ **Graphics over text.** Isn't it about time? With the DOM, you can layer objects and finally, place graphics right over your text! Figure 12-5 shows this long-awaited development.

✦ **Absolute positioning.** Until now, you have been used to relative positioning. On different screens, your graphics and text would be in different places. Now, for the first time, you can use the DOM to specify exactly at which pixel your images and text start.

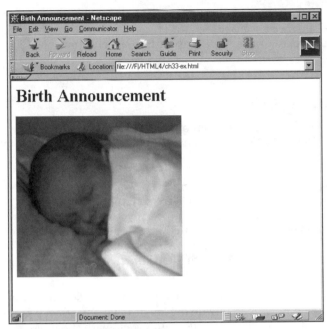

Figure 12-5: Graphics over text

CSS Level One

CSS level 1 pulls formatting information out of the HTML. Unfortunately, when CSS 1 was introduced, it was poorly supported by the two major browsers. In Version 4.0 of the browsers, CSS 1 is well-implemented. For the first time, you can format your paragraphs to have an indentation on the first line. Things taken for granted in print are possible with CSS 1.

The exciting thing about style sheets is, once you have one created that you like, you can apply it to all your documents and they will all look uniform. What kinds of things can you do with style sheets? Everything from the boring—have all paragraphs indented by a set amount (which, though it sounds boring, wasn't even possible before CSS 1)—to the exciting—have the first letter of a paragraph or a section span three lines of text, to look like old manuscripts or have a drop shadow. You can make your text look like a newspaper with the first line of text in all caps. If you resize your screen, it automatically fixes the text so the first line is still all caps, even if more words are now in the first line!

XML 1.0

eXtensible Markup Language (XML) is a way of using SGML to expand the number of elements available to you in the HTML DTD. While it is unlikely everyone will learn to write SGML to use XML, a few excellent resources are likely to make themselves available on the Web. People will copy what they find at these locations, paste them into their own documents, and will use XML without understanding all the fine points of SGML.

At publication, six XML user agents — read: browsers — were on the market. Now that the XML 1.0 specification has been recommended, more browsers should be supporting XML.

Unlike most additions to the HTML specification, which come from browser manufacturers, XML is coming from the SGML crowd and database devotees. XML should make the Web much richer. It also helps move the Web away from its dependence on HTML versions and browser versions.

Version independence

If a browser can process XML, meaning it isn't limited to processing the elements in the HTML DTD (for whatever version it claims to support), then perhaps Web surfers won't need to check constantly to see if they have the most recent browser version. This would be a huge improvement for Web developers, who could then use the newest elements without worrying about whether visitors have new enough browsers.

Increased flexibility means increased complexity

Why did HTML grow so fast? Because creating Web pages with HTML is easy. Sure, it is more complex now than it was in 1993, when HTML 1.0 was introduced, but even today, you don't have to use all the fancy features. You can publish a respectable page without learning a lot. XML certainly increases the flexibility of what you can publish, but at a cost. The biggest problem with XML will be that it is verbose and complex. Until end-user tools protect the majority of Web developers from the horrors of XML coding, XML won't really take off, except among the SGML-zealots who have been pushing it. And you know what you can expect from them: more complaints that it isn't as full-featured as SGML yet. Figure 12-6 shows the XML specification site.

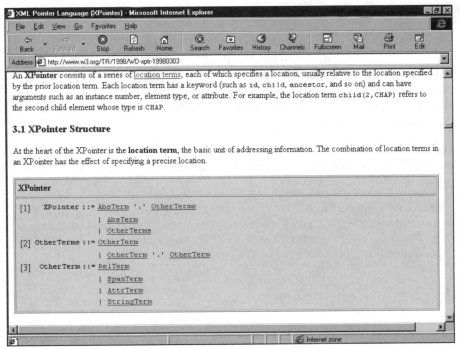

Figure 12-6: XML specification at the W3C site

From Here

Cross-Reference

Proceed to Chapter 13 and learn about browser versions and which browsers support which elements.

Go to Chapter 16 and begin learning about HTML structure in-depth.

Jump to Chapter 51 and learn more about the standardization process.

Summary

HTML has come a long way from the days all pages had black, Times Roman text on a gray background. Today, when you can place text over graphics, layer images, and define paragraphs with indentation. CSS and XML will help take Web design the rest of the way. XML may end the need to upgrade your browser regularly.

✦   ✦   ✦

Considering Browser Compatibility Issues

In This Chapter

Comparison of browsers by features

Discussion of tradeoffs of using newest HTML features

Discussion of installed base of browsers

Introduction to speech-synthesizing browsers

Y ou will learn many cool things in upcoming chapters that you can do to your Web page to make it sing and dance. But should you use them? Will every visitor to your site be able to see all these exciting things? This chapter recounts — browser by browser — what each browser can and can't do.

Considerations that come into play include the following: Which browser comes installed on the operating system that is shipping with new computers? What things do you simply need to use to make your page work the way you want?

This chapter helps you sort through the limitations of the installed base of browsers and the tradeoffs with using HTML features that aren't fully supported in older browsers.

First-Generation Browsers (1.0)

Mosaic 1.0 . . . Netscape 1.1 . . . what did these browsers do? Mosaic 1.0 supported only the most basic HTML elements. Using Mosaic 1.0, you couldn't see background images, tables, fonts, or frames (see Figure 13-1). Also, you could only see GIF files as inline images. If you wanted to show a JPEG image, you'd have to use a link from text or from a GIF image and show it as an out-of-line image.

Cross-Reference   If you don't know the difference between these two files types, don't worry. Chapter 34 tells you everything you need to know.

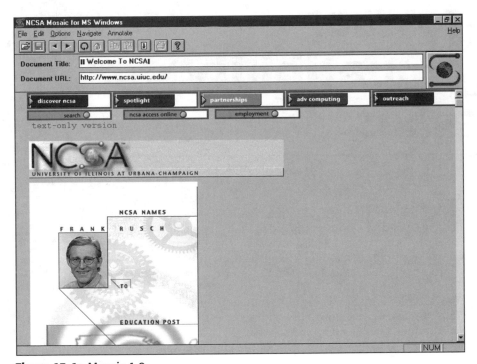

Figure 13-1: Mosaic 1.0

First-generation browsers were 16-bit jobs, which meant they would run under Windows 3.1, but they wouldn't run very well under Windows 95 or Windows NT. But say what you will about what they didn't do. They did get millions of people excited about the future prospects of the Web.

Inline images

What they did well, and what represented a change from the text-only browsers in use by the international physics community, was inline images. Someone sitting at a computer in Charlottesville, Virginia, could suddenly read a Web page of someone in Central Illinois and see pictures!

New sites of the week

One of the features of Mosaic 1.0, considered cool at the time—but humorous in retrospect—was a menu item entitled something like "New Sites of the Week." If you published a Web page and notified the folks at the National Center for Supercomputing Applications (NCSA), they would list your site. This list was initially only updated weekly. Not surprisingly, most of the new sites were located at universities. Having your site listed was cool. Imagine if you could get a list of new sites published every week these days, as shown in Figure 13-2. It would take a week just to read through the list!

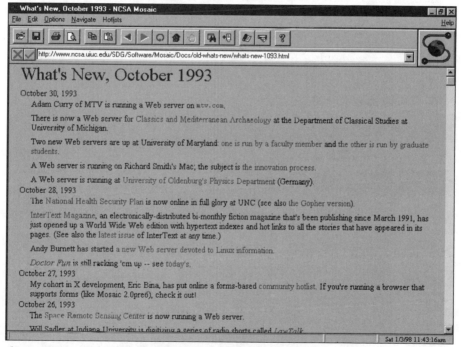

Figure 13-2: New sites of the week, circa October 1993!

Second-Generation Browsers (2.0)

Between the first-generation browsers and the second-generation browsers, the W3C was formed, Marc Andreesen left NCSA to help found Netscape Communications, and Microsoft joined the fray with Internet Explorer.

Believe it or not, many people are still using second-generation browsers; but they're probably not reading about HTML 4 and they don't even know what they are missing. If you are running Windows 3.1, you may still be running Netscape 2 or IE 2. Second-generation browsers didn't include the capability to check your mail, so in some work environments, the people who determine what software goes on desktops thought it may be wiser not to confuse users who may download all their mail from their mail server to their desk without realizing they'd done it. In these environments, Netscape 2 was a safer bet. Internet Explorer made its debut with Version 2.0. Figure 13-3 features Mosaic Version 2.0.

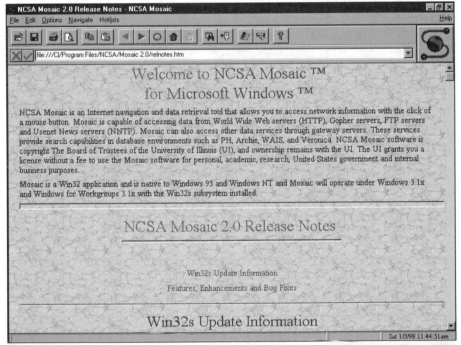

Figure 13-3: Mosaic 2.0 — Who could have guessed it would ever get better than this?

Customizing the colors

What made second-generation browsers so exciting was, suddenly, you could see background colors and background images. This increased the richness of the Web immeasurably. Printing in color has always been a luxury for businesses. On the Web, it became free and easy. Of course, not everyone browsing your page in 1994 would necessarily have a color monitor that could display more than 256 colors (or even a color monitor at all), but for those who knew how to use color to achieve an effect, the Web could be much more compelling.

In addition to changing the background color, you could suddenly change the text color, the link color, the visited link color, and the active link color. Corporate colors or school colors could be carried through a Web site. Very cool.

Forms

Another neat feature to come along in second-generation browsers was support for forms. Now Web sites could collect data and Web visitors felt like they were part of the action. The Web was still a small town. If you filled out a comments form on a site, you might even hear back from the Webmaster personally.

Not much changed in forms-support between second-generation browsers and third-generation browsers. It would take HTML 4 and the fourth generation of browsers to beef up support for forms.

JavaScript

Not everyone was ready for JavaScript when it was added to the panoply of choices Web developers had for souping up a page. When JavaScript first came on the scene, it was prone to abuse. Like all potentially great bells and whistles that could be added to a page, JavaScript was used for things it wasn't intended.

JavaScript has the potential to be powerful, because it runs on the client. This means it uses the power of the visitor's computer, instead of the power of the server. This also means data that gets processed doesn't have to travel across the network back and forth for processing to take place. Because of these facts, JavaScript is best used for validating fields and animating objects on the client. There is a server-side JavaScript, but that came along later. Of course, like any technology, JavaScript has limitations. See the sidebar for a discussion of those.

JavaScript limitations

JavaScript is a powerful scripting language, but it doesn't run on every version of every browser. Since it was introduced by Netscape, it makes sense that it initially ran better on Netscape. Netscape Navigator 2 supported JavaScript 1.0. Navigator 3 supported JavaScript 1.1; Navigator 4 supported JavaScript 1.2. In theory, Internet Explorer 3 supports JavaScript 1.0, but there are some slight variations on implementation from Netscape. Internet Explorer 4 supports JavaScript 1.2, but again, differently than Netscape. AOL version 4 understands JavaScript, but earlier versions don't.

Chapter 48 delves deeply into JavaScript and compatibility issues.

Tables

This was the beginning of real abuse of HTML. When codes were first introduced, they were used to create tables on Web pages. If you had data that would be more comprehensible in a table, you could put it into one. People went crazy with table border widths, but they basically used tables as they were intended to be used. Then someone realized if you could set border width to a half inch, you could set it to none.

Web designers began to put their text into tables. HTML-development tools started to do all their formatting with tables and Web-page source started getting long and ugly. This is about the time the cost of developing for the Web began to skyrocket. A page of HTML had so much markup in it, you could barely find the text. It became a daunting task to maintain.

Third-Generation Browsers (3.0)

This is when browsers began doing exciting things. Java? All third-generation browsers were Java-enabled. This expanded the range of things a browser could do but, because the Java Virtual Machine (Java VM) is still so slow in these browsers, developers remain hesitant to use much Java. The font element, which was standardized in HTML 3.2, worked in third-generation browsers.

The big development in third-generation browsers was frames! Framed sites began popping up all over. A lot of controversy still exists in Web developer circles about using frames. Second-generation browsers don't support them, but the consensus is definitely on the side of using frames. Chapter 30 talks about these issues and gives you what you need to know to build your own framed sites.

Third-generation browsers also saw the beginning of support for CSS. IE 3 supported a limited implementation of CSS. Netscape 3.0 didn't support CSS at all.

Java

Java is a programming language that is completely unrelated to JavaScript. Sun Microsystems created Java. Netscape created JavaScript. JavaScript had a different name originally, but when the Java hype took off, Netscape got smart and caught in on the wave.

Java, a *programming* language, can do all sorts of things JavaScript, a *scripting* language, can't do. For example, Java can access the server's file system. The interesting site-mapping tool described in Chapter 10, MAPA by Dynamic Diagrams, is written in Java. Java is like the little girl who had a little curl right in the middle of her forehead: When it is good, it is very, very good and when it is bad, it is horrid.

Partial implementation of CSS

Internet Explorer 3.0 supported a subset of CSS. This was enough to get people excited about style sheets, but not enough for most developers to move in that direction to the exclusion of the dreaded font element. Netscape didn't implement CSS at all. This was the beginning of the move by some Web surfers away from Netscape and toward Microsoft.

The other big market-share booster for Microsoft was bundling Internet Explorer with Windows 95 and Windows NT.

Frames

The improvement of frames greatly increased the control you had over your page. You could put a masthead at the top of your page with navigational controls, then make the rest of the page scroll under the masthead. This meant that a visitor to your site never had to scroll to get to navigational tools.

Despite what seemed like a no-brainer for better sites, there were drawbacks. Many people were still using second-generation browsers that didn't support frames. This meant you had to support a non-frames version of your whole site. Also, bookmarks sometimes set themselves to the inside page (the one that scrolls) instead of to the frameset (the one with all the frames in it), which means visitors could come to your site and not have *any* navigational tools (see Figure 13-4).

Font element

The font element was a mistake from the get-go. For this element to work properly, it had to be applied to every element on your page. The result may have been stunning (by the standards of people who were expecting everything to display in Times Roman font), but the cost was too high. Maintenance of pages became a nightmare.

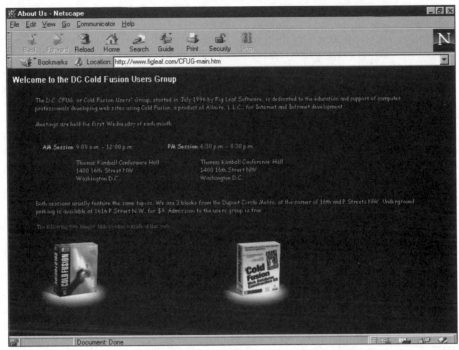

Figure 13-4: Arriving at an inside page with no navigational controls meant you didn't know there were other pages or how to get to them.

Web browser integrated with other desktop functions

Another twist to third-generation browsers was the understanding that people were spending an awful lot of time at their browsers and other desktop or network functions could be performed from the same software. Mail software became a standard part of third-generation browsers. Before then, you could send mail from the browser, but you couldn't read the mail you received in the browser window.

Fourth-Generation Browsers (4.0)

With fourth-generation browsers, you can see two distinct trends: the move toward the complete integration of the browser into the desktop and support for the change of presentation outside of the content of Web pages.

Separation of presentation from structure

Fourth-generation browsers completely support the HTML 4 Way. If you want to embed font elements throughout your document, you can, but fourth-generation browsers also support you if you want to move information about style into your style sheets. With the growing number of HTML elements available to a developer, the browsers have also become pickier about how they process HTML. Precision in defining structure is rewarded.

CSS 1 is supported in both Internet Explorer 4 and Netscape 4 (although not as well in Netscape 4).

Greater control over appearances and actions

Support for the Document Object Model (DOM) in fourth-generation browsers is a good sign. What would be an even better sign is uniform support. Right now, the JavaScript required to animate the DOM in Internet Explorer 4.0 is different from what is required in Netscape 4.0. A clever JavaScript programmer can sort it out, but it would be nice if you didn't have to do this.

Complete desktop integration

If you can surf the Web and send mail from your browser, wouldn't it make sense for you to be able to access your local files, run conferences, and write Web pages in your browser? Microsoft and Netscape are both heading in this direction, but each has a distinctly different take.

The Web is the platform

The folks at Netscape believe the Web is the platform, but they think the browser should run on your computer (what kind it is shouldn't matter) and then everything should run inside the browser. The focus, then, is on the browser as the operating system.

The Microsoft model

The Microsoft model is predictably different. They see the operating system as the browser. This has become something of a legal battle for Microsoft. The Department of Justice isn't happy with the way Microsoft has integrated Internet Explorer into its desktop. The standard installation of Internet Explorer 4 takes over your operating system, whether your operating system is Windows 95 or Windows NT. Microsoft claims Internet Explorer 4 is an operating system upgrade to Windows 95 and Windows NT.

Text-Only Browsers

For some applications, such as hand-held organizers, text-only browsing makes sense. For others, using Lynx (the original text-only browser) is a status symbol of being a UNIX nerd; see Figure 13-5 for DOSLynx. Visually impaired people can use text-only browsers attached to Braille output devices. Users with slow connect times also rely on text-only browsers.

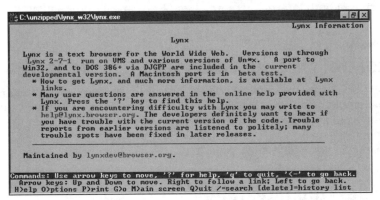

Figure 13-5: DOSLynx

As a Web developer, you should take the possibility that your visitors will use text-only browsers seriously. In every section about graphics or other objects, this book discusses the alt attribute. Setting it every time can help those who can't see your image — for whatever reason — know what they are missing.

Speech-Synthesizing Browsers

How long will it be before people insist on surfing the Web while driving, instead of flipping through the radio stations looking for a good song? The answer to this problem (where to put your eyes) is a speech-synthesizing browser. A version of CSS (Aural CSS) is currently being developed by the W3C to solve this problem. Figure 13-6 shows a phone-access system that uses speech synthesis.

Aural CSS, as currently written, is no cake-walk, but if your site may appeal to people in transit, then you must keep your own eyes open to see how the working version of Aural CSS develops (see Figure 13-7). Speech-synthesizing browsers can also help both the visually impaired and people who need to do research on the Web long after their eyes have given out for the day.

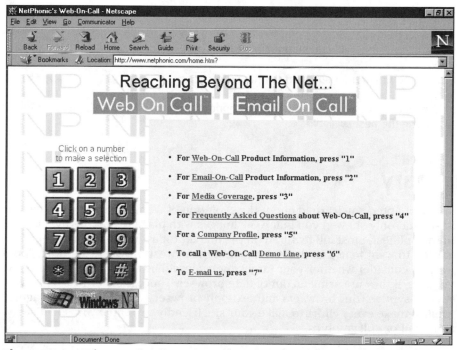

Figure 13-6: Web-on-Call delivers the Web over the phone — not a bad start

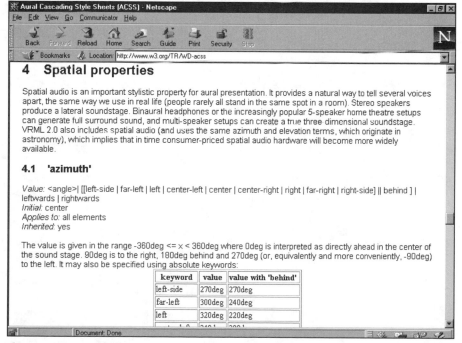

Figure 13-7: Aural CSS

From Here

Cross-
Reference

Jump to Chapter 48 and start learning JavaScript.

Jump to Chapter 23 and start learning CSS.

Proceed to Chapter 14 and start shopping for an HTML-development tool from among the best available.

Summary

In this chapter, you learned about the evolution of Web browsers from the most basic that only showed you inline GIF images with black text and gray backgrounds, to the spiffiest, most full-featured on the market today. While as a developer, it is natural to want to use all the features that the newest browsers support, you do want to consider whether your target audience will be able to view all your exciting features, if they are using an out-of-date browser. There is also the issue of whether speech-synthesizing browsers and text-only browsers can handle your pages. You'll want to make every effort to make your site friendly to people who can't see your animated or still graphics.

✦   ✦   ✦

Choosing an HTML Editor

In This Chapter

To WYSIWYG or not
to WYSIWYG?

Exploring HTML
editor features

Looking at HTML
editors

In the early days of the Web, everyone was stuck with just one option: Creating HTML with plain old *text editors* — simple word processing programs designed for writing software. This was, of course, part of the appeal of HTML: it could be created in a text editor. Compared to word processors, text editors are small, fast programs optimized for writing programming code. Although many people still prefer to use text editors to write HTML, those no-choice days are gone. Today you can choose from many HTML-creation programs.

The menu's full of cool, new options — so new, in fact, no consistent nomenclature exists (as yet) to describe them. This chapter uses the term *HTML editor* to describe *any* program including at least some features that help you write HTML, however simple or complex. The simplest programs are text editors souped up with a few HTML-savvy features. At the other extreme are expensive, big-ticket programs that enable you to create your pages in an entirely visual environment. Pros and cons exist to each approach. For a beginner, the visual environment is often the most painless way to get started.

This chapter discusses the features good Web-page development software should have and then moves on to review the gamut of programs. Included are both the HTML editors that provide a graphical environment for Web page creation and those that give you a place to type your HTML and content, providing a variety of cues and programs to assist with the HTML creation. Although you can find plenty of HTML editors available, be aware not all of them support the HTML 4 Way, the approach to HTML coding this book (and the World Wide Web consortium) advocates. They don't consistently separate presentation (formatting) from structure (HTML coding) and precious few support style sheets. But it's still early in the game for HTML 4-savvy editors to appear and future versions of these programs will do a better job. For now, you need to select a text editor with caution; many of them create code that doesn't conform to the HTML 4 specification.

To WYSIWYG or Not to WYSIWYG?

That's the question, and it's a biggie. On the one hand, you find *visual development environments*, which enable you to create fantastic-looking Web pages without writing any HTML. With these programs you see your HTML page just the way it will look when the browser displays it: that's why these programs are called *What You See Is What You Get* (WYSIWYG). On the other hand, you'll find *tag-based editors*, which force you to edit the HTML directly. These programs provide programs for entering and modifying HTML tags, but you need to know HTML to use a tag-based editor. What's at stake here?

Vocabulary

WYSIWYG. (pronounced *wiz-e-wig*) What You See Is What You Get

WYSIWYG editors: easy to use, but hands off

The HTML creation programs that give you a visual drag-and-drop environment for Web page creation are well-suited for beginners or for those who don't plan to use more advanced features in their pages. Using a program such as Netscape Composer, the WYSIWYG editor that comes with Netscape Communicator, you can quickly and easily create a nice-looking Web page.

But WYSIWYG editors exact a price for their ease of use:

✦ **Often, they don't include advanced features.** For example, Netscape Composer doesn't handle frames. That's ironic, because Netscape invented frames in the first place.

✦ **They often don't let you edit the HTML directly.** If you don't know HTML, that's a plus. However, experienced HTML authors know few WYSIWYG composers generate wholly satisfactory output. Often, they require some direct HTML *tweaking* (making some small but important changes) to get everything working (and looking) great.

✦ **They may introduce proprietary extensions that prevent your pages from working with all browsers.** If you can't see the HTML, you don't know what's in there. Microsoft's FrontPage Express, supplied gratis with Microsoft Internet Explorer 4.0, enables you to create scrolling marquees — but what you don't know is Netscape Navigator (and most other browsers except Internet Explorer) don't recognize the `MARQUEE` element, one of Microsoft's unilaterally introduced extensions.

✦ **They don't conform to the HTML 4 Way.** The current crop of WYSIWYG editors produces HTML conforming to an HTML 3.2 baseline, which doesn't separate presentation from content. A few incorporate style sheet features, but you need to know what you're doing to make sure these programs behave correctly.

The bottom line: For serious HTML, WYSIWYG editors won't cut it. Sooner or later, you realize you need to dive into the underlying HTML. At this point, you need a program that enables you to go *mano-a-mano* with the underlying code.

Getting serious: Tag-based programs

Tag-based editors don't hide the underlying HTML; instead, they stick it in your face. That's discomforting to beginners, but it's heaven to experienced HTML authors. Sooner or later, you need to see and directly edit the code — and this is particularly true if you want to write Real HTML 4, as this book advocates. You could use a simple text editor, such as the Windows Notepad utility, but you'll probably wind up using a tag-based editor. These programs are called *tag-based* because they provide easy-to-use tools for entering tags with a click of the mouse. For example, to code a heading, you select the heading text and click one of the heading buttons. The program enters the HTML tags automatically. This is easier (and less prone to error) than typing the tags yourself and it brings an added plus: You can manually tweak the underlying HTML, if you wish. And, more to this book's point, you can also make sure the code conforms to the HTML 4 Way.

What's the downside of a tag-based editor? You're not looking at your page the way browsers will display it. This makes it tough to enter and proofread text — all those HTML tags get in the way. Also, you don't immediately see the results of your coding. To see what your page looks like, you have to click an option that sends the page to a browser. If you find a mistake, you have to go back to the editor and make the change. Tag-based editors, in short, aren't very interactive.

What's the difference?

Want to see the difference between a WYSIWYG program and a tag-based editor? Look at Figure 14-1, which shows a WYSIWYG editor, and Figure 14-2, which shows a tag-based editor.

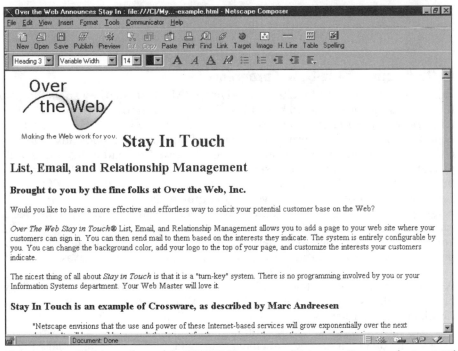

Figure 14-1: Simple Web page in WYSIWYG program (Netscape Communicator 4.03)

For example, if you're working in a tag-based editor, like the one shown in Figure 14-1 and you want to add a horizontal line in the middle of your page, you would place the cursor where you want the line to appear and then click the horizontal line tool. The program automatically enters the horizontal line and you see it right away on your page, just the way it's going to look when displayed by a browser.

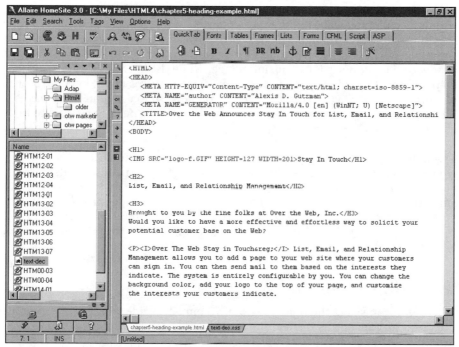

Figure 14-2: Same simple Web page in tag-based editor (HomeSite 3.0)

In a tag-based editor, you would scroll through your HTML to the point where you want to place a horizontal line and either type ⟨HR⟩ (that's the HTML tag that enters a horizontal line), or click a button indicating a horizontal rule tag should be added at that point in the page. You would then have to take the extra step of viewing your page in a browser (or a browser facsimile built into the editor) to see your horizontal line.

Exploring HTML Editor Features

Whether you choose a WYSIWYG or a tag-based editor to create your HTML, you'll be wise to spend some time exploring the various features offered by today's crop of HTML software. Depending on your needs, some of them may offer features and programs that will make your work go much more smoothly. On the other hand, you might get stuck with a program that doesn't do something you need done — and this means a lot more tedious, manual work for you.

Work-wise, creating your Web site may well be the tip of the iceberg. As soon as your site is up, you will want to make changes. Unlike a paper newsletter, which is printed, read, and then recycled, your Web site is expected to be, and always should be, fresh. One of the criteria for selecting a Web-page development program is how well it supports HTML maintenance. While the WYSIWYG programs may help you create a simple page faster, those same features might become more of a drawback once your site is up, when you need to make changes to pages. Whichever route you take, WYSIWYG or tag-based, you need to be able to make changes to your pages frequently.

The following sections explore some of the features found in today's HTML editors. To select the right features for your needs, you need to consider what you're planning to do. You won't necessarily need all the features listed. A handy summary is in Table 14-1. If you want to create a few simple pages, for instance, you won't need site maintenance features. But you won't want to live without those features if you plan to create a huge, complex site with dozens, or even hundreds, of Web pages.

Considerations

Before you can select the right program, you must decide what features you need. This section explains all the features we consider valuable in an HTML-development program.

Tip

While you might be tempted to go down Table 14-1 looking for the program with the most bullets under it, realize not all features are essential or even good. For example, if you are maintaining a site alone, collaborative development tools probably aren't necessary. If you publish your pages to an NT server and you have the NT drive on which you publish files mapped locally (as a drive letter of your local hard drive), then an integrated FTP client won't matter because you won't have to use it. If you use any server-side includes or scripting that is interpreted on the server, you can't use the "Open from the Web" feature without losing your scripting. Finally, an example of a downright annoying feature of some programs is *forced syntax compliance*. While you might want to enforce syntax compliance on others, you won't enjoy having it forced on you. The HTML standard is constantly evolving. If you are working with an editor that enforces compliance to a fixed HTML set of tags, then the editor will have to be upgraded to enable you to work in the newest HTML standard.

Note

Colored tags are a valuable feature to have in your HTML editor. With colored tags, each type of tag is displayed in a different color. For example, comments might be gray, tags related to tables might be green, tags related to scripts might be red, and so forth. This way, if you forget to close your comment, the rest of the code will be colored gray—a useful visual cue.

Some features, on the other hand, are absolutely essential. These include the capability to have multiple pages open for editing at the same time or to do multiple-file search-and-replace, and tag cues to tell you what attributes are available to the tag you are editing, colored tags, and the capability to add custom tags so sequences of tags you use frequently don't need to be added or cut and pasted.

Note Why will you fail to see your scripting if you open files with server-side scripting from the Web? Server-side scripting has already executed by the time you see the page. If you go to a page with server-side scripting (CGI scripts, server-side JavaScript, server-side Java, server-side includes, or Cold Fusion) and view the source, you won't see any of the code. Unlike client-side JavaScript — what most people think of when they think of JavaScript — and VBScript, these other types of scripts are interpreted on the server. This means by the time you view the page, you see only the results of what the script told the server to do, not the actual instructions (script) the server saw.

HTML 4 support

The HTML 4 Way separates presentation from structure. This is different from previous versions of HTML. Not all HTML-development programs encourage this dichotomy. Most development programs available at publication are not well-suited to the HTML dichotomy between structure and content. Even if you are happy with your HTML-development program, you might want to evaluate it in light of how well it supports this dichotomy.

Simple migration between editors

One of the nice things about HTML is, even if you create it in one tag-based editor, you can easily edit it in another tag-based editor. This means you can move between tag-based editors without having to perform file conversions, the way you would have to if you moved between word processing packages.

Many of the programs discussed in this chapter provide the capability to import your entire site. This means you can open the site you created with one program with a different program, if you find that program will make you more productive. If you are managing a growing site, this is a definite feature to remember.

One drawback of importing a site into a WYSIWYG editor is it will often use its own rules to make your HTML more cumbersome. When you evaluate HTML editors, be sure to open some of your existing pages in them to see what, if anything, each one does to the readability of your HTML. At the least, most of them will add a <META> tag to the top of the document, claiming credit for generating it.

On the CD-ROM Most of the editors discussed in this chapter are on the CD-ROM at the back of this book.

Wizards: A quick start

Some elements of Web pages — those that come in groups — are best created with wizards. *Wizards*, tools, dialog boxes, or whatever the marketing department wants to call them, are a great way to get something done quickly and accurately. The HTML page structure, tables, forms, style sheets, and channels fall into this category. The best programs give you the option of completing a simple dialog box or a series of simple dialog boxes to define these elements and then create the HTML for you. Figure 14-3 shows a Table Wizard.

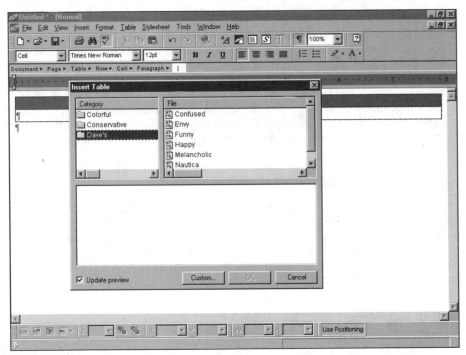

Figure 14-3: Table Wizard Dialog Box (iWrite)

Vocabulary

Channels. One of the interesting features the Version 4 browsers permit is the creation of "subscription to channels." Channels are basically a feature you can define in your page that enables visitors to indicate they want to receive any updates to your page or your site in the background. This means people who *subscribe* to your channel will always have a completely current version of your page loaded locally on their own clients.

Of all these wizards, the Style Sheet Wizard is the most essential. Figure 14-4 shows the HomeSite Style Sheet Wizard. You shouldn't be creating that many style sheets because the point of the style sheet is to apply the same one to your entire site. Still, you definitely won't want to memorize or look up the syntax everytime. Unfortunately, the Style Sheet Wizard is not yet pervasive in the programs discussed in the following. Another interesting and useful, but rare, wizard is the Channel Definition Wizard.

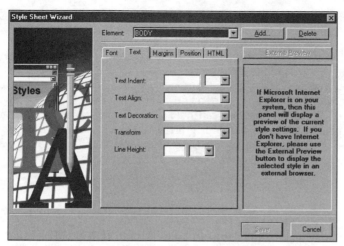

Figure 14-4: Useful dialog-box for Style Sheet Wizard (HomeSite 3.0)

Version control

Even the most organized Webmaster will appreciate support for version control, a feature that automatically assigns version numbers to each modified version of your pages. Before too long, you will find your mirror site (a copy of your site located elsewhere) doesn't perfectly mirror the source site (where the original version is stored). You might have made just one small change to a file on the server or from someone else's workstation. However you arrive at this moment of panic, version control can help you identify the most recent version of your HTML file.

Mirror site. A *mirror site* is either a place where you test your pages before publishing them to the public site or a copy of your public site. In either case, it is easy to find that your mirror site is not a perfect copy of your public site. Keeping the two in synch is facilitated by version-control software.

Unfortunately, few programs support this feature. One of the few that do is NetObjects Team Fusion, which is actually a collaborative development tool. You can purchase third-party products to fill this need, if you settle on a program that doesn't offer this valuable feature.

Version 2.0

Version control software helps you to compensate for the fact that you have too many demands on your time to keep track of the rapidly increasing demands on your brain. It also keeps a paper trail for you. Version 2.0 is a general-purpose version control program. If you are developing a Web site with a team, you will soon find you have multiple copies of pages in multiple locations. Version control software can help you sort out which is the most recent copy. It can also help you to manage your project by signing out pages to team members. Version 2.0 is brought to you by StarBase, the same folks who bring you StarTeam, and is available from the StarBase Web site (`www.starbase.com`).

Group collaboration programs

Only the lucky few get to make all decisions related to their Web sites. Most Web developers have to work with a team at some point. If you have a number of individuals working on your site, then this feature will ease your task. Group collaboration programs, while not yet pervasive in the programs discussed in the following, can make the process of team Web-site building easier.

Make yourself right at home: Customization

Any good Web-page development program enables you to customize it extensively. You should be able to see only the program bars you need. If you don't create forms, you don't need all the tags related to forms represented on your screen. These take up valuable space that could be used for the editor. You should also be able to create a custom color palette and see it or not, as you choose.

You may have strings of HTML you use frequently in combination. Wouldn't it be nice to click one button and have all those tags pasted right into your document? Whether this feature is marketed as *tag snippets* or *custom tags,* this is a nice feature to have.

Finally, the capability to create custom templates that provide the shell of your document without any additional typing—say, to provide metadata—is a nice feature to have. Fortunately, customization is widely available.

Open sesame

Where are your HTML files located? For most Webmasters, files will be located on a remote server and will only be available via FTP. For this reason, an integrated FTP client is usually essential to enhancing your productivity. If your server is an NT server and you have mapped a local drive to your server, this won't be an issue. If, in addition to the C: drive, the A: drive for your floppy and possibly a D: or E: drive for your CD-ROM, you also have some other letter of the alphabet mapped to a hard drive located on another computer, such as your Web server, you are using *drive mapping.* If you are working on Windows 95 or Windows NT and your Web server is on Windows NT, insist on it!

Mapping a local drive to your NT server. To do this, you have to be running Windows 95, Windows NT, or Mac OS. You also need access privileges to the server. Talk to your server administrator about getting these privileges and setting up your LMHOSTS and HOSTS files (not required for Mac OS) so you can save your files to your server as easily as you save them to a floppy disk. Licensing issues are also related to using this approach, but once you're set up, it does make things easier.

If you don't use server-side scripting or you don't know what it is, you will also want to take advantage of the "Open from the Web" feature. This enables you to open the page you want to edit without having to use FTP or sign onto your Web server. You get exactly what you would get if you opened the page with your browser and chose to save the source. Because you need FTP to save your files, when you are done editing, this feature isn't as valuable as an integrated FTP client.

If you are taking advantage of the "Open from the Web" feature, remember: you should make backup copies of all files before working. This way, if a program bombs, you can still retrieve the original file from the Web server.

Speaking of saving files, you might need the capability to save your files as either DOS, Mac, or UNIX files. The difference among these formats is the presence or absence of carriage returns (CR) or line feeds (LF). If you save the files in one format and open them in another, either you will have no end of line markers or you will have extra characters (^M) at the beginning of each line. If you develop your files on a PC and publish to an NT server, this won't be an issue for you.

You also need the capability to have more than one page open at once. Fortunately, support for multiple open documents is part of several of the programs.

Syntax compliance: How much is too much?

When selecting a Web-page creation program, you will find various levels of *syntax checking* (a feature that scrutinizes your code to make sure it's free from errors and conforms to HTML standards):

None	The program makes no attempt to check whether your HTML code conforms to HTML standards.
Continuous	Syntax checking can be turned on or off. When it is on, any errors or incomplete tags are marked in color, whether or not you are done with them.
On-demand built in	Syntax checking is only a click away. When you are ready to have your syntax checked, you can request it.
On-demand as a plug-in	After you install a plug-in (which may or may not cost more money), syntax checking is only a click away.
Forced continuous	Syntax checking is always, annoyingly, on.
Forced on-save	When you try to save, it forces you to correct any errors it finds.

The only unacceptable levels are "continuous" and "forced" anything. Can you imagine a word processor that wouldn't let you save a file that had a word it didn't recognize? This is the mentality behind forced syntax compliance. Continuous syntax checking is a waste of your processor. What is the point of telling you that you need a </CENTER> tag while you are still in the middle of typing the content you want centered? This feature is a lot like Microsoft Word's continuous spelling checker (offered in Versions 6, 7, and 97), which, gratefully, you can turn off.

You will want to check your syntax to make sure you comply with the latest set of rules, but you will want to do it on your schedule, not your editor's.

Another nice feature beginning to appear in these programs is support for browser-specific tags. Microsoft Internet Explorer and Netscape Navigator are not perfectly in synch when it comes to tag support. If you know your visitors are running a certain browser (for example, in an intranet) and that browser supports extra tags, it is nice to use those tags without being hassled by the syntax checker.

Tag assistance

A good HTML-development program will help you out with your tags — which attributes are available to the tag you are using — without imposing itself on you. A variety of ways can provide tag assistance. Some editors provide "tag completion," automatically filling in a </CENTER>, when you finish typing <CENTER>. Some editors offer visual assistance by color-coding the tags by type. While this may sound annoying, once you know what to look for, you will appreciate it. Some editors provide dialog boxes enabling you to fill in values for the attributes you want to include. The only truly time-wasting tag assistance in this set of programs is the "feature" that automatically inserts every attribute for the tag you select with the values of the attributes set to blank.

Viewing your work in progress

As you work in a tag-based editor, you want to see how your page is developing. It is convenient, but not essential, to have an internal browser in your development program. The alternative is to save your file and to open it locally from your browser or to publish it to your Web site if any server processing is required, and view it in your regular browser. If there is an internal browser, it should be accurate. An inaccurate internal browser is as bad as none at all. Best of all is the capability to select more than one internal browser of your choice.

Tip   To open a page on your local computer from your browser without publishing it to your remote server, select Open from the File menu and either choose File or Browse from the dialog box that pops up. Then identify the file you want to open and click Open.

Support for advanced tags

Server-side scripting may become a part of your Web site before you know it. If you want your visitors to be able to sign into your database to enter a contest on your site or to complete a survey, you need to use Cold Fusion, Active Server Pages, CGI, server-side Java, or server-side JavaScript.

If you are going to use JavaScript, applets, style sheets, or ActiveX controls, you want a development program that facilitates the use of these tags. You will get frustrated fast if you have to wrestle with your editor everytime you want to use one of these tools. Figure 14-5 shows the HoTMetaL Pro Wizard for adding ActiveX controls.

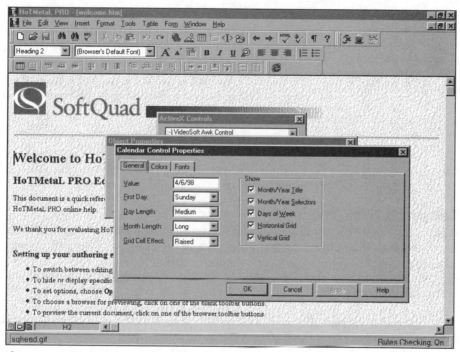

Figure 14-5: Inserting an ActiveX Control (made easy with HoTMetaL Pro)

Other niceties

Once you get used to these features, you'll find it hard to believe some of the programs don't include them all:

Automatic word wrapping — With this feature — a no-brainer, you would think — you can see your entire paragraph of text or all the attributes of your tag without having to scroll right.

Global find/replace — This feature searches all the files in your project or your site and makes changes. If you don't use style sheets, this is the only practical way you can make formatting changes that affect large numbers of pages, that is, unless you want to go into each one and make all the changes manually.

	This feature isn't as important if you're using style sheets, which enable you to define presentation styles for all the documents you link to it, but it is nice if you find you've been spelling the president's name wrong.
Link checking	Confirms all your links will work.
Link manager	Gives you some sort of graphical representation of the relationship between your pages.
Link repair	Automatically attempts to repair links that get broken from moving pages around in your directory tree.
Spell checking	Essential and, fortunately, universally available in these programs.
Site Manager	Shows you all the pages in your site in some graphically meaningful way.

Comparing HTML editors

By now you should have an idea of what features you need in an HTML editor. Use the column on the right to mark your needs and then compare your needs with what is available. All these programs can be downloaded from the Web for 15-, 30-, or 45-day evaluations. Take advantage of these downloads to find the program that works best for you.

The rest of this chapter discusses each of the programs in Table 14-1 in brief. Each description includes information on evaluation downloads, URLs for each company, and pricing.

Table 14-1
Comparison of HTML-development programs

	TextPad	Hot Dog Pro 4.5	HomeSite 3.0	HoTMetaL 4.0	iWrite	Dreamweaver	FrontPage 98	PageMill 3.0	HomePage 3.0	NetObjects Fusion 3 with TeamFusion
WYSIWYG	No	No	No	Yes	Yes	Yes	Yes	Yes	Yes	Yes
View source	Yes	Yes	Yes	Yes	Yes	Yes	Yes	Yes	Yes	No
Supports HTML 4.0 dichotomy	Yes	No	Yes	No	Yes	Yes	Yes	No	No	No
Imports a Web site	No	Yes	No	No	No	Yes	No	No	No	No
Web page importing	Yes	Yes	Yes	Yes	Yes	Yes	Yes	Yes	Yes	Yes
Wizards	No	Yes	Yes	Yes	Yes	Yes	Yes	Yes	Yes	Yes
Tables Wizard	No	Yes	Yes	Yes	Yes	Yes	Yes	Yes	Yes	Yes
Frames Wizard	No	Yes	Yes	Yes	Yes	Yes	Yes	Yes	Yes	Yes
Form Wizard	No	Yes	Yes	Yes	Yes	Yes	Yes	No	No	Yes
Style-sheets Wizard	No	Yes	No	Yes	Yes	Yes	Yes	No	No	No
Channel Wizard	No	Yes	No	No	No	No	Yes	No	No	No

Table 14-1 (continued)

	TextPad	Hot Dog Pro 4.5	HomeSite 3.0	HoTMetaL 4.0	iWrite	Dreamweaver	FrontPage 98	PageMill 3.0	HomePage 3.0	NetObjects Fusion 3 with TeamFusion
Image-Map creation	No	Yes	No	Yes	No	Yes	No	Yes	Yes	Yes
Version control	No	No	No	No	No	No	No	No	No	No
Collaborative site-creation tools	No	No	No	No	No	Yes	Yes	No	No	No
File Manager	No	Yes	Yes	No	No	Yes	Yes	Yes	Yes	No
Project Manager	No	Yes	Yes	Yes	No	Yes	Yes	Yes	No	No
Custom Tags	Yes	Yes	Yes	Yes	No	Yes	No	No	No	No
Customizable Interface	Yes	Yes	Yes	Yes	Yes	Yes	Yes	No	No	No
Customizable Templates	No	Yes	Yes	Yes	Yes	Yes	Yes	No	No	Yes
Integrated FTP client	No	Yes	Yes	Yes	Yes	Yes	Yes	Yes	Yes	Yes
Open files from Web	No	No	Yes	No	Yes	No	Yes	No	No	Yes
Multiple pages open at once	Yes	Yes	Yes	Yes	Yes	Yes	Yes	Yes	Yes	No

	TextPad	Hot Dog Pro 4.5	HomeSite 3.0	HoTMetaL 4.0	iWrite	Dream-weaver	FrontPage 98	PageMill 3.0	HomePage 3.0	NetObjects Fusion 3 with TeamFusion
Save files in multiple formats	No	Yes	Yes	No	No	No	No	No	No	No
Integrated syntax checker	No	Yes	Yes	Yes	No	Yes	No	No	No	No
Forced syntax compliance	No	No	No	No	No	Yes	No	No	No	No
Browser-specific tags	No	Yes	No	Yes	No	Yes	No	No	No	No
Tag cues	Yes	Yes	Yes	Yes	No	Yes	No	No	No	No
Tag completion	No	Yes	Yes	Yes	No	Yes	Yes	No	No	No
Colored Tags	No	No	Yes	Yes	No	Yes	Yes	Yes	Yes	No
Auto-detection of width and height for images	No	Yes	Yes	Yes	Yes	Yes	Yes	Yes	Yes	Yes
Internal browser	No	Yes	Yes	Yes	Yes	Yes	Yes	Yes	Yes	Yes

Table 14-1 (continued)

	TextPad	Hot Dog Pro 4.5	HomeSite 3.0	HoTMetaL 4.0	iWrite	Dream-weaver	FrontPage 98	PageMill 3.0	HomePage 3.0	NetObjects Fusion 3 with TeamFusion
Define multiple internal browsers	No	No	No	Yes	No	Yes	Yes	Yes	Yes	No
Accurate internal browser	No	Yes	Yes	Yes	Yes	Yes	Yes	Yes	Yes	No
External browser required	Yes	No	No	No	No	No	No	No	No	Yes
JavaScript	Yes	Yes	Yes	Yes (in additional software that ships)	Yes	Yes	Yes	Yes	No	Yes
Applets	No	Yes	Yes	Yes	Yes	Yes	Yes	Yes	Yes	Yes
ActiveX	No	No	Yes	Yes	Yes	Yes	Yes	Yes	No	Yes
Cold Fusion	Yes	No	Yes	No	No	Yes	No	No	No	No
CSS	Yes	Yes	Yes	Yes	Yes	Yes	Yes	No	No	Yes
Active Server Pages	No	Yes	Yes	No	No	No	Yes	No	No	Yes
Global find/replace capability	Yes	Yes	Yes	Yes	No	Yes	Yes	Yes	No	Yes
Link checking	No	Yes	Yes	Yes	No	Yes	Yes	Yes	No	Yes

	TextPad	Hot Dog Pro 4.5	HomeSite 3.0	HoTMetaL 4.0	iWrite	Dream-weaver	FrontPage 98	PageMill 3.0	HomePage 3.0	NetObjects Fusion 3 with TeamFusion
Link manager/ repair	No	Yes	No	Yes	No	Yes	Yes	Yes	Yes	Yes
Spell Checker	Yes	Yes	Yes	Yes	Yes	Yes	Yes	Yes	Yes	Yes
Site manager	No	Yes	No	Yes	No	Yes	Yes	Yes	Yes	Yes

Looking at HTML Editors

Now that you've examined the features HTML editors offer, look at some of the most popular programs. There's no such thing as a "best" HTML editor — but you should be able to find one just right for you.

TextPad

Available for Windows 3.1, Windows 95/98 and Windows NT, this is the most basic of text editors that supports HTML. If you want to write your own HTML from the ground up, this is your program — but it's strictly no frills. Without any wizards, syntax checking, integrated FTP client, or site management programs, you are truly on your own. But that's just where expert HTML coders want to be — and that's particularly true if you're writing True HTML 4. In some of the highest-powered Web production workshops, you'll be surprised to find expert HTML coders are using the lowest-powered software: The Windows Notepad utility, the program of choice for those who want to take the minimalist route to the max.

What does this program offer that the Windows Notepad doesn't? For one thing, an integrated spelling checker. That's a real benefit for professional Web publishing, in which spelling mistakes can't be tolerated. Also, you can create files larger than 32K, the current Notepad limit.

The Windows Notepad utility comes with several *clip libraries,* TextPad's name for their lists of HTML tags or JavaScript properties. Unfortunately, when you select a tag from the clip library, you get every attribute for that tag, with the value of the attribute blank, or worse yet, with a question mark where you might want to insert a value (see Figure 14-6). This feature is confusing unless you know what you're doing — and what's worse, it enters a lot of code into your documents you don't really need. Still, TextPad is fast and stable, and it's a genuine improvement over non-HTML-savvy text editors.

To get your copy of TextPad, access the program's Web site at `www.textpad.com`. A shareware product, TextPad will cost you $27 for the electronic version and $35 for the floppy disks.

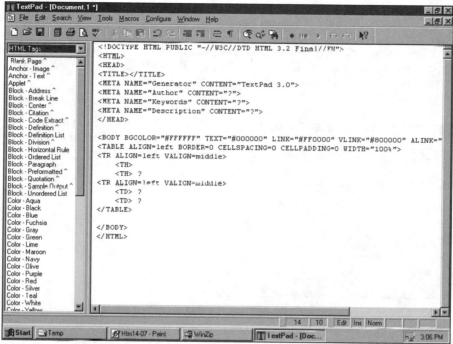

Figure 14-6: TextPad using the HTML-Forms clip library; notice every conceivable attribute for the <INPUT> tag is included, along with question marks for the <TABLE> tag.

Hot Dog Professional 4.5

The nicest thing about this program is things work the way you expect them to work. Available for Windows 95 and Windows NT, this impressive text-based HTML-development environment includes such features as page-building wizards, extensive customization, a channel definition wizard, support for tables, frames, and style sheets, split-screen view of the HTML and the page concurrently, and the capability to use HTML 4 the way it was intended to be used. HotDog Pro also uses something called *SuperToolz,* which is their marketing name for downloadable plug-ins, which are usually free. All the wizards are installed this way. This is a great feature if space is tight on your system.

Who fits the Hot Dog profile? Somebody who really wants to get into the nitty-gritty of actual HTML code, but doesn't want to hassle with tables, frames, forms, and other hard-to-code HTML elements (see Figure 14-7). An additional benefit is the program's interactive split-screen browser, which dynamically displays your changes. This feature alone makes HotDog a real plus when you're learning HTML; you see the results of your changes immediately, without having to switch to your browser.

HotDog Pro sells for $149.95, including a number of additional SuperToolz, such as an eVend InfoSeller SuperTool (for producing commerce sites that use the eVend standard), a JavaScript Editor SuperTool (for using JavaScript in your pages), a Java Text Effects SuperTool (for using JavaScript to animate text), and a Java Animation SuperTool (for Java animation). Check out the Web site at http://www.sausage.com/.

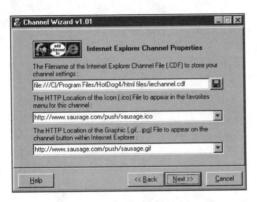

Figure 14-7: HotDog Pro 4.5 makes creating a channel simple with a Channel Wizard

HomeSite 3.0

HomeSite is one of the few products available that support the HTML 4 Way of developing a Web site. Most of the other programs rely heavily on tables to align elements on the page the way you want them, but not HomeSite.

Perhaps the most full-featured of HTML tag-based editors, HomeSite started off as shareware. It complements Allaire's Cold Fusion Web-to-database engine so well, Allaire bought the product and the programmer. HomeSite is also the text editor for the PC version of Dreamweaver. Useful features include:

✦ Powerful wizards — HTML structure, style sheets, tables, forms

✦ Internal, accurate, user-definable browser

✦ Tag coloring, tag completion, and tag cues (an irresistible threesome)

✦ Extensive customization of interface, templates, and tags

✦ Integrated on-demand syntax checking

✦ Integrated FTP client, with browsing of FTP directories

Who might enjoy using HomeSite? Someone who wants to see the HTML without having to endure the tedium of coding tables, form elements, and frames (see Figure 14-8). Also anyone who wants to use style sheets, but isn't familiar with all the properties. The extensively customizable interface make the program all your own in a matter of minutes.

This invaluable program, which runs on Windows 95 or Windows NT, is priced at $79 for the downloaded version and $89 for the CD-ROM — what a deal! It is available from Allaire on their Web site at www.allaire.com.

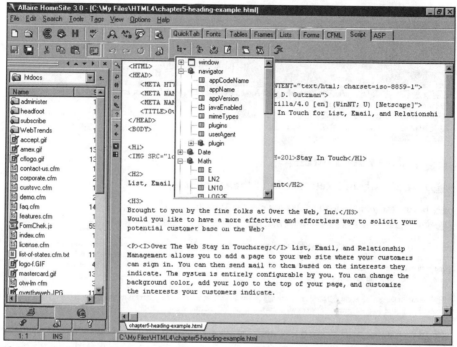

Figure 14-8: HomeSite with FTP-browsing in the left pane and the JavaScript tree open

HoTMetaL Pro 4.0

The folks at SoftQuad must develop a lot of Web sites, because they seem to have thought of about everything. HoTMetaL Pro 4.0, for Windows 95 and Windows NT, includes nearly every type of wizard:

✦ ActiveX Wizard

✦ Style-Sheets Wizard

✦ Site Wizard

✦ Table Wizard

✦ Frames Editor

✦ Form Wizard

The *tags-on view* is a great way to see your content without being overwhelmed by the HTML (see Figure 14-9). You can easily switch between WYSIWYG view, tags-on view, and HTML editing. Syntax checking, which defaults to continuous, can be set to on-demand.

If you want the best of both worlds — WYSIWYG and text-editing — but you aren't planning on using HTML 4 the way it was meant to be used, HoTMetaL may be the way to go. HoTMetaL, the annoying capitalization aside, is available from the SoftQuad Web site `www.softquad.com` for $129.

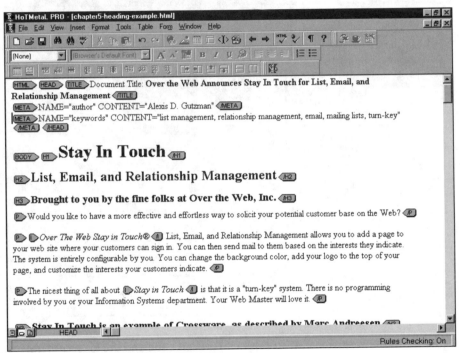

Figure 14-9: HoTMetaL Pro 4.0 in tags-on view

iWrite

iWrite (see Figure 14-10), was developed as an HTML 4 program from the ground up. Running on Windows 95 or Windows NT, it supports every HTML 4 feature — layers, objects, style sheets, JavaScript, and the document object model — like no other program reviewed here. iWrite has useful dialog boxes to help you define your styles, your images, and every other feature of your page. Its only weak point is lack of site, project, or file management programs. This aside, iWrite is the strongest page creation program out there. There is a WYSIWYG view, but it doesn't get in the way of the basic HTML.

Who will like iWrite? This program will appeal to anyone who wants to use all the features of HTML 4, in the HTML 4 Way. An adequate set of wizards gives you some assistance, but you have to know what you want to see and how you want to produce it before this program will interest you. And then you might not be able to put it away!

iWrite sells for $49 and is available from Xanthus at their Web site:
www.xanthus.com.

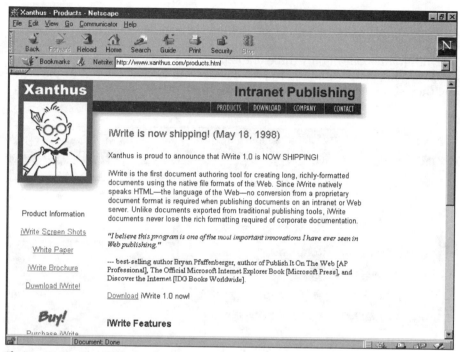

Figure 14-10: The iWrite Web site

Dreamweaver

This program is, indeed, a dream. You almost can't imagine a tool, system, or convention that isn't included in this incredible package. Dreamweaver was built with the HTML 4 model in mind and cleverly uses HomeSite 3.0 on the PC and BBEdit on the Mac as the text-editing programs for the WYSIWYG interface Macromedia provides. This results in a program that does everything it does well — whether on Windows 95, Windows NT, or the Mac.

The most appealing part of this program is the HTML the WYSIWYG interface produces is clean and utterly without the clutter of tables for formatting (respecting the HTML 4 Way). You could open the HTML file Dreamweaver produces in a simple text editor and it would look just like what you used to write.

Dreamweaver (see Figure 14-11), is a professional Web developer's program, as demonstrated by the price: $269 introductory, going up to $499, but this is one spiffy program. It includes a library where you can store scripts, HTML tag combinations, images, image maps, or whatever for use in all the other pages in your site. Making a change to the library item automatically changes the item in all the pages where it appears — like a server-side include.

To support animations and the Macromedia suite of programs (Director, Flash, Authorware), Dreamweaver includes a timeline feature.

This program is one of only three of the programs reviewed here that includes useful group collaboration tools. Entire books will be devoted to this package — and they should be. It is available from Macromedia (www.macromedia.com).

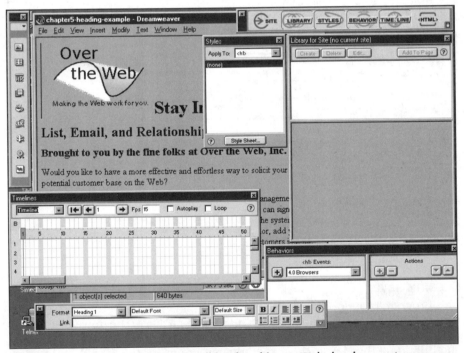

Figure 14-11: Dreamweaver may well be the ultimate Web development program.

FrontPage 98

FrontPage 98 (see Figure 14-12) is a huge step forward from FrontPage 97. This program gives you both WYSIWYG and text-based editing, on Windows 95, Windows NT, or the Mac. Additionally, you can define multiple internal browsers, including Netscape Navigator! The getting started wizards are powerful. And the HTML they produce is legible. There are several useful tools, such as site management, project management — including the capability to assign tasks to project team members — and link management. The nicest part of all is FrontPage 98 relies on the HTML 4 Way of doing things, rather than on tables, for attractive layout of pages.

FrontPage 98 appeals to both the beginner and the professional Web developer. It has a steep learning curve, but once you know it, you'll be very productive.

FrontPage also includes plenty of interactive features, such as database interaction, animation tools, a JavaScript Wizard, and an ActiveX Wizard. FrontPage 98 is available for $149 from Microsoft (www.microsoft.com).

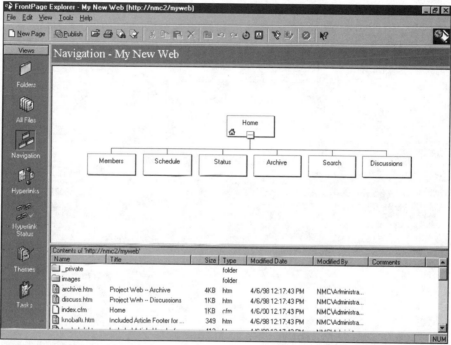

Figure 14-12: FrontPage 98 in Site View

HomePage 3.0

HomePage by Claris/FileMaker is an old war-horse in the world of HTML editors. HomePage 3.0 is available for the both the Mac and Windows platforms. While 3.0 still doesn't support style sheets, the HTML 4 dichotomy, or JavaScript, it is a nice editor for the basic Web page. What Version 3.0 added over Version 2.0 was complete integration with the FileMaker Pro database. If you have any data in a FileMaker Pro database you want to get to the Web, this is definitely your tool. HomePage 3.0 is available for $99.

PageMill 3.0

PageMill 3.0 (see Figure 14-13) is a big improvement over 2.0. While it still doesn't support style sheets or the HTML 4 dichotomy, it does include an enhanced site/file manager that gives you a graphical view of your site. At $99 for either the PC or the Mac from the Adobe Web site (www.adobe.com), it is competitively priced. PageMill 3.0 also works seamlessly with Photoshop and Photoshop LE, two of the most commonly used image manipulation packages.

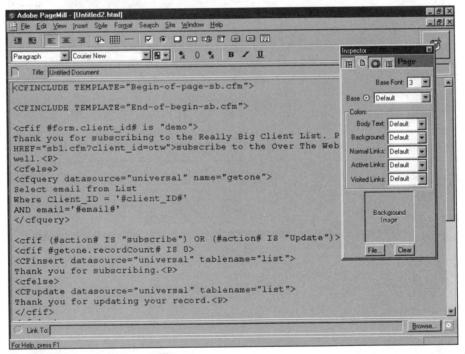

Figure 14-13: Adobe PageMill 3.0

NetObjects Fusion 3.0

NetObjects Fusion 3.0 is a huge improvement over NetObjects 2.0, which was still an excellent product. Fusion may be the most popular tool on the market for maintaining huge, distributed Web sites. With the addition of TeamFusion, Fusion 3.0 is an unbeatable software suite. Supported features are: team collaboration tools, version control, a WYSIWYG editing environment, and a tag-based editing environment, the most intuitive drag-and-drop editing environment of all the tools reviewed. Figure 14-14 shows NetObjects Fusion in Site View.

NetObjects Fusion is available for both the Mac and PC platforms for $295 or for $99 for the upgrade to 3.0 if you already own 2.0.

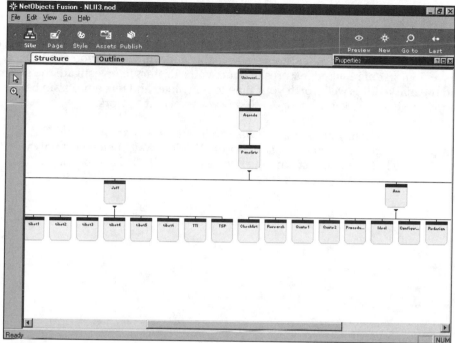

Figure 14-14: NetObjects Fusion in Site View

From Here

Cross-
Reference

With your HTML-development program in hand, you can proceed to develop your site's style and content. Before you jump ahead, though, take a moment to read about your Web server: What it does, what kind you have, and what you can make it do with server-side scripting, all in Chapter 15.

Ready to dive into HTML 4? Flip to Chapter 16, which explores the fundamentals of HTML document architecture. You'll learn some important distinctions to help you grasp HTML more quickly.

Want to see some CSS now? Jump to Chapter 23.

Summary

Before you can select the best Web page creation and editing program for you, you need to understand what features are available and which ones you need. Once you have your list of required features in hand, you can start to investigate the programs on the market. It is well worth your time to download and test a program before you purchase it so you know it works the way you expect it to work.

Whatever program you select, you want to be sure it works with the HTML 4 paradigm. If the program won't support the HTML 4 Way, then it certainly won't be there to help you deliver whatever comes next: HTML 5 and beyond.

✦　　✦　　✦

Understanding Server Options

The longer you support and maintain a Web site, the more fancy things you want to do there. What kind of fancy things? You may include server variables, such as the date the page was last modified or the URL of the page, or information stored in a database. Or, you may take information your visitors enter into your forms and use it to populate a database.

Before you can incorporate any of these, you need to understand the client-server model and processing options. This chapter gives you a solid understanding of what processing takes place where, what you must have installed to take advantage of server processing, what types of server processing software are available and how they work, and what you can take for granted on your server. This chapter also discusses particularities of both UNIX and NT servers.

The Client-Server Model

Lately, there's been a lot of press about the thin client model. The *thin client model* isn't a reference to a client of the Ford Modeling Agency, but rather a reference to the idea of putting less computing power on the desktop and more on the server. Since the late 1980s, the debate has raged over where computer power should reside: on the desktop (thick client) or on the server (thin client).

Before the late 1980s, most people who did any computer processing had dumb terminals on their desktops, which were hooked up to some sort of a mainframe computer. The *dumb terminal* was only a screen, a keyboard, and a wire. The wire connected to the mainframe, where all the processing took place. The keyboard enabled you to enter data. The screen enabled you to see data. In the beginning, all the power resided at the hub, in a big, expensive mainframe computer. (See Figure 15-1 for an example.)

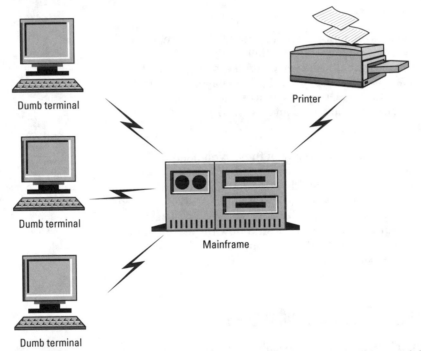

Figure 15-1: Dumb terminals and the mainframe at the center of the model

When personal computers (PCs) began to become affordable and useful software for PCs began to become available, businesses moved more processing from the center (the mainframe or server) to the periphery (the client). By the late 1990s, many offices had incredibly powerful computers on every desktop, far in excess of the power needed to do the kind of processing computer users were actually doing. This was the thick client model, as shown in Figure 15-2. Because middle-sized servers have become so powerful for far less than the cost of a mainframe, the server has replaced the mainframe at the center of the model.

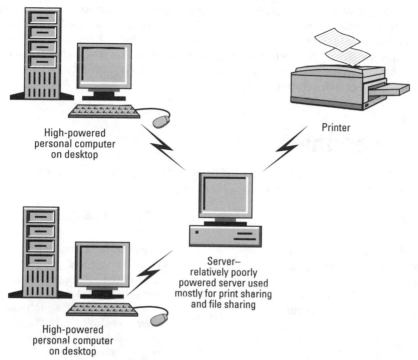

Figure 15-2: The thick client model with a lot of power on the desktop

The client-Web server model

The pendulum in business today is swinging back in the other direction to the idea of putting less power on the desktop and more on the server. Why? Several reasons:

✦ The growth of intranets, wherein many applications are delivered to the desktop via Web servers

✦ The continued need for shared files (and, thus, associated file servers)

✦ The realization that for most office applications, desktops don't need the processing power of the latest, greatest personal computers

✦ The availability of client-server software engineered to be run from a server

Processing: The crux of the issue

When you connect your computer to a server, where does the processing take place: on your desktop computer or on the server? That depends. When you request a Web page, if any processing is required other than serving the page, the processing usually takes place on the server. When you sign into your Web server to publish your files (using the FTP client you learned about in Chapter 6), the processing takes place on your desktop computer.

Cleverly designed Web applications can move some of the processing burden from the server to the client. Remember, in most Web applications, as the Webmaster, you are paying for the cost of processing on the server, but not on the client. The client computer belongs to the person visiting your site. The way to get the most bang for your Web-page buck is to move any processing you can from *your* server to *the visitor's* client workstation.

Client Processing

So how do you take advantage of client processing? First you must understand what you can and can't do using client processing.

What You Can Do

Validate data entry. If you have form fields on your page, you can make sure they contain the right kind of data before re-submitting them to the server. How does this save server processing? First, your server doesn't have to do the validation. Second, data will only be submitted once, when it is complete, saving your server the trouble of having to serve the same page (with error messages on it) multiple times to the same client.

Rearrange data on the page. This is new to HTML 4! If you are running a page that serves data from a database, you can save your server the trouble of having to serve the same data multiple times, sorted differently, by taking advantage of client-side processing. The

What You Can't Do

Serve a page. You can't serve a page using client processing. You can load another page that has already been downloaded with the current page, which can be a clever technique, but at some point all the data you display must come from the server (except for data collected from the visitor and data collected from the client workstation).

Deliver data from a database. The database has to reside on a server (either your own or another you have permission to read). The only way to get this data to the client is to deliver it from a server.

Collect data into a database. You have to get the data from the client's workstation back to the server. Client processing can't do this. The chapter on forms (Chapter 43) covers this in detail.

document-object model and client-side scripting will enable you to deliver all the data to the client one time and then give the client the option of seeing it different ways. Visitors don't need to know that instead of going out to your server every time they want to see the data rearranged, the processing takes place on their machine. This can take a real load off your server.

Date and time processing. Say you need to create a clock in a Web page. No good reason exists to run back to the server at set intervals when every client computer has a built-in clock. With client-side scripting, you can get at the local client variables, including the date and time, and process this data on the client side.

Measure visitor response. If you want to do any kind of testing of visitor response, you can administer the entire test in one or more pages, without returning to the server, until the test is complete. This includes dynamic testing, where the next question asked is based on the answer to the current question. For testing the time it takes for visitors to complete questions, nothing will be more accurate than client-side processing.

Read data from the visitor's computer. With few exceptions, you can't use client-side scripting to collect information about visitors or data from their machines. This kind of privacy safeguard for the Web surfer has contributed to the popularity and acceptability of client-side scripting. Other less innocuous technologies, such as ActiveX controls and Java applets, have failed to catch on as fast because they didn't safeguard the client workstation as well.

Write data to a client workstation. With the exception of cookies, which are covered later in this chapter, you can't write anything to your visitor's computer.

So how do you take advantage of client-side processing? Whenever you need to validate forms data, rearrange data on a page, perform date and time processing, or measure visitor response, you include a client-side script that does this using client power, rather than server power.

Cross-Reference Chapter 48 teaches you what you need to know about JavaScript, the most popular language for client-side processing, to do all these things.

Introducing Web Servers

What exactly is a Web server? A *Web server* is a patient program that sits on your server (that is, the physical machine dedicated to serving pages and performing other server functions) waiting to receive an HTTP request via TCP/IP. Helpful, huh?

Any server configured to handle communications via TCP/IP (the communications protocol of the Internet) has ports. These aren't physical ports, like the serial port and parallel ports on the back of your computer, but they serve the same purpose. All HTTP requests come through port 80 unless the server has been configured differently. *Port 80* is the default Web server port. This is how your server, which may be a file server, an applications server, and an FTP server, in addition to being a Web server, keeps it all straight.

When an HTTP request comes through port 80 to the Web server, the Web server finds the page requested, checks the permissions of the client making the request, and, if the client has the appropriate permission, serves the page. Permission? Aren't all requests for pages anonymous? Not exactly. Figure 15-3 illustrates the request process.

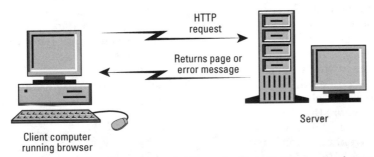

Figure 15-3: The client requests the page. Then the server evaluates the request and serves the page or an error message.

Permissions

Generally, HTTP requests are anonymous. What this really means is an account has been created on the Web server for HTTP requests. When a request comes through port 80, it is assumed to come from this account. Each file on the Web server has certain permissions associated with it. If the HTTP account (which may, in fact, be called *anonymous*) has adequate permission to read (or execute) that page, the Web server will serve that page.

All files and folders on a server have permissions associated with them. Whether or not you set them explicitly, they are there. Usually, when you create files on a server, they inherit the permissions of the directory in which you place them. The permissions for your directories are usually set by the systems administrator. If you are having problems getting your page to load or seeing images on your page, have the systems administrator check the permissions on your files and directories to make sure they are, in fact, universally readable and executable.

NT: Hidden permission

NT servers handle permissions a little differently. Really, it's sort of sneaky. If you are sitting at a Windows 95 or Windows NT client and you request a page from a Windows NT Web server, you won't necessarily be making the request under the guise of the anonymous account set up for HTTP requests. In fact, your browser has sent your login ID and password (encrypted, of course) to the Web server with your request. If your ID is a valid ID on the Web server, then you are permitted to see any files on the server you have read (or executed). You are also allowed to see all the files the anonymous account is permitted to see.

What if you are sitting at a non-Windows 95/NT client? Then, if you try to get to a page that isn't accessible to the anonymous HTTP account, you either get an error message indicating you don't have permission to get to the page or a dialog box asking you to sign in.

Is this a good thing? It is a great thing for intranets! This means you don't have to re-key your ID and password into your browser every time you want to see a secure page. It can be a headache for Web server administrators because that much more security information must be monitored. For the Webmaster, it means more testing is required. You must test your pages from both Windows 95 and NT clients and others, signed in as someone with less authority than yourself.

Server Processing

What kinds of processing are best performed on the server? Any kind of processing or interaction with databases or any data stored on the server. How does it work? The visitor requests a page from the Web server. The Web server knows the page contains something it can't process and hands off the page to the appropriate auxiliary software for processing. The software that performs auxiliary processing, which sometimes comes installed with the Web server, converts the page into HTML and hands it back to the Web server. The Web server serves the page. Figure 15-4 illustrates this concept.

What the Web server can't process

What can't the Web server process? Scripts, for one thing. Many proprietary flavors of server-side scripting exist. When a Web server comes across scripting that it recognizes isn't client-side scripting, it passes the page to the appropriate external software, which may be a middleware engine. Most often, pages with scripting not meant to be processed either by the client or by the server have different extensions. (Some you may have run across are in Table 15-1 later in this chapter.) Other times, the page has an extension of .html, but has a call to a script within the page. The Web server knows to hand this page to external software or a middleware engine (or has the processing capabilities built-in) when it comes to this code.

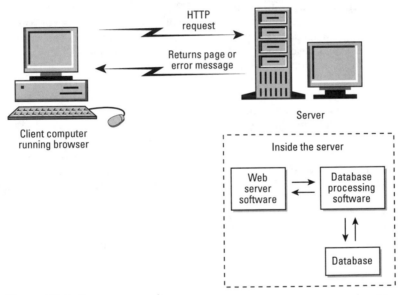

Figure 15-4: Server processing

Middleware. Software that sits outside the Web server software, but on the same physical server, which performs specialized processing related to the Web, but also related to other technologies, such as databases.

Converting scripts to HTML

How does the middleware or external software produce an HTML page? The reason server-side processing is necessary is for a page to be able to pull data out of a database and present it on a page or to write data taken from a form to a database. Usually when you write a page using a scripting language, you indicate all records that meet certain criteria should be written into the HTML and served to the client. The middleware or external software goes out to the database (usually using ODBC standards), reads the database, and formats the data with HTML. Then it returns the page to the Web server. The Web server recognizes the page as containing only HTML and serves it to the client.

Vocabulary

CGI script. The external software previously referred is usually a Common Gateway Interface script written in C, C++, or Perl. The compilers for these scripts are usually free. The CGI script does the same thing as the middleware, but usually requires a higher level of technical proficiency to accomplish it.

The History of Middleware

Up until about 1995, a standard for software that performed auxiliary processing existed. It was called the *Common Gateway Interface* (CGI). Every type of server-side processing required the Webmaster to write a script in either Perl, C, or C++. The script was saved with an extension of .cgi. When the Web server saw this extension, it read only the first line of the file and passed the script onto the appropriate compiler. Advantages to this system were: All three of these languages were commonly found on UNIX, most Web servers up until 1995 were UNIX-based, and compilers for all three of these languages were in the public domain and likely to be found on your UNIX server.

The disadvantages were and still are:

✦ All three of these languages are programming languages

✦ A single page of HTML may take pages of code to generate

✦ Making a change to the HTML on a page required a programmer

✦ Hours of programming produced relatively modest results

Today, many people who use CGI programs either use pre-existing programs and don't make any programming changes to them, pay their ISPs to make programming changes, or are hardcore programmers.

Unfortunately, no standard exists in middleware. Quite a number of different types of systems are available to you as a Web developer to produce high-quality server-side processing. Most middleware revolves around interacting with a database. The advantages of using modern middleware include fast development time and the availability of rapid-application development (RAD) tools for many of these products. The disadvantage is cost. Most of them are commercial software. If you administer your own server, you can choose which one you like best. If you are already using an ISP with which you are happy, you will probably use one of the RAD tools it provides. Table 15-1 shows common extensions used to indicate that external processing is required.

Cross-Reference

Chapter 14 compares HTML-development tools, some of which are RAD tools for middleware.

Extension	Language
.cgi	Common Gateway Interface (usually means the entire page is written in Perl and the result of the Perl script is a page of HTML)
.asp	Active server pages (proprietary to Microsoft)
.qry	Query page (proprietary to Tango)
.cfm	Cold Fusion markup language (proprietary to Allaire)
.js	Server-side JavaScript (used by Netscape servers for server-side processing)

Table 15-1
Extensions of Specific Languages

RAD. Rapid application development tools are productivity-enhancing if they allow:

✦ drag-and-drop access to data sources

✦ uniform-style application across all pages in your site or project

✦ multifile search-and-replace

✦ spelling check

✦ looking up of HTML tags

✦ auto-tag insertion

✦ wizards

✦ and all without creating messy code.

For more information about the `.shtml` extension, see Chapter 46, Building a Secure Site for Web Commerce.

Built-in middleware

The most popular type of server-side script processing comes built-in to the Web server. Two of the most popular commercial Web servers — Microsoft Internet Information Server and Netscape servers — use this approach. Internet Information Server (IIS) supports active server pages internally; Netscape servers support server-side JavaScript.

Built-in server-side script processing makes processing scripts transparent. For the server administrator, there is no additional software to install and configure. For the Web page developer, once you know what Web server software is running, you know what type of scripting you can use and you know it will work (as shown in Figure 15-5).

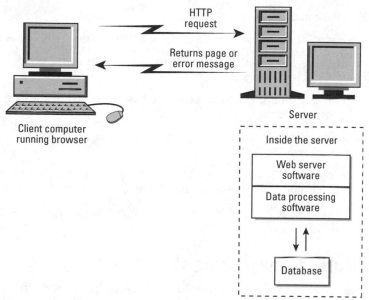

HTTP
request

Returns page or
error message

Client computer
running browser

Server

Inside the server

Web server
software

Data processing
software

Database

Figure 15-5: Built-in server-side script processing is transparent.

Stand-alone middleware

The alternative to built-in server-side script processing is stand-alone middleware. Why use stand-alone middleware? You may be running a Web server that doesn't include server-side scripting (other than CGI scripts). Another good reason exists. Some stand-alone middleware expands the processing power of your Web server to such a great extent, it is worth investing in another software program to get these extra benefits. What might these capabilities include? Sending e-mail from the Web site using data in a database, for one. See the following sidebar for more information.

Cold Fusion

Cold Fusion by Allaire is one product that greatly increases what your Web site can do without requiring any programming. Using a simple language, called *Cold Fusion Markup Language* (CFML), you can create powerful scripts you write right into your HTML pages. The Cold Fusion server returns the results of the script right into your page.

Some of the cool things you can do are:

✦ Schedule the generation of a page daily, hourly, or at whatever interval you choose.

✦ Pull content off other sites and parse it into your own format. (Get permission from the site owner before you try this.)

✦ Send mail to everyone in a database from a Web page based on criteria indicated on the form on the Web page.

✦ Insert records into a database. Update a database record. Read a database for records that meet certain criteria.

Cold Fusion is available for both NT and UNIX (Solaris) platforms. It works with ODBC-compliant databases. You can find out more from the Allaire Web site (`www.allaire.com`).

Rapid application development

The difference between easy-to-write and pain-to-maintain scripts is often the existence of an effective rapid application development environment. What is this? Essentially *rapid application development* (RAD) is a software program that makes it easy for you to write scripts. Microsoft includes support for active server pages in FrontPage. Netscape has a visual development environment for JavaScript, as shown in Figure 15-6. Allaire has Cold Fusion Studio for easy creation of Cold Fusion scripts.

Cookies

Cookies are small text files written to visitors' computers when they visit certain sites. These files allow the site to recognize visitors upon returning. Sometimes visitors want to be recognized and sometimes they don't.

As a Web developer, you can use cookies to identify visitors to your site. What can you do with this information?

✦ You can keep track of returning visitors.

✦ You can count new visitors.

✦ You can store visitors' preferences so they see what they told you they'd like to see.

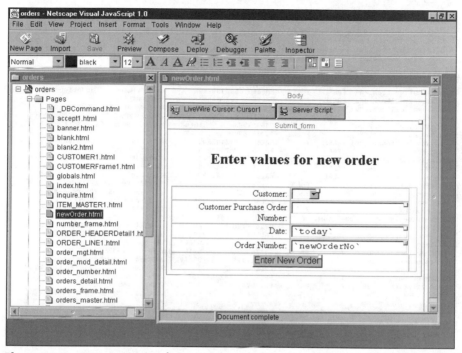

Figure 15-6: Netscape's visual development environment for JavaScript

Before you make the decision to use cookies, think about what kind of processing you want to do with this information. Writing a cookie is no work at all. Using the cookie effectively requires a lot more work.

The Web is a stateless system. A Web server doesn't know whether the same person has come to the Welcome page 100 times in a day or whether 100 different people have come once. This is why hit counts are so inaccurate. Cookies can change the stateless nature of the Web. If you know what you are doing with cookies, you can begin to collect valuable information about visitors to your site.

Cookies can also be abused. Many sites place cookies on visitors' pages and then do nothing with the data they are able to collect. Don't set cookies just because you can. You also need to remember visitors to your site have the option not to accept your cookies. You must make your site accessible even to people who don't want your cookies or can't save the cookie file (such as users at library computers or school computers). Figure 15-7 shows a typical cookie file.

```
cookies.txt - Notepad
File  Edit  Search  Help
# Netscape HTTP Cookie File
# http://www.netscape.com/newsref/std/cookie_spec.html
# This is a generated file!  Do not edit.

.msnbc.com             TRUE    /news/   FALSE   920448125             PX          0
e12.zdnet.com:8080     FALSE   /clear   FALSE   894560129             browser 808FD1F93516939C
www.alumni.caltech.edu FALSE   /~csc    FALSE   892384269             VisitorName    undefined
www.alumni.caltech.edu FALSE   /~csc    FALSE   892384447             WWHCount       2
www.alumni.caltech.edu FALSE   /~csc    FALSE   892384447             WWhenH  889796047548
www.eddiebauer.com     FALSE   /eb      FALSE   944035144             SHOPPERMANAGER%2FEB%5FCONTROL
.infoseek.com   TRUE   /        FALSE   916925983             InfoseekUserId  9B2BA358F0E355E88989(
www.cdw.com     FALSE  /        FALSE   1577858305            ID          47CR3RF9
pregnancy.miningco.com FALSE   /        FALSE   942187848             NGUserID       cf7a1833-311·
.imagine-inc.com       TRUE    /        FALSE   942191854             AccipiterId    FFFFFFFF*Def
www.miningco.com       FALSE   /        FALSE   942189026             NGUserID       cf7a6429-246·
search.miningco.com    FALSE   /        FALSE   942187635             NGUserID       cf7a6410-346·
pregnancy.tqn.com      FALSE   /        FALSE   942187640             NGUserID       cf7a1833-205·
.geocities.com  TRUE   /        FALSE   950960049             GeoId   1281605180788820840 4
.abcnews.com    TRUE   /        FALSE   1520498503            SWID    AA892903-B79B-11D1-AA56-00A0(
.preferences.com       TRUE    /        FALSE   1182140294            PreferencesID  B6KLL4E7u+yH:
www.previewtravel.com  FALSE   /        FALSE   942188989             NGUserID       c644F402-226:
destinations.previewtravel.com FALSE   /        FALSE   942188990             NGUserID       c644·
.abcnews.com    TRUE   /        FALSE   892641900             POLL2   1000000007C0000000000000000
www.idcresearch.com    FALSE   /        FALSE   1293753858            EGSOFT_ID      128.143.209·.:
.egghead.com    TRUE   /        FALSE   1577836625            ORDER_ENTRY    971231
.egghead.com    TRUE   /        FALSE   1577836625            SITE_USER_ID   27417533375545
.focalink.com   TRUE   /        FALSE   946641416             SB_ID   08883513120000573696104011925·
.linkexchange.com      TRUE    /        FALSE   942191812             SAFE_COOKIE    34f32e950414·
gm.preferences.com     TRUE    /        FALSE   1182140230            CPreferencesID iCJKXouxF1m+
.webauction.com TRUE   /        FALSE   967269410             AUCTION_TICKET yWf90a.c
.msnbc.com      TRUE   /        FALSE   937396925             MC1     GUID=a06670e2b2bc11d19d3f000·
```

Figure 15-7: A cookie file

Cross-Reference Chapter 54, Privacy, talks about cookies and how they can be used in a sinister manner to violate generally accepted rules of privacy.

Secure Servers

If you want to collect private information about your visitors or conduct any type of commerce, you need to set up a secure server. The term secure server is actually a misnomer. What is really secure on a *secure server* is the transmission of information but, because secure server is the expression everyone else uses, this book will also use this terminology.

How does a secure server work? When you go to a secure Web page, you will notice the lock on your browser (either in the lower left-hand corner of your screen on Netscape — or on the bottom toward the right part of your screen in Internet Explorer) is locked. By default, your browser gives you a warning every time you go to (or leave) a secure page, but you can turn off those annoying warnings (you may have already done this). Normally, only pages that show you confidential information (such as the value of your mutual fund portfolio) or pages into which you enter confidential information (such as your credit card number) are secure. When this page was sent to your browser, it was sent encrypted. This means people with a lot of time on their hands who were sniffing packets on the Internet couldn't open your packets to read what was sent. When you enter information on a secure form, it is, likewise, sent encrypted back to the server. The term *secure server* says nothing about how tight the security is on the server itself.

Four steps are involved in setting up a secure server:

1. **Get a secure key.** The *secure key* is what your server uses to send encrypted data. You can get a secure key from Verisign (`www.verisign.com`).

2. **Install the key on your Web server.** Your server will have a key manager (as shown in Figure 15-8) or a flat file, where you install the key you purchase from the certification authority.

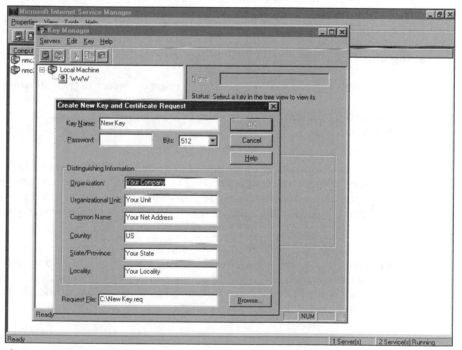

Figure 15-8: IIS Key Manager

3. **Publish your pages to the secure directory.** Your systems administrator will be able to tell you where the secure directory is on your server. Any pages that need to be secure should be published to that directory.

4. **Link to your secure pages using** `https://` **instead of** `http://`. When you link to pages in your secure directory, instead of using relative links, such as `commerce/buynow.html`, you need to use absolute links, such as `https://www.sellingstuff.com/commerce/buynow.html`. Notice this absolute link uses the `https` protocol rather than the `http` protocol.

In Depth

Secure Servers versus Secure Directories. Whether you will be required to publish all your secure pages in one directory or whether they can be anywhere on your server is really a policy issue. Just as with managing your media files, you may find placing all your secure pages (pages with which you communicate with the https protocol) in a single directory more convenient.

Looking at UNIX Servers

UNIX servers are the old war horses of the Web server world. UNIX servers make reliable Web servers. The only drawback to UNIX Web servers is the environment isn't as graphical as it is with NT servers (or Mac servers, for that matter). More and more tools have become available to make publishing to a UNIX server more straightforward, such as the FTP clients shown in Chapter 5.

If you are publishing to a UNIX server, you must be aware of the following things:

✦ **Capitalization matters.** When you link from one page to another or when you publish a page, `MyPage.html`, `mypage.html`, `MYPAGE.html`, `MyPage.HTML`, and `mypage.Html` are all different pages.

✦ **Scripts traditionally are published to your CGI-bin directory.** Unless your systems administrator tells you otherwise, assume any executable pages (that is, pages that require server-side processing) should be stored in your CGI-bin directory. If you are using any canned Perl scripts, this is where you are likely to find them.

✦ **Permissions.** You need read, write, and execute permissions to your directories and your files. Your directories and files will also have to be set so everyone has read and execute permissions. You can check your permissions by using some FTP clients or by using Telnet, if you are authorized access to your files via Telnet. (See Figure 15-9.)

File permissions

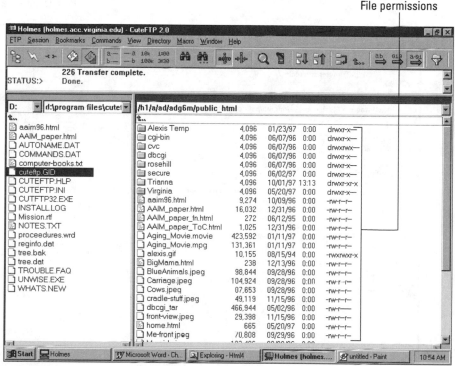

Figure 15-9: File permissions using CuteFTP

Looking at Windows NT Servers

Windows NT servers are newer to the field, but offer their users many advantages. The biggest advantage is the interface looks just like the PC that is probably sitting on your desk. For Windows 95, Windows 98, and Windows NT users, you can drag-and-drop into a Windows NT server environment as easily as you can onto your own local hard drive. Another advantage of publishing to a Windows NT Web server is capitalization doesn't matter. Unless you *wanted* Mypage.html to be a different page from MyPage.html, this is a real advantage!

A downside of publishing to a Windows NT server is you can't check file and directory permissions remotely (see Figure 15-10). This is a source of frustration for server administrators, as well. You must test thoroughly to be sure others can see your files and execute your scripts, because no one place exists where you can go to check your permissions. To make matters worse, if the permissions on a higher directory are too restrictive, you can't see a page even if the permissions for that directory and page are set appropriately. The only solution to this is to test, test, test!

Permissions blank

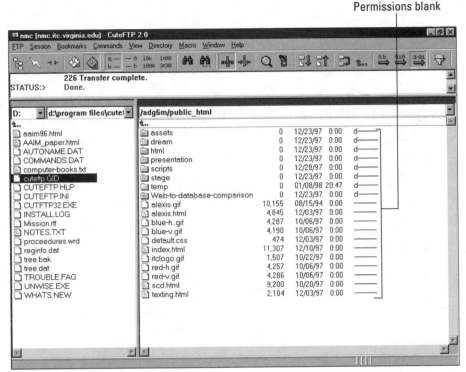

Figure 15-10: File permissions don't show up on NT.

From Here

Proceed to Part IV: "Developing Document Structure with HTML 4."

Jump to Chapter 44: "Accessing External Databases."

Jump to Chapter 46: "Building a Secure Site for Web Commerce."

Summary

In this chapter you learned about some of the fancier things you can do with your Web server. First, you learned about the client-server model and how you can use client-side processing to reduce the load on your server. You also learned about Web servers and permissions. Included were some tidbits about how you can use middleware to communicate with a database on your server.

You learned about how you can use cookies to do more sophisticated hit counting. Secure servers were also discussed, including the four steps you must take to implement a secure page on your site. Finally, you looked in-depth at UNIX and NT Web servers.

✦   ✦   ✦

Developing Document Structure with HTML 4

Understanding HTML Document Architecture

This chapter is about building the basic infrastructure of your page. Later, you learn about making everything look nice, but here you'll lay the foundation to build upon.

What's New in HTML 4?

HTML 4 introduces a number of new elements. They fall into the categories of frame elements, forms elements, annotation elements, table elements, and CSS-facilitating elements. One stray new element doesn't conveniently fall into any category — the BDO element — which gives you the ability to change text direction for an inline element. What this means is if the standard text direction of your document is left-to-right and you want to override that to display one sentence of a language requiring right-to-left directionality, you would use the BDO element.

Frames

Even though you may have been using frames for two years or engaged in heated debates about whether frames are a good way to structure a site, frames have never been an official part of the HTML specification until now. The W3C has finally embraced frames or at least recognized frames by adding the FRAME, FRAMESET, NOFRAMES, and IFRAME elements to the HTML 4.0 specification.

Framesets are what you use to define the presence of frames on your page. The IFRAME element is truly new to HTML and is a fabulous way to introduce an element to your page that stays consistent across pages. Unfortunately, the IFRAME element is not yet supported in both the major browsers, but the IFRAME element may well replace the FRAME element, once it is well-supported.

You can read more about the FRAMESET element, the FRAME element, and the IFRAME element in Chapter 30.

The IFRAME element is supported in Internet Explorer 3 and 4 and in Netscape 4.

Forms

A number of new elements have been introduced into the HTML specification to make forms more intuitive to the site visitor. The OPTGROUP element enables you to group your form fields in such a way that the visitor to your site should be able to navigate them more easily. Using style sheets, you can use one background color for the personal information form fields and another background color for the order form fields. The LABEL element gives you the opportunity to label each group of fields to process back on your server or to increase clarity to the visitor. The BUTTON element increases your flexibility when creating submit-type buttons at the bottom of your form.

Annotation

There are literary conventions that aren't currently supported in browsers, even though they may be useful. These include the capability to indicate what part of a text has been deleted and what part of a text has been inserted (for example, in drafting a law) using the DEL and INS elements. Other annotation-type elements are the ABBR (abbreviation) element, the ACRONYM element, and the Q (quote) element. None of these last three elements are currently displayed in any special way by browsers.

If you read more about these three elements, you can clearly see how they could come in handy. Check out Chapter 18 where they are discussed in detail.

Tables

You might have thought there wasn't anything you could imagine that would make tables any more attractive to you as a Web developer, but the new HTML 4 elements for tables have something for everyone. Even though the rest of HTML 4 moves formatting into style sheets, CSS1 doesn't support table formatting well, so the new elements are all about improving and simplifying table presentation. They include the COLGROUP, THEAD, TBODY, TFOOT, and LEGEND elements.

Facilitating CSS

The last group of new elements helps make CSS possible. These elements are the OBJECT element, which is how you incorporate images, sounds, movies, animations, and other types of multimedia into your page, and the SPAN element, which helps you define an area to which you want to apply a style from your style sheet.

What's gone from HTML 4.0?

Very little. As with any language, a few things fall by the wayside but many new terms become accepted. The only three obsoleted elements were associated with changing the way the text looked on the page to make it use fixed-width font. The way to do this in HTML 4 is probably the way you've been doing it all along — with the PRE element. The ways not to do it are with the LISTING element, the PLAINTEXT element, or the XMP element. Also, there are deprecated elements and attributes.

Vocabulary

Obsoleted. An obsoleted element is one that won't necessarily work in future versions of browsers. You should find ways to remove it from your pages now.

Deprecated. A deprecated element is one that will be obsoleted in the future. You can use it today without any negative consequences, but you might have to go through all your pages in a year or two to pull it when it gets obsoleted.

Components of HTML

This is probably a good time to review the basic building blocks of HTML. You learned them in Chapter 4, but that was a long time ago. To review, they are elements, attributes, and entities.

Elements

Elements are how you tell the browser what part of the page a certain segment of text is in your page. The browser isn't smart enough to know that if you leave a blank line in front of a few sentences of text and leave another blank line after the text, that is probably a paragraph. You tell it that is a paragraph by using the P element. If, instead, this text was a blockquote, you'd tell it using the BLOCKQUOTE element — and you'd be pleased the browser hadn't guessed wrong.

Cross-Reference

All the elements are listed in Appendix A.

Attributes

Attributes are how you dress up and customize your elements. Just about every element has at least two attributes. These are the id attribute and the class attribute. There are hundreds of other attributes, but each element only takes a few. Many of these they share in common. You'll soon find you remember which attributes go with which elements. HTML editors often provide a list of attributes for an element as part of tag hints.

Cross-Reference

You'll learn everything you want to know about the `id` attribute and the `class` attribute in Chapter 24. All the attributes are listed in Appendix B.

Entities

Entities enable you to display special characters on your page. Without entities, you can only display the characters you can type, minus the characters that have special meaning to HTML, such as less than (<), greater than (>), and ampersand (&). With entities, you can display the copyright symbol ©, the trademark symbol (™), the cent sign (¢), the symbols for other currencies (¥ yen, £ pound sterling), and hundreds of other characters, including letters and symbols from other alphabets.

Cross-Reference

All the entities are listed in Appendix C.

Block versus Inline Elements

Elements fall into two categories: block and inline. *Block elements* can contain other block elements and can also contain inline elements. *Inline elements* can only contain other inline elements. Block elements have more to do with the structure of your page. Inline elements are more about emphasis. Consider Table 16-1.

Table 16-1 Comparison of Block and Inline Elements	
Block elements	**Inline elements**
structure your document	add emphasis
define parts of your document	set a part of a block apart from the rest of the block
permit formatting	
take IDs and classes for purposes of style sheet formatting	
can contain other block elements	
can contain inline elements	

Examples of block elements are: P, HTML, BODY, and BLOCKQUOTE. Examples of inline elements are: B (bold), I (italics), Q (quote), and A (anchor).

Understanding Nesting

To make HTML work, you must learn to put block elements within other block elements and to put inline elements into other inline elements and into block elements. This process is called *nesting*. Consider the following nested list:

✦ This is the first bulleted item

✦ This is the second bulleted item

    1. This is a numbered item

    2. This is another numbered item

    3. This is a third numbered item

✦ This is the third and final bulleted item

The following HTML will create the same thing:

```
<UL>
   <LI> This is the first bulleted item
   <LI> This is the second bulleted item
   <OL>
       <LI> This is a numbered item
       <LI> This is another numbered item
       <LI> This is a third numbered item
   </OL>
   <LI> This is the third and final bulleted item
</UL>
```

First, you should know — and you may already know — that the rules about nesting are not enforced by all browsers. What this means is if you break them, there might not be any visible penalty *today*. In the future, as more elements are introduced, nesting rules will have to be more strictly enforced. Now the rules:

1. **Close your elements in the reverse of the order you opened them.** If you have a paragraph in which you identify a book title, which you both bold and italicize, you must close the inner element *before* you close the outer element.

   In the following example, notice the B element is the last one opened and, therefore, is the first one closed. The P element, which is the only block-level element, is the first one opened; therefore, it is the last one closed.

   ```
   <P>One book I can highly recommend is Dostoyevsky's
   <I><B>Crime and Punishment</B></I></P>.
   ```

2. **Always close inline elements before you close the block element that contains them.** This is a subset of the previous rule. But the consequences of breaking it can be visible on your page. If you fail to close an inline element when you intend to, you could end up with bolded or italicized and bolded text on the rest of your page.

3. **Sometimes opening a new block automatically closes the previous open block.** You need to play this by ear, but there are times when beginning a new block element automatically ends the previous block element. One time this absolutely works is with paragraphs. You simply can't put a P element within another P element. Go ahead and try it. When your browser sees the second P element, it automatically closes the first one. On the other hand, you certainly can put a list within another list. Starting a second UL element doesn't close the previous UL element. You can also put a P element into a UL element, which doesn't close it either.

Version Information

One part of your page isn't HTML at all—it's SGML. This is the first line of your file, which should contain version information. If you use an HTML editor, you will notice it may add the version information (or its best guess at the version information) to the beginning of your document. The version information tells the browser what set of rules to use when rendering the page. It won't recognize elements that aren't in the specification you use.

You can choose from three version statements in HTML 4:

1. **Strict.** This definition includes non-frames documents and none of the deprecated elements. If you choose to use this one, you must have extremely clean HTML.

```
<!DOCTYPE HTML PUBLIC "-//W3C//DTD HTML 4.0//EN"
"http://www.w3.org/TR/REC-html40/strict.dtd">
```

2. **Transitional.** This definition includes deprecated elements (the way people used to write HTML) and all the new HTML elements, but no frames elements. This is the one to use if you don't think you can control yourself or if you have to use deprecated elements to support a large base of visitors who will come from older versions of browsers.

```
<!DOCTYPE HTML PUBLIC "-//W3C//DTD HTML 4.0 Transitional//EN"
"http://www.w3.org/TR/REC-html40/loose.dtd">
```

3. **Frames.** This definition is the one you need to use if you use any of the frames elements. It also includes all the elements in the transitional version. This is the most flexible and you should use it if you don't know what you might put into your page.

```
<!DOCTYPE HTML PUBLIC "-//W3C//DTD HTML 4.0 Frameset//EN"
"http://www.w3.org/TR/REC-html40/frameset.dtd">
```

The HTML Element

The HTML element is the mother of all block-level elements. It contains the HEAD and the BODY. That said, it is optional, according to the HTML 4 specification, but older browsers will expect to see it. Your browser is smart enough to know — when it hits a HEAD element — that it is squarely in the middle of an HTML element. Putting it in is considered good form but no calamities will befall you if you leave it out (at least not any calamities related to the HTML element). The end tag is also optional.

HTML <HTML>

Start Tag:	Optional
Content:	HEAD
	BODY
End Tag:	Optional
Attributes:	Lang: language
	Dir: text direction
	Version: version (deprecated: should go on its own line)

```
<HTML>
<HEAD>
  <TITLE>This is the title</TITLE>
</HEAD>
<BODY>
    The body goes here.
</BODY>
</HTML>
```

The HEAD Element

Generally speaking, you'll want to include a HEAD element at the top of your document.

Head <HEAD>

Start Tag:	Optional
Content:	TITLE: title
	BASE: base directory for relative references
	META: meta elements
	SCRIPT: script
	STYLE: style element for internal style sheets
	LINK: link to external style sheets
	OBJECT: object

End Tag:	Optional
Attributes:	Lang: language
	Dir: text direction
	Profile: URL of meta data

```
<HEAD>
    <TITLE>A really spiffy page</TITLE>
    <META name="creator" content="John Q. Public">
</HEAD>
```

The META Element

Meta means *about*. This element is the place where you give information about your page. The META element is used by search engines to help index your page. The problem with the current scheme of META elements is no standard exists. This is about to change and a standard is being developed. Using META elements according to the new standard is highly recommended.

Meta	**<META>**
Start Tag:	Optional
Content:	Empty
End Tag:	Forbidden
Attributes:	http-equiv: http response header name
	name: metainformation name
	content: value associated with name
	scheme: select form of content usually used to provide helpful but noncritical information or to provide more context for the correct interpretation of metadata

Despite the fact that the META element is infinitely flexible, the way you use it is pretty straightforward. Here are some examples:

```
<META name="creator" content="Alexis D. Gutzman">
<META name="publisher" content="IDG Books Worldwide">
<META name="description" content="really fabulous resource
about developing Web sites using all the cool new features of
HTML 4.0">
```

For the most part, when you use the META element, you assign a value to the name attribute and to the content attribute.

Names

The Dublin Core Data Set (in Table 16-2) is the most widely accepted of the emerging standards and you will be safe to draw the values of your name attribute from it. You certainly don't need to include all of these; they are optional. Also, if you need to include one more than once — say, there are multiple contributors — then you can repeat an element.

	Table 16-2	
	The Dublin Core Data Set	
Purpose	***Value of name attribute***	***Explanation***
Title	title	The title of the page.
Author or Creator	creator	The person or organization responsible for creating the page.
Subject and Keywords	subject	The subject of the page or keywords that describe the content of the page. As much as possible, you are encouraged to use controlled vocabularies and formal classification schemas (like the kind used by a library).
Description	description	A narrative description or abstract of the page.
Publisher	publisher	The publisher (your employer, your university, your publisher).
Other Contributor	contributor	Anyone who has contributed to the content of the page.
Date	date	The date of publication. Consider using YYYY-MM-DD. This is no place to get creative.
Resource Type	type	The type of page this is: novel, poem, personal page, and so on. Really smart people are working on a standard for this.
Format	format	Don't use this yet. A standard is under development.
Resource Identifier	identifier	A unique number you associate with it so that no two documents at your URL have the same number.
Source	source	If your page was derived from a book, give the ISBN number of the book. Otherwise, don't worry about this one.
Language	language	Language of the page. Use the 2-digit code.

(continued)

Purpose	Value of name attribute	Explanation
Relation	relation	This is an experimental one. If your page has a formal relationship with another page, this is where you can specify it.
Coverage	coverage	Perhaps to be used for geographical specification; they aren't sure yet.
Rights Management	rights	You can use this to link to a copyright notice or to specify your copyright statement.

Table 16-2 *(continued)*

http-equiv

The previous name attributes are currently only good for search engines and people who want to view your source to see who else contributed to the creation of your fabulous page. The http-equiv attribute is something you can use instead of the name attribute that actually means something special to the browser that requested the page. The browser can use this data when displaying your page. A few examples are telling:

```
<META http-equiv="expires" content="Mon, 23 Mar 1998 20:00:00
EST">
<META http-equiv="Content-Type" content="text/html;
charset=ISO-8859-5">
<META http-equiv="refresh"
content="10,http://www.mycompany.com/home.html">
```

In the last example, the refresh rate is in seconds. This is something you might use if you want to show a splash screen briefly and then have the browser automatically load the Welcome page.

Additional HEAD Elements

What else can you put into the HEAD? A TITLE element, a BASE element, a SCRIPT element, a STYLE element, a LINK element, and an OBJECT element. You remember the TITLE element from Chapter 5. You should have one, and only one, of those. You use the TITLE element to title your document; it also shows up in search engines. The TITLE element shows up in the top of the browser, above the menus.

Title <TITLE>

Start Tag: Required

Content: Document title

End Tag: Required

Attributes: lang: language code (see Appendix D for a complete list), if different from the language code specified in the BODY element

dir: text direction, if different from that specified in the BODY element

The BASE element is a clever device you can make use of whether or not you are using a frameset. If you are using a frameset, you can use the BASE element to tell all references contained in your page to open in the same frame in which the current page is open. (This will make more sense in Chapter 30.) If you are not using frames, the BASE element is a way to say: "start looking for all relative references from this point." This can be convenient if all your relative references (in images and in links) start from two directories below the current page. You can avoid having all your URLs begin with "../../". It also makes things easier if you have to move a page later. You can make the BASE element the directory where the page used to reside so you needn't recode all the links.

Base <BASE>

Start Tag: Required

Content: Forbidden

End Tag: Forbidden

Attributes: target: frame name where you want all links in this page to open

href: URL to use as base point for all relative references

If you want to have a script that is event-driven in your page, then you should use the SCRIPT element in your HEAD to include it. An *event-driven script* is one that only gets called when a certain event occurs. Events can be created by visitor actions, by the clock, or by other things you set up The results of actions taken by the visitor — clicking a check box, for example — are the most common type of events.

You'll learn about JavaScript and writing scripts in Chapter 48.

Script <SCRIPT>

Start Tag: Required

Content: The script

End Tag: Required

Attributes: type: Scripting language; content type

If you want to include a style sheet within your page, which is *not* the recommended way, you can use a STYLE element to do this. The recommended way is to define the style sheet externally, in a text document with a .css extension, and link to it using the LINK element. The style sheet definition will look exactly the same, whether you define it in a SYTLE element or in an external file linked to your document by the LINK element.

Style `<STYLE>`

Start Tag:	Required
Content:	Style sheet definition
End Tag:	Required
Attributes:	`type`: content type, just as with the `SCRIPT` element
	`media`: screen, print, and so forth (not actually implemented yet, but a good idea)

Link `<LINK>`

Start Tag:	Required
Content:	Forbidden
End Tag:	Forbidden
Attributes:	`id, class, lang, dir, title, style`: as defined elsewhere in this chapter
	`events`: see Chapter 48
	`href`: URL for linked resource, such as external style sheet
	`hreflang`: language code for linked resource
	`type`: content type of href
	`rel`: forward link types
	`rev`: reverse link types
	`target`: target frame information
	`media`: for rendering on media
	`charset`: character encoding of linked media

```
<LINK href="styles/css1.css" type="text/css">
```

The BODY Element

The `BODY` element is the block-level element that holds nearly everything that shows up in your browser window. It can contain all the other block elements, except for `HEAD` and `HTML`.

Body `<BODY>`

Start Tag:	Optional
Content:	Document title
End Tag:	Optional

Attributes: `onload, onunload:` event, see Chapter 48

`background:` URL for background image (deprecated)

`text:` foreground color for text (deprecated)

`link:` foreground color for link (deprecated)

`vlink:` foreground color for visited link (deprecated)

`alink:` foreground color for active link (deprecated)

`id, class:` for style sheets

`lang, dir:` language and direction, as previously explained

`title:` title

`style:` style information

`bgcolor:` background color (deprecated)

Structure versus Presentation, Again

You will notice this book often lists all those nasty legacy attributes from HTML 3.2 that affect presentation right in your HTML code. Again, you should try to avoid using them as much as possible. Even though you may now be convinced you can live without style sheets and that CSS is something too complicated for your simple site, when the time comes to maintain your pages and you have to wrestle with all those nasty presentation attributes, you will regret it.

The HTML 4 Way is to separate presentation from structure. If you are dying to get to the interior decorating and you are willing to wait to learn how to build the structure, jump to Chapter 23 and get it out of your system now. If you are willing to deny yourself the pleasure of designing for the nonce and to stick with learning and applying the fundamentals, you will be rewarded later.

Making Your HTML as Readable as Possible

When you create your HTML, you can make sense of it most easily if you use a few typographical conventions. Consider implementing the following guidelines in your files:

✦ leave a blank line between block-level elements

✦ indent subordinate block-level elements

✦ indent any nested elements

✦ leave inline elements on the same line as the block in which they are contained

✦ format paragraphs as paragraphs (excepting the indent on the first line, which won't show up anyway)

✦ format lists as lists

✦ keep each cell on a table in its own line

This book scrupulously follows these guidelines because they make writing easy and maintaining easier. Most HTML editors also implement some sort of formatting of the HTML to make it easier to read.

CSS has its own rules about readability. Read all about them in Chapter 24.

From Here

Jump to Chapter 23 and get acquainted with style sheets.

Proceed to Chapter 17 and learn about structuring text with block-level elements and lists.

Summary

This chapter gave you a thorough explanation about the nitty-gritty of page structure. If you've made it this far, you won't have any problems with HTML. Much of what this chapter covered you needn't know for your first page, but if you made it through Chapter 16 of a book this size, you're obviously serious about your HTML.

You know what's new in HTML 4 and what's gone altogether. You learned the difference between a block element and an inline element. You know about nesting.

You learned about version information, the HTML element, the HEAD element — with the somewhat confusing META element and all its variations — and the other elements that can go in the head. You also learned the basics of the BODY element. Finally, you learned how to write your HTML so it will be readable and instantly make sense to you when you come back to it in six months.

✦　　✦　　✦

Structuring Text with Block-Level Elements and Lists

You are now squarely in the middle of building your Web page. The basic building blocks of a page are block-level elements. This chapter covers them all in detail. When you finish this chapter, you will have more than 50 percent of what you need to create most Web pages. This excludes your style sheet, which is covered in Part V.

This chapter steps up the pace a bit. If you weren't serious, you wouldn't have gotten here so, to some degree, the material will start to become more challenging. Don't worry, though, if you don't understand something. Everything glossed over here (or included in an example for purposes of demonstrating a topic) is covered in-depth later in the book. Focus on picking up the main points of this chapter; any stray items that pop up in examples are explained later.

Introducing Block-Level Elements

Block-level elements are the building blocks of your page. Most of your content will go into block-level elements (unless you use the HTML 3.2 Way of putting all your content into tables, which is highly discouraged). Block-level elements serve two purposes: they tell the browser what type of content is contained in the block and they enable you to define how that content is displayed in style sheets.

Defining content

Why is it important for the browser to know what type of content you have in your document? It isn't particularly important for today but, in the future, it might be. HTML is a subset of SGML, which is a way of marking up even the most obscure parts of text. A day could come when all Web pages are indexed to a degree we can't even imagine today. Perhaps some day the Web will resemble Xanadu, the vision of Ted Nelson where any snippet of text can be referenced anywhere else. Then it will matter that your blockquotes are contained in BLOCKQUOTE elements and your paragraphs are contained in P elements.

The other reason it's important is more and more levels of detail are being added to the HTML specification with every new version. You will have fewer changes to make to your pages to remain current if you define the content accurately when you create the page.

Dictating presentation

The other great reason to use block-level elements the way they were intended is to define the layout of your page. Block-level elements are easily formatted using style sheets. Without getting into a long explanation of style sheets definitions, consider the following style sheet:

```
BODY {
        background: #FFFFFF;
        margin-left: .5in;
        margin-right: .5in;
}

BLOCKQUOTE {
        padding: .5in;
}

P {
        text-indent: .5in;
}

UL {
        margin-left: 1in;

}

LI {
        margin-left: .25in;
}
```

What does this say? It tells most of the block elements in your document how to format themselves. Why is this so great? Because it is all in one place! If you want to change your style, you can do it in a central location: in your style sheet. If you cheat and use the BLOCKQUOTE element for all your paragraphs, because you want a half-inch margin of white space on either side of the text, you won't have any good way to change your style — say, right-justify the entire page — without going in by hand and editing all your HTML. And, if you want to add an actual blockquote to your page, you must nest BLOCKQUOTE elements. Not only will this not serve you well for the future, it also won't serve you well for today. You will do far more typing than you must just to get the look you want.

Creating Paragraphs: The P Element

If your document contains prose, you'll probably want to include it in a paragraph. Do you think all documents contain text? They needn't. You can use graphics or lists effectively to communicate many messages. Creating a paragraph is easy. In the past, you might have used only a <P> tag at the end of each paragraph. This works, but it can produce unpredictable results with style sheets. If you plan to use style sheets, you will be best off opening and closing all your paragraphs with the appropriate tags.

Paragraph <P>

Start Tag:	Required
Content:	Inline elements
	Text
End Tag:	Optional
Attributes:	id, class: used in conjunction with style sheets
	lang, dir: indicate language and text direction; better specified BODY element unless this element is an exception to the rest of the page
	title: title of this element
	style: define style here to override that in a style sheet
	align: alignment is deprecated; should be specified in style sheet
	events: see Chapter 48

Controlling Line Breaks and Spacing

HTML offers you two easy ways to break up your page visually: create white space and divide your page with lines. Many good reasons exist to use both these techniques. Generally speaking, more white space is better than less. Take advantage of white space to attract the visitor's eye.

Breaking up your page

You can use the BR element to break a line wherever you want to, even in the middle of a word. The BR element is an inline element, so it doesn't interfere with your block-level element. You can use the BR element within a block or between blocks.

**Break
**

Start Tag:	Required
Content:	Empty
End Tag:	Forbidden
Attributes:	id, class: used in conjunction with style sheets
	title: title of this element
	style: define style here to override that in a style sheet
	clear: deprecated; used to indicate where floating objects are to appear following the break; use style sheets, instead

The other way to break up your page is with horizontal lines. The HR element is just as easy to use as the BR element.

Horizontal Rule <HR>

Start Tag:	Required
Content:	Empty
End Tag:	Forbidden
Attributes:	id, class: used in conjunction with style sheets
	title: title of this element
	style: define style here to override that in a style sheet
	align: alignment is deprecated; use style sheets, instead
	noshade: deprecated; indicates the line shouldn't have a shadow, which is the default; use style sheets instead
	size: deprecated; used to define the height of the rule; use style sheets instead
	width: deprecated; used to define the length of the rule across the page (default is 100 percent of the width of the page); use style sheets instead
	events: see Chapter 48

Preventing a line break

At times, you will want to keep your line from breaking in the wrong place. You can prevent a line from breaking where you don't want it to by using a nonbreaking space. Both of these are entities. To add a nonbreaking space, use   as in:

```
The delegates signed the Constitution in September 1787.
```

This will force September and 1787 to appear on the same line. Be sure not to leave any spaces between September and   and 1787, or it won't work the way you expect.

Adding Headings

Headings are another easy way to break up your page. Notice how this book takes advantage of headings. They not only make it easier to read your page, but they make it easier for visitors to find what they need when they return to your page.

There are six levels of headings: H1, H2, H3, H4, H5, and H6. H1 is the most important; H6 is the least important. Use them in order of importance, not based on how they render in your browser. That's what style sheets are for.

Heading 1 <H1> through Heading 6 <H6>

Start Tag:	Required
Content:	Inline elements
End Tag:	Required
Attributes:	id, class: used in conjunction with style sheets
	lang, dir: indicate language and text direction; better specified BODY element unless this element is an exception to the rest of the page
	title: title of this element
	style: define style here to override that in a style sheet
	align: alignment is deprecated; should be specified in style sheet
	events: see Chapter 48

Creating Bulleted Lists: The UL Element

Lists are absolutely essential to good Web page design. Take advantage of lists to break up your page. The list type you see most commonly is the bulleted list. You create a bulleted list using the UL element. Every list worth its salt also has list items. The list items are created with the LI element. In fact, a list created with the UL element with no LI elements within it isn't a list at all!

Unordered List <UL>

Start Tag:	Required
Content:	List items
End Tag:	Required
Attributes:	id, class: used in conjunction with style sheets

lang, dir: indicate language and text direction; better specified BODY element unless this element is an exception to the rest of the page

title: title of this element

style: define style here to override that in a style sheet

type: deprecated; indicates the bullet type; should be specified in style sheet

compact: deprecated; tells the browser to display the list in a more compact way; results vary by browser

events: see Chapter 48

List items

Whether you are creating a bulleted list or a numbered list, you won't have anything in your list unless you use the LI element.

List Item <LI>

Start Tag:	Required
Content:	Inline elements
End Tag:	Optional
Attributes:	id, class: used in conjunction with style sheets

lang, dir: indicate language and text direction; better specified BODY element unless this element is an exception to the rest of the page

title: title of this element

style: define style here to override that in a style sheet

value: deprecated; used to tell the browser what number to associate with this list item (works only with numbered lists)

type: deprecated; indicates the bullet type; should be specified in style sheet; but even in a style sheet, you don't want to indicate the bullet type separately for each item in the list; this is better indicated in the list element

events: see Chapter 48

An example using UL follows:

```
Common symptoms of early pregnancy include:
<UL>
  <LI> nausea
  <LI> vomiting
  <LI> loss of appetite
  <LI> strange food cravings
  <LI> exhaustion
  <LI> mood swings
  <LI> crying for no reason
<UL>
```

Creating Numbered Lists: The OL Element

The other popular kind of list is the *ordered list,* which you can create using the OL element. The OL element is every bit as easy to create as the UL element. Again, you need an LI element for each item on your list.

Ordered List <OL>

Start Tag:	Required
Content:	List items
End Tag:	Required
Attributes:	id, class: used in conjunction with style sheets
	lang, dir: indicate language and text direction; better specified BODY element unless this element is an exception to the rest of the page
	title: title of this element
	style: define style here to override that in a style sheet
	type: deprecated; indicates the numbering style; should be specified in style sheet
	start: deprecated; tells the browser what number it should use to start the numbering; should be specified in style sheet
	compact: deprecated; tells the browser to display the list in a more compact way; results vary by browser
	events: see Chapter 48

An example using OL follows:

```
When you first get into your car, before you turn the key in
the ignition, be sure that:
<OL>
  <LI> Your seat is adjusted properly
  <LI> Your seatbelt is fastened
  <LI> Your rearview mirror is adjusted properly
  <LI> Your outside rearview mirror is adjusted properly
</OL>
```

Creating Definition Lists: The DL Element

The definition list is used far less frequently than the other two kinds of lists and it has three parts: the definition list (DL), the definition term (DT), and the definition description (DD). The DL element works just like the OL and UL elements. The DT element works much the same way as the LI element. The DD element is different: it contains the actual definition of the term. How this type of list renders depends on your browser.

Definition List <DL>

Start Tag:	Required
Content:	Definition terms
	Definition descriptions
End Tag:	Required
Attributes:	id, class: used in conjunction with style sheets
	lang, dir: indicate language and text direction; better specified BODY element unless this element is an exception to the rest of the page
	title: title of this element
	style: define style here to override that in a style sheet
	events: see Chapter 48

Definition Term <DT>

Start Tag:	Required
Content:	Inline elements
End Tag:	Optional
Attributes:	id, class: used in conjunction with style sheets
	lang, dir: indicate language and text direction; better specified BODY element unless this element is an exception to the rest of the page

title: title of this element

style: define style here to override that in a style sheet

events: see Chapter 48

Definition Description <DD>

Start Tag:	Required
Content:	Inline elements
End Tag:	Optional
Attributes:	id, class: used in conjunction with style sheets

lang, dir: indicate language and text direction; better specified BODY element unless this element is an exception to the rest of the page

title: title of this element

style: define style here to override that in a style sheet

events: see Chapter 48

Because you don't see too many definition lists, an example is in order:

```
<DL>
  <DT>chop
  <DD>to cut into random sized pieces
  <DT>grate
  <DD>to shred into small irregular strips
  <DT>dice
  <DD>to cut with a knife into regular-sized cubes
</DL>
```

This will render in your browser something like this:

chop

to cut into random-sized pieces

grate

to shred into small, irregular strips

dice

to cut with a knife into regular-sized cubes

You might want to use style sheets to make that look a little bit nicer.

Creating Indented Quotations: The BLOCKQUOTE

The BLOCKQUOTE has been one of the most misused elements. It should be used to quote a long passage of text and, in the past, to create white space on both sides of your paragraph. Worse yet, people have used nested BLOCKQUOTE elements to get even *more* white space on their pages.

The BLOCKQUOTE element is great for quoting long passages of text. It has an attribute called cite, which, while not currently processed by browsers, could prospectively be used to link to the page where the quote is found in its entirety.

Blockquote <BLOCKQUOTE>

Start Tag: Required

Content: Inline elements

End Tag: Required

Attributes: id, class: used in conjunction with style sheets

lang, dir: indicate language and text direction; better specified BODY element unless this element is an exception to the rest of the page

cite: URL of the quote if taken from the Web

title: title of this element

style: define style here to override that in a style sheet

events: see Chapter 48

Adding Preformatted Text

Sometimes you want to show text, but you want to give the browser no control over how it formats that text. The most common example of this is showing a code sample from a program or showing an HTML example. By using the PRE element, you can force the browser to use a fixed-width font. The browser also recognizes your end-of-line markers (when you hit return in your typing) to indicate the end of the line.

```
<P>The following is an example of how you use the PRE
element:</P>

<PRE>&lt;PRE&gt;Put the text you want to appear preformatted in
a PRE element.&lt;/PRE&gt;</PRE>
```

This will render as:

The following is an example of how you use the PRE element:

```
<PRE>Put the text you want to appear preformatted in a PRE
element.</PRE>
```

Preformatted text <PRE>

Start Tag:	Required
Content:	Inline elements
End Tag:	Required
Attributes:	id, class: used in conjunction with style sheets
	lang, dir: indicate language and text direction; better specified BODY element unless this element is an exception to the rest of the page
	width: suggested width that the block of preformatted text should be; currently ignored by most browsers
	title: title of this element
	style: define style here to override that in a style sheet
	events: see Chapter 48

Grouping Block Elements: The DIV Element

Just to tantalize you, you're now going to learn about the DIV element. The DIV *element* is how you group block-level elements to format them with a style sheet. Normally, you only create a style for an element, but the DIV element gives you greater flexibility by enabling you to create a zone that includes multiple block elements, whether those elements are nested, in which case, inheritance would come into play, or whether those blocks are consecutive. Consider the following example.

You have two paragraphs of text and an unnumbered list you want to draw attention to by adding a border and giving it a different background color. Without the DIV element, there is no way to put a border about multiple blocks, short of putting them all into one big cell in a table (ugly and messy). With the DIV element, you would create the following:

```
<DIV class="special">
<P>The reasons for using the DIV element are numerous:</P>
```

```
<UL>
<LI> to group block-level elements
<LI> to put a border around multiple block-level elements
<LI> to change the background color of multiple block-level
elements
</UL>

<P>Isn't HTML 4 grand?</P>
</DIV>
```

Then you would create a style sheet definition, ideally in your externally defined style sheet, to tell the browser this DIV element should have a yellow background and a blue border.

```
DIV.special {
        background: #FFFF00;
        border-top: ridge;
        border-bottom: ridge;
        border-left: ridge;
        border-right: ridge;
        padding: 15pt.;
}
```

Division <DIV>

Start Tag:	Required
Content:	Blocks
	Inline elements
End Tag:	Required
Attributes:	id, class: used in conjunction with style sheets
	lang, dir: indicate language and text direction; better specified BODY element unless this element is an exception to the rest of the page
	href: URL that gives more information about this element
	align: deprecated; use style sheets
	title: title of this element
	style: define style here to override that in a style sheet
	events: see Chapter 48

Nesting Block Elements

You might want to nest block-level elements occasionally but, in some conditions, you can't. You can't nest P elements because the presence of the second start tag for the P element will end the previous P element. You can, however, nest lists. This is a great thing, too. You can also nest paragraphs within lists. Consider the following:

```
<P>Suggestions for adding flavor to your low-fat recipes.</P>

<UL>

<LI> Always invite a member of the onion family to every dish!

    <UL>

    <LI> white onions
    <LI> Vidalia onions (in season)
    <LI> shallots, finely chopped
    <LI> purple onions as a garnish
    <LI> green onions for crunch

    </UL>

<LI> Use only freshly ground pepper; invest in an attractive
pepper mill.

<LI> Sprinkle your plain vegetables with a small amount of
freshly grated parmesan cheese—so much flavor for so little
fat.

</UL>
```

Which will render as:

Suggestions for adding flavor to your low-fat recipes.

Always invite a member of the onion family to every dish!

- white onions
- Vidalia onions (in season)
- shallots, finely chopped
- purple onions as a garnish
- green onions for crunch

Use only freshly ground pepper; invest in an attractive pepper mill.

Sprinkle your plain vegetables with a small amount of freshly grated parmesan cheese —so much flavor for so little fat.

You could, of course, spiff up the presentation of that subordinate list by using square bullets, as defined in your external style sheet, but what is shown is what will render in the absence of a style sheet.

From Here

Cross-Reference

Jump to Chapter 24 and start learning CSS syntax.

Proceed to Chapter 18 and master inline elements.

Summary

You learned a lot in this chapter: How to create all the basic block-level elements, how to nest elements, and how to create lists (all three kinds). You also got a taste of what the DIV element can do for your layout.

You learned how to break text, how not to break text, and how to insert preformatted text. You are well on your way to having mastered the essentials of HTML 4.

✦   ✦   ✦

Using Inline Elements and Special Characters

Inline elements enable you to specify the structure of your document further. They also enable you to add emphasis to specific words, in a way style sheets can't do. This chapter takes you through the details of inline elements and special characters. Included are information about using foreign languages, adding inline quotes, and using the SPAN element to change the presentation of a group of elements within a block.

Introducing Inline Elements

Inline elements are the parts of your document that fill the block elements. You may have a paragraph of text defined with the P element (a block-level element). Within the P element, you can define inline elements, such as quotes, book titles (to be italicized), words in a foreign language, words to which you'd like to draw attention (to be bolded), and special characters (such as a copyright symbol).

Inline elements give you the control to make these specific formatting changes within your block elements. Table 18-1 includes all inline elements.

Table 18-1
All Inline Elements

Element	Description	Deprecated	Logical or Physical
ABBR	abbreviated form		L
ACRONYM	instance of an acronym		L
B	bold		P
BIG	big		P
CITE	citation		L
CODE	computer code fragment		L
DEL	deleted text		L
DFN	instance definition		L
EM	emphasis		L
I	italics		P
INS	inserted text		L
KBD	text to be entered by the user		L
Q	quotation		L
S	strikeout	Deprecated (use DEL)	P
SAMP	sample of code		L
SMALL	small		P
SPAN	container for grouping within a block element		
STRIKE	strikeout	Deprecated (use DEL)	P
STRONG	strong		L
SUB	subscript		P
SUP	superscript		P
TT	teletype		P
U	underline	Deprecated (use DEL)	P
VAR	variable or program argument		L

All inline elements have a few things in common. They all require both start and end tags. They can all have other inline elements as part of their content. They can all be grouped for purposes of formatting with style sheets with the SPAN element.

Note

You can nest inline elements. All nestings are not valid. For instance, nesting a CODE element within a CITE element gives you unpredictable results. Even more important with inline elements than with block elements is that you close the elements in the reverse order they were opened.

Logical versus Physical Styles

There is more than one way to italicize text as it appears in your browser. You can use the straight-shootin' approach and use the I element, you can use the more indirect route and use the EM element, or you can use the CITE element because the phrase you want italicized is a book title. What is the difference? Whether you are using italics for the sake of using italics or whether you are using italics to convey some other information.

This is a philosophical discussion, really. Purists, from the SGML school, believe all text formatting is associated with some deeper meaning. You don't bold because you want bold, you bold because you want the words you think should be bolded to come across as stronger than the rest of the text. As it turns out, most browsers render the STRONG element the same as the BOLD element.

It doesn't reflect poorly on you either way. You can make your own call as to whether you use the physical inline elements or the logical inline elements. Table 18-2 shows physical styles; Table 18-3 shows logical styles.

	Table 18-2 **Physical Inline Elements**	
Element	*Description*	*Renders as*
B	bold	bold
I	italics	italics
S	strikeout	text with a line through it
SMALL	small	smaller than the regular font
STRIKE	strikeout	text with a line through it
SUB	subscript	text that falls below the baseline of the rest of the text
SUP	superscript	text whose baseline is above the baseline of the rest of the text
TT	teletype	fixed-width font
U	underline	underlined text (obsoleted: don't use this; it is too confusing because links are underlined)

	Table 18-3	
	Logical Inline Elements	
Element	*Description*	*Renders as*
ABBR	abbreviated form	nothing special
ACRONYM	acronym	nothing special
CITE	citation	italics (I)
CODE	code sample	fixed-width font (TT)
DEL	deleted text	text with a line through it (STRIKE or S); renders differently in IE and Netscape
DFN	definition	italics (I); renders differently in IE and Netscape
EM	emphasis	italics (I)
INS	inserted text	underlined (U); renders differently in IE and Netscape
KBD	code sample	fixed-width font (TT)
Q	quote	nothing special
SAMP	code sample	fixed-width font (TT)
STRONG	strong	bold (B)
VAR	program variable	italics (I)

Understanding Web Character Sets

The Web supports several character sets. This includes the standard English character set, the extended English character set—which includes all types of accents for the vowels, mathematical symbols, reference symbols, Greek letters—and internationalization characters. To include characters from any of these character sets, select the appropriate entity from Appendix C.

Adding Special Characters

What if you need to insert the copyright symbol? Use an entity. Entities can be inserted into inline elements or block elements. Remember to use an ampersand (&) at the beginning of the entity and a semicolon (;) at the end. The most common special characters are included in Table 18-4. A complete list of entities is available in Appendix C.

Table 18-4
Common Special Character Entities

Character Notation	Hex Notation	Entity Created
nbsp		nonbreak space
iexcl	&#161;	inverted exclamation mark
cent	&#162;	cent sign
pound	&#163;	pound sign
curren	&#164;	currency sign
yen	&#165;	yen sign
sect	&#167;	section sign
copy	&#169;	copyright sign
laquo	&#171;	left-pointing, double-angle quotation mark
not	&#172;	not sign
shy	&#173;	discretionary hyphen
reg	&#174;	registered trademark sign
deg	&#176;	degree sign
plusmn	&#177;	plus-or-minus sign
para	&#182;	paragraph sign
raquo	&#187;	right-pointing, double-angle quotation mark
frac14	&#188;	fraction one-quarter
frac12	&#189;	fraction one-half
frac34	&#190;	fraction three-quarters
iquest	&#191;	inverted question mark

Special Characters for Specific Jobs

If you are doing anything with math, you should be able to display the mathematical symbols. The most common of these are in Table 18-5.

Table 18-5
Common Mathematical Entities

Character Notation	Hex Notation	Entity Created
forall	&#8704;	for all
part	&#8706;	partial differential
exist	&#8707;	there exists
empty	&#8709;	empty set = null set = diameter
nabla	&#8711;	nabla = backward difference
isin	&#8712;	element of
notin	&#8713;	not an element of
ni	&#8715;	contains as member
prod	&#8719;	n-ary product = product sign
sum	&#8721;	n-ary sumation
minus	&#8722;	minus sign
lowast	&#8727;	asterisk operator
radic	&#8730;	square root = radical sign
prop	&#8733;	proportional to
infin	&#8734;	infinity
ang	&#8736;	angle
and	&#8743;	logical and = wedge
or	&#8744;	logical or = vee
cap	&#8745;	intersection = cap
cup	&#8746;	union = cup
int	&#8747;	integral
there4	&#8756;	therefore
sim	&#8764;	tilde operator = varies with = similar to
cong	&#8773;	approximately equal to
asymp	&#8776;	almost equal to = asymptotic to
ne	&#8800;	not equal to
equiv	&#8801;	identical to
le	&#8804;	less than or equal to

Character Notation	Hex Notation	Entity Created
ge	&#8805;	greater than or equal to
sub	&#8834;	subset of
sup	&#8835;	superset of
nsub	&#8836;	not a subset of
sube	&#8838;	subset of or equal to
supe	&#8839;	superset of or equal to
oplus	&#8853;	circled plus = direct sum
otimes	&#8855;	circled times = vector product
perp	&#8869;	up tack = orthogonal to = perpendicular
sdot	&#8901;	dot operator
lceil	&#8968;	left ceiling
rceil	&#8969;	right ceiling
lfloor	&#8970;	left floor
rfloor	&#8971;	right floor
lang	&#9001;	left-pointing angle bracket
rang	&#9002;	right-pointing angle bracket

How about if you need special punctuation symbols? See Table 18-6 for the most common entities that represent punctuation.

Table 18-6
Common Punctuation Entities

Character Notation	Hex Notation	Entity Created
bull	&#8226;	bullet = black small circle
hellip	&#8230;	horizontal ellipsis = three-dot leader
prime	&#8242;	prime = minutes = feet
Prime	&#8243;	double prime = seconds = inches
oline	&#8254;	overline = spacing overscore
frasl	&#8260;	fraction slash

Handling Foreign Languages

What if you need to include text from other languages? Greek? French (with its accents) or even Chinese? The first thing you must do is to define the base language for your page. You can do this in the HTML element itself. Your HTML element would look like this:

```
<HTML lang="EN">
```

The value of the lang attribute should be a valid two-character language code. If you then have a paragraph with a different language as the base — say Spanish — then you could identify the base language for that paragraph by putting a lang attribute into the P element like this:

```
<P lang="SP">
```

Sometimes you simply want to include a sentence or a word in another language. The SPAN element is most appropriate for those times. A complete list of language codes is in Appendix D.

Note   There is a lot more to showing foreign languages that require a different alphabet on your page. If you have only a sentence or two to display, your best bet is probably to use an image of the text. If you have a considerable amount of text to display in a language other than English — say Japanese — which uses Kanjii and Katakana, your visitors must run a Japanese operating system because Japanese, Chinese, and other character-based languages use a double-byte character set, quite different from the single-byte character set (ASCII) used for English. For more information about this complex topic, visit http://www.samsung.co.kr.

You probably noticed in the last chapter that most of the block-level elements include both lang and dir attributes. These often need to work together. Some languages are actually read right to left. HTML accommodates the creation of pages using these languages by rendering in the direction you dictate. You still create the text in a left-to-right direction, but it is rendered right-to-left, if you indicate, thus

```
<BODY lang="CH" dir="rtl">
```

would give you a body with a base language of Chinese and a text direction of right to left. In Chapter 16, an element called BDO was introduced as a new element. This is the bidirectional algorithm override element. It enables you to override the base direction. The dir attribute is mandatory for the BDO element.

Bi-Directional Algorithm Override <BDO>

Start Tag: Required

Content: Inline elements

End Tag:	Required
Attributes:	`dir`: Mandatory: `ltr` or `rtl`
	`id, class`: used in conjunction with style sheets
	`lang`: language
	`style`: for style sheets
	`title`: gives the element a title

Adding Quotes: The Q Element

The Q element is a prospective element. The Q element doesn't render as anything other than ordinary text, but it may someday in the future. The Q element is the inline equivalent of `BLOCKQUOTE` and takes the same attributes.

Quote `<Q>`	
Start Tag:	Required
Content:	Inline elements
End Tag:	Required
Attributes:	`id, class`: used in conjunction with style sheets
	`lang, dir`: indicate language and text direction
	`cite`: URL of the quote if taken from the Web
	`title`: title of this element
	`style`: define style here to override that in a style sheet
	`events`: see Chapter 48

Grouping Inline Elements: The SPAN Element

The SPAN element is the inline equivalent of the DIR element. You can group any number of elements within a block-level element or between block-level elements by enclosing them in a SPAN element.

The SPAN element can then use an `id` or a `class`, as defined in a style sheet, to change the look of the elements it encompasses. Suppose you want to change the background to yellow for part of some text (to make it look like it is highlighted). You can use the SPAN element as follows:

```
<P>It is very important to proofread <SPAN class="highlight">
all your text </SPAN> carefully. You can find examples of <SPAN
class="highlight">common misspellings in Table A4.</SPAN> As
Strunk and White always say, <SPAN class="highlight"><Q>"You
should always find time to proofread."</Q> Spell checking
simply is not enough.</SPAN></P>
```

This text would render as follows. The yellow background text is shown as underlined.

It is important to proofread <u>all your text</u> carefully. You can find examples of <u>common misspellings in Table A4.</u> As Strunk and White always say, <u>"You should always find time to proofread." Spell checking simply is not enough.</u>

And the style sheet would look like this:

```
SPAN.highlight {
            background: yellow}
```

From Here

Cross-Reference

Go to Chapter 24 and learn the CSS syntax.

Jump to Chapter 48 and learn about events and JavaScript.

Proceed to Chapter 19 and learn about hyperlinks.

Summary

This chapter covered the essentials of inline elements. You learned the difference between physical inline elements that actually make the browser render in a certain way and logical inline elements, which tell the browser what message you are trying to send with your text. You also learned about inline elements that currently don't render differently at all, such as ABBR, ACRONYM, and Q.

This chapter explained the use of entities in depth, including using them to display mathematical symbols, punctuation, and foreign languages. You learned about text language and direction. Finally, you learned about the SPAN element, which enables you to apply a style across inline elements.

✦   ✦   ✦

Adding Hyperlinks

Hyperlinks are what make your page really click! Without them you couldn't have a site (only a page) and the Web wouldn't be a Web at all. This chapter tells you everything you need to know about links — internal links, relative links, absolute links, FTP links — you name it.

When you complete this chapter, you will be able to create any kind of link you can find on the Web. You can even use an image on the CD-ROM at the back of this book to link from an image on your page to the IDG Books Worldwide page for this book.

Understanding Links

Links are what make the World Wide Web so interesting and so compelling. In the early days of the Web, a lot of people with pages didn't have much to say other than: "This is what I think is cool." What did they give you? A list of their favorite links. At one time, there were more links than pages.

Today, you have an amazing range of places to link. You can create your own *cool links* page or you can be more discriminating and only link to other places within your own sites and your own strategic alliances.

How do links work? Basically what a link does is tell the browser to load a new URL using the HTTP protocol (or another protocol, but more on that later). It's that simple.

URLs Dissected

Why is it so important to stop and analyze the parts of a URL? It isn't just to slow you down and keep the good stuff for later in the book. You need to understand the parts of a URL if you want to create links. Depending on the type of link you are using, you need to include different parts of the URL. This may be dry, but hang in there. The rest of the chapter assumes you have read this part.

Anatomy of a URL

A *uniform resource locator* (URL) has several parts (see Figure 19-1). There is the protocol, say, http://. When you loaded a page locally in Chapter 5, what appeared in place of http:// was file://. That is because the file you were opening was a local file; no protocol was necessary.

What comes next? The server name. There are two parts to the server name: the machine name and the domain name. If you have a domain with only one server, you've probably never given this any thought. Your server name is something like www.overtheweb.com. But if you are part of a large organization, like the University of Virginia, many, many servers exist within the virginia.edu domain. Each one has a different name: holmes.acc.virginia.edu, maewest.itc.virginia.edu, faraday.clas.virginia.edu.

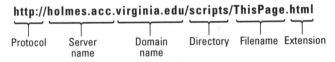

Figure 19-1: Anatomy of a URL

In addition to being able to have more than one server associated with one domain, you can have more than one domain reside on one physical server. An ISP may have hundreds of domains hosted from one physical server. How this is configured depends on the Web-server software running.

Following the server name comes the directory location on the server. This directory may be an actual directory, it may be a short name that maps to a longer directory name, or it may be a completely different name. For example, consider the following URL: http://watt.seas.virginia.edu/~bp/c34.html. The ~bp is the directory name. Does this mean there is a single directory directly under the root directory of watt.seas with the name ~bp? No. It means ~bp maps to some physical directory. This directory could be h1/users/bp/public_html or something even longer!

Finally, in the URL, you have the filename `something.html`. In fact, the extension on the file doesn't have to be `.html`. It should be appropriate for whatever type of file it is. If your file is an Active Server Pages (ASP) file, the extension would be `.asp`. If your URL is linking to a specific place on the current page or another page, you also need to include the anchor name of that place. If you don't include a valid anchor name, the page will load at the top. The anchor name begins with a pound sign (#).

Linking Local Pages with Relative File Names

The easiest kind of link to create is a link to a page in the same directory. Say you are currently working on a page you are going to publish as File1.html. You would like to link to another page you are going to publish into the same directory as File2.html. Here is all you need to create the link:

```
<A href="File2.html">Text that links</A>
```

Even though the browser always needs the fully qualified URL, it can figure out the rest of the URL from the current URL. All you need to provide is the file name. The browser assumes any information you leave out matches the information it used to get your current page. So if your visitor comes to your page at `http://this.domain.org/greatstuff/tidbits/File1.html`, his or her browser will turn your link of File2.html into `http://this.domain.org/greatstuff/tidbits/File2.html`.

Qualifying the URL

How does this work? The browser looks to see what page it is already on and then removes only the file name from the existing URL, adds the new file name onto the end of the URL, and requests the page. Pretty smart, eh?

The A element

Without even taking particular note of it, you just learned the A element, which you may remember from Chapter 5. When you want to link to a page, or to another location within the same page, all you need is the A element with the `href` attribute. In fact, the A element has several attributes. The two you use most often are `href` and `name`. `Href` gives the destination of the link; `name` names the anchor you are creating (more on that later).

Anchor <A>

Start Tag:	Required
Content:	Inline elements but no nesting of A elements
End Tag:	Required
Attributes:	`id`, `class`, `lang`, `dir`, `title`, `style`: previously defined

`href`: destination for a link

`hreflang`: language of the `href` attribute

`type`: content type of the link; most commonly "text/html"

`rel`: relationship in sequence of this `href`

`rev`: relationship in sequence of this `href`

`charset`: character encoding of the link

`shape`, `coords`: for imagemaps, see Chapter 36

`target`: identifies which frame in a frameset gets loaded with the contents of the `href`

`tabindex`, `accesskey`: for accessibility

`name`: name of an anchor

Linking to Pages in Other Directories

Of course, you can't spend your life linking only to other files within the same directory on the same server. Sometimes you simply must link to pages in other directories. When you do this, you can go one of two directions: up or down. Up means you will be going to a directory further up the directory structure or at least down a different leg of the directory structure than you are in currently. Down means you will go to a subdirectory of the directory you are in currently. The following helps make this clear:

```
Root

history

American          European

revolution  20thcent  WWI  WWII
```

If you are working on a page in the `history/american/revolution` directory and you want to link to a page in the `20thcent` directory, you would take advantage of double dots (`..`) to go up a directory. This means if you are working on a page, the ultimate URL of which will be `http://this.domain.org/history/American/revolution/index.html` and you want to link to a page in the `20thcent` directory, you would use the following `href` value:

```
<A href="../20thcent/index.html">Learn about the history of the
20th Century</A>
```

Be sure not to put a slash (`/`) before the double dots or it won't work. How would you point to a file called `index.html` in the WWI directory? Don't look ahead.

```
<A href="../../European/WWI/index.html">Learn about World War I
in Europe</A>
```

You can put as many sets of double dots as you need. However, at some point, it might be clearer just to use an absolute reference, which you learn about next.

Linking to External Pages

Relative references were covered in the last section. That is to say, all links were relative to the current page. When you link to pages outside your current server, you need to use absolute references. Absolute references do not depend on the location of the page that is linking to them. An *absolute reference* is simply a fully qualified URL. When you link to an external page, you use the URL as you would type it in the location window of your browser, if you wanted to open that page.

```
<A href- "http://my.domain.org/history/American/revolution/
index.html">Learn about the American Revolution</A>
```

In most browsers today, you don't actually need to type the protocol information (`http://`). If you simply type `my.domain.org/history/American/revolution`, you normally get the right page on your screen. Why? First, the browser assumes you are using the http protocol. Second, `index.html` (along with `default.html` or `home.html`) is one of the file names a server will serve if you don't tell it which page in a directory you want. Servers can be configured to serve any page as the default page; they frequently have a list and go down the list looking for the page defined as the default.

Tip

You can actually give your Web server a bit more information about your links to help them load faster. By putting a `/` at the end of a link, you tell the Web server the name is a *directory name*, and not a *filename*. This saves the Web server the trouble of looking for a file with that name. This will not work if your link is to a file name (`something.html`). In fact, it will result in a broken link.

In your absolute reference, however, you always need to give the protocol and the file name. So the following won't work:

```
<A href= "my.domain.org/history/American/revolution">Learn
about the American Revolution</A>
```

Because typing a URL incorrectly is so easy and then you end up with a broken link on your page, it is *highly recommended* you do bring up the page to which you want to link in your browser, copy the URL from the location window, and paste it into your HTML.

Linking to Locations on the Same Page

What if you have a long page, such as a FAQ, which by all the chunking rules you know you shouldn't break up into more than one page, perhaps because people will want to print it? How can you link to the middle of a page? You create a named anchor. A *named anchor* is simply a point on the page to which you can link directly.

```
<A name="Q21">Question 21</A>
```

The previous code creates a named anchor at Question 21. There are no rules about names, except they can't have spaces in them, so make up something you'll remember. Now if you want to link from somewhere else in the same page to Question 21, you use the following code:

```
<A href="#Q21">See also Question 21.</A>
```

If you want to link from somewhere else in another page in the same directory, you use the following code:

```
<A href="faq.html#Q21">See also Question 21 in the FAQ.</A>
```

You can, of course, link to a named anchor from pages in other directories or from pages on other servers. You should be able to figure out how to do this by now.

Cross-Reference

Chapter 30 explains frames and targets in detail.

In Depth

Does capitalization matter when you are creating links? It depends. If you are publishing to an NT server, no. If you are publishing to a UNIX server, yes. It definitely matters when you are linking to pages on other sites, because you don't know on what kind of server they reside. The easiest way to keep your own links straight on your own site is to pick a system and stick with it. Use all lowercase filenames and you shouldn't have a problem.

Link to Pages from Images

One feature you see on many pages is linking from images. Sometimes you can click an image and hyperlink to another page or to another place on the same page. Linking from an image is simple. An image is on the CD-ROM in the back of this book that you can use for this. This image is called HTML4.gif. To place this image on your page and link from that image to the IDG Books Worldwide page for this book, include the following code:

```
<A href="http://www.idgbooks.com/html4bible.html"><IMG
src="images/HTML4.gif"></A>
```

You just used the IMG element. The IMG element is covered in depth in Chapter 20. For now, just know you need to publish the image file from the CD to your images directory as binary (or raw data) for this to work.

How does this work? The image behaves exactly the same as the text would as the content of an A element. On older browsers, you might see a blue box around the image to indicate it links. But you'll learn how to turn that off when you get to Chapter 24 about style sheets.

Linking to Non-Web Data

What if you want to link to a file for your visitors to download? You can do this using the same A element.

```
<A href="http://www.yourserver.com/pub/contract.doc"> Download
the latest version of our contract.</A>
```

This works as long as it is in the pub directory and it is a file called contract.doc. When a visitor clicks this link, the browser asks what to do with this file. Once the browser gets it downloaded, the visitor can open it with any program that will open a .doc file. It's a good idea to give visitors a choice of ways to get at any file you want to download and also to give them a choice of formats including .rtf (rich text format). Check with your systems administrator to make sure permissions are right for this to work.

Tip

Better yet, create the document and save it as a .pdf file (portable document format) using Adobe Acrobat. Then visitors can see the document with all its formatting right on the screen and print it to a printer without needing to have the right word processor installed.

The BASE Element

What if you want to have many links to a different directory on the same server or you have to move your page to another directory, breaking all your links? HTML helps you out here by offering the BASE element. The BASE element goes into the HEAD element. It is easy to use. It tells any visiting browsers they should act as if this page is located in the BASE URL location for purposes of all relative references. An example helps:

You have 20 links on your page to other pages in your site. Your current page is called history/American/20thCentury/WWII/Pacific/thispage.html. Your links are mostly to pages in the history/European/WWII/Japan directory. So most of your links look something like this:

```
<A href="../../../../European/WWII/Japan/page1.html"> Click
here.</A>
```

Now, for some reason, you have to move this page to the history/Asian directory. Does this mean you must go through and recode all your links? No. You can simply add the following BASE element to your page:

```
<BASE
url="http://this.domain.org/history/American/20thCentury/WWII/
Pacific/">
```

Now all your relative links originate from the correct directory. This solves this immediate problem, but what you might want to do in the first place is to make all your links relative to the history directory. Then your BASE element would look like this:

```
<BASE url="http://this.domain.org/history/">
```

And your link would look like this:

```
<A href="European/WWII/Japan/page1.html"> Click here.</A>
```

Using the BASE element can make maintenance of your site much easier in the long run.

Adding a MAILTO Link

Have you ever clicked someone's e-mail address at the bottom of a page and had a mail window open? This is done with a mailto link. If you do use a mailto link, you should also give your e-mail address so people with nasty old browsers, or the stand-alone version of Navigator, can still send you e-mail. Here's how it works.

```
Contact me at<A href="mailto:info@yourdomain.org">
info@yourdomain.org.</A>
```

Where info@yourdomain.org is your e-mail address.

Bonus: Create a Link without Leaving Your Page

Isn't it risky to put links on your pages to other sites? Doesn't this mean you could be sending your visitors away, never to return? It is, indeed, risky, but you don't want to have a site without any links to the rest of the world. There is a way around this quandary. When you link to other locations, open up new windows! This means your own site is still there — it just ceases to be the active window.

```
<A href="http://other.site.com/relevant/index.html"
target="_blank">A strategic partner of ours</A>
```

The target attribute is set to _blank, which is a reserved target name. This attribute tells the browser to open a new, blank window the URL specified by the href attribute. You learn more about targets and reserved target names in Chapter 30, which is all about frames.

From Here

Jump to Chapter 30, Creating Frames.

Proceed to Chapter 20, Inserting Graphics and Other Objects.

Summary

In this chapter, you learned how to create all kinds of links: links to pages in the same directory on the same server, links to pages in different directories on the same servers, and links to pages on different servers. You also learned how to link images to pages. You learned how to create a mailto link and how to open a new page when you link to an external page, so the visitors don't leave your page altogether.

✦   ✦   ✦

Inserting Graphics and Other Objects

What is a Web page without graphics? This chapter takes you through the basics of inserting graphics and multimedia effectively into your pages. The IMG and OBJECT elements enable you to insert images and other types of multimedia into your pages.

A Quick Introduction to Graphics File Formats

Image files come in many formats. Fortunately, the Web only supports three formats: JPEG (Joint Photographic Experts Group), GIF (Graphics Interface Format, pronounced *jiff* by the inventor of the format, and *gif,* as in gift, by everyone else), and PNG (Portable Network Graphic). Initially, the Web only supported GIF images for inline viewing and JPEG images for out-of-line viewing. Today, you can use all three formats in the middle of your page. The Web uses these three types of graphics files because each format supports some type of compression.

JPEG

JPEG compresses your image by removing redundant data. It maintains the complete color spectrum of your image. If you have a photo of yourself in front of a tree or a beautiful sunset, JPEG is a good compression choice. In the tree photo, the slightly inaccurate re-creation of the leaf pattern is of little consequence. Because JPEG preserves all the colors, your tree and sunset are as lovely as the original when compressed with JPEG.

GIF

GIF, on the other hand, compresses your image by removing colors down to the 256-color palate. As a result, your GIF photo of a sunset probably has stripes (where one color ends and the next closest color begins), and your tree is also less vibrant. If you have an architectural drawing in which the straightness of the lines matters more than the background shade of sepia, then GIF is the proper format. Because this format handles line art skillfully, use GIFs to save text images.

PNG

PNG is the newest graphics file format supported on the Web. By using an exclusively designed algorithm, PNG provides the best overall quality. Only the newest browsers support PNG, however. If visitors view your page without the latest browser, they receive the broken-image graphic — unless you provide an alternate image.

Creating a graphic image

Many available software packages create graphics. Chapter 34 discusses your options for creating images and goes into greater detail about selecting the appropriate format.

Adding Inline Images with the IMG Element

Use the IMG element to add an image to your page simply. The IMG element includes everything you need in the start tag. IMG does not have content or end tags.

Image <IMG>

Start Tag:	Required
Content:	Empty
End Tag:	Forbidden
Attributes:	id, class: used in conjunction with style sheets
	lang, dir: indicate language and text direction
	src: URL of image
	alt: short description; used for text-only browsers
	longdesc: long description; used for text-only browsers

title: title of this element

style: define style here to override style sheet

usemap: URL of client-side image map

ismap: use server-side image map

height: height of image; use if overriding the actual image height

width: width of image; use if overriding the actual image width

align, hspace, vspace, border: deprecated; should be specified in style sheet

events: see Chapter 48

The two most important (and required) attributes are src and alt. Src specifies from where the image arrives. Even with an inline image, the image exists as a separate file, usually stored in your images directory. To support the shrinking number of text-only browsers, as well as the growing number of text-synthesizing browsers, include a useful alt attribute value. The alt attribute should contain a short, accurate description of the image's appearance. If you need a longer description, you should use the longdesc attribute.

Height and width serve two purposes. If you use an HTML editor to specify an image, the HTML editor automatically inserts the height and width attributes to facilitate quick page loading. In addition, if you want to load a small image and stretch it into a larger image, then use the height and width attributes.

Tip   Don't try to stretch a GIF image. Use JPEGs and PNGs for stretching instead.

Usemap and ismap are associated with image maps. Image maps are images with clickable areas — actually hyperlinks — under the image. Image maps are discussed fully in Chapter 36.

The following examples show how to use the IMG element:

```
<IMG class="logo" src="images/logo.gif" alt="Really Big Company
Logo">
```

This code inserts an image called logo.gif into your page. If you hold your mouse over the image using Internet Explorer 3 and above, or Netscape Navigator 4 and above, the words Really Big Company Logo pop up. The formatting — padding, borders, alignment, and text wrapping — of the image depends on your style sheet and the definition of the IMG class logo.

```
<IMG class="wrapped" src="images/stretch-box.gif"
alt="Concentric boxes" height="200" width="200">
```

The preceding code inserts an image called `stretch-box.gif`. The original image is 16×16 pixels, while the stretched image will be 200×200 pixels. If successful, stretching an image is a great way to minimize the load time of your page. The formatting of the image on the page depends on how the IMG class `"wrapped"` is defined in your style sheet.

Multimedia

A growing number of inline and external multimedia formats work on the Web. Some multimedia files play in your browser without any special plug-ins, while others require plug-ins. Multimedia files can include video, sound, animation, VRML (Virtual Reality Modeling Language), QuickTime VR, and a number of other formats.

As the page designer, remember that visitors to your site may need special software to load your page properly. You should include links to any plug-ins required for your page. Some of the more common multimedia file formats follow:

Extension	Description
.mov	movie
.wav	sound
.qtvr	QuickTime VR
.wrl	Worlds 3D VRML
.midi	sound
.dcr	Shockwave
.pdf	portable document format (Adobe)

Adding Inline Multimedia with the OBJECT Element

With more formats each requiring different information, adding multimedia is trickier than adding an image. Add multimedia to your page using the OBJECT element. Currently, most images are inserted into your page using the IMG element, but even images will eventually be inserted using the OBJECT element.

Object `<OBJECT>`

Start Tag:	Required
Content:	Alternate text
	other `OBJECT` elements
	one or more `PARAM` elements, description of what should appear
End Tag:	Required
Attributes:	`id`, `class`, `lang`, `dir`, `events`

`declare`: Boolean flag indicating the object is declared but should not be instantiated; if you use this attribute, you'll have to instantiate the object later with another `OBJECT` element

`classid`: URL of object's implementation; may be used either in conjunction with or instead of the data attribute, depending on the object

`codebase`: URL of base point for resolving relative references related to this object (specifically from the `classid`, `data`, and `archive` attributes)

`codetype`: content type of object specified in `classid` attribute in MIME format; saves time for a visitor downloading a content type that her browser can't render

`data`: URL of the object's data

`type`: MIME type of data specified in the `data` attribute; saves time for a visitor downloading a content type that her browser can't render

`archive`: list of URLs in space-delimited format that gives resources relative to the object's `classid` and `data` attributes; it may include the object's `classid` and `data` attributes; and the browser should preload the archive, which results in a quicker object load

`standby`: a message that the browser may show while loading the object

`title`: title of this element

`style`: define style here to override style sheet

`usemap`: URL of client-side image map

`name`: name for form submission

> height: height of object; use if overriding the actual image height
>
> width: width of object; use if overriding the actual image width
>
> align, hspace, vspace, border: deprecated; should be specified in style sheet
>
> tabindex: tabbing order (for forms)

The OBJECT element can be very confusing. Fortunately, you will probably never need to use all attributes at the same time.

The OBJECT element can be nested into a sort of pecking order. Your browser uses the first instance of the nested OBJECT element that it supports. If you, as a Web developer, put the spiffiest items first, then the visitor sees the coolest multimedia that her browser can support without realizing she is missing any items, as shown in the following example:

You want to include a model of a protein molecule for your cool chemistry site. The coolest model is the VRML version of the molecule, which is 3D and rotates and zooms at the visitor's discretion. Unfortunately, the visitor needs to have a computer that can handle 3D rendering and a VRML player installed. The next coolest way to show the model uses a QuickTime VR model of the molecule. This method enables the visitor to rotate the model without the ability to zoom and travel through the molecule. If the visitor can't even handle the QuickTime VR model, use an MPEG movie of the molecule bonding with another molecule. The last option is a GIF image of the molecule. For text-only browsers, settle for a short description in text of the molecule.

The following creates the nested OBJECT elements for this example:

```
<OBJECT
classid="http://nmc.itc.virginia.edu/nlii/Grisham/vrml/modelA1.
wrl" codetype="application/wrl" height="250" width="600">
  <OBJECT classid=
"http://nmc.itc.virginia.edu/qtvr/atp_synthase.qtvr"
codetype="application/quicktime">
      <OBJECT data="synthase.mpeg" type="application/mpeg">
          <OBJECT data="atp_synthase.gif" type="image/gif">
              You are missing the ATP Synthase molecule.
          </OBJECT>
      </OBJECT>
  </OBJECT>
</OBJECT>
```

Tips on Using Images Effectively

Good Web designers often debate when and how to use images. The two major issues with regards to images on your page are download time and visual clutter. No hard and fast rules about using images exist, but the following guidelines help:

1. **Use the lowest color depth appropriate for your application.** Chapter 34 discusses this issue in greater depth. In simple terms, don't save your black-and-white image in 16.7 million colors. If your image uses only primary colors, save it with the least color-palette baggage to reduce download time tremendously.

2. **Use the smallest image appropriate.** What are you trying to communicate with the image? You need to have a certain level of detail in your image to make your point, but try to keep images small. Crop them tightly and leave the white space on the page using padding in the style sheet.

3. **Use text instead of an text image,** if at all possible. If the your font is widely available (meaning it comes installed with Windows 95/98/NT with a reasonable facsimile available on the Mac), then use text; if not, use an image of text. (See Figures 20-1 and 20-2 for examples.)

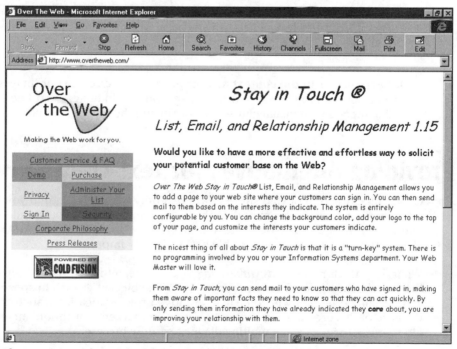

Figure 20-1: Using an image text is sometimes unavoidable.

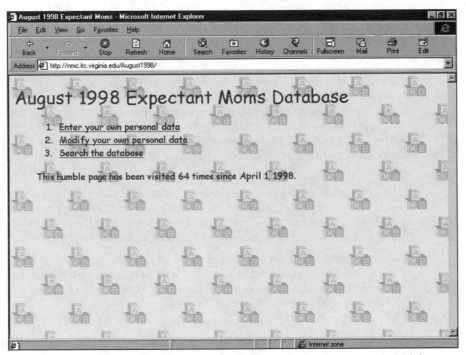

Figure 20-2: Use text, rather than an image, when the font you want is widely available.

4. **Keep images in the context of your page.** Make sure all your images contribute to the message of your page. Don't add images just because you like them. Avoid visual clutter by prioritizing the message of your page.

Providing Alternatives for Text-Only Browsers

Only a small fraction of Web surfers have text-only browsers. Should you bother to mark up your page to accommodate them? Probably not, but you should include alternatives for other reasons. The Americans with Disabilities Act (ADA) requires all government sites to be accessible to the visually impaired.

What does the term *speech-synthesizing browser* mean to you? If you only think of the visually impaired, broaden your horizon. The biggest growth in speech-synthesizing browsers will come in alternative browser locations, such as your car! Because of this growing segment of the browser market, you should include alternatives to images and multimedia for text-only browsers.

How can you make your Web page friendly to speech-synthesizing?

✦ **Use the** `alt` **attribute on every image.** Since speech-synthesizing browsers can't see your image, state your image contents.

✦ **Use text as the content of your** `OBJECT` **element.** Speech-synthesizing browsers skip the `OBJECT` element but process the content — the equivalent of `alt` text.

✦ **Never use the deprecated** `FONT` **element.** This element gives speech-synthesizing browsers fits. Use style sheets instead.

✦ **Use images only when absolutely necessary.** Use text instead of an image of text if possible. The image of text can be anti-aliased, but your ears-only visitors hear silence instead of your lovely image of text.

From Here

Cross-Reference

Go to Chapter 34 and learn about creating graphics for the Web.

Jump to Chapters 37 through 41 and learn about creating multimedia for the Web, including sound, video, ActiveX controls, and Java.

Proceed to Chapter 21, Adding Tables.

Summary

This chapter taught you how to add images and multimedia to your pages. You learned the `IMG` element and the dreaded `OBJECT` element. The examples provided with the `OBJECT` element should clarify its use. Finally, you learned about using images on your page effectively and accommodating text-only browsers.

✦   ✦   ✦

Adding Tables

Although tables have their place in a Web page, they should not format text. This chapter focuses on using tables in their intended manner: to display tabular data. For most of the other elements covered in this book, style sheets provide formatting. For tables, however, the style sheet model falls short. Because style sheets don't sufficiently support table formatting, tables include formatting information in the table definition.

This chapter covers everything from creating a basic table to grouping cells or columns to spanning cells or columns, and contains the most complete explanation of tables created with all available HTML 4 elements.

Introducing the HTML Table Model

HTML 4 adds to the potential formatting of tables on your Web page. For the first time, you can group rows and columns for purposes of formatting. Even though you have to include formatting in your table definition (unlike in the rest of HTML 4), you can include it at the group level, rather than at the cell or row level — a truly powerful feature.

In addition, you can group columns. To understand this profound change, examine the HTML 3.2 table model. Tables are created from left to right, top to bottom. The following table is defined in this order: A1, A2, A3, A4, B1, B2, B3, B4, C1, C2, C3, D1, D2, D3.

A1	A2	A3	A4
B1	B2	B3	B4
C1	C2	C3	
D1	D2		D3

If all the cells in the fourth column (A4, B4, and D3) had the same background color, that formatting information would have to be defined three times, once in each cell definition. Grouping formatting for rows would be easier, because all the cells in a row are defined together, but if you wanted to define formatting for all the rows except the first row, you'd have to put the definitions into each row.

What's new in HTML 4?

Using the COLGROUP element, you can group columns for purposes of formatting. As a result, you can define all the cells in a column to look the same without inserting formatting information into each cell. This feature is especially useful in terms of maintenance. If you change the background color of your page from your style sheet and find that the background color of one column doesn't match, you can change the formatting information only for that COLGROUP and have it reflected in every COLGROUP table cell.

In addition, the following set of elements in HTML 4 affects the formatting of rows: THEAD, TFOOT, and TBODY. You can define one or more rows as the THEAD, one or more rows as the TFOOT—the remaining rows take on the TBODY formatting.

Defining the Table

Create a table in HTML with the TABLE element. As with the UL, OL, and DL elements, however, this element alone won't achieve your desired results. You have to define table data in your table to see anything on your page.

Table <TABLE>

Start Tag:	Required
Content:	CAPTION
	COL
	COLGROUP
	THEAD
	TFOOT
	TBODY
	TR, TD
End Tag:	Required

Attributes:	`id`, `class`, `lang`, `dir`, `events`

`align`: deprecated; use style sheets

`cellpadding`: the amount of white space between the contents of a cell and its border

`cellspacing`: the amount of white space between cells and between cells and the outside borders of the table

`border`: the width in pixels of the frame around the table

`frame`: the side, if any, of the border of the table that is visible (see following choices)

`rules`: the rules, if any, that appear between cells (see following choices)

`width`: width of the table either in pixels or as a percentage of the window

`summary`: purpose of this table for speech-synthesizing browsers

The `frame` attribute takes one of the following values:

✦ **void** No sides. This is the default value.

✦ **above** The top side only.

✦ **below** The bottom side only.

✦ **hsides** The top and bottom sides only.

✦ **vsides** The left and right sides only.

✦ **lhs** The left-hand side only.

✦ **rhs** The right-hand side only.

✦ **border or box** All four sides.

The `rules` attribute takes one of the following values:

✦ **none** No rules. This is the default value.

✦ **groups** Rules appear between row groups and column groups only.

✦ **rows** Rules appear between rows only.

✦ **cols** Rules appear between columns only.

✦ **all** Rules appear between all rows and columns.

The following examples combine these interesting formatting options:

Row 1

Row 2

Row 3

frame="lhs", rules="rows"

Column 1	Column 2	Column 3

frame="above", rules="cols"

Column 1	Column 2	Column 3	Column 4	Column 5	Column 6

frame="void", rules="groups"

Adding Table Data

All data in a table goes into cells. A *cell* is created with the TD element or the TH element. Before you start defining cells, first set up rows into which the browser puts the cells. If you don't define rows to hold your cells, each cell will be its own row — meaning your table will be exactly one column wide. Create a row with the TR element.

Table Row <TR>

Start Tag: Required

Content: TD

TH

End Tag:	Optional
Attributes:	id, class, lang, dir, events, title, style

align: right, left, center, justify, char (these are not deprecated)

valign: top, middle, bottom, baseline (these are not deprecated)

char: indicate the character used for character alignment; default is decimal point

charoff: character offset from left when using character alignment

The TR element can contain both cell data and cell headers. To differentiate the two items, the cell headers are formatted in bold by your browser. To define the formatting for your header cells yourself, use the class attribute and define a class for your headers in your style sheet.

Table data <TD>

Start Tag:	Required
Content:	Cell data
End Tag:	Optional
Attributes:	id, class, lang, dir, events, title, style

align: right, left, center, justify, char (these are not deprecated)

valign: top, middle, bottom, baseline (these are not deprecated)

colspan: number of columns this cell spans (defaults to 1)

rowspan: number of rows this cell spans (defaults to 1)

abbr: abbreviated version of the cell's content

axis: a comma-delimited list of category names; used for associating each cell with a category in speech-synthesizing browsers

headers: ID that associates a header cell with table data; can be used for speech-synthesizing browsers, for grouping columns, or for style sheets

nowrap: deprecated; avoid wrapping text within this cell; can make cells very wide char: indicate the character to be used for character alignment; default is decimal point

charoff: character offset from left when using character alignment

bgcolor: deprecated; background color for this cell

width: deprecated; width of cell in pixels

height: deprecated; height of cell in pixels

Table heading <TH>

Start Tag:	Required
Content:	Cell heading
End Tag:	Optional
Attributes:	id, class, lang, dir, events, title, style

align: right, left, center, justify, char (these are *not* deprecated)

valign: top, middle, bottom, baseline (these are *not* deprecated)

colspan: number of columns this cell spans (defaults to 1)

rowspan: number of rows this cell spans (defaults to 1)

abbr: abbreviated version of the cell's content

axis: a comma-delimited list of category names; used for associating each cell with a category in speech-synthesizing browsers

headers: ID that associates a header cell with table data; can be used for speech-synthesizing browsers, for grouping columns, or for style sheets

scope: scope covered by header cell; valid values are row, column, rowgroup, colgroup

nowrap: deprecated; don't wrap text within this cell

width: deprecated; width of cell in pixels

height: deprecated; height of cell in pixels

After all the preceding definitions, you may be rethinking putting a table into your page to display tabular data. Don't get discouraged. The following simple example shows how to include a table on your page:

```
<TABLE border="1" frame="border" rules="all">
    <TR>
        <TH>
        <TH>Grams of Fat
        <TH>Grams of Protein
    <TR>
        <TH>Graham Crackers
        <TD align="center">1
        <TD align="center">0
    <TR>
        <TH>Raspberry Yogurt
        <TD align="center">2
        <TD align="center">9
    <TR>
        <TH>Turkey Breast
        <TD align="center">1
        <TD align="center">6
</TABLE>
```

This example generates a table that looks roughly like the following:

	Grams of Fat	Grams of Protein
Graham Crackers	1	0
Raspberry Yogurt	2	9
Turkey Breast	1	6

In reality, the borders crowd the text more than in this illustration. You can, of course, include cellpadding to keep the table from looking crowded, but this feature complicates the simple example.

The next example adds a few more features. This example uses the `align` attribute with the value set to "char" and the default alignment character is the decimal place. Neither of the two major browsers support character alignment, but this feature should be included in future versions. If you want to change the alignment character, add the `char` attribute and set it to the character on which you want to align.

```
<TABLE cellspacing="2" cellpadding="2" border="1" frame="box"
rules="cols">

<TR align="center">
  <TD>
  <TH>Chicago
  <TH>Washington, DC
  <TH>New York
  <TH>Charlottesville

<TR>
  <TH align="center">Breakfast
  <TD align="char">12.95
  <TD align="char">9.95
  <TD align="char">15.95
  <TD align="char">4.95

<TR>
  <TH align="center">Lunch
  <TD align="char">13.50
  <TD align="char">9.50
  <TD align="char">16.00
  <TD align="char">6.50

<TR>
  <TH align="center">Dinner
  <TD align="char">35.00
  <TD align="char">26.00
  <TD align="char">55.00
  <TD align="char">18.00

<TR>
  <TH align="center">Transportation
  <TD align="char">12.00
  <TD align="char">15.00
  <TD align="char">22.00
  <TD align="char">9.00

<TR>
  <TH align="center">Entertainment
  <TD align="char">45.00
  <TD align="char">45.00
  <TD align="char">75.00
  <TD align="char">20.00

<TR>
  <TH align="center">Total
  <TD align="char">118.45
  <TD align="char">105.45
  <TD align="char">183.95
  <TD align="char">58.45
</TABLE>
```

	Chicago	Washington, DC	New York	Charlottesville
Breakfast	12.95	9.95	15.95	4.95
Lunch	13.50	9.50	16.00	6.50
Dinner	35.00	26.00	55.00	18.00
Transportation	12.00	15.00	22.00	9.00
Entertainment	45.00	45.00	75.00	20.00
Total	118.45	105.45	183.95	58.45

Grouping Rows

HTML 4 enables you to group rows using the THEAD, TFOOT, and TBODY elements. When you create a table, you commonly have a header row (with cell headings), a number of rows with data, and then a footer row with totals, as in the preceding example.

If you use the THEAD, TFOOT, and TBODY elements, you must every element, even if you don't need the entire set. Although you must use them, you can leave them empty. The order in which they should appear is THEAD, TFOOT, and TBODY. Why in this particular order? The browser needs to be able to load both the header and the footer information before it loads the body, which could be hundreds of rows. Down the road, you will be able to fit the entire table in one screen with the body scrolling, or the browser automatically putting a header and a footer on each page, when it prints a long table.

Table header <THEAD>

Start Tag:	Required
Content:	TR
End Tag:	Optional
Attributes:	id, class, lang, dir, events, title, style
	align: right, left, center, justify, char (these are not deprecated)
	valign: top, middle, bottom, baseline (these are not deprecated)

Table footer `<TFOOT>`

Start Tag:	Required
Content:	`TR`
End Tag:	Optional
Attributes:	`id`, `class`, `lang`, `dir`, `events`, `title`, `style`
	`align`: right, left, center, justify, char (these are not deprecated)
	`valign`: top, middle, bottom, baseline (these are not deprecated)

Table body `<TBODY>`

Start Tag:	Required
Content:	`TR`
End Tag:	Optional
Attributes:	`id`, `class`, `lang`, `dir`, `events`, `title`, `style`
	`align`: right, left, center, justify, char (these are not deprecated)
	`valign`: top, middle, bottom, baseline (these are not deprecated)

These three elements improve the appearance of the code from the preceding costs and cities table. The table renders as follows in Internet Explorer 4 but won't work properly in Netscape 4 or earlier, which doesn't support these elements yet.

```
<TABLE cellspacing="2" cellpadding="2" border="1" frames="box"
rules="cols">

<THEAD align="center" class="table_header1">
<TR align="center">
   <TD>
        <TH>Chicago
        <TH>Washington, DC
        <TH>New York
        <TH>Charlottesville

<TFOOT align="char" class="table_footer1">
<TR>
   <TH align="center">Total
        <TD>118.45
        <TD>105.45
        <TD>183.95
        <TD>58.45
```

```
<TBODY align="char" class="table_body1">
<TR>
        <TH align="center">Breakfast
        <TD>12.95
        <TD>9.95
        <TD>15.95
        <TD>4.95

<TR>
        <TH align="center">Lunch
        <TD>13.50
        <TD>9.50
        <TD>16.00
        <TD>6.50

<TR>
        <TH align="center">Dinner
        <TD>35.00
        <TD>26.00
        <TD>55.00
        <TD>18.00

<TR>
        <TH align="center">Transportation
        <TD>12.00
        <TD>15.00
        <TD>22.00
        <TD>9.00

<TR>
        <TH align="center">Entertainment
        <TD>45.00
        <TD>45.00
        <TD>75.00
        <TD>20.00

</TABLE>
```

Several items in the preceding table definition may not have been clear in the first costs and cities table example. First, notice the align attributes. These attributes are the only version of align that are not deprecated, because the text cannot be formatted in any other way within a cell. In addition, the first costs and cities table contains more instances of the align attribute. Grouping the rows allowed the align="char" attribute-value pair to move from each TD element to the TBODY element. Because the TH elements for each row still have an align="center" attribute-value pair, this condition overrides the align attribute definition in the TBODY element. The headings should be centered, rather than decimal-aligned.

All three of the new elements in this example have defined classes. As a result, classes must be defined in the style sheets for these elements. The classes are called `table_header1`, `table_footer1`, and `table_body1`, respectively.

Align="char"

The `align` attribute appears in the preceding examples with a value of "char." What does this mean? The "char" value causes alignment over a set character. The default is the decimal. You can change the default by using an additional attribute called char. If you want to align a set of cells that all have slashes (/) over the slash, use the following code:

```
align="char" char="/"
```

You can further customize the alignment of the cell values by using the `charoff` attribute with a length (the number of pixels by which to offset the alignment), as in the following example:

```
align="char" char="/" charoff="15"
```

These uncommon usages are not supported by Version 4 or earlier of Netscape Navigator or Internet Explorer.

Defining Columns

Where do you define a column? Until now, you haven't defined any columns. The browser calculates the number of columns based on the number of cells defined in a row. If you put more cells into one row than into other rows, the results can be unpredictable. Each column element is not fully supported by the two major Version 4 browsers.

Browsers prefer an upfront definition of the columns. You can perform this task with the `COL` element.

Column `<COL>`

Start Tag:	Required
Content:	TR
End Tag:	Forbidden
Attributes:	`id`, `class`, `lang`, `dir`, `events`, `title`, `style`
	`span`: number of columns affected by `COL` attributes

width: column width

align: right, left, center, justify, char (these are not deprecated)

valign: top, middle, bottom, baseline (these are not deprecated)

For example, suppose you want to define a table with five columns of 100 pixels each. Use the following COL element at the top of your table definition before you start defining rows or row groups:

```
<COL span="5" width="100">
```

If those five columns don't share the same width, use the following code:

```
<COL width="15%">
<COL width="25%">
<COL span="3" width="20%">
```

If you want the browser to set the widths, use either of the following code examples:

```
<COL width="0*" span="5">
```

or

```
<COL span="5">
```

Grouping Columns

You may need to use the COLGROUP element, which can be used with or without the COL element.

Column group <COLGROUP>

Start Tag:	Required
Content:	TR
End Tag:	Optional
Attributes:	id, class, lang, dir, events, title, style
	span: number of columns included in group
	width: column width

align: right, left, center, justify, char (these are not deprecated)

valign: top, middle, bottom, baseline (these are not deprecated)

If you define all a group's columns in the same manner, use the COLGROUP to both group columns and define them as in the following code. This example creates a table with six columns, with the first three in one group, the next two in another group, the last one in a third group.

```
<COLGROUP span="3" style="group1">
<COLGROUP span="2" style="group2">
<COLGROUP span="1" style="group3">
```

If the first group has three columns of different widths, use the following code:

```
<COLGROUP span="3" style="group1">
  <COL width="75">
  <COL width="150">
  <COL width="100">
<COLGROUP span="2" style="group2">
<COLGROUP span="1" style="group3">
```

When you define the rest of your table, the fourth column will be formatted using style group2 without further instructions. The browser determines the fourth column in each row and applies the appropriate style.

Spanning Rows and Columns

Spanning rows and columns is easy, but all of these elements are not fully supported in both major Version 4 browsers. To span columns, simply add an attribute called colspan to any cell you want to span more than one column. Because the default is one, set the value of colspan to any number greater than one to create a cell that is the specified number of columns wide.

To span rows, use the rowspan attribute, which works in the same way as colspan. Keep an eye on the arrangement of your cells, though. In the following representation, only one cell should be defined in both the first and third rows for a proper result.

```
+-------------------------------+
| A1                            |
+-------+-------+---------------+
| B1    | B2    | B3            |
+-------+-------+               |
| C1    |       |               |
+-------+-------+---------------+
```

```
<TABLE border="1" frame="box" rules="all" cellspacing="2"
cellpadding="2">
<TR>
  <TD colspan="3">A1
<TR>
  <TD>B1
  <TD>B2
  <TD rowspan="2">B3
<TR>
  <TD colspan="2">C1
</TABLE>
```

Adding Finishing Touches to a Table

You can add two more elements to the table: a caption, created with the CAPTION element, and a summary, created with the summary attribute. Both features ease the comprehension of a table by speech-synthesizing browsers.

The CAPTION element must be defined immediately following the TABLE element start tag. The element's rendering depends on the particular browser.

Caption <CAPTION>

Start Tag:	Required
Content:	Caption to be displayed
End Tag:	Required
Attributes:	id, class, lang, dir, events, title, style
	align: deprecated; use style sheets

The summary attribute should be used as follows:

```
<TABLE summary="This table reflects the costs of living for a
day in major U.S. cities. It includes the costs of eating out
for breakfast, lunch, and dinner, the cost of transportation by
taxi, and the cost of entertainment in each city. Finally, it
shows totals for each city in the bottom row.">
<CAPTION>Daily Expenses for Travelers in Major U.S.
Cities</CAPTION>
```

Nesting Tables

Tables may be nested to produce interesting effects, such as the following example:

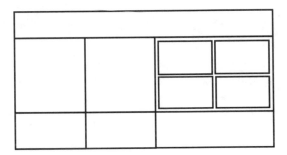

Because the TABLE element must have an end tag, no particular tricks exist for nesting tables. You may include a table within another table's cell or another table's row.

From Here

Jump to Chapter 31 to learn about formatting your page with CSS.

Proceed to Chapter 22 and learn about testing and validating your HTML.

Summary

This chapter taught you everything you could possibly want to know about tables in HTML 4. You first discover the table model in HTML. You also learned how to include defining tables as containers and defining rows and cells within tables.

To make your tables more interesting, you learned how to specify column groups and row groups. To format your data more effectively, you learned how to span rows and columns. Finally, you learned how to nest tables and add features to improve table rendering by speech-synthesizing browsers.

✦   ✦   ✦

Testing and Validating Your HTML

With the structure of your page in place, you should make sure it runs on any visiting browser. This chapter tells you how to make sure that your HTML is valid and properly renders. You discover common HTML mistakes, how to test your HTML, and how to validate your HTML on the Web using free software.

Watch for These Common HTML Mistakes

If you manage to avoid these common HTML mistakes, you have completed 80 percent of the steps needed for a valid HTML page. The most common HTML mistakes follow:

✦ **Failing to complete a tag.** Do all your elements have the necessary end tags? This element is particularly important for inline elements, such as bold and italics.

✦ **Failing to include a forward slash (/) in an end tag.** You may think you included an end tag, but the browser may see another start tag instead. Your browser isn't smart enough to figure out that the second occurrence of <B> in your paragraph should have been </B>.

✦ **Failing to close a comment.** If you fail to close a comment, everything after the comment's start tag disappears from your screen.

✦ **Improper nesting of tags.** This element won't always give you fits, but as more elements are added to HTML, expect browsers to get pickier. From now on, only publish pages with proper nesting so you won't have to fix those pages later.

✦ **Missing end quotes.** This mistake is tough to catch. If you don't watch your close quotes carefully, your browser thinks that the URL is another element.

Testing Your HTML

Check your HTML as you go by using an HTML editor (such as one introduced in Chapter 14) that uses tag coloring. If you can see the color of your tags, you can tell whether you have completed all your tags and comments. After getting comfortable with a tag-coloring HTML editor, you will find it invaluable.

To use the most simple and effective test, simply load your page into your browser to see whether it works. Just because your page looks great in your browser doesn't mean it looks great in every browser, however. Testing your HTML requires adherence to some guidelines. If you publish your page for access by anyone with any kind of browser from any platform, you want make sure it works properly for each configuration. Start with the checklist in Table 22-1.

Table 22-1 **Guidelines for Testing Your HTML**
Test from the most recent version of :
❏ Netscape Navigator
❏ Internet Explorer
❏ The AOL browser
Test from the previous version of:
❏ Netscape Navigator
❏ Internet Explorer
❏ The AOL browser
Test from all platforms:
❏ Windows 95/98/NT
❏ Windows 3.1
❏ Mac O/S
❏ UNIX platforms

Test with screen resolution set to:

❏ 640×480

❏ 800×600

❏ 1024×768

If your server is Windows NT, test from a machine in which you are logged on as another user, so that the security information is not passed through.

Why You Should Validate

Because you can't catch everything and your page's appearance will vary in different browsers, you should also validate your HTML.

What is validating?

Validating submits your HTML to rules-checking. You can validate your HTML on the software residing on your computer or the Web. When you validate your HTML, the validator returns listings of all the places in your page where your HTML does not comply to its rules. Many validators are available; if you build lots of pages, you'll probably want to purchase one that sits on your desktop. If you own an HTML editor, it may come with its own internal validator. Unfortunately, many of the validators on the market at time of publication do not support the HTML 4 rules.

Vocabulary

Validating. Passing your HTML through rules-checking software to identify where you have failed to close tags, where you have nested tags improperly, and where you have broken any other syntax rules that may affect how your page renders.

Why validate?

Although you create your page carefully, you should expect some mistakes to occur. HTML validating can help you:

1. To find blatant HTML errors (such as the preceding errors listed in "Watch for These Common HTML Mistakes"). Validating also finds misspellings in tags or attributes.

2. To find out whether your page complies with your rules. For example, have you used any deprecated attributes?

3. To find out if any parts of your page are difficult to render in speech-synthesizing browsers or Braille browsers.

4. To find out whether your page works with the major browsers.

Validating Your HTML

Many free validation services are available on the Web. At publication, a small number of these services supported HTML 4. Until support for the HTML 4 DTD is more common, the best place on the Web to validate your HTML 4.0 is the W3C's own validator (see Figure 22-1). Although the service is a bit verbose, it not only points out problems with your HTML but also suggests corrections (such as entity numbers).

You can find the W3C's validator on their Web site at `http://validator.w3.org/`.

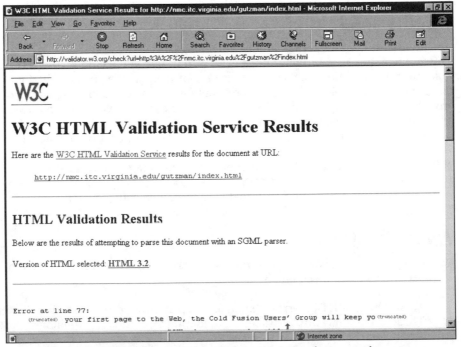

Figure 22-1: The W3C HTML validator gives helpful, if verbose, results.

What should you expect from HTML validation? (After all, validation may be built into your HTML editor, so you may not have to go too far to find out whether your code is compliant.) The following list describes the expected services:

✦ A list of errors in your HTML

✦ A list of any opened quotes without closure

✦ A list of nesting problems (usually listed as warnings, not as errors)

✦ A list of any place you used characters instead of entities (such as putting a > in your document)

If your HTML editor includes a validator, but does not include the HTML 4 rules, check with the manufacturer to see if an updated set of rules can be downloaded.

Assessing Usability

You have a beautifully designed page that now — thanks to the time you took to validate the HTML — complies with the DTD. But how long does it take to download? Will it work on every browser? How will speech-synthesizing browsers handle it?

Part of the impetus of the HTML 4 push for moving formatting out of the page is to increase the distribution of Web sites to nontraditional browsers, such as speech-synthesizing browsers and Braille browsers.

Bobby

A wonderful service available on the Web, called Bobby (http://www.cast.org), reviews your HTML just like a validator. Instead of returning a list of errors, however, it returns a list of places where you can make changes to your page to increase its usability by non-traditional browsers (see Figure 22-2). Bobby can also point out any rendering problems for your page in different browsers. Finally, Bobby calculates your page's download time along with other download statistics.

From Here

Cross-Reference

Jump to Chapter 43 to learn about delivering content via push technologies.

Proceed to Chapter 23 and jump into cascading style sheets.

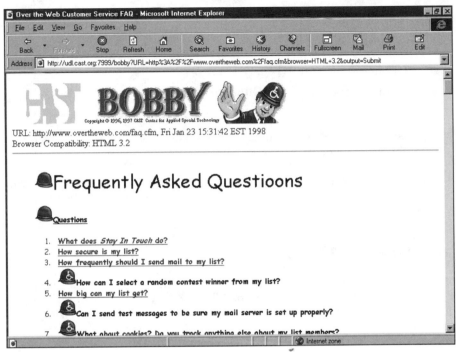

Figure 22-2: Results from Bobby

Summary

This chapter covered the fundamentals of testing and validating your HTML. You learned about resources for validating your HTML on the Web. You learned the most common HTML mistakes, how to check and test your HTML, and why you should validate. You also learned about assessing the usability of your HTML with the Bobby service.

✦   ✦   ✦

Enhancing Presentation with Style Sheets

◆ ◆ ◆ ◆

◆ ◆ ◆ ◆

Introducing Cascading Style Sheets

Perhaps the most exciting part of HTML 4 is its complete
support for cascading style sheets. Style sheets
completely change the model of HTML for the better. This
chapter explains why you need style sheets (even if you are
still a little bit afraid of them) and what they can do. It also
explains the cascading model of the style sheets and what
your choices are for creating style information to associate
with your page. You also get to see a few more examples of the
basic meat-and-potatoes kind of style sheet you will get used
to creating or modifying. Finally, you learn about browser-
compatibility issues related to style sheets.

Why Style Sheets Are Needed

The earlier chapters in this book alluded to all the great things
style sheets can do so many times that, if you haven't flipped
to this chapter to read ahead at least once, it's safe to say you
are a disciplined individual. Once you understand why you
need style sheets, you'll be hard pressed to believe you ever
lived without them.

On the Web, there is a lot of hype about a lot of things. Rarely
does any product or technology live up to the hype it
engenders. *Cascading style sheets* (CSS) are one of those rare
technologies.

HTML 3.2, with all its built-in formatting elements and attributes, made it a nightmare to create pages and even worse to maintain them. Web developers managing sites with hundreds or even thousands of pages had to face this problem daily. Style sheets directly addresses the problem of formatting information cluttering up your pages. With style sheets, all formatting information is moved from the HTML document to a style sheet (a text file with a `.css` extension). Any page that wants to use that format simply links to the style sheet. Any changes made to the master style sheet are automatically reflected in all pages that link to the style sheet. Now that is real power!

What Style Sheets Can Do

Style sheets can change the look of any element on your page. Element by element, you can define the way you want things to look in a style sheet. Your paragraphs will all take on the formatting you associate with the `P` element in your style sheet. If you want to define more than one look for an element, you can create classes of an element and assign the classes to the elements when you define them in the pages.

Say you have two types of paragraphs in your pages: normal and newspaper. The normal paragraphs should use a half-inch indent on the first line and leave quarter-inch of white space (padding) above them. The newspaper paragraphs should indent a quarter inch on the first line and leave two inches of white space on both the right and left sides. Style sheets can accomplish this easily. You, as the developer, simply define a regular `P` element in your style sheet to match the formatting you want your normal text paragraphs to have. Then you define another `P.newspaper` element (that is a `P` element with a `class` of newspaper) with the formatting you want your newspaper paragraphs to have. Whenever you come to a normal text paragraph, you use the regular `P` element. When you come to a newspaper paragraph, you use the `P` element with the `class` (an attribute) specified as "newspaper." What could be easier?

Grouping elements

Remember in Chapters 17 and 18, when you learned about grouping elements with the `DIV` (for block elements) and the `SPAN` (for inline elements) elements? Style sheets can also do something HTML 3.2 can't do, even with all those ugly, deprecated presentation elements. If you wanted to group two paragraphs, give them a background color in common, but different from the rest of the page, and put a nice thick border around them, you'd have to use tables in the way tables were never intended to be used. With style sheets, you can define a `DIV` class in your style sheet and by including them in the `DIV` element with the class set to whatever you called it in your style sheet, all this formatting will appear on your page. If you ever want to change the background color for that class of the `DIV` element, you can do this one time in one place, in your style sheet, and the changes will be reflected everywhere you used that `DIV` class.

Site face-lift

If nothing else you've read about style sheets thus far impresses you, this will. Imagine giving your site a complete face-lift in a morning. This might not sound impressive if your site is still only a handful of pages, but if your site has matured into the dozens, hundreds, or thousands of pages that many Webmasters have to maintain, this is truly revolutionary.

With style sheets, all the formatting information resides in one place. If you change the definitions in that one place, you can affect literally thousands of pages — however many link to the style sheet — in one fell swoop.

One day visitors come to your site and find a white background, left-justified text, blue headings, black text in Times Roman font. The next day they find a light blue background with the embossed logo of your company subtly woven into the background, navy headings in Verdana font, dark grey text in Verdana font, and the entire page is fully justified! That'll grab them!

Delegating page assembly without sacrificing design control

Wouldn't you love to implement a distributed team model to facilitate Web development in your organization? After all, the information you use in the pages comes from all over the organization. Why not just have them put all the material into Web pages directly? Before style sheets, about a million good reasons existed. Every which way a person can design a Web page is another reason not to let people who aren't part of the Web design team assemble their own pages. Who knows what they would look like?

But with style sheets, if people can be trained to use the H1–H6 elements and to markup their paragraphs with the P element, then most of the work can be done by a distributed team of people who are not necessarily Web designers. You can go in later, check their work, and add any tables. Most important of all, if they link to your style sheet, even if they don't do things exactly as you would have, their pages will look pretty much like the rest of the site.

The Cascading Model

So, what is this cascading business about? The cascading model depends on the idea that you can specify style sheets at more than one level. The lowest level style sheet takes precedence. For example, say your company has a corporate style sheet, called `corporate.css`. Your department might have its own style sheet called `hr.css`. Finally, you might want to create a specific style for a class of the `DIV` element, right in the HTML document. You could even define styles at the element level in the `BODY` of your page, but that isn't included in this example. How does this work?

In your HTML `HEAD` element, you would create a link to the corporate style sheet, then another link to the department style sheet. Following those, also in the `HEAD` element, you would define a style for the `DIV` element, using the `STYLE` element. Now, say the corporate style sheet had the following styles defined (to name a few):

✦ background tan

✦ text color brown

✦ font face Helvetica

✦ H1 is 22pt, H2 is 18pt, H3 is 16pt

Say the department had the following style defined (to name one):

✦ H2 is 20pt, H3 is 18pt, H4 is 16pt

And in the `STYLE` element in the `HEAD` element of your page, you define a `DIV` element with a class of highlight with a background of white and text color of black, with a black border.

What would show up in your document? Everything from the corporate style sheet that is not also defined in the department style sheet and everything in the department style sheet that is not defined in the `STYLE` element, and everything in the `STYLE` element that is not defined at the element level. The result would be:

✦ background tan

✦ text color brown

✦ font face Helvetica

✦ H2 is 20pt, H3 is 18pt, H4 is 16pt

✦ `DIV` class of highlight with a background color of white, text color of black, with a black border

Style Sheet Examples

Even though you may find a style sheet definition intimidating at first, don't fret; lots of great tools are available to help you create a syntactically correct style sheet. Refer to Chapter 14 for a list. A number of Web-based resources also exist for creating style sheets. Unlike pages, you won't be creating a lot of style sheets. You'll create one you like, use it for the majority of your pages, and modify it occasionally. If worse comes to worse, you could always start with one of the style sheets on the CD-ROM and modify it to meet your needs.

Here is an example style sheet. Explanations of things to notice are listed after the entire style sheet definition. Your style sheet doesn't need to contain all these rules (definitions of all these elements). You might just define a style for the body (one rule) and be content with the way your browser renders everything else.

```
BODY {
        font-family: "Book Antiqua", "Times New Roman", serif;
        color: #000040;
        background: #FFFF9F;
        padding: 1in;
}
A:LINK {
        color: #FF00FF;
}
A:VISITED {
        color: #808080;
}
BLOCKQUOTE {
        margin-left: 1in;
        margin right: 1in;
}
HR {
        height: 2pt;
}
P {
        text-indent: .5in;
}
P.double {
        text-indent: .5in;
        line-height: 24pt;
}
SPAN.highlight {
        color: #000080;
        background: #FFFF00;
}
```

The only difficult part about creating a style sheet is remembering the property names. For example, to indent a paragraph a half inch, you need to know that the property is `text-indent`, not `paragraph-indent`, or `indent-text`. If you can find a reasonably priced tool you like for creating style sheets (the previous one took advantage of the style sheet wizard in HomeSite 3.0), then you don't have to worry about the syntax; you can put your energy into creating the style sheet you want.

In the previous example, notice each element name (called a selector in style sheets) is followed by curly braces {, then comes a property followed by a colon and a value (called a declaration). With attributes, the syntax is

```
attribute = "value"
```

with style sheets, the syntax for a declaration is

```
property: value;
```

or

```
property: value, value, value;
```

Notice no quotes are around the value of the property in the style sheet (unless a single value more than one word in it, such as a font). Don't worry about learning all these rules right now. You get a more thorough explanation in the next chapter. Right now you should notice that for each element, you can define several different formatting features. The last two elements on the list also have class definitions: `P.double` and `SPAN.highlight`. Those would be used in your document as follows:

```
<P class="double">
```

and

```
<SPAN class="highlight">
```

What does this style sheet do?

1. It formats all the `BODY` elements with a light yellow (#000040) background and dark grey (#FFFF9F) text using a font of Book Antiqua or, if this is not available, Times New Roman or, if that is not available, any serif font, and it sets padding on the page of one inch.

2. It formats not yet visited links (`A:LINK`) to fuscia (#FF00FF).

3. It formats visited links (`A:VISITED`) to gray (#808080).

4. It formats blockquotes to have one-inch left and right margins, which would be added by the browser to the one-inch padding already defined in the `BODY` element.

5. It formats all horizontal rules to be two pixels tall.

6. It gives paragraphs a half-inch indentation on the first line.

7. It creates a paragraph class called double (`P.double`), which has the same half-inch indentation on the first line, but also includes double-spacing of text (line height: 24pt).

8. It also creates a `SPAN` class called highlight (`SPAN.highlight`), which will have a text color of navy blue (#000080) and a background color of bright yellow (#FFFF00).

Browser Compatibility Issues

What about actually using style sheets in browsers? Is all this stuff supported? Unfortunately, no. Internet Explorer 4 does the best job of implementing style sheets. Netscape 4 is significantly less supportive of style sheets, but does support many features of style sheets. Internet Explorer 3 also does a respectable job of supporting style sheets

What does this mean for you? If you are creating pages for an intranet and you know people using your pages will have IE 3 or 4, or Navigator 4, then you can test your pages on the platform you know people will be using, and only use the styles supported on that platform. However, if you are creating pages for the Internet, where you can't predict what kind of browser visitors will be using, you have three choices, recapped from Chapter 3:

✦ **Don't use style sheets.** Continue to design your pages with the deprecated HTML 3.2 elements and attributes and look forward to the day when browsers that support style sheets are more widely used.

✦ **Maintain two versions of your site.** Believe it or not, this is what many large, high-profile sites do. In Chapter 48 about JavaScript, you will learn how to test to see which browser a visitor is using so that you can automatically load the appropriate version of the page.

✦ **Use style sheets and to heck with the luddites who haven't upgraded.** They will, after all, be able to see your site; they just won't get the same design look that they should.

From Here

Cross-Reference Jump to Chapter 48 and learn about using JavaScript to test to see which version of which browser a visitor is using.

Proceed to Chapter 24 and learn the syntax of style sheets.

Summary

In this chapter you learned just why style sheets are so valuable. You learned what they can do that couldn't be done any way previously. You learned about the cascading model. You got a chance to analyze an example of a style sheet. You also learned enough about browser compatibility issues to understand that making a decision about using style sheets requires some analysis.

✦   ✦   ✦

Learning CSS Syntax

If you look at a style sheet and think you'll never get the hang of it, remember how you felt when you looked at HTML for the first time. Now you have no fear of it because you understand the rules; you know that even if you see an element you've never seen before, you can figure it out. CSS isn't any more difficult. It has a clear set of rules that unlike HTML, fits into one chapter. To help you along, a complete list of all the properties you can use in CSS is in Appendix G.

By the time you finish this chapter, you'll know the syntax of CSS, how CSS differs from HTML, and how to define and group CSS properties. You learn some shortcuts so your property definitions won't be quite as verbose as the example in the last chapter. You also learn about the box-formatting model CSS uses and about inheritance, which is why you don't need to redefine every property for every element. You also learn about defining classes and IDs, which enable you to add variety to different instances of the same element on the same page. Finally, you see the DIV and SPAN elements in action.

Anatomy of a Style Sheet

CSS has its own vocabulary. To understand what goes where in a style sheet, you need to understand what each item on the style sheet is called. A style sheet is composed of *rules*. This is a rule:

```
P {
        text-indent: 2cm;
        color: black;
        padding-top: .25in;
}
```

In the previous example, P is the *selector*. The selector could just as easily have been P.special, or P#123. A selector indicates to which elements, which class of elements, or which IDs of elements the rule applies.

A *rule* is made up of a selector with one or more declarations. Each of the three lines under the selector is a declaration. A *declaration* is composed of a property and one or more values. The *property* is separated from the value by a colon. Each declaration ends with a semi-colon. All the declarations are listed within curly braces.

Differences Between CSS and HTML Syntax

When learning HTML, you learned HTML has *elements* and that *elements have attributes*. CSS has selectors, which you should recognize, because they can be the same as the elements you use in HTML. In CSS, however, instead of the selectors having attributes, they have properties. The properties of CSS selectors, just like the attributes of HTML elements, have values.

Here is an example of an HTML element with one attribute:

```
<BODY dir="ltr">
This is my very short page.
</BODY>
```

and this is an example of a CSS selector with one declaration (property-value pair):

```
BODY {
      color: white;
}
```

You can see that just like an HTML element definition, the CSS selector has the element name in it. This is where the similarities end, though. In CSS, there are no angle brackets (<>). Instead, a CSS rule has curly braces around the declaration or declarations. The CSS selector name is not enclosed in any kind of markings.

There are no start or end tags, and no content. The reason for this should be obvious: CSS documents don't have anything rendered. They just have information *about* what is rendered in the HTML document. Instead, they have properties that describe how different parts of the element will be rendered. These properties have values, just like attributes in HTML have values. The attribute-value pair in HTML looks like this:

```
colspan="3"
```

In CSS, a property-value pair, which is called a *declaration*, looks like this:

```
color: white;
```

The three differences between defining attribute-value pairs and defining property-value pairs are:

1. A colon replaces the equal sign.

2. The value is not enclosed in double-quotes in CSS (unless the value is multiple words, as in a font name).

3. The pair is followed by a semi-colon.

Once you get used to those differences, you'll write declarations in CSS as deftly as you had been writing attributes in HTML.

Defining Properties

CSS is flexible. You can define a selector with one declaration or a selector with many declarations. You use the same syntax either way. The basic outline of a CSS rule is:

```
SELECTOR-NAME {
        property: value;     /* declaration */
        property: value;
        property: value;
}
```

If a value has multiple words, the value needs to be enclosed in double-quotes.

Here is an example of a style sheet with two rules:

```
BODY {
        font family: "Times New Roman",
    "Times Roman",
    serif;
        color: black;
        background: white;
        margin-left: .5in;
        margin-right: .5in;
}
P {
        text-indent: .5in;
        margin-top: .25in;
}
```

All it does is set the body of the document to have a white background with left and right margins of a half inch. It also sets the text to be black. The font-family property tells the browser to use the first font in the list that it finds on the client computer. Notice multiword font names, such as Book Antiqua and Times New Roman, each have double-quotes around them. The last name in the list is a font type, rather than a specific font. If neither of the first two fonts are on the client computer, it says, use any serif font. This style sheet also formats paragraphs to have an indentation on the first line of paragraphs of a half inch and a top margin of a quarter inch. This means a quarter inch of white space will be between paragraphs.

Grouping Properties

Here's another style sheet that defines the font family for headings:

```
H1 {
        font-family:  Helvetica,
                      Arial,
                      sans-serif;
}
H2 {
        font-family:  Helvetica,
                      Arial,
                      sans-serif;
}
H3 {
        font-family:  Helvetica,
                      Arial,
                      sans-serif;
}
```

What it says is headings H1, H2, and H3 should use Helvetica, if it is available, Arial, if Helvetica is not available, and any sans-serif font, if neither Helvetica nor Arial are available. To say all this takes a lot of space, though.

Fortunately, a more concise way exists. You can group property definitions by placing the element names into a comma-delimited list as follows:

```
H1, H2, H3 {
        font-family:  Helvetica,
                      Arial,
                      sans-serif;
}
```

Using this technique of grouping elements is a good way to save space, increase readability, and reduce the possibility of introducing errors.

Property Definition Shortcuts

You can define a lot of properties for fonts. Here is a style sheet excerpt to demonstrate this:

```
H3 {
        font-weight: bold;
        font-size: 16pt;
        line-height: 20pt;
        font-family: "Times New Roman";
        font-variant: normal;
        font-style: italic;
}
```

Fortunately, you can string this all into one property, called *font*, which shortens the definition considerably.

```
H3 {
        font: bold 16pt/20pt "Times New Roman" normal italic;
}
```

Once you get used to the shortcut, you'll never use the verbose definition again.

Box Formatting: The CSS Formatting Model

CSS uses a clever metaphor for helping you specify containers (block-level elements) on your page: the box. When you define formatting for your block-level elements — whether they be paragraphs, blockquotes, lists, images, or whatever — for purposes of CSS, you are defining formatting for a box. It doesn't care what is in the box, it just wants to format the box.

Box dimensions

The first thing the browser does is render the block-level element to determine what the physical dimensions of the element are, given the font selected for the element, the contents of the element, and any other internal formatting instructions supplied by the style sheet. Then the browser looks at the padding, the border, and the margins of the element to determine the space it actually requires on the page.

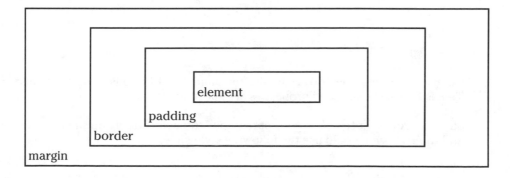

Padding is the distance between the outside edges of the element and the border. The *border* is a line or ridge. The *margin* is the distance between the border and the outer box of the next container. How you define the padding, border, and margin are described in detail in the following:

Padding

You don't need to define any padding, but if you are going to define a border, then you probably want to define padding so your element doesn't look too crowded. The default for an element is no padding. Figure 24-1 shows the same table with and without padding. You can see the one without padding looks crowded.

Figure 24-1: Tables with and without padding

Five properties are associated with padding. They are:

1. padding, which gives the same padding on all sides
2. padding-top
3. padding-right
4. padding-bottom
5. padding-left

Get used to seeing the -top, -right, -bottom, and -left additions to property names. This is how all box-related properties are specified.

Suppose you want to define your paragraphs to have padding on the top, the left, and the right; you could use the following style sheet:

```
P {
        padding-top: .5in;
        padding-right: .5in;
        padding-left: .5in;
}
```

Or you could use shorthand to write out the padding properties as follows:

```
P {
        padding: .5in .5in 0in .5in;
}
```

You can always string the top, right, bottom, and left properties together in that order. The same shorthand works for margins and borders. Notice no commas are between the items in the list.

Border

The default is to have no border on elements. You can define a border in two different ways. Either you can define the width, color and style of the border, by side, or you can define the width, color, and style for the box individually. Two examples follow:

```
BLOCKQUOTE {
        border-width: 1pt 1pt 0pt 1pt;
        border-color: black;
        border-style: solid;
}
```

In the previous example, a border is created for the top, right, and left sides of the list that is black, and solid.

```
BLOCKQUOTE {
        border-top: 1pt solid black;
        border right: 1pt solid black;
        border-left: 1pt solid black;
}
```

Both these examples create the same border. The border is inserted between the padding, if there is any, and the margin, if there is any. Valid values for border style are: none, dotted, dashed, solid, double, groove, ridge, inset, and outset.

Or, if you want to create a border that is the same on all four sides, you can use the border property:

```
BLOCKQUOTE {
        border: 1pt solid black;
}
```

Margins

Margins create white space outside of the border. Notice in Figure 24-1 the two tables are immediately adjacent to each other. This is because neither one has margins. Margins are created with the margin, margin-top, margin-right, margin-bottom, and margin-left properties. They work exactly the same as the padding property.

Understanding Inheritance

If you define a background color for the BODY of your document, you don't have to define the same background color for each P element. Why not? Inheritance. Elements within containers inherit characteristics of the containers in which they exist. A paragraph is a container, but it is also within a container — the BODY element. If you have an italicized word in your paragraph, you can expect that word to inherit the font, text color, text size, line spacing, and so forth of the paragraph (except it will be italicized); you can also expect the paragraph to inherit a few things from the BODY, such as background color, padding, margins, and anything else the P element doesn't specifically specify.

Inheritance is great. *Inheritance* enables you to define formatting only at the highest level. The formatting you define trickles down to the lower-level elements. An awareness of inheritance can keep you from specifying every property at every level.

Defining Classes

Classes are how you customize elements in your page. With classes, you can define more than one look for an element in your style sheet and then, in your page, you say which look you want to use. Classes are defined in your style sheet using the following notation:

```
P.first {
      font: bold 12pt/14pt "Times New Roman";
}
P.second {
      font: normal 12pt/12pt "Times New Roman";
}
```

To use these classes in your page, refer to them as follows:

```
<P class="first">This is a first-class paragraph.</P>
<P class="second">This is a second-class paragraph.</P>
```

Note the first class of P inherits all the formatting of P that it doesn't specifically override. The second class of P also inherits all the formatting of P that it doesn't specifically override. Classes first and second are not related to each other except they are both classes of the P element. You can make up your own names for classes.

Pseudo-Classes

When you are looking at a page and have already clicked one or more of the links on the page, you might notice the links you have already clicked are a different color from the links you have not yet clicked. You can define what you want those colors to be using pseudo-classes in style sheets. Even though *pseudo* means *fake* in Greek, these aren't really fake classes — they're predefined classes that already mean something to the browser. You can define pseudo-classes for three different types of links:

1. **A:link** for unvisited links

2. **A:visited** for visited links

3. **A:active** for the active link (that is, the link on which you are currently clicking)

If you want to add a regular class to the A element, you define the selector as A.first-class:link. Consider the following example:

```
A:link {
      color: red;
}
A:visited {
      color: blue;
}
A:active {
      color: green;
}
A.special:link {
      color: #FF33FF;   /* fuschia */
}
```

This style sheet has four rules. The first three define the colors of unvisited links, visited links, and active links. The last one will only be used when the class is specified as special; it specifies the color of unvisited links.

Defining IDs

You won't use IDs nearly as often as you use classes, but it's nice to know they are there if you need them. *IDs* are like classes, except they are not necessarily associated with elements. Isn't this contrary to the HTML 4 Way? Yes, but it's there if you need it. IDs are defined as follows:

```
#wide {
        letter-spacing: .4em;
}
```

And used as follows:

```
<H1 id="wide">This is a wide heading</H1>
<P id="wide">This is a paragraph of widely spaced text.</P>
```

As you can see, the ID-wide can be used with any element. It is recommended you use classes rather than IDs.

Grouping Elements with DIV and SPAN

In Chapters 17 and 18, you learned about using the DIV and SPAN elements to group block-level elements and inline elements, respectively. Now you can finally see how this works with style sheets. Consider the following style sheet rules:

```
DIV.important {
        background: red;
        font: bold 14pt/18pt Helvetica;
}
SPAN.incidental {
        font: normal 8pt/8pt Helvetica;
background: gray;
}
```

You can use them as follows:

```
<DIV class="important"><P>This is one very important
paragraph.</P>
<TABLE>
…table contents…
</TABLE>
<P>This is another important paragraph.</P></DIV>

<P>This is somewhat important. <SPAN class="incidental">And
this is really incidental.</SPAN> But you might want to
remember this fact.</P>
```

This creates two paragraphs with a table between them that have a background color of red and 14pt bold Helvetica text. Following this mess is another paragraph with formatting inherited from the BODY element, but the middle sentence has gray 8pt Helvetica text.

Comments in Style Sheets

Adding comments to your style sheets, just as you add comments to your HTML pages, is not a bad idea. Comments are defined in your style sheet using a different convention than in your pages. Look back to the sample code for the pseudo-classes style sheet. Notice next to the hexadecimal value #FF33FF, there is the following:

```
/* fuschia */
```

That is a comment in CSS. Adding a comment is little trouble when you create the style sheet; it is a lot more work to go back and remember what you meant when you defined the style sheet. If you use comments nowhere else, use them when you use hexadecimal notation for colors.

Comments are created with a /* preceding them and a */ following them.

From Here

Jump to Chapter 31, Understanding CSS Positioning Options.

Proceed to Chapter 25, Adding Styles to Your Web Page.

Summary

In this chapter you learned about the basics of CSS. You learned the vocabulary, the conventions, and differences between CSS and HTML syntax. You learned about defining properties, grouping properties, and defining properties using shortcuts. You learned about the CSS box model and about inheritance from containers to elements. You also learned about classes, pseudo-classes, and IDs. Finally, you learned about using the DIV and SPAN elements to group elements so they can all take advantage of the same formatting.

✦　　✦　　✦

Adding Styles to Your Web Pages

Now that you know why you should use a style sheet and how to write a style sheet, you need to know how to include style sheets in your page. This document takes you through the three options you have for adding styles to your page. With the cascading approach, you can actually use all three at the same time, but you probably don't want to do this, as you learn in this chapter.

Using an External Style Sheet

The preferred way to include styles in your page is to use an external style sheet. This is the only way to take advantage of all the benefits you have read about relating to using style sheets. If you use an external style sheet, then all your style information for all your pages is stored in one central place. If you want to give your site a face-lift, it's as easy as changing the external style sheet.

The LINK element

To use an external style sheet, simply create your style sheet and save it with a .css extension. Then link to it from the HEAD of your page using the LINK element. This is not the complete specification for the LINK element. The LINK element is used for other unrelated functions, which only confuse this use.

Cross-Reference For the complete specification of the LINK element, refer to Chapter 25.

Link `<LINK>`

Start Tag:	Required
Content:	Empty
End Tag:	Forbidden
Attributes:	`id`, `class`, `lang`, `dir`, `title`, `style`, `events`

`href`: URL of style sheet

`hreflang`: language of document specified in `href` attribute

`type`: MIME type of document specified in `href` attribute, usually "text/css"

Here is an example of the `LINK` element used to link to an external style sheet called `dec1997.css` that exists in the styles subdirectory:

```
<HEAD>
<LINK href="styles/dec1997.css" type="text/css">
</HEAD>
```

The `LINK` element, whether it is used for linking to an external style sheet or for some other purpose, must be located in the `HEAD` element.

Using a STYLE Element within the HEAD

If you are unhappy with any pre-existing style sheet or you don't want to store your styles in a separate style sheet for whatever reason, then you can store your complete style sheet in the `HEAD` element directly. How does this work? You put the rules (the statements that tell the browser how to render each element) directly into a `STYLE` element in the `HEAD`. As you can imagine, this could make your `HEAD` quite long.

The `STYLE` element has the following specification:

Style `<STYLE>`

Start Tag:	required
Content:	rules
End Tag:	required
Attributes:	`lang`, `dir`

`type`: MIME type, usually "text/css" (see Appendix E)

`media`: type of medium for which this style sheet is relevant; defaults to "screen"; must be a keyword or comma-delimited list of media keywords from list (see following valid list)

`title`: title of style information

No evidence exists that any browsers recognize the `media` attribute yet, but the valid `media` types are:

- ✦ **screen.** For computer screens.
- ✦ **tty.** For fixed-width terminal displays.
- ✦ **tv.** For televisions.
- ✦ **projection.** For projectors.
- ✦ **handheld.** For handheld devices.
- ✦ **print.** For print.
- ✦ **braille.** For braille-tactile feedback devices.
- ✦ **aural.** For speech synthesizers.
- ✦ **all.** For all devices.

The `STYLE` element is used as follows:

```
<HEAD>
<STYLE>
  BODY {
        color: black;
        background: white;
        padding-left: 1in;
        padding-right: 1in;
  }
  H1 {
        font: bold 24pt/30pt black;
  }
  P {
        text-indent: .5in;
  }
  A:link {
        color: blue;
  }
  A:visited {
        color: red;
  }
  A:active {
        color: yellow;
  }
  BLOCKQUOTE {
        margin-left: 1in;
        margin-right: 1in;
  }
</STYLE>
</HEAD>
```

Adding Inline Styles

Reasons may exist why you would want to add style information directly at the element level. You may have noticed nearly every element to which you have been introduced has had a `style` attribute. This attribute is used to define element-specific style information. The `style` attribute is used as follows:

```
<P style="text-indent: 1in; color: blue;">This paragraph has a
one inch indentation--twice the normal paragraph indentation--
on the first line and is rendered with blue text.</P>
```

Notice you don't need a selector (P) in the `style` attribute because you are only defining a rule for this instance of the element. You do need double quotes around the rules, as with any attribute value, and each descriptor does need to be followed by a semicolon.

The use of the `style` attribute is preferred to the use of the FONT element, which is deprecated in HTML 4, but it is not the ideal. Whenever possible, you should try to determine what formatting you need before you get to the element that needs special formatting and define a class for that element in your style sheet. The previous example could have been written instead as:

```
<P class="deep-blue">This paragraph has a one inch indentation-
-twice the normal paragraph indentation--on the first line and
is rendered with blue text.</P>
```

A rule would have to be in your style sheet as follows, as well:

```
P.deep-blue {
    text-indent: 1in;
    color: blue;
}
```

Either of these examples results in the same thing being rendered in the browser. Either one enables your page to be rendered easily in speech-synthesizing browsers. Both are vastly preferable to the HTML 3.2 method of using a clear GIF to indent the paragraph and then using the FONT element to change the text color to blue.

Using a Standardized Style Sheet

If after all these style sheets examples, you still don't feel comfortable writing your own style sheet, don't despair. Many standard style sheets are available. Most people get started writing HTML by copying pages with features they like and modifying the code to meet their needs. Most people who write Perl use this technique; most people who write JavaScript got started this way. Finding a style sheet you like and modifying it to meet your needs is no disgrace.

To help make it easier, the CD-ROM in the back of this book has several standard style sheets on it. Pick one that comes close to approximating the look you want and customize it to make it your own.

You might find your organization has its own style sheet, which you are expected to use. If this is the case, the powers that control the style sheet might not let you create special classes to accommodate your formatting needs. Fortunately, CSS has a way to help you get around any limitations this might present. Consider the following HTML, which refers to a corporate style sheet. It doesn't even matter what is in the style sheet for your purposes because you are required to use it and you are not allowed to change it.

```
<HTML>
<HEAD>
<LINK href="style/corporate.css" type="text/css">
</HEAD>

<BODY>

<H1>A heading</H1>

<P>This paragraph looks just the way they want it to look.</P>

<P>But I sure wish I could make this one look different.</P>

</BODY>
</HTML>
```

You can see the frustration you would encounter because you can't change the formatting of the second paragraph using the corporate style sheet you are provided. Given what you've learned in this chapter, you know two ways to get around this limitation. The first is to create a STYLE element in the HEAD element and create a class for the second paragraph.

```
<HTML>
<HEAD>
<LINK href="style/corporate.css" type="text/css">
<STYLE>
  P.different {
      color: blue;
      font-size: 14pt;
  }
</STYLE>
</HEAD>

<BODY>

<H1>A heading</H1>
```

```
<P>This paragraph looks just the way they want it to look.</P>

<P class="different">I'm so pleased that I can make this one
look different.</P>

</BODY>
</HTML>
```

The other way you learned is to put the style information directly into a `style` attribute in the P element.

```
<HTML>
<HEAD>
<LINK href="style/corporate.css" type="text/css">
</HEAD>

<BODY>

<H1>A heading</H1>

<P>This paragraph looks just the way they want it to look.</P>

<P style="color: blue; font-size: 14pt;">I'm so pleased that I
can make this one look different.</P>

</BODY>
</HTML>
```

There is one other way to take control of the look of your page at a micro level when you are forced to use a style sheet over which you have no control. This is to create another external style sheet and link to it in the HEAD following the link to the standard style sheet. For the previous example, where the customization you want to affect in formatting is minimal and only affects one element, either of the two methods of accomplishing this would be fine. Neither one substantially clutters your HTML. The first one is probably better, but the difference is minuscule. If, however, you want to create classes or change formatting for multiple elements, you probably want to move this formatting to your own style sheet, as shown in the following:

```
<HEAD>
<LINK href="style/corporate.css" type="text/css">
<LINK href="style/mine.css" type="text/css">
</HEAD>

<BODY>

<H1>A heading</H1>

<P>This paragraph looks just the way they want it to look.</P>
```

```
<P class="different">I'm so pleased that I can make this one
look different.</P>

</BODY>
</HTML>
```

You can actually include as many links to external style sheets as you need. Does the order matter? You bet! Because of the cascading rules discussed in the last chapter, the last style sheet specified can override all previous style sheets specified. If you are supposed to use a standard style sheet created by someone else, then you want to be careful not to override any of those styles. As with all style definitions, the lowest-level style defined has the highest priority. Conversely, the higher up a style is defined, the lower the priority.

Mixing the Approaches: An Example

The following example of combining style definitions should help make the concept of cascading style sheets and the use of classes, IDs, and inline style definitions clear. This is a long example, but it is one to which you can refer later if you have questions about your own implementation of style sheets.

```
Corporate.css

BODY {
    color: black;
    background: white;
    padding-left: 1in;
    padding-right: 1in;
}
H1 {
    font: bold 24pt/30pt black;
}
P {
    text-indent: .5in;
}
A:link {
    color: blue;
}
A:visited {
    color: red;
}
A:active {
    color: yellow;
}
BLOCKQUOTE {
    margin-left: 1in;
    margin-right: 1in;
}
```

```
mine.css

SPAN.special {
    color: red;
}

#wide {
    letter-spacing: .5em;
}
HR {
    width: 3pt;
    color: red;
}
```

The two external style sheets used in this example are defined previously. They are called `corporate.css` and `mine.css`. The HTML page is defined in the following:

```
<HTML>
<HEAD>
<LINK href="corporate.css" rel="stylesheet" type="text/css">
<LINK href="mine.css" rel="stylesheet" type="text/css">
<STYLE>
  H1#wide {
    line-height: 40pt;
  }
</STYLE>
</HEAD>

<BODY>
<H1 ID="wide">A page with <SPAN class="special">special</SPAN>
formatting</H1>
<P>This paragraph contains <SPAN id="wide">some rather widely-
spaced text.</SPAN></P>
<HR style="color: black">
<HR>
<P>This paragraph is normal, but you can <A
href="weird.html">link</A> to weird stuff from here.</P>
</BODY>

</HTML>
```

In the previous example, many conflicting instructions exist in the form of style information for the browser. How will it render?

The first H1 has an ID of wide. If you look at `mine.css`, you can see an ID of wide is defined that affects letter spacing. But this won't be used. Why? Because another ID of wide specific to the H1 element is defined in the STYLE element and that ID affects line height. Notice the H1 element also has a SPAN element with a class of special that affects one word. The special class is defined in `mine.css` and isn't overridden anywhere further down, so the word *special,* within the SPAN element, will be rendered as red.

The first paragraph also uses the SPAN element with an ID of wide. How will this render? It will use the ID wide defined in mine.css, because it isn't affected by the H1 element defined in the STYLE element.

The first HR element will render in black, because the style attribute is defined right there and will override the HR definition in mine.css. It will render with the width provided in mine.css, since the new definition doesn't specify the width. How about the second HR definition? Will it inherit the color of the previous HR element? No. It will render just as mine.css defines it because no style information overrides the style information in mine.css.

Finally, in the last paragraph, which doesn't have any style references, there is a link. How will the link render? Until the link is visited, it will render in blue as defined by A:link in corporate.css. Once it is visited, it will render in red, and when it is active, it will render in yellow. Nothing special must be done to the HTML to take advantage of the three pseudo-elements related to the A element.

From Here

 Jump to Chapter 31 and learn about absolute positioning in CSS.

Proceed to Chapter 26 and learn about adding colors and backgrounds to your pages.

Summary

In this chapter you got a crash course in using CSS in your page. You learned how to link to an external style sheet. You learned about using the STYLE element and you learned about using inline style definitions. You learned about using a standardized style sheet and how you can get around any limitations related to this. If you persevered, you also learned how cascading rules affect the implementation of styles in your page in a thorough example.

✦   ✦   ✦

Adding Colors and Backgrounds

The HTML 4 Way gives you lots of ways to change the colors on your screen. You can change text colors, background colors, and background images for everything on the page, or on an element-by-element basis. This chapter explains how your screen renders colors and why no two monitors look alike. It also discusses color palettes — the color information an image sends — including a color-safe palette that renders properly on both PCs and Macs. Next, you learn about color compatibility and why it's wise to choose your colors and stick with them. You learn how to define a background color and text colors. Finally, you learn how to add a background graphic and to specify whether it repeats.

How Your Monitor Creates Color

Computers use the RGB system to create colors. Don't be put off by another acronym; RGB stands for *Red-Green-Blue*. Basically, the computer can generate only red, green, or blue light. When it generates all three together, at full power, it produces white. When it generates none of them, it produces black. This is contrary to the way that artists think about color. White is usually the absence of color in art — but on your computer screen, white is what you get when you mix all the other colors together.

Hex notation

All information on your computer is passed in the form of binary data — a long string of ones and zeros — which is not a very useful way to convey information to people. A shorthand for the ones and zeros, *hexadecimal* (or *hex*) notation, offers people a way to discuss this information. The hexadecimal system assigns each digit a value between 0 and 15. The decimal system, the way we're used to counting, takes two digits to convey the numbers 10, 11, 12, 13, 14, and 15; hex substitutes letters for those six numbers. So, this is how you count from 0 to 15 in hex: 0, 1, 2, 3, 4, 5, 6, 7, 8, 9, *A, B, C, D, E, F.* If you want to count to 16, it's like going from 9 to 10 in the decimal system; to go from 15 to 16 in the hex system, you introduce a new digit. That's where it gets confusing. If 15 is *F*, then you write 16 as . 10 (pronounced "one-zero," *not ten*) in hex.

You frequently see numbers in hex like FF33A0. That might look like a foreign language, but it's a far sight easier to work with than 111111110011001110100000, which translates to the same thing! Here's the good news: You won't have to do math in hex to add colors to your page.

Introducing Color Codes

The computer projects color based on the intensity of red, green, and blue you tell it to provide. You tell it what intensity to provide by using *color codes* written in the hex system; you have already seen colors in this book defined in hex. In HTML, when you specify a color in hex, you need to precede the color code with a pound sign (#). Here are some easy ones: #000000 (no red, no green, no blue) is black; #FFFFFF (full-power red, full-power green, full-power blue) is white. Are you getting the hang of this? How about #FF0000? Red. #00FF00? Green. #0000FF? Blue.

Using English

At this point, there's more good news: You needn't use color codes to define your colors. All the colors in the previous section actually have English names that HTML recognizes. The problem with using English color names is only 16 of them are guaranteed to work. They are listed in Table 26-1.

Table 26-1	
English Names for Colors	
Color Name	**Hex Value**
Black	#000000
Green	#008000
Silver	#C0C0C0
Lime	#00FF00
Gray	#808080
Olive	#808000
White	#FFFFFF
Yellow	#FFFF00
Maroon	#800000
Navy	#000080
Red	#FF0000
Blue	#0000FF
Purple	#800080
Teal	#008080
Fuchsia	#FF00FF
Aqua	#00FFFF

Monitor-to-monitor variations

Have you ever noticed that a screen image you're used to seeing one way on your monitor will render in slightly different colors on another monitor? The reason is no absolute red exists in the computer world. There isn't even an absolute white. Depending on the tubes in your monitor, how old it is, how it is adjusted, and a few other things, white may be white, pinkish white, bluish white, greenish white, or just plain gray. Your eyes adjust to what they know ought to be white, but if you hold a white piece of paper up next to your monitor, you will see your monitor's idea of white probably isn't true white.

What does this mean to you as a designer? It means that although you want to select your colors carefully, you don't have control over how they render. You want to test them extensively on a number of different monitors — not just the same brand of monitor on ten different desks, although there will be a difference — but even on other platforms and brands of monitors.

Chapter 34 takes you through an explanation of bit depth you want to review before you select the colors for your site.

Color Palettes

Remember opening that box of 64 crayons as a child? That was a color palette of 64. It didn't seem limiting at the time. You had blue, green-blue, blue-green, green, and 60 other colors to choose from. If you had to limit yourself to a 64-color palette for your Web site, though, you'd be terribly frustrated. Fortunately, nearly everyone who visits your site with a browser that supports more than text is also likely to have a color monitor that supports at least 256 colors. Where does that number 256 come from? In the hex system, 100 (one-zero-zero) translates into 256 in the decimal system.

When you send information (such as a background image or information about the text color), you want to save time by using the palette on the visitor's system whenever possible, rather than sending another palette across the Web to the visitor's system. All computers have built-in color palettes — how convenient! — the only problem is that color palettes are not the same on all systems. A 256-color palette is available on both Macs and PCs, but only 216 of the colors are the same on both platforms. If you plan to use the built-in color palette on your visitors' computers, make sure your site is using a *color-safe* palette.

You can find the color-safe palette on the Web at `http://www.lynda.com/hex.html`.

Color-Compatibility Considerations

When you choose the colors for your background, background images, text color, and headings colors, you want to be sure that you are selecting them all from the same palette. If you select colors across palettes, there are two problems. The first is you need to send more palette information over the Web than necessary, slowing the download time of your page. The second is your colors might not match. Not every shade of blue goes with every shade of green. By keeping your color selection within a single palette, you are sure to avoid the problem of clashing shades, where some of your colors are considered warm, while others are considered cool.

Defining a Background Color

You are finally ready to start defining colors for your page. You saw in the previous chapters that you can define colors in your style sheet. You can define a background color for each element on your page, but unless you are doing that for some instructional purpose, you probably don't want to do that. Under normal circumstances, you define a background color for your BODY element and just let inheritance do its job so that every other element on the page ends up with the same background color.

By including a declaration like the one here in your style sheet, you can set the background color for any element:

```
background-color: #00AAAA;              /* light aqua */
```

The important thing to remember is the property is called background-color. If you are used to defining the background color directly in the BODY element, you are used to an attribute name of bgcolor.

Changing Default Text Colors

You can use style sheets to set text colors, as well. The property name to remember is *color*. By setting the color property for the BODY, all other elements will inherit that color. You can, of course, change the color of the text for any element by including the color property in a declaration like the one in the following, in that element's style sheet rule.

```
color: #FF33FF;        /* a loud shade of fuchsia */
```

You have already seen how text colors for links can be changed: You use the pseudo-elements related to the A element. In the style sheet that follows, the link color for links that have not yet been visited is yellow. The color for links that have been visited is gray; the color of the active link is blue. It sounds awful, but it wouldn't look bad if the background color were very dark.

```
A:link {
     color: yellow;
}
A:visited {
     color: gray;
}
A:active {
     color: blue;
}
```

Adding a Background Graphic

HTML 4 does a great favor for Web visitors by helping Web designers curb their natural desire for flash. For the first time, you can add a background graphic to your page that does not tile. The default is for all background images to tile. This means any image you assign to be your background image will automatically repeat itself until the screen is covered. This may or may not have been what you intended. If you aren't careful, the results can be horrendous.

Clever Web designers have always taken advantage of the tiling effect by specifying graphics that tile well, or tile invisibly, such as a marble effect, or clouds. An effect that can be stunning is creating a logo or the name of your company in a nice font and then using a graphics package — such as Photoshop — to emboss the image and then subduing the colors and letting that tile.

Adding a background image is a cinch in CSS:

```
BODY {
        background-color: white;
        background-image: url(../images/background.gif);
        background-repeat: no-repeat;
        background-attachment: scroll;
        background-position: top center;
}
```

A few things to note about these four background properties:

✦ `background-color` — This property determines the background color for your page. You want to make sure that the background color you select matches your background image color, if you have one.

✦ `background-image` — This property contains the URL of the background image. Notice that the URL is specified within parentheses with the keyword `url` preceding the parenthesis. This is how URLs are specified in CSS. You haven't seen this convention yet in this book.

✦ `background-repeat` — This property determines whether to repeat (that is, tile) the background image. Your choices are *repeat* (tile the way you are used to seeing background images tile), *repeat-x* (tile horizontally only), *repeat-y* (tile vertically only), or *no-repeat*.

✦ `background-attachment` — This property enables you to specify whether the background image moves with the text (that is, scrolls) or stays in one position relative to the page (remains fixed).

✦ `background-position` — You can specify two values for this property with a space between them: vertical position and horizontal position. You can specify them in terms of a percentage of the page, the distance on the page, or a keyword. All of the following are valid:

```
background-position: 10% 10%;
background-position: 1cm 3in;
background-position: top center;
background-position: 30% center;
```

Background shortcut

As with font definitions, you can define background properties together in one property called `background`. The `background` property is defined by this code:

```
background: background-color background-image background-repeat
background-attachment background-position
```

In the following valid examples of the `background` property, notice `background-position` is actually two values; a complete list of all the background properties is actually six values long. As with all shortcuts, you needn't include all the values.

```
background: white url(../images/logo-faded.gif) no-repeat
scroll center center;
background: url(../images/logo-faded.gif) 2cm center;
background: url(../images/logo-faded.gif) repeat-x fixed
10% center;
```

From Here

Jump to Chapter 34 and learn about bit depth in colors.

Proceed to Chapter 27 and learn about formatting paragraphs.

Summary

In this chapter, you learned about how your computer creates colors from zeros and ones. You learned a little bit about the hexadecimal system and how you can use it to define colors. You also learned about palettes and where to find system-safe palettes. Finally, you learned how to apply all this information to define a background color, text colors, and a background image that doesn't tile.

✦   ✦   ✦

Formatting Paragraphs

In this chapter, you learn about formatting paragraphs with the *box formatting model*. This CSS feature formats block-level elements of a document, including paragraphs. You learn about indenting text, controlling alignment, specifying line spacing, and controlling lists. You also learn how to add rules and borders.

Reviewing the CSS Box Formatting Model

You may recall the CSS box formatting model from Chapter 24: After a block-level object is rendered, the browser uses information in the style sheet to determine how to format around the box in which the object is rendered.

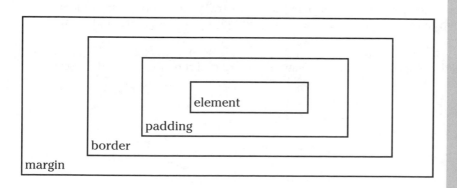

Padding summary

Padding—the white space between the element itself and the border (if there is one)—takes on the background color assigned to the element. These five properties are related to padding:

- ✦ padding-top
- ✦ padding-right
- ✦ padding-bottom
- ✦ padding-left
- ✦ padding

The first four take either a valid length or a percentage of the canvas. The fifth property, padding, is the shortcut for the first four. It can take between one and four values. It assumes that the values you provide are for the top, right, bottom, and left, in that order.

Margins summary

Margins take on the background color of the *parent element*—the container in which this block-level element is defined. For example, if the element being defined is a paragraph, the parent element might be the BODY element. Suppose two items are vertically aligned on the page, each with its own margin defined; for the top element, the margin would be the margin-bottom element, for the bottom element, it would be margin-top; the browser renders the two elements with a margin between them that equals the larger of these two margins, not the sum of the margins. For elements aligned horizontally, the browser renders each element with its own margin; it does not collapse the two margins into the greater of the two.

Five properties specify not only the margins, but also the white space between the border of the element (if it has one) and the margin of the next element. These properties are:

- ✦ margin-top
- ✦ margin-right
- ✦ margin-bottom
- ✦ margin-left
- ✦ margin

The margin properties work exactly the same as the padding properties.

Units of length

To define padding or margins, first you need to know what units you can use to define them. Many properties in CSS take lengths in both *relative units* and *absolute units*. The relative units are:

✦ **em** — (the height of the element's font)

✦ **ex** — (the height of the letter *x*)

✦ **px** — (pixels, which are measurable on the canvas)

The absolute units are:

✦ **in** — (inches)

✦ **cm** — (centimeters)

✦ **mm** — (millimeters)

✦ **pt** — (points; 72 points to an inch)

✦ **pc** — (picas; 12 points to a pica)

Adding Indentations

Another way to format your paragraph is to indent the first line of text, or outdent the first line of text. *Outdenting*, also known as creating a hanging indent, is when the first line of text hangs out into the margin and subsequent lines of text begin further in. You can define text indenting using the text-indent property as follows:

```
text-indent: .5in;

text-indent: 2cm;

text-indent: -8em;
```

Controlling Alignment

You might also want to control what is normally called text justification. CSS calls it *alignment*. Text alignment can be set to left, which is the default, center, right, or justify, which is full alignment.

The property is called `text-align`. Here are some examples:

```
text-align: left;

text-align: center;

text-align: justify;
```

Choosing Line Height

By default, your browser renders your font size with one pixel above the tallest letter and one pixel below the lowest-reaching letter. So, if you specify you want the font-size to be 12pt, the browser assumes line-spacing should be 14pt. You can, however, change that by using a greater `line-height` to spread out your text on the page.

The following example creates a paragraph with standard indentation and very tight line-spacing:

```
P {
   font-size: medium;
   line-height: 12pt;
}
```

Controlling Lists with Styles

You can use most of the properties listed earlier in this chapter to format your lists, as well. Each list item is formatted as its own block-level element, which means you can assign that element its own padding, borders, and margins. You can specify what bullets look like for unordered lists, the numbering system used for ordered lists, and (if you prefer) the image to be used as a bullet point. You can also specify whether the bullets are outdented (which is probably the way you're used to seeing them in lists), or flush with the left margin; if your text direction is right-to-left, your bullets can be flush with the right margin.

List style type

For ordered lists (OL), which typically have a number or a letter next to each list item, you can choose from among these types of list style:

✦ **decimal** — 1, 2, 3, 4, 5, and so on

✦ **lower-roman** — i, ii, iii, iv, v, and so on

✦ **upper-roman** — I, II, III, IV, V, and so on

✦ **lower-alpha** — a, b, c, d, e, and so on

✦ **upper-alpha** — A, B, C, D, E, and so on

For unordered lists, which typically have some shape of bullet next to each list item, you can choose between

✦ **disc** — standard solid circle

✦ **circle** — empty circle

✦ **square** — solid square

Some examples follow:

```
OL {
list-style-type: lower-alpha;    /* a, b, c, etc. */
}
UL {
      list-style-type: circle;
}
```

List style image

CSS enables you to specify an image instead of a disc, circle, or square for the bullet in unordered lists; you identify the image by its URL. The property is named `list-style-image`. If the browser can't find the URL of the image you have selected, it uses the style type you specified in the `list-style-type` property.

```
UL {
      list-style-type: square;
      list-style-image: url(../images/blue-box.gif);
}
```

List style position

The following example shows regular formatting of lists.

✦ Outside list item 1

has bullet outside the margin of subsequent lines

✦ Outside list item 2

has bullet outside the margin of subsequent lines

This is how you specify it:

```
UL {
          list-style: outside;
}
```

The next example shows compact formatting of lists:

✦ Inside list item 1

✦ has flush subsequent lines

✦ Inside list item 2

✦ has flush subsequent lines

You can specify compact formatting by using the CSS property called list-style. The code looks like this:

```
UL {
        list-style: inside;
}
```

Notice the property is associated with the UL element and not with the LI elements.

List style shorthand

As with many CSS property groups, you can use the list-style property to group your list formatting. The list-style property takes three values: the value of the list-style-type property, the value of the list-style-position property, and the value of the list-style-image property. The possible values of the three don't conflict; you can specify only one value — or any two values — and it will work. An example follows:

```
UL {
        list-style: square outside url(../images/blue-box.gif);
}
OL {
        list-style: decimal inside;
}
```

Adding Borders

Borders are a great way to break up your page and to draw attention to something important. CSS offers you superior flexibility when you specify which (if any) rules and borders you want to include with your box-formatted elements. You can choose border-width properties, a border-color property, a border-style property, and a variety of ways you can use shorthand notation to define borders.

Border width

You can use five properties to define the width of the border. They are `border-top-width`, `border-right-width`, `border-bottom-width`, `border-left-width`, and `border-width`. CSS is nothing if not predictable. You can specify any of the first four or you can use the fifth one to specify up to all four of the widths in shorthand, just as with the margin and padding properties.

If you specify one value for the `border-width` property, all four sides will be that width. If you specify two values for the `border-width` property, the top and bottom are assigned the first value, and the sides are assigned the second value. If you specify three values (and this is completely unintuitive), the top is assigned the first value, the sides are assigned the second value, and the bottom is assigned the third value.

In addition to specifying a valid length (using one of the measurements listed earlier), you can also use one of three keywords to instruct the browser to render your border width: `thin`, `medium`, and `thick`. The default is `medium`. An example of such a border rendering follows:

```
border-width: thin;          /* all 4 sides will be thin */
border-width: medium thick;  /* top, bottom medium, sides
thick */
border-width: 4px thin 2px;  /* top 4px, sides thin, bottom
2px */
border-width: 3mm 4mm 2mm 1mm; /* top, right, bottom, left, in
that order */
```

Border color

The `border-color` property takes up to four values; it works exactly like the `border-width` property. You can specify border color for all four sides at once or for each side individually. The property is called `border-color`. Here is what it looks like in action:

```
border-color: #FF0000;          /* makes all four borders red
*/
border-color: red blue red blue; /* makes top and bottom
borders red, sides blue */
border-color: yellow black;      /* makes top and bottom
yellow, sides black */
```

Border style

The `border-style` property tells the browser what kind of border to use. As with the `border-width` property, you can specify one to four values. Your choices are:

✦ **none** — No border; overrides `border-width` specification.

✦ **dotted** — Border is a dotted line. This is not yet implemented in Internet Explorer 4.

✦ **dashed** — Border is a dashed line. This is not yet implemented in Internet Explorer 4.

✦ **solid** — Border is a solid line (the default).

✦ **double** — Border is a double line. The `border-width` value specifies the total width of both lines and the white space between them.

✦ **groove** — Border is a 3D groove of the color assigned in `border-color` property.

✦ **ridge** — Border is a 3D ridge of the color assigned in `border-color` property.

✦ **inset** — Border is a 3D inset of the color assigned in `border-color` property.

✦ **outset** — Border is a 3D outset of the color assigned in `border-color` property.

```
border-style: solid none;     /* makes top and bottom solid,
none on sides */
border-style: ridge;        /* ridge on all four sides;
border-style: dotted dashed solid   /* top dotted, sides
dashed, bottom solid */
border-style: solid dotted double dashed   /* top, right,
bottom, left in that order */
```

Shorthand techniques

CSS provides several techniques for creating shorthand definitions related to borders. Four properties — `border-top`, `border-right`, `border-bottom`, and `border-left` — can be used to specify values for width, style, and color, in that order. A brief example follows:

```
border-top: thick dashed blue;
border-bottom: thick dashed red;
```

A `border` property can be used to set values for width, style, and color — but only if you want to assign the same values to all four sides, as in the following example:

```
border: thin solid black;      /* all four sides will be thin,
solid, and black */
border: 6px double yellow;      /* all four sides will be 6px,
double, and yellow */
```

From Here

Jump to Chapter 31 and learn about using CSS for absolute positioning.

Jump to Chapter 47 and learn about animating your page with JavaScript and the document-object model.

Proceed to Chapter 28 and learn about CSS and tables.

Summary

In this chapter, you reviewed the CSS box-formatting model. You learned more about specifying margins and padding for paragraphs. You learned the units of measurement to use when specifying many CSS property values. You also learned about including paragraph indentation, paragraph alignment, and the property that specifies line spacing. You learned about formatting lists, either with the bullet outdented or flush with the text. Finally, you learned about specifying borders for your block-level elements.

✦   ✦   ✦

Formatting Tables

In this chapter, you learn about using CSS to format tables. As you read in Chapter 21, about tables, CSS1 (the only version of CSS recommended by the W3C) does not provide as many ways to affect formatting of tables as it does formatting of other elements. Fortunately, the W3C is in the process of remedying this problem in CSS2, which was a working draft at publication time. This chapter incorporates both CSS1 and CSS2 to show you how to format every aspect of your HTML table.

Controlling Table Alignment

CSS provides the align property to enable you to specify table alignment. The align property for tables works exactly as it does for aligning paragraphs or any other block-level element. You can choose to align the table on the left, in the center, on the right, or fully justified across the canvas. You can specify the align property for the TABLE selector, for a class of the TABLE selector, or for an ID that affects the TABLE element.

```
TABLE {
        text-align: center;
}
TABLE.right-leaning {
        text-align: right;
}
TABLE#full {
        text-align: justify;
}
```

Setting Horizontal Cell Alignment

You can specify horizontal cell alignment in four places: at the cell level, at the row level, at the column level, or at the row group level.

At the cell level

Specifying alignment at the cell level is easy. Include the align attribute in the TD element. The problem with this is you could end up defining this attribute in every single cell. If you can define this attribute at a higher level, this can save you a lot of typing and reduce the chance of introducing errors into your TABLE definition.

```
<TABLE>
    <TR>
        <TH align="center">Vacation Location
        <TH align="center">Avg. Temp.
        <TH align="center">Package Deal
    <TR>
        <TD align="left">Ireland
        <TD align="char" char="&deg;">68&deg;
        <TD align="char" char=".">$799.95
    <TR>
        <TD align="left">Greek Islands
        <TD align="char" char="&deg;">84&deg;
        <TD align="char" char=".">$649.95
    <TR>
        <TD align="left">Cancun
        <TD align="char" char="&deg;">85&deg;
        <TD align="char" char=".">$729.99
</TABLE>
```

Using CSS, you can move some of this formatting into classes. There is no character alignment in CSS, so some formatting would have to remain in the HTML. The style sheet would look like this:

```
TD.left {
        align: left;
}
TH.center {
        align: center;
}
```

And the HTML would look like this:

```
<TABLE>
    <TR>
        <TH class="center">Vacation Location
        <TH class="center">Avg. Temp.
        <TH class="center">Package Deal
    <TR>
```

```
            <TD class="left">Ireland
            <TD align="char" char="&deg;">68&deg;
            <TD align="char" char=".">$799.95
        <TR>
            <TD class="left">Greek Islands
            <TD align="char" char="&deg;">84&deg;
            <TD align="char" char=".">$649.95
        <TR>
            <TD class="left">Cancun
            <TD align="char" char="&deg;">85&deg;
            <TD align="char" char=".">$729.99
    </TABLE>
```

At the row level

As you can see in the previous example, defining alignment at the cell level is impractical. Especially for the first row, where every cell has the same class. Moving alignment to the cell level makes more sense. The style sheet would now look like this:

```
TD.left {
        text-align: left;
}
TR.center TH.center {
        text-align: center;
}
```

And the HTML would look like this:

```
<TABLE>
        <TR class="center">
            <TH>Vacation Location
            <TH>Avg. Temp.
            <TH>Package Deal
        <TR>
            <TD align="left">Ireland
            <TD align="char" char="&deg;">68&deg;
            <TD align="char" char=".">$799.95
        <TR>
            <TD align="left">Greek Islands
            <TD align="char" char="&deg;">84&deg;
            <TD align="char" char=".">$649.95
        <TR>
            <TD align="left">Cancun
            <TD align="char" char="&deg;">85&deg;
            <TD align="char" char=".">$729.99
    </TABLE>
```

Notice the alignment for the first row was moved from the cell level to the row level. Already, the HTML looks better.

At the column level

Unfortunately, none of the other rows lend themselves to moving the alignment attribute to the row level. But all of them share column formatting. They all have a left column with left alignment, a center column with character alignment — where the character on which they would like to align being the degree sign (°), which is defined using the ° entity — and a right column with character alignment that lines up on the decimal point.

To take advantage of column level alignment, you have to define columns. The previous example doesn't define columns, but the following example does. All the alignment formatting for rows after the first row is moved to the column level. The style sheet needs to be modified to look like this:

```
COL.left TD.left {
        text-align: left;
}
TR.center TH.center {
        text-align: center;
}
```

Because no character alignment is in CSS, the formatting for the second and third columns would still need to be specified in the HTML.

```
<TABLE>
    <COL class="left">
    <COL align="char" char="&deg;">
    <COL align="char" char=".">
    <TR align="center">
        <TH>Vacation Location
        <TH>Avg. Temp.
        <TH>Package Deal
    <TR>
        <TD>Ireland
        <TD>68&deg;
        <TD>$799.95
    <TR>
        <TD>Greek Islands
        <TD>84&deg;
        <TD>$649.95
    <TR>
        <TD>Cancun
        <TD>85&deg;
        <TD>$729.99
</TABLE>
```

Even though the first row would be affected by the alignment formatting defined at the column level, the row level alignment overrides the column level formatting, so all the cells in the first row will have center alignment. Finally, the HTML looks like something you probably wouldn't mind maintaining.

At the row group level or column group level

The previous example doesn't lend itself to the use of the THEAD, TFOOT, TBODY, or COLGROUP elements to specify alignment, but you can specify alignment at either the row group level or the column group level.

```
COLGROUP.center {
        text-align: center;
}
TBODY.right {
        text-align: right;
}
```

Setting Vertical Cell Alignment

New to CSS2 is the vertical-align property. You can specify vertical alignment (called *valign* in HTML 3.2) in your style sheet to apply to TD elements. You may use a keyword from the list or you may specify a percentage value. The keywords are:

✦ **top.** Sets the top of the cell to align with the top of the row in which the cell is defined.

✦ **middle.** Sets the middle of the cell to align with the middle of the row in which the cell is defined.

✦ **bottom.** Sets the bottom of the cell to align with the bottom of the row in which the cell is defined.

✦ **baseline.** This is a relative specification. The baseline of the row is the baseline of the top line of the text in the row. The baseline of the top line of text in the row depends on the font sizes used in each of the cells. The browser determines the baseline of the first row of text and aligns the baseline of the text in this cell with the baseline of the row.

✦ **sub.** This subscripts the cell.

✦ **super.** This superscripts the cell.

✦ **text-top.** Aligns the top of the cell with the top of the font of the highest text in that row.

✦ **text-bottom.** Aligns the bottom of the cell with the bottom of the font of the lowest text in that row.

```
TD.mid {
        vertical-align: middle;
}
```

Specifying Table and Cell Widths

You can specify widths for both the table and individual cells. With cell specifications, specify width at the column level or at the cell level. For both cells and tables, you can either specify widths as absolute values or as relative values.

Absolute values

Before you decide to specify your table width using absolute values, be sure you know how each cell will render. Otherwise, you could end up with cells that aren't wide enough to hold an entire word. Tables neither do a good job of breaking words at the syllable nor do they hyphenate your words when you specify too small a width for cells. In fact, if you specify an absolute value for cell height and an absolute value for cell width, your cell might be too small to display all your text. In this case, the text might spill over into the next cell, crossing rules!

Vocabulary
antidisestablishmentarianis m

When you specify absolute widths, you are specifying them in pixels. A screen can be 640 pixels wide, 800 pixels wide, or 1,024 pixels wide (even more for super-high resolution monitors), but the browser will not always be set to fill the entire screen. You have no way of predicting how wide the browser window will be. The attribute used for specifying width is the width attribute.

```
<TABLE width="200">
      <COl width="100">
      <COL width="50" span="2">
      ... rest of table...
</TABLE>
```

In the previous example, the table is set to 200 pixels, the first column is 100 pixels wide, the second and third columns are each 50 pixels wide. Normally, you wouldn't specify both TABLE width and COL width absolutely.

Relative values

Whenever possible, you want to use relative values to specify table width. You can specify the table width as a percentage of the screen.

```
<TABLE width="40%">
      ... rest of table...
</TABLE>
```

You can also specify relative cell widths within a table for which you have specified an absolute width. The example in the section on absolute widths would probably be better defined as:

```
<TABLE width="200">
    <COL width="50%">
    <COL width="25%" span="2">
    ... rest of table...
</TABLE>
```

Another way to define cell widths is to use the 0* value. The 0* value is the way you instruct the browser to use the minimum width necessary.

```
<TABLE>
    <COL width="0*">
    <COL width="100" span="2">
    ... rest of table...
</TABLE>
```

Specifying width in style sheets

You can also use style sheets to specify widths. The property is called width. The last two examples could be reworked, using style sheets into:

```
<TABLE class="this-one">
    <COL ID="half">
    <COL ID="quarter" span="2">
    ... rest of table...
</TABLE>
<TABLE>
    <COL class="min">
    <COL class="this-one" span="2">
    ... rest of table...
</TABLE>
```

The style sheet for these two tables would look like this:

```
TABLE.this-one {
        width: 200;
}
#half {
        width: 50%;
}
#quarter {
        width: 25%;
}
COL.min {
        width: 0*;
}
COL.this-one {
        width: 100;
}
```

Adding Cell Spacing

You can specify cell spacing within the table. The property is called *cell spacing* (cell spacing as an attribute of the TABLE element). *Cell spacing* is the space between the border on the inside of one cell and the border on the inside of the next cell or the outside border of the table. When you define borders, actually borders are around each cell and a separate border is around the entire table. If they are thin and there is no cell spacing, it will look like it is one line that surrounds the cells and attaches to the border around the table. The more cell spacing you define, the clearer it will be these are separate lines.

The previous table has no cell spacing.

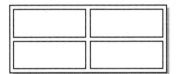

The previous table has cell spacing. The spacing attribute is defined as part of the TABLE element:

```
<TABLE cellspacing="3">
```

Or, as part of a style sheet:

```
TABLE {
        cell-spacing: 3
}
```

New to CSS2, you can specify different values for horizontal space between cells and for vertical space between cells. The first value supplied to the cell-spacing property is for horizontal cell spacing; the second is for vertical cell spacing. If you provide only one, it applies to both kinds of cell spacing.

Also new to CSS2, you can collapse borders, removing the cell spacing altogether. This makes your table look more like a table appears in a word-processing document. The property is called border-collapse. This applies only to table elements: TABLE, COLGROUP, COL, THEAD, TFOOT, TBODY, TR, TH, TD.

```
TABLE {
        border-collapse: collapse;
}
```

The default value of border-collapse is "separate". You can choose between the "collapse" and the "separate" keywords.

Defining Cell Padding

Cell padding can be defined at the TABLE level, the column group or column level, the row group or row level, or the cell level. Cell padding is the white space between the contents of a cell and the borders of a cell. By default, browsers render tables without any cell padding. This tends to make the widest element in each cell look crowded.

The property is the same padding property used to define padding for any block-level element that takes advantage of the box formatting model.

```
TABLE {
        padding: 1em;
}
```

Even if you specify an absolute width for a table or a cell, the padding attribute has an effect. If you specify an absolute width and padding, the browser will make the width of the cell in which the contents appear smaller, allowing room for the padding.

Using Colors in Tables

Within a table, there are several elements to which you can assign color. These include the borders, the rules, the background color, and the text color. You can specify all these things as the same for a table or you can specify different colors for every rule, border, cell text color, and cell background color. The properties are the same as for the rest of CSS: color, background-color, and the variations on the border/border-color property.

```
COLGROUP {
        border: thin solid black;
        background-color: white;
        color: black;
}
COLGROUP.highlight {
        border-left: thick solid blue;
        background-color: yellow;
        color: navy;
}
```

Defining Rules and Borders

By default, tables in HTML have a border-width set to zero. This means all rules and borders are turned off. If you take the small action of setting border-width to 1, you will suddenly have both borders and rules.

Rules are the lines between cells. The capability to define these independently of the border, which is the line around the table, is new to HTML 4. The three attributes for defining borders are: rules, frame, and border. The border attribute defines the width of the frame and rules; the value must be defined as a valid measurement using the units listed in Chapter 27.

The frame attribute takes a keyword value; valid values are:

✦ **void.** No borders are displayed on the table; this is the default value.

✦ **above.** Only a top border is displayed.

✦ **below.** Only the bottom border is displayed.

✦ **hsides.** The top and bottom borders are displayed.

✦ **vsides.** The right and left borders are displayed.

✦ **lhs.** Only the left-hand side border is displayed.

✦ **rhs.** Only the right-hand side border is displayed.

✦ **box.** All four sides are displayed.

✦ **border.** All four sides are displayed.

The rules attribute also takes a keyword value. The rules attribute specifies internal lines. Valid values for the rules attribute are:

✦ **none.** No rules are displayed. This is the default value.

✦ **group.** Rules are displayed only between groups.

✦ **rows.** Rules are displayed between rows.

✦ **cols.** Rules are displayed between columns.

✦ **all.** Rules are displayed between all cells.

From Here

Cross-Reference

Jump to Chapter 31 and learn about CSS absolute positioning tricks.

Proceed to Chapter 29 to learn about using CSS to define fonts.

Summary

Using a combination of CSS1, CSS2, and HTML 4, you can define the formatting of your tables. Controlling table alignment, horizontal alignment of cell contents in your cells, and vertical alignment of cell contents in your rows is relatively straightforward. In this chapter, you learned about specifying table and cell widths as both relative and absolute values. You also learned about cell spacing, cell padding, defining rules and borders, and defining colors in tables.

✦   ✦   ✦

Adding Fonts

CSS gives you incredible flexibility in defining fonts for your pages. You can specify multiple font faces, sizes for each element, the width between letters, and the spacing between words. You can even add interesting typographical effects, such as all caps on the first line (which many magazines and newspapers use), and a first letter that spans multiple lines. This chapter explains how to create all these effects using CSS.

Introducing Fonts

Most people think of fonts as letters. Fonts are really the representation of letters with *glyphs* (pictures). The letters a b c can look very different in Arial (a b c), Times New Roman (a b c), and Lucida Console (a b c). Even though the letters are the same, the glyphs are different.

Caution

The two major font families are *serif* and *sans serif*. Serif fonts include little decorations on the edges of letters. The most common serif font is Times Roman or Times New Roman, depending on your platform. Sans serif (meaning without serif) fonts are much plainer. In the paragraph that shows font examples, Arial and Lucida Console are sans serif fonts.

When you send text over the Internet, normally you send only your choices of the letters that make up the text. The recipient's browser renders your text by using whatever font face and size its owner has configured it to use. Until recently, you couldn't send the choice of font — and you certainly couldn't send the actual font. With CSS, Web authors have increasing control over font choice.

One reason text renders so quickly in your browser is nothing more than choices of letters — not the actual glyphs — are sent to your computer. With CSS, the Web developer now has three possible choices:

✦ Send text without specifying a font

✦ Send text that specifies which font the browser should use (usually as a list of choices in case the first choice isn't present)

✦ Send the text with the URL of a *downloadable* font (which requires specialized software).

Fonts versus the image of fonts

Most Web developers who want to include fonts other than those commonly available create their text as graphics and send graphics instead of text. This approach can substantially slow down the load time of their pages. On the upside, it does guarantee anyone with a graphics-capable browser will see the font the same way. If you want to show a small amount of a foreign language, using an image of text is probably the best way to go; your visitors need not load a special font set or run any particular operating system.

Using Local Fonts

If you decided you don't want to be stuck using the default font on the system — and you don't want to play games with creating images of text instead of sending the text — then you may want to take advantage of the CSS capability that specifies which local fonts the system ought to use. Because you can't know which fonts are installed on the browser — and you can't even know whether the browser is a PC, a Mac, or something else (unless you are developing for an intranet) — CSS gives you the option of specifying a list of fonts from which the browser can select. It will use the first listed font that matches one currently installed. To be even more thorough, after specifying each specific font name you would prefer the browser use, you can specify font family names; doing so ensures that if none of your specified fonts is present, the browser selects something that at least looks similar.

Font-Selection Considerations

There are two major factors to consider when selecting the fonts for your page. The first relates to aesthetics:

✦ Do the fonts on the page work together?

✦ How many different fonts work on one page?

✦ Should you mix serif and sans serif fonts?

The second question relates directly to whether the browser can re-create the page as you initially conceived it.

The aesthetics of font selection

Different fonts connote different qualities. Do you want the artistic sweep of a cursive font such as Brush Script? Do you want the clean lines of a sans serif font such as Helvetica? There are good reasons to use just about any font, but you'll want to make sure the font you select helps convey your message, rather than getting in the way of it.

Consider whether to use the same font for headings as you do for paragraph text. Serif fonts such as Times Roman (which have little hooks on the ends of the letters) are easier to read. Sans serif fonts such as Helvetica are cleaner looking and leave more white space. For these reasons, many people choose to use serif fonts for paragraph text and sans serif text for headings. You can use more than one font family in your document, but normally it's wise to avoid using more than two font families in one document. Too many font families can contribute to a cluttered or disorganized look.

Availability of local fonts

Even if you can create the perfect page, with just the right fonts, on your local system, what can you do to ensure that the browser renders your page as you would like it to be rendered? You can send a list of fonts you would like the browser to use, and the browser will use the first one in your list that it has. You aren't limited in how many you can list. If the default browser font would be noticeably worse, you would be well advised to list every font that would work well.

Controlling Font Selection

You can use the font-family property to indicate which font you want the browser to use. You can identify specific fonts, font families (serif, sans serif, cursive, fantasy, monospace), or both. If you list both, include the font families at the end so the browser will look for the most precise match before it uses a generic font family.

```
P {
        font-family: "Bookman Antiqua", Georgia, "Times New
Roman", "Times Roman", Times, serif;
}
```

The rule just given tells the browser the paragraph text should be rendered with Bookman Antiqua font; if that is not available, Georgia; if Georgia is not available, Times New Roman; if Times New Roman is not available, Times Roman; if Times Roman is not available, Times — or, if none of those fonts are available, any serif font. Note, any font name with more than one word in it should be contained in double quotes.

Internet Explorer does a pretty good job of handling font families. It does provide a script font when you specify cursive, but it gives you the same thing for fantasy as for sans serif. Netscape gives you sans serif for both cursive and fantasy font families. However, if you specify "Comic Sans MS" font (which is part of the fantasy family), it will work on both Netscape and Internet Explorer. The moral of the story: Specify the exact font you want used; don't rely on font families.

Choosing Font Sizes

You can set the font size with the font-size property. Setting the font size is useful because you can be sure the browser will lay out headings as you want them to appear. Normally, H6 elements render the same as regular paragraph text. You can change this and give greater importance to H6 elements by increasing the font size, changing the font style, or increasing the line height.

The font-size property takes a value in points (pt):

```
H6 {
        font-size: 14pt;
}
```

Using Condensed and Expanded Fonts

You can condense and expand fonts both horizontally — by spreading out the letters or the words — or vertically — by increasing or decreasing the white space between lines, using CSS. Table 29-1 shows each type of property at work.

Condensing and expanding horizontally

To condense or expand fonts horizontally (meaning the letters appear closer to each other than they normally would), use the letter-spacing property to add to the default value of space between letters.

Table 29-1
Expanding and condensing lines, words, and letter spacing

CSS for expanding letter spacing	P.wide { letter-spacing: .5pt; }
Example	this is an example of increased letter spacing
CSS for condensing letter spacing	P.narrow {letter-spacing: -.8pt; }
Example	this is an example of decreased letter spacing

CSS for condensing space between rows	P.crowded {
	line-height: 10pt;
	}

Example	this is an example of decreased line height; notice the lines really crowd each other.

CSS for expanding space between rows	P.spread-out {
	line-height: 18pt;
	}

Example	this is an example of increased line height; notice the lines are a bit more spread out.

CSS for expanding space between words	P.speaking-slowly {
	 word-spacing: 1em;
	}

Example	this is an example of expanded word spacing

```
H1 {
      letter-spacing: .2em;
 }
```

In this example, the letter spacing will be increased by .2em for H1 elements.

```
P.legal {
      letter-spacing: -.2em;
 }
```

In the previous example, the letter spacing will be decreased by .2em for P elements with a class of "legal."

You can also expand or condense fonts by increasing or decreasing the white space between words. The property for this is called *word spacing*. It works like letter spacing, which adds to the default amount of white space between words.

```
P.spread-out {
     letter-spacing: .2em;
     word-spacing: .5em;
}
```

The previous example creates a class called *spread out,* in which there is an extra .2em of space between letters and an extra .5em of space between words.

Tip

If you spread out letters, you probably want to spread out words as well, or it might not be clear where one word ends and the next one begins.

Condensing and expanding vertically

Condensing or expanding text on the page vertically — that is, leaving more or less white space between lines — is easily accomplished with the line-height property. By default, line height is two pixels greater than font-size. For example, if you have a 12pt font for your paragraph text, the browser will automatically render the text with 14pt line height — 12 points for the letter and one blank point to provide blank space at both the top and bottom of the letter. If you want to condense the line height, you can do so by specifying a line height less than 2 points greater than the font size. If you want to increase the white space between lines, increase the line height to more than two points greater than the font size.

```
P {
     font-size: 12pt;
     line-height: 14pt;
}
P.double {
     font-size: 12pt;
     line-height: 24pt;
}
P.smooshed {
     font-size: 12pt;
     line-height: 12pt;
}
```

For clarity in this example, the font size is repeated for each class, but it needn't be repeated. The double class double spaces the 12pt text. The smooshed class leaves no white space between lines.

Adding Small Caps and Other Decorations

There are two very cool things you can do with CSS. They take advantage of the pseudo-elements called first-line and first-letter. You learned about pseudo classes in Chapter 24; pseudo-classes are related to the A element. The descriptors for these classes (A:link, A:visited, A:active) can be assigned their own values to customize the look of linked text further.

Changing the first line

Pseudo-elements relate to the typographical layout of your page. The property called first-line enables you to simulate newspapers and magazines, which often apply a different typographical effect to the first line of text in a paragraph (all caps, for example).

```
P.first:first-line {
        font-style: small-caps;
}
```

When you have this rule in your style sheet, you can use the following HTML:

```
<P class="first">In Chicago today, it was announced that people
with more money live in nicer neighborhoods.</P>
```

This approach would render text similar to the following example in your browser:

IN CHICAGO TODAY, IT WAS announced
that people with more money live in
nicer neighborhoods.

Changing the first letter

The property called first-letter enables you to create text with a first letter that extends below the first line. For example, in many magazines, the first letter of the first paragraph in an article is two lines high.

```
P.drop-cap:first-letter {
        font-size: 36pt;
        float: left;
}
```

With this rule in your style sheet, you can use the following HTML:

```
<P class="drop-cap">In Chicago today, it was announced that
people with more money live in nicer neighborhoods.</P>
```

In a browser that supports this feature (which currently excludes both Netscape 4 and Internet Explorer 4), the code just given renders like this:

In Chicago today, it was announced
that people with more money live
in nicer neighborhoods.

From Here

Jump to Chapter 31, Understanding CSS Positioning Options.

Jump to Chapter 33, Cool CSS Positioning Tips and Tricks.

Proceed to Chapter 30, Creating Frames.

Summary

In this chapter, you learned about specifying the fonts you want used with your Web page. You also learned fonts are really pictures of letters called *glyphs*. This chapter discussed the factors you should consider when selecting fonts and the number of font faces you probably don't want to exceed. You learned to specify font size, font spacing (both horizontally and vertically), and you learned to add very cool text decorations, such as all caps on the first line, or a first letter that spans several rows.

✦   ✦   ✦

Creating Frames

Frames are an exciting, though controversial, way to enhance the navigational possibilities of your page. Frames give you an interesting kind of control over the layout of your site because parts of your page can remain static, while other parts change. This chapter explains how frames work, why they are controversial, and how best to use them. Finally, at the end of this chapter is a section about a newcomer to frames, the inline frame, which adds frames to your site in a way that doesn't carry all the liabilities of traditional frames.

Introducing Frames

Frames are a way of dividing your browser window so it can hold more than one logical page. When you create a framed site, the page has a URL, then each frame within the page has its own URL. Because each frame within a framed site has its own URL, you can load other pages into only a part of your browser, keeping the rest of your frames static.

Figure 30-1 shows one way of dividing your site using frames. This is a common way. At the top, in the banner, you put the site name, logo, ads, and so on. In the lower-left frame, the navigational tools (buttons, a table, or text) are placed. Finally, the content goes in the main frame. The content can change, but banner and navigational tools frames stay the same.

Banner runs across top of page; doesn't change regardless of what is loaded into main frame

Navigational tools go here; don't change regardless of what is loaded into main frame

Content goes here (main frame)

Figure 30-1: Sample layout for a framed site

Problems with Framed Sites

Why are framed sites controversial?

✦ **Older browsers can't load frames**. Netscape 2 and earlier can't handle frames. Are many people still using browsers that don't support frames? No. This reason, while once persuasive, is now all but irrelevant.

✦ **Some sites use frames for evil.** This has given many legitimate sites a bad name. How does this work? They create a frameset document with a base target of their main frame (content frame). This allows their ads and their banners to stay on the page regardless of which links you select. The only way to get out of this frame is to type in a new URL (or use a bookmark), find a URL that has a target specified of _top, which you learn about later in this chapter, or close the browser and start over.

✦ **Bookmarks don't always get set properly for framed sites.** For example, AOL 3.0 sets the bookmark to the main frame location (or the last of the URLs loaded into the frameset), rather than setting the bookmark to the master document. This means the next time you load the bookmark, you get an unframed page, with no navigational tools and no banner.

✦ **Navigation can be confusing to some visitors.** Because anything can load in any of the two or more frames, some visitors are confused when they click a link in one frame and the contents of a different frame change.

✦ **Too much scrolling is required.** Poorly designed framed sites require the visitor to scroll in more than one frame. Especially confusing is a framed site where the navigational controls are in a frame that requires scrolling. Above all else, if they are in their own frame, the navigational controls should all be visible at all times without scrolling.

Does this mean you should avoid frames? The authors of this book are split on this topic, which reflects the rest of the Web-developer world. Frames have their problems and the new IFRAME element can help you avoid some of them, but some things you simply can't do without frames, so they also have their place.

Developing the Master Frame Document

So how does the browser know it needs to load more than one URL and where to put each one? You create a master frame document. Instead of a BODY element, you create a FRAMESET element or in the previous example, nested FRAMESET elements.

The master frame document is a standard HTML document, but there is no BODY element. Instead, there is a HEAD (and you should include all the usual HEAD information, including META elements, and a TITLE element), and a FRAMESET element. The FRAMESET element is defined as follows:

Frameset <FRAMESET>

Start Tag: Required

Content: FRAMESET, FRAME, and
              NOFRAMES elements

End Tag: Required

Attributes: id, class, title, style: defined previously

rows: used to indicate the widths of the rows in order from top to bottom; the default is 100%, meaning one row; you can specify the widths in pixels, a percentage of the browser window, or relative width

cols: used to indicate the widths of the columns in order from left to right; the default is 100%, meaning one column; you can specify the widths in pixels, a percentage of the canvas, or relative width

events: defined in Chapter 48

Rows only

If you define only rows, you will have a framed document that looks like Figure 30-2.

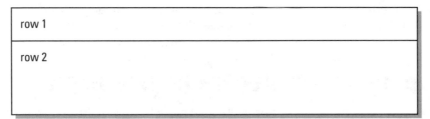

Figure 30-2: A framed page with two rows

The widths of the rows in Figure 30-2 would be determined by the values you specify in the rows attribute. The following FRAMESET shows using a percentage to indicate the size (pixels and relative sizes are discussed in the Columns Only section).

```
<FRAMESET rows="15%, 85%">
</FRAMESET>
```

Columns only

Or, you might want to define a framed document with only columns, as in Figure 30-3.

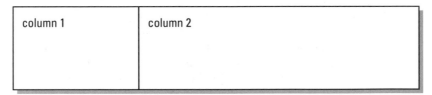

Figure 30-3: A framed page with two columns

The widths of the columns in Figure 30-3 would be determined by the values you specify in the cols attribute. The following FRAMESET might have created Figure 30-3. The number 200 indicates the number of pixels (which might be dictated by the width of a graphic you are including in that column). The asterisk (*) tells the browser to use the rest of the space for the second column.

```
<FRAMESET cols="200, *">
</FRAMESET>
```

Both rows and columns

If you define both rows and columns, you end up with a grid-like framed document. Figure 30-4 is one example of a framed document with both rows and columns.

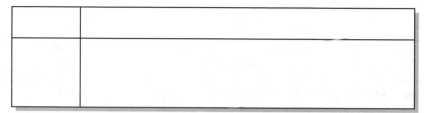

Figure 30-4: A framed document with both rows and columns

Figure 30-4 might have been created with the following HTML:

```
<FRAMESET cols="200, *" rows="1*, 5*">
</FRAMESET>
```

In the previous definition, the first column will be 200 pixels wide, regardless of how wide the page is. The second column will be the rest of the page. The first row will be one part of the height of the page; the second column will be five parts of the height of the page. The browser will calculate that the page must be divided into six parts and assigned to the rows in that proportion. The 1*, and 5* mean 1 part and 5 parts, respectively.

Relative versus Absolute widths and heights. You can define cols and rows using both relative and absolute measurements. If you use absolute measurements, you need to know exactly how many pixels you want the width or height. If you use relative measurement, you specify the percentage or the proportion of the browser window you want the frame to take.

A warning is in order about using absolute values for frame widths. If you specify an absolute column width and visitors to your site don't have their browser in full-screen mode, they might only see the left-hand column and not even realize a right-hand column (or more than one) exists. If possible, use relative values for column widths and row heights.

Nested FRAMESETs

What if you want to create a framed document, like the example in Figure 30-1? After all, that is probably the most common model on the Web today. Use nested FRAMESETs. The outer FRAMESET will define the rows. The inner FRAMESET divides the second row into two columns.

```
<FRAMESET rows="20%, 80%">
        ... FRAME element for first row ...
        <FRAMESET cols="25%, 75%">
            ... FRAME element for first column ...
            ... FRAME element for second column ...
        </FRAMESET>
</FRAMESET>
```

Targets

The browser needs to know three things. First, how much space you want it to allocate for each of your frames. You have already told it with the FRAMESET element. Second, how you want to refer to each of those frames: as target names. And third, how to populate each of those frames initially.

With the FRAME element, one of the attributes is name. With the name, you specify how you want to refer to the frame. This is called the *target name* of the frame. You can direct other links into this target. For example, if you have navigational tools in one frame, you can have the destination of those links load into your main frame by specifying the target attribute on the A element.

Consider the following master frame document:

```
<HTML>

<HEAD>
  <TITLE>This is the title of my site</TITLE>
  ... lots of META elements here ...
</HEAD>

<FRAMESET rows="200, *">
  <!-- creates first row as banner -->
  <FRAME name="banner" src="banner1.html">

  <FRAMESET cols="25%, 75%">
    <!-- creates column on left for navigational tools -->
    <FRAME name="navigate" src="navigational-tools.html">

    <!-- creates main frame for content -->
    <FRAME name="main" src="home.html">

  </FRAMESFT>

</FRAMESET>

</HTML>
```

Now, look at a possible version of navigational-tools.html, the file with the navigation buttons, in this case text, and the links. Notice how the A element for each of the links includes a target attribute directing the results of the link to load into the main frame.

```
<HTML>

<HEAD>
  ... TITLE and META elements here ...
</HEAD>
```

```
<BODY>
  <A href="products.html" target="main">Products and
Solutions</A>
  <A href="custsvc.html" target="main">Customer Service</A>
  <A href="white.html" target="main">White Papers</A>
  <A href="jobs.html" target="main">Job Postings</A>
</BODY>

</HTML>
```

Reserved target names

You must start your `target` names with letters. After that, you can use any of the regular, acceptable characters. Some `target` names begin with underscore (_). These are the reserved `target` names HTML makes available to help you with your frames. Using reserved names gives you a way to reference your frames relatively. Even if you change the `target` names of your frames, the reserved names still work.

✦ **_blank.** This causes the results of the link to be loaded into a new browser window. Unless the document referred to by the `src` attribute is a master frame document, the new page won't use frames.

✦ **_self.** This causes the results of the link to be loaded into the same frame as the `A` element, which created the link. In the previous example, you would use the _self target for links you have within the main frame.

✦ **_parent.** This causes the results of the link to be loaded into the `FRAMESET` parent of the current frame. If there is no `FRAMESET` parent, the results of the link are loaded into the same frame.

✦ **_top.** This causes the results of the link to be loaded into the full browser window, canceling frames. When would you want to use this? If you have a "back to home" link on the bottom of your main screen, you'd want it to point to the master frame document with a target of _top. This way, you wouldn't end up with the problem of unintentionally nested frames.

Creating FRAMEs

Finally, having told the browser how much space to allocate for each frame and having given each frame a name, you need to tell the browser what to put into each frame. You do this with the `FRAME` element. You've already seen the `FRAME` element at work.

Frame `<FRAME>`

Start Tag: Required

Content: Empty

End Tag:	Forbidden
Attributes:	`id, class, title, style`: defined previously

`name`: used to indicate the name to be associated with this frame (the target name)

`src`: used to specify what should initially be loaded into this frame

`frameborder`: tells browser to draw a border around this frame (1 - the default value), or not to (0); if the adjoining frame has a frameborder, it will appear between the unbordered frame and the bordered frame

`marginwidth`: width of margin in pixels (margin between frame contents and borders on sides)

`marginheight`: height of margin in pixels (margin between frame contents and borders on top and bottom)

`noresize`: Boolean attribute (meaning if you want to indicate noresize, you just include the attribute without a value) that tells the browser this frame is not resizable by the visitor

`scrolling`: There are three values for this attribute: yes, no, auto. Choose no if you know the contents of the frame will always fit into the frame (say you have column width and row height set in pixels to fit the image in the frame). Choose yes if you want there always to be a scroll bar on the side of this frame. Choose auto if you want the browser only to display a scroll bar if the content doesn't fit into the frame.

You must define a `FRAME` element for each frame you want to create. The `FRAMESET` element tells the browser how many frames and how much space to give them. The `FRAME` element names each frame and gives it an initial value.

When defining `FRAME`s, you can specify URLs using either relative or absolute file names. Just as with any other reference element (`A` or `IMG`), you can specify both local and remote file names. Local file names are probably better referred to with relative file names. Remote file names required fully qualified URLs.

Enhancing Navigability

Frames are a great way to ensure visitors always have navigational tools right on the screen where they can see them. Right? Not necessarily. One thing you should be cautious about is creating a page you plan to use only in the main frame and have it be indexed by a search index as a stand-alone page. Why is this a problem? Because when visitors come to that page from a search engine, they have no way to get to the rest of your site. Does this mean you need to put navigational tools on every page? Not necessarily. What you should have on every page is a link back to the front page of your site. That link must have a `target` of _top to work properly.

If you don't include a `target` of _top, you will have a problem with your site self-nesting, when anyone clicks that link when the main page is actually part of the framed site.

Figure 30-5: Your framed site

If your site looks like Figure 30-5, and someone clicks the [Go to Home Page] link you rightly have at the bottom of every page, but you forget the `target="_top"` attribute-value pair in your link, visitors get the results shown in Figure 30-6.

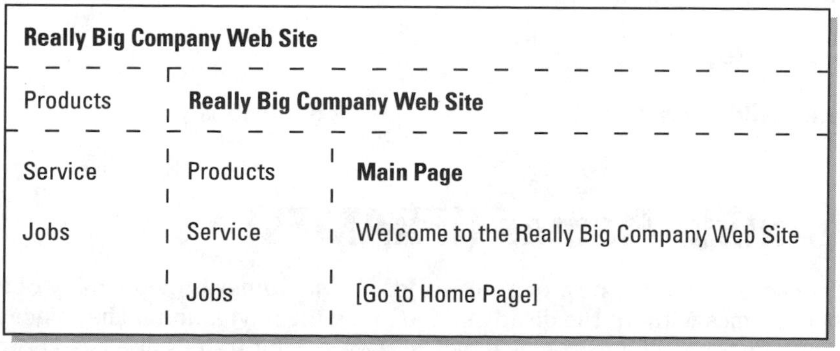

Figure 30-6: Your framed site with unintentional nesting

NOFRAMES

You can place one more element in your FRAMESET element. This is the NOFRAMES element. The NOFRAMES element is one you should include in the outermost FRAMESET, after you have defined all your other FRAMESETs and FRAMEs. NOFRAMES contains the page you want your visitors to get if their browsers don't support frames. It could be as simple as a message telling them to upgrade their browsers to see your site.

Note   If you do use the NOFRAMES element, and you should, be sure the text you include is something you wouldn't mind seeing on a Search Engine Results page. Search engines are notorious for using this text as your synopsis when indexing a site. This won't help attract visitors to your site.

```
<NOFRAMES>

Over the Web provides robust, turn-key modules for your
professional Web site.  The Over the Web site is only
accessible with a frames-capable browser. Please upgrade your
browser at one of the following locations:<BR>
<UL>
<LI><A href="http://www.netscape.com/">Netscape
Communications</A>
<LI><A href="http://www.microsoft.com/ie">Microsoft</A>
<LI><A href="http://www.aol.com">America Online</A>
</UL>
</NOFRAMES>
```

More likely, it will be the front page for the scaled-down version of your site that doesn't require frames. It's up to you to decide if the expense is justified to maintain a non-frames version of your site.

No frames <NOFRAMES>

Start Tag: Required

Content: HTML for non-frames page

End Tag: Required

Attributes: Id, class, title, style   defined previously

Adding Inline Frames (IFRAMEs)

Inline frames give you the best of both worlds. *Inline frames* provide many of the benefits of frames without the disadvantage of having navigation taking place in more than one frame. Inline frames look like they are not frames at all. No border is between an inline frame and the rest of the page. They also do not have the capability to have independent scrolling.

An inline frame is like a server-side include. You refer to the HTML file you want to appear in the inline frame and when the page is rendered, it appears as if the inline frame were part of the main HTML document.

Vocabulary
a b c

Server-side include. A *server-side include* is a clever way to reuse HTML. If all your pages take advantage of the same header and footer, you can put the header HTML and the footer HTML into separate HTML files and *call* them from all your documents. The syntax of using a server-side include varies from Web server to Web server, so check with your systems administrator if you want to use these. When the page is rendered in the browser, the server-side include HTML (the HTML in the separate file) appears in the main HTML document as if it were typed there. The advantage of using a server-side include is you can change only the HTML in the server-side include and have it reflected on every page that calls the server-side include.

The principal disadvantage of using inline frames is they are not well-supported by the browsers in use. Inline frames are a recent addition to the HTML elements. Currently, inline frames are only supported by Internet Explorer 4.

Inline `<INLINE>`

Start Tag: Required

Content: Empty

End Tag: Required

Attributes: `id, class, title, style` defined previously

`longdesc`: long text description of this element; useful for text-synthesizing browsers

`name`: name of this element; useful for scripting

`src`: required; the URL of the page you want inserted into the inline frame

`frameborder`: defaults to "1"; set to "0" if you don't want a border

`marginwidth`: width of margin in pixels for both sides

`marginheight`: height of margin in pixels for top and bottom

`scrolling`: yes, no, or auto; you only need to worry about this if you set the height and width to be smaller than the known contents of the URL height: height of the inline frame in pixels

width: width of the inline frame in pixels

align: deprecated; used to specify alignment on the page

From Here

Cross-Reference Proceed to Chapter 31 to learn about CSS positioning options.

Summary

In this chapter you learned about frames. You learned how framed documents work—with a master frame document, targets, and frames. You learned how to define horizontal frames, vertical frames, or some combination of both. This chapter also discussed how your screen gets divided: using absolute measurements, percentages, or fractions of the screen. You learned about naming your frames, directing the results of links into specific frames (targets), and reserved target names. This chapter also covered how to define the initial values of your frames.

One of the controversial aspects of frames is that all browsers don't support them. Using the NOFRAMES element, you learned how you can make this problem transparent to your site visitors. Finally, you learned about inline frames and how they help you get around some of the drawbacks of using traditional frames.

✦   ✦   ✦

Lay It Out Like the Pros

Understanding CSS Positioning Options

In the last few chapters of Part IV, you learned much of what you need to know to use CSS. In this chapter, you learn about positioning options available to you in CSS. This chapter focuses on the five properties that give you complete control over how your elements are positioned on the page. The positioning properties—display, float, clear, position, and z-index—give you the power to position your text and graphics relatively, absolutely, or using some combination of the two.

The display Property

The display property is one you already take for granted. All elements have a display property. You can use the default display property or set your own. You can also use the display property to make elements appear and disappear on your page. Dynamic HTML, which is just JavaScript and CSS with the document object model, takes advantage of the display property to have objects appear and disappear without reloading the page.

There are six valid values for the display property:

1. **block.** All block elements have a default display value of block. You can make an inline element behave like a block element by setting the value of the display property to block.

2. **inline.** All inline elements have a default display value of inline. You can, of course, change this.

3. **list-item.** List items are sort of a hybrid between `block` elements and `inline` elements. You probably noticed the chapters that discussed lists beat around the bush on what type of element lists and list items are. A list item is treated as a `block` element with an added list-item marker.

4. **compact.** You can set list items to compact, if you want them to attempt to take up less space on the page.

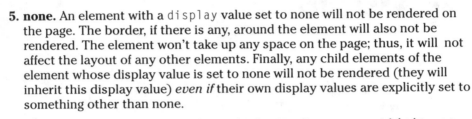

Cross-Reference

See Chapter 17 for an example of compact definition of lists.

5. **none.** An element with a `display` value set to none will not be rendered on the page. The border, if there is any, around the element will also not be rendered. The element won't take up any space on the page; thus, it will not affect the layout of any other elements. Finally, any child elements of the element whose display value is set to none will not be rendered (they will inherit this display value) *even if* their own display values are explicitly set to something other than none.

Cross-Reference

Chapter 48 about JavaScript explains why the `display` property might be set to none.

6. **run-in.** No elements have a default value of run-in. First the rules and then an example. Setting the display value of an element to run-in has the following effect: If the following element is not of type block, is floating, or is positioned absolutely, the run-in element will be rendered as a block element. Otherwise, the run-in element will be rendered as if it were part of the following element, which means, as if it were inline with the following element. This doesn't work in Version 4 or earlier browsers.

```
H6.run-in {

    display: run-in;
    font-variant: bold;
        }
H6:after.run-in {
    content: ". ";
        }
```

```
<H6 class="run-in">Run-in</H6>
<P>No elements have a default value of run-in. Setting the
display value of an element to run-in has the effect you are
seeing in this example.</P>
```

The previous example, using the style sheet rules immediately preceding it, will be rendered as follows:

Run-in. No elements have a default value of run-in. Setting the display value of an element to run-in has the effect you see in this example.

The float Property

It is not unusual to want to arrange your page so one or more elements, most commonly an image, appear next to (rather than above or below) other elements. The following HTML and CSS create the effect you see in Figure 31-1:

```
IMG.icon {
      padding: 20px;
      float: left;
}

<HTML>
<HEAD>
  <LINK rel="stylesheet" type="text/css" href="ch31.css">
  <TITLE>Chapter 31 Examples</TITLE>
</HEAD>

<BODY>
<H1>Chapter 31 Examples</H1>

<IMG class="icon" src="../public_html/itclogo.gif">

<P>It is common to want to have images appear on the same line
as your text. In this example, the float property of the IMG
class icon is set to "left" to achieve this effect. More text
is required in this example so that you can see that the text
continues to wrap around the image. This is that additional
text that is required. By now, the example should have enough
text to make the point. Just in case, another sentence will
provide additional text for puposes of making this point. This
will be the last sentence.</P>

</BODY>
</HTML>
```

Float values

The float property has three values: left, right, and none. Setting the value of the float property to none (the default value) results in the element not floating at all. In the previous example, the page would instead be rendered as seen in Figure 31-2.

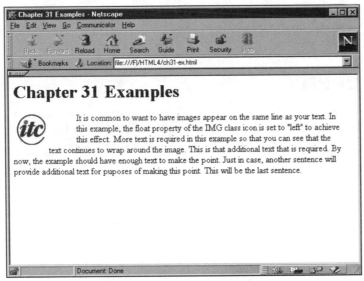

Figure 31-1: Using the `float` property to wrap text around an image.

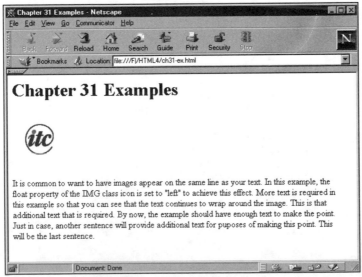

Figure 31-2: Setting the `float` property to none results in no floating.

The clear Property

The clear property works in conjunction with the float property. While the float property is applied to the object you want to wrap around, the clear property is applied to the object you want to do the wrapping. The default value for the clear property is none. This means both the right and the left side of the element are allowed to have a floating object next to it.

The clear property working with the float property

```
IMG.icon {
        padding: 20px;
        float: left;
}
IMG.icon2 {
        padding: 20px;
        float: right;
}
P {
        clear: none;
}


<BODY>
<H1>Chapter 31 Examples</H1>
<IMG class="icon" src="../public_html/itclogo.gif">
<IMG class="icon2" src="../public_html/itclogo.gif">

<P>It is common to want to have images appear on the same line
as your text. In this example, the float property of the IMG
class icon is set to "left" to achieve this effect. More text
is required in this example so that you can see that the text
continues to wrap around the image. This is that additional
text that is required. By now, the example should have enough
text to make the point. Just in case, another sentence will
provide additional text for purposes of making this point. This
will be the last sentence.</P>

</BODY>
```

In the previous example, there are two icon classes. One positions an image as floating to the left of the nonfloating element. The other positions an image as floating to the right of the nonfloating element: in this case, the P element. Notice both the images must appear *before* the nonfloating element. If they don't, the nonfloating element only wraps around the first image and the second image appears on a line by itself after the nonfloating element. The results of the previous example can be seen in Figures 31-3 and 31-4. The same example is shown in both Netscape and Internet Explorer so you can see both browsers render the same thing slightly differently. Specifically, Internet Explorer seems not to respect the padding property. Netscape graduates the text around the image.

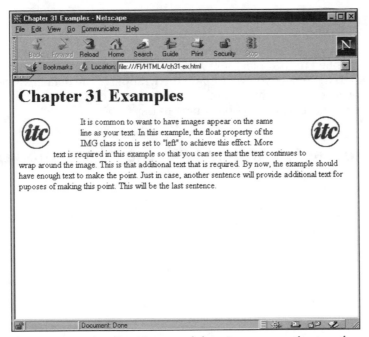

Figure 31-3: Using the `float` and the `clear` properties together (in Netscape)

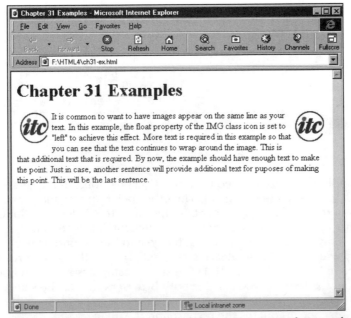

Figure 31-4: Using the `float` and the `clear` properties together (in Internet Explorer)

In Figure 31-5, the clear property of the nonfloating element (P) is set to left. This prevents anything from floating to the left of the P element. In this example, however, because both images (being the same image) are the same height, the second image (with a class of icon2) floats to the right on the page parallel to the first image.

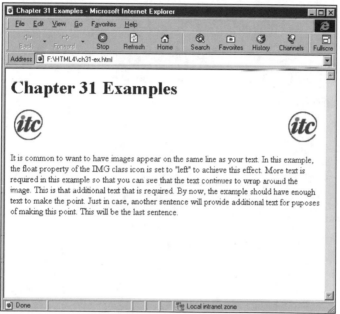

Figure 31-5: Floating with the clear property set to left

The results in Figure 31-5 are not exactly what were intended. If what was wanted was for the second image to float to the right of the text and the first image to be positioned above the text, then the float property of the first image must also be turned off (set to none, commented out, or deleted from the style sheet). The resultant style sheet would look like this:

```
IMG.icon {
     padding: 20px;
     /* float: left; */
}

IMG.icon2 {
     padding: 20px;
     float: right;
}
```

```
P {
        clear: left;
}
```

And the results of this style sheet, with the HTML previously given, can be seen in Figure 31-6.

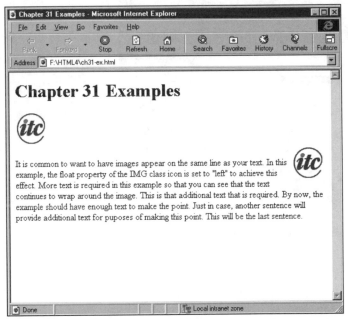

Figure 31-6: Using the `float` and `clear` properties properly to achieve desired results

The position Property

The fourth of the five properties you can use to control positioning with CSS is the `position` property. The `position` property takes one of three values.

✦ **normal.** This is the default value. Normal position simply means the rules you have learned thus far about CSS will apply to your element and it will be rendered in a position based on the values you assign to it and the values of the previous normal elements.

✦ **relative.** This means relative to the position the element would have if it were defined as a statically positioned element. All children elements are positioned with this new relative position as their starting point. When positioning elements with the relative position, overlaying or obscuring other elements is possible.

✦ **absolute.** When you define an element as absolutely positioned, it is not included in the calculations used to position other elements on the page. The element is simply put where you tell it to be put. All children elements of this element are positioned relatively to this absolute position. When using absolute positioning, it is possible to overlay or obscure other elements.

The z-index Property

The z-index property is a wonderful addition to CSS. It enables you to position elements in the third dimension: depth. Figure 31-7 shows the three dimensions.

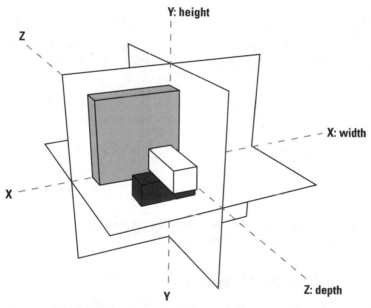

Figure 31-7: The three dimensions

Why would you want to position elements with the z-index property?

✦ To layer graphics, each of which are links, to save space, or to create an interesting visual effect.

✦ To layer text over an image.

✦ To hide graphics for use later, using JavaScript, when you can simply change the z-index of an object and have it magically appear.

Understanding Relative Positioning

In CSS, relative positioning has two possible meanings. Most Web designers think of relative positioning as when they position an element using the `float` property (formerly the `valign` and `align` attributes) or by changing the margins or padding on an element to scoot it one way or another. Generally speaking, *relative positioning* is positioning the element using any means other than absolute positioning. All the properties you have learned about CSS in this chapter and in previous chapters have been about relative positioning, which CSS2 now confusingly calls *static positioning*.

To make matters more interesting, CSS introduced the `position` property, which you can set to "relative." This enables you to move an element by some offset from the position at which it would have been positioned if you had allowed the browser to position it using all the previous properties you defined for it and for preceding elements.

To unconvolute the previous sentence, these are the plain-English steps the browser goes through to position an element not defined as absolutely positioned:

1. calculate the internal size of the box associated with each element (see Chapter 30 for information about boxes)

2. calculate the size of each element's box, including padding, borders, and margins

3. calculate the position of each element's box on the page based on the amount of space taken up by each previous box

Relative to relative positioning

If you choose to set the value of the position property to "relative," then the browser takes a fourth step to calculate the position of the element. After calculating the starting point for that box, the browser calculates where — relative to that starting point — using the relative offset you have indicated, you want the element positioned.

Understanding Absolute Positioning

When you position an element with absolute positioning, the browser only takes the first two steps previously listed. After it has calculated the size of the box, it renders that box exactly where you tell it. You risk overlaying other elements, if you are not careful, but it can be used to create stunning layout effects.

Combining Relative and Absolute Positioning

You can combine relative and absolute positioning in CSS, but you must do so thoughtfully or you will end up with your text running over your graphics, or your graphics overlaying your text.

The easiest way to combine relative and absolute positioning is to define the first element on your page — say, an image of known dimensions — as absolutely positioned near the top-left of the page, or wherever you want it positioned, and then to define the rest of your page as being relative to that offset (the dimensions of the absolutely positioned element).

Other options for combining relative and absolute positioning include positioning an element to the right or left of the body of your page and limiting the width of the rest of the elements in your page by using the width attribute.

You learn more specific applications of both relative and absolute positioning in Chapter 33.

From Here

Jump to Chapter 47 and learn about the Document Object Model (DOM), which is essential to dynamic HTML.

Proceed to Chapter 32 to learn about positioning and sizing graphics.

Summary

In this chapter you learned advanced CSS. You learned the five essential layout properties: display, float, clear, position, and z-index. You learned how relative positioning differs from static positioning and how they both differ from absolute positioning. You also learned how to combine relative and absolute positioning.

✦   ✦   ✦

Positioning Graphics and Text

In This Chapter

Specifying the
location of an image

Defining text
positions

Floating text around
an image (floating an
image next to text)

I n this chapter, you learn more tricks to give you control over the layout of your page using CSS and HTML together. Specifically, you learn how to have an image appear in the location of your choice. This chapter explains how to position your text where you want it to appear and how to wrap your text around floating graphics. Many examples help jog your own creativity.

Specifying Image Location

In the previous chapters, you learned enough CSS to specify where on the page an image should be located. In fact, you learned more than one way to do this.

Using frames

One way to assure your image ends up where you want it is to use frames. If you plan to create a framed site anyway, then the thought of using frames may already have occurred to you. Consider placing an image in the upper right-hand corner of the screen. If you use frames, you can be sure the graphic will never move.

Your HTML might look like this:

```
<FRAMESET rows="200, *">
   <FRAMESET cols="*, 200">
       <FRAME name="banner" src="banner.html"
frameborder="0">
```

```
            <FRAME src="image.gif" scrolling="no" frameborder="0">
        </FRAMESET>
        <FRAME name="main" src="home.html">
    </FRAMESET>
```

Your image, called `image.gif`, in the previous example, should be exactly 200×200 pixels. By setting the scrolling attribute to "no," you are assured a scroll bar won't be to the right of your image. By setting the frameborder attribute to zero for both the columns in the first row of the page, you are assured a border won't be around the banner or around the image next to the banner.

Using CSS with absolute positioning

Another way to specify the position of an image is to use the CSS position property with a value of absolute. You can use this method to position one or more graphics on the page. The problem with this technique is it requires careful planning to make sure the elements positioned as static (or relative) don't run over your absolutely positioned element — in this case, an image. You can also use absolute positioning to position subtle graphics in a case where you want the text run right across the images.

Consider the following CSS:

```
IMG.no1 {
        position: absolute;
        top: 200;
        right: auto;
        bottom: auto;
        left: 350;
}
IMG.no2 {
        position: absolute;
        top: 800;
        right: auto;
        bottom: auto;
        left: 350;
}
```

Notice both images have absolute positioning. Any images with a class of no1 (probably only one) will be positioned with the upper left-hand corner of the page at 200, 300 pixels from the upper left-hand corner of the page. Any images with a class of no2 will be positioned with upper left-hand corner of the image at 800, 350 pixels from the upper left-hand corner of the page.

	200	
350	Placement of image with class of no1	
	600	
	Placement of image with class of no2	

The resulting page will look like that in Figure 32-1. Notice you only see one image. Because the absolute position of the second image (no2) is 800 pixels down the page and the viewable area is less than that, the second image will only be visible when you scroll down the page.

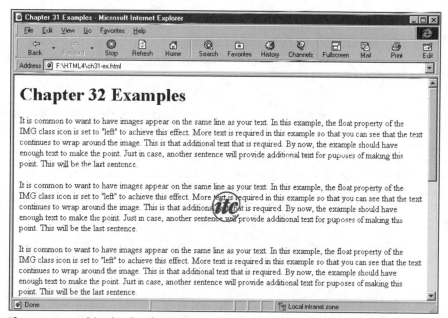

Figure 32-1: This absolutely positioned image has text overlaying the image.

Using CSS with relative positioning

Figure 32-2 uses relative positioning to place the image to the left of the text.

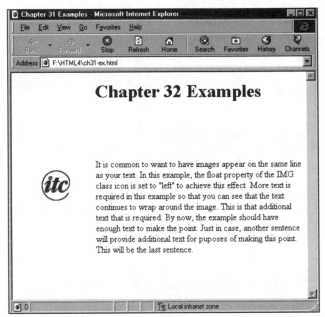

Figure 32-2: Relative positioning places the image to the left of the body of text.

Look at the style sheet and notice the BODY element is formatted with a 150-pixel left-hand border. This leaves room to relatively position the image next to the text. What about all that white space above the paragraph? This is because when you use relative positioning for one element, all subsequent elements are positioned based on that element's normal position. What does this mean? It means the browser leaves space for the image *above* the paragraph of text, even though the image is positioned *next to* the paragraph of text. If you have multiple paragraphs, this could be ugly.

```
P.thisone {
     position: normal;
}

IMG.relative {
     position: relative;
     left: -100;
     top: 100;
}

BODY {
     margin-left: 150;
}
```

Using CSS to float the image

If the float property had been used instead, the result would have been Figure 32-3.

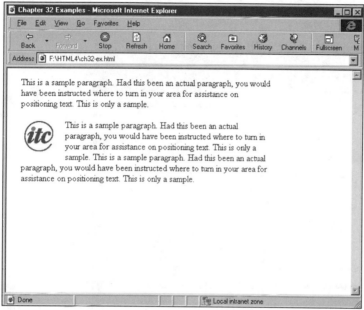

Figure 32-3: The float property wraps the text around the image.

Notice the text wraps around the image, rather than giving you a clean left margin. Either look has its place, depending on the look you desire. The CSS for Figure 32-3 follows:

```
IMG.icon {
        float: left;
}

P {
        margin-left: 15px;
}
```

Defining Text Positions

How can you put text where you want it? You have several choices in formatting your text. You can format your text by modifying the padding and margin of the text element itself, as in Figure 32-4.

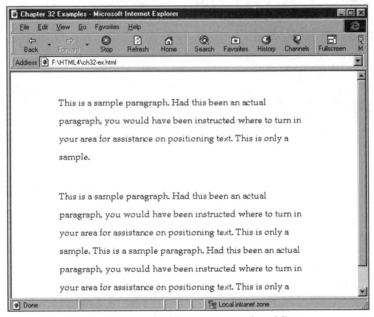

Figure 32-4: Text formatted with margins and padding

The CSS that follows was used to create the simple effects you see in Figure 32-4:

```
P {
        margin-top: 1cm;
        line-height: 200%;
        font-family: "Book Antiqua";
        padding: 0 2cm;
}
```

Changing the BODY element

Another option you have for formatting your page—so the text appears where you want it—is to change the formatting of the BODY element. Figure 32-5 uses BODY element formatting.

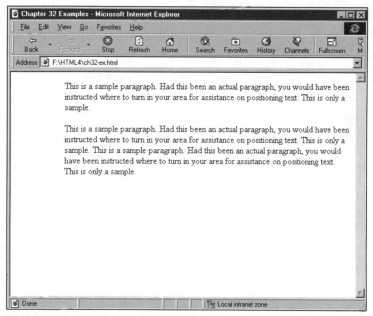

Figure 32-5: Text formatting with the BODY element

Figure 32-5 was created with the following CSS:

```
BODY {
        margin-left: 1in;
}
```

If you wanted to add page decorations to the left margin, you could put it in the one-inch left-hand margin. Or, you could use an absolutely positioned graphic, with a negative horizontal position, to put in that space.

Positioning text with relative positioning

You might have a need to pull text out of the body of the page, to draw attention to it for some reason. Figure 32-6 uses relative positioning to pull a paragraph of text out of the body of page and draw attention to it.

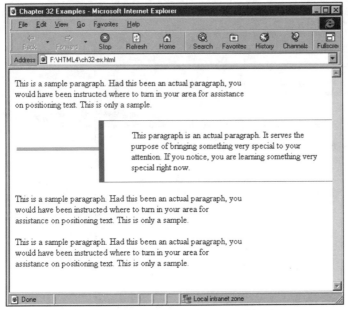

Figure 32-6: Text formatted with relative positioning

The following CSS was used to create Figure 32-6:

```
IMG.icon {
       float: left;
       position: relative;
       top: 36pt;
}

BODY {
       margin-right: 1.5in;
}

P.pull {
       position: relative;
       padding: 1em 1em 1em 3em;
       left: 150px;
```

```
        top: auto;
        text-indent: -154px;
        border-left: red .25cm solid;
        border-top: red 1px solid;
        border-bottom: red 1px solid;
    }
```

The graphic image you see (three thin parallel red lines) to the left of the paragraph, which is offset to the right, is really only a 1 pixel × 5 pixel graphic. It is stretched to the width you see by changing the width parameter associated with the IMG element.

Floating an Image Next to Text

In Figure 32-7, you can see the same boring text and the same boring images are rearranged, so the text floats around the image, first to the right of the image and then to the left.

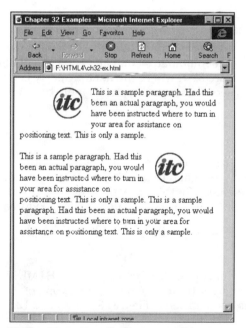

Figure 32-7: Text floating around images

The CSS used to create this effect follows:

```
IMG.left {
      float: left;
      margin-left: 1.5cm;
      margin-right: 10pt;
}

IMG.right {
      float: right;
      margin-right: 1.5cm;
      margin-left: 10pt;
}
```

Tips on floating text

The float property is not perfectly implemented in either Internet Explorer 4 or Netscape 4. Generally, Internet Explorer supports more of the CSS properties more fully. Some combinations of properties give strange and unpredictable results, so you need to test your work carefully.

Floating both the text and the image

Figure 32-8 is the result of applying the float property to both the P elements and the IMG elements. In Internet Explorer, this combination had no visible effect and the result looked exactly the same as Figure 32-7, where the float property is only applied to the IMG element. As you can see, Netscape does not handle this combination well.

Floating only the text

Neither browser wants to have the float property assigned to the text. Both browsers want to have the float property assigned to the IMG element. The result of applying the float element to the text element (in this case, the P element) varies by browser, but is equally unappealing in both browsers, as can be seen in Figures 32-9 and 32-10.

The order of the HTML matters

If you use the same CSS used effectively in Figure 32-6, but change the HTML so the IMG element appears *after* the P elements, for both P elements, then you get different and unsatisfactory results, as you can see in Figures 32-11 and 32-12.

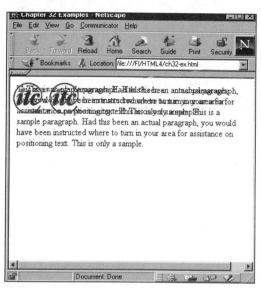

Figure 32-8: Netscape has problems with the float property being applied to both the P element and the IMG element.

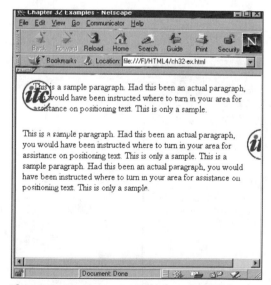

Figure 32-9: Netscape can't handle floating when the float property is applied to the text, rather than to the IMG element.

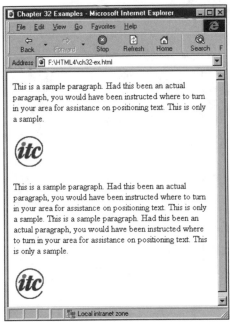

Figure 32-10: Internet Explorer doesn't even try to float anything when the float property is applied to the text, rather than to the image.

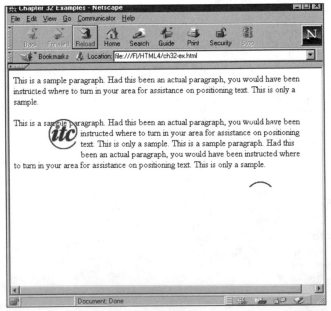

Figure 32-11: Netscape chokes if the IMG element is listed in your HTML after the P element.

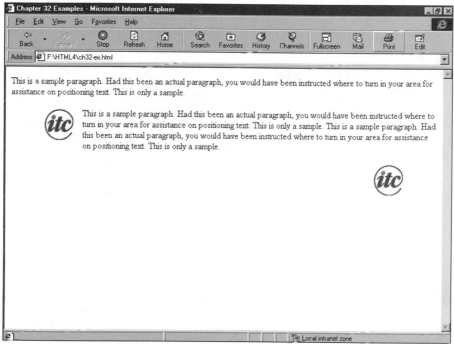

Figure 32-12: Internet Explorer doesn't seem to understand the IMG element should float next to the preceding P element, even when the IMG element will be floating to the right of the P element.

From Here

Cross-Reference

Jump to Chapter 34 and learn how to create still graphics for the Web.

Proceed to Chapter 33 and learn more cool CSS positioning tips and tricks.

Summary

In this chapter, you learned how to position text and graphics using a variety of techniques, including frames, the position property, the float property, changing margins and padding of text blocks, and changing margins of the BODY element. You also learned some of the implementation shortcomings of the two leading browsers: Internet Explorer 4 and Netscape 4.

✦　　✦　　✦

Cool CSS Positioning Tips and Tricks

In this chapter, you see more CSS positioning tricks. Specifically, you learn how to lay out your page in ways that simply weren't possible before CSS. You learn how to create newspaper columns. You see how (finally!) you can superimpose text over graphics to title your image or to annotate your image. You also learn how to create pull quotes. This chapter assumes you have read (and understood) all previous chapters about CSS.

Creating Columns of Text

You can use CSS to create columns of text. For a brief moment in time, one draft of the CSS2 specification, which is not final as this book goes to press, included a property for real newspaper columns. It enabled you to create text columns that dynamically resized themselves to fit on the page. It decided how much of the text should go in the first column and how much should go in subsequent columns, so each column was the same length. Unfortunately, this property, called `columns`, along with a host of related properties that permitted customization of columns, has been dropped from the CSS2 specification.

Fortunately, you can still create columns of text with CSS, but you simply must do more of the work yourself. To create columns of text, you must use the `DIV` element (you will recall this is used to format and group multiple block-level elements). You also need most of the following properties in your style sheet:

   ✦ **width.** This property tells the browser how wide to make each column. You can use a percentage or a value. Generally, using a percentage is safer, in case the browser window isn't open in full-screen mode.

✦ **float.** This property puts the text column either on the right or the left. Even though the only official values available to you for this property are right, left, or none, Internet Explorer does support a center value for this property.

✦ **border.** If you want to put a `border` between your columns of text, you can use one or more of the border properties to do this.

✦ **margin.** You might need either margins or padding to format your text columns to your satisfaction.

✦ **padding.** `Padding` can help provide white space between the column of text and the border, if you use one.

✦ **text-align.** You can use the `text-align` property to fully justify your text, so neither the left nor the right edge of the text is jagged. If you want the text to look like newspaper text, you definitely want to set `text-align` to justify.

Figure 33-1 shows two sample columns created using CSS.

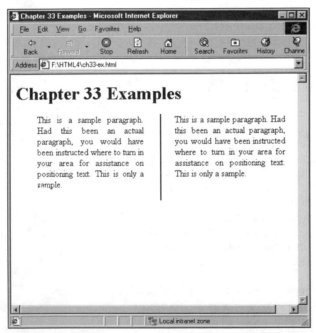

Figure 33-1: Creating text columns with CSS

The HTML used to create these columns is simple:

```
<BODY>
<H1>Chapter 33 Examples</H1>
```

```
<DIV class="left"><P>This is a sample paragraph. Had this been
an actual paragraph, you would have been instructed where to
turn in your area for assistance on positioning text. This is
only a sample.<P></DIV>

<DIV class="right"><P>This is a sample paragraph. Had this been
an actual paragraph, you would have been instructed where to
turn in your area for assistance on positioning text. This is
only a sample.<P></DIV>

</BODY>
```

The CSS used to create the columns is a bit more interesting:

```
DIV.left {
      width: 45%;
      text-align: Justify;
      float: left;
      padding-right: 0.3in;
      border-right: solid thin;
      margin-left: 1cm;
}

DIV.right {
      width: 45%;
      text-align: Justify;
      float: right;
      padding-left: 0.25in;
      margin-right: 1cm;
}
```

Notice only the left column has a border. You could just as easily have put the border on the left-hand side of the right column. In either case, you must be careful not to use the margin property to create white space on the side on which you have the border. Use padding on that side instead (remember, the border is drawn between the margin and the padding).

Netscape 4 doesn't support this implementation of the float property.

Superimposing Text and Graphics

The z-index property, mentioned briefly in Chapter 31, is just the ticket for layering text and graphics, only text, or only graphics. In Figure 33-2, the z-index property is used to superimpose text — in this case, a caption, on an image.

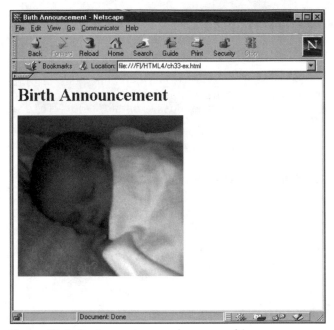

Figure 33-2: Text superimposed on a graphic

Again, the HTML is simple:

```
<H1>Birth Announcement</H1>

<img class="under" src="../images/bed.jpeg" width=295
height=286 alt="baby sleeping" border="0">

<P class="over">Cute kid, eh?</P>

</BODY>
```

The CSS uses the z-index property, which layers the element with the lower z-index value on top of elements with higher z-index values.

```
IMG.under {
      position: absolute;
      top: 10;
      left: 20;
      z-index: 300;
}
P.over {
      position: absolute;
      z-index: 100;
```

```
        font-size: 18pt;
        font-family: sans-serif;
        top: 320;
        left: 20;
        color: Fuchsia;
    }
```

The `z-index` property is not implemented in Internet Explorer 4.

Creating Pull Quotes

Not much has been written about creating pull quotes, but they can be an attractive addition to your Web page. *Pull quotes* can draw attention to a few key words or sentences that summarize a thought, thus giving the visitor a quick idea of the point of the page. This is especially important if a lot of text is on the page. Web visitors have become used to gleaning the message of the page from a combination of things, of which text is only a small part. Some visitors won't sit still to read an entire page of text unless you can grab them with a snappy quote. Pull quotes can do this for you.

Figure 33-3 shows an effective use of columns and pull quotes together.

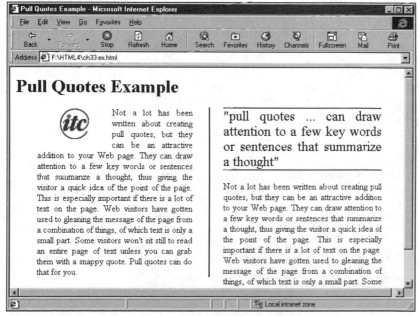

Figure 33-3: Pull quotes used in combination with columns

The HTML, as you've become used to seeing, is simple:

```
<BODY>

<H1>Pull Quotes Example</H1>

<DIV class="left"><IMG class="icon"
src="../public_html/itclogo.gif">

<P>Not a lot has been written about creating pull quotes, but
they can be an attractive addition to your Web page. They can
draw attention to a few key words or sentences that summarize
a thought, thus giving the visitor a quick idea of the point
of the page. This is especially important if there is a lot
of text on the page. Web visitors have gotten used to gleaning
the message of the page from a combination of things, of which
text is only a small part. Some visitors won't sit still to
read an entire page of text unless you can grab them with a
snappy quote. Pull quotes can do that for you.</P></DIV>

<DIV class="right">
<P class="pull">"pull quotes ... can draw attention to a few
key words or sentences that summarize a thought"</P>

<P>Not a lot has been written about creating pull quotes, but
they can be an attractive addition to your Web page. They can
draw attention to a few key words or sentences that summarize
a thought, thus giving the visitor a quick idea of the point
of the page. This is especially important if there is a lot of
text on the page. Web visitors have gotten used to gleaning the
message of the page from a combination of things, of which text
is only a small part. Some visitors won't sit still to read an
entire page of text unless you can grab them with a snappy
quote. Pull quotes can do that for you.</P></DIV>

</BODY>
```

The CSS is more complicated:

```
DIV.left {
       width: 45%;
       text-align: Justify;
       float: left;
       padding-right: 0.3in;
       border-right: solid thin;
       margin-left: 1cm;
}

DIV.right {
       width: 45%;
       text-align: Justify;
       float: right;
```

```
        padding-left: 0.25in;
        margin-right: 1cm;
}

IMG.icon {
        float: left;
        margin-left: 1cm;
        margin-right: 1cm;
}

P.pull {
        font: 18pt Helvetica blue;
        border-top: thin blue solid;
        border-bottom: thin blue solid;
}
```

The DIV.left and DIV.right rules should look familiar. The IMG.icon rule also has nothing new. Notice the CSS for the pull class of the P element doesn't use any advanced CSS properties. Notice, too, the float value of the DIV.left rule is "left." Also notice the float property of the IMG.icon rule is "left." Because the DIV element contains the IMG element (in the previous HTML), this means you can float an element within another floated element.

None of this works in Netscape 4, due to its lack of support for the float element. Figure 33-4 shows how Netscape handles this example.

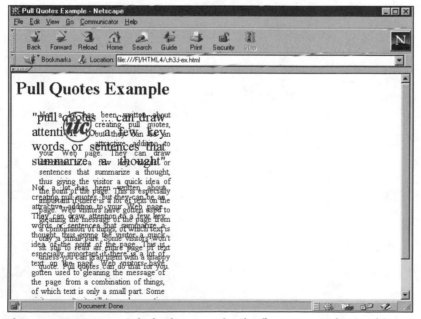

Figure 33-4: Netscape's lack of support for the float property leaves this page unintelligible.

From Here

Go to Chapter 36, Designing and Implementing Imagemaps.

Jump to Chapter 47, Introducing the Document Object Model.

Proceed to Chapter 34, Creating Still Graphics for the Web.

Summary

This chapter has given you some ideas of the interesting ways you can use the CSS properties you learned in the previous chapters. It introduced layering of text and graphics with the z-index property. It showed you how to create text columns with the width and float properties. It also demonstrated how to create pull quotes to draw attention to a phrase or sentence from a body of text. You are now fully armed to write CSS. Part VII shows you how to add sensory excitement and interactivity.

✦   ✦   ✦

Adding Sensory Excitement and Interactivity

Creating Still Graphics for the Web

You have been working with images for about 400 pages now. In this chapter, you learn how to *create* images. You learn about your choices for file formats. You also learn about color depth (bit depth) and what you can do — between file format selection and bit-depth reduction — to shrink the size of your file so it downloads quickly. This chapter also shows you how to create graphics using two popular tools, how to capture graphics you like from elsewhere, how to create image previews, and how to create transparent GIFs.

Understanding Graphics File Formats

Web browsers support — to some degree — three graphics file formats: GIF, JPEG, and PNG. All three of these graphics file formats use some form of compression to store your image.

Why compression?

Uncompressed images can be large. Consider Table 34-1, which compares image dimensions, number of colors, and file size for some sample uncompressed images.

Table 34-1
Uncompressed image file size comparison by image dimensions and number of colors

Dimensions	Colors	File size
1" x 1"	2	9K
1" x 1"	256	9K
1" x 1"	16.7 million	18K
2" x 2"	2	16K
2" x 2"	256	24K
2" x 2"	16.7 million	63K
3" x 3"	2	16K
3" x 3"	256	49K
3" x 3"	16.7 million	139K

As you can see, with file sizes like this, you would have to limit yourself to mighty tiny images, or two-color, such as black and white, images. Or, you could compress the files.

Figures 34-1 to 34-9 show these images with compression. Even though these are only black and white images, to look good, they still require a lot of shades of gray.

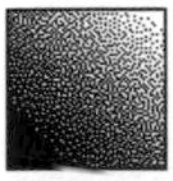

Figure 34-1: This 1×1-inch image uses only two colors: black and white

Figure 34-2: The same 1×1-inch image using 256 colors: all shades of gray

Figure 34-3: The same 1×1-inch image using 16.7 million colors

Figure 34-4: This 2×2-inch image uses only two colors: black and white

Figure 34-5: The same 2×2-inch image uses 256 colors; obviously a big improvement

Figure 34-6: The same 2×2-inch image uses 16.7 colors; notice there is no color striping as in the previous image

Figure 34-7: This 3×3-inch image uses two colors

Figure 34-8: The same 3×3-inch image uses 256 colors

Figure 34-9: The same 3×3-inch image uses 16.7 million colors, which looks nicest, but make too large of a file size

Compression options

When you implement file compression, you either have to throw away some information about the image or find a way to store the existing information about the image in a more intelligent manner. GIF files throw away some color information. JPEG files throw away some information about the image itself. PNG files store the information using a more intelligent algorithm.

GIF

GIF was the earliest format in use in inline images on the Web. Version 1 browsers could open GIF images inline, but required JPEG images be opened out-of-line. GIF uses a compression scheme — called *LZW compression* — that predates CompuServe, even though you might see it called CompuServe GIF. CompuServe implemented LZW compression, thinking it was in the public sphere and then found out it was proprietary. A lot of lawyers sorted it out.

How does GIF work? Simply, GIF indexes images to an 8-bit palette. The system palette is 256 colors. Before you can save your file in GIF format, the utility you are using simply makes its best guess at mapping all your colors to one of the 256 colors in an 8-bit palette.

Is a reduction in color depth a problem? That depends. GIF uses dithering to achieve colors between two colors on the palette. Even with dithering, however, GIF images of a sunset will have stripes of color, where a smooth gradation would be more natural. GIF images also tend to have more cartoonish colors because flesh tones aren't part of the palette. A GIF image of a drawing, say, of a checkerboard, however, will look just fine.

See Chapter 35 for a lesson in creating animated GIFs. Transparent GIFs are discussed at the end of this chapter.

System Palette. The system palette is the 256 colors your monitor will be able to display if you set your video board only to show 256 colors. These colors differ from a PC to a Mac.

JPEG

JPEG takes a different approach. JPEG, in case you are curious, stands for the *Joint Photographic Experts Group,* the name of the group that created the standard. With JPEG, you get to keep all your colors, but you don't get to keep all the data about the image. What kind of images lend themselves to being compressed with JPEG? A tree. If you take a photo of a pine tree, the acorns are in specific places, but when the image is compressed and decompressed (opened on your Web page), the computer has to approximate where those acorns went, because it had to throw away some of the data. Is this a problem? Not with most photos of most pine trees. Faces also take well to JPEG because the colors are all there; faces in GIF can look unnatural because of the color loss.

Every generation 3 and 4 browser can handle inline JPEGs. JPEGs are also ideal for showing gradient filled graphics (when the color changes gradually from one color to another). The same graphic would suffer enormously under the GIF compression because all those in-between colors wouldn't be there.

What suffers under JPEG compression? Text, schematic drawings, and any line art. Of course, with JPEG, you can select the level of compression (usually either as a percentage or as Maximum, High, Medium, or Low). You generally want to use the maximum compression level your image can handle without losing image quality. You won't know how much compression your image can handle without loss until you try it at different levels of compression.

Lossy versus Lossless. File formats that implement compression schemes that discard information about the image are called *lossy* file formats. Both GIF, which discards color information, and JPEG, which discards image information, are lossy file formats. File formats that don't discard any information about an image are called *lossless.* PNG is a lossless compression scheme.

PNG

The *Portable Network Graphics,* or PNG format, was developed exclusively for the Web and is in the public domain. The PNG format takes advantage of a clever way of storing the information about the image so you don't lose color and you don't lose image quality; it is a lossless format. The only drawback is, because the standard is so new, PNG graphics are only supported by fourth-generation and later browsers. Eventually, PNG will replace GIFs for many color-rich still image files. Only GIFs can support animation and transparency.

Understanding Color Depth

In the computer world, everything is black or white, on or off. Computers operate in the base two system, so when creating colors, your choices of colors are base two numbers. A *bit* is a representation of on or off (1 or 0). One-bit color uses a two-color palette (2^1). Two-bit color uses a four-color palette (2^2). Eight-bit color uses a 256 color palette (2^8). Thirty-two-bit color uses a 16.7 million color palette (2^{32}).

Vocabulary

Browser-safe color palette. Between the two system palettes, there are 216 colors in common. This is called the *216-browser-safe palette.* By limiting your graphics to colors from this palette, you can be sure the browser won't have to guess or dither to achieve the color you want.

Palettes

You might be thinking: *Two colors: that's not so bad. An artist can do a lot with two colors; think of the ways you can blend them.* Unfortunately, this isn't how computers work. When you select a color palette, you get only the colors in that palette, not any blends of colors in that palette.

When you create an image, you want to balance the quality of the image against the file size of the image. When you send an image file over the Internet to a Web page, you send either information about the palette or you send the actual palette. With GIF files, you send a color look-up table (CLUT) with the image. With JPEG files, you send a palette. As you can imagine, this makes the files considerably larger.

Enhancing Downloading Speed

The bandwidth conservation society was created to help with these problems. You can find their useful Web site at `http://www.infohiway.com/faster/index.html`. What can you do to insure your pages download quickly? There are a few things:

✦ limit image file sizes

✦ limit the number of images

✦ reuse images as much as possible so images can be loaded from cache

✦ use frames so only part of the browser windows need to reload

✦ use text rather than images, where possible; see Figure 34-10 for an example of changing the colors of cells in a table to approximate a graphic image

Image file sizes

You can limit image file sizes

✦ by using the maximum compression your image will take.

✦ by using the smallest bit-depth your image can stand.

✦ by minimizing the dimensions of your image on the page.

Test your pages at 640×480, 800×600, and 1028×764 to see how they will look to different visitors. Often an image that renders well at 1028×764, and doesn't dominate the page, looks huge and overbearing at 640×480.

Number of images

How many images is the right number? You may be surprised to learn that sometimes very small images with white space between them load faster than one large image.

Take advantage of white space to contribute to your images. You can use two intelligent techniques to get more image for the byte. By changing the background color to match the background color of your images, you can keep your images smaller. By anti-aliasing the text against that background to blend the edges into the background color, you can achieve the look of one large graphic with multiple small — and fast to load — images.

Reuse images

Reusing images is as simple as having a single graphic for "home" on all your pages. Have a single bullet graphic (if you can't stand to use the standard bullet) for every bullet on every page. Why does this help your pages load faster? Your browser will check to see whether an image it needs is already in cache and load the image from cache, if it can. This reduces the number of bytes that actually need to be downloaded.

Use frames

How can using frames speed download time? After the initial frameset loads, the browser will usually be loading one new frame at a time. Also, because the images are probably part of the banner and/or the navigational tools, the frame that does reload is less likely to be image-intensive.

Tip

By putting all or most of the images into one of your frames and the mostly text-based content into your main frame, you can save visitors having to load the images more than once. After the initial load, subsequent loads will be faster.

Use text rather than images

You've read this elsewhere in the book. You can use tricks when using text to make it look somewhat like an image. Consider Figure 34-10, for example. Instead of using a graphic with boxes and buttons in the left frame (this is a frameset page) for navigation, it uses a table with each cell assigned a different background color. You can assign each cell a different text color. You can even assign each cell a different font, if that would contribute to the message of the navigational tools.

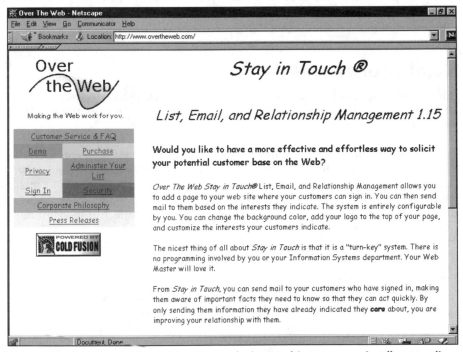

Figure 34-10: Use a table with text instead of a graphic to create visually appealing navigational tools.

Creating Graphics

If you want to create top-notch graphics, the tool of choice among professionals is Adobe Photoshop, available for the Mac, the PC, and the SGI computer. Freeware and shareware software programs also are available that perform subsets of the functions performed by Photoshop. Photoshop LE, the light version, ships with many scanners.

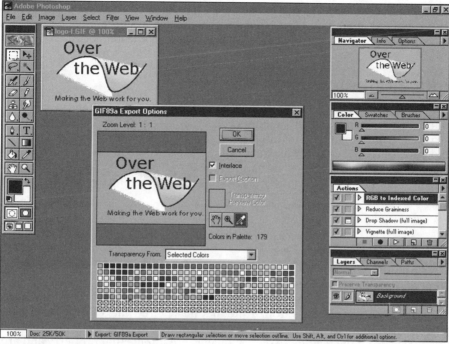

Figure 34-11: Adobe Photoshop

Essential functions

What should your graphics package be able to do? For existing images, such as photographs, you want to sharpen, blur, and perform some special effects on the image (posterize, swirl, mosaic). For images you create on the screen, you want to create your own custom palette (so you can send as few colors as you need). You also need some basic artist tools, such as a paint brush, a pencil, a spray can, and a magnifying glass for magnifying part of the image to see it better.

Regardless of whether the image is made by hand or based on a photograph or clipart, you need the following capabilities:

✦ to reduce the bit-depth of any image you want to save as GIF

✦ to index the color of the image so you can save the image to GIF

✦ to save the image as an interlaced GIF

✦ to save the image as a transparent GIF

✦ to save the image as a PNG file

✦ to save the image as a progressive JPEG, which is discussed at the end of this chapter

Progressive JPEG. Progressive JPEGs are a nice addition to a Web page. They work the same as Interlaced GIFs. Before the entire image has become downloaded, you can begin to see the image. Then the images slowly come into focus.

Free alternatives

If you aren't ready to commit to a $500 software package to get all these great functions, you can work with a number of small, free software packages and services that do many of the things previously listed for you. On the Web, you can find sites that turn your TIF file into a GIF, or make your GIF an interlaced GIF. The tradeoff is the time. Finding, learning, and using a variety of small packages to solve all your imaging needs obviously takes longer than learning one package and using it on your desktop.

Capturing Graphics

What about taking graphics you like from another site? This is generally not an okay thing to do. Unless you have explicit permission from the creator of the images — say, you are taking graphics from a site that makes free images available or you have written permission from the owner of the site — you are essentially stealing the images from the legitimate owner. Images are intellectual property and are protected by copyright laws. Most people won't take you to court, but you are still a thief.

Just because an image is on a Web page doesn't mean it is in the public domain. Yes, it gets downloaded onto your own computer (into cache), and, yes, your browser gives you the ability to save the image as a local file (using the right mouse button or prolonged clicking it on a Mac), but it still doesn't mean you own the image or the right to use the image. If you see something you like on another page, write to the page owner and ask if he or she owns the image and if you can use it. Chances are, the owner will be flattered by your request. Be sure that person owns the image or permission won't mean anything (if the image was stolen from somewhere else).

Chapter 52 discusses copyright, trademark, and other intellectual property issues at length.

Progressive JPEGs and Interlaced GIFs

Once upon a time on the Web, you had to wait for an image to finish loading before you knew what it was. Today, you can save your files using the Progressive JPEG format or the Interlaced GIF format and watch the image come into focus as it loads.

The advantage to this approach is a visitor to your site knows roughly what an image is before the entire image has downloaded. If download times are long, say, due to a poor Internet connection, the visitor to the site can actually take a link off the page before the image has finished loading without having missed anything.

Finally, these two image formats are good because the visitor participates in the download time. Instead of waiting for the page to download — sitting idly by — the visitor waits for the page to download while watching the images become clearer. This is more of a reward for waiting — and less of a sense of waiting — for the visitor.

How they work

The sense of "coming into focus" that these types of images provide is the result of the way the images are stored. Progressive JPEGs and Interlaced GIFs download only every eighth line at first, then every fourth line, then every second line, and then, finally, the odd-numbered lines. The result is the image goes from blurry to focused.

You create a Progressive JPEG or an Interlaced GIF by saving it into this format. In Photoshop, when you save a file as a GIF file, it asks you whether you want the file to be normal or interlaced. Freeware packages are also available that convert your regular JPEGs and GIFs into Progressive JPEGs and Interlaced GIFs.

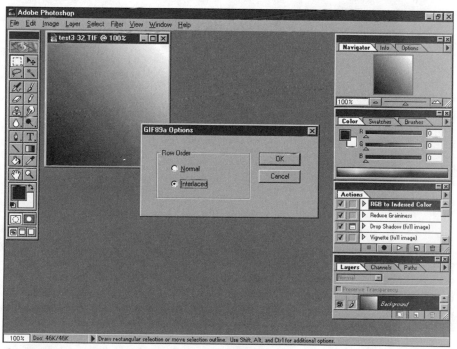

Figure 34-12: Adobe Photoshop asks you whether you want your GIF file to have rows interlaced or normal.

Using Transparent GIFs

Transparent GIFs are a wonderful invention that enable your image to blend into your background or to float over your page. The effect of a transparent GIF on a page can be magical. By setting the page background color to the same color as the outline of the image or to one of the colors of the image, transparent GIFs can contribute to a light, airy look to a page.

Transparent GIFs work by having one or more colors of your choosing set not to appear. Whatever color you set as the transparent color, depending on how you do it will be transparent, when rendered in the browser. This can result in the cut-out parts of letters also being clear — say, the hole in the middle of an *O*. The danger to this effect is if you have a part of your image that should be white — say, the whites of a cartoon character's eyes, and you set the transparent color to white and put the image on a yellow background — then the cartoon character will look like he has jaundice or hepatitis (yellow whites to his eyes). You can create transparent GIFs using The Imaging Machine (`http://www.vrl.com/Imaging`), as shown in Figure 34-13.

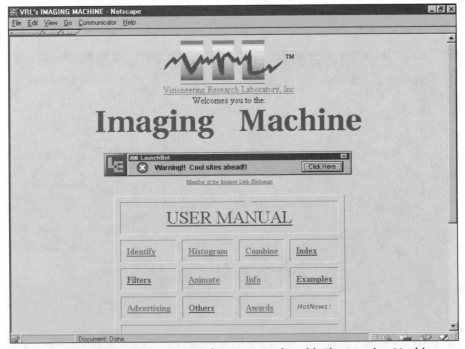

Figure 34-13: Transparent GIFs are a breeze to make with The Imaging Machine.

From Here

Jump to Chapter 38, Producing and Adding Video.

Proceed to Chapter 35, Creating Animated Graphics for the Web.

Summary

In this chapter, you learned most of what you should know to use images in your pages. You learned about the compression choices you have for images. You learned about color palettes and bit depth. This chapter also discussed clever tricks for increasing the download speed of your page, such as using frames and reusing images.

You learned a few things about creating graphics and the tools you can use to do this. You also were warned about copyright issues related to using graphics from other peoples' sites. You learned about Progressive JPEGs and Interlaced GIFs, about transparent GIFs, and about tools for creating these interesting types of images.

✦　　✦　　✦

Creating Animated Graphics for the Web

Creating an animated image for the Web is incredibly simple. Those banner ads you see with animation are both simple to create and relatively small to load, compared to old-fashioned animations. This chapter takes you through what you need to know to create animated GIFs (the most popular type of animation on the Web). It also discusses other options you have for more sophisticated animations.

Introducing Animated GIFs

Animated GIFs are an easy way to add motion to your Web page without any programming, using only the simplest of tools. Animated GIFs are like slide shows. The steps involved are simple:

1. Plan the animation.

2. Create the individual frames of the slides in your favorite image creation tool.

3. String your images together into a long "filmstrip" using a GIF animation tool.

4. Modify the animated GIF properties, such as palette information, number of times you want the images to loop (once, 20 times, or continuously), and image size.

5. Export your animated GIF from the animation tool to a .GIF file.

6. Add your animation to your HTML using the IMAGE element.

Planning Your Animation

As with anything else, planning is essential to creating effective animated GIFs. Suppose you wanted to animate a stick figure jumping up into the air, and then landing and doing a flip. Because you want this to be a loop, you also need to get the stick figure back the starting point gracefully, so the loop can begin again.

How many images do you need? Figure 35-1 is the starting point.

Figure 35-1: This is the starting point for stick art animation.

Then the figure must squat to get some momentum for a big jump. Figures 35-2 and 35-3 capture the squat and the jump.

Figure 35-2: The stick figure squats.

Figure 35-3: The stick figure jumps.

How should the stick figure land? The easiest thing would be to land the stick figure back in the squat from which it started and use this as the beginning motion for the big flip. Figure 35-2 can be reused for the landing position. This means it is time for the flipping figures. Figures 35-4 and 35-5 show the flip.

Figure 35-4: The stick figure begins its flip.

Figure 35-5: The stick figure completes its flip.

Again, the stick figure needs to land. Fortunately, the squatting figure can be reused, by just moving the squatting character over to the right in your image editor. The standing figure (Figure 35-1) can also be moved to the right in your image editor to make the stick figure stand where it should have landed. The two figures created are shown in Figures 35-6 and 35-7.

Figure 35-6: The stick figure begins its flip.

Figure 35-7: The stick figure completes its flip.

If an animated GIF weren't a loop, the animation would end there. But because the character needs to get back to the beginning, another squat and the two flipping frames, in reverse order, of course, will return it to the beginning.

Creating the Animation

Creating the animation requires a bit of artistic talent and a lot of imagination. Just as when you were a child and you created flip books of animation, each image should be only a slight variation of the previous image. You want to be careful not to use too much motion in your animation because the size of the file will grow as the number of still images in your animation grows. By limiting the dimensions of the images and the bit-depth, however, you can help limit the size of the file.

Note   Your animated GIF has *frames*. Within each frame there can be one or more *images*. You can create interesting effects by changing the size of the image in the frame to make it appear to be getting closer or farther away.

You want to follow some guidelines when creating your animations:

✦ keep all frames the same size

✦ keep colors to a minimum

✦ limit the amount of motion from one image to the next

✦ limit the number of frames

As with anything else, you need to plan your animation carefully so the effect you desire is achieved in a reasonable number of images. When you export the animation from the animation tool, you can specify the file be a vertical row of images or a horizontal row of images. The effect can be different depending on which direction you choose.

Because the previous example uses simple stick figures, creating the animation is pretty fast.

Using a GIF Animation Editor

Plenty of useful GIF animation editors are available. You can do a search on the Web to find the most recent tools available. At one site, you can create your own animated GIF banner with text of your choosing.

An easy and relatively inexpensive tool is Gamani's GIF Movie Gear 2.0 (see Figure 35-8). It is $30 shareware available from `http://www.gamani.com`. It takes care of all the settings you might want to manipulate, without requiring you to learn anything technical about animated GIFs. Everything takes place in well-documented dialog boxes.

On the CD-ROM   You can find a 30-day version of GIF Movie Gear 2.51 on the CD-ROM in the back of this book.

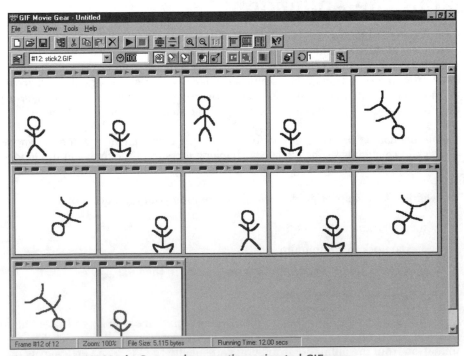

Figure 35-8: GIF Movie Gear makes creating animated GIFs easy.

In Figure 35-8, the animated GIF uses the seven still frames shown in Figures 35-1 to 35-7. Some of them are reused, which saves time in creating the images. The filmstrip is created as a horizontal strip because the action of the animations is mostly horizontal. It could have been just as easily set as a vertical strip.

You can do everything from optimizing the palette, to sizing the frames, to setting the number of loops using GIF Movie Gear. You can preview your animated GIF right in Movie Gear. When you are satisfied, you can export the file to a .GIF file for use in your Web pages.

Including an Animated GIF on Your Page

Including an animated GIF on your page is just like including any other GIF on a page. You use the IMG element. The following HTML is all you need to include the GIF, which is included on the CD-ROM:

```
<IMG src="patrice.gif" width="144" height="144" alt="stick
figure acrobatics">
```

You could also make this animated GIF a link to another page by including the IMG element within an A element.

Testing Your Animation

As with everything else on your page, you want to test your animation from your browser and from a variety of other browsers, to make sure it works as you expect. You also want to run your page through Bobby, which is discussed in Chapter 22, to make sure the download time for your page with the animation is reasonable. Finally, you want to be sure to use the alt attribute of the IMG element so visitors looking at your page with a browser that doesn't support animated GIFs know what they are missing.

More Animation Options

You can use other techniques to add animation to your page. Some of your options include:

✦ Shockwave/Flash

✦ Movies

✦ Java

✦ ActiveX controls

Shockwave/Flash

Shockwave and Flash are a proprietary animation system owned by Macromedia. To create a shockwave or a flash file, you need to use either Authorware or Director. To play a shockwave or a flash file, your site visitors need to have a special plug-in loaded.

Chapter 39 discusses Shockwave and Flash in more detail.

Movies

Another way to add motion to your page is to add a movie. The problem with most movie files is they tend to be considerably larger than animated GIF files. This means they take a lot of time to download — although you can do things to get them to start playing before they complete the download — and they take up a lot of space on your server. Movies will run in most browsers without any additional plug-ins.

Chapter 38 discusses video in more detail.

Java applets

If you are comfortable with programming, you might find Java to your liking. With Java, you can create more than just simple animations. Generally, when you work with Java, you work with a dataset and some actions on a dataset. The previous stick figure animation wouldn't be well-suited to a Java animation. Java files tend to be small, but sometimes run slowly. Additionally, the visitor to your site must have a Java-enabled browser.

Chapter 41 discusses Java Applets in more detail.

ActiveX controls

ActiveX controls can give you lots of interesting animation effects without a lot of work. The only real work involved is locating them. Plenty of ActiveX controls are available (free or for a small fee). Once you find them, you include the reference to them in your HTML and visitors to your site — if their browsers can handle it — can see your interesting animation effects with relatively little work. The downside of ActiveX controls is they install software directly on the visitor's computer. Cautious visitors won't give your page permission to install the control.

Chapter 40 discusses ActiveX controls in more detail.

From Here

Jump to Chapter 38 and learn about creating video for the Web.

Jump to Chapter 39 and learn about plug-ins you can use to spice up your Web page.

Proceed to Chapter 36 and learn about designing and implementing imagemaps.

Summary

In this chapter you learned how to create animated GIFs for your page. You need a basic image editor (anything that can create an image and save it as a GIF), a GIF animation editor, and some imagination. The most important thing is planning your animation well, so it works as you expect. You also learned about alternatives for adding animation and motion to your page.

✦   ✦   ✦

Designing and Implementing Imagemaps

Imagemaps are images with clickable regions under them. An imagemap can be a wonderful way to make a visually appealing page interactive. Or, it can be slow-to-load and confusing, if not done properly. This chapter helps you to do it right. You learn about both server-side and client-side imagemaps. You also learn about the tools you can use for creating imagemaps. Finally, you learn about testing your imagemaps and adding alternative text to increase their effectiveness.

Introducing Imagemaps

Imagemaps work by having an image with defined regions under the image. Each of those regions is associated with a link just as with the other linking elements, such as LINK and A. The browser or the server calculates the regions under the image based on the shape associated with each region, the dimensions of the region, and the anchor point of the region, which is where the region starts — usually from the upper left-hand corner of the image.

Imagemaps can be effective ways of communicating information without excessive reliance on text, possibly making a site accessible to people for whom English is a foreign language or to small children. This theory breaks down if your site design includes any destination pages that rely on text in English, which almost all sites do. In any case, you can use a large site map for a single transit page, but you risk incurring the ire of your visitors if you put too many large, slow-to-load imagemaps on your site.

Imagemap Design

Imagemaps can be a valuable addition to your site or they can be an annoyance to your site visitor. How can you know? You can review some questions to see if your application of an imagemap is likely to elicit favorable responses or to anger visitors.

1. **Did you keep the imagemap size to a minimum?** You might be thinking you want your initial imagemap to fill a screen. What size screen? You certainly want to design for a 640×480 screen, to keep the image size down and to guarantee everyone can see the whole image. Even if your image is well-compressed, you are still talking about a large image. Why not use one or more smaller images with some white space between them and plenty of white space around the margins of the page?

2. **Can you navigate around your site another way, other than the imagemap?** You definitely want to make sure another way exists. The simplest and least glamorous way is to enclose the names of the pages you are linking to within square brackets [like this].

3. **Can people with their browsers set _not_ to load images still navigate through your site?** This relates to the previous question. In the worst case, you will have visitors to your site who don't see any of your images. Can they navigate?

4. **Is it obvious what the _hot_ regions of your imagemaps link to?** Think of the average sign for a ladies room in a nice grocery store. It usually has the word _women_ (wanting not to offend women who aren't ladies?), an illustration of a wheelchair, and an illustration of a baby in a diaper. What does this tell you? Previously the sign also had a stick figure with a skirt on, but that went the way of the word _ladies_. Those illustrations tell you the bathroom is wheelchair-accessible and it has a changing station for babies. These signs are as clear as can be. The images that are part of the hot regions of your imagemaps need to be just as clear. If you have any doubt that your hot regions accurately and adequately convey where they link to, do user testing. Find people who aren't part of the Web design group, who aren't necessarily experts on your product line, and watch them click around. Can they find what they want right away?

5. **Is there `alt` text for each hot region?** The `alt` attribute should be populated for each region so if visitors have any doubt where a link goes, they can place their cursors over the region and read the `alt` text.

Server-Side versus Client-Side Imagemaps

Imagemaps can either run on the browser or on the server. They look identical, regardless of where the processing takes place. In the earlier days of the Web, when most Web pages were published by systems administrators or UNIX gurus, server-side imagemaps were the thing to do. Today, when most pages are published by clients of ISPs, server-side imagemaps are a nightmare for systems administrators. The preferred method of delivering an imagemap is with a client-side imagemap.

Server-side imagemaps usually require root permission to write to files shared by everyone on the server. You can see why that model doesn't scale well. Server-side imagemaps also put some processing that can be delegated to the visitor's computer back on the server. This doesn't fit the model of distributed computing most systems administrators are pursuing.

Client-side imagemaps are easy to create and plenty of free or inexpensive tools can help you create them. The information the browser needs is all included in the HTML or in a separate file referred to by the HTML. The imagemapping tool creates this for you based on the regions you draw on the image you are using.

Some of the HTML editors reviewed in Chapter 14 have imagemapping tools built into them.

Developing Graphics for Imagemaps

What kind of images lend themselves to becoming imagemaps? You can use any kind of image, with any shape of hot regions, but the more complex the shapes of your regions, the more work you must do mapping the image. The important thing is the regions give site visitors a clear idea of where they are linking to.

Toolbars

There is an application of imagemaps you might not have considered. Some sites use narrow toolbars with links to the essential pages on their sites. Figure 36-1 is an example of this.

The toolbar in Figure 36-1 is small and attractive. It fits conveniently between the heading of a page or the banner of a page, if there is one, and the content. The toolbar can also be placed at the bottom of the page, to facilitate navigation.

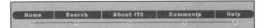

Figure 36-1: This is a toolbar as an imagemap.

Using an Imagemap Editor

Plenty of inexpensive image mapping tools are available. One nice one is MapEdit, by Boutell.com. This is shareware that can be downloaded as a 30-day trial version and can be purchased for $25. It runs on just about every platform including Win95/98/NT, Mac, and UNIX varieties.

Figure 36-2 shows MapEdit in use.

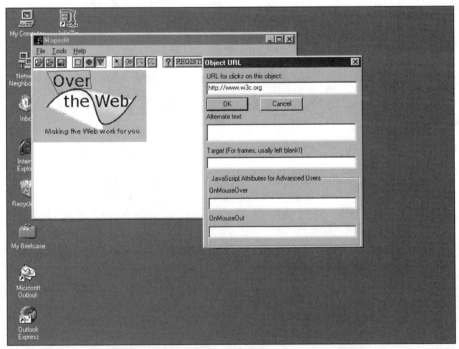

Figure 36-2: MapEdit creates clickable regions under your images.

In Depth   The major drawback to the way MapEdit works is it only opens `.htm`, `.html`, and `.asp` files, even though plenty of other file extensions might actually be Web pages (such as `.cfm`, `.cgi`, and so forth). If a lot of your Web pages have an extension other than `.html`, `.htm`, or `.asp`, you will want to find a different image mapping program.

With MapEdit, you define regions right on top of your image using either a circle drawing object, a rectangle drawing object, or a free-form drawing tool. For each region you define, you have a dialog box that requests the URL for the link, alt text for a text description of the link destination, and a target name, if the destination of the link is supposed to populate a frame.

The MAP Element

Essential to creating an imagemap are the MAP element and the AREA element. The MAP element tells the imagemap this is where information about clickable regions begins.

Map <MAP>

Start Tag:	Required
Content:	AREA elements
End Tag:	Required
Attributes:	id, class, lang, dir: defined elsewhere
	name: required; contains name associated with the usemap attribute of the IMG element
	alt: alternate text

The AREA Element

The AREA element defines the regions within the imagemap that link to other pages.

Area <AREA>

Start Tag:	Required
Content:	Empty
End Tag:	Forbidden
Attributes:	id, class, lang, dir: defined elsewhere
	shape: "rect"; some browsers support other shapes, but this is the only one in the HTML 4 spec
	coords: coordinates that define the beginning point of the shape and the dimensions of the shape
	href: URL of the link

nohref: Boolean attribute that indicates there is no link

tabindex, accesskey: see Chapter 42

alt: alternate text (recommended)

events: see Chapter 48

The Anatomy of an Imagemap

For the image in Figure 36-1, the toolbar, the HTML looks like this:

```
<A HREF="http://www.itc.virginia.edu/images/navbar.map/">
<IMG width="436" height="52" border=0
src="http://www.itc.virginia.edu/images/navbar.gif"
ismap usemap="#navbar" alt="ITCWeb" ></A>

<MAP name="navbar">
<AREA shape="rect" coords="2,11,77,43"
href="http://www.itc.virginia.edu/itcweb/home.html"
alt="ITCWeb Home">
<AREA shape="rect" coords="77,11,162,43"
href="http://www.itc.virginia.edu/itcweb/search/home.html"
alt="Search">
<AREA shape="rect" coords="162,12,260,43"
href="http://www.itc.virginia.edu/department/home.html"
alt="About ITC">
<AREA shape="rect" coords="260,12,363,43"
href="http://www.itc.virginia.edu/itcweb/comments/home.html"
alt="Comments">
<AREA shape="rect" coords="364,12,436,43"
href="http://www.itc.virginia.edu/itcweb/help/home.html"
alt="Help">
</MAP>
```

You should recognize some of the elements. To begin with, an A element is at the very top. Within this is the IMG element for the graphic used, which is the same one you see in Figure 36-1. There is also an ismap attribute, which is Boolean (meaning if it is present, it is on, otherwise it is off), which indicates this is the image for an imagemap. The next attribute, usemap, gives the URL of the map to be used. You've seen the pound sign (#) before. It indicates the map to be used is located within the current document. It could just as easily have given a file name or any other valid URL. Finally, there is the alt attribute, which you definitely want to use.

Adding Alternate Text

As you have just read, it is important to include text in the alt attribute, describing where each of your links leads. This isn't the place to give the URL; this isn't useful. This is the place to give a short text description of what will be found at that page.

Where should you include alternate text? In the AREA element for each link and again in the IMG element. The IMG element's alt text will be shown whenever the cursor is positioned at a point that isn't part of one of the hot regions. If the cursor is over a hot region, the alt text for that AREA element will be displayed.

From Here

Go to Chapter 39 and learn about incorporating plug-ins.

Jump to Chapter 41 and learn about adding Java applets.

Proceed to Chapter 37 and learn about producing and adding sounds.

Summary

In this chapter, you learned all about imagemaps. The most important thing about imagemaps isn't where the hot regions are, it's what the image contains to direct visitors to the correct links. This chapter gave you some guidelines for designing imagemaps. It also explained how to design graphics to meet these guidelines. You learned about client-side imagemaps, server-side imagemaps, and why systems administrators much prefer you use client-side imagemaps. You learned about using an imagemap editor and about the importance of adding alternate text. Finally, you learned about the MAP and AREA elements and the anatomy of an imagemap.

✦　　✦　　✦

Producing and Adding Sounds

Adding sounds to your Web pages is not particularly
difficult. There are advantages of adding sound to your
pages, but equally good reasons exist not to put sound in your
pages. This chapter talks about how digital audio works, what
sound formats work on the Web, how audio compression
works, how streaming audio differs from regular audio, how to
obtain and record sound files, how to use sound editing
software, and, finally, how to add sound to your page with the
OBJECT element and the EMBED element.

Understanding Digital Audio

Digital audio tries to represent sound, which is inherently
analog, being a wave, with ones and zeros. When you digitize
sound waves, you take samples of the wave at certain intervals.
Just as with images, you can select the precision of the sound
captured by setting the bit-depth of the sound file. Eight-bit
sound divides the spectrum into 256 levels. Sixteen-bit gives
you 65,536 levels. There is also 32-bit sound, but it is not going
to run over the Web and it is not highly accessible to client
workstations because so few truly 32-bit sound cards exist.

The quality of sound your computer produces is dependent
on five things:

1. the quality of equipment used to record the sound

2. the bit-depth of the recorded sound

3. the frequency of sampling (sample rate)

4. whether the sound is recorded in mono or stereo (the
   number of channels)

5. the quality of equipment in the machine playing the
   sound back

As with images and other types of multimedia files, the quality of the deliverable has to be balanced against the file size. You want to deliver the maximum quality sound for the minimum file size. Compression can help to some degree.

Recording equipment

Several factors figure into the quality of the sound you record. One is the recording environment. If you are going to record voice, you'll want to record in a room with good acoustics. You also need to be sure the bit-depth of the recording equipment is at least as high as the bit-depth at which you are recording. A smart system won't even let you think you can record 16-bit stereo sound on an 8-bit mono system.

Recording bit-depth

The *bit-depth* of the sound recording indicates how precisely the sound that occurs at the moment of sampling is recorded. As with color palettes, the number of sounds you can choose between is limited to one from the palette you select. For 8-bit sounds, the sampled sound will be one of 256. For 16-bit sound, the sampled sound will be one of 65,536 sounds. Table 37-1 shows bit-depth and sample rates for common types of digitized sound.

Table 37-1 Sample rates and bit-depth for common types of digitized sound				
Quality	*Sample Rate (KHz)*	*Bits per Sample*	*Mono/ Stereo*	*Data Rate (uncompressed) (KBytes/sec)*
Telephone	8	8	Mono	8
AM Radio	11.025	8	Mono	11.0
FM Radio	22.050	16	Stereo	88.2
CD	44.1	16	Stereo	176.4
DAT	48	16	Stereo	192.0

Sample rate

Sample rates are measured in kilohertz (KHz). The more frequently you sample sound, the higher the sample rate, the more like the original sound your digitized sound will sound. Of course, the more frequently you sample, the more information you have to store to represent the original sound and the larger the file size.

Mono versus stereo

The difference between mono and stereo is the number of channels of sound in the file. For stereo, there is exactly twice as much data. Why does twice as much data exist? Because you are sending two channels of information: one for the left speaker and one for the right speaker.

Do you want to use stereo sound? This depends on two things: file size and likely equipment of the end user. Do you expect site visitors to have stereo playback equipment? If not, it doesn't matter. The real question is whether the sound you are delivering is audio for its own sake, in which the quality of the sound really matters, or whether the sound is part of something bigger, in which case, mono is probably fine.

Play-back equipment

All this business about bit depth, sample rates, and mono versus stereo don't mean much if the people trying to play back your sound has an old or low-quality sound card. If people playing back your sound don't have a 16-bit sound card, they can't possibly play back all 65,536 sounds in the 16-bit spectrum. Their computers will automatically choose the next closest sound from the 256 sounds in the 8-bit spectrum. Bad speakers and a slow processor — that can't recreate the sound at the proper sample rate — can also result in inferior sound quality.

Introducing Sound File Formats

Four sound formats frequently used on the Web are:

1. **.WAV** This is the original Windows file format. Although it used to be proprietary to Windows, you can actually play it now under any of the newer browsers, even on a Mac or on UNIX.

2. **.AIF (or .AIFF) Audio Interchange File Format** This common audio file format is also cross-platform, but doesn't take advantage of any compression.

3. **.AU** The original Sun standard, it enables you to make tiny sound files.

4. **.MPEG MPEG Audio Layer 3** (.MP3) is part of the MPEG2 standard. With it, you can create small files while maintaining a pretty high sound quality. It is nonproprietary. You can achieve compression rates of 1:10 or 1:12 with CD-quality sound. On the downside, it does require a special player. A lot of record companies are using this because you can put up CD-quality files. Streamworks player will play streamed files. You also need special software to compress your audio files into .MP3 format.

Other ways exist to put sound on the Web, including Shockwave, RealAudio, and QuickTime, but they are proprietary. They require plug-in software (as does .MP3), which can inconvenience your site visitors enough so they don't bother to get the plug-in or to hear the audio files you put so much time into creating.

Introducing Streaming Audio

Streaming audio has caught on so well everyone wants to call their product *streaming*. Consequently, two possible things are meant by the term *streaming audio*. Both kinds of streaming audio enable the visitor to your site to begin hearing the audio file before it finishes downloading, which is the usual way you listen to audio files on the Web.

The first involves a special server that delivers the audio over the Web using a proprietary protocol (not HTTP) to get it to the desktop. It also requires a special plug-in for the browser. The most popular streaming audio server on the market is the RealAudio server. You can learn more about it and about the technology in general at the RealAudio Web site at www.realaudio.com.

The other kind of streaming audio does take advantage of the HTTP protocol, so for lack of a better name, it is called *HTTP Streaming*.

Streaming audio is a big improvement over traditional audio, because the sound file can begin to play before it has completed downloading. Normally, a sound file won't begin playing until the entire file has downloaded. This was part of the reason for the initial impatience with audio on the Web.

How does streaming audio work? When you save a file for streaming, all the basic file format information is front-loaded in the file. This means the first things the browser computer receives about the audio file is enough information to begin playing immediately. In a nonstreaming file, the audio file information is spread out along the length of the file, so the receiving computer can't begin to play the file until the entire file is downloaded.

If you are going to use either kind of streaming audio, you might also have to make changes to the MIME type on your server. Check with your systems administrator to see if your server can handle the MIME type you will be using.

Obtaining Sound Files

You can legally obtain public domain digital music at some sites, but many of the sources you might consider using can get you into trouble with lawyers. You may not obtain sound files by capturing music off your favorite CDs, the radio, or cassettes. You may obtain sound files by recording your own musical works or your own voice, or by purchasing licensed production music or sound effects.

Will you get caught if you use music you obtain illegally or you own legally, but you distribute illegally (and this is what you are doing when you publish music, even music you own) on the Web? Probably. There are Web agents — software programs that crawl around the Web looking for sound files belonging to different recording companies — and these agents have been successful at locating illegally distributed music being published by even the most harmless organizations.

Being hassled by a big-name law firm in New York City with a "cease-and-desist order" is only half the trouble. If you are using music because you think it adds something spicy to your site — say, the theme music from *Mission Impossible* — it will be obvious to visitors to your site, unless your site appears affiliated with the movie in some way, that you have stolen the music and are using it illegally. Does this make your site look professional? No.

Recording Sound Files

If you choose to use a professional sound-editing tool, such as Sound Edit 16, you can record directly into that. Or, you can use whatever sound-recording software comes installed with your sound card. You do need a sound card and an input jack or CD-ROM. Because you know you shouldn't record music off your CD, you won't actually be using any music from your CD collection, but you might be using *clip sounds,* which are like clip art in that you can re-use them if you purchase the CD on which they are distributed.

Figure 37-1 shows the screen for Sound Edit 16 when you are recording sound. You can set the sample rate, the bit-depth, and mono versus stereo. The controls for record, stop, pause, and so forth should look familiar, if you have ever played a CD on your computer.

Editing Sound Files and Adding Filters

Sound-editing software, unlike image-editing software, isn't usually cheap or free. One free package runs on the Mac, called SoundHack, which does a respectable job. One of the more reasonably-prices packages is Sound Edit 16, by Macromedia. What can you do with your sound files? You can add noise, remove noise, add filters, such as the effect that you were singing the national anthem in a football stadium (or in space!).

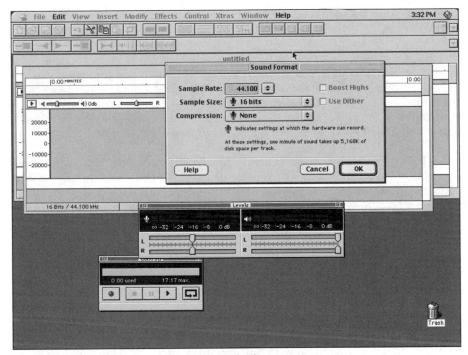

Figure 37-1: Recording sound with Sound Edit 16

Sound Edit 16 makes it easy to add special effects to your sound files. Just as easy is removing loud breath sounds from a voice recording and adding pauses. Figure 37-2 shows the list of filters you can apply in Sound Edit 16.

Compressing Sound Files

Once you have made all the trade-off decisions about your audio files, bit depth, sample rate, and mono versus stereo, you can still use compression to reduce the file size. Many compression schemes are available. Probably the two seen most often are MPEG Audio layer 3 (also known as MP3) and RealAudio.

RealAudio is proprietary, but is widely used and the compression tool is free, as is the plug-in. MP3 is not proprietary. The MPEG standard is probably the future of free audio on the Web. Their Web site (www.mpeg.org) is a treasure trove of information about audio compression and video compression, along with tools for delivering both on the Web.

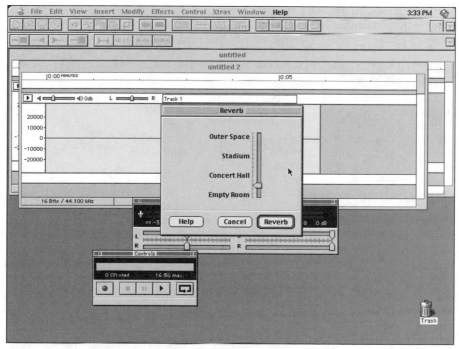

Figure 37-2: Adding effects with Sound Edit 16

Other compression standards exist, but they are not as compatible across platforms and your site visitors might have trouble playing the files back.

Adding Sound Files to Your Page

You have two choices for adding sound to your page with HTML: You can add inline sound, which starts to play as soon as your page loads, or you can add out-of-line sound that plays as a result of some action on the part of the visitor.

Inline sound

The official HTML 4 specification indicates inline sound should be created with the OBJECT element but, as of publication, the OBJECT element did not work to deliver sound in any of the major browsers. You can add inline sound using the EMBED element (which is deprecated, but works with all major browsers), with the value of the src attribute being the URL for the sound file. You'll also want to use the loop attribute to indicate how many times to play the sound in the background. If you want the sound to play ad nauseum, you can set the value of loop to "infinite" (which should probably be "ad nauseum" to make it clear to Web authors this is the effect of playing a loop of sound an infinite number of times).

```
<EMBED src="media/sound/annoying-beep.mpeg" loop="infinite"
autostart="true">
```

Or, the official way, with the OBJECT element:

```
<OBJECT data="media/sound/annoying-beep.mpeg"
type="application/mpeg">This is an annoying beep.</OBJECT>
```

Out-of-line sound

The alternative to inline sound is the preferred method of delivering sound, which is delivering sound only when the visitor to your page requests it. Many record stores on the Web let you play snippets from songs on albums they are selling. It wouldn't make sense to show a list of albums (based on your selection criteria) and then start playing snippets from all the songs from all the albums in a row. Out-of-line sound gives the visitor to your site the option to listen to your audio file or to browse in silence.

Adding out-of-line sound to your page is as simple as using the A element and pointing to the sound file with the href attribute.

```
<A href="media/sound/elvis-impersonation.wav" alt="me singing
Blue Christmas with the stadium filter">Listen to me singing
Blue Christmas at the Meadowlands</A>
```

From Here

Cross-Reference

Jump to Chapter 39 and learn about plug-ins.

Jump to Chapter 40 and learn about ActiveX controls.

Proceed to Chapter 38 and learn about creating video and adding it to your page.

Summary

In this chapter you learned how digital audio works, what the variables are that make for a better or a worse recording, and why even the best recording may play back poorly on a visitor's computer. You learned about sound file formats and why streaming audio is a good idea. You also endured a stern lecture about why you shouldn't use unauthorized sound files, even if you think you can get away with it.

This chapter discussed Sound Edit 16, which you can use both to record and edit the sound, along with adding effects and filters. As with most multimedia objects, you must understand quality decisions, sample rate, and bit depth to deliver the best quality sound for the smallest file size to your site visitors. Finally, you learned about your two options for adding sound to your Web page, and why out-of-line is probably the better approach.

✦   ✦   ✦

Producing and Adding Video

Digital video has made tremendous strides in the last five years. This is a complex science that doesn't lend itself to a thorough explanation in one short chapter. While this chapter introduces you to the fundamentals of digital video, the list of what it doesn't cover is almost as long as the list of what it does cover. This chapter defines the terms you will come across in making buying decisions about video hardware and software. More important, this chapter is full of references to other more comprehensive sources, most notably, magazines that include up-to-the-minute reviews of hardware and software.

The short version is if you are serious about putting high-quality video on your Web site, you must either devote a tremendous amount of time and a lot of money to the undertaking or you should hire a company dedicated to video compression to take your edited analog video and convert it into a Web-ready format. If you simply want to produce the kind of video — small frame size and choppy — you see on most Web pages, this chapter gets you started nicely. In any case, you need to know the vocabulary and the anatomy of digital video.

Introduction to Digital Video

Video is by nature an analog product. Converting analog video into ones and zeros has always been fraught with challenges. With still images, you have a similar problem: how to store colors and shapes as ones and zeros in as little space as possible, while retaining as clear a copy of the original image as possible. With video you have the added dimension of movement.

With film, motion is created by showing a series of still images in rapid succession. The more images in a given time interval, the more fluid the motion. If you start with clear still images and add fluid motion, you have top-quality video or film.

When digitizing video, you have to consider the size of the frame and the number of colors (2, if just black and white, 256, or even 1.7 million), as in capturing still images. Just as with film, you also have to decide how many still images will be seen in a given interval of time. With digital video, you also must think about compression of the images and the motion. That compression can take two forms: compression within each frame or compression between frames.

Expectations

If you spend a lot of time on the Web, your expectations are probably pretty humble. You'll settle for postage-stamp size video that plays relatively smoothly. This is what most sites deliver today. Fortunately, the current state of video compression and delivery can help you deliver better video than this. A number of excellent products are available for desktop computing to help you produce results at better than the postage-stamp level for a consumer's budget. The resources listed at the end of this chapter point you to the state-of-the-art technology.

Garbage in, garbage out

As with many other components, with video, the quality of the digital video you produce is highly correlated with the quality of the analog with which you have to begin. While you can take high-quality analog video and still produce junk in digital form, you can't take bad analog video and produce clear, sharp digital video.

The Anatomy of Digital Video

Digital video takes advantage of the best of imaging technologies and a thing or two from audio technologies. Digital video, at its most basic level, is a collection of still images that are sequenced. Intelligent compression schemes exist that you can apply to allow the video to be compressed both within each frame and between frames.

The problem with digital video has always been the compression versus file size trade-off. If the file is too big, the computer trying to play the file will be unable to play the frames at the rate they were intended to play. If the file is compressed too much, the computer won't have the power to decompress in real-time, producing the same playback problem.

Regardless of how you compress video files, capturing and editing video can require huge wedges of disk space for even the shortest snippet of video. Video capture, editing, and compression require special hardware and software not often found on regular desktop computers.

Three factors dictate video quality: frame rate, frame size, and compression technology. Compression technologies are discussed in their own section later in this chapter.

Frame rate

The *frame rate* is measured in frames per second. Full-motion video is considered 30 frames per second (fps). Films are 29.75 fps. Most video shown over the Web is played at 15fps. The more frames you show per second, the larger the file you need to send, but the smoother the motion.

Frame size

The *frame size* is measured in pixels and indicates the amount of screen space your movie will fill. Common frame sizes are 80×60, 160×120, 176×144, 240×180, 320×240, and 352×288. Video delivered over the Web is rarely 640×480 or full-screen because the file sizes become prohibitive. This kind of video is usually reserved for CD-ROMs or DVD.

Introducing Video File Formats

Few video formats work on the Web. These include:

✦ **.MOV.** This is the original movie format of the Web. It isn't owned by anyone and it doesn't require any special plug-ins to play it back. On the downside, it also doesn't use good compression, so file sizes can be large.

✦ **.QT.** The QuickTime architecture is owned by Apple computers. Playback requires a special plug-in, which you probably already have on your Mac, but you have to download on your PC.

✦ **.MPG.** MPEG, the standard set by the Motion Picture Experts' Group, is probably the best, nonproprietary standard available for video on the Web. Compressing your video as MPG will take a while, but the results can be pretty impressive.

Introducing Streaming Video

Streaming video works just like streaming audio. When you compress video normally, the video file contains all the movie information, frame by frame, for the entire movie in order. In parallel with this information is information about the file: the file type, the file size, and compression information. The problem with normal video compression is, for the browser to begin to play the movie, it has to receive all the information about the file first.

Streaming video moves all the information about the file to the front of the file. This means the first information the browser receives is the information it needs to get the computer ready to play a movie. Once the actual movie starts to download, the browser is ready to start playing it as it arrives. Obviously, if the file is too big or if the frame rate can't be met by the download speed, then the movie won't play back properly. Used properly, however, streaming video can be a valuable addition to your Web site.

Video Compression Schemes

Essentially two kinds of video compression exist: intraframe and interframe. *Intraframe compression* takes advantage of the kind of compression you are used to with images. It compresses each frame as well as it can. Interframe compression actually compresses between frames. The amount of *guessing* you let the computer do between frames affects how smoothly the video plays back. This also affects the size of the file. Obviously, if you can drop half the frames and still have a decent video, your file size will be much smaller.

Capturing Analog Video

Capturing analog video requires some playback device, such as a VCR if your source video is on VHS tape, or a camcorder if your source video was recorded that way. Capturing analog video also requires video in jacks on the video board of your computer. Unless you have an AV Mac, you need to purchase a special video capture board for your computer. The video capture board will likely take S-video, an 8-pin mini DIN connector or an RCA phono jack.

Capturing digital video is something of an art. Depending on the software you use, you have to adjust from 2 to about 30 settings in the software. You also want to make sure your disk is defragmented or, better yet, that you have a separate hard drive you can reformat between each session of video capture. Capturing video can take up a lot of hard drive space. Sometimes you'll want 30 frames from one part of a tape and then another 30 from another part. Finding the exact starting and ending frames can require capturing far more video and then editing it.

Editing Digital Video

Editing digital video is definitely the fun part. One relatively easy-to-use software package is Adobe Premiere. When editing, you can add interesting (or annoying) transitions from one frame to the next. Figure 38-1 shows a list of transitions.

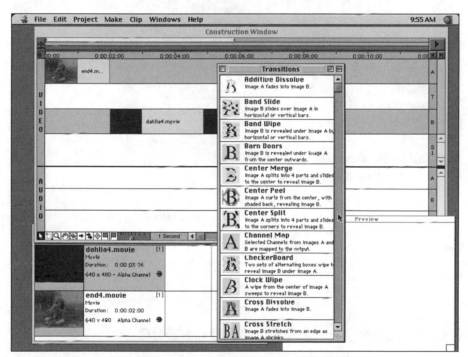

Figure 38-1: Adobe Premiere enables you to choose the transitions.

Another feature you want your video editing software to have is titling capabilities. You might want to add scrolling credits at the end or a title at the beginning. Figure 38-2 shows the movie being titled in Premiere.

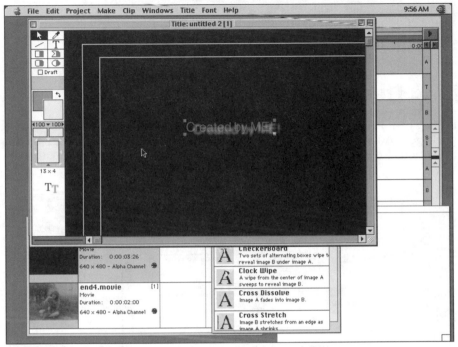

Figure 38-2: Titling with Premiere

Finally, when you are done with your editing, you kick off the compression process (see Figure 38-3) and go home for the night. Frequently, the compression will take overnight. The length of time it takes depends on the power of the computer on which you are compressing, the type of compression, the length of the video, and the frame rate.

Adding Video Files to Your Page

Video is usually added as out-of-line video, meaning to see the video, the site visitor must take an action. However, you can create inline video, which is added with the OBJECT element. The OBJECT element is discussed in depth in the next chapter. Out-of-line video is added with the familiar A element. Examples for both follow:

Inline movies

```
<OBJECT data="media/movies/cool.mpeg"
type="application/mpeg">Sorry you can't see this movie. It is
pretty cool.
</OBJECT>
```

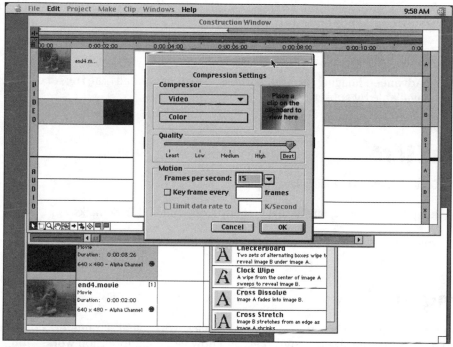

Figure 38-3: Making compression selections in Premiere

Out-of-line movies

```
<A href="media/movies/cool.mpeg" alt="Very cool movie">Click
here to see a cool movie</A>
```

Invaluable Resources

AV Video Multimedia Producer (http://www.kipinet.com) available by subscription or on newsstands.

NewMedia (http://www.newmedia.com) available by subscription or on newsstands.

Interactivity (http://www.interactivitymag.com) available by subscription or on newsstands.

Digital Video (http://www.dv.com) available by subscription or on newsstands.

Videography (no Web address; e-mail `videography@psn.com`) available by subscription or on newsstands.

Emedia (no Web address; e-mail `r.manis@mf.kable.com`) available by subscription.

Advanced Imaging (no Web address; e-mail `advancedimaging@erols.com`) available by subscription.

From Here

Go to Chapter 41, Adding Java Applets.

Jump to Chapter 52, Intellectual Property: Copyright and Trademarks.

Proceed to Chapter 39, Incorporating Plug-Ins.

Summary

In this chapter, you learned how digital movies work, what parameters contribute to the quality and size of movie files, and how video compression works. You learned about capturing and editing video, and about including video in your Web sites. Many alternative ways to creating video on your page require plug-ins. These are discussed in Chapter 39.

✦　　✦　　✦

Incorporating Plug-Ins

Plug-ins offer you the ability to add many diverse types of media to your Web pages. Many of the desktop software packages you may use daily have plug-ins that enable the results of your work to be seen on the Web. Far too many types of plug-ins exist for this chapter to list all of them. (The day this chapter was written, Netscape had 176 shipping plug-ins!)

Reviewing the OBJECT Element

The OBJECT element is one of the most versatile elements in HTML. You can use it to include inline graphics, audio, video, Java applets, and plug-ins in your page. Even though it has many attributes, you rarely need more than a few for any instance of the element. Because this book aims to be comprehensive, you can find the complete OBJECT element definition in Chapter 20.

The main attributes you need to include inline plug-ins with the OBJECT element are data and type. For example, to include an inline VRML model, you would use the following HTML:

```
<OBJECT data="media/3D/music.wrl"
type="world/wrl">

Too bad you don't have a VRML plug-in. You can
find one at <A href="http://www.netscape.com/
comprod/products/navigator/version_2.0/plugins
/3d_and_animation.html" alt="Netscape plug-in
download center">the Netscape plug-in download
center</A>.

</OBJECT>
```

Visitors to your site would have to have a plug-in that recognized the MIME type "world/wrl."

How Plug-Ins Work

It's like magic. You download a plug-in and you install it. Then you come across a page with an application requiring that plug-in and voila! Your browser runs that application just as if that functionality was built into the browser. How does the browser know which plug-in to use?

The answer is MIME types. Your computer has a list of MIME types it recognizes. Where does this list come from? Every time you install a software package, your computer adds this MIME type to the list. It uses this same list to assign a special icon to a file when you look at a file listing.

In Netscape, you can define a new MIME type manually, by going into Edit, and then Preferences, and then Navigator, and then Applications. In Figure 39-1, you see is a list of MIME types. A MIME type consists of the file extension (so the computer knows which files to associate with this MIME type on a PC or on UNIX), the category of file (audio, video, application, image, and so forth), and the application that should be used to open the file. For Macs, there aren't any file extensions.

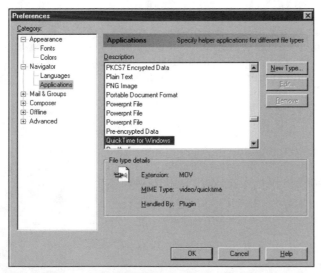

Figure 39-1: Setting MIME types manually in Netscape

In Internet Explorer, you actually set the MIME types and define new MIME types in the operating system, from any file listing (see Figure 39-2). If you go into an Explorer window (right-mouse click the Start button and choose Explore), and then select View, and then Options, and click the File Types tab, you see a list of valid MIME types for your computer.

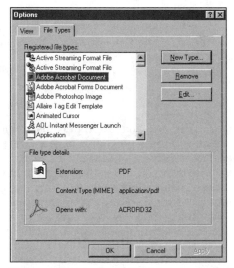

Figure 39-2: Setting MIME types manually
for Internet Explorer

Plug-in Pluses and Minuses

Plug-ins can be a rich addition to your site. They add interesting visual stimuli and are relatively quick to develop. As you read previously, adding an inline plug-in to your page is as simple as adding the OBJECT element. Adding an out-of-line plug-in to your page uses the familiar A element.

Plug-ins can do so much, so easily, why would a Web author want to avoid them at all? The major drawback to plug-ins is visitors to your site might decide not to download the plug-in and would miss whatever exciting visual/aural stimuli you prepared for them. If a large portion of the message on your page is contained in a file requiring a plug-in, then you risk failing to communicate that message to much of your audience.

Plug-ins are best used in intranets, where you have some control over (or at least a knowledge of) the setup of each of the computers likely to visit your page. The other relatively safe environment in which to use a plug-in is on a site where the same information is offered in another format, say, text. Many news sites rely primarily on text to convey their messages, but offer video or audio to supplement the message of the text.

The page design you want to avoid is a page where the only element on the page is your plug-in. This annoys people to whom you haven't yet given enough information to be convinced they should go to the trouble of getting the plug-in and installing it. The other thing you want to make sure you do is to provide a direct link to the site providing the plug-in, so people don't have to search for the plug-in.

Adding Plug-Ins

Plug-ins can be divided into several categories: 3D and animation plug-ins, audio and video plug-ins, discipline-specific plug-ins, business plug-ins, image viewers, and presentation plug-ins. Often, the effects achieved with plug-ins can be achieved equally well with either JavaScript or Java. The drawback to using programming, specifically Java, is that the development time is much longer than simply using a plug-in. Frequently you must purchase additional software to implement a plug-in. Sometimes, your systems administrator must make changes to the server to accommodate new MIME types, because the Web server must also be familiar with the MIME type.

3D and animation plug-ins

If you want to take advantage of vector graphics or 3D models, you need a plug-in for now. Future versions of browsers undoubtedly will include support for vector graphics but, even then, not all visitors to your site will have the latest browser.

Cosmo Worlds and World View

The most popular 3D plug-in is the one that has been around the longest: Cosmo Worlds by SGI (see Figure 39-3). This runs on PCs or UNIX. If you want to display 3D models on a Mac, you can use World View by Intervista. The nonproprietary standard you can use to create 3D models is VRML. Creating sophisticated 3D models without some sort of tool is difficult and time-consuming. Cosmo Create, also by SGI, is the most powerful tool for creating 3D models in VRML, the most commonly used 3D modeling language used on the Web.

Shockwave and Flash

Shockwave and Flash are plug-ins by Macromedia. Not surprisingly, these plug-ins support files created by Macromedia's own products: Director, Authorware, and Flash (see Figure 39-4). You can create impressive interactive animations and applications with Authorware and Director. Flash creates vector graphics.

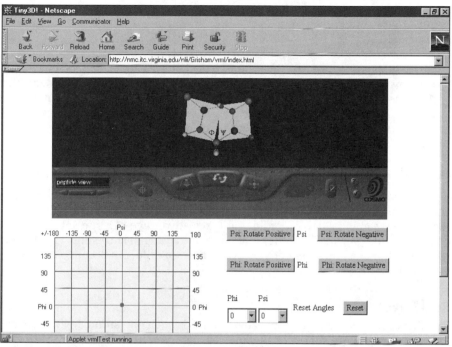

Figure 39-3: Cosmo Worlds enables you to travel through a 3D model of your creation — in this case, a molecule.

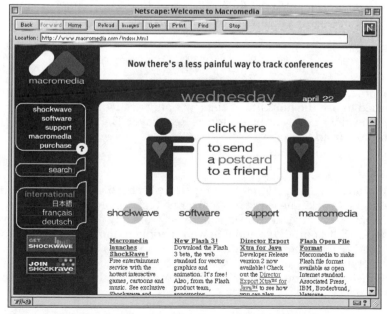

Figure 39-4: Shockwave plays Director and Authorware files.

Why would you want to use Flash as a plug-in when you can create graphics that display inline without any plug-ins? Vector graphics are an efficient way to deliver graphics to the Web.

In Depth

Vector graphics files are small because, instead of a file containing the image, the file contains only the equations that create the images (remember geometry class?). Also, the graphics created by the equations are infinitely scalable without any loss of quality. Expect to see much more of vector graphics on the Web as Version 5 browsers support this format for inline graphics.

Audio and video plug-ins

Both audio and video can be played by the Version 3 and 4 browsers without any special plug-ins. If you want to use fancier video or audio tools, however, including real-time streaming video or audio that takes advantage of a special server, you need a special plug-in. The other reason to use a plug-in is to show QuickTimeVR movies, which can be an effective way to show an object in 3D or to navigate around a space.

RealPlayer

RealPlayer by RealNetworks, Inc. kills two birds with one stone. If you are using either the RealAudio server or the RealVideo server, RealPlayer is all your site visitors need. Either of these technologies, while relatively expensive to implement, result in excellent image/sound quality delivered in real-time without those pesky download delays. Another advantage to this technology is the browser computer reuses cache when downloading the files. This means the entire video or audio file doesn't reside on the visitor's computer at any given time, saving the visitor precious hard drive space.

NetShow

NetShow is another streaming video application. NetShow is seen more commonly on sites designed to use the full suite of elements only available to Internet Explorer. NetShow does nearly as nice a job as RealPlayer The NetShow server is available at no cost from Microsoft.

QuickTimeVR

QuickTimeVR is a video application that competes with both video products and 3D modeling products. QuickTime is the original video technology used on Macs. QuickTimeVR can be effective at showing an object from any perspective. Say you are creating an exhibit of products and you want people to move the objects so they can look at the objects from all sides. How would you do this? You might create a movie of the object, as you move it (or move around it, depending on its size), but how fast should you move? What if visitors want to linger at a certain perspective? QuickTimeVR solves all this by creating a cylinder of images, woven together so viewers can turn the cylinder, looking at any angle, and then move the object so they can look at any other angle, as in Figure 39-5. The same can be done with panoramas: QuickTimeVR can create a seamless view of the Grand Canyon from the middle. In addition to giving viewers control over the speed of the "movie" and the navigation, QuickTimeVR creates relatively small files — compared to real movies — so this is a winner from every perspective.

Figure 39-5: QuickTimeVR shows an object from all angles.

Discipline-specific plug-ins

For some fields, such as Chemistry, incredibly powerful plug-ins enable you to express an idea or equation with such brevity, you just can't avoid using plug-ins. If your discipline is something other than Chemistry, look and see if there isn't some plug-in to make your life easier before you embark on a Java program to solve your display problems.

Chime

Chime by Chemscape is one of these plug-ins. You might not need to represent molecules but, if you did, this would be the product to use. Figure 39-6 shows a protein molecule that is fully navigable. The viewer can zoom into the molecule, rotate the molecule, and so forth. Sure, you could write a program in Java that would achieve these results, but not in the code required to create the same molecule with Chime.

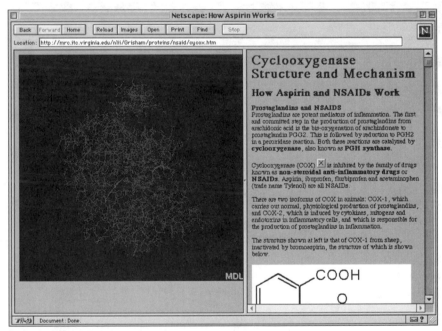

Figure 39-6: Chime shows navigable chemical models in 3D.

```
<OBJECT border="0" src="p53_dna.pdb" name="p53_1"
align="abscenter" display3D="wireframe" color3d ="chain"
height="400" width="400" color = "chain">A very cool protein
molecule</OBJECT>
```

Business plug-ins

Probably the single most popular plug-in in use on the Web is the Acrobat Reader, which displays Portable Document Format (PDF) files. *PDF* is Adobe's own format for saving formatted files for printing. Who uses PDF files on the Web? The IRS for one. Nearly any tax form you could possibly want is available on the IRS Web site (`http://www.irs.gov`). The beauty of PDF is the file can be printed the way it was intended. If you take a form and recreate it on the Web (in HTML), you can't be sure where page breaks will fall. If you take a form and create a PDF file with it, then everyone who opens it can print it to look exactly the same.

Acrobat Reader

To create PDF files, you need to purchase one of the Adobe products that creates PDF files. Adobe Acrobat ($295) is the basic package you need if you want to publish documents in PDF format. Figure 39-7 is an example of what a PDF file would look like on your screen. If you already use Adobe Illustrator to create documents, you can export directly from Illustrator into the PDF format. For most documents, which you create in your favorite word processor or scan in using OCR, you need Acrobat. Using the Acrobat Writer, you can "print" any document to PDF format. If you have a document in postscript format, Distiller converts it into PDF. You can even edit a file you have converted into PDF format using Adobe Exchange.

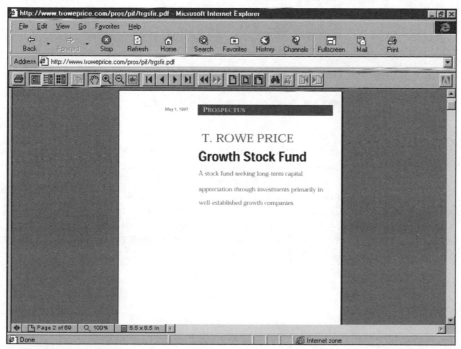

Figure 39-7: Mutual Fund companies put their IRA application forms on the Web in PDF format.

Testing Your Plug-In

As with everything else you publish on your Web site, you should test your plug-ins extensively. You want to test them from multiple platforms, using both Internet Explorer, Netscape, and AOL. In fact, you probably want to test your plug-in from a computer that doesn't already have the plug-in installed. This way, you can go through the process many of your site visitors will go through:

1. **Arrive at your page and get notification you need a plug-in.**

2. **Follow the link on your page to get the plug-in.** This link should open a new window so the visitor doesn't lose your page.

Use an A element to link with the value of the `target` attribute set to "blank" to open a new window for the plug-in page.

3. **Download and install the plug-in.** Does it require restarting the browser? You want to know this so you can tell the visitor to bookmark your page before quitting the browser. You might also want to tell the visitor on your page how long a download takes and what is involved in installation.

4. **Play the plug-in on your page.** Does it require reloading the page? You want to mention this somewhere.

Configuring Your Server

For some plug-ins, the server needs some special information. For the Chime plug-in, for example, the server must be notified some special MIME types exist. When you use a plug-in, be sure you have read all the documentation on the plug-in site, so you know if any changes must be made to your server. The odd thing about these server changes is, if you had played the same plug-in from a CD on your desktop, you wouldn't need any new MIME types. No good rule exists about when you will need to have your systems administrator make MIME type changes to your server. You have to read the documentation and do some testing yourself to see if your plug-ins will play from your server.

From Here

Jump to Chapter 43, Creating Subscriptions with the Channel Definition Format.

Proceed to Chapter 40, Adding ActiveX Controls.

Summary

In this chapter you learned about some of the powerful effects you can add with plug-ins. This chapter discussed how they work, using MIME types, and how you include them in your Web page, using the OBJECT element. You also learned about the pros and cons of using plug-ins and why you will want to include the same information in an alternate form for people who don't bother to go out and get the plug-ins. You learned about some of the hottest plug-ins on the Web today, how to test your plug-ins, and a bit about configuring your server for plug-ins that require the server to know about its MIME type.

✦   ✦   ✦

Adding ActiveX Controls

Netscape was first on the scene with plug-ins. ActiveX controls are Microsoft's answer to plug-ins. ActiveX controls, while they run under Netscape as well, were designed to add functionality to Internet Explorer 3 and higher. Just like plug-ins, before visitors to your site can use an ActiveX control on your Web page, they must download it.

What kind of functionality can ActiveX controls add to your page? Nearly any kind you can imagine and program. ActiveX controls are written in regular programming languages, using one of the Microsoft Software Development Kits (SDKs). Many ActiveX controls are available at no cost. Others can be licensed from the developers. Many resources are on the Web for finding both these kinds of controls. If you still can't find the one you want, you can write one yourself.

ActiveX controls are easily inserted into your Web page using the ActiveX control pad, which is available at no cost from the Microsoft Web site (`http://www.microsoft.com/ workshop/author/cpad/`). With the ActiveX control pad, all the parameters that need to be set for the ActiveX control you are inserting can be set using a point-and-click dialog box ad, as shown in Figure 40-1.

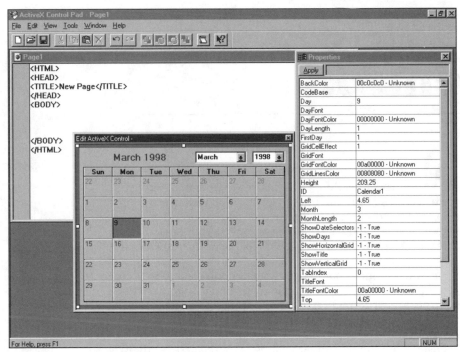

Figure 40-1: The ActiveX control pad

Introducing ActiveX

ActiveX is Microsoft's solution for letting Web developers add their own functionality to Internet Explorer. *ActiveX* is a marketing name for a set of technologies based on COM (the Component Object Model). ActiveX controls run under Netscape as well, but they require a Netscape ActiveX control to do so. Programmers, writing in traditional second-generation languages, such as C, C++, Visual Basic, and Java, can write ActiveX controls. By taking advantage of existing OLE architecture, ActiveX controls are smaller than regular programs or Java Applets, and they are optimized for download and execution. In addition, they register themselves on the client computer.

Unlike pages with plug-ins, pages with ActiveX control initiate the download of the ActiveX control. The beauty of this approach is visitors to the page don't need to know anything about anything. They can simply accept or refuse the download.

Licensing for ActiveX controls can be complicated. Some ActiveX controls are freely distributable. Some require licensing from the author. In these cases, you must get a license file to place on your server so the ActiveX control will run properly. Of course, if you write your own, you needn't worry about licensing issues.

ActiveX Pluses and Minuses

ActiveX has its advantages over plug-ins. The biggest advantage is to the site visitor. Visitors to the site needn't know anything to accept the ActiveX control. All they need to do is click the word *Accept* to have the ActiveX control download.

ActiveX controls exist that don't support specific commercial technologies. The vast majority of Netscape plug-ins were written — like the Acrobat Reader and Real Player — to facilitate distribution of proprietary media standards over the Internet. ActiveX controls tend to focus more on performing a specific task (running a clock, displaying a calendar, showing a stock ticker) than on delivering technologies.

One downside of ActiveX controls is, while ActiveX controls aren't necessarily difficult to implement, they are more complicated to implement than a plug-in. Another disadvantage of ActiveX controls, which is the same as the disadvantage of plug-ins, is people can choose not to accept the download of the plug-in. When this happens, your page might have a big hole in it or it might not function properly.

Mac Support

The biggest minus to ActiveX controls is they don't run on Macs. If you are building an application for the Internet or, more specifically, for education, this is an insuperable obstacle to using ActiveX controls. You can do something to get around this major hole in ActiveX design. See the section "Getting Around the Mac Problem" later in this chapter.

Understanding the ActiveX Security Model

How safe is it to use ActiveX controls? That depends. The ActiveX security model relies on the goodwill of the ActiveX control programmer. ActiveX controls are inherently dangerous. The ActiveX security model enables the programmer to have full and free control of your computer. This makes ActiveX controls powerful. They can read, write, and edit files. This also makes ActiveX controls potentially *very* dangerous. Because ActiveX controls have unrestrained access to your computer, no limit exists to the damage they can do. There is no logging of the actions ActiveX controls take, so there is no way later to trace which controls, if any, caused system problems you are having.

The Microsoft answer to the cavalier approach ActiveX controls take to security is all controls will be digitally signed by the distributor, and you, as the site visitor, have the power to accept or refuse controls, based on whether you trust the distributor. Is this enough? No. What if the programmer, whom you trust, accidentally leaves a security hole on your system and another site you go to knows about this and takes advantage of it? Once you accept an ActiveX control, it gets installed on your system and stays there. Any site you subsequently arrive at can use this control, even if you never granted it explicit permission to do so.

What does all this mean to you as a Web developer? It means you want to be careful about using other ActiveX controls you come across — even if you think they're perfectly safe — because you may unwittingly contribute to problems on your visitors' computers. It also means you will understand why so many people who come to your site choose not to accept your controls. Visitors need to look after the integrity of their own computers.

When can this security model be a good thing? If you are developing for an intranet, you can write ActiveX controls that perform powerful actions on client computers, without having to install that software manually on every computer. Be sure to test your controls carefully, especially if they affect the file system at all.

Finding ActiveX Controls

Chances are, you'll start your foray into using ActiveX controls by using ones others have written. Lots of places are on the Web where you can find sources of controls. Some of these controls have licensing costs associated with them, but you can find out about this when you identify the controls you want to use.

Dozens of sites consider themselves resources for ActiveX controls. One place to start is the Browser Watch site (http://browserwatch.internet.com/activex.html). Although you may find 20 sites that list controls, you will find they all list basically the same controls. Browser Watch does a nice job of directing you to the control without numbing your senses with visual clutter and advertising in the process.

In Depth

Publicizing your own controls. If you find no one has written the control you need and you are brave enough to take this on yourself, you might want to have your own control listed on these sites. Each site has its own form for submitting your ActiveX control information.

Incorporating ActiveX Controls

There are two parts to including an ActiveX control on your page, once you identify the one you want. The first involves the OBJECT element. You insert the ActiveX control with the OBJECT element, which you've seen before (defined in Chapter 20). Even though over a dozen attributes exist for the OBJECT element, most of the time, you only need four of them. You also need an indeterminate number of PARAM elements.

```
<OBJECT id="Calendar1" width=372 height=279
 classid="CLSID:8E27C92B-1264-101C-8A2F-040224009C02">
  <PARAM name="_Version" value="458752">
  <PARAM name="_ExtentX" value="9843">
  <PARAM name="_ExtentY" value="7382">
  <PARAM name="_StockProps" value="1">
  <PARAM name="BackColor" value="12632256">
  <PARAM name="Year" value="1998">
  <PARAM name="Month" value="3">
  <PARAM name="Day" value="9">
</OBJECT>
```

In the previous example, which inserts the calendar ActiveX control into your Web page, only four attributes of the OBJECT element are needed.

```
<OBJECT id="ShockwaveFlash1" width="192" height="192"
 classid="CLSID:D27CDB6E-AE6D-11CF-96B8-444553540000">
  <PARAM name="Movie" value="">
  <PARAM name="Src" value="">
  <PARAM name="WMode" value="Window">
  <PARAM name="Play" value="-1">
  <PARAM name="Loop" value="-1">
```

```
    <PARAM name="Quality" value="AutoLow">
    <PARAM name="SAlign" value="">
    <PARAM name="Menu" value="-1">
    <PARAM name="Base" value="">
    <PARAM name="Scale" value="ShowAll">
    <PARAM name="DeviceFont" value="0">
    <PARAM name="EmbedMovie" value="0">
    <PARAM name="BGColor" value="">
</OBJECT>
```

In the previous example, which inserts the Shockwave ActiveX control, again only four attributes are needed.

Tip

The `classid` **attribute.** Where do you get that long, nasty `classid` attribute? You get this information, which is the unique identifier for that ActiveX control, from the owner of the control. Depending on the licensing of the control, you can sometimes copy the source of a control you find on a page you like. If licensing restrictions exist, then this approach won't work and the control won't run on your page.

Defining Options (Parameters)

How many parameters do you need for an ActiveX control? This depends on the control. For some controls, no parameters exist. For others, there can be ten or more. You can find out about the parameters you have to set wherever you find out about the control.

How do you set parameters? With the PARAM element, as shown in Table 40-1.

Table 40-1 Parameter (PARAM)		
Start Tag:	required	
Content:	empty	
End Tag:	forbidden	
Attributes:	id	document-wide unique ID; optional
	name	name of the parameter; defined by the ActiveX control
	value	value associated with the parameter specified by the name attribute
	valuetype	how to interpret the value: data or ref or object; data is the default, ref indicates the value is a URL, object indicates the ID of another object defined in this page
	type	MIME type of parameter

Getting Around the Mac Problem

The easiest thing you can do is to nest OBJECT elements. Place the OBJECT you most want your visitors to use in the outermost OBJECT element. Then, after your PARAM elements, place the next OBJECT element you would want them to use. Finally, within your last choice OBJECT element, you can include alternate text explaining what they are missing.

```
<OBJECT id="ShockwaveFlash1" width=192 height=192
 classid="CLSID:D27CDB6E-AE6D-11CF-96B8-444553540000">
  <PARAM name="Movie" value="mymovie.dcr">
  <PARAM name="Src" value="">
  <PARAM name="WMode" value="Window">
  <PARAM name="Play" value="-1">
  <PARAM name="Loop" value="-1">
  <PARAM name="Quality" value="AutoLow">
  <PARAM name="SAlign" value="">
  <PARAM name="Menu" value="-1">
  <PARAM name="Base" value="">
  <PARAM name="Scale" value="ShowAll">
  <PARAM name="DeviceFont" value="0">
  <PARAM name="EmbedMovie" value="0">
  <PARAM name="BGColor" value="">
        <OBJECT name="veryshocked.dcr"
type="application/futuresplash">
This is a very nice Shockwave animation. You should consider
downloading the plug-in for this at <A
href="http://www.macromedia.com" alt="Macromedia">the
Macromedia site</A>.
      </OBJECT>
</OBJECT>
```

Testing Your Control

In every chapter, when this book discusses testing your work, you hear you need to test from more than one browser. This is extra important when using ActiveX controls because they weren't really designed to run in Netscape. ActiveX controls also aren't natively supported in AOL or in IE browsers prior to Version 2. To test your control, you want to start by testing your control from a computer that doesn't already have the control installed. This is the only way to check and make sure the control downloads and installs itself properly. You also want to test your control on multiple PC operating systems to make sure it works properly. Because ActiveX doesn't run on Macs reliably, you needn't worry about testing it on a Mac, but you will want to include alternate text between your OBJECT begin and end tags explaining what the viewer is missing.

From Here

Jump to Chapter 48 and learn about another way to make your pages interactive: with JavaScript.

Proceed to Chapter 41 and learn about Java Applets.

Summary

In this chapter you learned about the pros and cons of ActiveX controls. You learned how they differ from plug-ins and how the security model (or lack thereof) works.

You also learned ActiveX controls aren't your best choice if you anticipate any of the visitors to your site might be using Macs. This chapter gave you resources for finding ActiveX controls on the Web and for publicizing your own, if you choose to write any yourself. Finally, you learned how the OBJECT element and PARAM element are used to define an ActiveX control within your Web page. Testing an ActiveX control is similar to testing a plug-in.

✦   ✦   ✦

Adding Java Applets

Java! What technology has produced more hype than Java? Is it merited? Will it really change the face of computing? This chapter won't cover much about that, but it can help you understand what Java applets can do for your Web page today. It explains how Java differs from plug-ins and ActiveX controls, the other ways of adding extra functionality to your Web page. You learn about the Java security model, which is much stricter than the ActiveX or plug-in security model. You also learn how to insert a Java applet into your page.

Introducing Java

Java is a way to add additional functionality to your browser. Because it downloads within the browser page and doesn't operate outside of the browser's operating space, it doesn't require permission from the page visitor before it can run. Visitors can set their browsers not to accept any Java applets, but this isn't all that common. As long as visitors to your page have a Java-enabled browser and the patience to wait for the applet to start, they will get your Java applet.

Java is a nonproprietary software standard developed by Sun Microsystems. Java is an open standard, intended to take the best of C++ — stripping out the most convoluted parts, such as memory management, which Java handles automatically — and simplifying it. Java is fully supported in both Microsoft Internet Explorer and Netscape Navigator.

Java is what is called an *object-oriented programming language.* Note two things about this catch phrase: First, *object-oriented* means a program is designed around the data. This only means something if you understand the old way of programming—procedure-oriented programming—where the program was designed around what it did, not around the data. Second, Java is a programming language. Java is not for the faint-hearted. If you are not a programmer, this probably isn't how you want to begin. JavaScript, which is completely unrelated to Java, is a better starting point for aspiring programmers.

Two kinds of Java actually exist: server-side Java and client-side Java. This chapter only discusses client-side Java, which is inserted into your page as an applet. Server-side Java enables your page to talk to a database or to perform advanced server functions. Server-side Java doesn't have all the constraints on what it can and can't do that client-side Java has. Server-side Java uses the full power of the Java programming language.

Java Plusses and Minuses

Why would anyone want to use Java? Java is a safe way to add limited functionality to your browser. Java uses a much tighter security model, so people are less worried about what kind of damage it will do to their computers. Consequently, more people have their browsers set to accept Java applets than have their browsers set to accept (or are willing to accept) ActiveX controls.

So, what can Java do? It can read the local file system, meaning it can show you the contents of a local file, and it can perform animations. Java can create new windows within the existing browser and it can perform certain actions based on the position of the mouse.

The biggest drawback to using Java applets is you have to write a program. The beauty of the Web and the reason it has grown so fast is that creating Web pages doesn't require any special programming skills or training. Anyone can write HTML, as this book shows. Java applets return to the programming model of delivering functionality. When you program, you have to test thoroughly to make sure there aren't any unintended consequences to your actions. With HTML, most of the mistakes you can make are immediately visible and easily corrected.

Programming Java is time-consuming and requires special skills. It is often faster to find a plug-in or ActiveX control to do the same thing or to find a way to provide comparable functionality without programming.

The Java virtual machine

Why else might you not want to use Java? Speed, or lack thereof. Java is a clever programming language, but this cleverness results in decreased performance in a network environment. Java is designed to run on any platform. When you compile Java (as you normally do with any programming language), instead of being compiled into machine language, which is specific to the platform on which you are compiling, Java is compiled into byte-code, which is generic and platform-independent.

That byte-code is what is sent over the network to your browser. Your browser has a virtual machine built into it that compiles the byte-code into machine language before it runs. The time saved by the programmer in writing the code only once and having it run on every platform is spent by everyone who ever tries to run the program on his own virtual machine.

The Just-In-Time compiler

Virtual machines, through the use of Just-In-Time compilers, are getting faster. Perhaps as desktop machines get faster you won't notice the time it takes to run the byte-code through the virtual machine to get the machine code but, today, it is slow. Some of your site visitors will get impatient and stop the download, not understanding why it takes so long.

Understanding the Java Security Model

The Java security model is much safer for the casual Web visitor. While the ActiveX security model and the plug-ins security model rely on the intelligence of the user and the goodwill and competence of the programmer, the Java security model relies on the sandbox.

Everything that takes place within a Java applet takes place within a sandbox that constrains the Java applet. The Java applet can't act on anything outside of this sandbox in any permanent way. What can a Java applet do?

✦ Access the CPU

✦ Work within the limited space the browser uses

✦ Read input from the mouse or keyboard when the mouse has clicked within the applet window

✦ Work within the browser's windowing system

✦ Create new windows within the browser

Where can even this tight security fail the user? If the sandbox security is not implemented properly by the browser developers, then the Java applet could presumably take advantage of any security hole they created.

Overall, the Java security model is much tighter than the ActiveX security model. ActiveX can write to your file system, potentially corrupting essential system files. Java can't touch your file system. Java can view your file system, but can't make any changes to it.

Java Development Tools

Many Java development tools are on the market. Two with wide popularity for good reasons are Microsoft's Visual J++ (see Figure 41-1) and Visual Cafe for Java by Symantec (see Figure 41-2).

Microsoft Visual J++ isn't completely compatible with Netscape. Sun Microsystems writes the Java standard. Microsoft's standard isn't completely compatible with Sun's standard. To make matters worse, Netscape is behind on the Java standard, meaning Netscape 4 requires a patch to run the 1.1 Versions of Java.

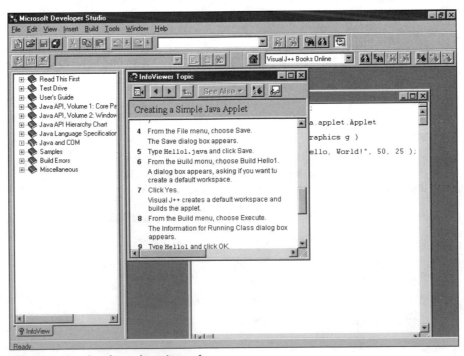

Figure 41-1: Visual J++ by Microsoft

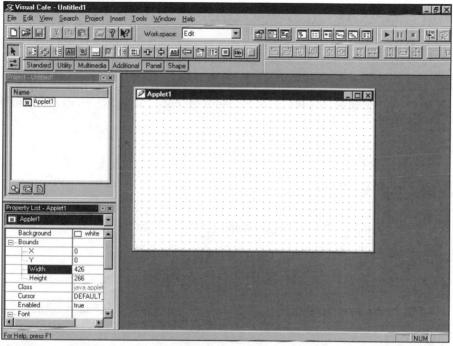

Figure 41-2: Visual Cafe for Java by Symantec

If you do anything that is more than a basic applet, you must choose which browser it runs on because they are so incompatible. Also, for anything more than the basic sandbox application, you need to get a digital signature (which gives you more control over the system, like an ActiveX control), from Verisign. If you want digital signatures for both Microsoft and Netscape, you have to buy both separately. Then you have to get the digital signature tool from either Netscape or Microsoft (each is application-specific).

Java SDK

You can get the software development kit (SDK) at www.javasoft.com. It has all the libraries, instructions, and Java tools that work on the command line. The JavaSoft site is the place to go for information about writing Java and adding Java applets to your pages.

Incorporating Java Applets

Not surprisingly, Java applets can be included in your Web page with the OBJECT element (defined in its entirety in Chapter 20). Before HTML 4, Java applets were routinely inserted with the APPLET element, but that is deprecated in HTML 4. Because the OBJECT element doesn't work with every browser, this chapter gives you examples of how to include an applet with both the APPLET element and the OBJECT element.

```
<APPLET code=graph.class width=760 height=470>
<PARAM name= "title"    value = "Hanes-Woolf Kinetics">
<PARAM name="xLabel" value = "[S]">
<PARAM name="yLabel" value = "[S]/v">
<PARAM name="xUnits" value = "mM">
<PARAM name="yUnits" value = "sec/micro-mole">
<PARAM name="imageName" value = "hw.gif">
<PARAM name="scaleX" value = ".2">
<PARAM name="scaleY" value = ".01">
<PARAM name="quadrants" value = "2">
</APPLET>
```

You only need a few attributes of the OBJECT element for your Java applet definitions. Implementing an applet with the OBJECT element isn't supported yet in either Netscape 4 or Internet Explorer 4.

```
<OBJECT
classid="http://nmc.itc.virginia.edu/nlii/grisham/kinetics/hw/
graph.class" width=760 height=470 type="application/java-
archive">
<PARAM name = "title" value = "Hanes-Woolf Kinetics">
<PARAM name = "xLabel" value = "[S]">
<PARAM name = "yLabel" value = "[S]/v">
<PARAM name = "xUnits" value = "mM">
<PARAM name = "yUnits" value = "sec/micro-mole">
<PARAM name = "imageName" value = "hw.gif">
<PARAM name = "scaleX" value = ".2">
<PARAM name = "scaleY" value = ".01">
<PARAM name = "quadrants" value = "2">
</OBJECT>
```

Defining Options (Parameters)

As with ActiveX controls, Java applets take parameters in the PARAM element. Important to note is the PARAM names must exactly match what the Java applet is looking for. The values assigned to these names must also be of the correct type.

See Chapter 40 for a more thorough explanation of how the PARAM element works.

Testing Your Applet

Testing on your Java applet needs to be performed on both your local workstation (before you include it on your page) and on your Web page. The best place to do your first round of testing is in the Java development tool you use.

When you are confident your Java applet does what you want it to do, you can upload it to your server. Your Java applet must reside in a directory with execute permissions. Most of your pages only require read permission, but because the Java applet is executable code, your directory also must permit execution. If your applet won't run at all, check with your systems administrator to see whether you have execute permissions on that directory.

As with everything else on your pages, you should test your Java applet from a variety of platforms, from more than one browser. If any unusual behavior occurs in any of these environments, you should warn visitors and refer them to a configuration that works. Not every implementation of Java on every platform works consistently.

Introducing Server-Side Java

What can you do with server-side Java? Server-side Java enables your Web pages to interact with your Web server. Pretty much anything you can do with CGI (Common Gateway Interface) scripts, Perl, or server-side JavaScript, you can do with server-side Java. Using the JDBC (Java database connector), you can have your Web page communicate with a database, returning dynamic pages based on the information entered. You can also create and read files on the server.

 If you already know Java, this may be a way to perform server functions, such as those discussed in Chapter 42, Creating Forms, or in Chapter 46, Building a Secure Site for Web Commerce. Many of the back-end tools you can purchase for your server, including some that perform database access, are written in Java.

From Here

Go to Chapter 44, Accessing External Databases.

Jump to Chapter 48, Introducing JavaScript (which bears no relation to Java except to confuse a lot of people).

Proceed to Chapter 42, Creating Forms.

Summary

Java applets can add functionality to your pages. They generally adhere to a tight security model that doesn't permit them to do any damage to your machine. Signed applets can be given (by you) permissions to act on your machine like ActiveX controls. Unfortunately, Java isn't yet truly cross-platform; applets you write to run under Internet Explorer won't necessarily work under Netscape. Chapter 44 discusses how you can access external databases with your form data. Server-side Java is one technology that enables you to do this.

✦　　✦　　✦

Creating Forms

The face of the Web changed dramatically when Web forms became possible. Unfortunately, forms haven't changed much since then. This chapter teaches you about all the basic controls forms can include. It covers how forms processing works, what your choices are, and what you can do with the data you collect.

In addition to all the existing form fields you've seen before, HTML 4 introduces a few new form-related elements, including the feature that enables you to link a field to the caption for that field. This chapter discusses all these new elements with examples.

Introducing Forms

Forms are a way of collecting information from your site visitors. What you collect, how you collect it, and how you process it vary from site to site and from application to application.

How does it work?

1. You place data-entry fields on your Web page. They can include text fields, radio buttons, check boxes, text area fields (for more extensive data entry), and other buttons, such as submit and reset buttons.

2. Your site visitors fill in the fields from their own computers and click a button.

3. The information typed by the visitor is sent over the Internet to your server.

4. Your server takes action on the data.

5. Ideally, you provide your visitors with a screen confirming you have received the data and that some action will be taken on the data.

You can do fancier things, such as send a confirming message by e-mail, sending yourself a notice that someone is using your form, or entering the data this visitor submits directly into a database.

Understanding Form Processing

Before you start designing your form, consider what you want to do with your data. The form design is visual, but until you know how you are going to use the data, you probably don't want to request the data.

What can you do with the data you collect from a form? All options fall into one of three categories:

1. Save the data for further processing.

2. Return information to the visitor.

3. Take other action (such as financial transactions).

Saving the data for further processing

You might want to do this if you require people to register for your site or if you want to collect names for a mailing list. You could store the data in a database to verify the visitor is registered before giving access on subsequent visits. You might run a raffle on your page with a prize randomly awarded to people who sign in to your site. You might require people to sign in before they download your free software or newsletter. In any case, you need to collect certain data and store it on your server — either in a database or in a flat file.

Return information to the visitor

You could perform processing based on the data. For example, you might search through a list of books to find books that match the visitor's list of favorite types of stories. If the processing doesn't require any input from the server, then this processing is better performed using client-side processing. If, however, your processing requires access to data that resides on the server, such as a search of a card catalog, a search of a site index, or a search of an inventory database, then you can use the data provided by the visitor to perform server-side processing against existing data.

This is probably the most common and acceptable use of forms on the Web. People aren't as likely to question or resent providing information when they can expect to get information they are seeking. You need to be reasonable with what kind of information you require your visitors to enter. Few people will give you a social security number or credit card information to do a site search.

Take other action

If someone comes to your site to purchase something, that visitor will expect to provide certain types of information, including personal information, payment information, and shipping information. One of the processing decisions you must make is whether you will collect and retain the payment information on the server or whether you will send the information offline to a place where it is less vulnerable to be reached by hackers. In either case, you'll collect information using a form, or a series of forms, and all your site visitor will normally receive back is confirmation the purchase was completed.

Cross-Reference

For more information about collecting and processing information about site visitors, see Chapter 46, Building a Secure Site for Web Commerce.

Inserting the FORM

There are two parts to the form: the first is the FORM element and the second is the fields or controls that accept data. Without a FORM element, your form may appear to look just right when you test it, but it will never work.

Form <FORM>	
Start Tag:	Required
Content:	Inline elements
	Form field elements
End Tag:	Required
Attributes:	id, class, lang, title, style: previously defined
	action: the URL of the script for processing the data or a mailto address if the action is just to mail the data
	method: how the data is to be sent to the script
	enctype: what types of files will be accepted if one or more of form fields accept file uploads
	target: the target name of the frame within the frameset, if your script is a frameset
	events: see Chapter 48

The two attributes you see used most frequently are action and method.

```
<FORM method="dosomething.cfm" action="post">
... form fields here ...
</FORM>
```

Action

Action tells the form where to send the data it collects. Without an action, your data won't be sent anywhere. Ideally, your action will be the URL of a file containing a script that does something with this data or the URL of a page containing server-side processing.

If you start sniffing through other people's HTML (using view source in your browser), you will notice a lot of action attributes don't call scripts. What they do instead is send e-mail, using the mailto: method. How does this work? Instead of a URL, you specify your e-mail address preceded by "mailto:." This tells your browser to send this data to your e-mail address.

Is this a good thing? It depends. This is easy to do. You can have a "functional" form on your Web page in minutes. But does this really do you any good? Not if you expect a high volume of traffic to your site. If a lot of people use your form, you may soon be inundated by data you don't have the capacity to process. If you expect only a few people to complete your form each week, then you may have time to process this data manually.

The bottom line is you should have a real script to process your data if you expect to do anything serious with your form.

Method

The `method` attribute indicates how you want the data to be sent. Your choices are "get" and "post." When you use the "get" method, you send the data as part of the URL. You are limited to 100 characters with the "get" method. This means if you have a lot of form data or if your form data might approach 100 characters — and one text area could exceed 100 characters if you don't set it up properly — then you can't use the "get" method.

With the "post" method, no limits exist on the number of characters you can send. Also, the values of all the input fields aren't displayed on the location line of the browser, the way they are with the "get" method. Generally speaking, the "post" method is the preferred method of sending form data to a script.

In Depth   Have you ever noticed when you do a search at a search engine that the URL in your location window gets very long with strange codes? This is because search engines use `method="get"`.

Adding Controls

Controls are the generic name for all the form fields you can add to your page: the second necessary component of the form. You can add nine types of controls. They do everything from enabling a person completing your form to enter text to accepting yes or no answers from that person, to enabling that person to choose one or more items from a list you provide. Controls also give you the buttons the person completing your form needs to click to submit the data.

You must know what type of data you need to receive from your form before you create controls. Table 42-1 shows what controls can help you collect values for each type of data.

Table 42-1
List of Controls by Type of Data Desired

Type of Data to Be Collected	What Will Be Displayed on the Form	Control to Use	Value String Returned to Script
text data to be processed or evaluated	text entry field the size of which is defined using the `size` attribute	INPUT type="text" name="text1"	text1="the text entered"
text data (as lengthy comments)	a large text area field for data entry the size of which is defined using the `rows` and `cols` attributes	TEXTAREA name="textarea1"	textarea1="very long text string. May include punctuation."
text data that needs to be protected from view, such as password data	text entry field, but characters typed appear as either asterisks or dots	INPUT type="password" name="password1"	password1="visible text"
yes/no data (actually returns a value only if the value is "yes")	check box unchecked unless the `checked` attribute is present	INPUT type="check box " name="box1" value="yes"	box1="yes" (returned only if the box is checked)
one value from a short list of choices	radio button unchecked unless the `checked` attribute is present	INPUT type="radio" name="set1" value="first"	set1="first" (returned only if the radio button is checked)
one value from a long list of choices	drop-down list of choices	SELECT name = "dropdown1" OPTION value= "first"	dropdown1
multiple values from a long list of choices	scrollable list of choices; the visitor must hold down a special key while selecting every choice after the first; list will be the length specified in the `size` attribute; must include multiple attribute	SELECT name= "dropdown1" size="8" multiple OPTION value="first" OPTION value="second"	dropdown1="first, second"
upload a file	text entry field for name of file along with a Browse button to view files on the client computer	INPUT type="file" accept="application/ msword"	contents of file will be uploaded to server if `enctype` attribute is included on `FORM` element

(continued)

Table 42-1 (*continued*)			
Type of Data to Be Collected	*What Will Be Displayed on the Form*	*Control to Use*	*Value String Returned to Script*
button	submit form, reset form, or take other action	INPUT type="submit" or INPUT type="reset" or INPUT type="image" alt="click to submit" or BUTTON	no data is sent; buttons execute actions but do not send their own data; they just cause the other data to be sent or cleared

INPUT Element

The most general type of control is the INPUT element. The INPUT element is incredibly flexible. It can be used to create standard text fields, password fields, check boxes, radio buttons, submit buttons, reset buttons, file input fields, hidden fields, image fields, and general purpose buttons.

Input <INPUT>

Start Tag: Required

Content: Empty

End Tag: Forbidden

Attributes: id, class, lang, dir, title, style: previously defined

name: name to be associated with this data when it is sent to the script

value: value to be sent for this form field

alt: alternate text to be associated with this form field

checked: Boolean variable used to indicate a check box or radio button should be checked when the page is painted

disabled: Boolean variable used to indicate a check box or a radio button should be grayed out when the page is painted

readonly: Boolean variable that allows a text or password to be seen, but not edited

size: indicates the size of the field for text and password fields when the page is painted

maxlength: indicates the maximum number of characters that will be accepted as data for text and password fields src: URL of images for fields that have images associated with them

usemap: URL of imagemap to be used for client-side imagemaps

tabindex: the number of this field in the tabbing order

accept: for file uploads, this is the list of MIME types that will be accepted

accesskey: the shortcut key associated with this field for accessibility

events: see Chapter 48

Type attribute

The INPUT element is incredibly flexible, thus the long list of attributes that are associated with it. Because you will never need all these attributes in one instance of the INPUT element, it makes more sense to discuss the INPUT element by type. Each of the type values are associated with their own different fields.

Text

The text value for the type attribute is what you use to define text input fields. The other attributes you might want to include are:

name So the value of this field entered will have a name when it arrives at the script. If only one field is in the form, a name isn't necessary.

size The size of the field you want the site visitor to see on the screen, when the page is painted.

maxlength The maximum number of characters you are willing to accept as the value of this field.

alt Alternate text you want associated with this field.

tabindex The number you want this field to be in the tabbing order.

accesskey The keyboard character you want associated with this field as a shortcut.

Note

This is not yet implemented in any of the major browsers. Also, it is not yet clear how this shortcut key will work if the key you assign to the shortcut is already a shortcut key for the browser. For example, Ctl-R (or ⌘-R on a Mac) will reload the page in most browsers.

Password

When you want a text input field to accept data you don't want anyone else to see, that is, password data, you can use the password value for the type attribute. The other attributes you might want to include are the same as those you might want to include for the text type value.

Tip

If you need to have a visitor enter a password, you probably want to include two password fields to enable the visitor to retype the password. You might also want to include a JavaScript to check and make sure the value of both password fields is the same before leaving the page. This will save you the trouble of doing server processing to confirm the password.

Cross-Reference

See Chapter 50 for a JavaScript example that checks the value of data entered.

Check box

The check box value for the `type` attribute enables you to take a yes or no answer from the person completing the form. Note, if a check box isn't checked, either by you when you define the check box or when the visitor completes the form, then *no data* is sent for this field. This means you won't actually receive "yes" or a "no" as an answer to a question. If the question is "May we sell your e-mail address to spam merchants?" and you associate this check box with the name "spam," then you will only receive the field called *spam,* with whatever value you give it in the value attribute if the box is checked. If the person does not check the box, the field "spam" won't be sent to the script at all.

You will want to include at least a few of the following attributes when you define a check box:

name So the script will know to what question or statement the person indicated yes.

value If you want a particular value associated with this field name. Because the field is only sent when the value is yes, the name and value pair will always be the same when they are sent. But for some scripts, having the name and value pair is more convenient than having only the field name.

alt Alternate text you want associated with this field.

checked If you want the check box to be checked when the page is painted by the browser, then you want to include this Boolean attribute.

disabled If you want the check box field to be grayed out when the page is painted, then include this Boolean attribute. You can then enable the field later using JavaScript and the document object model, as explained in Chapters 47 and 48.

tabindex The number you want this field in the tabbing order.

accesskey The keyboard character you want associated with this field as a shortcut. See the previous note on `text` type fields for more details about this.

Radio

A *radio button* is similar to a check box, in that the site visitor can't make up the value of the field. But unlike the check box, the radio button—or rather a set of radio buttons—enable you to give the visitor a choice of one option from a list of options. Radio buttons are created in sets. When one button of a set is checked, then the other buttons in that set can't be checked. A good example of this is payment information: either you are paying by Visa, Mastercard, or American Express. Radio buttons are perfectly suited to collect this type of data.

You create a set of radio buttons by assigning the same `name` attribute to all the buttons. Then, so you know which button was associated with which value, you assign a unique value to the `value` attribute of each radio button. For three buttons in a set, the skeletal HTML might look like this:

```
Which of the three colors in the United States flag is your
favorite?<BR>
<RADIO name="flag" value="red" checked> red
<RADIO name="flag" value="white"> white
<RADIO name="flag" value="blue"> blue
```

In the previous example, the button next to the word "red" is checked. One of the three values will be sent with the field name "flag" to the script. The site visitor cannot leave this field blank.

You may also want to include the `alt`, `disabled`, `tabindex`, and `accesskey` attributes, which are defined in the previous Check box section.

File

You can let site visitors upload files to your server, such as images or resumes, using the file value of the `type` attribute. This is actually a bit trickier than the other types of the `INPUT` element because you must be sure to include the `enctype` attribute for the `FORM` element or it won't work. The `accept` attribute of the `INPUT` element limits the MIME types your server will accept. Telling people what types of files they can upload is a good idea, so they won't get an unhelpful message from the server and think your form is broken.

Note   File uploading with the file `type` of the `INPUT` element doesn't work with all servers. Check with your systems administrator to see whether it will work on your server. It does generally work with NT servers.

Uploading files is easy for visitors if they are using any of the late version browsers, except for Internet Explorer 3. IE 3 has a bug and won't display the "Browse" button next to the text entry field. This means visitors must type in the exact path name of the file on their computers for the upload to work. Of course, a patch is on the Microsoft site, but this is little solace to your visitor who can't figure out how to use your form.

The following HTML shows the essentials for creating a form that accepts files for uploads. In this example, the Web page is for an employment agency. It only accepts resumes in Microsoft Word format. The `get` method will not work with file uploads.

```
<FORM action="upload-resume.cgi" method="post"
enctype="multipart/form-data">
```

```
Upload your resume by finding it on your local hard drive,
using the Browse button below. Remember that your resume must
be in Microsoft Word format, with a filename that includes
.doc.<BR>

Full name as it appears on the resume: <INPUT type="text"
name="full_name" size="30" maxlength="50"><BR>

Social security number: <INPUT type="text" name="ssn" size="15"
maxlength="11"><BR>

Resume file: <INPUT type="file" name="resume" size="30"
accept="application/msword"><BR>

<INPUT type="submit" value="Send Your Resume Now!">

<INPUT type="reset" value="Reset Form">

</FORM>
```

Notice in the previous form, no special action is required to create the "Browse" button for the file upload. The browser creates this automatically when it sees the input type is file.

Hidden

What is the point of putting a hidden form field on your page? After all, who can fill in a field if it's hidden? Actually, a *hidden field* isn't really a form field, but a way to pass data from one page to another. For many good reasons, you may want to pass data from one page of your site to another. For example, you may have asked for information from the visitor already on a previous page that you don't want to ask for again. By using a hidden field, you can pass that data onto your script without the visitor even being aware of it. You might also include a hidden field to ensure the script is really receiving data from your form, rather than from another page (someone trying to break into your system). Or, if a script is multipurpose, you might include a hidden field to tell the script which action, from the multiple actions it can perform, you want it to take.

In any case, your basic hidden field looks like this:

```
<INPUT type="hidden" name="this_page" value="page1.html">
```

The hidden field doesn't show up on your page at all. You would have to view the source for the page to know the field is even there. Also, the hidden field must be placed between the FORM element's begin and end tags or it won't be sent with the rest of the data.

Submit or reset

Input types of submit or reset create buttons that either submit the form data to the script indicated in the action attribute of the FORM element or reset all the fields to the values you assigned to them using the value attributes.

You can specify what text appears in your button by setting the value attribute. The following code shows three different ways to create a submit button that says "Purchase!" on it. The GIF file called "purchase-image.gif" contains an image that says "Purchase!"

```
<INPUT type="submit" value="Purchase!">

<INPUT type="image" src="images/purchase-image.gif"
alt="Purchase!">

<BUTTON type="submit">Purchase!<IMG src="images/purchase-
image.gif" alt="Purchase!"></BUTTON>
```

Image

The *image value* of the type attribute enables you to create a submit button that uses an image instead of just text to be the button. This can be more visually appealing, but it can also be more confusing. People are used to buttons on the Web looking a certain way. Unless you make your image look *buttonish,* you risk having people complete your form and then not knowing how to submit the data.

Creating an image button is easy:

```
<INPUT type="image" src="images/accept.gif" alt="Accept">
```

Button

The button value of the type attribute is yet another way to create a button on your page. In case you lost count, this is the fourth way to do this using the INPUT element alone! The *button value* of the type attribute is a way to execute client-side scripts, rather than the standard submit or reset actions of the other buttons.

Client-side scripts usually use JavaScript or VBScript. One type of button you might want to include would be a button that checks to make sure a password meets your criteria. By including a button labeled "Check Password" next to two password entry fields, you can perform this type of verification on the client's machine even before you send the data across the network.

The following HTML shows how you might do this. The JavaScript in this example is called "TestPasswords()". What it does is confirm the passwords in both password fields match each other and are of a certain length, don't use the same letter repeatedly, and a few other things. If the password doesn't pass the tests, a message is returned to the visitor with instructions on which rules weren't met.

```
<FORM action="password-change.cfm" method="post">

Enter your old password here: <INPUT type="password" name="old-
password" size="12" maxlength="12"><BR>

Enter your new password here: <INPUT type="password" name="new-
pwd1" size="12" maxlength="12"><BR>

Please re-enter your new password: <INPUT type="password"
name="new-pwd2" size="12" maxlength="12"><BR>

<INPUT type="button" value="Check new passwords"
onclick="TestPasswords()">
<INPUT type="reset">
<INPUT type="submit" value="Submit passwords for change">

</FORM>
```

BUTTON Element

To add a bit more confusion to the whole discussion of buttons, in addition to the four ways you can create buttons using the INPUT element, the W3C has created the BUTTON element. New to HTML 4, the BUTTON element is supposed to give you more flexibility in creating buttons. It is hoped the browsers will implement the BUTTON element in such a way that both text buttons and image buttons actually recess when clicked, the way most menu buttons do in normal desktop applications.

Button <BUTTON>

Start Tag:	Required
Content:	Inline elements
End Tag:	Required
Attributes:	id, class, lang, dir, title, style: previously defined
	name: name to be associated with the data sent to the script (optional)
	value: value sent to the script (optional)
	type: submit, reset, or button
	disabled: for use with JavaScript and the document-object model
	tabindex: a number assigning the tabbing order through form
	accesskey: shortcut key to access button for accessibility purposes
	events: see Chapter 48

Why would you ever use the BUTTON element when you can create buttons in four other ways, including buttons with images in them? The BUTTON element is far more flexible than any of the other ways of creating buttons. Additionally, the INPUT element's variations of buttons don't actually depress on the page the way people expect button to depress when they are clicked. HTML 4 specifies browsers should support the BUTTON element by having a button take action when it is clicked.

The BUTTON element has several attributes, but you rarely need more than the type attribute. Defining a button with the BUTTON element is different from defining a button with the INPUT element because the BUTTON element takes content. It also requires an end tag. You include an image as the button in the BUTTON element by including the IMG element between the start tag and the end tag. You should also include text in the content so, if for some reason the image doesn't load, text is available to indicate what the button does.

Two examples of buttons created with the BUTTON element follow:

```
<BUTTON type="submit">Click here to submit!<IMG
src="images/submit.gif"></BUTTON>

<BUTTON type="button" onclick="ValidateForm()">Validate form
before submitting</BUTTON>
```

SELECT, OPTION, and OPTGROUP Elements

The HTML 4 specification tremendously enhances what you can do with the standard drop-down list, known in HTML as the *select list*. The select list is created with the SELECT element and the OPTION element. HTML 4 introduces the OPTGROUP element, which enables you to group OPTION elements so your standard drop-down list looks more like a directory listing than like the drop-down lists you are used to seeing, with a single, long listing of all the options.

Figure 42-1 shows two types of select lists. The first is the standard select list with a drop-down box. You can select one item from a list that can be as long as you wish. The second shows a select list that actually looks like a scrollable list. Notice eight lines are visible. In this list, you can choose more than one from the eight items. As of publication, none of the major browsers supported the OPTGROUP element, so you have to see how this is supported on your own desktop.

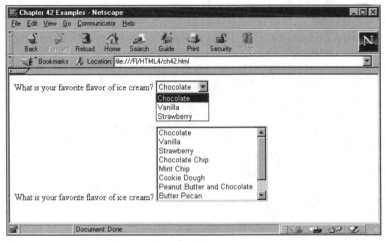

Figure 42-1: Two different types of select lists

SELECT Element

The SELECT element is the structure in which you build a select list. A select list should have a name, but doesn't generally demand any of the other attributes available to it. A SELECT element must have at least one OPTION element in it.

Select <SELECT>

Start Tag: Required

Content: OPTGROUP, OPTION elements text

End Tag: Required

Attributes: id, class, lang, dir, title, style: previously defined

name: name associated with the value or values returned to the script

size: if this is to be a scrollable list instead of a drop-down list, you must specify the number of rows to be visible with the size attribute

multiple: Boolean value that indicates more than one value may be selected; must be used in conjunction with the size attribute

disabled: for use with JavaScript and the DOM

tabindex: indicates tabbing order in form; a number

events: see Chapter 48

Two examples of the SELECT element in action appear later in this section.

OPTION Element

For each item on the select list you want your visitors to be able to select, you need an instance of the OPTION element.

Option <OPTION>

Start Tag:	Required
Content:	Text
End Tag:	Optional
Attributes:	id, class, lang, dir, title, style: previously defined
	selected: indicates the drop-down list or scrollable list will begin with this item in focus or highlighted
	disabled: for use with JavaScript and the DOM
	label: to be sent as the value of this selection; should be used if the contents of the OPTION element are too long to be useful for processing
	value: the initial value of the choice; normally the same as the contents of the OPTION element

The OPTION element is straightforward. For each item you want in your drop-down list, you create an OPTION element. In the example in Figure 42-1, the following HTML was used to create the drop-down list.

```
What is your favorite flavor of ice cream?
<SELECT name="test1">
      <OPTION>Chocolate
      < OPTION >Vanilla
      < OPTION >Strawberry
</ SELECT >
```

Using attributes

If one of the flavors had been called "Very Berry Razzmatazz Strawberry" and you didn't want to send all this information to the script, you could have used the following OPTION element (in addition to the previous ones).

```
<OPTION label="Strawberry">Very Berry Razzmatazz Strawberry
```

If you don't include a label attribute, the contents of the OPTION element will be sent as the value selected. Notice, even though an end tag is optional, it isn't generally used.

If you wanted the select list to start off with the word "Vanilla" in view, instead of just having the first OPTION element in the list in view, you could have used the selected attribute.

```
<OPTION selected>Vanilla
```

OPTGROUP element

The OPTGROUP, once it is fully implemented, will make select lists much more powerful and flexible. The OPTGROUP is intended to work like the drop-down menus you see at the top of most applications. It is a way of organizing your select lists.

Option Group <OPTGROUP>	
Start Tag:	Required
Content:	OPTION elements
End Tag:	Required
Attributes:	id, class, lang, dir, title, style: previously defined
	disabled: for use with JavaScript and the DOM
	label: to appear in the select list as the title of this group

HTML 4 does not allow for nested OPTGROUP elements, but it won't be surprising to see the major browsers implement it anyway. Currently, none of the major browsers implement the OPTGROUP element.

Unlike the OPTION element, where the label attribute is optional and is used only if the contents of the element are too long to send and process, the label attribute on the OPTGROUP element is necessary if you want the group heading to appear in the list. Also, unlike the OPTION element, the visitor can't select the label of the OPTGROUP as the value to send to the script. The OPTGROUP only leads to a list of options. All the selectable options must be in OPTION elements.

If you wanted to create a select list with the following groups:

"What is your favorite frozen dessert?"

Ice Cream

Chocolate

Vanilla

Strawberry

Chocolate Chip

Mint Chip

Cookie Dough

Peanut Butter and Chocolate

Sorbet

Raspberry

Lemon

Lime

Frozen Yogurt

Vanilla

Chocolate

Peanut Butter

Raspberry

the HTML would be:

```
What is your favorite frozen dessert?
<SELECT name="test3" multiple size="8">
      <OPTGROUP label="Ice Cream">
      <OPTION>Chocolate
      <OPTION>Vanilla
      <OPTION>Strawberry
      <OPTION>Chocolate Chip
      <OPTION>Mint Chip
      <OPTION>Cookie Dough
      <OPTION>Peanut Butter and Chocolate
      </OPTGROUP>
      <OPTGROUP label="Sorbet">
      <OPTION>Raspberry
      <OPTION>Lemon
      <OPTION>Lime
      </OPTGROUP>
      <OPTGROUP label="Frozen Yogurt">
      <OPTION>Vanilla
      <OPTION>Chocolate
      <OPTION>Peanut Butter
      <OPTION>Raspberry
      </OPTGROUP>
</SELECT>
```

TEXTAREA Element

The TEXTAREA element is a way to accept free-form text from your visitors. If you want to accept suggestions or lengthy text, this is the control to use.

Text Area <TEXTAREA>

Start Tag: Required

Content: Initial text to appear in TEXTAREA

End Tag: Required

Attributes:	id, class, lang, dir, title, style: previously defined
	name: name associated with the value or values returned to the script
	rows: number of rows of text permitted
	cols: number of columns of text visible
	disabled: for use with JavaScript and the DOM
	readonly: shows contents of TEXTAREA element, but doesn't allow editing
	tabindex: number indicating tab order in form
	accesskey: shortcut key for accessibility
	events: see Chapter 48

Text areas are easy to create. To define one that has 4 visible rows and is 60 columns wide, with initial text of "enter your comments here," you would use the following HTML:

```
<TEXTAREA name="comments1" rows="4" cols="60">Enter your
comments here.</TEXTAREA>
```

LABEL Element

The LABEL element is one of the elements new to HTML 4. Its absence has been noted. When you create most form controls, such as text fields, select lists, check boxes, there is some text, such as the question to which the control is the answer, that isn't attached in any way to the actual control. The LABEL element enables you to attach that text to the control.

Why would you want to attach text to a control? So site visitors can click the text, as well as the control (such as a tiny check box), as they can when they are in most desktop applications. Because the text associated with a control may not be immediately adjacent to a control—when using tables for formatting, for example, associating text with a control is a little bit tricky.

Label <LABEL>	
Start Tag:	Required
Content:	Text
End Tag:	Required
Attributes:	id, class, lang, dir, title, style: previously defined
	for: indicates the ID value of the control with which it is associated

accesskey: shortcut key for accessibility

events: see Chapter 48

The LABEL element (not to be confused with the label attribute of the OPTION and OPTGROUP elements) is attached to the text you want associated with a control. Here are the steps involved in assigning text to a control:

1. Use the id attribute of the form control to assign an ID to the form field.

2. Place the text you want associated with the form control within a LABEL element.

3. Assign the for attribute of the LABEL element to match the value of the id in the form control.

Here is a relatively complex example using tables for formatting a form.

```
<FORM action="do-something.cgi" method="post">

<TABLE>
<TR>
<TD align="right"><LABEL for="fname">Please enter your first
name</LABEL>
<TD><INPUT type="text" name="first_name" id="fname">
<TR>
<TD align="right"><LABEL for="lname">Please enter your last
name</LABEL>
<TD><INPUT type="text" name="last_name" id="lname">
<TR>
<TD align="right"><LABEL for="spam">May we sell your personal
data to spammers?</LABEL>
<TD><INPUT type="check box" name="spam" value="yes" id="spam">
<TR>
<TD align="right"><LABEL for="comments">Please enter any
comments you have about our site</LABEL>
<TD><TEXTAREA name="comments" id="comments" rows="4"
columns="40">Enter your comments here</TEXTAREA>
<TR>
<TD><INPUT type="submit" value="Send this now">
<INPUT type="reset" value="Clear">
</TABLE>

</FORM>
```

Notice the id and the name can be the same, but they needn't be the same.

FIELDSET and LEGEND Elements

The FIELDSET and LEGEND elements work together; they are both new to HTML 4. The FIELDSET is strictly a structural element; its presence or absence doesn't affect the way your page is rendered. The LEGEND element is an added convenience for visitors "seeing" your Web page with their ears.

Fieldset <FIELDSET>

Start Tag: Required

Content: LEGEND element

Inline elements

End Tag: Required

Attributes: id, class, lang, dir, title, style: previously defined

Legend <LEGEND>

Start Tag: Required

Content: Text of the legend

End Tag: Required

Attributes: id, class, lang, dir, title, style: previously defined

accesskey: shortcut key for accessibility

Neither of these elements would be difficult to implement. The FIELDSET element should surround related fields so they are grouped. The LEGEND element immediately follows the FIELDSET element with a descriptive title for the FIELDSET.

Form Processing Options

Today, more options for processing your data are on the server than this book can cover. Just a few of the options available to you include:

Common Gateway Interface Scripts (CGI scripts). This is the oldest type of server-side processing. You can write your program/script in Perl or C, or by using a shell script. This is still the most common type of script running on UNIX servers.

Server-side JavaScript. JavaScript is a widely known scripting language. It can, in fact, be used for full-scale, object-oriented programs. Netscape has introduced servers that include server-side JavaScript processing. Because of the popularity of JavaScript, other Web server manufacturers are sure to follow suit.

Server-side Java. Java has almost caught up with the hype associated with it when it was first introduced. You can use Java on your server to perform many form-processing functions. If you know Java and your Web server supports server-side Java (Microsoft Internet Information Server does not), then this is a good option. If you don't know Java, much easier ways exist to accomplish server-side processing of forms.

Cold Fusion. This is not yet a mainstream product, but it should be. Cold Fusion, by Allaire, is the easiest way to add server-side processing to your pages. In only minutes, you can have a form on your page that collects data into a database and sends out confirmation mail. New features are constantly being added to this product to make it even more useful.

Active Server Pages. This is the Microsoft standard. If you are already running the Microsoft Web server (Internet Information Server), and you are using Microsoft Office, implementing Active Server Pages on your site is only a small step. Front Page 98, the Microsoft Web authoring tool, makes this even easier.

Dealing with Form Data

What is the best way to handle form data? With a script or program. Ideally, you will know how you are planning to use each piece of data you request before you request it. Then, you will have a program or script in place that acts on the data when you first publish your form onto your site.

When you create your form, you need to give some thought to how each piece of data returned will be used. If you don't plan to look at or respond to comments, don't ask for them. You will probably find that if you have multiple-word responses to questions in select lists, working with shortened versions of these responses using the label attribute in the OPTION element will be easier, as shown here:

```
<OPTION label="girl colors">Red, pink, fuschia, yellow, or
orange
```

Where the question might have been: "In what colors do you prefer to dress your daughter?"

If you make use of check boxes or radio buttons, remember that a value is only sent when the check box or radio button is checked. This means even from a long set of check boxes, it is possible no values will be returned. Your script must be able to deal with the absence of data as data in itself.

What if you don't know how to write a script, but you still want to collect data? You can use a mailto:.

Mailto:

With your e-mail address as the action of the script, a *mailto*: will send the field names (as set by you in the name attributes) and their values to you via e-mail. The problem with this technique is, while you have the data, you don't have the data in any particularly useful form. All that is returned to you is a list with each line containing a field name and the value entered for that field.

```
last_name = Miller
first_name = John
email = miller@somewhere.org
color = blue
flavor = Mint Chip
music = Meatloaf
```

Even worse than having the data returned in a difficult-to-process format, the mailto: doesn't always return the fields in the order they were completed. For these reasons, the mailto: should be used only when you really do plan for the data to go no further than your mailbox.

From Here

Cross-Reference

Jump to Chapter 44 and learn about accessing external databases.

Jump to Chapter 46 and learn about building a secure site for Web commerce.

Proceed to Chapter 43 and learn about creating subscriptions with the Channel Definition Format.

Summary

Forms enable you to take input from your site visitor for processing on your server. If you want to add a site search, sell anything, or take a survey, you must learn how to put form fields on your page. A lot of flexibility exists in creating forms. Also, some new elements are part of the HTML 4 specification, which give you more control over buttons and enable you to group your fields. And more accessibility features are in HTML 4, such as the `tabindex` attribute and the `accesskey` attribute.

The most important thing to know about forms is you must have plans for processing your data or you are wasting your visitors' time in collecting data. Before you put up a form, be sure you have plans to use the data wisely.

✦   ✦   ✦

Creating Subscriptions with the Channel Definition Format

Push technology was going to revolutionize the way people used the Web. Despite the hype, push technology never materialized as promised. One of the problems with early push technology was no standard existed. If you wanted to use push technology—which is better entitled *smart pull*—you had to get a client that supported it and then the server from which you wanted to pull also had to support it. Or, you could use an agent to search the Web for you, pulling down new pages that met your criteria. Either way was cumbersome and nonstandard.

The *Channel Definition Format* (CDF) is an attempt by Microsoft to standardize the world of push technology. Some push vendors have signed up to support the standard, but Netscape has not. Netscape promotes its own proprietary subscription format, which this book does not discuss at length.

Introducing Push Options

What is push technology? *Push* (also known as *server-push/client-pull*) *technology* is the idea that citizens of the Web can define their interests on their own computers in some sort of channel client. Then that client can go out to the Web at regular intervals and download only the material of interest to Web citizens. This idea was good, but it hasn't been implemented with much success.

What push has come to mean in actuality is the same citizens of the Web (sometimes called *Webizens* or *Netizens*) subscribing to channels that interest them. At regular intervals, the client software can go only to those channel sites and download the latest updates to pages.

Nothing new

The truth about push technology is nothing new is there. Push uses the HTTP protocol to get pages off a server (or multiple servers). The difference between push and other means of getting at Web pages is with push, you set up some preferences up-front (or as you go) and the pages are *precached* (a fancy expression for downloaded) to your client during low-use times. You don't have to wait for the download; it happens in the background.

Two kinds of push technology exist — those using keywords and those using subscriptions. In *keywords,* you define what keywords you want included, just as if you were at a search engine page performing a regular search. The client that sits on your computer communicates during nonpeak hours with a central server, which has agents crawling and indexing the Web. Your client queries that server for any new pages it has found during the last period you defined in your search criteria (day, week, month, whatever). It returns the page descriptions and URLs of all the pages matching your criteria, just like a search engine. Then you can scroll through the pages it returns and load any that sound interesting into your browser. As you can see, there isn't much being *pushed* in this scenario.

The second kind of push technology uses channels.

Channels

Here the television analogy is appropriate. *Channels* are Web destinations to which you can subscribe. Why would you subscribe? So the contents of a site can be precached onto your desktop during nonpeak hours (when the Web won't keep your unattended computer waiting). What can a channel include? Anything that goes into a Web page can be part of a channel. A channel is simply a preloaded bookmark. If you do take advantage of channels, you'll find when you go to a channel to which you subscribed, it loads instantly. Why? Because it is loading from cache memory.

If you want to follow all the late-breaking developments at Netscape and you visit their site daily to find out anyway, why not subscribe to the Netscape channel? This way, when you do visit their site, it will load instantly.

What is the downside of channels? If you subscribe to too many, your cache could become dangerously large. When you subscribe to a channel, you are prompted with a setting for the size of cache you are willing to allow this channel to occupy. The default (on Netcaster) is 1MB. If you subscribe to 30 channels and each one uses up 30MB of cache, you could quickly have a lot of garbage on your machine.

Marketing with Push

From a Web developer's perspective, you want to know how you can get your page before as many of the right people as possible. Unfortunately, the first kind of push technology doesn't facilitate your marketing efforts any more than does a search engine. Changing your content — at least a little bit everyday — helps your page appear in more results lists, but pretty much every page on the Web using the META clements successfully has the same chances of being found.

Using channels, however, can help you set your site off from the rest. Most Web sites don't take advantage of channels and subscriptions. Consequently, those that do — mostly sports, entertainment, and news sites — set themselves apart.

You can be especially successful in getting your visitors to subscribe if you meet the following criteria:

✦ Give your visitors a compelling reason to download and install a Version 4 or higher browser, so the client software is built into the browser.

✦ Host a newsgroup or chat room on your site that is both relevant to the rest of your site and will engage visitors.

✦ Keep your content current.

✦ Link to other sites with current content.

Introducing Channel Definition Format

The closest thing to a standard for channel definition is the Channel Definition Format (CDF), which has been proposed by Microsoft. *CDF* certainly has the potential to be the most successful solution to the different, proprietary approaches to delivering push content because it is based on the XML standard. The XML standard is the W3C's proposal for making the Web more extensible (that's where the *X* comes from in XML: *eXtensible Markup Language*).

Don't expect the CDF to be roundly endorsed by any governing body — this doesn't happen too often on the Web — but you can develop your own channels with it. The CDF is up and working in IE 4 and it is easy to use. Best of all, some Web-development tools (notably HotDogPro) have channel wizards, which take you through the creation of the Channel Definition File (.cdf file).

The Channel definition has three parts: the channel, the items, and the schedule. All this information goes into the .cdf file.

CDF (XML) syntax

The CDF is based on XML. This means, even though CDF has elements and attributes, like HTML, it won't look exactly the same. In CDF, each element is contained in angle brackets (<>) but, instead of having a start tag and an end tag, there is only one tag, with a slash (/) right before the close to the angle brackets. An example helps to clarify this:

```
<LOGO HREF="http://www.overtheweb.com/images/wave.ico"
STYLE="icon" />
```

The previous is the tag for the LOGO element. There are two attributes: href and style.

The CHANNEL element is an HTML element that contains the actual channel definition as its content. Within the CHANNEL element, you want to include — as a minimum — the two graphics that are part of your channel: a title and an abstract.

Images

If your channel definition has nothing else, it must have two graphics:

1. A 16 pixel × 16 pixel icon, stored in an .ICO file (referred to as an "icon")

2. A 32 pixel × 80 pixel graphic image, stored as a .GIF file or a .JPEG file (an "image")

You can also have an optional wide image, which is 32 pixels × 194 pixels, and is also either .GIF or .JPEG. This last type of image is referred to as "image-wide."

Images are included in your channel using the LOGO element, which is defined using XML syntax. The LOGO element has two attributes: href, which gives the URL of the image, and style, which can be one of three values: icon, image, or image-wide.

```
<LOGO href="http://www.somesite.com/images/pict1.ico"
style="icon" />
```

```
<LOGO href="http://www.somesite.com/images/pict2.gif"
style="image" />
<LOGO href="http://www.somesite.com/images/big-pict.gif"
style="image-wide" />
```

Title

The title of your channel will be included in a regular old HTML TITLE element:

```
<TITLE>Sample Channel Created for Chapter 43</TITLE>
```

Abstract

The abstract of your channel will be included in an HTML ABSTRACT element:

```
<ABSTRACT>This channel will give you the examples that you need
to create a channel, as described in Chapter 43 of the HTML 4
Bible.</ABSTRACT>
```

Scheduling precaching of your channel

The CDF offers an HTML element called SCHEDULE, which you can use to indicate the frequency with which your page is updated. This information tells the client workstation how frequently to check the server to see whether the content has changed. The SCHEDULE element has three attributes: startdate, stopdate, and timezone. The content of the SCHEDULE element is a series of XML elements: INTERVALTIME, EARLIESTTIME, and LATESTTIME. You needn't use them all. Only use the ones you need.

Both the date attributes take a date in the format of YYYY-MM-DDTHH:mm, where YYYY is the 4-digit year, MM is the 2-digit month, DD is the 2-digit day, *T* is the letter "T" indicating the time formatting is beginning, HH is the 2-digit hour, and, finally, mm is the 2-digit minutes.

```
<SCHEDULE startdate="1998-04-01T14:00"></SCHEDULE>
```

In the preceding example, the schedule would be good starting on April 1, 1998, at 2PM. It would not have an end date.

For the timezone attribute, the timezone is indicated relative to Greenwich Mean Time. Thus, Eastern Standard Time is "+5." To add this to the previous example:

```
<SCHEDULE startdate="1998-04-01T14:00"
TIMEZONE="+5"></SCHEDULE>
```

The XML elements, INTERVALTIME, EARLIESTTIME, and LATESTTIME all take one or more of the following interval attributes: day, hour, min.

To complete the previous example:

```
<SCHEDULE startdate="1998-04-01T14:00">
  <INTERVALTIME day="7" />
  <EARLIESTTIME hour="4" min="30" />
  <LATESTTIME hour="8" min="30" />
</SCHEDULE>
```

Items

Items are hierarchical nodes within the channel. Items are also where the content that belongs to your subscription is defined. One channel can have multiple items within it. You can define items to make the channel more easily navigable for subscribers. For example, you can define a channel that points to your home page and then have items that point to technical resources, customer service, a chat room, and so forth.

The other thing you can do with items is to specify the number of levels the client should precache (meaning the number of levels down links), and the usage of the channel. The usage can be either "Channel" or "ScreenSaver."

```
<ITEM href="http://www.somesite.com/images/screensaver.html"
level="1">
  <USAGE value="ScreenSaver"></USAGE>
</ITEM>
```

You can specify as many items as you need. In the previous example, the item is a screensaver.

Complete example

Creating a subscription doesn't require the detail given in the previous example. A subscription can be as simple as:

```
<CHANNEL href="http://www.mychannel.com" level="3">
  <LOGO href="http://www.mychannel.com/images/logo.ico"
image="icon" />
  <LOGO href="http://www.mychannel.com/images/pict1.gif"
image="image" />
  <TITLE>This is the title</TITLE>
  <ABSTRACT>This is the abstract</ABSTRACT>
  <SCHEDULE starttime="1998-05-20" timezone="+6">
      <INTERVALTIME day="7" />
  </SCHEDULE>
  <ITEM href="http://www.mychannel.com" level="1">
      <USAGE value="ScreenSaver"></USAGE>
  </ITEM>
</CHANNEL>
```

Subscribing to a Channel

What does it mean to subscribe to a channel? The word *subscribe* isn't as apt as the word *channel* in the television analogy. In fact, subscribing to a channel involves no more than having your client copy the .cdf file so it knows where to get the pages that constitute the channel and the frequency information found in the SCHEDULE element. In Internet Explorer 4, you can do this by selecting "Add to Favorites" from the "Favorites" menu.

Creating a subscription page

From a developer's perspective, you want to create a button on your "subscription information" page. This page should explain what is involved in subscribing to anyone who is thinking of subscribing, The page should explain how frequently you will update the site, the advantages of subscribing, and the technical requirements to subscribe (see Figure 43-1). In the case of the previous CDF example, subscribers must have Internet Explorer 4 as their browser.

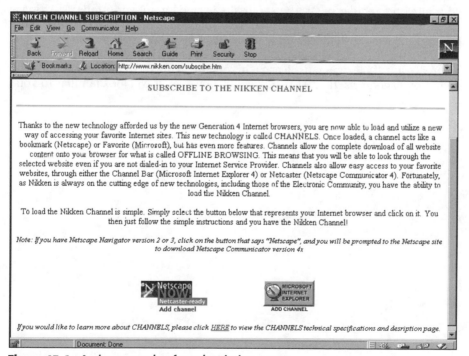

Figure 43-1: A nice example of a subscription page

To create the subscription, create an image on which the visitor can click and then place that image within an `anchor` element that refers to your .cdf file.

```
<A href="mychannel.cdf" alt="Subscribe to this channel"><IMG
src="images/subscribe.gif"></A>
```

From Here

Jump to Chapter 48 and learn about JavaScript.

Proceed to Chapter 44, Accessing External Databases.

Summary

Channels can be a great service to visitors to your site. If you, in fact, have content that is updated regularly and your visitors want to be apprised of the changes to your site on a regular basis, then your site is ripe for subscriptions. Creating a channel is relatively simple. One standard (if you can call it that) is the Channel Definition Format, which is simply a text file stored in a .cdf file.

To create a .cdf file, you must learn a bit of XML syntax. Because most of the channel definition is comprised of HTML elements, however, it will look familiar to you.

✦   ✦   ✦

Accessing External Databases

The Web-to-database interface is the best thing to happen to the Web since inline graphics. So many ways exist to connect your Web page to a database, this chapter can't begin to discuss all the options available today. Instead, this chapter discusses how the Web-to-database interface works, what types of software are available for this interface, and how they work. Finally, the chapter focuses on four of the technologies that work well.

Understanding Databases

Databases have been around for a long time. Properly used, databases are an efficient way to store data so redundancy is removed. On UNIX, most databases are text files with indexes. This chapter should be of particular interest to you if your organization already has data in a database.

Regardless of how much data is in your database, the most important things you should know about that data is how to get at it, meaning what the unique keys are to the data and how to modify it, again using the unique keys.

Tables

A database is made up of *tables*. Tables hold *rows* of data. Rows of data in a database are similar to rows of data in a spreadsheet. Tables also have *fields*. Each field in a database is similar to a column of data in a spreadsheet. If one field is for e-mail addresses, then for every row of data, either an e-mail address will be in that field or it will be blank. Tables are related to each other with keys.

Keys

A *key* is a value associated with one row in a table. Usually, a key is unique, meaning a key can only be associated with one row. A social security number would be a unique key. While a last name could be used as a key, it would not always be a unique key. Frequently, a database assigns its own unique value to each row to insure all keys are, indeed, unique.

Relationships

So far, nothing about databases makes them any more powerful than spreadsheets. It is the relationships you can create between tables that makes them powerful. A *normalized* database consists of multiple tables related to each other by keys so the same data isn't stored more than once, such as name and address information.

Common databases

The most common enterprise databases are Oracle, Sybase, and SQL server. The most common desktop database is Microsoft Access.

 Vocabulary
Enterprise Database. An *enterprise database* is one that resides on a server and can be accessed from multiple clients and multiple applications, concurrently.

 Vocabulary
Desktop Database. A *desktop database* is one that resides on the user's desktop. It is only intended for use by an individual or from the Web, depending on the interface, for a low volume of transactions.

ODBC

Databases can talk to each other and to Web servers using the Open Database Connectivity Standard (ODBC). *ODBC* is a set of rules databases agree to obey. It is like *Esperanto* (the language that was supposed to become the universal language, which no one actually speaks). Most databases, and software that interacts with databases, know this language and can communicate with each other using this language. You needn't worry about how it works; you only need to know whether your database is ODBC-compliant and whether your Web server or database-to-Web engine is ODBC-compliant. If they both are, then you have the tools you need to start building a Web-to-database interface.

If your database or your database-to-Web engine are not ODBC-compliant (such as File Maker Pro), then you must use the proprietary system this database has available for communicating with the Web. In the case of File Maker Pro, there is one. Not every non-ODBC-compliant database makes such a tool available. Even if your non-ODBC-compliant database has a way to get data to and from the Web, it will probably not be a scalable, enterprising solution. The most robust solutions — the ones that can handle the most traffic — tend to be ODBC-compliant.

The Web-to-Database Interface

To understand how the Web-to-database interface works, it helps to review how data is normally delivered to a client workstation, in a browser, via the Web (using the HTTP protocol, to be specific). Figure 44-1 shows the client workstation (on the left) requesting a page (using the HTTP protocol) from a Web server (on the right). The Web server receives the request and, if it can find the page requested and, if the client workstation meets any security restrictions that may exist on the page, the server delivers the page to the client workstation (using the HTTP protocol).

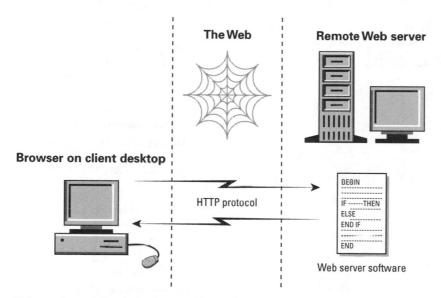

Figure 44-1: Delivering a page with no database interaction

Requesting data

When database interaction is required, a few more steps need to take place on the server. Figure 44-2 shows the client workstation (on the left) requesting a page (using the HTTP protocol) from a Web server (on the right). In this case, the page has a file extension of something other than .HTML (or .HTM), indicating to the Web server that some special type of action is required. The Web server determines whether it can handle the processing by itself or whether it needs to pass this page onto another software package. How does it know whether to pass on the page and where to pass the page? By checking the MIME type of the page requested.

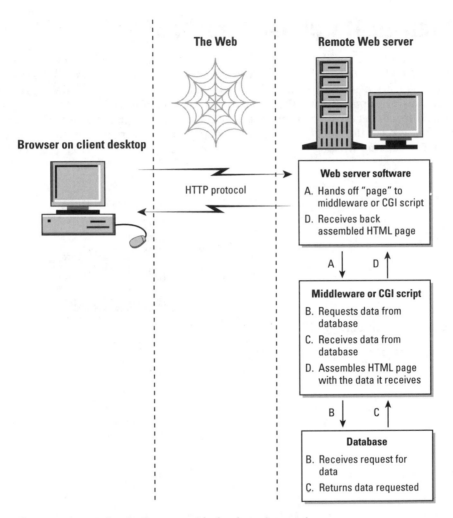

Figure 44-2: Delivering a page with database interaction

Communicating with the database

If the MIME type of the page requested is not supported by the Web server software, the page is handed off to the appropriate application, referred to as the Web-to-Database Engine, based on the MIME type. This application communicates with the database (usually in ODBC) to perform one of three actions:

1. **Search for data**. From the Web page, the visitor can indicate search criteria and only receive back data that matches those criteria.

2. **Add new data to the database.** From the Web page, the visitor can enter new data that will be added to the database.

3. **Modify existing data in the database.** From the Web page, the visitor can modify existing data — say, updating his address or phone number — or changing the inventory by making a purchase.

If the MIME type of the page requested is supported by the Web server, then it processes the request and communicates with the database directly. The choice of actions will still be one from the preceding list.

Returning results

Finally, the Web-to-Database Engine has the results of its communications with the database and can format those results into HTML, which is easily understood by the Web server (again, this can all take place within the Web server software, if the Web-server software supports the MIME type of the page requested). The Web server delivers the results of the action on the database to the client workstation.

Conclusions from the Web-to-database interaction

Important to note about this entire transaction are:

✦ The workstation doesn't perform any extra processing.

✦ The Web server or Web server and Web-to-Database Engine combination communicate with the database transparently.

✦ The database can actually reside on a different computer than the Web server and Web-to-Database Engine.

That last observation is the most salient. You can leave your database wherever it normally resides and communicate — via ODBC — across a network, with that database. This enormously expands your options for Web-to-database interaction.

Note

A significant performance penalty can occur when the Web server software resides on a different physical machine from the database. You must do extensive testing before implementing this approach. One way around this slow-down is to copy (nightly or more often, if necessary) the data from the remotely located database to a mirror copy of the database located on your Web server machine. How well this work-around actually works depends on the location of the database, the size of the database, and the processing power of both machines.

Options for Accessing Database Data

Now that you understand how the interface between the Web server and the database works, you should understand what kind of choices you have for delivering this service on your own Web server. Because the Web server side of the processing has three components — the Web server, the Web-to-Database Engine, and the database — you can purchase three different combinations of products to meet these needs.

1. **Three stand-alone components.** Stand-alone Web server, stand-alone Web-to-Database Engine, and stand-alone database.

2. **Dual-purpose Web server and stand-alone database.**

3. **Stand-alone Web server and dual-purpose database.**

Three stand-alone components

Using three stand-alone components gives you the greatest flexibility in creating your applications. Chances are, your Web server has already been selected for you and is running on your server. For most people, this is half the equation in selecting complementary products. The other half of the equation is the database, which you probably already have in place, populated with your business data. This leaves you with the decision of which solution to use to connect your Web server to your database.

If your database is ODBC, then the hands-down best middleware on the market is Cold Fusion, by Allaire (www.allaire.com). Using Cold Fusion, you can script interaction with the database right in your Web pages. The scripting language is Cold Fusion Markup Language (CFML) and looks like HTML. The Cold Fusion Web-to-Database Engine processes the CFML tags and returns the data from the database to the Web server, as in Figure 44-2.

Cold Fusion is available in both a workgroup edition, which works with desktop databases, such as Fox Pro and Access, and an Enterprise version, which works with enterprise databases such as Oracle, Sybase, Paradox, and SQL Server. Cold Fusion for Workgroups runs on Windows NT Server. Cold Fusion Enterprise Edition runs on both Windows NT server and UNIX servers.

Dual-purpose Web server and stand-alone database

When would you want to use a dual-purpose Web server? When it is free and already installed on your Web server. Microsoft Internet Information Server (IIS) supports Active Server Pages (.ASP files), which can be processed right in the IIS Web server.

When would you want to use a stand-alone Web server (that is, not use the built-in functionality of the Web server to process some form of database-interaction pages)? When you want to perform more actions than the freeware/middleware included with the Web server will provide.

One function you might want to perform from your database-interaction script is to send a confirmation message to the visitor's e-mail account confirming certain action has been taken. With IIS, you can't do this without purchasing additional COM objects, so your free solution is no longer free. With Cold Fusion, which you must purchase up-front, it is included.

Other dual-purpose Web servers include the Netscape Enterprise servers, which process server-side JavaScript, and O'Reilly servers, which process server-side Java, VBScript, JScript, Perl, or Python. If you decide to use either of those technologies, you won't have to purchase separate middleware. Whichever direction you take, you want to make sure the middleware you select is compatible with your database.

Stand-alone Web server and dual-purpose database

Why would you want to use a dual-purpose database that doubles as middleware? When it is built into your database. Netiva is one company that offers such a product. File Maker Pro is another such product. Netiva, unlike most other dual-purpose databases, can handle enterprise-level traffic. Most of the other dual-purpose databases are designed for low volume.

External Database Access Without Programming

Today, many ways exist to perform basic interactions with a database without programming. Using FrontPage, Microsoft's Web-development tool, you can create interactive Web pages with Access without programming. If your back-end database is File Maker Pro, Claris HomePage communicates directly with it, in a seamless, drag-and-drop environment. Regardless of the back-end database, as long as it is ODBC-compliant, you can use Tango, which is both the middleware and the editor, to create data-based Web pages without programming.

Only a few of the products on the market meet these needs. The market is quite crowded now. In the next few years, it could winnow down to the few best-of-breed products. For this reason, you want to make sure you select your products carefully.

External Database Access with SQL

To get the maximum flexibility when interacting with your database, you want to get your hands on the code and do the programming or the scripting yourself. Most middleware uses SQL, not to be confused with the Microsoft product by the same name, which is the structured query language for communicating with a database.

The problem with SQL is it is not standard. Whichever database you select will have its own slight variation on SQL, which you must learn to get data in to or out of the database. To perform the three previous tasks, which you might want to perform on your data, you can use statements similar to the following ones, where the name of the data source name (the ODBC name for the database) is "Inventory" and the field names are "Partno," "Description," "Quantity," and "Cost," and the unique key is "Partno."

Search for data.

```
Select * from Inventory
  Where Description = '%description%'
```

Add new data to the database.

```
Insert into Inventory (Partno, Description, Quantity, Cost)
  Values ('Partno', 'Description', Quantity, Cost)
```

Modify existing data in the database.

```
Update Inventory
  Set Description = 'Description'
      Quantity = 'Quantity'
      Cost = 'Cost'
  Where Partno = 'Partno'
```

From Here

Go to Chapter 46, Building a Secure Site for Web Commerce.

Jump to Chapter 48, Introducing JavaScript.

Proceed to Chapter 45, Building a Community: Incorporating Discussion Groups Chat.

Summary

Communicating with a database can be a bit of a hurdle to set up, but nothing enriches your Web pages like access to current, real-time data your visitors want to see. Creating static Web pages that reflect database data accurately is impossible, so if you want your visitors to get at your real-time database data, you must take the time to get this up and running. Once you are operational, the maintenance costs of these products are negligible.

Before you purchase products to get your Web server to communicate with your database, you want to see both if your Web server includes middleware and if this middleware is adequate to meet your needs. You also want to confirm your database can handle the volume of traffic you expect your site to receive.

Once you select your tools, you can determine whether you will be satisfied creating your data-based Web pages with nonprogramming tools or whether you should get your hands dirty with SQL.

✦　　✦　　✦

Building a Community: Incorporating Discussion Groups and Chat

Before a World Wide Web existed, clever individuals had already figured out how to congregate in a virtual space for discussion and socializing. These places were called *newsgroups*. They still exist today as part of the Usenet system. You can use this same concept — of allowing people on your site to talk to each other in a structured setting — or a real-time version of this concept on your page to develop a virtual community.

When you put a threaded discussion group into your Web page, you won't use any of the Usenet newsgroups that already exist. Instead, you'll create a threaded discussion group. This chapter explains how you can use threaded discussion groups and real-time chatting to make your site interactive and vital.

Introducing Threaded Discussion Groups and Chat

Newsgroups are like bulletin boards. You can post messages anyone else in the world can read and then anyone can respond to your messages either on the bulletin board or by e-mail. Over 28,000 newsgroups are on the Web today that are part of the Usenet system. They have names like `comp.lang.java.beans` and `misc.kids.pregnancy`. Both major browsers have newsreaders built into them (in Netscape, it is called *Collabra*; in Internet Explorer, it is called *Outlook Express*).

When you post a message on a newsgroup, if that message doesn't directly relate to what others have been talking about (although it should be related to the broad topic of the group), that is called a new *thread*. Most people want to read newsgroups by threads. This way, they can read the messages only in the threads that interest them.

 Vocabulary

Threaded discussion group. A *threaded discussion group* is like a newsgroup except it runs off your Web server, instead of running as part of the Usenet. Your visitors don't need any special software to participate in your threaded discussion group (also referred to as a *forum*).

Chatting is the real-time equivalent of newsgroups. Unlike newsgroups, where messages get posted to a virtual bulletin board for anyone to see, with *chat rooms,* the message is addressed to someone else in the room and scrolls off the screen in a short time. In chat rooms, anyone else in the room can see what you are saying, even if it is addressed to one specific person. While threaded discussion groups usually maintain the messages for a few days to a few weeks, chat discussions go away within minutes.

Applications of threaded discussion groups

Why would you want to add a newsgroup to your page? For many reasons. By creating a newsgroup, you can have a place where people can come and discuss your product or service, or tangentially related topics. The newsgroup you add to your page won't be a Usenet newsgroup (such as `misc.legal.computing`), but a threaded discussion group of your own creation.

What you do when you create a threaded discussion group on your site is create a community on your site. You give visitors a reason to return. They know information might change daily, even if you aren't the one changing the information. You enable your visitors to contribute to the content of your site.

Consider two sites that use threaded discussion groups effectively: `www.gund.com` (Figure 45-1) and `www.allaire.com` (Figure 45-2).

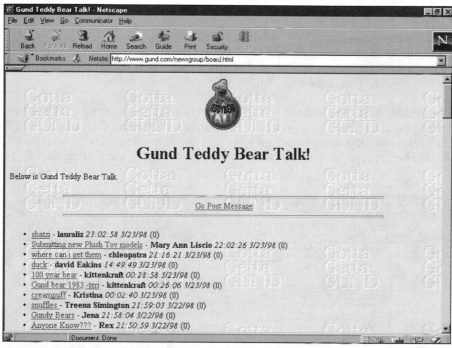

Figure 45-1: The Gund site is a discussion group for teddy bear collectors.

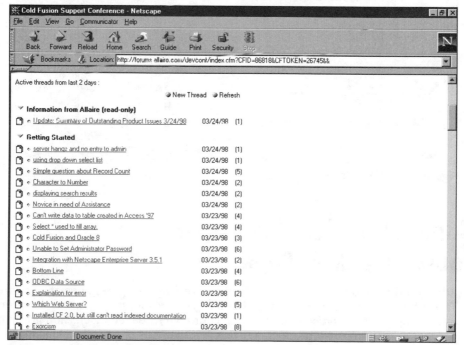

Figure 45-2: Allaire provides all support for its products on a forum.

Applications of chat rooms

Chat rooms are better suited to highly subjective, emotional discussions with strangers than to sorting out the facts is a clear, rational way. Thus, you are more likely to see chat rooms on political or news sites, where everyone is entitled to an opinion and no one cares who's right.

The MSNBC news site (shown in Figure 45-3) uses chat rooms to hash out breaking political stories. Discussions can be heated, so if you want to maintain a semblance of control over the discussions on your site, be advised to stick to threaded discussion groups, where you can even pull threads that wander far afield.

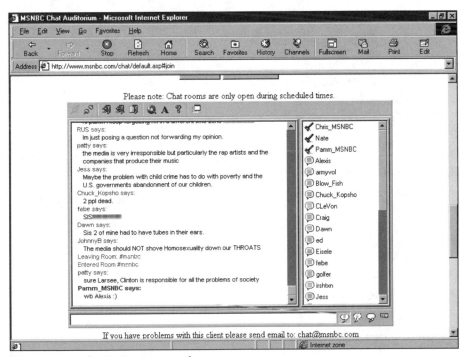

Figure 45-3: The MSNBC News chat room

Adding Threaded Discussion Groups to a Web Page

Adding a threaded discussion group to your Web page requires special software. The software interacts with either a database, where messages posted are stored, or a flat file, with an index. You can write your own threaded discussion group or purchase an off-the-shelf product. Forums, by Allaire, is one product that can add a threaded discussion group to your site. Figure 45-4 shows how settings are configured in forums (the software by Allaire).

Check with your systems administrator to see if forums, or some other software that provides threaded discussion groups, already exist on your server. Each package is different but, generally, you should be able to modify the following settings to customize the interface so the discussion group page matches the rest of your site:

✦ Background color or graphics

✦ Button color or graphics

✦ Fonts

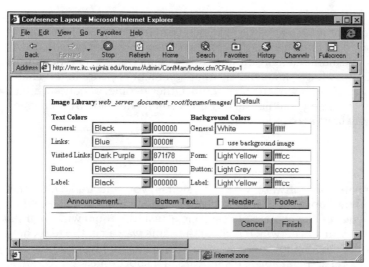

Figure 45-4: Setting the look of the discussion group in forums

In addition, you want to administer the discussion group, so if someone begins a thread that bashes your site or your product — as opposed to asking questions — you can pull that thread or, at least, pull those messages. Here are some settings you want to make:

✦ Number of threads permitted

✦ Number of discussion groups permitted (so you can have more than one newsgroup — perhaps one for each product you produce)

✦ Ability to moderate the threads and pull inappropriate threads or messages

✦ Password protection for administrative privileges

Adding Chat to a Web Page

Several products are on the market that enable you to add chat rooms to your Web page. In most cases, chat rooms require more client-side processing than do discussion groups. Discussion groups are entirely server-based activities. Chat rooms are usually Java-based. This means they rely on your visitors to have Java-compatible browsers.

Text chat

The usual kind of chat room is text-based. Each person creates a nickname before entering the chat room and then all the comments made by that person are preceded by the nickname. When you want to say something, you type your comment in and press Enter. Immediately, that comment appears in the chat window of everyone who is "in" the chat room. Other people, of course, are talking concurrently. By the time you finish answering a comment made by someone else, that comment may have scrolled off the screen.

Visual chat

With graphical chat-room software, when you sign in, you select an avatar that represents you in the room. You can be a beautiful woman or Pinocchio. When you enter the room, you see the avatars of everyone else in the room with their names under them. When you speak (which is done the same way as in the text chat), your dialogue may appear in a bubble over your head or in a scrolling text box, as with a text chat. In either case, the dialogue disappears in a short time.

When you first enter a chat room, it takes a moment to get your bearings, figure out what everyone is talking about, and decide who makes any sense to you. Some people live in chat rooms and spend all their time there inciting riots. You want to avoid those people. You also want to avoid attracting those people to your site.

Creating Community

One way to create a loyal following of visitors who return to your site with regularity is to create a sense of community. Adding discussion groups and chat rooms to your site are the tactical methods of creating community, but you need to think back to the strategic goals of attracting a crowd.

Will people come to your Web site because you have fancy features like a discussion group or a chat room? Probably not. Heck, the Web is full of fun places to waste time. You need to find a way to set your site apart because of something visitors can only get from your threaded discussion group or chat room.

Your first thought may be that people will come to your site to talk about your products, but this may be a bit optimistic. Look at the Gund site (see Figure 45-1). The discussion group there is about collecting teddy bears (and other stuffed animals). Gund happens to make teddy bears, but they don't limit discussion on their site to their own creatures. The Gund site is a general meeting place for collectors of stuffed critters.

What can you offer?

What can you offer from a discussion group or chat room? In the case of Allaire, all free customer support is offered only on their forum. This certainly attracts a crowd. They make sure every question is answered in short order. They also offer an archive of old questions for searching, if you don't feel bold enough to post your own question or you don't want to look stupid.

Can you offer a service that is only available from a threaded discussion group or chat room? Some of the parenting sites on the Web have chat rooms and threaded discussion groups where parents ask questions of other parents. How to get their children to sleep through the night? Which brand of stroller is best? How to get the kids to stop fighting? Parents flock to sites where they can share their concerns and get their questions answered quickly by both experts and peers.

A big-name columnist

Perhaps you have a celebrity who could publish a column on your site, such as Danny Goodman, author of the *JavaScript Bible* (IDG Books Worldwide, 1998), who publishes the JavaScript Apostle column on the Netscape site. People know of Goodman, own his books, and visit the Netscape DevEdge site to see what he has to say about late-breaking technologies.

Celebrities can attract people to your site because people already feel they "know" them. Visitors come to learn more about their area of expertise and to get closer to them.

Consider ABC News. After *This Week with Sam Donaldson and Cokie Roberts*, a Sunday morning political talk show, they often have one of their roundtable regulars go online on the ABC News Web site to chat with the viewers.

Talk with a professional

Perhaps you can offer a certain number of hours a week when a professional in your field will be online taking questions. Whether your field is cooking, car repair, quilting, or oncology, people will be delighted to have a chance to get their questions answered by a real professional.

This type of discussion doesn't lend itself to a chat room, but by taking submitted questions and answering them in real-time, publishing the answers right to the Web site, you can create a vibrancy and interactivity that people will return for again and again.

Beyond Chat and Threaded Discussion Groups

Another way to create a community on your site is to offer resources that are hard to find elsewhere. Many people make the mistake of offering links to resources rather than offering the actual resources. When you offer links to resources, you give people a reason to leave your site. When you offer resources, you give people a reason to come to your site and stay. A threaded discussion group can be a resource — for example, if visitors can actually get samples of code, get answers as to why their specific problems are happening and how to fix them, and get these answers and solutions in a timely manner, then you have offered a real resource and these visitors will return.

An expert in the field, who can give tips on how to use your technology in ways others hadn't considered, can be a valuable resource. A regular column that keeps visitors to your site apprised of how new developments in technology will affect your products and services certainly will be a valuable resource.

What kind of services can you offer that attracts your visitors? Perhaps you can create instructions for doing slightly less than your product does at little or no cost. This way, when your visitors are ready to buy or need the extra features your product offers, they will already feel favorably disposed because of the free resources you have offered. One resource — nearly pervasive among software developers — is offering a light version of the software at no charge.

From Here

Cross-Reference

Jump to Chapter 50, Creating Interactive Documents.

Proceed to Chapter 46, Building a Secure Site for Web Commerce.

Summary

Creating a community on your Web site is an excellent way to develop a dedicated following of site visitors. Creating a community is not particularly difficult but, unfortunately, few sites take advantage of this avenue of increased traffic.

Web site development is frequently left to the techies who know how to do fancy things with technical tools. They get bogged down in the tactical side of assembling a Web site without giving much thought to the strategy of creating community as a means of developing a loyal following. Threaded discussion groups and chat rooms can help enhance traffic on your site, but only if you are truly offering the visitors something they can't get otherwise. Celebrity columnists and area professionals can help create a vibrant community on your site.

✦   ✦   ✦

Building a Secure Site for Web Commerce

Web commerce is big, big business and it is only getting bigger. Businesses that ignore this avenue of sales and marketing do so at their own peril. Conducting business on the Web does have technical hurdles, but each one can be surmounted. This chapter takes you through the security risks of conducting business on the Web and the steps you can take to maximize the security on your site. Security for commerce is trustworthy and efficient. This chapter helps you take advantage of the best out there today.

Introduction to Security

If you are going to conduct commerce on your site, you need to be sure everything related to the transactions visitors perform is secure. Several things must be secured before you can safely tell your customers you have made every effort to protect their personal and payment information.

Security is related to data. You need to ensure, as well as possible, the data entered by your visitors is never compromised. The easiest way to see where you must have security is to follow the data through a transaction, as shown in Figure 46-1.

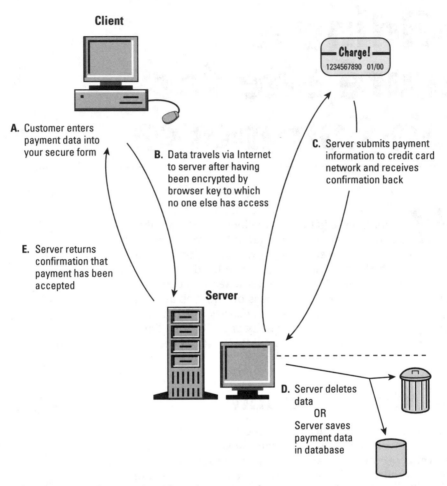

Client

A. Customer enters payment data into your secure form

B. Data travels via Internet to server after having been encrypted by browser key to which no one else has access

C. Server submits payment information to credit card network and receives confirmation back

E. Server returns confirmation that payment has been accepted

Charge!
1234567890 01/00

Server

D. Server deletes data
OR
Server saves payment data in database

Figure 46-1: Following data though a transaction

On the left in Figure 46-1, customers enter personal information, including payment information, into your sales form on your site. When the form is complete, they click the "Submit" button and the information travels across the Internet to your server. Once the data is on your server, you perform certain actions against it, including possibly submitting the payment information to a credit card network. Then you may or may not keep the payment information on your server, or move it to another server not connected to the Internet, depending on whether you have future plans for this data.

So, where is this data in danger? When can someone get to this data? In any of the following places:

✦ While being transmitted across the Internet from the customer's computer to your server.

✦ While sitting on your server or in a database, if you choose to leave it there.

✦ While being submitted to a credit card network.

Security Across the Internet

The most hyped of all possible security holes on the Web is the danger your data might be intercepted in transit between the client workstation and the server. When your data is travelling across the Internet, it is completely unprotected. Your data travels across "public" wires put in place by the federal government, educational institutions, and private network providers.

What are the risks to your data when it is travelling across public wires? Packet-sniffing software. Packet-sniffing software is a reality. *Packet-sniffing software* is software that gets planted somewhere along the Internet. Every packet of network data (remember, the TCP/IP protocol packages your data into little packets with addressing information on each packet) travels through this software without the sender or the receiver even knowing the data has been sniffed. The packet-sniffing software tries to evaluate whether the data is worth mirroring to another server — the home server of nefarious software.

The packet-sniffing software could theoretically identify which data is payment data and grab only those packets. In practice, a reported case of credit card fraud from data sniffed off the Internet has never occurred.

Security on the Server

Another place where your data is in jeopardy is while it sits on your Web server. Even though your Web server may be right there in your office, the fact that your Web server — with all the data it contains — is attached to the Internet means your data is at risk.

A good hacker can break into most Web servers. Whether this hacker can get at your payment information on the server depends on other factors.

Security When Submitting Payment Information

If your payment information is submitted to a credit card network over any public wires, your payment information may be in jeopardy from the same risks as those previously listed related to transmitting data over the Internet. Fortunately, most credit card networks make use of private phone lines. When a merchant submits to a credit card network, this normally must be done by modem or by leased line.

Plugging Security Holes

Fortunately, good ways exist to plug the security holes described. The best way to safeguard your data while it is travelling over the Internet is to encrypt it. This solution is called, confusingly, "implementing a secure server," and is described in the following. It would seem implementing a secure server would protect data on the server, but protecting data on the server is another problem altogether.

To keep or not to keep payment information

The second security hole previously discussed relates to whether you keep payment information after submitting it for processing and, if you do, where you store it. This is by far the most difficult security hole to plug. The easiest solution is that implemented by most retail establishments: don't keep payment information.

Whichever solution you implement, your server should always have the most recent version of the operating system and server software available (betas excluded). All service packs, upgrades, and patches should be applied. Even when you have all the patches in place, you can't be sure someone still won't break into your server. Many of those patches were created as a result of holes other hackers discovered or created.

When you maintain a database of customers, it is natural to keep such information as name, e-mail address, address, areas of interest, products purchased, and, unfortunately, payment information. This is the least safe setup for your data. From most secure to least secure, the following list gives options for keeping your data from the eyes of hackers:

> **Do not keep payment information.** If you don't have payment information in your possession, it can't be stolen from you. Many customers assume their payment information will only be used for that purchase and won't be kept by you. In most cases, you have no use for that information after the initial transaction. If you bill monthly for a service, you need to keep payment information and you should consider the next most secure option.

Keep payment information on a separate computer that does not communicate with any network. Manually move payment information (sneaker-net) on a floppy disk or a Zip disk from your server to a freestanding, non-networked computer nightly. This is a hassle, but it is the safest way to keep payment information, if you must keep payment information. In the worst case, if you are hacked, the hacker will only get at one day's worth of payment information.

Keep payment information on a separate computer that communicates with the network via some protocol other than TCP/IP. TCP/IP is the protocol of the Web. Most hackers come into your network (and break through your firewall) using the TCP/IP protocol. If you can use some other protocol, say IPX or NetBEUI, to move data from your server to another computer and that other computer doesn't support TCP/IP, then the hackers must be very clever to get at the valuable data.

Keep payment information on a separate computer that does not serve as a server. If you must keep payment data and you must keep it on a computer connected to the network, keep it on a computer that doesn't serve as any kind of a server. If all file sharing is turned off on that computer and the only access to the hard drive is by sitting in front of the monitor, then your data will be relatively safe. There are, of course, hackers who can take advantage of operating system bugs to make your computer sharable, but it will take someone with an impressive skill set to get into your data without sitting in front of the computer.

Keep payment information on a server, but in a separate database from the rest of your customer information. Most stores swipe a card and submit payment information, but don't keep a copy of enough information to make fraudulent purchases. The copy of the receipt they keep has the card number and expiration date with a signature, but no address information. The least you can do to protect your payment data is not to store it with the rest of the personal data most merchants require to make a sale. If you want to use a credit card either over the phone or on the Web, you normally have to provide a valid card number, expiration date, card holder name, and billing address. If all this data can't be found in one place on your server, then a hacker will have far more difficulty getting at your payment data and submitting false charges.

Keep payment information on a server together with the rest of your customer information. This is what most Web sites that transact commerce, which keep payment information, do today. It will take more hackers and more publicity of hackers — the kind most merchants are too embarrassed to provide — to bring awareness of the danger of this system design to the attention of Web merchants.

Credit card submission

The final security hole previously described related transmitting payment information to a credit card network. The best suggestion here is, if you have a choice, submit by modem or by leased line, rather than over the Internet. It may seem more expensive or more complicated, but you can't recover the trust you lose from your customers if their data is stolen and used for ill while it is in your hands.

Understanding Secure Servers

A *secure server* is any Web server with a digital server certificate installed on it. What does this do for you? Alone, it does nothing. A secure server doesn't secure your transmissions and it doesn't secure your data. If you want to submit encrypted transmissions, however, having a digital certificate on your server is a must.

Most of the major Web servers support becoming a secure server. How you implement a secure server depends on which Web server software you are running. The basic idea is the same, though. You install a digital server certificate — according to your server software directions — and instruct your secure pages to communicate using the secure HTTP (https://) protocol.

Digital Server Certificates

A *digital certificate* is a file produced by a certifying authority. Verisign is the biggest of the certifying authorities (www.verisign.com). To get a digital certificate, you must prove to the certifying authority you are who you say you are (having a Dunn & Bradstreet number helps). Once they are convinced of the legitimacy of your operation and you pay a substantial sum of money, they issue you a digital certificate.

Vocabulary

Secure Sockets Layer (SSL). *Secure Sockets Layer* is a technology developed by Netscape to allow the secure transmission of data across the Internet. It relies on the establishment of a trust relationship between the client and the Web server, and then the establishment of a session-specific encryption key, and finally, establishment of an encrypted system of transmission between the client and the Web server. Figure 46-2 shows the sequence of events more clearly.

Now that you have a digital certificate, you can begin the process of implementing secure transmissions using the SSL. Fortunately, all the technical stuff is done for you by the server. The procedures for using secure transmissions are shown in Figure 46-2.

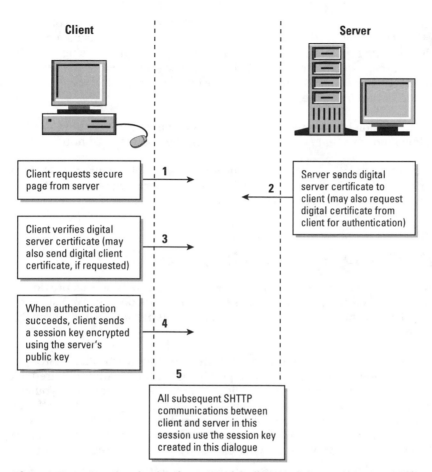

Figure 46-2: Communication between the client and the server using SSL

Security Protocol Options

The protocol used for secure transmissions is the *SHTTP protocol*. When you link to a page that is to be sent in a secure manner, you need to use the SHTTP protocol explicitly. Data sent with the SHTTP protocol is encrypted using either the private key generated by the client or with the public key sent as part of authentication by the server.

To keep the data as secure as possible, the SSL standard uses asynchronous encryption. Data sent from the server to the client is encrypted using a public 1024-bit key. Data sent from the client to the server is encrypted using the private 1024-bit secure session key created by the client and submitted to the server, itself encrypted with the public key of the server, when authentication was first established between the client and the server.

The secure session key is only valid for that session between the client and the server. It is unique to that session and automatically expires in 24 hours.

In Depth

The 1024-bit encryption is weapons-grade encryption. Until recently, the U.S. federal government wouldn't allow browser makers to export their 1024-bit encryption technology. People in other countries had to settle for 512-bit encryption.

Implementing Your Secure Site

A bit more is involved in getting a secure server certificate than was previously explained. How you go about taking these steps depends on your Web server software, but somehow you (or your systems administrator) must go through all these steps.

1. **Generate key pair file and a request file.** This involves walking through the steps on your server software and providing the information required in a dialog box to generate a key pair file and a request file. Normally, you are required to provide a name and a password for the key, the bit length of the encryption to be used (normally 1024), the name of your company, the organizational unit within your company, your domain name, your country code, your state or province, your city, and the name of the request file.

2. **Request a secure server certificate from a certification authority.** You can usually do this online at the Web site of the certification authority. You are required to provide proof your company or organization exists and they follow up with a phone call.

3. **Install the certificate on your Web server.** Again, this depends on your Web server software, but can be as easy as selecting "Install Certificate" from the menu and walking through the dialog boxes.

4. **Move your secure files to your secure document directory.** Any files you want transmitted using SSL need to be placed into your secure directory. This would include your secure forms, account balance information, and so forth.

5. **Link to those files using the SHTTP protocol.** Now you have to go back to all the places in your site where you link to the page that is now part of your secure site. This includes all A elements and FORM elements that have action attributes. You probably used relative addressing to link to these secure pages. Now you need to change all those relative references to absolute references using the SHTTP protocol. So, a link that looked like:

```
<A href="page1.html">Go to a secure page</A>
```

would now look like:

```
<A href="shttp://my.site.com/secure/page1.html">Go to a
secure page</A>
```

From Here

Jump to Chapter 48, Introducing JavaScript.

If you haven't already jumped ahead, your self-control is amazing. To learn about the Document Object Model, proceed to Chapter 47.

Summary

While transacting business on the Web may seem intimidating at first, none of the obstacles should stop you. Basically, your data is in jeopardy in three places. You can take steps to ensure you have protected your data in each of those three places. Secure sockets layer transmissions are safe. Implementing a secure server with a secure server certificate is not that much work.

The costs are relatively modest and the profit potential is huge. If your business isn't already planning to move to some Web-based commerce, it should start thinking about it now.

✦   ✦   ✦

Building Dynamic Pages with JavaScript

Introducing the Document Object Model

Dynamic HTML. It sounds so sexy, doesn't it? In fact, dynamic HTML is nothing more than a set of technologies about which you've already heard a bit. The document object model (DOM), JavaScript, cascading style sheets (CSS), and the eXtensible Markup Language (XML) are collectively referred to as *dynamic HTML*. This chapter takes you through the revolutionary changes the DOM brings to Web site development.

What the Document Object Model Is

The *Document Object Model* (DOM) is a way of making any part of your Web page addressable with JavaScript, VBScript, or any other scripting or programming language. What does this mean? This means suddenly you can do things on your Web page you couldn't do before! What kinds of things? Exciting things like:

- ✦ redraw a page without reloading the page.
- ✦ move images and text around the page without using a movie or animation.
- ✦ create dynamic forms that automatically ask the next question based on the answers to the previous questions.
- ✦ create a dynamic table of contents.

✦ show and hide levels of detail based on visitor input without the page having to be reloaded.

✦ change the color of text or an image as the cursor moves over it.

All these changes to your page are loaded with your page when it loads in the first place. They can all take place without the page being reloaded. They go a long way toward making your page act like a regular application.

None of the new, exciting things you can do with your page can be done without learning a scripting language, however. You also need to learn about events. Because JavaScript is the most widely implemented and the most widely used, this book shows all the examples using JavaScript.

Why DOM Is Needed

Without the DOM, the Web would never be more than a series of static magazine pages. Sure, some pages would look pretty sexy with moving video or access to real-time data from a database but, essentially, everything you would ever see on a page would be the same, regardless of how you interact with the page. With the DOM, the Web becomes an application on your desktop, just like other software you buy at the store. On CD-ROM, every Web site can be fully functional software that responds to your mouse as you roll it over words, including menus that open and close, and that dynamically responds to where you click a page.

What would the alternative be to the DOM? You've probably seen it. If you want to add the same kind of interactivity you get from the DOM, JavaScript, and CSS to your page, you must use Java. This might be great for programmers, but because most sites aren't published by programmers, it would spell — in short order — the end of the rapid growth and instant accessibility of the Web.

Introducing the DOM Specification

The DOM by itself doesn't do anything. The DOM is a way to address any object on your page through scripting. In fact, the very name — document object model — changes the vocabulary used in discussing Web pages. In previous chapters, each *thing* on your page was referred to as an *element*. Now, with the document object model, suddenly everything becomes an *object*. What's the difference? If you had to identify one, you could say an element is something you define and an object is something you act upon. Once the browser has rendered all your elements, they become objects that you can move around.

The word *object* comes from the programming world—object-oriented programming—to be specific. JavaScript is an example of an object-oriented scripting language.

Cross-Reference   Chapter 48 covers JavaScript in more depth. If you want to read the DOM specification—not for the faint-hearted—visit http://www.w3.org/TR/WD-DOM/.

Objects are anything rendered on your Web page. How do things get onto your Web page? By being defined in HTML, the way you learned in the preceding chapters.

Name, rank, and serial number

In the DOM, every object can be referred to either by name or by its relationship to other objects on the page. You may have noticed nearly every element in the HTML 4 specification had name as one of its attributes. You can use this attribute to assign a name that won't be of any use anywhere except in the script, using the DOM.

Why would you use one method of referencing an object over the other? Table 47-1 gives a few of the common applications you might want to create with the DOM and JavaScript. For each, it indicates whether you would probably want to reference the objects involved in the application by name or by relationship.

Table 47-1 Referencing objects by name or by relationship for various applications		
Application	**by Name**	**by Relationship**
Processing a form	√	
Displaying/Hiding a table of contents or other nested list		√
Animating an object	√	
Processing a fieldset from a database		√

The general rule as to how to refer to an object in your script is: If you need the script to scale to fit one or an infinite number of instances of that object—such as with a table of contents or when processing a fieldset from a database, where you may not know the exact layout of the data—you want to refer to objects by relationship. Otherwise, you can safely refer to objects by name.

All in the family

Relationships between objects are patterned after relationships between family members. An object can have a parent, a child or children, and one or more siblings. Sibling objects share a parent. The Adam and Eve of this family is the *document* object. The document object has no parent, for example, in a list defined as follows:

```
<OL name="this-list">
<LI name="first-child">
<LI name="second-child">
  <OL name="third-child">
       <LI name="first-grandchild">
       <LI name="second-grandchild">
  </OL>
<OL>
```

First-child, second-child, and third-child are all children of this list; they are also siblings. Third-child has two children of its own. It is not typical to name lists or to name list items but, for this example, it makes the relationships clearer.

All objects within a document are referenced by what type of object they are and what occurrence of this type of object they are. For example, if you had four images (specifically, four instances of the IMG element) on your page and you want to refer to the last one, you'd address it as "image #4." In DOM, the first instance of a object type is the 0th instance. So to refer to image #4, you'd actually use image 3.

Referencing objects

Referring to objects in the DOM is relatively simple. If you have a named object, you can refer to it as itself. Consider the following HTML, which defines the object:

```
<IMG src="images/nice-pic.gif" name="pic1">
```

Now, you can easily refer to the previous object created in JavaScript. In the following equation, a new object called *newobj* is being created that is equivalent to pic1, previously defined.

```
newobj = pic1;
```

If the element definition had omitted the name attribute — for whatever reason — the HTML would look instead, like this:

```
<IMG src="images/nice-pic.gif">
```

And as the page author, you must know which instance of an IMG element you were referring to (actually, using JavaScript, you could find this out if you knew the value of the src attribute, but the more complex stuff comes later) and then you could refer to the image using the relative method of addressing. In this example, the object previously defined is the first instance of an image on the page.

```
newobj = document.all.image(0);
```

Property is 9/10ths of the Law

In addition to being able to refer to an object by name using the DOM, you can also determine or *set* the value of attributes of the element using the DOM. Do this by getting at an object's *properties*. Every object has properties. With few exceptions, the object's properties parallel the object's attributes. Only the newest elements don't have properties, such as the STYLE element. Despite the fact that formatting attributes, such as the align attribute, are deprecated in most elements (tables being one case where there are no alternatives, because CSS doesn't support table formatting well), properties exist to determine the values of even some deprecated attributes.

The display property

Notice in addition to querying the value of a property, you can also change the value of the property. This is the power of the DOM. After a page has been loaded, you can change the value of an element's attributes by changing the properties of the object. As you may recall learning in Chapter 24, CSS elements have a display attribute. The three common values are "" (empty value), "none" (meaning not visible and taking up no space on the page), and "hidden" (meaning not visible, but taking up space on the page anyway). If you want to set an object as invisible and not to take up any space on the page — in other words, to disappear as if it had never been there — after the page has been loaded, usually as the result of an event, you can use the following JavaScript code:

```
document.all.image(0).display = "none";
```

Notice the property name is tacked onto the end of the object name. In this case, the object is being referred to by relationship. From the object name, you can tell this is the first image on the page. The next example refers to the object by name.

```
cat-on-roof.display = "none";
```

The object was named *cat-on-roof,* but you can't tell what kind of object it is from the JavaScript alone. Whatever kind of object it is, it will be rendered invisible and the rest of the page will be redrawn, so this invisible object doesn't take up any space on the page as a result of this JavaScript.

The style property

Another attribute nearly pervasive in HTML 4 elements is the `style`. Using the `style` property and subproperties of the `style` property, you can change anything about the look of an element you can set with CSS and the `style` attribute. What kinds of things can you set?

✦ `style.color` changes the color of the object.

✦ `style.textDecoration` changes the text to be underlined, overlined, struckthrough (line-through), or to blink.

✦ `style.fontFamily` changes the font of the text.

✦ `style.fontSize` changes the size of the text.

In addition to those in the list, you can change almost every property CSS can affect. The fastest way to apply style qualities to an object is to define a style within the `HEAD` element and to apply the entire style by name. In the following example, you can see the `STYLE` element in the `HEAD`, and then the JavaScript you would use to set the style of an object to a different value.

```
<HEAD>
<STYLE>
  beginning {
color: black;
font-family: Helvetica;
font-size: 12pt;
}
alternate {
color: red;
font-family: Helvetica;
font-size: 14pt;
}
</STYLE>

<!-- and later on in the document, in the JavaScript, you would
use the following code -->
document.all.div(4).style = alternate;
<!-- more JavaScript would follow, then the rest of the rest of
the page definition -->
```

Notice the DOM object is assigned directly to the name of the style.

Positions everyone

One of the more interesting and spicy things you can do with the DOM is to add animations to your page via scripting, rather than by creating an animation using, say, Director and then having your site visitors download the Shockwave plug-in to show the animation. With the DOM, animations are nothing more than an object with its position continually redefined. Because you can set the screen position of an object using CSS — the horizontal and vertical positions, and the z-index — you can create a loop in JavaScript that moves the object by simply changing one or more of those positions. Chapter 48 shows an example of an animation in JavaScript. The key DOM component to the JavaScript is shown in the following:

```
document.all.image(0).left = document.image(0).left + 10;
```

By putting the previous statement into a loop, the image would move smoothly across the page. You probably want to make sure the image doesn't continue to move to the right, right off the screen, by making sure the value of `document.image(0).left` never exceeds a set value (say, 770), and when it does reach or exceed this value, to set it back to the starting value of the animation.

Objects Defined in the DOM

Every element in HTML has an associated object name in DOM. To refer to objects by relationship, as previously described, you need to know what each object is called. For the most part, you'll find these names obvious, perhaps exactly what you would have guessed — had you guessed — in some cases, the names are not intuitive; these nonintuitive cases will be noted specially.

Objects in the document

Not all these object names are the same on all browsers. Not all object properties work on all browsers. Later in this chapter, the controversial subject of browser incompatibility is discussed at greater length.

The most comprehensive reference guide to the objects in the DOM is available at the Microsoft site (`http://www.microsoft.com/msdn/sdk/inetsdk/help/dhtml/references/objects/objects.htm#om40_objects`). Unfortunately, Netscape does not offer a similar comprehensive guide to its use of the DOM.

Sometimes people write HTML pages leaving out what would seem critical elements, such as the HTML element, the HEAD element, and the BODY element. Fortunately, the DOM still creates objects for these elements, even when they are only assumed to be there. Otherwise, there would be no document object from which to refer to all the other objects on the page.

Browser Wars

While the DOM is promising and can make your site do some interesting things, due to significant browser incompatibilities—unless you are writing your site for an intranet, where you know for sure which browser every visitor will be running— you are better off following the developments closely at this time, rather than trying to implement the DOM today. Right now, Internet Explorer and Netscape require different scripts to do the same thing.

While Microsoft references every object on the page under the document object with the object name document.all.objectName, where objectName is the name of the specific object on the page, Netscape uses document.layerName.object Name where the layerName, is the name you give to the LAYER element (unique to Netscape) on which the object resides. The CSS standard for layering objects in 3D is to use z-index as a property of a style. You can see this scripting for cross-browser compatibility requires two entirely different sets of scripts.

Another difference between the implementation of Netscape and Microsoft is Microsoft opens every single element of the page, even those that have not yet been included in the DOM to scripting. Microsoft has positioned Internet Explorer, through the use of ActiveX controls, the DCOM, and DOM to be the platform of choice for application delivery. Netscape, on the other hand, seems to be dragging its feet in implementing scriptable objects. Not all the objects in the DOM are scriptable in Netscape.

From Here

Cross-Reference

Jump to Chapter 49 to learn about building dynamic forms.

Proceed to Chapter 48 and learn enough JavaScript to be dangerous with the DOM.

Summary

The DOM is the greatest thing to hit the Web since forms. It adds a whole new dimension of functionality to Web sites. Together with CSS (especially the capability to place objects in all three dimensions) and JavaScript, the DOM can literally make your page dance. Thanks to the DOM, every element of your page is completely addressable. In addition, the DOM demands every browser redraw the page dynamically, meaning if you change the definition of an element after the page has been rendered, the browser will redraw the page without the page having to be reloaded.

You can address objects on your page either by name—if they have names and you know them—or by relationship (the child of my parent's third sibling). The exciting thing about the DOM is you take actions on objects by changing their properties; it is this simple. Properties correspond almost identically to attributes in the HTML definition of the object.

Unfortunately, the conclusion to this chapter of the DOM is not as rosy as it should be. Microsoft and Netscape haven't implemented the DOM the same way. In fact, before a DOM existed, there were just two browser makers trying to offer some level of scripting to their developers. Microsoft goes beyond what the DOM demands while Netscape falls short. Everyone hopes the next version of these two browsers will fully (and identically) support the DOM.

✦   ✦   ✦

Introducing JavaScript

JavaScript is the most widely used scripting language on the Web. Originally developed by Netscape, JavaScript has now grown beyond the realm of anything Netscape can control and is supported natively by all the major browsers. With the Document Object Model (DOM), you can use JavaScript to animate, display, or hide any part of your page. Unfortunately, JavaScript isn't completely standard yet, but this should get straightened out as the DOM is implemented in both the major browsers.

This chapter introduces you to all the components that make up JavaScript: syntax, events, event handlers, properties, methods, functions, and the magical *this,* which enables you to pass data from a form to a script. Even with the mechanics under your belt, however, there is nothing like an example to demonstrate how its done. Chapter 49 provides JavaScript examples of the concepts described in this chapter.

What JavaScript Is — and Isn't

JavaScript is an object-oriented scripting language. With JavaScript, you can manipulate many variables and objects on your page. With JavaScript and the DOM, you can change the value of all the properties of all the objects on your page. Because the DOM requires browsers to redraw pages in response to events, JavaScript becomes far more powerful with the DOM.

Pre-DOM

Before the DOM, JavaScript could do only a few things:

✦ **Populate a field on the screen with a value.** For example, your script could determine the local time of the client and automatically populate the date field of a form the visitor was completing.

✦ **Collect system variables.** Because the functionality of the browsers vary and so many versions of browsers are in use today, it is common for a JavaScript program to determine which version of which browser is running before loading a page. Using this technique, the page can even call a different, more appropriate page for that browser. The JavaScript can even determine the IP address of the client computer.

✦ **Validate data on a form.** If the data is validated, the JavaScript would usually do nothing, allowing the form data to be passed to the page designated by the `action` attribute of the `FORM` element. If the data did not validate, JavaScript would write an appropriate message into a pop-up box. In either case, the JavaScript couldn't change the color of the field in error or put a red arrow next to the mandatory field that wasn't populated without reloading the page.

Post-DOM

After the DOM, the world is your oyster! A few of the things you might want to do with JavaScript now are:

✦ **Create a real-time clock with a working second hand.** A DOM-compliant browser redraws the part of the page that has changed without the need for the page to reload.

✦ **Create a dynamic form that displays only the relevant fields, based on the information already provided.** For example, if the visitor answers an insurance form question about whether any family member has died before age 55 with a "yes" (checking that check box), then a set of questions about which relatives and how they died would appear. If a visitor answers that question with a "no," then the next question to appear might be to ask whether the visitor uses tobacco or illegal drugs. This helps the form maker avoid such techniques as "If no, skip to question 13."

✦ **Reward certain screen interactions, such as answering a series of trivia questions correctly by providing a congratulatory animation.** The JavaScript can both evaluate the results of the quiz and animate a still image (or a series of images) without reloading the page and without requiring additional actions by the visitor, such as clicking a "see results" button.

✦ **Dynamically sort the results of a database fieldset based on the sort order requested by the visitor** *without communicating with the server*. Collecting certain data from a database for display on the client doesn't require any JavaScript; this is basically a server process. But enabling the client to sort the data in useful ways — once the search has been performed against the database — is something JavaScript can now do with the DOM.

Remaining limitations

Even with all JavaScript can do, things still exist it can't do. JavaScript is limited to a *sandbox* in the browser, just as the original unsigned Java Applets were. JavaScript still cannot:

✦ **Manipulate files on the client computer.** JavaScript can't create files, write to existing files, or delete files, except within the cache allocated to the browser.

✦ **Execute any operations outside of the browser.** JavaScript can't kick off an installation file or initiate a download.

These limitations may seem a handicap for developers, but they are in place to safeguard the site visitor. Right now, few Web citizens fear JavaScript. Because of the limitations built into JavaScript, there hasn't been any big security scare from the visitor's point of view. This is unlike cookies, Java, and ActiveX. Many visitors have disabled the capability for their browsers to accept any of those technologies, for fear of rogue programs. JavaScript would do well to avoid any similar security scare. If the price for this is some modest limitations, then it is probably worth the price.

JavaScript versus Other Scripting Languages

JavaScript is completely unrelated to Java. Java is a programming language that was developed by Sun Microsystems to be a cross-platform, full-featured application-development language. JavaScript is a scripting language that Netscape developed to enable Web developers to add scripting to their pages in Netscape Navigator.

Microsoft created VBScript to do the same thing within Internet Explorer, but Netscape had the momentum (and capitalized greatly from the name similarity with Java and all the publicity Java was receiving). Consequently, Microsoft added complete support for JavaScript to Internet Explorer.

You may hear of one more scripting language occasionally. It is called *Tcl* (Tool Command Language, pronounced *tickle*). Tcl was developed by Sun Microsystems (the Java people). With Tcl, you can write *Tclets* (pronounced *ticklets*), which are just Tcl applets. Tcl is the UNIX programmer's answer to JavaScript. It has only been around for six years, but it does seem to be catching on in certain communities. Strangely (or not), Sun has a Netscape plug-in for Tcl, but no plug-in or ActiveX control that allows Tcl to run under Internet Explorer.

JavaScript Execution

When does a JavaScript execute? That depends. Some scripts, such as those that populate fields when the page first loads or those that query system variables to determine which version of a page to load, execute before the page loads. Then scripts execute based on some action taken by the visitor to the page, such as validating a form before submitting it or writing additional form fields to the page based on answers to previous questions. Scripts that execute based on visitor actions are called *event-driven scripts*. Events are discussed in detail in an upcoming section.

The choice of when the script executes is yours. If you want the script to execute when the page loads, you place the script into the BODY element. If you want the script to execute based on events, you place the script into the HEAD element. Having both kinds of scripts is permissible.

JavaScript Rules

Before you jump into the syntax of JavaScript, you need to know a few things.

JavaScript is case-sensitive. This means the following three statements are not the same thing:

```
redDog = 4;
RedDog = 4;
reddog = 4;
```

In the preceding three lines of code, you have either created three variables or set three separate variables to 4.

1. **All lines of JavaScript need to end with a semicolon.** Some of your lines of code will be more than one line. You can format your lines however you want, inserting line breaks wherever it is convenient so your code is easy to read. Remember to put a semi-colon at the end of each line; then the browser knows when the line ends.

2. **Events, event handlers, properties, functions, methods, and DOM properties and methods use special capitalization.** You've already seen this unusual capitalization system. The first letter of the first word is in lowercase and then each subsequent word has the first letter capitalized. There are no hyphens or underscores. Some examples of this are document.all.image(0). onMouseOver, ifValid(), and redDog.

3. **Rules for naming variables.** Variables in JavaScript are like variables in any other programming or scripting language. Variables in JavaScript are simply containers for holding data. If you want to store data temporarily, or until you can move it into a container that gets displayed on the page somewhere, you create a variable. Unlike some programming languages, you needn't define your variables before you use them. The first time the variable name appears, the script recognizes this as a new variable and assigns a type to it (integer, number, character, and so on) based on the value you give it.

You need to watch for some things:

- Variable names are case-sensitive.
- Variable names must begin with an alphabetic character or an underscore. Subsequent characters in the name can be alphabetic, numeric, or underscore (notice hyphens aren't allowed).
- Variables cannot be JavaScript keywords.
- Variables can be any length, but your fingers will get tired of typing 32-character variable names. Make names long enough to be meaningful, but short enough to type accurately.

Introducing Events

You have seen the word *events* in nearly every element definition in this book. An *event* is any action taken by the visitor sitting at the browser. An event can also be caused by the browser, such as when the page finishes loading. Every movement of the mouse, every click of the mouse, every keystroke can generate an event. As a developer, you must decide what kinds of actions you want to take based on events. Acting on events requires *event handlers*, which are discussed later on in this chapter.

The major scriptable events are shown in Table 48-1.

Table 48-1
Scriptable Events

Event	Trigger
load	This event is triggered when the page is loaded.
unload	This event is triggered when the page is unloaded (usually when another page is called).
mouseOver	This event is triggered when the mouse goes over an object on the page.
mouseOut	This event is triggered when the mouse is *no longer* over an object it was formerly over.
mouseDown	This event is triggered when a visitor clicks (only the downstroke of the mouse) on an object.
mouseUp	This event is triggered when visitors release the mouse button they have depressed. Most systems handle only the mouseUp event, rather than both the mouseDown and mouseUp, or only the mouseDown. If visitors start to click (triggering a mouseDown), and then move the mouse off of the object (triggering a mouseOut), and then release the button (triggering a mouseUp), then normally visitors don't want any action taken.
click	This event is triggered when visitors both click and release an object.
dblClick	This event is rarely used in Web pages because Web pages rely on single clicks, but you can capture and act on a double click, as well.
keyPress	This event is triggered when a keyboard key is depressed and released.
keyDown	This event is triggered when a keyboard key is depressed.
keyUp	This event is triggered when a keyboard key is released.
focus	This event is triggered only in forms, when the cursor moves to highlight a field (either by tabbing to that field, by using a mouse to place the cursor at that field, or by using an access key to bring the focus to that field).
blur	This event is triggered only in forms when the cursor is moved away from a field that was formerly in focus.
submit	This event is only triggered in forms when the object clicked is a BUTTON element with a `type` of "submit" or an INPUT element with a `type` of "submit."
reset	This event is only triggered in forms when the object clicked is a BUTTON element with a type of "reset" or an INPUT element with a `type` of "reset."
change	This event is only triggered in forms when the contents of the object in focus is changed and then the focus leaves this object. In other words, if an input field has today's date in it and the visitor changes the date and tabs to another field or clicks another field, then the change event is triggered.

As a developer, you must know what events you can trap. Then you need to think about what events you need to trap and how you want your page to behave, based on those events.

Event Handlers

As you can see, events are happening every time visitors move their mouse across your page, even if they never click anything. Think of all the mouseOver events this might generate. Does your browser actually send all those events somewhere to be processed? Luckily, no. The browser only pays attention to the ones you tell it to notice. It does this by looking for event handlers. *Event handlers* are attributes you can include in the definitions of your HTML elements.

```
<INPUT type="submit" value="Buy Now!" onSubmit="return
ifValid(this.form)">
```

The previous submit button executes the JavaScript function *ifValid()* before submitting the form. If the *ifValid()* function validates all the data, then it returns *true* and the form is submitted using the action attribute of the FORM element. If the function returns *false,* meaning one or more fields didn't validate, then the function returns some useful information (which you must program into the function yourself), and the form is not submitted.

```
<INPUT type="checkbox" name="Family_History" value="yes"
onClick="determineFamilyHistory()">
```

With the previously defined check box, if it is clicked, regardless of whether it is clicked to be selected or clicked to be deselected, a function called determineFamilyHistory() is called. *DetermineFamilyHistory()* (which the mythical programmer has written) looks at the value of the variable called Family_History to determine whether the value is "yes" or "no." If the answer is "yes," it writes additional fields to the page to request additional details about the family history.

Table 48-2 shows all the event handlers, what event they trap, and with what elements you can use them, if limitations exist.

Properties

Properties in JavaScript are exactly the same as properties in the DOM. Of course, since JavaScript existed before the DOM, there are JavaScript properties that exist outside the DOM. Most properties can be either viewed or changed. Some properties can only be viewed. This isn't the place for the complete list of properties in JavaScript — for this, see the wonderful and comprehensive *JavaScript Bible*, by Danny Goodman, IDG Books Worldwide — but a few properties will help you get the idea of how they are used.

Table 48-2
Event Handlers

Event Handler	Triggered on . . .	Element Limitations, if Any
onLoad	page finished loading	BODY, FRAMESET
onUnload	page unloading (or another page loading into the same window or frame)	BODY, FRAMESET
onMouseOver	mouse being over an object	
onMouseOut	mouse being moved off of an object	
onMouseDown	mouse being depressed	
onMouseUp	mouse being released	
onClick	mouse being depressed and released	
onDblClick	mouse being clicked twice	
onKeyPress	keyboard key being depressed and released	
onKeyDown	keyboard key being depressed	
onKeyUp	keyboard key being released	
onFocus	form field being highlighted either by tabbing, by an access key, or |by clicking in the field	INPUT, SELECT, BUTTON, TEXTAREA
onBlur	form field losing the focus by tabbing out of the field, by an access key, or by clicking another form field	INPUT, SELECT, BUTTON, TEXTAREA
onSubmit	submit button being clicked or pressed	INPUT, BUTTON
onReset	reset button being clicked	INPUT, BUTTON
onChange	the value of any field being changed and then that field losing focus	INPUT, SELECT, TEXTAREA

You access properties in JavaScript by appending the property name to the object name. For example, if you have a check box called *box1*, you might take some action based on whether it is selected. In this case, the object name is *box1* and the property name is *checked*.

```
if (box1.checked)
{take some action }
```

Another property you might want to check is the *length* property of a set of radio buttons. Recall that radio buttons usually occur in sets (one name is associated with multiple buttons, only one of which can be checked at one time). If you want to check to see which button is checked, you might want to loop through all the buttons. Even if you don't know how many buttons there are, you can loop through the list by checking each button from the 0th to the last in the list (the last in the list is the value of the object.length property). In this example, *buttonSet* is the name of the radio button set.

```
for (var i = 0; i < buttonSet.length; i++)
     {take some action}
```

One of the properties that make the DOM so exciting is the *display* property, which is now part of CSS. In the following example, the display property is set to "none" when *box1* is checked.

```
if (box1.checked)
{document.all.form[0].button[3].display == "none"}
```

Methods

What if you want to force an event? Say, as a result of a check box being checked, you want to jump to another page? Or, as a result of an item in a select list being selected, you want to take an action? Sometimes, you don't want to wait for a visitor to click a button, especially if only one field is in the form. Methods are ways to force events.

Not all methods work with all elements, but the methods available to you are the same as the events listed previously. A method is always shown followed by parentheses, because a method takes an action on something. For example, `focus(box1)` brings focus to whatever object is called *box1*.

How do you call a method? From anywhere in a script or from an event handler in your element definition. One example of each follows:

```
if (box1.checked)
        {focus(document.all.testform.newname)}

<INPUT type="checkbox"
onClick="focus(document.all.testform.newname)">
```

Notice in both examples, the method simply acts on whatever is in the parentheses. Generally, methods are used only in forms and the objects of the methods (what they act on) are also in forms. Using the focus() method is a good way to move the visitor to the correct next field for data entry.

Functions

Most of what you want to do with JavaScript, you write yourself in functions. *Functions* act on some data, so function names are also followed by parentheses. Methods are the freebie actions you can take in JavaScript without doing any real work. Everything else you need your scripts to do requires the sweat of your own brow.

Functions are where the rubber meets the road in JavaScript. Because JavaScript is an event-driven language, most of your functions will be called either by events handlers or by other functions. For purposes of illustration, follow this pseudocode example. *Pseudocode* is English that represents code, rather than the actual code. The syntax presented here is not actual JavaScript. Learning both the logic and the syntax at the same time is confusing so, first, follow the logic. The same example is shown with the actual JavaScript in Chapter 49.

The page in this example asks a series of mutually exclusive questions. Depending on the answers to the questions, it shows follow-up questions. In this example, the page is supposed to accept the names of expected twins, as part of an expectant mom's database. Before it can accept the twins' names, however, it needs to know whether the twins are both boys, both girls, or one of each.

HTML definition:

```
Q1. Are the twins both boys?
    If yes, call bothBoys()
Q2. Are the twins both girls?
    If yes, call bothGirls()
    If no and no to Q1, call oneOfEach()
```

JavaScript:

```
function bothBoys()
    change display property of Q2 so that it is hidden
    call showBoy1()
    call showBoy2()
function bothGirls()
    call showGirl1()
    call showGirl2()
function oneOfEach()
    call showBoy1()
    call showGirl1()
function showBoy1()
    change display property of Boy1 fields so that it shows
function showBoy2()
    change display property of Boy2 fields so that it shows
function showGirl1()
    change display property of Girl1 fields so that it shows
function showGirl2()
    change display property of Girl2 fields so that it shows
```

The actual JavaScript and HTML for this example is in Chapter 49. It is slightly more complex to demonstrate more scripting possibilities.

Passing Data from the Page to the Script

In the previous example, what form fields will be used in the HTML to accept the answers to the questions posed in Q1 and Q2 is not clear. Check boxes are out because, if the answer to both questions is "no," then neither will be checked, no visitor action will be taken, no events will be created, and the form fields for accepting the names will never appear. The two working options are radio buttons, with both Q1 and Q2 having two buttons: One each for "yes" and "no," and a select list with two options, "yes" and "no."

Either of these choices requires data be passed from the page to the script. Notice all the functions in the previous example have those parentheses following them? Well, this is where you put the data you want to pass. On the HTML definition, you put the data you want to send; on the JavaScript side, you put what you want to call the data when you receive it. This sounds simple enough, but how can you put data the visitor hasn't yet entered into the function name to send it from the page to the script? Obviously, you can't. JavaScript has a way of getting around this: it is called *this*.

This

No, this isn't one of those "Who's On First" routines. JavaScript enables you to send the contents of a form field, after it is entered, or if any action is taken on the field by the visitor, by using the reserved word *this*. What *this* sends is the value of only that field. If you need to send the contents of the entire form, say, from the onSubmit event handler to validate data before you submit it, you can say *this.form*. So, if you want to send the value of Q1 radio buttons to the script, you could use the following HTML:

```
Q1. Are the twins both boys: <BR>
<INPUT type="radio" name="bothBoys" onClick="form(this)"> Yes
<BR>
<INPUT type="radio" name="bothBoys" onClick="form(this)"> No
<BR>
```

If you want to validate an entire form, when the *submit* button was clicked, you could use the following HTML:

```
<INPUT type="submit" value="Send Now!"
onSubmit="validateAll(this.form)">
```

This submit button would submit the names and values of all the form fields to a function of your own creation called *validateAll*.

What the script sees

Sending the value of the bothBoys radio button in the previous example is the same as telling the script to use the value of the object `document.form[0].bothBoys`. You can see using this property name in every reference in this script could get cumbersome fast. Instead, when you send the value of bothBoys using the *this* reserved word, you can choose what you want to call the field within the script.

Being able to call the field whatever you want is important. Notice the showBoy1() function is called by two other functions. If `showBoy1()` acted on data, rather than just displaying (or rather unhiding) form fields, then you would have to create two different versions of the same function, one to act on each specific object. This wouldn't be at all efficient. Instead, you can create a variable to hold the value of the object you are processing in the script until you return it to the page.

```
function bothBoys ( boys2 ) {
  if (boys2 = "yes") {
      document.all.bothGirls.display = "none";
      showBoy1 ();
      showBoy2 ();
  }
}
```

Notice in the function definition line, you are told whatever data comes into the bothBoys function will be called *boys2* while it is inside the function. JavaScript simply creates a container of the type of the data sent to it. In this example, the variable *boys2* is only referred to once. Even so, it is far more convenient to refer to the value of *boys2*, than to refer to the entire object name.

Sending form data

When you send the entire contents of a form to a script to be validated, you will be grateful for the *this* reserved word. Here is an example of a possible *validateAll()* function for a short form.

```
function validateAll (myform) {
  validText(myform.first_name);
  validText(myform.last_name);
  validEmail(myform.email);
  validPhone(myform.phone);
}
```

Without the *this* reserved word, your script would be far more verbose and prone to error.

Adding Scripts with the SCRIPT Element

Now that you have an idea what you put into your JavaScript, you must understand how to insert your JavaScript into your page. HTML offers the SCRIPT element. If you want the script to be event-driven, include the SCRIPT element in the HEAD. If you want the script to execute when the page first loads, you include the script in the BODY element. You can have both types of scripts.

Even after you insert your SCRIPT elements, you still need to decide where to put your script. You can put the script into the SCRIPT element, but you needn't. If your script is long or if it uses functions you want other scripts to use, you can put your script into an external text file and link to it with the SCRIPT element's src attribute. For JavaScript scripts, the file extension is usually .JS.

A note about JavaScript-challenged browsers

Although most browsers in use are JavaScript capable, "hiding" your scripts from JavaScript-challenged browsers is still considered good form. You can easily do this by commenting out the actual contents of your script. A browser will ignore any tags it doesn't recognize, so the JavaScript-challenged browser will see the <SCRIPT> tag and ignore it, and then it will see a big, long comment (that actually contains your script), so it will ignore that, too, and then it will see the </SCRIPT> tag and ignore that.

Script `<SCRIPT>`

Start Tag:	Required
Content:	Script statements
End Tag:	Required
Attributes:	`charset`: defaults to charset in version declaration
	`type`: content type of scripting language (for example, "text/javascript")
	`language`: deprecated; replaced by *type*
	`src`: URL of the script if it is in an external file
	`defer`: Boolean variable that indicates this script is event-driven and the browser needn't take any actions upon loading the page

The JavaScript-capable browser, on the other hand, won't be fazed by HTML comments. It knows once it is within a `SCRIPT` element, the only comments that count are JavaScript comments (enclosed between /* and */), so it will process the script just as it should.

Testing and Debugging JavaScript

You almost can't avoid testing and debugging JavaScript. When you load a page with JavaScript, the first thing the browser does is review the script for syntax. Anything it doesn't like, it tells you about — right then and there. Then, as you try to execute the script, it finds *and reports* every error it finds along the way.

JavaScript is interpreted, rather than compiled. This means, instead of ever giving you a single, long listing of errors, it tells you about them, one annoying pop-up box at a time. If you have never come to a site where your browser reported a JavaScript error in your days of surfing the Web, then you must be pretty new at this. Some sites have different errors on different days.

Even after you figure out what all your errors are and fix them to your satisfaction, a good idea is to try clicking fields in an order that doesn't make sense, to be sure things work as they should even when visitors do unexpected things.

From Here

Jump to Chapter 50, Creating Interactive Documents.

Proceed to Chapter 49, Building Dynamic Forms.

Summary

JavaScript is a powerful scripting language that enables you to manipulate your page in all sorts of exciting ways, thanks to the DOM. This chapter covered the mechanics of JavaScript, but you won't really know how to use it until you see it in action. The next two chapters show examples of JavaScript in use to do things you might want to do on your page today.

✦　　✦　　✦

Building Dynamic Forms

JavaScript gives you client-side processing power. What this means is you can perform some initial processing of form data before the data ever leaves the client's workstation. This saves you time (less network travel) and server-processing power. Using JavaScript, you can be sure no form data is submitted until all the fields are completed to your satisfaction.

In the previous chapter, you saw an example of a dynamic form, where an initial short form loads when the page is drawn and then as the short form is populated, more fields that are appropriate to what has already been completed, appear. In this chapter, you learn how to write the JavaScript for that form, including the ever-important field: validation.

Form Objects and Events

You only need to script a handful of form elements to make your form dynamic and to test for valid input. This chapter isn't intended as the complete reference guide to JavaScript. Rather than listing every property that is part of an object, it lists the ones you are most likely to see, with examples.

INPUT type ="text" and INPUT type ="password"

Description	accepts single-line entry of text
Properties used most often	className, defaultValue, maxLength, name, size, style, title, value
Methods used most often	blur, click, focus
Collections	all, children, filters
Events	onblur, onchange, onclick, onfocus, ondblclick, onkeypress, onkeydown, onkeyup

```
object.className = "newClass"
```

All these examples use the generic object name *object*. In reality, you would use either the object's relative name or the variable name you assigned to the object in the function. This example sets the value of the class attribute to "newClass", which has presumably been defined elsewhere.

```
object.defaultValue = "Enter your name here."
```

The default value of the text box, that is the text that appears in the box when the page is redrawn, now is "Enter your name here." The value of the size attribute would have to be pretty large to accommodate all this text.

```
object.maxLength = 25
```

This statement sets the value of the maxLength attribute to 25 from whatever it was previously.

```
if (object.name="LastName") {
  object.size = 15}
```

In this example, if the name attribute of the object is "LastName", then the size attribute gets set to 15.

```
object.style.display = "none"
```

This statement makes the object invisible. Notice the property is style.display. The style property can take any of many different properties, most of which are discussed in the section about cascading style sheets. Pretty much, if you can set the property in CSS, you can change it with JavaScript.

INPUT type="checkbox"

Description	accepts yes or no (true or false); only transmits any data when the value is yes or true
Properties used most often	checked, class, name, style, title, value
Methods used most often	blur, click, focus
Collections	all, children, filters
Events	onblur, onchange, onclick, onfocus, ondblclick

```
if (object.checked) {
      object.title = "This box is checked."}
else {
      object.title ="This box is not checked."}
```

In this example, the `title` property is changed to change the value of the *tooltip* that appears in a pop-up box over the check box, when the mouse is held over the check box.

```
if (object.type = "checkbox") {
object.value = "Red"}
```

In this example, if the object is of type "checkbox," meaning it was defined in HTML as type="checkbox", then the value associated with it is set to "Red".

INPUT type="radio"

Description	accepts one value from a set of possible values
Properties used most often	checked, class, name, style, title, type, value
Methods used most often	blur, click, focus
Collections	all, children, filters
Events	onblur, onchange, onclick, onfocus, ondblclick

```
if (object.defaultChecked) {
      object.value = "default"}
```

In this example, if the object was defined in HTML with the Boolean attribute of `checked`, then the value of the value property is set to "default".

INPUT type="submit"

Description	accepts one value from a set of possible values
Properties used most often	name, style, title, type, value
Methods used most often	blur, click, focus
Collections	all, children, filters
Events	onblur, onchange, onclick, onfocus, ondblclick, onmouseover

```
<INPUT type="submit" value="Done" onclick="return
validateAll(this.form)">
```

In the previous example, when the "Done" button is clicked, all the data from the form is sent to the `validateAll()` function, where it is validated. As a result of the validation, either true or false is returned to the `INPUT` statement. If the form data validates, true is returned and the data is submitted to the form. If the form data does not validate, false is returned and one or more error messages are generated, based on how the `validateAll()` function is designed.

The Form

You've seen all the HTML elements by now. So, without much explanation, this is the form on which all our scripting is based. Take a close look at it so you understand what it displays.

You will be asked for your mother's maiden name as a password to your record. You can use another password, if you prefer; just remember what it is so you can modify your record later, if you must.

```
<form action="CH49-2.html" method="POST">
<table width="600">

<tr><td colspan="2" align="center"><b>About the Mom</b>

<tr>
      <td align="RIGHT">First name:
      <td><input type="Text" name="first_name" size="18">

<tr>
      <td align="RIGHT">Last name:
      <td><input type="Text" name="last_name" size="25">
```

```
<tr>
        <td align="RIGHT">Email address:
        <td><input type="Text" name="email" size="20">

<tr>
        <td align="RIGHT">Country:
        <td><input type="Text" name="Country" value="USA"
size="5">

<tr>
        <td align="RIGHT">Web page address:
        <td><input type="Text" name="web_page" size="30">

<tr>
        <td align-"RIGHT">Date of Birth (mm/dd/yy):
        <td><input type="Text" name="dob" size="12">

<tr><td colspan="2"><hr>
<tr><td colspan="2" align="center"><b>About the Siblings</b>

<tr>
        <td align="RIGHT">Are there any siblings?
        <td><input type="checkbox" name="siblings" size="25">

<tr>
  <td align="RIGHT">If so, how many?
  <td><select name="count">
        <option>0
        <option>1
        <option>2
        <option>3
        <option>4
        <option>5
        </select>

<tr><td colspan="2"><hr>
<tr><td colspan="2" align="center"><b>About the Baby or
Babies</b><tr>
<tr>
  <td align="RIGHT">Due date (mm/dd/yy):
  <td><input type="Text" name="due_date" size="12">

<tr>
  <td align="RIGHT">Twins?
  <td><input type="Checkbox" name="twins">

<tr>
  <td align="RIGHT">Sex known scientifically?
  <td><input type="Checkbox" name="sex_for_sure">

<DIV class="Known" style="display: none">
<tr>
  <td align="RIGHT" valign="top">Know to be:
```

```
   <td><input type="radio" name="known_sex" value="b">
Boy(s)<BR>
   <input type="radio" name="known_sex" value="g"> Girl(s)<BR>
   <DIV class="Both" style="display: none">
   <input type="radio" name="known_sex" value="s"> One of each
(twins only)
   </DIV>
</DIV>

<DIV class="Guessed" style="display: none">
<tr>
   <td align="RIGHT" valign="top">Guessed to be:
   <td><input type="radio" name="guessed_sex" value="b"> Boy<BR>
   <input type="radio" name="guessed_sex" value="g"> Girl
</DIV>

<DIV class="Twins" style="display: none">
   <DIV class="boys" style="display: none">
<tr>
   <td align="RIGHT">Boys' Names (first and middle)
   <td><input type="Text" name="A_first_name" size="18">
<input type="Text" name="A_middle_name" size="18">
   <tr>
   <td>
   <td><input type="Text" name="B_first_name" size="18">
<input type="Text" name="B_middle_name" size="18">
   </DIV>

   <DIV class="girls" style="display: none">
<tr>
   <td align="RIGHT">Girls' Names (first and middle)
   <td><input type="Text" name="A_first_name" size="18">
<input type="Text" name="A_middle_name" size="18">
   <tr>
   <td>
   <td><input type="Text" name="B_first_name" size="18">
<input type="Text" name="B_middle_name" size="18">
   </DIV>

   <DIV class="both" style="display: none">
<tr>
   <td align="RIGHT">Childrens' Names (first and middle)
   <td>Boy <input type="Text" name="A_first_name" size="18">
<input type="Text" name="A_middle_name" size="18">
   <tr>
   <td>
   <td>Girl <input type="Text" name="B_first_name" size="18">
<input type="Text" name="B_middle_name" size="18">
   </DIV>
<input type="hidden" name="A_sex">
<input type="hidden" name="B_sex">
</DIV>
```

```
<tr><td><input type="Submit" value="Proceed" onclick="return
validateAll(this.form)">
<input type="reset" value="Clear">
</table>
</form>
```

In the previous form, you can see most of the end of the form is contained in `DIV` elements with the display property set to "none" in the `style` attributes. Using JavaScript, you selectively turn on some of these fields, depending on the values of check boxes. This form could be far more extensive, asking for siblings' names, based on whether there are siblings, and dynamically generating the correct number of names boxes for siblings based on the number of siblings but, for purposes of example, it has plenty of material to script and validate.

In Figure 49-1, all the elements set to invisible (display: "none") in the HTML are visible. This is to make it obvious for now, that all those fields are there. In Figure 49-2, you see the form as it would load initially, based on the HTML definition given previously.

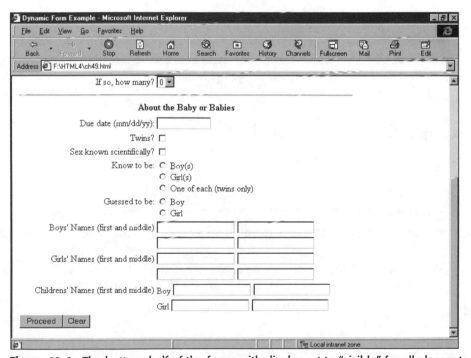

Figure 49-1: The bottom-half of the form, with display set to "visible" for all elements

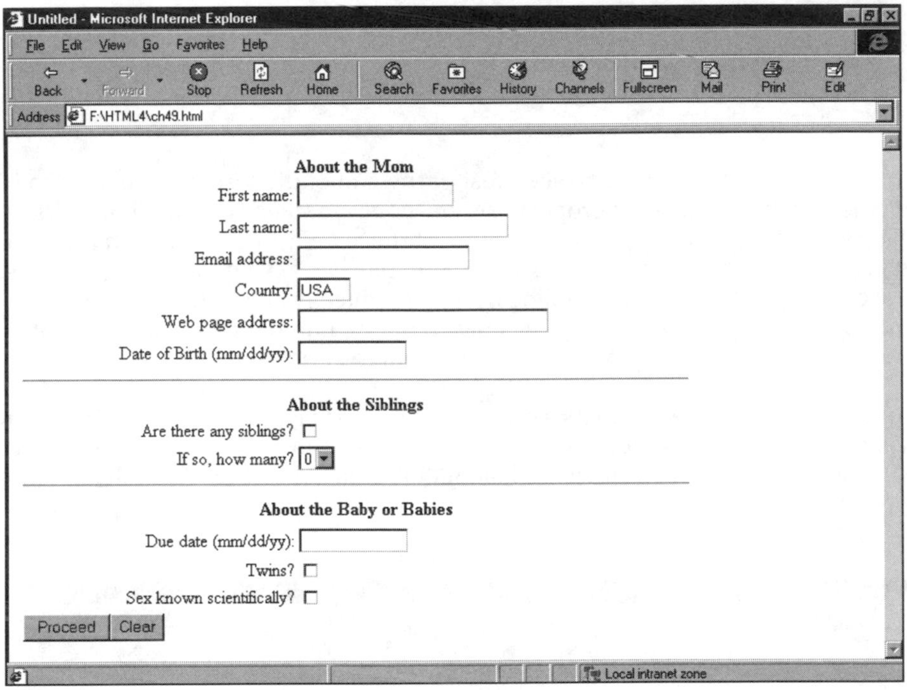

Figure 49-2: The form with hidden fields actually hidden

Testing for Valid Input

What kinds of input might you want to validate?

✦ that a field has data.

✦ that a field has numerical data, for example, a phone number.

✦ that a field has a valid date (formatted according to the specification you give in the instructions).

✦ that an e-mail address has some character string followed by an @ followed by some character string with one or more periods, but no spaces.

✦ that a Web address doesn't have any spaces in it.

In the previous form, you should check for two of the things in this list.

Passing the form data to the script

In the previous HTML, the submit button has an event handler on it. This event handler passes the form data `onclick="return validateAll(this.form)"`. What this statement does is to pass the entire contents of the form into a single variable. What is the variable it is passed into? You can't know until you look at the JavaScript:

```
function validateAll ( el ) {
if (isEmpty(el.first_name) || isEmpty(el.lastname)) {
  return false}
[do more stuff]
}
```

This is how the script begins. Notice you can avoid the long references to form fields by passing the entire form into a single variable. Each element within the form can referred to either by name, if you know it, or by its index value in the series of elements in the form. Because the element names are known in this example, names will be used.

Notice the `if` statement sends the `first_name` form field to the `isEmpty()` function. The double pipes (||) mean *or*.

Checking that data exists

This is the easiest thing to do. Every variable, regardless of where it comes from, has a built-in property called `length`. You can use the `length` property to determine how many characters are in a variable.

```
function isEmpty( el ){
return ((el == null) || (el.length == 0))
}
```

Checking for a valid e-mail address

An e-mail address should contain some character string without spaces, then an @, and then another character string without spaces, but with at least one period followed by at least two characters. Those rules won't guarantee the e-mail address is valid; `mickey@disney.com` would pass this test, but might not be a valid address.

```
function validateEmail(email) {
  if (isEmpty(email)) {        // email empty?
      alert("Enter your email address, please.");
      return false;
      }

  if (email.indexOf(" ",0) != -1) {  // space within name?
      alert("No spaces are permitted in an email address.");
      return false;
      }

  var atsignPos = email.indexOf("@", 0)  // check for @
  if (atsignPos == -1) {
      alert("Enter a valid email address with an @, please.");
      return false;
      }

  if (email.indexOf(".", atsignPos) == -1) {  // check for .
// after @
      alert ("Enter a valid email domain after the @,
please.");
      return false;
      }

  return true;
  }
```

Notice the first thing checked in the previous function is whether the e-mail variable is empty. The isEmpty() function from the previous example is used to check to see whether the variable is empty. Whenever possible, you want to reuse functions.

The other things this example include are:

✦ **Comments.** Comments are preceded by two slashes (//). Everything to the right of the two slashes is ignored by JavaScript. Even so, commenting your JavaScript is a good idea, so you remember what you wanted it to do the next time you return to it.

✦ **Alerts.** An alert sends a pop-up box to the screen with a message. The pop-up box has an OK button to make it go away.

✦ **The** indexOf() **function.** JavaScript has many built-in functions, including indexOf(). What this function does is to tell you at which position in the string (the variable is the string) a certain character occurs. If the character is not in the string, the function returns a value of –1. So, to test to determine whether a certain character occurs within the string, we test to see whether the function returns –1.

Making Parts of Forms Appear or Disappear

One of the powerful things about HTML 4 and the DOM is the capability to make parts of a form appear or disappear. Prior to HTML 4, you would have to use multiple pages or multiple frames within a page to ask the right follow-up questions based on the initial questions asked. In the previous example, the number of form fields and titles on form fields depends on whether there are twins. To do this before HTML 4, CSS, and the DOM, you would have to place the check boxes asking about twins and whether the sex is known scientifically on the first page, and then the question about what the sex is/are would go on a second page; and, finally, the boxes for accepting the names of the children would go on the third page. You can see the new way is much more elegant.

Appear

As long as the form fields have already been defined within a `DIV` element, and the `DIV` element is created with a `display` value of none, making the form fields or, actually, that entire part of the page, appear is relatively simple.

```
makeAppear (item) {
item.style.display = "visible";
}
```

Disappear

Conversely, making the same item disappear is as simple as setting the display property to none.

```
makeDisappear (item) {
   item.style.display = "none";
   }
```

Resources

This chapter could not begin to scratch the surface of what JavaScript can do. If you really want to know JavaScript, look at one or more of the following resources. They are invaluable to the authors:

JavaScript Bible, by Danny Goodman (IDG Books Worldwide, 1998)

The JavaScript Guide to Netscape Navigator Version 4.0, published and distributed by Netscape, and other up-to-the-minute JavaScript documentation: `http://developer.netscape.com/tech/javascript/index.html?content=/docs/manuals/javascript.html`

Microsoft's DHTML Reference Guide online at `http://www.microsoft.com/msdn/sdk/inetsdk/help/dhtml/references/objects/objects.htm#om40_objects`

Web Techniques magazine, available on newsstands.

From Here

Cross-Reference

Jump to Chapter 51 and learn why none of the new tricks work as you expect them to work across both major browsers: standardization.

Proceed to Chapter 50 and follow another example of using JavaScript with the DOM to create an exciting interactive Web page.

Summary

The day forms appeared on the Web, the face of the Web changed forever. With forms, you can take information from visitors, as well as give it to them. Taking in data, however, has always been risky. What if they give you junk? What if they leave fields blank? What if they format the data wrong? You didn't used to have to think about these things until the data was sent to your server. But this has changed. With JavaScript and client-side processing, you can guarantee nothing arrives at your server until it is in a condition to be entered into your database (or wherever you put it).

To make your forms even more exciting, you can use the DOM to make fields magically appear based on the data entered by the visitor. How often have you seen a form that said, "If no, skip to Q. 14." With the DOM, you can make those decisions for visitors and only show them the questions they need to answer.

✦   ✦   ✦

Creating Interactive Documents

The DOM and JavaScript make it possible for the contents of a browser page to resemble closely the interactivity and responsiveness of any other application on your desktop. When you see a file listing on your desktop, you can show or hide the files and folders within a given directory. With the DOM and JavaScript, you can simulate these types of dynamic responses to user interaction.

In the previous chapter, the interactive form example showed how form fields could be made to appear and disappear based on user interaction with other form fields. In this chapter, you see how JavaScript and the DOM can be used to create a dynamic table of contents, one in which each subsection is visible or invisible, based on actions taken by the user.

Defining Hidden Text

JavaScript is a powerful language. JavaScript enables you to define HTML elements right from the script, even if you don't define those elements in your HTML body. This probably isn't the way you want to do things, however. Why not?

✦ Maintaining the page later is more difficult

✦ Writing the page in the first place takes longer

✦ Testing the page is more difficult

The best way to create hidden text is to include anything you want hidden right in your HTML and then to define it with a style of `display: none`. In the previous chapter, this is how the form fields that are initially hidden are created.

```
<DIV CLASS="leveltwo" STYLE="display:none">
    <H2>Defining Hidden Text</H2>
    <H2>Bringing Hidden Text Into View</H2>
    <H2>Designing an Interactive Table of Contents</H2>
    <H2>Dynamically Modifying Styles</H2>
</DIV>
```

In this example, these four lines of H2 text will not appear until the `display` property is set to something other than "none."

Bringing Hidden Text Into View

To make your hidden text display, all you must do is turn the display property of the DIV element that contains your hidden text to "visible" or "" (empty quotes). The following JavaScript turns the previous hidden text into visible text or visible text into hidden text. In the first line, an `if` statement tests to see whether the element is visible. If the text is visible (`style.display==""`), then JavaScript makes the text invisible. If the text is invisible (`style.display=="none"`), then JavaScript sets the text to be visible.

```
        if (thisChild.style.display == "" )
        thisChild.style.display = "none";
else
        thisChild.style.display = "";
```

`thisChild` is the variable name assigned to the H2 entries listed in this example.

Designing an Interactive Table of Contents

In this example, the table of contents dynamically shows and hides section headings within Chapters 49 and this chapter. Figures 50-1 and 50-2 show the table of contents in this example fully collapsed and fully revealed.

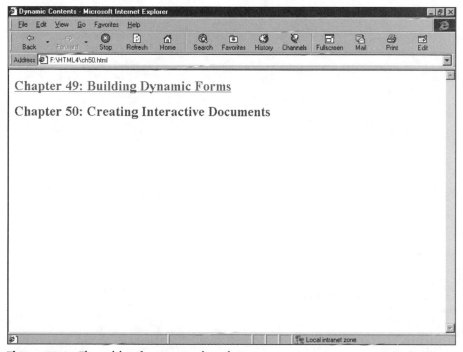

Figure 50-1: The table of contents closed

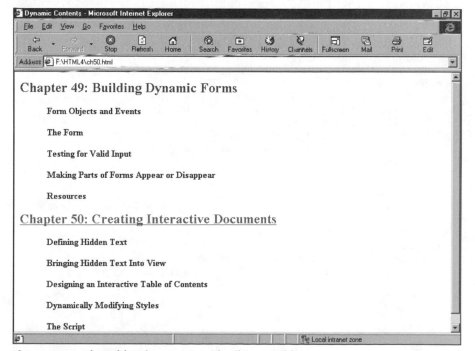

Figure 50-2: The table of contents with all text visible

The HTML used to accomplish this is listed in the following:

```
<HTML>
<HEAD>
<TITLE>Dynamic Contents</TITLE>

<STYLE TYPE="text/css">
        H1 {
color: blue;
font-size:18pt;
}
        H2 {
color: black;
font-size: 12pt;
}
        DIV.leveltwo {
margin-left: 0.5in;
}
</STYLE>
<SCRIPT Language="JavaScript">
<!--
... script goes here ...
-->
</SCRIPT>
</HEAD>
<BODY>

<DIV class="levelone" STYLE="position:absolute; width:550">
<DIV> <!-- although this DIV has no apparent purpose, it needs
to be here -->
<H1 onMouseOver="onLevelOne( this );"
  onMouseOut="notOnLevelOne( this );"
  onClick="hideContents( this );">Chapter 49: Building Dynamic
Forms</H1>
   <DIV CLASS="leveltwo" STYLE="display:none">
        <H2>Form Objects and Events</H2>
        <H2>The Form</H2>
        <H2>Testing for Valid Input</H2>
        <H2>Making Parts of Forms Appear or Disappear</H2>
        <H2>Resources</H2>
   </DIV>

</DIV> <!-- close for DIV with no apparent purpose -->

<DIV> <!-- DIV with no apparent purpose -->
<H1 onMouseOver="onLevelOne( this );"
  onMouseOut="notOnLevelOne( this );"
  onClick="hideContents( this );">Chapter 50: Creating
Interactive Documents</H1>
```

```
<DIV CLASS="leveltwo" STYLE="display:none">
    <H2>Defining Hidden Text</H2>
    <H2>Bringing Hidden Text Into View</H2>
    <H2>Designing an Interactive Table of Contents</H2>
    <H2>Dynamically Modifying Styles</H2>
    <H2>The Script</H2>
</DIV>

</DIV> <!-- close for DIV with no apparent purpose -->
</DIV> <!-- close for levelone DIV -->

</BODY>
</HTML>
```

Note these few things about this HTML listing:

✦ **The styles are defined right in the** HEAD, rather than in a separate style sheet.

✦ **The script is missing.** Because this requires its own explanation, it will be outlined later in this chapter.

✦ **Everything is contained in** DIV **elements.** You can pretty much divide the page into a series of nested DIV elements. This is important to the way formatting works, as well as in the way text is made to appear and disappear. In fact, if you strip out all the rest of the content, you have the following sets of DIV elements:

```
<DIV class="levelone">
  <DIV>
        <DIV class="leveltwo">
        </DIV>
      </DIV>
    <DIV>
        <DIV class="leveltwo">
        </DIV>
      </DIV>
</DIV>
```

✦ **Some of the** DIVs **have no apparent purpose.** We want to give you a good explanation for why they are needed, but we can't. This script simply won't work properly without them.

✦ **The** H1 **elements have three event handlers on them:** onMouseOver(), onMouseOut(), **and** onClick(). The first event handler, onMouseOver(), enables your script to do something when the mouse is over the contents of the H1 element — in this case, change the text color. The second event handler, onMouseOut(), enables your script to do something when the mouse is no longer over the contents of the H1 element — in this case, return to the original text color. The final event handler, `onClick()`, is the one you are most used to seeing. It actually calls the function that shows or hides the contents.

✦ **This example includes the actual text that will show and hide.** It would be more common actually to pull the text to be used in this table of contents from an external file or database. Exactly how you would do this depends on the technology you are using, which would be specific to your Web server.

Dynamically Modifying Styles

The presence of the `onMouseOver()` and `onMouseOut()` event handlers in the previous HTML suggest we can make changes to the contents of those elements or to other elements on the page based on where the mouse is. In fact, what we do in this example is change the color and decoration of the text in the H1 elements. Of course, you could change anything about the styles of the H1 elements.

The style definition of the H1 element is:

```
H1 {
color: blue;
font-size:18pt;
}
```

Changing the value of the color property to red and adding a text decoration of underline is easily accomplished in JavaScript:

```
function onLevelOne( el ){
  el.style.color = "red";
  el.style.textDecoration = "underline";
  return;
}
```

Changing the style back to the original style is just as simple:

```
function notOnLevelOne( el ){
  el.style.color = "blue";
  el.style.textDecoration = "none";
  return;
}
```

The Script

Finally, here is the entire JavaScript you need to include in the SCRIPT element in the previous HTML. Most of it should look familiar.

```
function onLevelOne( el ){
  el.style.color = "red";
  el.style.textDecoration = "underline";
  return;
}

function notOnLevelOne( el ){
  el.style.color = "blue";
  el.style.textDecoration = "none";
  return;
}

function hideContents( el ){
  var elParent = el.parentElement;
  var childrenCount = elParent.children.length;
  var thisChild = 0;
  for( i = 0; i<childrenCount; i++ ){
      thisChild = elParent.children(i);
      if (thisChild != el ){
          if (thisChild.style.display == "" )
              thisChild.style.display = "none";
          else
              thisChild.style.display = "";
      }
  }
  return;
}
```

The only function that should look unfamiliar to you is hideContents(). This function loops through all the children of the element that calls it (this means it loops through all the DIV elements nested within the DIV element of the element that calls it) and changes the display property for each one.

As mentioned in the previous two chapters, JavaScript and the implementation of the DOM vary for Microsoft Internet Explorer and Netscape Navigator. This example only works properly in Internet Explorer 4 and above.

From Here

Cross-Reference

Jump to Chapter 52, Intellectual Property: Copyright and Trademarks, and learn how to protect your own, and how not to get into trouble for violating someone else's, rights.

Proceed to Chapter 51, Standardization, and learn why nothing seems to work in both major browsers and when, if ever, you can expect this to change.

Summary

With all this exposure to JavaScript, you are well-armed to make your pages dance. If you want to script your pages to the hilt, though, be well-advised to consult the resources listed at the end of Chapter 49. They contain additional valuable examples.

In this chapter, you saw a simple example of a folding table of contents. Some of the properties should have looked familiar to you, but you saw them used in new ways. The complete working example in this chapter can be used as a jumping-off point for your own dynamic Web page.

✦   ✦   ✦

Web Publishing Issues

Standardization

Standardization is the name of the game on the
Web. Because everyone agrees Web pages should
be loaded using the HTTP protocol, every browser can
load every standard Web page. When people or companies
stop conforming to the standard or, more frequently,
develop new standards in areas that aren't yet well
developed, standardization becomes a problem.

This chapter sorts the thorny history of standardization.
You learn why so many things (JavaScript, the DOM, Java
implementation, and CSS implementation) aren't yet standard
between the major browsers. You also learn a bit about the
process that exists within the W3C for creating standards.

Introduction to Standardization

This chapter is being written in reverse order. First, you
read about the rational process in place to insure every
new technology is compatible with every existing technology
and that all the major players in these industries sing songs
holding hands. Then you read about the actual process an
individual company goes through to bring a new technology
to market before its competitors get it done. This includes all
the compelling reasons why a company can't stop and wait for
everyone else to agree (and catch up) with what it is doing. By
the end of this chapter, you understand why standardization
rarely precedes technical innovation and why developers will
always be in a position of having to make tradeoffs between
universal access to their page (by every browser that has
ever been written) and implementing the latest, coolest
technologies. Finally, you see, eventually, after a technology
has aged a bit and is no longer the hottest technology out, all
the players can come together and agree on a standard.

Understanding the Standardization Process

The process of setting standards for Web-related technologies is run by the World Wide Web Consortium (W3C) based at MIT in the U.S. and at INRIA in Europe. The W3C is led by Tim Berners-Lee, "creator of the World Wide Web," as the W3C pages tell you repeatedly. The W3C is a consortium. The vocabulary used to define a *consortium,* how it runs, and how it works is a study in nonconfrontation. The person who runs it is a *director.* The people who get paid to do what Berners-Lee says are his *team.* The companies that pay to participate and get a vote in what is decided are *members.* When the W3C is thinking about setting a standard for a technology, it *initiates an activity.* When a W3C committee has decided upon what it thinks is a standard, it issues a *proposed recommendation.* After the membership votes to support the proposed recommendation, it becomes a *recommendation.*

No wonder the W3C doesn't claim to have any enforcement power. With a passive vocabulary like this, it couldn't enforce a bedtime!

Participation in the standardization practice is similar to participation in social activities. If you are going to show up, you'd better behave according to accepted norms. Throwing a tantrum at a meeting about the standards for a technology about which you feel strongly is strictly frowned upon by the members.

Activities

If a member of the W3C (members are universities, corporations, and organizations, but not individuals) thinks the W3C should look into setting a standard, and then members can initiate an activity. Members may initiate activities both for technologies and for social issues affected by technology. If the W3C agrees some interest exists in this activity, then committees and mailing lists are formed to determine which direction that technology should go.

The Activity Proposal needs to answer some hard questions:

✦ What is the market? Who are the major players? Who stands to benefit from a standard? Are the players and the beneficiaries members of the W3C or will they join? Is the market new, growing, or a niche market? What alternatives to this technology are there? Who owns these technologies?

✦ How many resources of the W3C will this need?

✦ What is the scope of the project?

✦ Is there a deadline? What are the timelines?

✦ Are there any intellectual property conflicts?

✦ Is anyone else setting standards for this technology? Will there be a conflict? Whom will this affect?

✦ Is an activity already in place that covers this technology?

Groups

If an activity proposal is accepted by the director, then a working group is formed to begin work on the activity. The goal of most *working groups* is to produce a statement or a proposed recommendation. The composition of the working group is important. Any technology company in any way affected by the recommendations regarding an activity will want to be part of this working group. You can bet both Netscape and Microsoft were represented on the HTML 4 working group. Only members can participate in working groups for activities.

Consensus

Not surprisingly, the W3C operates by consensus. A working group must address the concerns of all participants and make an effort to resolve them before reaching a conclusion. A simple majority rule is not enough. The idea is the working group hashes through every possibility until either everyone is in agreement, the people who dissent are convinced the position arrived at is the best possible position given the constraints, or the people in the minority think the problem is no longer worth fighting over.

This philosophy protects small start-ups that come to the table with new technology to protect. It gives every party — whether Sun, Microsoft, or Midge's New Technology Company — an equal weight.

Proposed recommendations

Not all activity proposals result in proposed recommendations, but many do. When a working group has resolved the conflict raised by its membership and has drafted what it thinks is a pretty good attempt to set a standard, it publishes what is called a *proposed recommendation*. A proposed recommendation — even working drafts that are developed along the way — is published to the W3C Web site. Most materials you purchase in bookstores explaining the newest technologies are actually written with the working drafts or the proposed recommendations as the reference materials.

Voting

By following the process of consensus building that takes place during the drafting of the proposed recommendation, the hope is all major conflicts have been resolved by the time the proposed recommendation is issued. During the voting period, all members of the W3C — whether or not they participated on the working group (and most won't have) — vote on the proposed recommendation.

At the end of the voting period, the director, ever the facilitator of good will, has three choices:

1. Issue the proposed recommendation as a recommendation
2. Reject the proposed recommendation
3. Issue the proposed recommendation with comments

When members vote, they can make comments in addition to their vote. If the comments are substantial, especially if the comments that accompany no votes are substantial, then the director will not accept the proposed recommendation as a recommendation. Thus far, the process of consensus has been effective in dealing with the comments of members *before* the activity is no longer a draft; most proposed recommendations do become recommendations.

Recommendations

Even after all these steps are taken to ensure the viewpoint of every member is heard, considered, and incorporated as much as possible, the conclusions regarding standardization the W3C reaches are still only recommendations. Why? First, the W3C is an international standards body and does not yet have access to U.N. troops to enforce its resolutions. Second, all companies in the community of corporations are trying to develop the best new technologies without antagonizing *you*, the developer. Making up new and different ways to do the same thing, just to be different, doesn't serve the company's own interests. Each company is best served by having the largest pool of developers developing in that technology. This logic enticed Microsoft to offer native support for JavaScript in its Internet Explorer browsers. (Of course, Microsoft's native support isn't the same as Netscape's.) Companies that insist on "my way or the highway" often find themselves on the shoulder — alone.

Players in the Standardization Process

So who gets a vote when the W3C asks? Members of the W3C. Membership in the W3C isn't exclusive, however. Any organization or company can join. Of course, a rather high membership fee exists, which pays the administrative costs of running the W3C.

Who would want to get involved in the W3C? Technology vendors, content providers, corporate users, research laboratories, standards bodies, universities, and governments. If you develop a new technology, you need to be at the table when the standards for related technologies are being set. Otherwise, you run the risk of being written right out of the standard. If your operations are affected by new technologies, then you want to be on the working group, pushing for that standard in which you've already invested. If you develop content that makes use of new technologies, then you want to be well-positioned to know what resources you need to have in place when a new standard is implemented.

The major players, of course, are Microsoft and Netscape. They develop the browsers most widely used to visit Web sites. America Online (AOL) is another big player, but it competes with the Big Two differently. Microsoft and Netscape both want to see standards set that:

✦ are backward-compatible with their own browsers.

✦ make use of the newest technologies they are implementing—the way they are implementing them.

✦ don't require them to add any features or elements coined by their competitors.

But realistically, both browsers want to meet all the needs of the developers. If you, as a developer, find your site looks much better with one browser than with another, you may finally put a "Best Viewed with …" logo on your page and call it a day, rather than trying to make a silk purse out of a sow's ear with the other browser.

It might surprise you to learn Microsoft has been far quicker to adopt the technologies developed by others than has Netscape. Despite the bad rap Microsoft receives for its anticompetitive practices (so says Senator Arlen Specter), Microsoft implemented JavaScript as soon as it was clear this was what developers preferred (over its own VBScript). Netscape invented JavaScript, but it still hasn't opened everything in its browsers to scripting with the DOM, the way Microsoft has.

The Extensions Game

How do you get the standards set in your favor? You create extensions you know aren't standard and implement them on your browser. If they catch up in the developer community, the other browser maker will be forced to become compliant with the de facto standard you have set. At this point, if the W3C accepts it, this is just icing.

Consider the FONT element. The FONT element has never been part of an official W3C specification, but Netscape introduced it, Microsoft adopted it, and until CSS is fully and uniformly implemented in both browsers, it will continue to give the best results for formatting text available. At some point, standardization is irrelevant. Finally, with the HTML 4 specification, the W3C recognized the FONT element just enough to deprecate it!

Consider the MARQUEE element. What's that, you ask? It *was* an element introduced by Microsoft that scrolled any text it contained across the screen, just like a marquee on a bank. It never caught on. Microsoft browsers were such a small share of the market at that time, not too many developers wanted to bet the farm on an element that wouldn't be seen by most Web visitors.

Where Is Netscape Headed?

The platform *is* the browser. Netscape was the first to embrace the concept of *crossware*, which is software that runs over the Internet. Crossware is installed from the Internet, upgraded from the Internet, and communicates with a server or other clients over the Internet.

In addition, the real *operating system* of crossware is the browser, not the computer's operating system! If the world moves toward software that runs only within the browser, then the platform on which the browser resides will be irrelevant. Netscape sees the browser sitting on the operating system, which lives and breathes only to server the browser.

Communicator suite

The Netscape Communicator suite already includes many business applications, such as messaging, e-mail, a calendar, and conferencing software. Netscape has put its money where its mouth is. All of its software is installed by a download from the Web.

So, if Netscape becomes the de facto operating system for millions of business applications, where does that leave Microsoft? With competition for the first time in a long time.

CORBA

Because Netscape now gives away its browsers, it must have something to sell or the company won't be in business much longer. What Netscape sells is *Web servers*. This is a tough market to be in, though, because so many other people are *giving* their servers away free. To help make Netscape's servers stand out above the crowd, Netscape has introduced its own standard for component-based, cross-platform, networked applications. This standard, the *Common Object Request Broker Architecture* (CORBA), allows components written in different languages to talk to each other over the network.

Where Is Microsoft Headed?

But Microsoft isn't worried. Microsoft's vision isn't so different from Netscape's vision. It, too, sees the browser as being the real platform.

Internet Explorer

Where Microsoft got into trouble recently was when it tried to make its Internet Explorer 4 browser just another *feature* of the operating system. In Microsoft's world, the operating system *owns* the browser and serves it as it would any other component of the operating system.

Microsoft's vision is bigger than just the world of desktop operating systems. Microsoft also has servers to sell. But instead of implementing CORBA, Microsoft's servers run DCOM.

DCOM

The *Distributed Component Object Model* (DCOM) is based on the Component Object Model (COM) on which ActiveX is based. The *COM* is a system of standards to which all COM-compliant applications must adhere. By meeting these standards, any COM application can talk to any other COM application. DCOM is an open standard, which means no one company *owns* the rules for COM. DCOM was actually developed by a consortium of businesses, including IBM, Sun, HP, and DEC.

How does DCOM differ from COM? DCOM takes COM over networks. DCOM uses existing protocols to move data from servers to clients and back again. DCOM works on both servers and clients. Another advantage to DCOM is you can write the components in any programming language, as long as you comply with the standards. Finally, many commercially available DCOM components exist, so if you do decide to implement DCOM in your shop, you don't have to write all the programs yourself.

From Here

Cross-Reference

Jump to Chapter 54 about privacy and learn what you may be sacrificing to all this standardization.

Proceed to Chapter 52, Intellectual Property: Copyright and Trademarks.

Summary

Standards are a Web developers dream. Oh, for the day when you can implement a fabulous new technology and *know* it will work on all platforms on all browsers in the same way. But, alas, that day will never come. Browser makers and other purveyors of technology don't make money by finishing neck-and-neck with their competitors. They need to be the first one across the finish line to deliver on a new technology.

Even with the W3C spelling out standards as fast as they can, it will never be able to anticipate technology to such a degree that the standards precede the technology. XML is a good attempt at this but, until it is implemented, the jury is still out.

All you can hope for is, within a reasonable period of time *after* a new technology is introduced, the competitive browser makers will implement it in a reasonably similar fashion. W3C or no W3C, the market is still the primary factor that drives standardization in this industry.

✦   ✦   ✦

Intellectual Property: Copyright and Trademarks

◆　◆　◆　◆

In This Chapter

Understanding intellectual property

What can you legally copy?

Copyright infringement and fair use

Plagiarism

Obtaining permission for use

Legal resources on the Web

◆　◆　◆　◆

When people think of the Web, they think of things being free and accessible but, in fact, most of the content on the Web enjoys protection under the law. Most people know they can't scan in the contents of a chapter of this book and publish it on the Web without breaking the law. But many people don't realize copying a Web page from another site or even a portion of a page (as little as a single "Go" button) is just as illegal.

The guidance provided in this book won't get you far in a court of law. This chapter is designed to keep you out of court. The guidelines provided are intentionally conservative. Will you necessarily get caught if you violate copyright laws? Of course not, but you might get caught and have to spend a lot of money on lawyers to defend yourself. Protection for intellectual property isn't just a nice idea; it's the law.

Understanding Intellectual Property

Just as there are people whose livelihood depends on the creation of physical property, there are people whose livelihood depends on the creation of intellectual property. A writer's work shouldn't be taken without compensation, any more than a carpenter's work should be taken without compensation.

What intellectual property includes

Intellectual property includes a fairly broad category of materials:

- ✦ book manuscripts
- ✦ poetry
- ✦ movie scripts
- ✦ patents
- ✦ logos
- ✦ shoe designs
- ✦ operating system software
- ✦ photographs

- ✦ architectural drawings
- ✦ refrigerator designs
- ✦ musical scores
- ✦ computer applications
- ✦ a plant hybrid
- ✦ computer graphics
- ✦ cartoons

This list is by no means comprehensive; it is only intended to give you an idea of how comprehensive the category of intellectual property is. In addition to the specific things listed previously, intellectual property includes anything that can be copyrighted, trademarked, or patented.

The difference most people concoct to defend using someone else's intellectual property in an unauthorized way is when you take intellectual property, you still leave the creator with his or her copy, so no harm done, right? Wrong.

While patents and trademarks must be applied for with the U.S. government's Office of Copyright and Trademark, protection for copyrights is far more liberal. Anything to which you affix the word *Copyright* and the year are considered copyrighted and entitled to protection under the law.

Understanding Public Domain

The alternative to copyright is public domain. Just because something is published on the Web doesn't mean it is in the public domain. Some works are automatically in the public domain. These include:

A work for which the copyright has expired. Copyrights aren't perpetual.

Anything published by the federal government. You can't copyright a tax form, for example.

Things that can't be copyrighted. Even though some things can't be copyrighted — slogans, titles, short phrases (bumper sticker material), names, and so on — they can be trademarked. Registering a trademark is a more complicated process, but trademarked materials are protected from duplication, as are copyrighted materials.

The copyright was forfeited. This is unusual, so don't count on it. You'd still have to hire a lawyer to prove this in court.

The copyright was abandoned. Abandoning the copyright takes more work than creating it. If people want to abandon their copyrights and place their intellectual property into the public domain, they can attach a statement to their work indicating anyone who wishes to may display the work. If the statement reads something like "This article is Copyright *this year* by *the author*, it may be freely redistributed in its entirety provided that this copyright notice is not removed....," then the copyright was *not* abandoned.

You can copy anything in the public domain without restraint. If a work specifies you may copy it, but you must retain attribution — for example, a site with colorful backgrounds for downloading says you can use the backgrounds for noncommercial use as long as you give credit to the creator — then unless you include attribution on the pages where you use the background, you are in violation of copyright.

The other time you can copy and reuse otherwise copyrighted material is when you are using it for fair use.

Fair Use versus Copyright Infringement

Few legal concepts are hazier than fair use. *Fair use* is when you use an otherwise copyrighted work without the permission of the creator, in an unauthorized way, but without violating copyright laws, right?

What does *not* (necessarily) constitute fair use is easier to say:

Reproduction of copyrighted material for educational use. This is probably the most misunderstood part of fair use. Many educators believe if they copy a chapter of a book without permission and make enough copies for everyone in the class, because this is for education, somehow it's fair use. It isn't. If you want to copy a chapter of a book for anything other than your own personal use, you need the permission of the copyright holder.

Reproduction of copyrighted material for noncommercial use. Copying a graphic you like for your personal home page—just because your home page isn't a commercial site—isn't fair use. If you want to use someone's graphic for your personal home page, write to the owner and ask for permission. Most creators will be flattered and give you permission.

Copying and republishing material you find on another site onto your site. Just because it is published on the Web doesn't mean it is fair game for reproduction. The owners of the material retain the right to that material even if they let you look at it on their site and the technology lets you copy it from their site.

All of these are copyright infringements. So what is fair use, anyway?

Fair use

Fair use is a subjective thing. The original statute is worded vaguely and the courts have sanctioned it using a variety of criteria. Unfortunately, you do have to go to court to prove fair use or, rather, to have a judge agree your interpretation of what fair use is legitimate.

Some of the factors that have contributed to a decision in favor of fair use include:

The effect such use may have on the potential market for the work. Even if the work hasn't yet been marketed, if it were marketed, how its market would be affected.

The amount and proportion of the work used. That is, if you use only 5 percent of a work, you're more likely to fall into fair use than if you use 80 percent of the work, but no specific percentage guarantees your usage will be determined fair use. Different sources give different guidelines as to how many photos from a book you can use or how many words from an article you can use, but the law simply doesn't specify a number.

The nature of the work used. If the work is fiction, you are generally limited more. If the work is nonfiction, you are generally given more liberty. If you want to argue with a paragraph of a nonfiction article, quoting it for that purpose would generally be considered fair use. Copyright is intended to protect the free exchange of ideas.

The purpose and character of the use. In this factor, educational use does have a leg up over commercial use, but the law doesn't make a distinction between commercial and noncommercial use and that alone does not make a use fair use.

Copyright infringement

If a work isn't in the public domain and you aren't using it under fair use guidelines, is it necessarily copyright infringement? No. The other two ways to avoid violating copyright, trademark, and patent laws are:

1. **Purchase the right to use it.** This seems rather obvious. Most people create intellectual property in anticipation of making money from it. If people are willing to extend the right to use their work to you for money, then you aren't in violation of anything. Just be sure when you purchase something for use on the Web (which is actually redistribution), you have specific permission to do so. For example, you can't put music from a commercial CD on the Web without permission. For most works, when you buy them, you only buy the right to use and enjoy them yourself; you don't buy the right to reproduce them, which is what publishing them on the Web is.

2. **Request the right to use it in writing.** For some things, such as cool animations you see on other Web pages, you just need to request permission to use the work on your own page, in writing (e-mail is fine) from the copyright owner. If the copyright owner doesn't mind, then you are in the clear.

Pretty much every other way you can think of to use intellectual property is considered copyright, trademark, or patent infringement.

Plagiarism

Give credit where credit is due. If you can remember this simple statement, you'll go far to avoid getting into trouble for plagiarism. You probably learned about plagiarism when writing a term paper in high school. If you quote what someone else had to say directly, you should attribute it to that person. If you take the essence of what someone else had to say and rephrase it, you should still attribute it to that person if it is an original idea or a newly discovered fact.

The easiest way to avoid plagiarism on the Web is to link to sites that support the point you want to make. Saying "*Great Web Books Review* gave the *HTML 4 Bible* five stars!!!" is not plagiarism, but it is more effective to say this and then link to the *Great Web Books Review* site where the quote actually originated. If you link to the site where you found the original quote if, in fact, you found it on the Web, then you are not likely to be accused of plagiarism.

People suspect plagiarism when they believe you have a reason to claim what someone else said first as your own original thought. If you show where you got the idea by providing a link to that page, then you dispel most concerns about plagiarism.

Derivative Works

Copyright laws not only protect the original work created by the author; copyright laws also protect the derivative works. *Derivative works* include works based heavily on the original work. If you paraphrase an entire article, without critical comment, this is a derivative work. You would be in violation of copyright to publish it.

Obtaining Permission for Use

Staying out of trouble is the name of the game in the copyright world. Why do most artists and authors create? In thought-provoking interviews with Brian Lamb on C-SPAN, authors say, "because it had to be said." But the reality for most is much simpler: to gain exposure and to make money. Does this mean they don't want you using their materials? Absolutely not. Most creators will let you use their work either for money or for recognition.

What isn't a derivative work?

You can safely do a few things to an original work to prevent having it fall into the category of derivative work.

✦ **Parody.** A parody based on an original work is not considered an original work.

✦ **Criticize or critique.** If you review an original work and make critical comments about the work, you can include short appropriate excerpts from the work to demonstrate your points.

✦ **Restate only the facts, where the facts weren't anyone's original thought.** If a fire occurs in your town and the television news reports the facts, you can safely re-report the facts in your own words for publication without worrying you might be creating a derivative work. You can't copyright facts.

For recognition

Because you now realize you can't use other people's stuff without violating copyright laws, you must find a way to get people to agree to let you use their materials free. The golden carrot that will entice most creators is recognition. Let's consider an example:

You come across a Web site with a fabulous background graphic. This is the Web site of a student organization at a university. You know you could probably take it and never get caught, because chances are the students who created this site can't afford to find you or to hire lawyers to sue you. But you are an honorable person. You've read this chapter and you understand intellectual property, so you decide to send mail to the address on the screen, where it says "maintained by..." and to request permission to use the background.

Chances are, the aspiring graphical artists in the preceding example would be flattered to have you use their background but, just to be sure, you could offer to mention the artists and their e-mail address or personal Web site somewhere in your site under credits. This costs you nothing and wins you future goodwill with artists whose work you like.

For money

Shocking, but true, is sometimes you have to pay for things even on the information superhighway (does anyone other than Al Gore call it this anymore?). If graphics you want to use are found on a commercial site—either one in the business of selling graphics or somewhere else—you may have to provide the other kind of incentive to get authors to give you permission to use their work: money.

Legal Resources on the Web

Many resources on the Web focus on copyright and fair use. Some of them are published by law firms that specialize in electronic intellectual property law. Some of them are published by legal organizations. Some of them are published by universities.

One excellent resource (see Figure 52-1) is provided by the Institute for Learning Technologies at Columbia University (`http://www.ilt.columbia.edu/projects/copyright/index.html`).

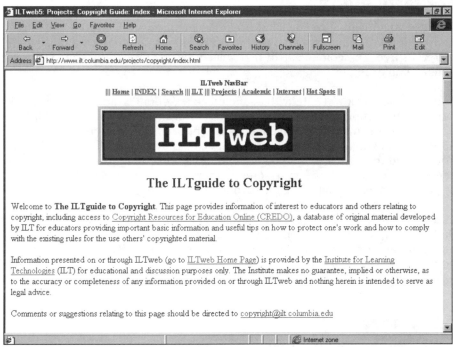

Figure 52-1: Columbia University's Institute for Learning Technologies Guide to Copyright

From Here

Cross-Reference

Jump to Chapter 54, Privacy.

Proceed to Chapter 53, Pornography, Indecency, and Obscenity.

Summary

Intellectual property—which includes a broad spectrum of materials—is protected by the law and judges who have not been afraid to enforce those laws. As a developer on the Web, you have a double interest in copyright laws: you want to be sure your own site is protected from theft and you want to be sure anything you publish on your site isn't in violation of someone else's copyright.

You can use other people's materials with permission and you can also use materials in the public domain. A third category, called fair use, is a lot thornier. Unfortunately, you can't be sure you are really protected by fair use guidelines until you get a judge to agree with you, and that can be an expensive proposition.

Fortunately, excellent resources are on the Web that can help you stay out of trouble and out of court. Your best defense in copyright — as in tax law — is to be as conservative as possible in interpreting the law. The other philosophy that will keep you out of trouble is to create everything that goes on your page yourself (or hire an artist or content provider).

✦   ✦   ✦

Pornography, Indecency, and Obscenity

The Web has turned out to be an attractive forum for vendors of the gamut of adult entertainment (smut), commonly referred to as pornography, indecency, and obscenity, depending on which law you are reading. Because of the concern about protecting children from these materials in a medium that is completely unrestricted, many governments and organizations have tried different approaches to make certain sites either illegal or inaccessible. Governments want to be sure they are addressing the concerns of parents to have a safe place for their children to surf. Libraries want to protect free speech, but avoid attracting perverts to their World Wide Web sites or having their computer centers become public-access peepshows. Finally, free-speech activists worry various types of controls — in the interest of keeping smut from the eyes of children — will make otherwise legal materials inaccessible to adults.

This chapter addresses the relevant laws regarding obscenity in the U.S. This chapter also briefly reviews the one major failed attempt of the U.S. government to create broad-based restrictions on Internet content. Even without clear laws governing the Internet, however, parents can still do things to protect their own children today. This chapter discusses the most popular software available for identifying and restricting Internet activity. Finally, we review what will probably be the best long-term strategy for protecting people from inappropriate material: the W3C's PICS initiative.

> ## 18 U.S. Code § 1465. Transportation Matters for Sale or Distribution
>
> Whoever knowingly transports in interstate or foreign commerce for the purpose of sale or distribution, or knowingly travels in interstate commerce, or uses a facility or means of interstate commerce for the purpose of transporting obscene material in interstate or foreign commerce, any obscene, lewd, lascivious, or filthy book, pamphlet, picture, film, paper, letter, writing, print, silhouette, drawing, figure, image, cast, phonograph recording, electrical transcription or other article capable of producing sound or any other matter of indecent or immoral character, shall be fined under this title or imprisoned not more than five years, or both.
>
> The transportation as aforesaid of two or more copies of any publication or two or more of any article of the character described above, or a combined total of five such publications and articles, shall create a presumption that such publications or articles are intended for sale or distribution, but such presumption shall be rebuttable.

Understanding Obscenity Law

Laws about pornography, indecency, and obscenity are almost as difficult to interpret and, thus, to guess, as copyright laws. They are, however, enforced. The most common way people are prosecuted under federal law for obscenity is via the law about transportation of obscene matters across state lines. This law is quoted in its entirety in the following sidebar.

What is filthy?

The statute quoted in the sidebar uses colorful language: *obscene, lewd, lascivious,* and *filthy.* But what do those words mean? This depends on the jury that hears the case.

Obscenity is difficult to define because not everyone finds the same material obscene. What was considered obscene 30 years ago can be seen on television commercials during prime time (Victoria's Secret models dancing across the screen in underwear).

In addition to this federal law, innumerable state and local laws govern use and distribution of obscene materials. If you tread into the area of obscenity involving minors, the stack of laws gets even taller.

Even if you live in the most liberal community in the land, where anything goes, you may be subject to the laws of a conservative community.

Which community sets the standards?

The courts have stated repeatedly that the standards are set by the community in which the obscene materials are received. This means the definitions of obscene, lewd, lascivious, and filthy will be determined by people who do not necessarily share the opinions of you and all your open-minded friends.

The Supreme Court, in *Miller v. California*, in 1973, created a three-prong test for obscenity. It asked whether:

✦ the average person applying contemporary community standards would find the work, taken as a whole, appeals to the prurient interest.

✦ the work depicts or describes, in a patently offensive way, sexual conduct specifically defined by applicable state law.

✦ the work, taken as a whole, lacks serious literary, artistic, political, or scientific value.

Given that these standards vary from community to community and the previously stated law about transportation of obscene materials across state lines doesn't specifically include transmission of materials by phone or by computer network, the U.S. Congress wanted to make one clear law to straighten all this out. It was concerned that even with relatively strict laws on the book, any competent eight-year-old could see graphic pornography on the Internet. Its answer to this problem was the Communications Decency Act of 1995.

The Communications Decency Act

The Web changed color overnight with the threat of the Communications Decency Act (CDA). Suddenly, the most popular color for a site was black with a blue ribbon, to show how the CDA would darken the heretofore free avenues of communication.

What did the CDA do? For the most part, it specified things that were already illegal in other media were now also illegal on the Web, but it was vague. Consider the following activity, which was punishable by up to two years in jail:

"[Any person who] makes a telephone call or utilizes a telecommunications device, whether or not conversation or communication ensues, without disclosing his identity and with intent to annoy, abuse, threaten, or harass any person at the called number or who receives the communication;"

Does this mean flaming someone on a newsgroup from an anonymous account lands you two years in the pen?

Or, how about this one:

> "…initiates the transmission of any comment, request, suggestion, proposal, image, or other communication which is obscene or indecent knowing that the recipient of the communication is under 18 years of age regardless of whether the maker of such communication placed the call or initiated the communication;"

This could cover many of the posts on the `misc.kids.breastfeeding` newsgroup, where woman who are trying to breast-feed their children write in with explicit questions about how to position a child at the breast. If a mother under age 18 were to write and ask for assistance, apparently providing such assistance would be illegal. Depending on the community standards involved in its interpretation, it might also cover a Web page posted by a breast-feeding advocacy group or a page published by a hospital women's center giving instructions for performing monthly breast self-exams.

Current Status of the CDA

The CDA was passed by both houses of Congress, signed into law by President Clinton, and immediately hauled into court, where it was found unconstitutional. Because of the vague, broad language of the act, the CDA was found to violate the First Amendment's protection of free speech.

Because of the bad press the CDA received, a change of the act being revived in its current state is unlikely. More likely, you will see bits and pieces of it inserted into other telecommunications bills to try to outlaw the most egregious activities and the activities that fall more into the *annoying* category than into the *dangerous* category will remain legal. As it is, most of the truly dangerous activities are already illegal.

Choices for Blocking Inappropriate Materials

Fortunately, many options exist to protect your children — and yourself — from receiving inappropriate materials. If you have spent much time surfing the Web, you know you needn't look for pornography to find it. Many sites pedaling adult materials intentionally mislabel themselves so people stumble across their materials in the hope of finding a broader audience. In looking for a list of area codes for the U.S., one of the authors of this book stumbled upon a site with a domain name that appeared to be for one of the companies that puts out phone books. Instead, the site contained manipulated photographs of the president actively involved in sadomasochistic sex. Oops!

Here are five ways to keep materials you don't want from your computer. Unfortunately, almost all involve relying on someone else's judgment.

1. Blocking sites (by IP address) you know or you believe contain inappropriate materials

2. Blocking URLs (pages only) you know or you believe contain inappropriate materials

3. Filtering pages by keyword so pages containing one or more keywords won't download onto your computer

4. Letting site authors label their own pages with keywords (Metadata) and then permitting only sites that rate themselves as appropriate — by whatever system is used — to download

5. Having a third-party label sites as appropriate or inappropriate for different audiences

Each of these approaches is discussed in greater detail in the following. Each of these systems requires either specialized software that works in conjunction with a browser or an enhanced browser that can handle some filtering functions.

Blocking sites (IP addresses)

This is perhaps the most general approach to keeping smut (used broadly) off your computer. With this system, either you or some trusted third-party (a school or church group) could locate a list of IP addresses associated with whatever material you want to keep off your computer. Even the Flat-Earth Society could publish a list of IP addresses its members might find offensive and this list could be imported into screening software, which is either built into the browser or works with the browser to keep those pages from downloading. With this system, you could prevent having any pages from these sites ever download onto your computer.

The first obvious problem is you have to trust the organization making the list. Are they really prohibiting what you want prohibited and permitting what you want permitted? The second problem is, in this system, all pages within a given domain name, whether or not they are problematic, would be excluded as part of an excluded site. In the previous example, with the Flat-Earth Society, if any part of the Discovery Channel's highly acclaimed Web site contained a reference to the earth as spherical, every page would be banned.

Blocking URLs

A slight improvement on the previous system is a system where each page within a site would be reviewed and labeled as appropriate or inappropriate individually. This would obviously be a tremendously greater task for any organization that wanted to get involved in this business, but it would prevent the problem previously discussed with the Discovery Channel site.

Neither of these systems listed — blocking by site or blocking by URL — gets at the constantly changing nature of the Web. Aggressive pornography merchants could get around these systems by creating new domain names as soon as they find themselves on one or more lists. For the small administrative fee and hassle of registering a new domain name, they would remain visible to the world.

Filtering by keyword

To solve the problem created by the knowledge that content of the Web changes daily, you would have to scan a document for certain words or images while it is in the process of downloading to your computer, without letting you see it until it passes your tests. This system is usually called *keyword filtering*. In this system, the parent (or other authority figure, which may include a manager in an office) creates a file of keywords that either are forbidden or are forbidden in certain combinations. The browser or a third-party software would make this easy to do.

If you want to prevent images or text about naked women, you could have a keyword list that included the following filtering rules: nude & naked, naked & breast, nude & topless. If you only included *breast* on the list, many health information pages about breast cancer would be excluded, as would many recipes for chicken breasts.

The problem with a system that filters by keyword is it assumes text is on the page. A smart and aggressive pornography merchant would convert all his controversial text into GIF files, so a phrase like "hot hot hot all nude girls!!!" would be a graphical image. The rest of the page might be images or harmless sounding payment information. Filtering software wouldn't catch this because it can't read images.

Self-labeling

Fortunately, your list of options doesn't end there. The W3C, in its usual international, self-reliant way, has suggested a system of metadata be implemented to permit page authors to label their own sites. This system is referred to as the Platform for Internet Content Selection (PICS).

In the previous systems, the line between the labeling and the filtering is blurred. In fact, two components exist for most systems of controlling the delivery of content. Those are

- ✦ **Labeling the material.** You, some trusted organization reviewing the material, or the authors of the material decide for whom it might be appropriate, into what categories of interest the material might fall, and possibly what type of material it is. The *Dewey decimal system* is a labeling system most people recognize as effective.

- ✦ **Filtering the material.** Either based on the labels available or based on keyword rules created by the recipient, the materials are either permitted or forbidden to the owner of the computer.

The self-labeling approach doesn't address the filtering side of the equation at all. All it does is try to give you, as the recipient of the page, the maximum latitude in selecting appropriate sites for viewing without relying excessively on governments or third parties to make decisions for you. This system of self-labels presupposes a standard vocabulary and syntax. The W3C or another organization could develop the syntax and vocabulary with which everyone would label their own sites. As with the Dewey decimal system, there are standards as to which numbers mean what types of subjects. Once these are established, everyone could label their own sites according to these standards.

In fact, you would probably need several scales on which to label or rate the material. The motion picture industry is stuck with a single system — G, PG, PG-13, R, NR — that groups all kinds of possibly offensive material — violence, language, nudity — into one ranking. The Web system would probably want to have different scales for at least those three categories. In addition, the Web system would want to have a labeling system indicating what the site contained that might actually make searches more effective.

Third-party labeling

Of course, the problem with self-labeling is page authors might lie and indicate their sites are appropriate for audiences for whom they clearly aren't appropriate. A possible way around this problem is for third-parties to get involved in generating their own labels of sites. This creates a system where you could find a site labeled (rather than just permitted or denied) by more than one organization. As with book reviews, you wouldn't have to give permission for others to label your site, so multiple labels with conflicting information might appear.

Site-Blocking Software

Right now, you can purchase software that implements one or more of the solutions previously described to keep your children safe from inappropriate content. These commercial software packages take advantage of a variety of technologies to determine what "inappropriate material" is. In one case, Surf Watch, the software comes with a subscription that automatically updates your list of forbidden sites based on background communications with the manufacturer's servers. Consequently, your blocked-site list is never out-of-date. This approach combines the labeling and the filtering into one easy step.

Another approach, one used by Net Nanny, is to give you the power to specify which keywords you want filtered from download. Both these packages also cover newsgroups and other methods of getting content from the Internet to your computer.

Using Site-Coding Standards

Site-coding standards rely on the two-part system of labels and filtering rules being created, maintained by, and stored in two separate places. Unfortunately, there isn't a single standard for labeling your site. The W3C, through the PICS, sets the syntax to be used when creating labels, but leaves it to other organizations to create the categories (or dimensions) for rating a site and the scale on which it is to be rated.

Two of the major systems for categorizing a site are the RSAC system, published by the Recreational Software Advisory Council, and the much more comprehensive SafeSurf rating system, which includes quite a few categories for rating. The categories included in the SafeSurf system are: age range, profanity, heterosexual themes, homosexual themes, nudity, violence, sex violence and profanity, intolerance of another person's racial, religious, or gender background, glorifying drug use, other adult themes, gambling, and general information. Within those categories, the scale usually includes values from "subtle innuendo" to "detailed graphic," depending on the category.

Both these labeling systems are put forth by rating services — organizations that are, themselves — third-parties that participate in labeling the sites of others. Within the PICS standard, you can place labeling information in three places:

1. **Within the HTML document** HEAD, **using the** META **element.** The syntax of the META element, for these purposes, is

   ```
   <META http-equiv="PICS-Label" content='specificlabel'>
   ```

   where *specificlabel* is particular to the rating system you are using. Naturally, only the author of the HTML document would have the rights to put the labeling information directly into the document.

2. **In a separate header file that gets transmitted with the HTML page.** The author of the document could place the labeling information into a separate header file, as an alternative to placing the information into the HTML document itself.

3. **In a separate file, which is located at a URL on the server of the rating service.** For ratings services, this is the only option. Anyone who wanted to take advantage of these ratings would have to know the URL of the rating service to request these labels be applied.

Creating a Profile for Filtering

From a parent's or librarian's perspective, what matters is that you create an appropriate profile that will filter out what you want forbidden and permit what you want included. You will need to understand PICSRules to do this. The complete PICSRules specification is located at http://www.w3.org/TR/REC-PICSRules.

The PICSRules are fairly simple to implement. Unfortunately, at this point, none of the major browsers support them. What follows is a sample PICSRules document. The URLs are made up and any resemblance between these names and actual URLs is pure coincidence.

```
(PicsRule-1.1
  (
  Policy (RejectByURL ("http://*@www.hotbabes.com:*/*"
          "http://www.childporn.com:*/*"

          "http://www.gratuitiousviolence.com:*/*")
  Policy (AcceptIf "otherwise")
  )
)
```

Summary

A lot of material is on the Web that you probably don't want to see yourself, let alone have your children see and, unfortunately, some of it is intentionally labeled in such a way that it will surely be seen by people who aren't looking for it. The U.S. government tried to pass a law that would cover a multitude of materials and make it illegal to post this material in a place where it might be seen by a minor. The Communications Decency Act was doomed from the start. Even if the courts hadn't declared it unconstitutional, all this Act would have done is drive businesses that wanted to violate it out of the country to countries with more liberal laws. Even though offenders are prosecuted where the pornography is received, it is difficult to prosecute people who don't live in the U.S. for anything less than murder.

Fortunately, better options than just outlawing certain types of materials are available. The W3C has suggested a Platform for Internet Content Selection (PICS) initiative that will allow people to label their own sites or the sites of anyone else, based on criteria established by other organizations. The result of this system is an increase in responsibility on site authors for labeling the content of their sites, an increase in the input that third-parties have in steering their members toward material appropriate for themselves and their families, and an increase in the control Web surfers have in dictating what does and doesn't get loaded onto their machines by themselves or by members of their families.

While the PICS standards haven't been implemented on any of the major browsers, they will undoubtedly provide the best long-term, self-censorship system for the Internet. Execution of the PICSRules profiles are anticipated to be implemented within a short period of time.

✦   ✦   ✦

Privacy

How much information should you provide? How much information should you require your site visitors to provide? What is being done with this information you provide? What should you do or not do with the information you collect? These questions are asked daily by both Web site visitors and Webmasters. While no standards are in place that can assure your Web visitors you won't do anything underhanded with their data (or that a site you visit won't do anything underhanded with your data), in the near future, both standards and well-recognized organizations will guarantee those standards are in one place and are enforced. And none of these improvements in the world of privacy will be brought to you by any government action or agency.

This chapter discusses what privacy means on the Web, what technologies are most often used to undermine a privacy, and what it is exactly that people mean by privacy. The chapter also discuss the standards proposed by the W3C, another excellent contribution, by the way. Finally it discusses what you can do today to publicize and guarantee (to your visitors' satisfaction) you respect their privacy.

Introducing Privacy on the Internet

The Web relies on the HTTP protocol, which is a stateless protocol. Consequently, every request for a page is completely unrelated to every other request. So, then, this will be a one-paragraph chapter, right? If the Web server with which you communicate doesn't know whether ten successive requests for pages come from the same client, from three different clients, or from ten different clients, then privacy is a moot point, right? Wrong. Simple techniques that change the stateless nature of the Web have become commonplace on the Web. Now, from the Web server's point of view, it sees which requests for pages come from each client. It sees sessions with clients that begin the first time a visitor requests a page from that server until some period of inactivity between the server and the client elapses (sometimes as brief a period as 20 minutes). It can even create persistent sessions with clients, where it never forgets a client has requested a page from a server.

Unlike in previous chapters, where the common expression was "a client visits a Web site," the terminology used in this chapter is the more accurate: "a client requests a page from a Web server."

Privacy of What?

What exactly is it you need to keep private? Or, put differently: what is it sites want to collect and what will they do with it that is so awful? This is the real question. If all a server can collect about you is your IP address (that might even be temporary if you dial into an ISP) and which of its pages you requested, so what? Even if it knows which pages you requested from it over a long period of time, you are just a number to it (say, 128.143.209.211) that it can't connect to your name, your phone number, your credit card, number, or anything.

Unfortunately, this isn't the entire story. Again, using simple techniques, Web sites can plant tiny text files on your computer — called *cookies* — that can be used to track where you've been and can even be associated with your personal information, once you enter it somewhere.

The way the Web works today, every time you enter your own personal information into a Web site, even just to enter a raffle for a toaster, your information can be disseminated to many other sites without your knowledge or consent. If you enter your payment information, your files are that much more attractive for resale.

Privacy-Intrusive Technologies on the Web

The simple technologies that create a *state* (an ongoing relationship between the client and the server) in a previously stateless environment work in conjunction with the client software, the browser. This means either Netscape or Microsoft are actually facilitating the server potentially invading your privacy. How do companies and organizations invade your privacy? Almost without exception, they begin by leaving a cookie on your computer (more to follow). This by itself isn't evil. What may get under your skin, however, is how some sites have come to use cookies. Examples range from mildly intrusive to grossly intrusive.

Cookies are nothing more than single lines in little text files. If you search your computer for a file called cookie.txt (or cookie on a Mac), you will probably find one. You can view the contents of your cookie file in any text reader. You will not, however, necessarily make sense of it. Cookies are usually encrypted when they are written so more information can be stored in less space (and so you don't know exactly what they have on you).

In most cases, the cookie created by a server has nothing more than your unique ID. In some cases, the cookie has personal information you have entered that enables you to "customize" this site. The next time you go to the site and it refers to you by name, you can be pretty sure the server didn't actually recognize you, but simply looked in your cookie file to see what you said your name was and what you said your preferences were.

Of course, all the major browsers give you the power to refuse cookies, either outright or as a result of a prompt. Most people don't find them particularly offensive and many sites don't work if you don't let the server set the cookie, so most visitors to sites will continue to grant permission for cookies to be written. Sometimes sites collaborate so a cookie set by one site can be read by a number of other sites.

Cross-Reference

Chapter 15 discusses underhanded uses of cookies.

Principles of Privacy Protection

What does protecting your privacy mean? Generally, the rule is privacy protection involves someone you trust not sharing your information without your knowledge and consent. That's how most personal relationships work: you only share your private thoughts with people you trust and, even then, you trust them not to repeat your thoughts to others. Sometimes you even need to stipulate what a friend can and cannot repeat to others.

Right now, you have few assurances any site on the Web won't share your information with anyone else. Several organizations are trying to change that. Of course, one is the W3C.

The Platform for Privacy Preferences

The W3C has developed a standard for privacy on the Web called the Platform for Privacy Preferences, which has been endowed with yet another acronym: P3P. The *P3P* is a clever system, which, once implemented, will enable you to specify a profile of information on your browser and a set of conditions under which servers may use your profile information. When you contact a server to request a page, the server will communicate with the browser what information it would like to have and how it will use it. If the server agrees to your limitations and doesn't want any more information than you want to provide, then you can see pages on the server without taking any further actions. If the server would like to use your information for some other purposes, you are asked to agree to its terms. If you agree, you continue to browse the site. If you decline their terms, then your browsing experience may be limited by the server or discontinued altogether. If the server wants additional information you haven't included in your profile, then it queries you and you can provide the information or not. Again, your browsing may be limited based on whether you agree to or decline to agree to the terms of the server.

Explaining Your Privacy Policy

Until the P3P standards have been implemented, you can and should state your privacy policy clearly on your site. You should also implement policies on your server to protect the data of visitors, just as you promised. And you should consider joining one of the independent organizations that guarantees you comply with a certain level of protection for the data you collect from your visitors (see Figure 54-1). To help assure their members comply with their stated policies, these organizations audit member servers for compliance.

In exchange for membership in, and compliance with, the standards of one of these independent organizations, you have the right to display the logo of the organization you join on your site. For now, not too many people recognize the logos of these organizations, which means the credibility the logos of these organizations currently buy you is limited but, over time, as these logos become more prevalent, visitors will come to expect a guarantee that your privacy policy is enforced and audited.

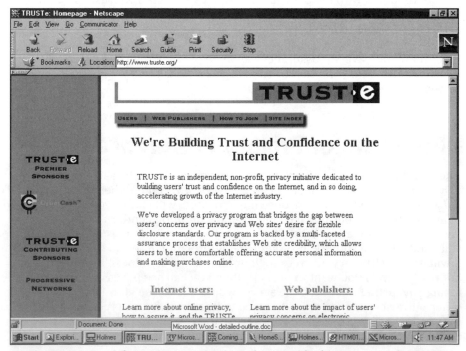

Figure 54-1: One of the major organizations that provide this guarantee is TRUSTe.

Summary

Privacy, or lack thereof, on the Web has become an increasingly controversial topic. Millions of people visit sites every day. How much of their activity is being tracked? This is impossible to say. What is known is an entire industry has materialized to track the habits of Web citizens both at the macro level (which sites are visited the most and at what times) and at the micro level (what the specific preferences and surfing habits of an individual are). For the most part, the technologies that facilitate getting these types of questions answered are not particularly sophisticated.

The technology predominant in tracking Web visitor behavior at the micro level is the cookie. As harmless as this sounds, cookies can be used to track every move of a Web visitor. The W3C has developed the P3P to help protect Web visitors from a variety of privacy infringements that are becoming increasingly common on the Web. Until the standards of the P3P are in place, your best bet is to publicize and enforce your privacy policy clearly on your Web site.

✦   ✦   ✦

Defamation and Libel

Defamation is basically trying to ruin someone else's good reputation. You see it all the time on newsgroups and e-mail discussion groups, where one person's controversial post becomes fodder for another person's personal attacks, which may be only marginally related to the original post. Fortunately, most defamation on the Web never makes it into the courts. Most attempts at disparaging another person's reputation are handled between the parties in the public courts of public opinion: on the newsgroups and e-mail discussion groups.

But the courts have historically recognized cases exist where the power is not equally shared between the defamer and the defamed. In these cases, and where there is money to be had from the defamer, the courts have been willing to protect the reputation of the little guy against the big, bad, publisher of libel. In this chapter, you learn the legal definitions of defamation and libel and a bit about why so few libel cases from the Internet make it into the courts. You also learn what is and isn't libel. Finally, you learn about why carriers of these communications aren't necessarily responsible for the defamation they contain.

Understanding Defamation and Libel

Defamation is a broad legal concept that includes both slander (spoken) and libel (written). *Black's Law Dictionary, 5/E,* defines defamation as:

Holding up of a person to ridicule, scorn, or contempt in a respectable and considerable part of the community; may be criminal as well as civil. This includes both libel and slander.

Defamation is that which tends to injure reputation; to diminish the esteem, respect, or goodwill or confidence in which the plaintiff is held, or to excite adverse, derogatory or unpleasant feelings or opinions against him. Statement which exposes person to contempt, hatred, ridicule or obloquy. *McGowen v. Prentice La. App.* The unprivileged publication of false statements which naturally and proximately result in injury to another. *Wolfson v. Kirk Fla. App 273.*

A communication is defamatory if it tends so to harm the reputation of another as to lower him in the estimation of the community or to deter third persons from associating or dealing with him. The meaning of a communication is that which the recipient correctly or mistakenly but reasonably understands that it was intended to express.

Defamation is an old legal concept that protects you from people who want to ruin your reputation or your good standing within a community. In reading the previous definition, you may notice a not insubstantial amount of correspondence takes place on some newsgroups — where flame wars are common — which might be construed as defamation.

Putting it in writing

The law protects you from both spoken and written defamation. When the defamation is in writing, it is called *libel. Black's Law Dictionary, 5/E,* defines libel as:

A method of defamation expressed by print, writing, pictures, or signs. In its most general sense, any publication that is injurious to the reputation of another. A false and unprivileged publication in writing of defamatory material. *Bright v. Los Angeles United School District, 51 Cal. App. 3rd 852, 124.* A malicious written or printed publication which tends to blacken a person's reputation or expose him to public hatred, contempt, or ridicule, or to injure him in his business or profession. *Corabi v. Curtis Pub. Co. 441 Pa. 432.*

Accusation in writing or printing against the character of a person which affects his reputation in that it tends to hold him up to ridicule, contempt, shame, disgrace, or obloquy, to degrade him in the estimation of the community, to induce an evil opinion of him in the minds of right-thinking persons, to make him an object of reproach, to diminish his respectability or abridge his comforts, to change his position in society for the worse, to dishonor or discredit him in the estimation of the public, or his friends and acquaintances, or to deprive him of friendly intercourse in society, or to cause him to be shunned or avoided, or where it is charged that one has violated his public duty as a public officer. Almost any languages which upon its face has a natural tendency to injure a man's reputation, either generally or with respect to his occupation. *Washer v. Bank of America National Trust and Savings Association.*

There can be no presumption of malice or bad faith consistent with freedom of the press under First Amend., U.S. Const., if plaintiff is a public figure. Malice must be proved on a showing that defendant published material either knowing it to be false or recklessly without regard as to whether it is true or false. *N.Y. Times v. Sullivan, 376 U.S. 254.*

The key concepts to retain from this rather lengthy definition are that libel:

✦ must be in print, writing, pictures, or signs.

✦ must diminish someone's respectability. This means someone who is not respected to begin with can't be libeled. Calling a convicted prostitute a *slut* in writing wouldn't necessarily be libel. Writing the same thing about a woman with a sterling reputation very well might be.

✦ the standard is much tougher when you are writing about public figures. Public figures must prove you maliciously published something about them, which you knew not to be true, to prove libel. In other words, your First Amendment right to free speech is broader regarding what you can say about public figures.

What Is Libelous — and What Is Not

Only a court can decide what is truly libelous but, in the meantime, you can spend lots of money and time with a lawyer either proving what you said *isn't*, or proving what someone else said *is*.

So, then, how do you decide what is libelous? Well, as with tax law, you are often safest to take the most conservative approach. If something might be construed as libel, don't include it on your page.

Repeating a libelous statement

You might be surprised to learn that repeating something someone else says that is libelous is libelous. You can smear the reputation of another person even by quoting what someone else says. That someone else said it first — and you are only quoting them — does not diminish your responsibility. You are still contributing to the perception of this person that others have.

Public figures

The courts have long distinguished between saying or printing nasty things about private citizens and saying or writing critical things about public figures. In 1964, the U.S. Supreme Court heard a case involving libel against a public figure. Justice Brennan, writing for the court, had this to say:

> "We consider this case against the background of a profound national commitment to the principle that debate on public issues should be uninhibited, robust, and wide-open, and that it may well include vehement, caustic, and sometimes unpleasantly sharp attacks on government and public officials." He added: ". . . erroneous statement is inevitable in free debate."

The court concluded that a public figure must prove actual malice to win a libel case. Actual malice is a much stricter standard than just trying to ruin someone's reputation. *Actual malice* must involve proof the statement was made with "knowledge that it was false or with reckless disregard of whether it was false or not."

Who is a public figure? It used to be only public officials were public figures, but the courts have slowly broadened the use of the title public figure to include Hollywood stars and members of the press. How else would grocery store tabloids get away with the things they attribute to the celebrities they discuss?

Rule of thumb

If you want to stay out of your lawyer's office and the courts, follow The Golden Rule (or one of the golden rules, anyway): If you can't say something nice, don't say anything at all. Product reviews can be effective when comparisons are made between products and all the check marks are only in one column. The same is true of individuals. Your intelligent audience can read between the lines and figure out your withholding of praise is the same as a put-down, without getting you into trouble. After all, you can't be sued to failing to compliment someone. That simply isn't covered by libel law.

The Net: The Great Equalizer

Despite all the defamation that goes on the Internet, especially on newsgroups, remarkably few lawsuits have occurred involving libel. Why? The biggest reason is it simply is not cost-effective to sue someone who doesn't have any money. Civil suits award dollars, not prison time.

If some moron on a newsgroup flames what you have to say by calling you nasty names and questioning your integrity and abilities, you can flame right back. Most right-thinking people don't need a lawyer's intervention to right this kind of situation. This is actually one of the things the courts consider when evaluating libel claims: what is your ability to defend yourself against the libel? In the case of newsgroups, you have the exact power as the defamer (unless it is moderated and he or she is the moderator).

Public figures are better able to defend themselves from defamation because they have greater access to distribution channels; they can hold press conferences and get free media coverage. Private individuals are protected by the law because they aren't in any position to defend themselves. But the Internet changes all this. To defend themselves, everyone can publish a Web site. Defending yourself in a newsgroup is even easier.

Discussion of Recent Cases

The only really hot case involving libel was between two parties with vastly different power. One, CompuServe, was accused by the other, Cubby, of carrying defamatory materials about itself on its public forums. In this case, the mere fact that CompuServe hosted the discussion got it hauled into court.

A rather complex relationship was actually involved. CompuServe contracted with a company called CCI, which contracted with Rumorville to provide certain publications on one of its public forums. In one of the publications, Rumorville said nasty things about Cubby, which was an up-and-coming competitor to Rumorville. Both were creating the same type of publication. Cubby sued Rumorville and CompuServe (for carrying Rumorville) for libel.

To the great relief of ISPs everywhere, the suit was dismissed because CompuServe was a *distributor*, rather than a *publisher*, of Rumorville, much the same way you wouldn't blame a newsstand for carrying defamatory comments in a newspaper it sold. Certainly booksellers couldn't be expected to know what was and wasn't libelous in every book they sold.

This case, called *Cubby v. CompuServe,* dates from 1991 and is one of the few cases aimed at the Internet and the Web. You can read more about it — this includes finding a link to the complete transcript from the appeal — and other law-related Web sites at CounselQuest's Web site: http://www.counselquest.com/ z-cyber.htm#cases.

Summary

Despite the volume of information disseminated on the Web and the Internet, surprisingly few legal cases have involved defamation and libel and these new communications media. One of the major reasons for this is the preference of the courts, when it comes to remedying libel, is the affected parties work it out between themselves. The law protects the defamed parties if they have fewer resources than the defamer. Thus, a newspaper that defamed a private individual would be at risk.

Public figures are, to a large degree, exempt from coverage by libel laws for two reasons: They have greater access to the media to correct the inaccurate statements and, in the interest of free speech, sometimes public figures must come under stricter scrutiny in the discussion of public issues.

The Internet levels the playing field. Suddenly, everyone can be a publisher. You no longer need to own a printing press and a stable of paperboys to get out your word. Because anyone can publish on the Internet for little or no cost, the courts and the sensible people who have been defamed have let the medium used to create the problem be the medium used to remedy the problem.

In *Cubby v. CompuServe,* CompuServe was sued because Cubby was defamed on one of its public forums in such a way that Cubby had no way to counter the defamation. CompuServe won because the courts interpreted CompuServe's actions as equivalent to the distributor of the defamatory remarks, rather than as the publisher of those defamatory remarks.

✦   ✦   ✦

Appendixes

HTML 4 Elements Reference

This appendix provides a reference guide to all the elements defined in the HTML 4.0 strict, transitional, and frameset flavors. Deprecated elements are shaded. See Appendix B for an explanation of attributes and their permissible values.

A

PURPOSE	Inserts a hyperlink
TYPE	Inline
NESTED WITHIN	BODY
START TAG	Required
END TAG	Required
CONTENT	Contains inline elements and text
ATTRIBUTES	id = "name" (OPTIONAL) class = "name" (OPTIONAL) style = "style" (OPTIONAL) title = "name" (OPTIONAL) lang = "language" (OPTIONAL) dir = (rtl, ltr) (OPTIONAL) accesskey = "character" (OPTIONAL) charset = "charset" (OPTIONAL) href = "url" (OPTIONAL) href = "langcode" (OPTIONAL rel = "link-type" (OPTIONAL) rev = "link-type" (OPTIONAL) tabindex = "number" (OPTIONAL)

target = "(_blank, _self, _parent, _top, or name)"
(OPTIONAL)
onclick = "script" (OPTIONAL)
ondblclick = "script" (OPTIONAL)
onkeydown = "script" (OPTIONAL)
onkeypress = "script" (OPTIONAL)
onkeyup = "script" (OPTIONAL)
onmousedown = "script" (OPTIONAL)
onmousemove = "script" (OPTIONAL)
onmouseup = "script" (OPTIONAL)
onblur = "script" (OPTIONAL)
onfocus = "script" (OPTIONAL)

EXAMPLE

```
<A href =
"http://www.yahoo.com">Yahoo!</A>
```

TIP   Make sure you surround the URL with quotation
                         marks.

ABBR

PURPOSE   Indicates an abbreviation

TYPE   Inline

NESTED WITHIN   Any BLOCK element

START TAG   Required

END TAG   Required

CONTENT   Text

ATTRIBUTES   id = "name" (OPTIONAL)
                    class = "name" (OPTIONAL)
                    style = "style" (OPTIONAL)
                    title = "name" (OPTIONAL)
                    lang = "language" (OPTIONAL)
                    dir = (rtl, ltr) (OPTIONAL)
                    onclick = "script" (OPTIONAL)
                    ondblclick = "script" (OPTIONAL)
                    onkeydown = "script" (OPTIONAL)
                    onkeypress = "script" (OPTIONAL)
                    onkeyup = "script" (OPTIONAL)
                    onmousedown = "script" (OPTIONAL)
                    onmousemove = "script" (OPTIONAL)
                    onmouseup = "script" (OPTIONAL)

EXAMPLE   `<ABBR title = "Incorporated">Inc.</ABBR>`

TIP   Use the title attribute so users can see what the
                    spelled-out version of the abbreviation looks like.

ACRONYM

PURPOSE	Indicates an acronym
TYPE	Inline
NESTED WITHIN	Any BLOCK element
START TAG	Required
END TAG	Required
CONTENT	Text
ATTRIBUTES	id = "name" (OPTIONAL) class = "name" (OPTIONAL) style = "style" (OPTIONAL) title = "name" (OPTIONAL) lang = "language" (OPTIONAL) dir = (rtl, ltr) (OPTIONAL) onclick = "script" (OPTIONAL) ondblclick = "script" (OPTIONAL) onkeydown = "script" (OPTIONAL) onkeypress = "script" (OPTIONAL) onkeyup = "script" (OPTIONAL) onmousedown = "script" (OPTIONAL) onmousemove = "script" (OPTIONAL) onmouseup = "script" (OPTIONAL)
EXAMPLE	`<ABBR title = "World Wide Web">WWW</ABBR>`
TIP	Use the `title` attribute so users can see what the spelled-out version of the acronym looks like.

ADDRESS

PURPOSE	Provides information about the author
TYPE	Inline
NESTED WITHIN	Any BLOCK element
START TAG	Required
END TAG	Required
CONTENT	Text
ATTRIBUTES	id = "name" (OPTIONAL) class = "name" (OPTIONAL) style = "style" (OPTIONAL) title = "name" (OPTIONAL)

lang = "language" (OPTIONAL)
dir = (rtl, ltr) (OPTIONAL)
onclick = "script" (OPTIONAL)
ondblclick = "script" (OPTIONAL)
onkeydown = "script" (OPTIONAL)
onkeypress = "script" (OPTIONAL)
onkeyup = "script" (OPTIONAL)
onmousedown = "script" (OPTIONAL)
onmousemove = "script" (OPTIONAL)
onmouseup = "script" (OPTIONAL)

EXAMPLE

```
<ADDRESS>John Doe
(<A HREF = "mailto:jd@bogus.org>
jd@bogus.org</A>)</ADDRESS>
```

TIP

Place this element at the bottom of your page to indicate who's responsible for its maintenance. Use a `mailto` URL (as shown) to incorporate a clickable e-mail link. Usually rendered in italics.

APPLET (Deprecated)

PURPOSE

Incorporates a Java applet

TYPE

Inline

NESTED WITHIN

`BODY` element

START TAG

Required

END TAG

Required

CONTENT

None

ATTRIBUTES

id = "name" (OPTIONAL)
class = "name" (OPTIONAL)
style = "stylc" (OPTIONAL)
title = "name" (OPTIONAL)
archive = "CDATA" (OPTIONAL)
code = "CDATA" (REQUIRED)
codebase = "url" (OPTIONAL)
object = "CDATA" (OPTIONAL)
alt = "text" (OPTIONAL)
name = "CDATA" (OPTIONAL)
width = "length" (REQUIRED)
height = "length" (REQUIRED)
align = "(top, middle, bottom, left, right)"
hspace = "pixels"
vspace = "pixels"

EXAMPLE	`<APPLET code = "tic-tac-toe.class" width = "500 height = "500">Play tic-tac-toe!</APPLET>`
TIP	To conform to the strict flavor of HTML 4, use the `OBJECT` element instead.

AREA

PURPOSE	Defines regions in a client-side imagemap
TYPE	Inline
NESTED WITHIN	`MAP` element
START TAG	Required
END TAG	Forbidden
CONTENT	Empty
ATTRIBUTES	id = "name" (OPTIONAL)
	class = "name" (OPTIONAL)
	style = "style" (OPTIONAL)
	title = "name" (OPTIONAL)
	shape = "(rect, circle, poly, default)" (OPTIONAL)
	coords = "comma-separated list of lengths" (OPTIONAL)
	href = "url" (OPTIONAL)
	nohref (OPTIONAL)
	alt = "text" (REQUIRED)
	tabindex = "number" (OPTIONAL)
	accesskey = "character" (OPTIONAL)
	onclick = "script" (OPTIONAL)
	ondblclick = "script" (OPTIONAL)
	onkeydown = "script" (OPTIONAL)
	onkeypress = "script" (OPTIONAL)
	onkeyup = "script" (OPTIONAL)
	onmousedown = "script" (OPTIONAL)
	onmousemove = "script" (OPTIONAL)
	onmouseup = "script" (OPTIONAL)
	onblur = "script" (OPTIONAL)
	onfocus = "script" (OPTIONAL)
EXAMPLE	`<MAP name = "mymap">`
	`<AREA href = "page1.html"`

```
                               alt = "Page 1"
                               shape = "circle"
                               coords = "184,200,60"
                          </AREA>
                          </MAP>
```

TIP   The code for client-side imagemaps is generated by
                          imagemap editors.

B

PURPOSE   Bold emphasis

TYPE   Inline

NESTED WITHIN   Any BLOCK element

START TAG   Required

END TAG   Required

CONTENT   Text

ATTRIBUTES   id = "name" (OPTIONAL)
                          class = "name" (OPTIONAL)
                          style = "style" (OPTIONAL)
                          title = "name" (OPTIONAL)
                          onclick = "script" (OPTIONAL)
                          ondblclick = "script" (OPTIONAL)
                          onkeydown = "script" (OPTIONAL)
                          onkeypress = "script" (OPTIONAL)
                          onkeyup = "script" (OPTIONAL)
                          onmousedown = "script" (OPTIONAL)
                          onmousemove = "script" (OPTIONAL)
                          onmouseup = "script" (OPTIONAL)

EXAMPLE   `<B>Text in bold</B>`

TIP   Be careful to close this element properly.

BASE

PURPOSE   Specifies an absolute URL to use as the basis for
                          resolving relative URLs in your document

TYPE   inline

NESTED WITHIN   HEAD element

START TAG   Required

END TAG	Forbidden
CONTENT	Empty
ATTRIBUTES	href = "url"
EXAMPLE	`<BASE = "www.myserver.org/myhome/">`
TIP	Always use relative URLs within your document and specify the base with this element. You can then move your document easily by making one change (to the `BASE` element).

BASEFONT (Deprecated)

PURPOSE	Sets the default font, font size, and color for the entire document
TYPE	Inline
NESTED WITHIN	`BODY`
START TAG	Required
END TAG	Forbidden
CONTENT	Empty
ATTRIBUTES	id = "name" (OPTIONAL) size = "CDATA" (OPTIONAL) color = "color" (OPTIONAL) face = "CDATA" (OPTIONAL)
EXAMPLE	`<BASEFONT face = "Helvetica" color = "silver" size = "4">`
TIP	You can change the font locally using the `FONT` element.

BDO

PURPOSE	Overrides the default text direction
TYPE	Inline
NESTED WITHIN	Any `BLOCK` element
START TAG	Required
END TAG	Required
CONTENT	Text

ATTRIBUTES	id = "name" (OPTIONAL)
	class = "name" (OPTIONAL)
	style = "style" (OPTIONAL)
	title = "name" (OPTIONAL)
	lang = "language" (OPTIONAL)
	dir = (rtl, ltr) (REQUIRED)
EXAMPLE	`<BDO dir = "ltr">Here's some English amidst a language requiring right-to-left presentation.</BDO>`
TIP	You can set the whole document's text direction using the `dir` attribute in the `HTML` element.

BIG

PURPOSE	Displays text in a large font
TYPE	Inline
NESTED WITHIN	Any `BLOCK` element
START TAG	Required
END TAG	Required
CONTENT	Text
ATTRIBUTES	id = "name" (OPTIONAL)
	class = "name" (OPTIONAL)
	style = "style" (OPTIONAL)
	title = "name" (OPTIONAL)
	onclick = "script" (OPTIONAL)
	ondblclick = "script" (OPTIONAL)
	onkeydown = "script" (OPTIONAL)
	onkeypress = "script" (OPTIONAL)
	onkeyup = "script" (OPTIONAL)
	onmousedown = "script" (OPTIONAL)
	onmousemove = "script" (OPTIONAL)
	onmouseup = "script" (OPTIONAL)
EXAMPLE	`<BIG>Text in a large font</BIG>`
TIP	Be careful to close this element properly.

BLOCKQUOTE

PURPOSE	Indents an extended quotation
TYPE	Block
NESTED WITHIN	BODY element
START TAG	Required
END TAG	Required
CONTENT	Text
ATTRIBUTES	id = "name" (OPTIONAL)
	class = "name" (OPTIONAL)
	style = "style" (OPTIONAL)
	title = "name" (OPTIONAL)
	lang = "language" (OPTIONAL)
	dir = (rtl, ltr) (OPTIONAL)
	cite = "url" (OPTIONAL)
	onclick = "script" (OPTIONAL)
	ondblclick = "script" (OPTIONAL)
	onkeydown = "script" (OPTIONAL)
	onkeypress = "script" (OPTIONAL)
	onkeyup = "script" (OPTIONAL)
	onmousedown = "script" (OPTIONAL)
	onmousemove = "script" (OPTIONAL)
	onmouseup = "script" (OPTIONAL)
EXAMPLE	`<BLOCKQUOTE>Here's a long quotation.</BLOCKQUOTE>`
TIP	You can use the Q element for inline quotations.

BODY

PURPOSE	Provides a container for all the text and elements that appear onscreen within the browser window
TYPE	Block
NESTED WITHIN	HTML element
START TAG	Optional
END TAG	Optional
CONTENT	Block elements
ATTRIBUTES	Strict DTD:
	id = "name" (OPTIONAL)
	class = "name" (OPTIONAL)
	style = "CSS style definition" (OPTIONAL)
	title = "name" (OPTIONAL)

lang = "language code" (OPTIONAL)
dir = (rtl, ltr) (OPTIONAL)

Transitional DTD (deprecated):
background = "url" (OPTIONAL)
text = "color" (OPTIONAL)
link = "color" (OPTIONAL)
vlink = "color" (OPTIONAL)
alink = "color" (OPTIONAL)
onclick = "script" (OPTIONAL)
ondblclick = "script" (OPTIONAL)
onkeydown = "script" (OPTIONAL)
onkeypress = "script" (OPTIONAL)
onkeyup = "script" (OPTIONAL)
onmousedown = "script" (OPTIONAL)
onmousemove = "script" (OPTIONAL)
onmouseup = "script" (OPTIONAL)
onload = "script" (OPTIONAL)
onunload = "script" (OPTIONAL)

NOTE	Although the BODY tags are optional, you shouldn't omit them.

EXAMPLE	`<BODY>`
	`<H1>Sailing the Southern Chesapeake Bay</H1>`
	`</BODY>`

TIP	Use substantive title words to increase chance of detection by Web search engines.

BR

PURPOSE	Inserts a line break at the element's position
TYPE	Inline
NESTED WITHIN	BODY
START TAG	Required
END TAG	Forbidden
CONTENT	Empty (no content permitted)
ATTRIBUTES	Strict DTD: id = "name" (OPTIONAL) class = "name" (OPTIONAL) style = "style" (OPTIONAL)

title = "name" (OPTIONAL)

Transitional DTD:
clear = "(none, left, right, all)"

EXAMPLE

```
I will put a line break <BR>
here.
```

DON'T FORGET   Enter blank lines with `<BR>`, not `<P>`.

BUTTON

PURPOSE   Creates a button with definable text on the button face

TYPE   Inline

NESTED WITHIN   FORM element

START TAG   Required

END TAG   Required

CONTENT   Text (displayed on button face)

ATTRIBUTES
id = "name" (OPTIONAL)
class = "name" (OPTIONAL)
style = "style" (OPTIONAL)
title = "name" (OPTIONAL)
lang = "language" (OPTIONAL)
dir = (rtl, ltr) (OPTIONAL)
name = "CDATA" (OPTIONAL)
value = "CDATA" (OPTIONAL)
type = "(button, submit, reset)" (OPTIONAL)
disabled (OPTIONAL)
tabindex = "number" (OPTIONAL)
accesskey = "character" (OPTIONAL)
onclick = "script" (OPTIONAL)
ondblclick = "script" (OPTIONAL)
onkeydown = "script" (OPTIONAL)
onkeypress = "script" (OPTIONAL)
onkeyup = "script" (OPTIONAL)
onmousedown = "script" (OPTIONAL)
onmousemove = "script" (OPTIONAL)
onmouseup = "script" (OPTIONAL)
onblur = "script" (OPTIONAL)
onfocus = "script" (OPTIONAL)

EXAMPLE	`<BUTTON type = "submit" name = "submit">Send It!</BUTTON>`
TIP	If you want to specify the text on the button face, use this element instead of `INPUT`.

CAPTION

PURPOSE	Creates a caption for a table
TYPE	Inline
NESTED WITHIN	`TABLE` element
START TAG	Required
END TAG	Required
CONTENT	Text
ATTRIBUTES	Strict DTD: id = "name" (OPTIONAL) class = "name" (OPTIONAL) style = "style" (OPTIONAL) title = "name" (OPTIONAL) lang = "language" (OPTIONAL) dir = (rtl, ltr) (OPTIONAL) onclick = "script" (OPTIONAL) ondblclick = "script" (OPTIONAL) onkeydown = "script" (OPTIONAL) onkeypress = "script" (OPTIONAL) onkeyup = "script" (OPTIONAL) onmousedown = "script" (OPTIONAL) onmousemove = "script" (OPTIONAL) onmouseup = "script" (OPTIONAL) Transitional DTD: align = "(top, bottom, left, right)"
EXAMPLE	`<CAPTION>Table 19.3 Expected vs. Actual Values</CAPTION>`
TIP	You must use this immediately after the `TABLE` element's start tag. You can specify only one caption per table.

CENTER (Deprecated)

PURPOSE	Centers the text enclosed within the tags
TYPE	Inline

NESTED WITHIN	Any `BLOCK` element
START TAG	Required
END TAG	Required
CONTENT	Text
ATTRIBUTES	id = "name" (OPTIONAL)
	class = "name" (OPTIONAL)
	style = "style" (OPTIONAL)
	title = "name" (OPTIONAL)
	lang = "language" (OPTIONAL)
	dir = (rtl, ltr) (OPTIONAL)
	onclick = "script" (OPTIONAL)
	ondblclick = "script" (OPTIONAL)
	onkeydown = "script" (OPTIONAL)
	onkeypress = "script" (OPTIONAL)
	onkeyup = "script" (OPTIONAL)
	onmousedown = "script" (OPTIONAL)
	onmousemove = "script" (OPTIONAL)
	onmouseup = "script" (OPTIONAL)
EXAMPLE	`<CENTER>This text is centered.</CAPTION>`
TIP	Use DIV align = "center" instead, or style sheets.

CITE

PURPOSE	Marks a cited work
TYPE	Inline
NESTED WITHIN	Any `BLOCK` element
START TAG	Required
END TAG	Required
CONTENT	Text
ATTRIBUTES	id = "name" (OPTIONAL)
	class = "name" (OPTIONAL)
	style = "style" (OPTIONAL)
	title = "name" (OPTIONAL)
	lang = "language" (OPTIONAL)
	dir = (rtl, ltr) (OPTIONAL)
	onclick = "script" (OPTIONAL)
	ondblclick = "script" (OPTIONAL)
	onkeydown = "script" (OPTIONAL)
	onkeypress = "script" (OPTIONAL)

onkeyup = "script" (OPTIONAL)
onmousedown = "script" (OPTIONAL)
onmousemove = "script" (OPTIONAL)
onmouseup = "script" (OPTIONAL)

EXAMPLE	`<CITE>Leaves of Grass</CITE> by Walt Whitman`
TIP	Usually rendered in italics.

CODE

PURPOSE	Identifies text as computer code
TYPE	Inline
NESTED WITHIN	Any `BLOCK` element
START TAG	Required
END TAG	Required
CONTENT	Text
ATTRIBUTES	id = "name" (OPTIONAL)
	class = "name" (OPTIONAL)
	style = "style" (OPTIONAL)
	title = "name" (OPTIONAL)
	lang = "language" (OPTIONAL)
	dir = (rtl, ltr) (OPTIONAL)
	onclick = "script" (OPTIONAL)
	ondblclick = "script" (OPTIONAL)
	onkeydown = "script" (OPTIONAL)
	onkeypress = "script" (OPTIONAL)
	onkeyup = "script" (OPTIONAL)
	onmousedown = "script" (OPTIONAL)
	onmousemove = "script" (OPTIONAL)
	onmouseup = "script" (OPTIONAL)
EXAMPLE	`<CODE>dowhile book-done = "no"</CODE>`
TIP	Usually rendered in a monospace font and indistinguishable from `KBD`, `SAMP`, `TT`, and `VAR`.

COL

PURPOSE	Identifies individual columns so you can assign attributes to them
TYPE	Block

NESTED WITHIN	COLGROUP element
START TAG	Required
END TAG	Forbidden
CONTENT	Empty
ATTRIBUTES	id = "name" (OPTIONAL)
	class = "name" (OPTIONAL)
	style = "style" (OPTIONAL)
	title = "name" (OPTIONAL)
	lang = "language" (OPTIONAL)
	dir = (rtl, ltr) (OPTIONAL)
	span = "number" (OPTIONAL>
	width = "lengths" (OPTIONAL)
	onclick = "script" (OPTIONAL)
	ondblclick = "script" (OPTIONAL)
	onkeydown = "script" (OPTIONAL)
	onkeypress = "script" (OPTIONAL)
	onkeyup = "script" (OPTIONAL)
	onmousedown = "script" (OPTIONAL)
	onmousemove = "script" (OPTIONAL)
	onmouseup = "script" (OPTIONAL)
EXAMPLE	`<COL width = 20 span = 3>`
TIP	This is an empty element that contains attributes only. To create columns, specify TD elements within a TR element.

COLGROUP

PURPOSE	Groups columns and sets default alignments
TYPE	Inline
NESTED WITHIN	TABLE element
START TAG	Required
END TAG	Forbidden
CONTENT	Empty
ATTRIBUTES	id = "name" (OPTIONAL)
	class = "name" (OPTIONAL)
	style = "style" (OPTIONAL)
	title = "name" (OPTIONAL)
	lang = "language" (OPTIONAL)
	dir = (rtl, ltr) (OPTIONAL)

	span = "number" (OPTIONAL>
	width = "lengths" (OPTIONAL)
	align = "(left, center, right, justify, char)"
	char = "character"
	charoff = "length"
	valign = "(top, middle, bottom, baseline)"
	onclick = "script" (OPTIONAL)
	ondblclick = "script" (OPTIONAL)
	onkeydown = "script" (OPTIONAL)
	onkeypress = "script" (OPTIONAL)
	onkeyup = "script" (OPTIONAL)
	onmousedown = "script" (OPTIONAL)
	onmousemove = "script" (OPTIONAL)
	onmouseup = "script" (OPTIONAL)
EXAMPLE	`<COL width =  20 span = 3>`
TIP	This is an empty element that contains attributes only. To create columns, specify `TD` elements within a `TR` element. To define the attributes of individual columns and override `COLGROUP`, use `COL`.

DD

PURPOSE	Identifies a definition in a definition list
TYPE	Block
NESTED WITHIN	`DL` element
START TAG	Required
END TAG	Optional
CONTENT	Text and inline elements
ATTRIBUTES	id = "name" (OPTIONAL)
	class = "name" (OPTIONAL)
	style = "style" (OPTIONAL)
	title = "name" (OPTIONAL)
	lang = "language" (OPTIONAL)
	dir = (rtl, ltr) (OPTIONAL)
	onclick = "script" (OPTIONAL)
	ondblclick = "script" (OPTIONAL)
	onkeydown = "script" (OPTIONAL)
	onkeypress = "script" (OPTIONAL)
	onkeyup = "script" (OPTIONAL)
	onmousedown = "script" (OPTIONAL)

	onmousemove = "script" (OPTIONAL) onmouseup = "script" (OPTIONAL)
EXAMPLE	`<DD>Here is the definition of the term.</DD>`
TIP	Use `DD` within a `DL` list. For the term, use `DT`.

DEL

PURPOSE	Indicates deleted text in a legal or political document
TYPE	Inline
NESTED WITHIN	Any `BLOCK` element
START TAG	Required
END TAG	Required
CONTENT	Text and inline elements (no block elements permitted)
ATTRIBUTES	id = "name" (OPTIONAL) class = "name" (OPTIONAL) style = "style" (OPTIONAL) title = "name" (OPTIONAL) lang = "language" (OPTIONAL) dir = (rtl, ltr) (OPTIONAL) cite = "url" (OPTIONAL) datetime = "YYYYMMDD" onclick = "script" (OPTIONAL) ondblclick = "script" (OPTIONAL) onkeydown = "script" (OPTIONAL) onkeypress = "script" (OPTIONAL) onkeyup = "script" (OPTIONAL) onmousedown = "script" (OPTIONAL) onmousemove = "script" (OPTIONAL) onmouseup = "script" (OPTIONAL)
EXAMPLE	We can support `<DEL>10</DEL><INS>12</INS>` positions.
TIP	Use `INS` to show what's inserted in place of the deleted text.

DFN

PURPOSE	Indicates the defining instance of a term

TYPE	Inline
NESTED WITHIN	Any `BLOCK` element
START TAG	Required
END TAG	Required
CONTENT	Text
ATTRIBUTES	id = "name" (OPTIONAL) class = "name" (OPTIONAL) style = "style" (OPTIONAL) title = "name" (OPTIONAL) lang = "language" (OPTIONAL) dir = (rtl, ltr) (OPTIONAL) onclick = "script" (OPTIONAL) ondblclick = "script" (OPTIONAL) onkeydown = "script" (OPTIONAL) onkeypress = "script" (OPTIONAL) onkeyup = "script" (OPTIONAL) onmousedown = "script" (OPTIONAL) onmousemove = "script" (OPTIONAL) onmouseup = "script" (OPTIONAL)
EXAMPLE	`<DFN>anime</DFN> refers to a distinctive Japanese tradition of cartoon animation.`
TIP	Use `DL`, `DD`, and `DT` for a definition list.

DIR (Deprecated)

PURPOSE	This element was originally intended for multicolumn directory listings, but browsers render it as an unordered list (`UL`)
TYPE	block
NESTED WITHIN	`BODY`
START TAG	Required
END TAG	Required
CONTENT	Text and inline elements
ATTRIBUTES	id = "name" (OPTIONAL) class = "name" (OPTIONAL) style = "style" (OPTIONAL) title = "name" (OPTIONAL) lang = "language" (OPTIONAL)

	dir = (rtl, ltr) (OPTIONAL) onclick = "script" (OPTIONAL) ondblclick = "script" (OPTIONAL) onkeydown = "script" (OPTIONAL) onkeypress = "script" (OPTIONAL) onkeyup = "script" (OPTIONAL) onmousedown = "script" (OPTIONAL) onmousemove = "script" (OPTIONAL) onmouseup = "script" (OPTIONAL)

EXAMPLE	`<DIR>`
	`  <LI>Item 1`
	`  <LI>Item 2`
	`  <LI>Item 3`
	`  </DIR>`

TIP	Use UL instead.

DIV

PURPOSE	Provides a means for grouping elements and assigning attributes to the group
TYPE	Block
NESTED WITHIN	BODY
START TAG	Required
END TAG	Required
CONTENT	Block elements
ATTRIBUTES	id = "name" (OPTIONAL) class = "name" (OPTIONAL) style = "style" (OPTIONAL) title = "name" (OPTIONAL) lang = "language" (OPTIONAL) dir = (rtl, ltr) (OPTIONAL) href = "url" onclick = "script" (OPTIONAL) ondblclick = "script" (OPTIONAL) onkeydown = "script" (OPTIONAL) onkeypress = "script" (OPTIONAL) onkeyup = "script" (OPTIONAL) onmousedown = "script" (OPTIONAL) onmousemove = "script" (OPTIONAL) onmouseup = "script" (OPTIONAL)

| EXAMPLE | ```
<DIV>
  <H1>Heading</H1>
  <P>Paragraph 1</P>
</DIV>
``` |
| TIP | Use SPAN to group inline elements. Note, browsers generally place a line break before a DIV element, but impose no other presentation attributes. |

DT

PURPOSE	Creates a definition list
TYPE	Block
NESTED WITHIN	DL element
START TAG	Required
END TAG	Required
CONTENT	Text and inline elements
ATTRIBUTES	id = "name" (OPTIONAL)
	class = "name" (OPTIONAL)
	style = "style" (OPTIONAL)
	title = "name" (OPTIONAL)
	lang = "language" (OPTIONAL)
	dir = (rtl, ltr) (OPTIONAL)
	onclick = "script" (OPTIONAL)
	ondblclick = "script" (OPTIONAL)
	onkeydown = "script" (OPTIONAL)
	onkeypress = "script" (OPTIONAL)
	onkeyup = "script" (OPTIONAL)
	onmousedown = "script" (OPTIONAL)
	onmousemove = "script" (OPTIONAL)
	onmouseup = "script" (OPTIONAL)
| EXAMPLE | ```
<DL>
  <DT>term 1
  <DD>definition of term 1
</DL>
``` |
| TIP | Use DT within a DL list. Use DD for the definition. |

DT

PURPOSE	In a definition list, identifies a defined term
TYPE	Block
NESTED WITHIN	DL element
START TAG	Required
END TAG	Optional
CONTENT	Text and inline elements
ATTRIBUTES	id = "name" (OPTIONAL) class = "name" (OPTIONAL) style = "style" (OPTIONAL) title = "name" (OPTIONAL) lang = "language" (OPTIONAL) dir = (rtl, ltr) (OPTIONAL) onclick = "script" (OPTIONAL) ondblclick = "script" (OPTIONAL) onkeydown = "script" (OPTIONAL) onkeypress = "script" (OPTIONAL) onkeyup = "script" (OPTIONAL) onmousedown = "script" (OPTIONAL) onmousemove = "script" (OPTIONAL) onmouseup = "script" (OPTIONAL)
EXAMPLE	`<DT>antidisestablishmentarianism</DT>`
TIP	Use DT within a DL list. Use DD for the definition.

DFN

PURPOSE	Marks the defining instance of a term
TYPE	Inline
NESTED WITHIN	Any BLOCK element
START TAG	Required
END TAG	Required
CONTENT	Text
ATTRIBUTES	id = "name" (OPTIONAL) class = "name" (OPTIONAL) style = "style" (OPTIONAL) title = "name" (OPTIONAL)

lang = "language" (OPTIONAL)
dir = (rtl, ltr) (OPTIONAL)
onclick = "script" (OPTIONAL)
ondblclick = "script" (OPTIONAL)
onkeydown = "script" (OPTIONAL)
onkeypress = "script" (OPTIONAL)
onkeyup = "script" (OPTIONAL)
onmousedown = "script" (OPTIONAL)
onmousemove = "script" (OPTIONAL)
onmouseup = "script" (OPTIONAL)

EXAMPLE `<DFN>User agent</DFN> is the uptown word for e-mail program.`

TIP Usually rendered in bold.

EM

PURPOSE Marks text for emphasis

TYPE Inline

NESTED WITHIN Any `BLOCK` element

START TAG Required

END TAG Required

CONTENT Text

ATTRIBUTES id = "name" (OPTIONAL)
class = "name" (OPTIONAL)
style = "style" (OPTIONAL)
title = "name" (OPTIONAL)
lang = "language" (OPTIONAL)
dir = (rtl, ltr) (OPTIONAL)
onclick = "script" (OPTIONAL)
ondblclick = "script" (OPTIONAL)
onkeydown = "script" (OPTIONAL)
onkeypress = "script" (OPTIONAL)
onkeyup = "script" (OPTIONAL)
onmousedown = "script" (OPTIONAL)
onmousemove = "script" (OPTIONAL)
onmouseup = "script" (OPTIONAL)

EXAMPLE `Do this <EM>right now</EM>.`

TIP Usually rendered in italics.

FIELDSET

PURPOSE	In a form, groups thematically related elements
TYPE	Block
NESTED WITHIN	BODY element
START TAG	Required
END TAG	Required
CONTENT	Contains HTML elements and text
ATTRIBUTES	Strict DTD: id = "name" (OPTIONAL) class = "name" (OPTIONAL) style = "CSS style definition" (OPTIONAL) title = "name" (OPTIONAL) lang = "language code" (OPTIONAL) dir = (rtl, ltr) (OPTIONAL) onclick = "script" (OPTIONAL) ondblclick = "script" (OPTIONAL) onkeydown = "script" (OPTIONAL) onkeypress = "script" (OPTIONAL) onkeyup = "script" (OPTIONAL) onmousedown = "script" (OPTIONAL) onmousemove = "script" (OPTIONAL) onmouseup = "script" (OPTIONAL) Transitional DTD: align = "top, bottom, left, right" (OPTIONAL)

EXAMPLE	`<FORM>`
	`<FIELDSET>`
	`  <LEGEND>Title of Subsection of`
	`Form</LEGEND>`
	`   <INPUT>`
	`   <INPUT>`
	`   <INPUT>`
	`</FIELDSET>`
	`</FORM>`

TIP	Use LEGEND to provide a title for the group.

FONT (Deprecated)

PURPOSE	Defines presentation styles for fonts
TYPE	Inline

NESTED WITHIN	Any `BLOCK` element
START TAG	Required
END TAG	Required
CONTENT	text and other inline elements
ATTRIBUTES	id = "name" (OPTIONAL)
	class = "name" (OPTIONAL)
	style = "style" (OPTIONAL)
	title = "name" (OPTIONAL)
	lang = "language" (OPTIONAL)
	dir = (rtl, ltr) (OPTIONAL)
	size = "CDATA " (OPTIONAL)
	color = "color" (OPTIONAL)
	face = "CDATA" (OPTIONAL)
	onclick = "script" (OPTIONAL)
	ondblclick = "script" (OPTIONAL)
	onkeydown = "script" (OPTIONAL)
	onkeypress = "script" (OPTIONAL)
	onkeyup = "script" (OPTIONAL)
	onmousedown = "script" (OPTIONAL)
	onmousemove = "script" (OPTIONAL)
	onmouseup = "script" (OPTIONAL)
EXAMPLE	`<FONT face = "Times Roman" size = "5">`
TIP	Define font presentation styles with style sheets.

FORM

PURPOSE	Creates a form for user input
TYPE	Block
NESTED WITHIN	`BODY`
START TAG	Required
END TAG	Required
CONTENT	Input and Select elements; text
ATTRIBUTES	id = "name" (OPTIONAL)
	class = "name" (OPTIONAL)
	style = "style" (OPTIONAL)
	title = "name" (OPTIONAL)
	lang = "language" (OPTIONAL)
	dir = (rtl, ltr) (OPTIONAL)
	action = "url" (REQUIRED)

method = "(get, post)" (default = "get")
enctype = "MIME type" (OPTIONAL)
onclick = "script" (OPTIONAL)
ondblclick = "script" (OPTIONAL)
onkeydown = "script" (OPTIONAL)
onkeypress = "script" (OPTIONAL)
onkeyup = "script" (OPTIONAL)
onmousedown = "script" (OPTIONAL)
onmousemove = "script" (OPTIONAL)
onmouseup = "script" (OPTIONAL)
onsubmit = "script" (OPTIONAL)
onreset = "script" (OPTIONAL)

EXAMPLE

```
<FORM action = "script.cgi">
  <INPUT type = "text" size = "60" >
</FORM>
```

TIP

Forms don't do anything unless the output is directed to a program that can decode and process the submitted information.

FRAME

PURPOSE

Specifies the document to be loaded into a frame

TYPE

Inline

NESTED WITHIN

FRAMESET

START TAG

Required

END TAG

Forbidden

CONTENT

Empty

ATTRIBUTES

id = "name" (OPTIONAL)
class = "name" (OPTIONAL)
style = "style" (OPTIONAL)
title = "name" (OPTIONAL)
lang = "language" (OPTIONAL)
dir = (rtl, ltr) (OPTIONAL)
src = "url" (OPTIONAL)
longdesc = "url" (OPTIONAL)
name = "CDATA" (OPTIONAL)
frameborder = "(1, 0)" (OPTIONAL)
marginwidth = "pixels" (OPTIONAL)
marginheight = "pixels" (OPTIONAL)
noresize (OPTIONAL)

scrolling = "(yes, no, auto)" (OPTIONAL)
target = "(_blank, _self, _parent, _top, or name)"
    (OPTIONAL)

EXAMPLE	```<FRAMESET cols = "15%, *">```
	  ```<FRAME src = "navaids.htm">```
	  ```<FRAME src = "page1.htm">```
	```</FRAMESET>```

TIP	Don't use a `BODY` element on a page containing frame elements or the frames won't work.

FRAMESET

PURPOSE	Defines frame sizes and positions in a framed document
TYPE	N/A
NESTED WITHIN	`HTML`
START TAG	Required
END TAG	Required
CONTENT	`FRAME` **elements**
ATTRIBUTES	id = "name" (OPTIONAL) class = "name" (OPTIONAL) style = "style" (OPTIONAL) title = "name" (OPTIONAL) rows = "comma-separated list of lengths" (OPTIONAL) cols = "comma-separated list of lengths" (OPTIONAL) onload = "script" (OPTIONAL) onunload = "script" (OPTIONAL)

EXAMPLE	```<FRAMESET cols = "15%, *">```
	  ```<FRAME src = "navaids.htm">```
	  ```<FRAME src = "page1.htm">```
	```</FRAMESET>```

TIP	Don't use a `BODY` element on a page containing frame elements or the frames won't work.

H1 through H6

PURPOSE	Marks the enclosed text as a heading, ranging from most prominent (H1) to least prominent (H6)
TYPE	Block
NESTED WITHIN	BODY element
START TAG	Required
END TAG	Required
CONTENT	Contains HTML elements and text
ATTRIBUTES	Strict DTD: id = "name" (OPTIONAL) class = "name" (OPTIONAL) style = "CSS style definition" (OPTIONAL) title = "name" (OPTIONAL) lang = "language code" (OPTIONAL) dir = (rtl, ltr) (OPTIONAL) onclick = "script" (OPTIONAL) ondblclick = "script" (OPTIONAL) onkeydown = "script" (OPTIONAL) onkeypress = "script" (OPTIONAL) onkeyup = "script" (OPTIONAL) onmousedown = "script" (OPTIONAL) onmousemove = "script" (OPTIONAL) onmouseup = "script" (OPTIONAL) Transitional DTD: align - "left, center, right, justify" (OPTIONAL)
EXAMPLE	`<H1>This is a major heading</H1>`
TIP	The H1 element appears to be the document's title, so it's wise to use it for this purpose. Note, heading levels H4 through H6 are rarely used.

HEAD

PURPOSE	Demarcates an area containing elements describing the document's contents, including the TITLE
NESTED WITHIN	HTML element
START TAG	Optional
END TAG	Optional

CONTENT	Can contain the SCRIPT, STYLE, META, LINK, OBJECT, TITLE, and BASE elements
ATTRIBUTES	profile = "url" (OPTIONAL) lang = "language-code" OPTIONAL dir = (ltr | rtl) OPTIONAL

EXAMPLE	`<HEAD>`
	`<TITLE>Sailing the Southern Chesapeake Bay</TITLE>`
	`</HEAD>`

TIP	The most important function of the HEAD element is to provide a home for the TITLE element.

HTML

PURPOSE	Demarcates the portion of the document containing HTML
NESTED WITHIN	None (encloses all other elements)
START TAG	Optional
END TAG	Optional
CONTENT	Contains HTML elements and text
ATTRIBUTES:	lang = "language-code" OPTIONAL dir = (ltr | rtl) OPTIONAL

EXAMPLE:	`<HTML>`
	`   [all other elements]`
	`</HTML>`

TIP	Although these tags are optional, it's good form to include them.

HR

PURPOSE	Inserts a horizontal rule
TYPE	Inline
NESTED WITHIN	Any BLOCK element
START TAG	Required
END TAG	Required
CONTENT	Text and inline elements (no block elements permitted)

ATTRIBUTES	Strict DTD:
	id = "name" (OPTIONAL)
	class = "name" (OPTIONAL)
	style = "style" (OPTIONAL)
	title = "name" (OPTIONAL)
	lang = "language" (OPTIONAL)
	dir = (rtl, ltr) (OPTIONAL)
	cite = "url" (OPTIONAL)
	datetime = "YYYYMMDD"
	onclick = "script" (OPTIONAL)
	ondblclick = "script" (OPTIONAL)
	onkeydown = "script" (OPTIONAL)
	onkeypress = "script" (OPTIONAL)
	onkeyup = "script" (OPTIONAL)
	onmousedown = "script" (OPTIONAL)
	onmousemove = "script" (OPTIONAL)
	onmouseup = "script" (OPTIONAL)
	Transitional DTD (deprecated):
	align = "(left, center, right)"
	noshade
	size = "pixels"
	width = "pixels"
EXAMPLE	`<P>A paragraph</P>`
	`<HR>`
	`<P>Another paragraph</P>`
TIP	Use style sheets to assign presentation attributes to rules.

I

PURPOSE	Italic emphasis
TYPE	Inline
NESTED WITHIN	Any `BLOCK` element
START TAG	Required
END TAG	Required
CONTENT	Text
ATTRIBUTES	id = "name" (OPTIONAL)
	class = "name" (OPTIONAL)
	style = "style" (OPTIONAL)
	title = "name" (OPTIONAL)

onclick = "script" (OPTIONAL)
ondblclick = "script" (OPTIONAL)
onkeydown = "script" (OPTIONAL)
onkeypress = "script" (OPTIONAL)
onkeyup = "script" (OPTIONAL)
onmousedown = "script" (OPTIONAL)
onmousemove = "script" (OPTIONAL)
onmouseup = "script" (OPTIONAL)

EXAMPLE
`<I>Text in italics</I>`

TIP
Be careful to close this element properly.

IFRAME

PURPOSE
Creates an inline subwindow in which you can insert another document

TYPE
Inline

NESTED WITHIN
Any `BLOCK` element

START TAG
Required

END TAG
Required

CONTENT
Text and inline elements (no Block elements permitted)

ATTRIBUTES
id = "name" (OPTIONAL)
class = "name" (OPTIONAL)
style = "style" (OPTIONAL)
title = "name" (OPTIONAL)
lang = "language" (OPTIONAL)
dir = (rtl, ltr) (OPTIONAL)
longdesc = "url" (OPTIONAL)
name = "CDATA" (OPTIONAL)
src = "url" (OPTIONAL)
frameborder = "(1,0)" (OPTIONAL)
marginwidth = "pixels" (OPTIONAL)
marginheight = "pixels" (OPTIONAL)
scrolling = "(yes, no, auto)" (OPTIONAL)
align = "(top, mid`d`le, bottom, left, right")
(OPTIONAL)

EXAMPLE
`<IFRAME src = "insert.html" width = 200`
`height = 300 scrolling = "yes" frameborder`
`= "0">Your browser doesn't support frames.`
`However, you can visit the <A href =`
`"insert.html"> document </A> that would`
`have been shown here.`

TIP	Place text to be viewed by nonframe browsers between the tags.

IMG

PURPOSE	Inserts a graphic at the tag's location
TYPE	Inline
NESTED WITHIN	BODY
START TAG	Required
END TAG	Forbidden
CONTENT	Empty
ATTRIBUTES	Strict DTD: id = "name" (OPTIONAL) class = "name" (OPTIONAL) style = "style" (OPTIONAL) title = "name" (OPTIONAL) src = "url" (REQUIRED) alt = "CDATA" (REQUIRED) longdesc = "url" (OPTIONAL) onclick = "script" (OPTIONAL) ondblclick = "script" (OPTIONAL) onkeydown = "script" (OPTIONAL) onkeypress = "script" (OPTIONAL) onkeyup = "script" (OPTIONAL) onmousedown = "script" (OPTIONAL) onmousemove = "script" (OPTIONAL) onmouseup = "script" (OPTIONAL) Transitional DTD (deprecated): width = "length" (OPTIONAL) height – "length" (OPTIONAL) vspace = "length" (OPTIONAL) hspace = "length" (OPTIONAL) borders = "pixels" (OPTIONAL) align = "(bottom, middle, top, left, right)" (OPTIONAL)
EXAMPLE	`<IMG source = "picture.gif" alt = "A picture of my sailboat.">`

INPUT

PURPOSE	Accepts user input within a form
TYPE	Inline
NESTED WITHIN	FORM
START TAG	Required
END TAG	Forbidden
CONTENT	Empty
ATTRIBUTES	id = "name" (OPTIONAL)
	class = "name" (OPTIONAL)
	style = "style" (OPTIONAL)
	title = "name" (OPTIONAL)
	lang = "language" (OPTIONAL)
	dir = (rtl, ltr) (OPTIONAL)
	type = "(text, password, check box, radio, submit, reset, file, hidden, image, button)" (REQUIRED)
	name = "CDATA" (OPTIONAL)
	value = "CDATA" (OPTIONAL)
	checked (OPTIONAL)
	disabled (OPTIONAL)
	readonly (OPTIONAL)
	size = "CDATA" (OPTIONAL)
	maxlength = "number" (OPTIONAL)
	src = "url" (OPTIONAL)
	alt = "CDATA" (OPTIONAL)
	usemap = "url" (OPTIONAL)
	tabindex = "number" (OPTIONAL)
	accesskey = "character" (OPTIONAL)
	onclick = "script" (OPTIONAL)
	ondblclick = "script" (OPTIONAL)
	onkeydown = "script" (OPTIONAL)
	onkeypress = "script" (OPTIONAL)
	onkeyup = "script" (OPTIONAL)
	onmousedown = "script" (OPTIONAL)
	onmousemove = "script" (OPTIONAL)
	onmouseup = "script" (OPTIONAL)
	onblur = "script" (OPTIONAL)
	onfocus = "script" (OPTIONAL)
	onchange = "script" (OPTIONAL)
	onselect = "script" (OPTIONAL)
EXAMPLE	`<INPUT type = "text" size = "60" >`

TIP	Many of the attributes have specific meanings for a given input type. For example, in a text input box, the `size` attribute governs the length of the box displayed onscreen.

INS

PURPOSE	Indicates inserted text in a legal or political document
TYPE	Inline
NESTED WITHIN	Any `BLOCK` element
START TAG	Required
END TAG	Required
CONTENT	Text and inline elements (no Block elements permitted)
ATTRIBUTES	id = "name" (OPTIONAL) class = "name" (OPTIONAL) style = "style" (OPTIONAL) title = "name" (OPTIONAL) lang = "language" (OPTIONAL) dir = (rtl, ltr) (OPTIONAL) cite = "url" (OPTIONAL) datetime = "YYYYMMDD" (OPTIONAL) onclick = "script" (OPTIONAL) ondblclick = "script" (OPTIONAL) onkeydown = "script" (OPTIONAL) onkeypress = "script" (OPTIONAL) onkeyup = "script" (OPTIONAL) onmousedown = "script" (OPTIONAL) onmousemove = "script" (OPTIONAL) onmouseup = "script" (OPTIONAL)
EXAMPLE	`We can support <DEL>10</DEL><INS>12</INS> positions.`
TIP	Use `DEL` to show what's deleted.

ISINDEX (Deprecated)

PURPOSE	Creates a single-line text input control for server-enabled searches
TYPE	Inline

NESTED WITHIN	Any `BLOCK` element
START TAG	Required
END TAG	Forbidden
CONTENT	Empty
ATTRIBUTES	id = "name" (OPTIONAL) class = "name" (OPTIONAL) style = "style" (OPTIONAL) title = "name" (OPTIONAL) lang = "language" (OPTIONAL) dir = (rtl, ltr) (OPTIONAL) prompt = "text"
EXAMPLE	`<ISINDEX prompt = "Enter your search terms here" >`
TIP	Use Form elements instead.

KBD

PURPOSE	Displays text to be entered by the user as input
TYPE	Inline
NESTED WITHIN	Any `BLOCK` element
START TAG	Required
END TAG	Required
CONTENT	Text
ATTRIBUTES	id = "name" (OPTIONAL) class = "name" (OPTIONAL) style = "style" (OPTIONAL) title = "name" (OPTIONAL) onclick = "script" (OPTIONAL) ondblclick = "script" (OPTIONAL) onkeydown = "script" (OPTIONAL) onkeypress = "script" (OPTIONAL) onkeyup = "script" (OPTIONAL) onmousedown = "script" (OPTIONAL) onmousemove = "script" (OPTIONAL) onmouseup = "script" (OPTIONAL)
EXAMPLE	`In the user name text box, type` `<KBD>anonymous</KBD>.`
TIP	Usually rendered in a monospace font and indistinguishable from `CODE`, `SAMP` `TT`, and `VAR`.

LABEL

PURPOSE	Associates text with a control so when the user passes the mouse pointer over the control, the focus (selection) passes to the associated control
TYPE	Inline
NESTED WITHIN	FORM
START TAG	Required
END TAG	Required
CONTENT	Text and Input controls
ATTRIBUTES	id = "name" (OPTIONAL) class = "name" (OPTIONAL) style = "style" (OPTIONAL) title = "name" (OPTIONAL) lang = "language" (OPTIONAL) dir = (rtl, ltr) (OPTIONAL) for = "id of another element" accesskey = "character" onclick = "script" (OPTIONAL) ondblclick = "script" (OPTIONAL) onkeydown = "script" (OPTIONAL) onkeypress = "script" (OPTIONAL) onkeyup = "script" (OPTIONAL) onmousedown = "script" (OPTIONAL) onmousemove = "script" (OPTIONAL) onmouseup = "script" (OPTIONAL) onblur = "script" (OPTIONAL) onfocus = "script" (OPTIONAL)

EXAMPLE	`<LABEL>Please type the date (DD/MM/YYYY).`
	`  <INPUT type = "text">`
	`</LABEL>`

TIP	In a table, use the for attribute to specify the ID of the associated control.

LEGEND

PURPOSE	In a form, provides a title for a thematically related group of elements established with the LEGEND element
TYPE	Inline

NESTED WITHIN	LEGEND element
START TAG	Required
END TAG	Required
CONTENT	Contains HTML elements and text
ATTRIBUTES	Strict DTD: id = "name" (OPTIONAL) class = "name" (OPTIONAL) style = "CSS style definition" (OPTIONAL) title = "name" (OPTIONAL) lang = "language code" (OPTIONAL) dir = (rtl, ltr) (OPTIONAL) accesskey = "character" (OPTIONAL) onclick = "script" (OPTIONAL) ondblclick = "script" (OPTIONAL) onkeydown = "script" (OPTIONAL) onkeypress = "script" (OPTIONAL) onkeyup = "script" (OPTIONAL) onmousedown = "script" (OPTIONAL) onmousemove = "script" (OPTIONAL) onmouseup = "script" (OPTIONAL) Transitional DTD: align = "top, bottom, left, right" (OPTIONAL)

EXAMPLE

```
<FORM>
   <FIELDSET>
        <LEGEND>Title of Subsection of
               Form</LEGEND>
        <INPUT>
        <INPUT>
        <INPUT>
   </FIELDSET>
</FORM>
```

TIP   Use LEGEND within a FIELDSET element.

LI

TYPE	Block
PURPOSE	Defines an item in a list
NESTED WITHIN	UL, OL, DIR, MENU
START TAG	Required

END TAG	Optional
CONTENT	LI elements for each line of list
ATTRIBUTES	Strict DTD: id = "name" (OPTIONAL) class = "name" (OPTIONAL) style = "style" (OPTIONAL) title = "name" (OPTIONAL) lang = "language" (OPTIONAL) dir = (rtl, ltr) (OPTIONAL) onclick = "script" (OPTIONAL) ondblclick = "script" (OPTIONAL) onkeydown = "script" (OPTIONAL) onkeypress = "script" (OPTIONAL) onkeyup = "script" (OPTIONAL) onmousedown = "script" (OPTIONAL) onmousemove = "script" (OPTIONAL) onmouseup = "script" (OPTIONAL) Transitional DTD (deprecated): type = "(disc, square, circle)" (OPTIONAL)

EXAMPLE

```
<UL>
    <LI>Here's the first item in the list.
    <LI>Here's the second item in the list.
    <LI>Here's the third item in the list.
</UL>
```

TIP	The end tag is optional.

LINK

PURPOSE	Defines the relationship between two linked documents
TYPE	Block
NESTED WITHIN	HEAD element
START TAG	Required
END TAG	Forbidden
CONTENT	Empty
ATTRIBUTES	id = "name" (OPTIONAL) class = "name" (OPTIONAL) style = "CSS style definition" (OPTIONAL) title = "name" (OPTIONAL)

lang = "language code" (OPTIONAL)
dir = (rtl, ltr) (OPTIONAL)
charset = "character set" (OPTIONAL)
href = "url" (OPTIONAL)
hreflang = "language code" (OPTIONAL)
type = "MIMEtype" (OPTIONAL)
target = "(_blank, _self, _parent, _top, or frame name)
rel = "(alternate, stylesheet, start, next, prev,
   contents, index, glossary, copyright, chapter,
   section, subsection, appendix, help, bookmark)"
   rev = "(alternate, stylesheet, start, next, prev,
   contents, index, glossary, copyright, chapter,
   section, subsection, appendix, help, bookmark)"
media = "(screen, tty, tv, projection, handheld, print,
   braille, aural, all")

EXAMPLE

```
<LINK rel = "stylesheet" type =
"text/css">
```

TIP

The various forward and backward link types aren't recognized by most browsers.

MAP

PURPOSE   Creates a client-side imagemap

TYPE   Inline

NESTED WITHIN   `BODY`

START TAG   Required

END TAG   Required

CONTENT   `AREA` or `A` elements with text

ATTRIBUTES   id = "name" (OPTIONAL)
class = "name" (OPTIONAL)
style = "style" (OPTIONAL)
title = "name" (OPTIONAL)
lang = "language" (OPTIONAL)
dir = (rtl, ltr) (OPTIONAL)
name = "CDATA"
onclick = "script" (OPTIONAL)
ondblclick = "script" (OPTIONAL)
onkeydown = "script" (OPTIONAL)
onkeypress = "script" (OPTIONAL)
onkeyup = "script" (OPTIONAL)
onmousedown = "script" (OPTIONAL)

	onmousemove = "script" (OPTIONAL)
	onmouseup = "script" (OPTIONAL)
EXAMPLE	```<MAP name = "navigation">```
	``` <AREA href = "page1.html shape = "rect"```
	```coords = "0,0, 118, 28">```
	``` <AREA href = "page2.html" shape = rect```
	```coords = "184, 0, 276, 28">```
	```</MAP>```
TIP	Define the map with AREA.

MENU (Deprecated)

PURPOSE	Creates a single-column menu list
TYPE	Block
NESTED WITHIN	BODY
START TAG	Required
END TAG	Required
CONTENT	LI elements, inline elements, and text
ATTRIBUTES	id = "name" (OPTIONAL)
	class = "name" (OPTIONAL)
	style = "style" (OPTIONAL)
	title = "name" (OPTIONAL)
	lang = "language" (OPTIONAL)
	dir = (rtl, ltr) (OPTIONAL)
	name = "CDATA"
	onclick = "script" (OPTIONAL)
	ondblclick = "script" (OPTIONAL)
	onkeydown = "script" (OPTIONAL)
	onkeypress = "script" (OPTIONAL)
	onkeyup = "script" (OPTIONAL)
	onmousedown = "script" (OPTIONAL)
	onmousemove = "script" (OPTIONAL)
	onmouseup = "script" (OPTIONAL)
EXAMPLE	```<MENU>```
	``` <LI>Item 1```
	``` <LI>Item 2```
	``` <LI>Item 3```
	```</MENU>```
TIP	Use UL instead.

META

PURPOSE	Creates a client-side imagemap
TYPE	N/A
NESTED WITHIN	BODY
START TAG	Required
END TAG	Forbidden
CONTENT	Empty
ATTRIBUTES	id = "name" (OPTIONAL) class = "name" (OPTIONAL) style = "style" (OPTIONAL) title = "name" (OPTIONAL) lang = "language" (OPTIONAL) dir = (rtl, ltr) (OPTIONAL) http-equiv = "text" name = "text" content = "CDATA" scheme = "CDATA"
EXAMPLE	`<META name = "keywords" content = "Chesapeake Bay, cruising, sailing, marinas">`
TIP	A number of content description schemes are under development, but most browsers don't yet recognize them.

NOFRAMES

PURPOSE	Displays text for browsers incapable of displaying frames
TYPE	Block
NESTED WITHIN	BODY
START TAG	Required
END TAG	Optional
CONTENT	Block elements, inline elements, and text
ATTRIBUTES	id = "name" (OPTIONAL) class = "name" (OPTIONAL) style = "style" (OPTIONAL)

title = "name" (OPTIONAL)
lang = "language" (OPTIONAL)
dir = (rtl, ltr) (OPTIONAL)

EXAMPLE	`<NOFRAMES>Your browser doesn't handle frames. Sorry!</NOFRAMES>`
TIP	Be sure to include this element when you create a main frames page. Include links to the pages that would have been displayed by a forms-capable browser.

NOSCRIPT

PURPOSE	Displays text for browsers that don't support scripting
TYPE	Block
NESTED WITHIN	`BODY`
START TAG	Required
END TAG	Optional
CONTENT	Block elements, inline elements, and text
ATTRIBUTES	id = "name" (OPTIONAL) class = "name" (OPTIONAL) style = "style" (OPTIONAL) title = "name" (OPTIONAL) lang = "language" (OPTIONAL) dir = (rtl, ltr) (OPTIONAL)
EXAMPLE	`<NOSCRIPT>Your browser doesn't handle scripts. Sorry!</NOSCRIPT>`
TIP	Be sure to include this element when you add a script to your document. Explain what the script does.

OBJECT

PURPOSE	Inserts a type of data not natively supported by the browser, such as a Java applet, script, or font data. For images, use `IMG`.

TYPE	Block
NESTED WITHIN	BODY
START TAG	Required
END TAG	Optional
CONTENT	Contains inline elements and text; cannot contain block elements
ATTRIBUTES:	id = "name" (OPTIONAL)
	class = "name" (OPTIONAL)
	style = "style" (OPTIONAL)
	title = "name" (OPTIONAL)
	lang = "language" (OPTIONAL)
	dir = (rtl, ltr) (OPTIONAL)
	title = "CDATA" (OPTIONAL)
	tabindex = "number" (OPTIONAL)
	classid = "url" (OPTIONAL)
	codebase = "url" (OPTIONAL)
	declare (OPTIONAL)
	data = "url" (OPTIONAL)
	type = "MIME type" (OPTIONAL)
	codetype = "MIMEtype" (OPTIONAL)
	archive = "url" (OPTIONAL)
	standby = "text" (OPTIONAL)
	height = "length" (OPTIONAL)
	width = "length" (OPTIONAL)
	usemap = "url" (OPTIONAL)
	name = "CDATA" (OPTIONAL)
	tabindex = "number" (OPTIONAL)
	border = "pixels" (OPTIONAL)
	hspace = "length" (OPTIONAL)
	vspace = "length" (OPTIONAL)
	align = "(bottom, middle, top)" (OPTIONAL)
	onclick = "script" (OPTIONAL)
	ondblclick = "script" (OPTIONAL)
	onkeydown = "script" (OPTIONAL)
	onkeypress = "script" (OPTIONAL)
	onkeyup = "script" (OPTIONAL)
	onmousedown = "script" (OPTIONAL)
	onmousemove = "script" (OPTIONAL)
	onmouseup = "script" (OPTIONAL)

EXAMPLE	`<OBJECT classid = = "stupid.applet.class">`
	`  <PARAM name = "whirl" value = `
	`"incessantly">`

```
Your browser doesn't support Java.
</OBJECT>
```

TIP   Between the tags, place text that will appear only in browsers that don't support the data type.

OL

PURPOSE	Creates a numbered list
TYPE	Block
NESTED WITHIN	BODY
START TAG	Required
END TAG	Required
CONTENT	LI elements
ATTRIBUTES	Strict DTD: id = "name" (OPTIONAL) class = "name" (OPTIONAL) style = "style" (OPTIONAL) title = "name" (OPTIONAL) lang = "language" (OPTIONAL) dir = (rtl, ltr) (OPTIONAL) onclick = "script" (OPTIONAL) ondblclick = "script" (OPTIONAL) onkeydown = "script" (OPTIONAL) onkeypress = "script" (OPTIONAL) onkeyup = "script" (OPTIONAL) onmousedown = "script" (OPTIONAL) onmousemove = "script" (OPTIONAL) onmouseup = "script" (OPTIONAL) Transitional DTD: type = "(disc, square, or circle)" (OPTIONAL) start = "number" (OPTIONAL) value = "number" (OPTIONAL) compact

EXAMPLE
```
<OL>
  <LI>Item 1
  <LI>Item 2
</OL>
```

TIP   Define the list style with style sheets.

OPTGROUP

PURPOSE	In a form, defines a group of items in a drop-down menu created with SELECT.
TYPE	Inline
NESTED WITHIN	FORM
START TAG	Required
END TAG	Optional
CONTENT	Text
ATTRIBUTES	id = "name" (OPTIONAL)
	class = "name" (OPTIONAL)
	style = "style" (OPTIONAL)
	title = "name" (OPTIONAL)
	lang = "language" (OPTIONAL)
	dir = (rtl, ltr) (OPTIONAL)
	disabled (OPTIONAL
	label = "text" (REQUIRED)
	onclick = "script" (OPTIONAL)
	ondblclick = "script" (OPTIONAL)
	onkeydown = "script" (OPTIONAL)
	onkeypress = "script" (OPTIONAL)
	onkeyup = "script" (OPTIONAL)
	onmousedown = "script" (OPTIONAL)
	onmousemove = "script" (OPTIONAL)
	onmouseup = "script" (OPTIONAL)

EXAMPLE

```
<SELECT name = "hull-length">
    <OPTGROUP label = "Hull Length">
        <OPTION selected value = "34'">34'
        <OPTION>36'
        <OPTION>40'
    </OPTGROUP>
    <OPTGROUP label = "Year">
        <OPTION selected value = "1988">1988
        <OPTION>1989
        <OPTION>1990>
    </OPTGROUP>
</SELECT>
```

TIP   Define the items to appear in the menu by using OPTGROUP and OPTION.

OPTION

PURPOSE   In a form, defines an item in a drop-down menu
                       created with SELECT

TYPE   Inline

NESTED WITHIN   FORM

START TAG   Required

END TAG   Optional

CONTENT   Text

ATTRIBUTES   id = "name" (OPTIONAL)
                       class = "name" (OPTIONAL)
                       style = "style" (OPTIONAL)
                       title = "name" (OPTIONAL)
                       lang = "language" (OPTIONAL)
                       dir = (rtl, ltr) (OPTIONAL)
                       selected (OPTIONAL)
                       disabled (OPTIONAL
                       label = "text" (OPTIONAL)
                       value = "CDATA" (OPTIONAL)
                       onclick = "script" (OPTIONAL)
                       ondblclick = "script" (OPTIONAL)
                       onkeydown = "script" (OPTIONAL)
                       onkeypress = "script" (OPTIONAL)
                       onkeyup = "script" (OPTIONAL)
                       onmousedown = "script" (OPTIONAL)
                       onmousemove = "script" (OPTIONAL)
                       onmouseup = "script" (OPTIONAL)

EXAMPLE
```
<SELECT name = "hull-length">
   <OPTGROUP label = "Hull Length">
       <OPTION selected value = "34'">34'
       <OPTION>36'
       <OPTION>40'
   </OPTGROUP>
   <OPTGROUP label = "Year">
       <OPTION selected value = "1988">1988
       <OPTION>1989
       <OPTION>1990>
   </OPTGROUP>
</SELECT>
```

| TIP | Define the items to appear in the menu by using `OPTGROUP` and `OPTION`. |

P

PURPOSE	Defines a paragraph of `body` text (generally with a blank line above the paragraph)
TYPE	Block
NESTED WITHIN	`BODY`
START TAG	Required
END TAG	Optional
CONTENT	Contains inline elements and text — cannot contain block elements
ATTRIBUTES	Strict DTD: id = "name" (OPTIONAL) class = "name" (OPTIONAL) style = "style" (OPTIONAL) title = "name" (OPTIONAL) lang = "language" (OPTIONAL) dir = (rtl, ltr) (OPTIONAL) onclick = "script" (OPTIONAL) ondblclick = "script" (OPTIONAL) onkeydown = "script" (OPTIONAL) onkeypress = "script" (OPTIONAL) onkeyup = "script" (OPTIONAL) onmousedown = "script" (OPTIONAL) onmousemove = "script" (OPTIONAL) onmouseup = "script" (OPTIONAL) Transitional DTD: align = "(left, center, right, justify)"
EXAMPLE	`<P>This is a text paragraph</P>`
TIP	For good form, begin each paragraph with `<P>` and close with `</P>`. Do not use `<P>` to enter blank lines.

PARAM

PURPOSE	Defines run-time settings for an object
TYPE	Inline
NESTED WITHIN	OBJECT
START TAG	Required
END TAG	Forbidden
CONTENT	Empty
ATTRIBUTES:	id = "name" (REQUIRED) name = "CDATA" (OPTIONAL) value = "CDATA" (OPTIONAL) valuetype = "(data, ref, or object)" type = "MIME type"

EXAMPLE

```
<OBJECT classid = = "stupid.applet.class">
  <PARAM name = "whirl" value =
"incessantly">
  Your browser doesn't support Java.
</OBJECT>
```

TIP — Check the applet's documentation to find out how to set the run-time settings (parameters).

PRE

TYPE	Inline
PURPOSE	Preserves spaces and line breaks as they are typed
NESTED WITHIN	BODY
START TAG	Required
END TAG	Required
CONTENT	Contains HTML elements and text (but see the following note)
ATTRIBUTES	width = "number" (OPTIONAL) id = "name" (OPTIONAL) class = "name" (OPTIONAL) style = "style" (OPTIONAL) title = "name" (OPTIONAL) lang = "language" (OPTIONAL) dir = (rtl, ltr) (OPTIONAL) onclick = "script" (OPTIONAL)

	ondblclick = "script" (OPTIONAL) onkeydown = "script" (OPTIONAL) onkeypress = "script" (OPTIONAL) onkeyup = "script" (OPTIONAL) onmousedown = "script" (OPTIONAL) onmousemove = "script" (OPTIONAL) onmouseup = "script" (OPTIONAL)
NOTE	You can't use IMG, OBJECT, BIG, SMALL, SUB, or SUP within a PRE element.

EXAMPLE	`<PRE>`
	`This`
	`text     will     preserve     its`
	`bizarre`
	`        spacing</PRE>`

TIP	To align characters correctly, consider using a monospace font.

Q

PURPOSE	Marks an inline quotation
TYPE	Inline
NESTED WITHIN	Any BLOCK element
START TAG	Required
END TAG	Required
CONTENT	Text
ATTRIBUTES	id = "name" (OPTIONAL) class = "name" (OPTIONAL) style = "style" (OPTIONAL) title = "name" (OPTIONAL) lang = "language" (OPTIONAL) dir = (rtl, ltr) (OPTIONAL) cite = "url" (OPTIONAL) onclick = "script" (OPTIONAL) ondblclick = "script" (OPTIONAL) onkeydown = "script" (OPTIONAL) onkeypress = "script" (OPTIONAL) onkeyup = "script" (OPTIONAL) onmousedown = "script" (OPTIONAL) onmousemove = "script" (OPTIONAL) onmouseup = "script" (OPTIONAL)

EXAMPLE	`<Q cite = "source.html">Here's a quotation.</Q>`
TIP	You can use the `BLOCKQUOTE` element for longer (indented) quotations. If you use `Q`, don't use quotation marks. They're supplied by the browser in a way that's sensitive to the document's language code.

S (Deprecated)

PURPOSE	Displays text in strikethrough font
TYPE	Inline
NESTED WITHIN	Any `BLOCK` element
START TAG	Required
END TAG	Required
CONTENT	Text
ATTRIBUTES	id = "name" (OPTIONAL) class = "name" (OPTIONAL) style = "style" (OPTIONAL) title = "name" (OPTIONAL)
EXAMPLE	`<S>Text in a strikethrough font</S>`
TIP	Be careful to close this element properly.

SAMP

PURPOSE	Identifies computer output
TYPE	Inline
NESTED WITHIN	Any `BLOCK` element
START TAG	Required
END TAG	Required
CONTENT	Text
ATTRIBUTES	id = "name" (OPTIONAL) class = "name" (OPTIONAL) style = "style" (OPTIONAL) title = "name" (OPTIONAL) lang = "language" (OPTIONAL) dir = (rtl, ltr) (OPTIONAL)

cite = "url" (OPTIONAL)
onclick = "script" (OPTIONAL)
ondblclick = "script" (OPTIONAL)
onkeydown = "script" (OPTIONAL)
onkeypress = "script" (OPTIONAL)
onkeyup = "script" (OPTIONAL)
onmousedown = "script" (OPTIONAL)
onmousemove = "script" (OPTIONAL)
onmouseup = "script" (OPTIONAL)

EXAMPLE

```
Wait until you see <SAMP>fatal
error</SAMP> on the screen; then panic.
```

TIP

Usually rendered in a monospace font.

SCRIPT

PURPOSE

Contains a script

TYPE

Inline

NESTED WITHIN

`BODY`

START TAG

Required

END TAG

Required

CONTENT

A script in a language, such as JavaScript.

ATTRIBUTES:

Strict DTD:
type = "MIME type" (REQUIRED)
charset = "character set"
src = "url"
defer

Transitional DTD (deprecated):
language = "scripting language"

EXAMPLE

```
<SCRIPT type = "text/javascript">
  <!-- hide your script within HTML
  comment tags -->
</SCRIPT>
```

TIP

Hide your script within comment tags so it won't be
displayed by older browsers.

SELECT

PURPOSE	In a form, creates a drop-down menu
TYPE	Inline
NESTED WITHIN	FORM
START TAG	Required
END TAG	Required
CONTENT	OPTGROUP or OPTION elements
ATTRIBUTES	id = "name" (OPTIONAL)
	class = "name" (OPTIONAL)
	style = "style" (OPTIONAL)
	title = "name" (OPTIONAL)
	lang = "language" (OPTIONAL)
	dir = (rtl, ltr) (OPTIONAL)
	name = "CDATA"
	size = "number" (OPTIONAL)
	multiple (OPTIONAL)
	disabled (OPTIONAL)
	tabindex = "number"
	onclick = "script" (OPTIONAL)
	ondblclick = "script" (OPTIONAL)
	onkeydown = "script" (OPTIONAL)
	onkeypress = "script" (OPTIONAL)
	onkeyup = "script" (OPTIONAL)
	onmousedown = "script" (OPTIONAL)
	onmousemove = "script" (OPTIONAL)
	onmouscup = "script" (OPTIONAL)
	onblur = "script" (OPTIONAL)
	onfocus = "script" (OPTIONAL)
	onchange = "script" (OPTIONAL)

EXAMPLE

```
<SELECT name = "hull-length">
  <OPTGROUP label = "Hull Length">
      <OPTION selected value = "34'">34'
      <OPTION>36'
      <OPTION>40'
  </OPTGROUP>
  <OPTGROUP label = "Year">
      <OPTION selected value = "1988">1988
      <OPTION>1989
      <OPTION>1990>
  </OPTGROUP>
</SELECT>
```

TIP	Define the items to appear in the menu by using OPTGROUP and OPTION.

SMALL

PURPOSE	Displays text in a "small" font size
TYPE	Inline
NESTED WITHIN	Any BLOCK element
START TAG	Required
END TAG	Required
CONTENT	Text
ATTRIBUTES	id = "name" (OPTIONAL)
	class = "name" (OPTIONAL)
	style = "style" (OPTIONAL)
	title = "name" (OPTIONAL)
	lang = "language" (OPTIONAL)
	dir = (rtl, ltr) (OPTIONAL)
	onclick = "script" (OPTIONAL)
	ondblclick = "script" (OPTIONAL)
	onkeydown = "script" (OPTIONAL)
	onkeypress = "script" (OPTIONAL)
	onkeyup = "script" (OPTIONAL)
	onmousedown = "script" (OPTIONAL)
	onmousemove = "script" (OPTIONAL)
	onmouseup = "script" (OPTIONAL)
EXAMPLE	`<SMALL>Use as directed. Call physician if condition persists.</SMALL>`
TIP	You can use the BIG element to render text in a "large" size.

SPAN

PURPOSE	Encloses text within a generic inline element that you can define with style sheets
TYPE	Inline
NESTED WITHIN	Any BLOCK element
START TAG	Required
END TAG	Required

CONTENT	Block elements
ATTRIBUTES	id = "name" (OPTIONAL)
	class = "name" (OPTIONAL)
	style = "style" (OPTIONAL)
	title = "name" (OPTIONAL)
	lang = "language" (OPTIONAL)
	dir = (rtl, ltr) (OPTIONAL)
	href = "url"
	onclick = "script" (OPTIONAL)
	ondblclick = "script" (OPTIONAL)
	onkeydown = "script" (OPTIONAL)
	onkeypress = "script" (OPTIONAL)
	onkeyup = "script" (OPTIONAL)
	onmousedown = "script" (OPTIONAL)
	onmousemove = "script" (OPTIONAL)
	onmouseup = "script" (OPTIONAL)
EXAMPLE	`<SPAN class = "bibliography">Book Title</SPAN>`
TIP	Use `DIV` to group and define block elements.

STRIKE (Deprecated)

PURPOSE	Displays text in strikethrough font
TYPE	Inline
NESTED WITHIN	Any `BLOCK` element
START TAG	Required
END TAG	Required
CONTENT	Text
ATTRIBUTES	id = "name" (OPTIONAL)
	class = "name" (OPTIONAL)
	style = "style" (OPTIONAL)
	title = "name" (OPTIONAL)
	onclick = "script" (OPTIONAL)
	ondblclick = "script" (OPTIONAL)
	onkeydown = "script" (OPTIONAL)
	onkeypress = "script" (OPTIONAL)
	onkeyup = "script" (OPTIONAL)
	onmousedown = "script" (OPTIONAL)
	onmousemove = "script" (OPTIONAL)
	onmouseup = "script" (OPTIONAL)

EXAMPLE	`<S>Text in a strikethrough font</S>`
TIP	Be careful to close this element properly.

STRONG

PURPOSE	Marks text for emphasis
TYPE	Inline
NESTED WITHIN	Any `BLOCK` element
START TAG	Required
END TAG	Required
CONTENT	Text
ATTRIBUTES	id = "name" (OPTIONAL)
	class = "name" (OPTIONAL)
	style = "style" (OPTIONAL)
	title = "name" (OPTIONAL)
	lang = "language" (OPTIONAL)
	dir = (rtl, ltr) (OPTIONAL)
	cite = "url" (OPTIONAL)
	onclick = "script" (OPTIONAL)
	ondblclick = "script" (OPTIONAL)
	onkeydown = "script" (OPTIONAL)
	onkeypress = "script" (OPTIONAL)
	onkeyup = "script" (OPTIONAL)
	onmousedown = "script" (OPTIONAL)
	onmousemove = "script" (OPTIONAL)
	onmouseup = "script" (OPTIONAL)
EXAMPLE	`Do this <STRONG>right now</STRONG>.`
TIP	Usually rendered in boldface.

STYLE

TYPE	Inline
PURPOSE	Defines the style to be associated with an `HTML` element throughout the document
NESTED WITHIN	`HEAD`
START TAG	Required

END TAG	Required
CONTENT	CDATA (style sheet)
ATTRIBUTES	type = "CDATA" (REQUIRED) media = "MIME type" (OPTIONAL)

EXAMPLE	`<STYLE type = "text/css">`
	  `H1 {text-align: center; font-family:`
	`Helvetica; color: red; font-style: italic}`
	`</STYLE>`

TIP	Define the type as text/css.

TABLE

PURPOSE	Creates a table
TYPE	Inline
NESTED WITHIN	`COLGROUP` element
START TAG	Required
END TAG	Required
CONTENT	Table tags and text
ATTRIBUTES	Strict DTD: id = "name" (OPTIONAL) class = "name" (OPTIONAL) style = "style" (OPTIONAL) title = "name" (OPTIONAL) lang = "language" (OPTIONAL) dir = (rtl, ltr) (OPTIONAL) summary = "text" (OPTIONAL) width = "length" (OPTIONAL) border = "pixels" (OPTIONAL) frame = "(void, above, below, hsides, lhs, rhs, vsides, box, border)" (OPTIONAL) rules = "(none, groups, rows, cols, all)" (OPTIONAL) cellspacing = "length" (OPTIONAL) cellpadding = "length" (OPTIONAL) onclick = "script" (OPTIONAL) ondblclick = "script" (OPTIONAL) onkeydown = "script" (OPTIONAL) onkeypress = "script" (OPTIONAL) onkeyup = "script" (OPTIONAL) onmousedown = "script" (OPTIONAL)

onmousemove = "script" (OPTIONAL)
onmouseup = "script" (OPTIONAL)

Transitional DTD (deprecated):
align = "(left, center, right)"

EXAMPLE

```
<TABLE>
  <TR>
      <TD>Cell 1
      <TD>Cell 2
  </TR>
</TABLE>
```

TIP

Use the summary attribute to specify a brief summary of the table for people using nongraphical browsers.

TBODY

PURPOSE

Creates a table `body` that scrolls within a fixed table header (see `THEAD`) and table footer (`TFOOT`)

TYPE

Inline

NESTED WITHIN

`TABLE` element

START TAG

Optional

END TAG

Optional

CONTENT

Table tags and text

ATTRIBUTES

id = "name" (OPTIONAL)
class = "name" (OPTIONAL)
style = "style" (OPTIONAL)
title = "name" (OPTIONAL)
lang = "language" (OPTIONAL)
dir = (rtl, ltr) (OPTIONAL)
align = "(left, center, right, justify, char)"
char = "character"
charoff = "length"
valign = "(top, middle, bottom, baseline)"
onclick = "script" (OPTIONAL)
ondblclick = "script" (OPTIONAL)
onkeydown = "script" (OPTIONAL)
onkeypress = "script" (OPTIONAL)
onkeyup = "script" (OPTIONAL)
onmousedown = "script" (OPTIONAL)

	onmousemove = "script" (OPTIONAL) onmouseup = "script" (OPTIONAL)
EXAMPLE	``` <THEAD> <TR> <TH>Header 1 <TH>Header 2 </TR> </THEAD> <TBODY> <TR> <TD>Item 1 <TD>Item 2 </TR> </TBODY> ```
TIP	Note, THEAD must contain the same number of columns as the table body and THEAD. TFOOT must appear before TBODY.

TD

PURPOSE	Creates a table cell
TYPE	Inline
NESTED WITHIN	TR element
START TAG	Required
END TAG	Optional
CONTENT	Table tags and text
ATTRIBUTES	Strict DTD: id = "name" (OPTIONAL) class = "name" (OPTIONAL) style - "style" (OPTIONAL) title = "name" (OPTIONAL) lang = "language" (OPTIONAL) dir = (rtl, ltr) (OPTIONAL) axis = "text" (OPTIONAL) headers = "ID list" (OPTIONAL) scope = "(row, col, rowgroup, colgroup)" rowspan = "number" (OPTIONAL) colspan = "number" (OPTIONAL) align = "(left, center, right, justify, char)" char = "character"

charoff = "length"
valign = "(top, middle, bottom, baseline)"

Transitional DTD (deprecated):
nowrap (OPTIONAL)
width = "length" (OPTIONAL)
height = "length"
onclick = "script" (OPTIONAL)
ondblclick = "script" (OPTIONAL)
onkeydown = "script" (OPTIONAL)
onkeypress = "script" (OPTIONAL)
onkeyup = "script" (OPTIONAL)
onmousedown = "script" (OPTIONAL)
onmousemove = "script" (OPTIONAL)
onmouseup = "script" (OPTIONAL)

EXAMPLE	`<TR>`
	  `<TD>Cell 1`
	  `<TD>Cell 2`
	`</TR>`

TIP	You can omit the end tag.

TEXTAREA

PURPOSE	In a form, creates a multiline text entry box
TYPE	Block
NESTED WITHIN	`FORM`
START TAG	Required
END TAG	Required
CONTENT	Text
ATTRIBUTES	id = "name" (OPTIONAL) class = "name" (OPTIONAL) style = "style" (OPTIONAL) title = "name" (OPTIONAL) lang = "language" (OPTIONAL) name = "CDATA" (OPTIONAL) rows = "number" (REQUIRED) cols = "number" (REQUIRED) disabled (OPTIONAL) readonly (OPTIONAL) tabindex = "number" (OPTIONAL) accesskey = "character" (OPTIONAL)

onclick = "script" (OPTIONAL)
ondblclick = "script" (OPTIONAL)
onkeydown = "script" (OPTIONAL)
onkeypress = "script" (OPTIONAL)
onkeyup = "script" (OPTIONAL)
onmousedown = "script" (OPTIONAL)
onmousemove = "script" (OPTIONAL)
onmouseup = "script" (OPTIONAL)
onblur = "script" (OPTIONAL)
onfocus = "script" (OPTIONAL)
onchange = "script" (OPTIONAL)
onselect = "script" (OPTIONAL)

EXAMPLE

`<TEXTAREA rows = "16 cols = "65" name = "comments">`

TIP

Use `<INPUT type = "text">` to create a one-line text box.

TH

PURPOSE

Creates a table header cell

TYPE

Inline

NESTED WITHIN

TR element

START TAG

Required

END TAG

Optional

CONTENT

Table tags and text

ATTRIBUTES

Strict DTD:
id = "name" (OPTIONAL)
class = "name" (OPTIONAL)
style = "style" (OPTIONAL)
title = "namc" (OPTIONAL)
lang = "language" (OPTIONAL)
dir = (rtl, ltr) (OPTIONAL)
axis = "text" (OPTIONAL)
headers = "ID list" (OPTIONAL)
scope = "(row, col, rowgroup, colgroup)"
rowspan = "number" (OPTIONAL)
colspan = "number" (OPTIONAL)
align = "(left, center, right, justify, char)"
char = "character"
charoff = "length"
valign = "(top, middle, bottom, baseline)"

Transitional DTD (deprecated):
nowrap (OPTIONAL)
width = "length" (OPTIONAL)
height = "length"

EXAMPLE

```
<TR>
  <TH>Header 1
  <TH>Header 2
</TR>
<TR>
  <TD>Item 1
  <TD>Item 2
</TR>
```

TIP

You can omit the end tag. Most browsers render the contents of header cells in bold.

THEAD

PURPOSE

Creates a table header that conforming browsers will prevent from scrolling

TYPE

Inline

NESTED WITHIN

TR element

START TAG

Required

END TAG

Optional

CONTENT

Table tags and text

ATTRIBUTES

id = "name" (OPTIONAL)
class = "name" (OPTIONAL)
style = "style" (OPTIONAL)
title = "name" (OPTIONAL)
lang = "language" (OPTIONAL)
dir = (rtl, ltr) (OPTIONAL)
align = "(left, center, right, justify, char)"
char = "character"
charoff = "length"
valign = "(top, middle, bottom, baseline)"
onclick = "script" (OPTIONAL)
ondblclick = "script" (OPTIONAL)
onkeydown = "script" (OPTIONAL)
onkeypress = "script" (OPTIONAL)
onkeyup = "script" (OPTIONAL)

	onmousedown = "script" (OPTIONAL) onmousemove = "script" (OPTIONAL) onmouseup = "script" (OPTIONAL)
| EXAMPLE | ```
<THEAD>
  <TR>
      <TH>Header 1
      <TH>Header 2
  </TR>
</THEAD>
<TBODY
  <TR>
      <TD>Item 1
      <TD>Item 2
  </TR>
</TBODY>
``` |
| TIP | Note, THEAD must contain the same number of columns as the table body and TFOOT. |

TFOOT

PURPOSE	Creates a table footer that conforming browsers will prevent from scrolling
TYPE	Inline
NESTED WITHIN	TR element
START TAG	Required
END TAG	Optional
CONTENT	Table tags and text
ATTRIBUTES	id = "name" (OPTIONAL) class = "name" (OPTIONAL) style = "style" (OPTIONAL) title = "name" (OPTIONAL) lang = "language" (OPTIONAL) dir = (rtl, ltr) (OPTIONAL) align = "(left, center, right, justify, char)" char = "character" charoff = "length" valign = "(top, middle, bottom, baseline)" onclick = "script" (OPTIONAL) ondblclick = "script" (OPTIONAL) onkeydown = "script" (OPTIONAL) onkeypress = "script" (OPTIONAL)
```

<table>
<tr><td></td><td>onkeyup = "script" (OPTIONAL)
onmousedown = "script" (OPTIONAL)
onmousemove = "script" (OPTIONAL)
onmouseup = "script" (OPTIONAL)</td></tr>
</table>

EXAMPLE	

```
<TFOOT>
  <TR>
      <TH>Header 1
      <TH>Header 2
  </TR>
</THEAD>
<TBODY>
  <TR>
      <TD>Item 1
      <TD>Item 2
  </TR>
</TBODY>
```

TIP	Note, THEAD must contain the same number of columns as the table body and THEAD. TFOOT must appear before TBODY.

TITLE

PURPOSE	Enables you to specify title text that appears on the browser's title bar (but not in the document itself)
NESTED WITHIN	HEAD element
START TAG	Required
END TAG	Required
CONTENT	CDATA; entities are permitted but no elements
NOTE	All other elements are excluded. You can't add character formatting (such as boldface) or any other presentation within the TITLE element.
EXAMPLE	`<TITLE>Sailing the Southern Chesapeake Bay</TITLE>`
TIP	Use substantive title words to increase chance of detection by Web search engines.

TR

PURPOSE	Creates a table row
TYPE	Inline
NESTED WITHIN	TR element
START TAG	Required
END TAG	Optional
CONTENT	Table tags and text
ATTRIBUTES	id = "name" (OPTIONAL)
	class = "name" (OPTIONAL)
	style = "style" (OPTIONAL)
	title = "name" (OPTIONAL)
	lang = "language" (OPTIONAL)
	dir = (rtl, ltr) (OPTIONAL)
	align = "(left, center, right, justify, char)"
	char = "character"
	charoff = "length"
	valign = "(top, middle, bottom, baseline)"
	onclick = "script" (OPTIONAL)
	ondblclick = "script" (OPTIONAL)
	onkeydown = "script" (OPTIONAL)
	onkeypress = "script" (OPTIONAL)
	onkeyup = "script" (OPTIONAL)
	onmousedown = "script" (OPTIONAL)
	onmousemove = "script" (OPTIONAL)
	onmouseup = "script" (OPTIONAL)

EXAMPLE

```
<TR>
    <TD>Cell 1
    <TD>Cell 2
</TR>
```

TIP   You can omit the end tag.

TT

PURPOSE	Displays text in a monospace font
TYPE	Inline
NESTED WITHIN	Any BLOCK element
START TAG	Required
END TAG	Required

CONTENT	Text
ATTRIBUTES	id = "name" (OPTIONAL)
	class = "name" (OPTIONAL)
	style = "style" (OPTIONAL)
	title = "name" (OPTIONAL)
	onclick = "script" (OPTIONAL)
	ondblclick = "script" (OPTIONAL)
	onkeydown = "script" (OPTIONAL)
	onkeypress = "script" (OPTIONAL)
	onkeyup = "script" (OPTIONAL)
	onmousedown = "script" (OPTIONAL)
	onmousemove = "script" (OPTIONAL)
	onmouseup = "script" (OPTIONAL)
EXAMPLE	`<TT>Text in a large font</TT>`
TIP	Usually rendered in a monospace font and indistinguishable from `CODE`, `KBD`, `SAMP`, and `VAR`.

U (Deprecated)

PURPOSE	Displays text with underlining
TYPE	Inline
NESTED WITHIN	Any `BLOCK` element
START TAG	Required
END TAG	Required
CONTENT	Text
ATTRIBUTES	id = "name" (OPTIONAL)
	class = "name" (OPTIONAL)
	style = "style" (OPTIONAL)
	title = "name" (OPTIONAL)
	onclick = "script" (OPTIONAL)
	ondblclick = "script" (OPTIONAL)
	onkeydown = "script" (OPTIONAL)
	onkeypress = "script" (OPTIONAL)
	onkeyup = "script" (OPTIONAL)
	onmousedown = "script" (OPTIONAL)
	onmousemove = "script" (OPTIONAL)
	onmouseup = "script" (OPTIONAL)
EXAMPLE	`<U>Underlined</U>`

TIP   Avoid this element. Users may confuse underlined
                        text with hyperlinks.

UL

PURPOSE   Creates a numbered list

TYPE   Block

NESTED WITHIN   BODY

START TAG   Required

END TAG   Required

CONTENT   LI elements

ATTRIBUTES   Strict DTD:
                        id = "name" (OPTIONAL)
                        class = "name" (OPTIONAL)
                        style = "style" (OPTIONAL)
                        title = "name" (OPTIONAL)
                        lang = "language" (OPTIONAL)
                        dir = (rtl, ltr) (OPTIONAL)
                        onclick = "script" (OPTIONAL)
                        ondblclick = "script" (OPTIONAL)
                        onkeydown = "script" (OPTIONAL)
                        onkeypress = "script" (OPTIONAL)
                        onkeyup = "script" (OPTIONAL)
                        onmousedown = "script" (OPTIONAL)
                        onmousemove = "script" (OPTIONAL)
                        onmouseup = "script" (OPTIONAL)

                        Transitional DTD:
                        type = "(disc, square, or circle)" (OPTIONAL)
                        start = "number" (OPTIONAL)
                        value = "number" (OPTIONAL)
                        compact

EXAMPLE
```
<OL>
   <LI>Item 1
   <LI>Item 2
</OL>
```

TIP   Define the list style with style sheets.

VAR

PURPOSE	Marks text as a variable in a computer program
TYPE	Inline
NESTED WITHIN	Any BLOCK element
START TAG	Required
END TAG	Required
CONTENT	Text
ATTRIBUTES	id = "name" (OPTIONAL)
	class = "name" (OPTIONAL)
	style = "style" (OPTIONAL)
	title = "name" (OPTIONAL)
	lang = "language" (OPTIONAL)
	dir = (rtl, ltr) (OPTIONAL)
	cite = "url" (OPTIONAL)
	onclick = "script" (OPTIONAL)
	ondblclick = "script" (OPTIONAL)
	onkeydown = "script" (OPTIONAL)
	onkeypress = "script" (OPTIONAL)
	onkeyup = "script" (OPTIONAL)
	onmousedown = "script" (OPTIONAL)
	onmousemove = "script" (OPTIONAL)
	onmouseup = "script" (OPTIONAL)
EXAMPLE	`<VAR>x = "19"</VAR>`
TIP	Usually rendered in a monospace font and indistinguishable from CODE, SAMP TT, and VAR.

✦   ✦   ✦

HTML 4 Attributes Reference

Attribute	Used in	Valid value	Purpose
abbr	TD, TH	text	abbreviation for header cell
accept-charset	FORM	character set	list of supported code character sets
accept	INPUT	MIME types	list of MIME types for file upload
accesskey	A, AREA, BUTTON, INPUT, LABEL, LEGEND, TEXTAREA	character	character to press to bring focus to element
action	FORM	URL	form handler program
align	CAPTION	top, bottom, left, right	alignment relative to table
align	APPLET, IFRAME, IMG, INPUT, OBJECT	top, middle, bottom, left, right	vertical or horizontal alignment
align	LEGEND	top, bottom, left, right	relative to fieldset
align	TABLE	left, center, right	relative to window

(continued)

Attribute	Used in	Valid value	Purpose
align	HR	left, center, right	
align	DIV, H1, H2, H3, H4, H5, H6, P	left, center, right, justify	text alignment
align	COL, COLGROUP, TBODY, TD, TFOOT, TH, THEAD, TR	left, center, right, justify, char	table alignment
alink	BODY	color	color of selected links
alt	APPLET	text	text description
alt	AREA, IMG	text	text description
alt	INPUT	CDATA	text description
archive	OBJECT	URL	space separated archive list
archive	APPLET	CDATA	comma separated archive list
axis	TD, TH	CDATA	groups of related headers
BACKGROUND	BODY	URL	image for document background
bgcolor	TABLE	color	background cell color
bgcolor	TR	color	background row color
bgcolor	TD, TH	color	background cell color
bgcolor	BODY	color	document background color
border	IMG, OBJECT	length	link border width
border	TABLE	pixels	controls frame width around table
cellpadding	TABLE	length	spacing within cells
cellspacing	TABLE	length	spacing between cells
char	COL, COLGROUP, TBODY, TD, TFOOT, TH, THEAD, TR	character	alignment character

Attribute	Used in	Valid value	Purpose
charoff	COL, COLGROUP, BODY, TD, TFOOT, TH, THEAD, TR	length	offset for alignment character
charset	A, LINK, SCRIPT	character set code	code for character set of linked resource
checked	INPUT	checked	Boolean value for radio buttons and check boxes
cite	BLOCKQUOTE, Q	URL	source document
cite	DEL, INS	URL	info on reason for deletion or insertion
class	All elements except BASE, BASEFONT, HEAD, HTML, META, PARAM, SCRIPT, STYLE, TITLE	CDATA	space-separated list of class names
CLASSID	OBJECT	URL	location of code
clear	BR	left, all, right, none	control of text flow next to floated object
code	APPLET	CDATA	location of code
codebase	OBJECT	URL	base URL for object
codebase	APPLET	URL	base URL for applet
codetype	OBJECT	MIME type	MIME type of code
color	BASEFONT, FONT	color	text color
cols	FRAMESET	lengths in comma-separated list	list of lengths
cols	TEXTAREA	number	width of text box
colspan	TD, TH	number	number of cols spanned by cell
compact	DIR, MENU DL, OL, UL	compact	smaller list size
content	META	CDATA	type of content

(continued)

Attribute	Used in	Valid value	Purpose
coords	A, AREA	lengths in comma-separated list	coordinates of imagemap areas
data	OBJECT	URL	reference to object's data
datetime	DEL, INS	YYYY-MM-DD Thh:mm:ssTZD	date, time, and time zone in ISO format
declare	OBJECT	declare	declare but don't run
defer	SCRIPT	defer	optionally run later
dir	All elements except APPLET, BASE, BASEFONT, BDO, BR, FRAME, FRAMESET, HR, IFRAME, PARAM, SCRIPT	ltr, rtl	text direction
dir	BDO	ltr, rtl	text direction
disabled	BUTTON, INPUT, OPTGROUP, OPTION, SELECT, TEXTAREA	disabled	Boolean value to disable this option
enctype	FORM	MIME type	encoding type
face	BASEFONT, FONT	CDATA	comma-separated list of font names
for	LABEL	ID name	matches field ID value
frame	TABLE	void, above, below, hsides, lhs, rhs, vsides, box, border	part to display
frameborder	FRAME, IFRAME	1, 0	borders on or off
headers	TD, TH	ID names	space-separated list of IDs for header cells
height	IFRAME	length	frame height
height	IMG, OBJECT	length	override height
height	APPLET	length	initial height
height	TD, TH	pixels	height for cell

Attribute	Used in	Valid value	Purpose
href	A, AREA, LINK	URL	URL for linked resource
href	BASE	URL	base URL
hreflang	A, LINK	language code	language code
hspace	APPLET, IMG, OBJECT	pixels	horizontal gutter
http-equiv	META	text	HTTP response header name
id	All elements except BASE, HEAD, HTML, META, SCRIPT, STYLE, TITLE	ID name	document-wide unique ID
ismap	IMG	ismap	use server-side image map
label	OPTION, OPTGROUP	text	for use in hierarchical drop-down menus
lang	All elements except APPLET, BASE, BASEFONT, BR, FRAME, FRAMESET, HR, IFRAME, PARAM SCRIPT	language code	specifies language
language	SCRIPT	CDATA	script language name
link	BODY	color	color of links
longdesc	IMG, FRAME, IFRAME	URL	link to long description
marginheight	FRAME, IFRAME	pixels	margin height
marginwidth	FRAME, IFRAME	pixels	margin width
maxlength	INPUT	number	max chars for text fields
media	STYLE, LINK	screen, tty, tv, projection, handheld, print, braille, aural, all	media type
method	FORM	get, post	HTTP method used to submit the form

(continued)

Attribute	Used in	Valid value	Purpose
multiple	SELECT	multiple	Boolean value to enable multiple selections in drop-down list
name	BUTTON, TEXTAREA	CDATA	names input object
name	APPLET	CDATA	allows applets to find each other
name	SELECT	CDATA	names the field
name	FRAME, IFRAME	CDATA	name of target frame
name	A	CDATA	name of destination
name	INPUT, OBJECT	CDATA	name of form field
name	MAP	CDATA	name of map
name	PARAM	CDATA	name of applet parameter
name	META	text	name of metainformation field
nohref	AREA	nohref	Boolean value to set region to no action
noresize	FRAME	noresize	deny frame resize
noshade	HR	noshade	Boolean value to turn off 3D effects
nowrap	TD, TH	nowrap	Boolean value to turn off word wrap
object	APPLET	CDATA	serialized applet file
onblur	A, AREA, BUTTON, INPUT, LABEL, SELECT, TEXTAREA	script	event: loss of focus on element (pointer moved away)
onchange	INPUT, SELECT, TEXTAREA	script	event: value changed
onclick	All elements except APPLET, BASE, BASEFONT, BDO, BR, FONT, FRAME, FRAMESET, HEAD, HTML, IFRAME, ISINDEX, META, PARAM, SCRIPT, STYLE, TITLE	script	event: mouse click on element

Attribute	Used in	Valid value	Purpose
ondblclick	All elements except APPLET, BASE, BASEFONT, BDO, BR, FONT, FRAME, FRAMESET, HEAD, HTML, IFRAME, ISINDEX, META, PARAM, SCRIPT, STYLE, TITLE	script	event: double-click element
onfocus	A, AREA, BUTTON, INPUT, LABEL, SELECT, TEXTAREA	script	event: element selected (receives focus)
onkeydown	All elements except APPLET, BASE, BASEFONT, BDO, BR, FONT, FRAME, FRAMESET, HEAD, HTML, IFRAME, ISINDEX, META, PARAM, SCRIPT, STYLE, TITLE	script	event: key pressed
onkeypress	All elements except APPLET, BASE, BASEFONT, BDO, BR, FONT, FRAME, FRAMESET, HEAD, HTML, IFRAME, ISINDEX, META, PARAM, SCRIPT, STYLE, TITLE	script	event: key pressed and released
onkeyup	All elements except APPLET, BASE, BASEFONT, BDO, BR, FONT, FRAME, FRAMESET, HEAD, HTML, IFRAME, ISINDEX, META, PARAM, SCRIPT, STYLE, TITLE	script	event: key released

(continued)

Attribute	Used in	Valid value	Purpose
onload	FRAMESET	script	all frames loaded
onload	BODY	script	document loaded
onmousedown	All elements except APPLET, BASE, BASEFONT, BDO, BR, FONT, FRAME, FRAMESET, HEAD, HTML, IFRAME, ISINDEX, META, PARAM, SCRIPT, STYLE, TITLE	script	event: mouse button depressed
onmousemove	All elements except APPLET, BASE, BASEFONT, BDO, BR, FONT, FRAME, FRAMESET, HEAD, HTML, IFRAME, ISINDEX, META, PARAM, SCRIPT, STYLE, TITLE	script	event: mouse pointer moved
onmouseover	All elements except APPLET, BASE, BASEFONT, BDO, BR, FONT, FRAME, FRAMESET, HEAD, HTML, IFRAME, ISINDEX, META, PARAM, SCRIPT, STYLE, TITLE	script	event: mouse pointer moved over element
onmouseup	All elements except APPLET, BASE, BASEFONT, BDO, BR, FONT, FRAME, FRAMESET, HEAD, HTML, IFRAME, ISINDEX, META, PARAM, SCRIPT, STYLE, TITLE	script	event: mouse button released

Attribute	Used in	Valid value	Purpose
onreset	FORM	script	event: form reset
onselect	INPUT, TEXTAREA	script	event: text selected
onsubmit	FORM	script	event: form submitted
onunload	FRAMESET	script	event: frames removed
onunload	BODY	script	event: document removed
profile	HEAD	URL	explanation of meta information
prompt	ISINDEX	text	prompt message
readonly	TEXTAREA INPUT	readonly	user cannot modify
rel	A, LINK	alternate, stylesheet, start, next, prev, contents, index, glossary, copyright, chapter, section, subsection, appendix, help, bookmark	forward link types
rev	A, LINK	alternate, stylesheet, start, next, prev, contents, index, glossary, copyright, chapter, section, subsection, appendix, help, bookmark	reverse link types
rows	FRAMESET	lengths	comma-separated list of lengths
rows	TEXTAREA	number	height (in lines) of text entry area
rowspan	TD, TH	number	rows spanned by cell
rules	TABLE	none, groups	rulings between rows and cols
scheme	META	CDATA	form of content
scope	TD, TH	row, col, rowgroup, colgroup	location of headers

(continued)

Attribute	Used in	Valid value	Purpose
scrolling	FRAME	yes, no, auto	scrollbar in frame
selected	OPTION	selected	Boolean value to set selected option in drop-down list box
shape	A, AREA	rect, circle, poly, default	set imagemap area shape
size	HR	pixels	size of rule
size	FONT	CDATA	relative font size
size	INPUT	CDATA	varies by field
size	BASEFONT	CDATA	base font size
size	SELECT	number	rows visible
span	COL	number	number of columns modified by attributes
span	COLGROUP	number	number of columns in group
src	SCRIPT	URL	location of external script
src	INPUT	URL	location of image
src	FRAME, IFRAME	URL	location of frame content
src	IMG	URL	location of image
standby	OBJECT	text	message to show while loading
start	OL	number	starting number
style	All elements except BASE, BASEFONT, HEAD, HTML, META, PARAM, SCRIPT, STYLE, TITLE	style definition	inline style definition
summary	TABLE	text	for speech output
tabindex	A, AREA, BUTTON, INPUT, OBJECT, SELECT, TEXTAREA	number	position in tab order
target	A, AREA, BASE, FORM, LINK	target name or _blank, _self, _top, _parent	display in frame
text	BODY	color	default text color
title	STYLE	text	title

Attribute	Used in	Valid value	Purpose
title	All elements except BASE, BASEFONT, HEAD, HTML, META, PARAM, SCRIPT, STYLE, TITLE	text	text to display in tool tip
type	A, LINK OBJECT, PARAM, SCRIPT, STYLE	MIME type	content type of data
type	INPUT	text, password, check box, radio, submit, reset, file, hidden, image, button	type of input control
type	LI, UL	disc, square, circle	bullet style
type	OL	1, a, A, i, I	number style
type	BUTTON	button, submit, reset	type of button
usemap	IMG, INPUT, OBJECT	URL	client-side imagemap
valign	COL, COLGROUP, TBODY, TD, TFOOT, TH, THEAD, TR	top, middle, bottom, baseline	vertical alignment
value	OPTION	CDATA	default content of form control
value	PARAM	CDATA	value of parameter
value	BUTTON	CDATA	sent to server when submitted
value	LI	number	reset sequence number
valuetype	PARAM, OBJECT	CDATA, DATA, REF, OBJECT	type of data
version	HTML	CDATA	HTML version
vlink	BODY	color	color of visited links

(continued)

Attribute	Used in	Valid value	Purpose
vspace	APPLET, IMG, OBJECT	pixels	size of vertical gutter
width	HR	length	width of rule
width	IFRAME	length	frame width
width	IMG, OBJECT	length	override width
width	TABLE	length	table width
width	APPLET	length	initial width of applet
width	COL, COLGROUP	space-separated list of lengths	width of columns
width	TD, TH	pixels	cell width
width	PRE	number	line length

✦   ✦   ✦

HTML 4 Entities Reference

Character Appearance	Character Name	Entity Code	Mnemonic
&	ampersand	&#38;	&amp;
«	angle quotation mark, left	&#171;	&laquo;
»	angle quotation mark, right	&#187;	&raquo;
|	broken vertical bar	&#166;	&brvbar;
Á	capital A, acute accent	&#193;	&Aacute;
Â	capital A, circumflex accent	&#194;	&Acirc;
Ä	capital A, dieresis or umlaut mark	&#196;	&Auml;
À	capital A, grave accent	&#192;	&Agrave;
Å	capital A, ring	&#197;	&Aring;
Ã	capital A, tilde	&#195;	&Atilde;
Æ	capital AE diphthong (ligature)	&#198;	&AElig;
Ç	capital C, cedilla	&#199;	&Ccedil;

(continued)

Character Appearance	Character Name	Entity Code	Mnemonic
É	capital E, acute accent	&#201;	&Eacute;
Ê	capital E, circumflex accent	&#202;	&Ecirc;
Ë	capital E, dieresis or umlaut mark	&#203;	&Euml;
È	capital E, grave accent	&#200;	&Egrave;
Ð	capital Eth, Icelandic	&#208;	&ETH;
Í	capital I, acute accent	&#205;	&Iacute;
Î	capital I, circumflex accent	&#206;	&Icirc;
Ï	capital I, dieresis or umlaut mark	&#207;	&Iuml;
Ì	capital I, grave accent	&#204;	&Igrave;
Ñ	capital N, tilde	&#209;	&Ntilde;
Ó	capital O, acute accent	&#211;	&Oacute;
Ô	capital O, circumflex accent	&#212;	&Ocirc;
Ö	capital O, dieresis or umlaut mark	&#214;	&Ouml;
Ò	capital O, grave accent	&#210;	&Ograve;
Ø	capital O, slash	&#216;	&Oslash;
Õ	capital O, tilde	&#213;	&Otilde;

Character Appearance	Character Name	Entity Code	Mnemonic
Þ	capital THORN, Icelandic	&#222;	&THORN;
Ú	capital U, acute accent	&#218;	&Uacute;
Û	capital U, circumflex accent	&#219;	&Ucirc;
Ü	capital U, dieresis or umlaut mark	&#220;	&Uuml;
Ù	capital U, grave accent	&#217;	&Ugrave;
Ý	capital Y, acute accent	&#221;	&Yacute;
¢	cent sign	&#162;	&cent;
®	circled R registered sign	&#174;	&reg;
©	copyright sign	&#169;	&copy;
¤	currency sign	&#164;	&curren;
°	degree sign	&#176;	&deg;
÷	division sign	&#247;	&divide;
ª	feminine ordinal indicator	&#170;	&ordf;
½	fraction 1/2	&#189;	&frac12;
¼	fraction 1/4	&#188;	&frac14;
¾	fraction 3/4	&#190;	&frac34;
>	greater-than sign	&#61;	&gt;
¡	inverted exclamation mark	&#161;	&iexcl;

(continued)

Character Appearance	Character Name	Entity Code	Mnemonic
¿	inverted question mark	&#191;	&iquest;
<	less-than sign	&#60;	&lt;
º	masculine ordinal indicator	&#186;	&ordm;
µ	micro sign	&#181;	&micro;
·	middle dot	&#183;	&middot;
x	multiplication sign	&#215;	&times;
¬	negation sign	&#172;	&not;
	non-breaking space		
¶	paragraph sign	&#182;	&para;
±	plus-or-minus sign	&#177;	&plusmn;
£	pound sign	&#163;	&pound;
"	quotation mark	&#34;	&quot;
§	section sign	&#167;	&sect;
á	small a, acute accent	&#225;	&aacute;
â	small a, circumflex accent	&#226;	&acirc;
ä	small a, dieresis or umlaut mark	&#228;	&auml;
à	small a, grave accent	&#224;	&agrave;
å	small a, ring	&#229;	&aring;
ã	small a, tilde	&#227;	&atilde;

Character Appearance	Character Name	Entity Code	Mnemonic
æ	small ae diphthong (ligature)	&#230;	&aelig;
ç	small c, cedilla	&#231;	&ccedil;
é	small e, acute accent	&#233;	&eacute;
ê	small e, circumflex accent	&#234;	&ecirc;
ë	small e, dieresis or umlaut mark	&#235;	&euml;
è	small e, grave accent	&#232;	&egrave;
ð	small eth, Icelandic	&#240;	&eth;
í	small i, acute accent	&#237;	&iacute;
î	small i, circumflex accent	&#238;	&icirc;
ï	small i, dieresis or umlaut mark	&#239;	&iuml;
ì	small i, grave accent	&#236;	&igrave;
ñ	small n, tilde	&#241;	&ntilde;
ó	small o, acute accent	&#243;	&oacute;
ô	small o, circumflex accent	&#244;	&ocirc;
ö	small o, dieresis or umlaut mark	&#246;	&ouml;
ò	small o, grave accent	&#242;	&ograve;

(continued)

Character Appearance	Character Name	Entity Code	Mnemonic
ø	small o, slash	&#248;	&oslash;
õ	small o, tilde	&#245;	&otilde;
ß	small sharp s, German (sz ligature)	&#223;	&szlig;
þ	small thorn, Icelandic	&#254;	&thorn;
ú	small u, acute accent	&#250;	&uacute;
û	small u, circumflex accent	&#251;	&ucirc;
ü	small u, dieresis or umlaut mark	&#252;	&uuml;
ù	small u, grave accent	&#249;	&ugrave;
ý	small y, acute accent	&#253;	&yacute;
ÿ	small y, dieresis or umlaut mark	&#255;	&yuml;
-	soft hyphen	&#173;	&shy;
´	spacing acute	&#180;	&acute;
¸	spacing ccdilla	&#184;	&cedil;
¨	spacing diaresis	&#168;	&uml;
¯	spacing macron	&#175;	&macr;
1	superscript 1	&#185;	&sup1;
2	superscript 2	&#178;	&sup2;
3	superscript 3	&#179;	&sup3;
¥	yen sign	&#165;	&yen;

✦   ✦   ✦

Language Codes Reference

Language Family	Language	Name Code
	Bislama	BI[not given]
Amerindian	Aymara	AY
Amerindian	Guarani	GN
Amerindian	Quechua	QU
Asian	Bhutani	DZ
Asian	Burmese	MY
Asian	Cambodian	KM
Asian	Chinese	ZH
Asian	Japanese	JA
Asian	Korean	KO
Asian	Laothian	LO
Asian	Thai	TH
Asian	Tibetan	BO
Asian	Vietnamese	VI
Baltic	Latvian; Lettish	LV
Baltic	Lithuanian	LT
Basque	Basque	EU
Celtic	Breton	BR
Celtic	Irish	GA
celtic	ScotsGAELIC	GD
Celtic	Welsh	CY
Dravidian	Kannada	KN
Dravidian	Malayalam	ML

(continued)

Language Family	Language	Name Code
Dravidian	Tamil	TA
Dravidian	Telugu	TE
Eskimo	Greenlandic	KL
Eskimo	Inupiak	IK
Finno-ugric	Estonian	ET
Finno-ugric	Finnish	FI
Finno-ugric	Hungarian	HU
Germanic	Afrikaans	AF
Germanic	Danish	DA
Germanic	Dutch	NL
Germanic	English	EN
Germanic	Faroese	FO
Germanic	Frisian	FY
Germanic	German	DE
Germanic	Icelandic	IS
Germanic	Norwegian	NO
Germanic	Swedish	SV
Germanic	Yiddish	JI
Hamitic	Afan (Oromo)	OM
Hamitic	Afar	AA
Hamitic	Somali	SO
Ibero-Caucasian	Abkhazian	AB
Ibero-caucasian	Georgian	KA
Indian	Assamese	AS
Indian	Bengali; Bangla	BN
Indian	Bihari	BH
Indian	Gujarati	GU
Indian	Hindi	HI
Indian	Kashmiri	KS
Indian	Marathi	MR
Indian	Nepali	NE
Indian	Oriya	OR

Language Family	Language	Name Code
Indian	Punjabi	PA
Indian	Sanskrit	SA
Indian	Sindhi	SD
Indian	Singhalese	SI
Indian	Urdu	UR
Indo-european (other)	Albanian	SQ
Indo-european (other)	Armenian	HY
International aux.	Esperanto	EO
International aux.	Interlingua	IA
International aux.	Interlingue	IE
International aux.	Volapuk	VO
Iranian	Kurdish	KU
Iranian	Pashto; Pushto	PS
iranian	Persian (Farsi)	FA
Iranian	Tajik	TG
Latin/greek	Greek	EL
Latin/greek	Latin	LA
Negro-african	Hausa	HA
Negro-african	Kinyarwanda	RW
Negro-african	Kurundi	RN
Negro-african	Lingala	LN
Negro-african	Sangho	SG
Negro-african	Sesotho	ST
Negro-african	Setswana	TN
Negro-african	Shona	SN
Negro-african	Siswati	SS
Negro-african	Swahili	SW
Negro-african	Tsonga	TS
Negro-african	Twi	TW
Negro-african	Wolof	WO

(continued)

Language Family	Language	Name Code
Negro-african	Xhosa	XH
Negro-african	Yoruba	YO
Negro-african	Zulu	ZU
Oceanic/indonesian	Fiji	FJ
Oceanic/indonesian	Indonesian	IN
Oceanic/indonesian	Javanese	JV
Oceanic/indonesian	Malagasy	MG
Oceanic/indonesian	Malay	MS
Oceanic/indonesian	Maori	MI
Oceanic/indonesian	Samoan	SM
Oceanic/indonesian	Sundanese	SU
Oceanic/indonesian	Tagalog	TL
Oceanic/indonesian	Tonga	TO
Romance	Catalan	CA
Romance	Corsican	CO
Romance	French	FR
Romance	Galician	GL
Romance	Italian	IT
Romance	Moldavian	MO
Romance	Occitan	OC
Romance	Portuguese	PT
Romance	Rhaeto-romance	RM
Romance	Romanian	RO
Romance	Spanish	ES
Semitic	Amharic	AM
Semitic	Arabic	AR
Semitic	Hebrew	IW
Semitic	Maltese	MT
Semitic	Tigrinya	TI
Slavic	Bulgarian	BG

Language Family	Language	Name Code
Slavic	Byelorussian	BE
Slavic	Croatian	HR
Slavic	Czech	CS
Slavic	Macedonian	MK
Slavic	Polish	PL
Slavic	Russian	RU
Slavic	Serbian	SR
Slavic	Serbo-Croatian	SH
Slavic	Slovak	SK
Slavic	Slovenian	SL
Slavic	Ukrainian	UK
Turkic/altaic	Azerbaijani	AZ
Turkic/altaic	Bashkir	BA
Turkic/altaic	Kazakh	KK
Turkic/altaic	Kirghiz	KY
Turkic/altaic	Tatar	TT
Turkic/altaic	Turkish	TR
Turkic/altaic	Turkmen	TK
Turkic/altaic	Uzbek	UZ

✦   ✦   ✦

MIME Types Reference

MIME Content Type	File Extension	Description
application/msword	doc	Microsoft Word document
application/octet-stream	bin dms lha lzh exe class	Executable program
application/pdf	pdf	Adobe Acrobat document
application/postscript	ai eps ps	PostScript document
application/powerpoint	ppt	Microsoft PowerPoint document
application/rtf	rtf	Microsoft Rich Text Format document
application/x-compress	Z	UNIX compress file
application/x-gtar	gtar	tar archive (GNU format)
application/x-gzip	gz	gzip archive
application/x-shockwave-flash	swf	MacroMedia ShockWave Flash animation
application/x-tar	tar	tar archive (4.3BSD)
application/zip	zip	WinZip archive
audio/basic	au snd	Sun/NeXT sound
audio/mpeg	mpga mp2	MPEG sound
audio/x-aiff	aif aiff aifc	Silicon Graphics sound

(continued)

MIME Content Type	File Extension	Description
audio/x-midi	mid midi rmf	MIDI audio format
audio/x-pn-realaudio	ram ra	Real Audio sound
audio/x-pn-realaudio-plugin	rpm	Real Audio plug-in
audio/x-wav	wav	Microsoft Windows sound
image/cgm	cgm	Computer Graphics Metafile
image/gif	gif	CompuServe GIF image
image/jpeg	jpeg jpg jpe	JPEG image
image/png	png	PNG image
image/tiff	tiff tif	TIFF image
image/x-pict	pict	Macintosh PICT image
text/css	css	CSS style sheet
text/html	html htm	HTML document
text/javascript	js ls mocha	JavaScript script
text/plain	txt	ASCII text
text/richtext	rtx	Microsoft Rich Text format
text/tab-separated-values	tsv	tab-separated values
text/vbscript	vbx	Visual Basic script
text/sgml	sgml sgm	SGML document
video/mpeg	mpeg mpg mpe	MPEG video
video/quicktime	qt mov	QuickTime video
video/x-msvideo	avi	Windows (AVI) video
x-world/x-vrml	wrl vrml	VRML (3D) world

✦   ✦   ✦

Hex Notations Reference

When indicating you would like to assign one of these colors, you must use the Hex notation. The color provided in the Description column is so you know approximately how the hex code will appear.

Description	Hex Code
White	#FFFFFF
Red	#FF0000
Green	#00FF00
Blue	#0000FF
Magenta	#FF00FF
Cyan	#00FFFF
Yellow	#FFFF00
Black	#000000
Aquamarine	#70DB93
Chocolate	#5C3317
BlueViolet	#9F5F9F
Brass	#B5A642
Bright Gold	#D9D919
Brown	#A62A2A

Description	Hex Code
Bronze	#8C7853
Bronzell	#A67D3D
Cadet Blue	#5F9F9F
Cool Copper	#D98719
Copper	#B87333
Coral	#FF7F00
Cornflower Blue	#42426F
Dark Brown	#5C4033
Dark Green	#2F4F2F
Dark Green Copper	#4A766E
Dark Olive Green	#4F4F2F
Dark Orchid	#9932CD
Dark Purple	#871F78
Dark Slate Blue	#6B238E
Dark Slate Grey	#2F4F4F
Dark Tan	#97694F
Dark Turquoise	#7093DB
Dark Wood	#855E42
Dim Grey	#545454
Dusty Rose	#856363
Feldspar	#D19275
Firebrick	#8E2323
Faded Brown	#F5CCB0

Description	Hex Code
Forest Green	#238E23
Gold	#CD7F32
Goldenrod	#DBDB70
Grey	#C0C0C0
Green Copper	#527F76
Green Yellow	#93DB70
Hunter Green	#215E21
Indian Red	#4E2F2F
Khaki	#9F9F5F
Light Blue	#C0D9D9
Light Grey	#A8A8A8
Light Steel Blue	#8F8FBD
Light Wood	#E9C2A6
Lime Green	#32CD32
Mandarian Orange	#E47833
Maroon	#8E236B
Medium Aquamarine	#32CD99
Medium Blue	#3232CD
Medium Forest Green	#6B8E23
Medium Goldenrod	#EAEAAE
Medium Orchid	#9370DB
Medium Sea Green	#426F42
Medium Slate Blue	#7F00FF

Description	Hex Code
Medium Spring Green	#7FFF00
Medium Turquoise	#70DBDB
Medium Violet Red	#DB7093
Medium Wood	#A68064
Midnight Blue	#2F2F4F
Navy Blue	#23238E
Neon Blue	#4D4DFF
Neon Pink	#FF6EC7
New Midnight Blue	#00009C
New Tan	#EBC79E
Old Gold	#CFB53B
Orange	#FF7F00
Orange Red	#FF2400
Orchid	#DB70DB
Pale Green	#8FBC8F
Pink	#BC8F8F
Plum	#EAADEA
Quartz	#D9D9F3
Rich Blue	#5959AB
Salmon	#6F4242
Scarlet	#8C1717
Sea Green	#238E68
Semi-Sweet Chocolate	#6B4226

Description	Hex Code
Sienna	#8E6B23
Silver	#E6E8FA
Sky Blue	#3299CC
Slate Blue	#007FFF
Spicy Pink	#FF1CAE
Spring Green	#00FF7F
Steel Blue	#236B8E
Summer Sky	#38B0DE
Tan	#DB9370
Thistle	#D8BFD8
Turquoise	#ADEAEA
Very Dark Brown	#5C4033
Very Light Grey	#CDCDCD
Violet	#4F2F4F
Violet Red	#CC3299
Wheat	#D8D8BF
Yellow Green	#99CC32

✦   ✦   ✦

Cascading Style Sheets Reference

Backgrounds and Color

color

PURPOSE	Specifies the foreground color of an element.
INHERITED	Yes
VALUES	Color code or mnemonic
DEFAULT	Defined by browser
USED IN	All elements
SUPPORT	MSIE 3.0/Win95: Yes
	MSIE 4.0/Win95: Yes
	NN4.0/Win95: Yes
	MSIE 3.0/Mac OS: Yes
	MSIE 4.0/Mac OS: Yes
	NN4.0/Mac OS: Yes
EXAMPLE	`{ color: #C0C0C0 } or { color: red }`
TIP	You can specify values using color codes or color mnemonics.

background

PURPOSE	Provides a shorthand method for grouping background properties.
INHERITED	Yes
VALUES	You can specify any of the values used for background-color, background-image, background-repeat, background-attachment, or background-position.
DEFAULT	Not defined
USED IN	All elements
SUPPORT	MSIE 3.0/Win95: Yes
	MSIE 4.0/Win95: Yes
	NN4.0/Win95: Yes
	MSIE 3.0/Mac OS: Yes
	MSIE 4.0/Mac OS: Yes
	NN4.0/Mac OS: Yes
EXAMPLE	`{ background: url(picture.gif) repeat fixed }`
TIP	This is a handy way to set background properties without much typing. Note, some browsers may not support all the background properties.

background-color

PURPOSE	Specifies the background color of an element.
INHERITED	Yes
VALUES	Color code or mnemonic
DEFAULT	Defined by browser
USED IN	All elements

SUPPORT	MSIE 3.0/Win95:
	MSIE 4.0/Win95: Yes
	NN4.0/Win95: Yes
	MSIE 3.0/Mac OS: No
	MSIE 4.0/Mac OS: Yes
	NN4.0/Mac OS: Yes
EXAMPLE	`{ color: #C0C0C0 } or { color: red }`
TIP	You can specify values using color codes or color mnemonics (see Appendix F).

background-Image

PURPOSE	Inserts a graphic in an element's background.
INHERITED	Yes
VALUES	Color code or mnemonic
DEFAULT	Defined by browser
USED IN	All elements
SUPPORT	MSIE 3.0/Win95: Yes
	MSIE 4.0/Win95: Yes
	NN4.0/Win95: Yes
	MSIE 3.0/Mac OS: No
	MSIE 4.0/Mac OS: Yes
	NN4.0/Mac OS: Yes
EXAMPLE	`{ background-image: url(picture.gif)}`
TIP	Note the syntax for including URLs; it differs from the way you include URLs in HTML statements. Use caution with this property; current implementations are buggy.

background-repeat

PURPOSE	Specifies how a background image is repeated.
INHERITED	Yes
VALUES	*repeat, repeat-x, repeat-y,* or *no-repeat.* Repeat repeats the image both horizontally and vertically. Repeat-*x* repeats the image horizontally, while repeat-*y* repeats the image vertically.
DEFAULT	Repeat
USED IN	All elements
SUPPORT	MSIE 3.0/Win95: No
	MSIE 4.0/Win95: Yes
	NN4.0/Win95: Yes
	MSIE 3.0/Mac OS: No
	MSIE 4.0/Mac OS: Yes
	NN4.0/Mac OS: Yes
EXAMPLE	`{ background-repeat: repeat-x }`
TIP	If a browser doesn't recognize this property (but does handle others, you get a repeated graphic).

background-attachment

PURPOSE	Determines whether the background image scrolls with the content or remains fixed.
INHERITED	Yes
VALUES	Scroll or fixed
DEFAULT	Defined by browser
USED IN	All elements

SUPPORT	MSIE 3.0/Win95: No
	MSIE 4.0/Win95: Yes
	NN4.0/Win95: No
	MSIE 3.0/Mac OS: No
	MSIE 4.0/Mac OS: Yes
	NN4.0/Mac OS: No

EXAMPLE   `{ background-attachment: fixed }`

TIP   This property isn't widely supported, but it isn't risky to use; if a browser doesn't recognize it, it scrolls the image with the text. This property isn't supported by Netscape Navigator 4.

background-position

PURPOSE   Specifies the position of the background graphic within an element.

INHERITED   Yes

VALUES   You can specify the position in several different ways. The easiest way uses keywords (top left, top center, right top, left center, center, right center, bottom left, bottom center, and bottom right). You can also type two percentages to express the distance from the left and the distance from the top, respectively; 50 percent 100 percent is the same as bottom center. You can also type measurements for an absolute position from the left and top, respectively (see the examples).

DEFAULT   Defined by browser

USED IN   All elements

SUPPORT   MSIE 3.0/Win95: No

                        MSIE 4.0/Win95: Yes

                        NN4.0/Win95: No

MSIE 3.0/Mac OS: No

MSIE 4.0/Mac OS: No

NN4.0/Mac OS: No

EXAMPLE

```
{ background-position: top center }{
background-position: 50% 0% }{ background
position: 48pt 60pt }
```

TIP   This property is not supported by Netscape Navigator 4.

Box Properties

border

PURPOSE   Provides a shorthand means of specifying all types of
                    properties for all borders.

INHERITED   Yes

VALUES   Specify any value used in the border color or border width
                    properties.

DEFAULT   0

USED IN   Replaced and block-level elements

SUPPORT   MSIE 3.0/Win95: No

                    MSIE 4.0/Win95: Yes

                    NN4.0/Win95: Yes

                    MSIE 3.0/Mac OS: No

                    MSIE 4.0/Mac OS: Yes

                    NN4.0/Mac OS: Yes

EXAMPLE   `{ border: 1pt blue }`

TIP   If you type just one measurement, it applies to all four
                    borders.

border-color

PURPOSE	Provides a shorthand means of specifying color settings for all borders.
INHERITED	Yes
VALUES	Specify colors for the top, right, bottom, and left borders, in that order. If you specify only one value, it applies to all four sides.
DEFAULT	Not defined
USED IN	Replaced and block-level elements
SUPPORT	MSIE 3.0/Win95: Yes
	MSIE 4.0/Win95: Yes
	NN4.0/Win95: Yes
	MSIE 3.0/Mac OS: Yes
	MSIE 4.0/Mac OS: Yes
	NN4.0/Mac OS: Yes
EXAMPLE	`{ border-color: red }`
TIP	If you specify just one value, it applies to all four margins.

border-bottom-color

PURPOSE	Specifies the color of the box's bottom border.
INHERITED	Yes
VALUES	Specify a color code or mnemonic (see Appendix F).
DEFAULT	Value of the color property for the current element
USED IN	Replaced and block-level elements
SUPPORT	MSIE 3.0/Win95: No

MSIE 4.0/Win95: Yes

NN4.0/Win95: Yes

MSIE 3.0/Mac OS: No

MSIE 4.0/Mac OS: Yes

NN4.0/Mac OS: Yes

EXAMPLE   { border-bottom-color: silver }

TIP   You can use the border property to set the border
                          properties for all four sides at once.

border-left-color

PURPOSE   Specifies the color of the box's left border.

INHERITED   Yes

VALUES   Specify a color code or mnemonic (see Appendix F).

DEFAULT   Value of the color property for the current element

USED IN   Replaced and block-level elements

SUPPORT   MSIE 3.0/Win95: No

                          MSIE 4.0/Win95: Yes

                          NN4.0/Win95: Yes

                          MSIE 3.0/Mac OS: No

                          MSIE 4.0/Mac OS: Yes

                          NN4.0/Mac OS: Yes

EXAMPLE   { border-left-color: red }

TIP   You can use the border property to set the border
                          properties for all four sides at once.

border-right-color

PURPOSE	Specifies the width of the box's right border.
INHERITED	Yes
VALUES	Specify a color code or mnemonic (see Appendix F).
DEFAULT	Value of the color property for the current element
USED IN	Replaced and block-level elements
SUPPORT	MSIE 3.0/Win95: No
	MSIE 4.0/Win95: Yes
	NN4.0/Win95: Yes
	MSIE 3.0/Mac OS: No
	MSIE 4.0/Mac OS: Yes
	NN4.0/Mac OS: Yes
EXAMPLE	`{ border-right-color: red }`
TIP	You can use the border property to set the border properties for all four sides at once.

border-top-color

PURPOSE	Specifies the color of the box's top border.
INHERITED	Yes
VALUES	Specify a color code or mnemonic (see Appendix F).
DEFAULT	Value of the color property for the current element
USED IN	Replaced and block-level elements
SUPPORT	MSIE 3.0/Win95: No
	MSIE 4.0/Win95: Yes

NN4.0/Win95: Yes

MSIE 3.0/Mac OS: No

MSIE 4.0/Mac OS: Yes

NN4.0/Mac OS: Yes

EXAMPLE   `{ border-top-color: blue }`

TIP   You can use the border property to set the border
                        properties for all four sides at once.

border-style

PURPOSE   Provides a shorthand means of specifying color settings for
                        all borders.

INHERITED   Yes

VALUES   Specify styles for the top, right, bottom, and left borders,
                        in that order. If you specify only one value, it applies to
                        all four sides. You can choose from none, dotted, dashed,
                        solid, double, groove, ridge, inset, outset.

DEFAULT   Not defined

USED IN   Replaced and block-level elements

SUPPORT   MSIE 3.0/Win95: Yes

                        MSIE 4.0/Win95: Yes

                        NN4.0/Win95: Yes

                        MSIE 3.0/Mac OS: Yes

                        MSIE 4.0/Mac OS: Yes

                        NN4.0/Mac OS: Yes

EXAMPLE   `{ border-style: double}`

TIP   If you specify just one value, it applies to all four margins.

border-bottom-style

PURPOSE	Specifies the color of the box's bottom border.
INHERITED	Yes
VALUES	none, dotted, dashed, solid, double, groove, ridge, inset, outset.
DEFAULT	Value of the color property for the current element
USED IN	Replaced and block-level elements
SUPPORT	MSIE 3.0/Win95: No
	MSIE 4.0/Win95: Yes
	NN4.0/Win95: Yes
	MSIE 3.0/Mac OS: No
	MSIE 4.0/Mac OS: Yes
	NN4.0/Mac OS: Yes
EXAMPLE	`{ border-bottom-style: dashed }`
TIP	You can use the border property to set the border properties for all four sides at once. This property isn't supported by Netscape Navigator 4; you must use the same properties for all four borders. Note that neither Netscape Navigator nor Microsoft Internet Explorer support dashed or dotted border styles.

border-left-style

PURPOSE	Specifies the color of the box's left border.
INHERITED	Yes
VALUES	none, dotted, dashed, solid, double, groove, ridge, inset, outset.
DEFAULT	Value of the color property for the current element

USED IN	Replaced and block-level elements
SUPPORT	MSIE 3.0/Win95: No
	MSIE 4.0/Win95: Yes
	NN4.0/Win95: Yes
	MSIE 3.0/Mac OS: No
	MSIE 4.0/Mac OS: Yes
	NN4.0/Mac OS: Yes
EXAMPLE	`{ border-left-style: groove }`
TIP	You can use the border property to set the border properties for all four sides at once.

border-right-style

PURPOSE	Specifies the width of the box's right border.
INHERITED	Yes
VALUES	none, dotted, dashed, solid, double, groove, ridge, inset, outset.
DEFAULT	Value of the color property for the current element
USED IN	Replaced and block-level elements
SUPPORT	MSIE 3.0/Win95: No
	MSIE 4.0/Win95: Yes
	NN4.0/Win95: Yes
	MSIE 3.0/Mac OS: No
	MSIE 4.0/Mac OS: Yes
	NN4.0/Mac OS: Yes
EXAMPLE	`{ border-right-style: inset }`
TIP	You can use the border property to set the border properties for all four sides at once.

border-top-style

PURPOSE	Specifies the color of the box's top border.
INHERITED	Yes
VALUES	none, dotted, dashed, solid, double, groove, ridge, inset, outset.
DEFAULT	Value of the color property for the current element
USED IN	Replaced and block-level elements
SUPPORT	MSIE 3.0/Win95: No
	MSIE 4.0/Win95: Yes
	NN4.0/Win95: Yes
	MSIE 3.0/Mac OS: No
	MSIE 4.0/Mac OS: Yes
	NN4.0/Mac OS: Yes
EXAMPLE	`{ border-top-style: groove }`
TIP	You can use the border property to set the border properties for all four sides at once.

border-width

PURPOSE	Provides a shorthand means of specifying width settings for all borders.
INHERITED	Yes
VALUES	Specify lengths for the top, right, bottom, and left borders, in that order. If you specify only one value, it applies to all four sides.
DEFAULT	Not defined
USED IN	Replaced and block-level elements

SUPPORT	MSIE 3.0/Win95: Yes
	MSIE 4.0/Win95: Yes
	NN4.0/Win95: No
	MSIE 3.0/Mac OS: Yes
	MSIE 4.0/Mac OS: Yes
	NN4.0/Mac OS: Yes
EXAMPLE	`{ border-width: 1pt }`
TIP	If you specify just one value, it applies to all four margins.

border-bottom-width

PURPOSE	Specifies the width of the box's bottom border.
INHERITED	Yes
VALUES	Specify thin, medium, or thick, or type a length.
DEFAULT	0
USED IN	Replaced and block-level elements
SUPPORT	MSIE 3.0/Win95: No
	MSIE 4.0/Win95: Yes
	NN4.0/Win95: No
	MSIE 3.0/Mac OS: No
	MSIE 4.0/Mac OS: Yes
	NN4.0/Mac OS: Yes
EXAMPLE	`{ margin-left: 0.5in }`
TIP	You can use the border property to set the border properties for all four sides at once. This property isn't supported by Netscape Navigator 4; you must use the same properties for all four borders.

border-left-width

PURPOSE	Specifies the width of the box's left border.
INHERITED	Yes
VALUES	Specify thin, medium, or thick, or type a length.
DEFAULT	0
USED IN	Replaced and block-level elements
SUPPORT	MSIE 3.0/Win95: No
	MSIE 4.0/Win95: Yes
	NN4.0/Win95: No
	MSIE 3.0/Mac OS: No
	MSIE 4.0/Mac OS: Yes
	NN4.0/Mac OS: Yes
EXAMPLE	`{ border-left-width: 0.5in }`
TIP	You can use the border property to set the border properties for all four sides at once. This property isn't supported by Netscape Navigator 4; you must use the same properties for all four borders.

border-right-width

PURPOSE	Specifies the width of the box's right border.
INHERITED	Yes
VALUES	Specify thin, medium, or thick, or type a length.
DEFAULT	0
USED IN	Replaced and block-level elements
SUPPORT	MSIE 3.0/Win95: No

MSIE 4.0/Win95: Yes

NN4.0/Win95: No

MSIE 3.0/Mac OS: No

MSIE 4.0/Mac OS: Yes

NN4.0/Mac OS: Yes

EXAMPLE   `{ border-right-width: 0.5in }`

TIP   You can use the border property to set the border
                   properties for all four sides at once. This property isn't
                   supported by Netscape Navigator 4; you must use the same
                   properties for all four borders.

border-top-width

PURPOSE   Specifies the width of the box's top border.

INHERITED   Yes

VALUES   Specify thin, medium, or thick, or type a length.

DEFAULT   0

USED IN   Replaced and block-level elements

SUPPORT   MSIE 3.0/Win95: No

                   MSIE 4.0/Win95: Yes

                   NN4.0/Win95: No

                   MSIE 3.0/Mac OS: No

                   MSIE 4.0/Mac OS: Yes

                   NN4.0/Mac OS: Yes

EXAMPLE   `{ border-top-width: 0.5in }`

TIP   You can use the border property to set the border
                   properties for all four sides at once. This property isn't
                   supported by Netscape Navigator 4; you must use the same
                   properties for all four borders.

height

PURPOSE	Specifies the height of an element.
INHERITED	No
VALUES	Specify a length or a percentage of the containing block, or auto.
DEFAULT	auto
USED IN	Replaced and block-level elements
SUPPORT	MSIE 3.0/Win95: Yes
	MSIE 4.0/Win95: Yes
	NN4.0/Win95: Yes
	MSIE 3.0/Mac OS: Yes
	MSIE 4.0/Mac OS: Yes
	NN4.0/Mac OS: Yes
EXAMPLE	`{ width: 50%}`
TIP	If the height is set to auto, the height is determined by the intrinsic height of the element.

margin

PURPOSE	Provides a shorthand means of specifying settings for all margins.
INHERITED	Yes
VALUES	Specify lengths for the top, right, bottom, and left margins, in that order. If you specify only one value, it applies to all four sides.
DEFAULT	Not defined
USED IN	Replaced and block-level elements

SUPPORT	MSIE 3.0/Win95: Yes
	MSIE 4.0/Win95: Yes
	NN4.0/Win95: No
	MSIE 3.0/Mac OS: Yes
	MSIE 4.0/Mac OS: Yes
	NN4.0/Mac OS: Yes
EXAMPLE	`{ margin: 0.5in }`
TIP	If you specify just one value, it applies to all four margins.

margin-bottom

PURPOSE	Specifies the width of the box's bottom margin.
INHERITED	Yes
VALUES	Specify a length or a percentage of the containing block.
DEFAULT	0
USED IN	Replaced and block-level elements
SUPPORT	MSIE 3.0/Win95: Yes
	MSIE 4.0/Win95: Yes
	NN4.0/Win95: No
	MSIE 3.0/Mac OS: Yes
	MSIE 4.0/Mac OS: Yes
	NN4.0/Mac OS: Yes
EXAMPLE	`{ margin-bottom: 0.5in }`
TIP	You can use the margin property to set the margin for all four sides at once.

margin-left

PURPOSE	Specifies the width of the box's left margin.
INHERITED	Yes
VALUES	Specify a length or a percentage of the containing block.
DEFAULT	0
USED IN	Replaced and block-level elements
SUPPORT	MSIE 3.0/Win95: Yes
	MSIE 4.0/Win95: Yes
	NN4.0/Win95: Yes
	MSIE 3.0/Mac OS: Yes
	MSIE 4.0/Mac OS: Yes
	NN4.0/Mac OS: Yes
EXAMPLE	`{ margin-left: 0.5in }`
TIP	You can use the margin property to set the margin for all four sides at once.

margin-right

PURPOSE	Specifies the width of the box's right margin.
INHERITED	Yes
VALUES	Specify a length or a percentage of the containing block.
DEFAULT	0
USED IN	Replaced and block-level elements
SUPPORT	MSIE 3.0/Win95: Yes
	MSIE 4.0/Win95: Yes

NN4.0/Win95: Yes

MSIE 3.0/Mac OS: Yes

MSIE 4.0/Mac OS: Yes

NN4.0/Mac OS: Yes

EXAMPLE   `{ margin-right: 0.5in }`

TIP   You can use the margin property to set the margin for all
                         four sides at once.

margin-top

PURPOSE   Specifies the width of the box's top margin.

INHERITED   Yes

VALUES   Specify a length or a percentage of the containing block.

DEFAULT   0

USED IN   Replaced and block-level elements

SUPPORT   MSIE 3.0/Win95: Yes

                         MSIE 4.0/Win95: Yes

                         NN4.0/Win95: Yes

                         MSIE 3.0/Mac OS: Yes

                         MSIE 4.0/Mac OS: Ycs

                         NN4.0/Mac OS: Yes

EXAMPLE   `{ margin-top: 0.5in }`

TIP   You can use the margin property to set the margin for all
                         four sides at once.

max-height

PURPOSE	Specifies the maximum height of an element.
INHERITED	No
VALUES	Specify a length or a percentage of the containing block, or auto.
DEFAULT	0
USED IN	Replaced and block-level elements
SUPPORT	MSIE 3.0/Win95: Yes
	MSIE 4.0/Win95: Yes
	NN4.0/Win95: Yes
	MSIE 3.0/Mac OS: Yes
	MSIE 4.0/Mac OS: Yes
	NN4.0/Mac OS: Yes
EXAMPLE	`{ max-height: 50%}`
TIP	You can also set the minimum height of an element (with min-height).

min-height

PURPOSE	Specifies the minimum height of an element.
INHERITED	No
VALUES	Specify a length or a percentage of the containing block, or auto.
DEFAULT	0
USED IN	Replaced and block-level elements
SUPPORT	MSIE 3.0/Win95: Yes

MSIE 4.0/Win95: Yes

NN4.0/Win95: Yes

MSIE 3.0/Mac OS: Yes

MSIE 4.0/Mac OS: Yes

NN4.0/Mac OS: Yes

EXAMPLE   `{ max-height: 50%}`

TIP   You can also set the maximum height of an element (with max-height).

max-width

PURPOSE   Specifies the maximum width of an element.

INHERITED   No

VALUES   Specify a length or a percentage of the containing block, or auto.

DEFAULT   0

USED IN   Replaced and block-level elements

SUPPORT   MSIE 3.0/Win95: Yes

MSIE 4.0/Win95: Yes

NN4.0/Win95: Yes

MSIE 3.0/Mac OS: Yes

MSIE 4.0/Mac OS: Yes

NN4.0/Mac OS: Yes

EXAMPLE   `{ max-width: 50%}`

TIP   You can also set the minimum width of an element (with min-width).

min-width

PURPOSE	Specifies the minimum width of an element.
INHERITED	No
VALUES	Specify a length or a percentage of the containing block, or auto.
DEFAULT	0
USED IN	Replaced and block-level elements
SUPPORT	MSIE 3.0/Win95: Yes
	MSIE 4.0/Win95: Yes
	NN4.0/Win95: Yes
	MSIE 3.0/Mac OS: Yes
	MSIE 4.0/Mac OS: Yes
	NN4.0/Mac OS: Yes
EXAMPLE	`{ max-width: 50%}`
TIP	You can also set the maximum width of an element (with max-width).

padding

PURPOSE	Provides a shorthand means of specifying settings for all paddings.
INHERITED	Yes
VALUES	Specify lengths for the top, right, bottom, and left paddings, in that order. If you specify only one value, it applies to all four sides.
DEFAULT	Not defined
USED IN	Replaced and block-level elements

SUPPORT	MSIE 3.0/Win95: Yes
	MSIE 4.0/Win95: Yes
	NN4.0/Win95: Yes
	MSIE 3.0/Mac OS: Yes
	MSIE 4.0/Mac OS: Yes
	NN4.0/Mac OS: Yes
EXAMPLE	{ padding: 0.25in }
TIP	If you specify just one value, it applies to all four paddings.

padding-bottom

PURPOSE	Specifies the width of the box's bottom padding.
INHERITED	Yes
VALUES	Specify a length or a percentage of the containing block.
DEFAULT	0
USED IN	Replaced and block-level elements
SUPPORT	MSIE 3.0/Win95: Yes
	MSIE 4.0/Win95: Yes
	NN4.0/Win95: Yes
	MSIE 3.0/Mac OS: Yes
	MSIE 4.0/Mac OS: Yes
	NN4.0/Mac OS: Yes
EXAMPLE	{ padding-bottom: 0.5in }
TIP	You can use the padding property to set the padding for all four sides at once.

padding-left

PURPOSE	Specifies the width of the box's left padding.
INHERITED	Yes
VALUES	Specify a length or a percentage of the containing block.
DEFAULT	0
USED IN	Replaced and block-level elements
SUPPORT	MSIE 3.0/Win95: Yes
	MSIE 4.0/Win95: Yes
	NN4.0/Win95: Yes
	MSIE 3.0/Mac OS: Yes
	MSIE 4.0/Mac OS: Yes
	NN4.0/Mac OS: Yes
EXAMPLE	`{ padding-left: 0.5in }`
TIP	You can use the padding property to set the padding for all four sides at once.

padding-right

PURPOSE	Specifies the width of the box's right padding.
INHERITED	Yes
VALUES	Specify a length or a percentage of the containing block.
DEFAULT	0
USED IN	Replaced and block-level elements
SUPPORT	MSIE 3.0/Win95: Yes
	MSIE 4.0/Win95: Yes

NN4.0/Win95: Yes

MSIE 3.0/Mac OS: Yes

MSIE 4.0/Mac OS: Yes

NN4.0/Mac OS: Yes

EXAMPLE   `{ padding-right: 0.5in }`

TIP   You can use the padding property to set the padding for all four sides at once.

padding-top

PURPOSE   Specifies the width of the box's top padding.

INHERITED   Yes

VALUES   Specify a length or a percentage of the containing block.

DEFAULT   0

USED IN   Replaced and block-level elements

SUPPORT   MSIE 3.0/Win95: Yes

                  MSIE 4.0/Win95: Yes

                  NN4.0/Win95: Yes

                  MSIE 3.0/Mac OS: Yes

                  MSIE 4.0/Mac OS: Yes

                  NN4.0/Mac OS: Yes

EXAMPLE   `{ padding-top: 0.5in }`

TIP   You can use the padding property to set the padding for all four sides at once.

width

PURPOSE	Specifies the width of an element.
INHERITED	No
VALUES	Specify a length or a percentage of the containing block, or auto.
DEFAULT	auto
USED IN	Replaced and block-level elements
SUPPORT	MSIE 3.0/Win95: Yes
	MSIE 4.0/Win95: Yes
	NN4.0/Win95: Yes
	MSIE 3.0/Mac OS: Yes
	MSIE 4.0/Mac OS: Yes
	NN4.0/Mac OS: Yes
EXAMPLE	`{ width: 50%}`
TIP	If the width is set to auto, the width is determined by the intrinsic width of the element.

Display Properties

cursor

PURPOSE	Affects the appearance of the mouse pointer as it moves over an object.
INHERITED	Yes
VALUES	auto, crosshair, default, hand, move, e-resize, ne-resize, nw-resize, n-resize, se-resize, sw-resize, s-resize, w-resize, text, wait, help.

DEFAULT	auto
USED IN	All elements
SUPPORT	MSIE 3.0/Win95: No
	MSIE 4.0/Win95: Yes
	NN4.0/Win95: No
	MSIE 3.0/Mac OS: No
	MSIE 4.0/Mac OS: Yes
	NN4.0/Mac OS: No
EXAMPLE	`{ cursor: crosshair }`
TIP	This is a cool property because it doesn't require any scripting, but produces dynamic results.

display

PURPOSE	Specifies that an object should be hidden in such a way that its space is *not* visible even though the content is not.
INHERITED	Yes
VALUES	none (hides the element), block (display as a block element), inline (display as an inline element), list-item (display as a list item).
DEFAULT	Not defined
USED IN	TABLE, INPUT, TEXTAREA, INPUT type="button", DIV, SPAN, IFRAME, IMG, BODY
SUPPORT	MSIE 3.0/Win95: No
	MSIE 4.0/Win95: No
	NN4.0/Win95: Yes
	MSIE 3.0/Mac OS: No

MSIE 4.0/Mac OS: Yes

NN4.0/Mac OS: No

EXAMPLE   { display: none }

TIP   To hide an element so that the element's space is still
                   visible, use the visibility property.

visibility

PURPOSE   Specifies that an object should be hidden in such a way
                   that its space is visible even though the content is not.

INHERITED   Yes

VALUES   inherit (takes on visibility properties of enclosing element),
                   visible, or hidden

DEFAULT   Not defined

USED IN   inherit

SUPPORT   MSIE 3.0/Win95: No

                   MSIE 4.0/Win95: No

                   NN4.0/Win95: No

                   MSIE 3.0/Mac OS: No

                   MSIE 4.0/Mac OS: No

                   NN4.0/Mac OS: No

EXAMPLE   { visibility: hidden }

TIP   To hide an element so the element's space is also hidden,
                   use the display property.

Font Properties

font

PURPOSE	Provides a shorthand method for indicating two or more font properties.
INHERITED	Yes
VALUES	List font properties in a list.
DEFAULT	Not defined
USED IN	All elements
SUPPORT	MSIE 3.0/Win95: Yes
	MSIE 4.0/Win95: Yes
	NN4.0/Win95: Yes
	MSIE 3.0/Mac OS: Yes
	MSIE 4.0/Mac OS: Yes
	NN4.0/Mac OS: Yes
EXAMPLE	`{ font: 14pt Arial bold}`
TIP	If the font name requires two or more words (such as Times Roman), place the name in quotes.

font-family

PURPOSE	Define font typeface and alternates (in order of preference).
INHERITED	Yes
VALUES	Font names or font family names, in a comma-separated list (in order of preference). Font family names: serif, sans-serif, cursive, fantasy, monospace.
DEFAULT	Determined by browser

USED IN	All elements
SUPPORT	MSIE 3.0/Win95: Yes
	MSIE 4.0/Win95: Yes
	NN4.0/Win95: Yes
	MSIE 3.0/Mac OS: Yes
	MSIE 4.0/Mac OS: Yes
	NN4.0/Mac OS: Yes
EXAMPLE	`{ font-family: Helvetica, Arial, "sans-serif" }`
TIP	If the font name requires two or more words (such as Times Roman), place the name in quotes.

font-size

PURPOSE	Defines font size
INHERITED	Yes
VALUES	Absolute sizes (xx-small, x-small, small, medium, large, x-large, or xx-large); relative sizes (larger or smaller), font size measurement in pts, in.cm, px, or em), or percentage in relation to parent element.
DEFAULT	Medium
USED IN	All elements
SUPPORT	MSIE 3.0/Win95: Yes
	MSIE 4.0/Win95: Yes
	NN4.0/Win95: Yes
	MSIE 3.0/Mac OS: Yes
	MSIE 4.0/Mac OS: Yes
	NN4.0/Mac OS: Yes

EXAMPLE	`{ font-size: 14pt }`
TIP	Because of inconsistent browser support, avoid using em, ex, or percentage measurements.

font-style

PURPOSE	Defines emphasis options for text.
INHERITED	Yes
VALUES	normal, italic, or oblique.
DEFAULT	normal
USED IN	All elements
SUPPORT	MSIE 3.0/Win95: Yes
	MSIE 4.0/Win95: Yes
	NN4.0/Win95: Yes
EXAMPLE	`{ font-style: italic }`
TIP	Oblique is not widely supported.

font-variant

PURPOSE	Enables font variations such as small caps.
INHERITED	Yes
VALUES	normal or small-caps.
DEFAULT	normal
USED IN	All elements
SUPPORT	MSIE 3.0/Win95: No
	MSIE 4.0/Win95: Yes
	NN4.0/Win95: No

MSIE 3.0/Mac OS: No

MSIE 4.0/Mac OS: No

NN4.0/Mac OS: No

EXAMPLE { font-variant: small-caps }

TIP This style is not widely supported.

font-weight

PURPOSE Determines weight (boldness) of font.

INHERITED Yes

VALUES normal or bold. You can also specify a numerical weight ranging from 100 (light) to 900 (dark), or relative weights (bolder or lighter).

DEFAULT normal

USED IN All elements

SUPPORT MSIE 3.0/Win95: Yes

MSIE 4.0/Win95: Yes

NN4.0/Win95: Yes

MSIE 3.0/Mac OS: Yes

MSIE 4.0/Mac OS: Yes

NN4.0/Mac OS: Yes

EXAMPLE { font-style: bold }

TIP Only the normal and bold values are widely supported.

@font-face (CSS Level 2)

PURPOSE Indicates name and location of a downloadable font.

INHERITED	No
VALUES	Include a font-family descriptor and the URL of the downloadable file, as shown in the following example.
DEFAULT	Determined by browser
USED IN	All elements
SUPPORT	Microsoft Internet Explorer Version 4
EXAMPLE	`@font-face { font-family: Verdana; src: url (http://www.fictitious.org/verdana.eot) }`
TIP	This property is not expected to come into widespread use until Version 5 browsers appear.

Positioning Properties (CSS Level 2)

bottom

PURPOSE	Specifies an offset from the bottom of a positioned element's reference box.
INHERITED	No
VALUES	Specify a length or percentage of the reference box's width.
DEFAULT	0
USED IN	All elements
SUPPORT	MSIE 3.0/Win95: No
	MSIE 4.0/Win95: Yes
	NN4.0/Win95: No
	MSIE 3.0/Mac OS: No
	MSIE 4.0/Mac OS: Yes
	NN4.0/Mac OS: No

EXAMPLE	`{ bottom: 0.5in }`
TIP	If you don't specify a height for an absolutely positioned element (using the height property), the width is determined by the top and bottom properties.

clear

PURPOSE	Determines whether an element will allow floating elements on its left side, its right side, or both sides.
INHERITED	No
VALUES	left, right, both, or none.
DEFAULT	none
USED IN	All elements
SUPPORT	MSIE 3.0/Win95: No
	MSIE 4.0/Win95: Yes
	NN4.0/Win95: No
	MSIE 3.0/Mac OS: No
	MSIE 4.0/Mac OS: Yes
	NN4.0/Mac OS: No
EXAMPLE	`{ clear: left }`
TIP	Positioning properties are supported only by Microsoft Internet Explorer Version 4.

float

PURPOSE	Floats an element to the left or right, so text flows around it.
INHERITED	No
VALUES	left, right, or none.

DEFAULT	none
USED IN	All elements
SUPPORT	MSIE 3.0/Win95: No
	MSIE 4.0/Win95: Yes
	NN4.0/Win95: No
	MSIE 3.0/Mac OS: No
	MSIE 4.0/Mac OS: Yes
	NN4.0/Mac OS: No
EXAMPLE	`{ float: left }`
TIP	Works inconsistently between Netscape Navigator 4 and Microsoft Internet Explorer 4.

left

PURPOSE	Specifies an offset from the left of a positioned element's reference box.
INHERITED	No
VALUES	Specify a length or percentage of the reference box's width.
DEFAULT	0
USED IN	All elements
SUPPORT	MSIE 3.0/Win95: No
	MSIE 4.0/Win95: Yes
	NN4.0/Win95: No
	MSIE 3.0/Mac OS: No
	MSIE 4.0/Mac OS: Yes
	NN4.0/Mac OS: No

EXAMPLE   `{ left: 0.5in }`

TIP   If you don't specify a width for an absolutely positioned
                 element (using the width property), the width is
                 determined by the left and right properties.

position

PURPOSE   Determines whether an element flows with the text (static),
                 occupies a fixed position (absolute), or flows in relation to
                 an absolutely positioned element (relative).

INHERITED   No

VALUES   absolute, relative, or static.

DEFAULT   normal

USED IN   All elements

SUPPORT   MSIE 3.0/Win95: No

                 MSIE 4.0/Win95: Yes

                 NN4.0/Win95: No

                 MSIE 3.0/Mac OS: No

                 MSIE 4.0/Mac OS: Yes

                 NN4.0/Mac OS: No

EXAMPLE   `{ position: absolute }`

TIP   Positioning properties are supported only by Microsoft
                 Internet Explorer Version 4.

right

PURPOSE   Specifies an offset from the right of a positioned element's
                 reference box.

INHERITED   No

VALUES	Specify a length or percentage of the reference box's width.
DEFAULT	0
USED IN	All elements
SUPPORT	MSIE 3.0/Win95: No
	MSIE 4.0/Win95: Yes
	NN4.0/Win95: No
	MSIE 3.0/Mac OS: No
	MSIE 4.0/Mac OS: Yes
	NN4.0/Mac OS: No
EXAMPLE	`{ right: 0.5in }`
TIP	If you don't specify a width for an absolutely positioned element (using the width property), the width is determined by the left and right properties.

top

PURPOSE	Specifies an offset from the top of a positioned element's reference box.
INHERITED	No
VALUES	Specify a length or percentage of the reference box's width.
DEFAULT	0
USED IN	All elements
SUPPORT	MSIE 3.0/Win95: No
	MSIE 4.0/Win95: Yes
	NN4.0/Win95: Yes
	MSIE 3.0/Mac OS: No

MSIE 4.0/Mac OS: Yes

NN4.0/Mac OS: Yes

EXAMPLE   `{ top: 0.5in }`

TIP   If you don't specify a height for an absolutely positioned
                           element (using the height property), the width is
                           determined by the top and bottom properties.

z-index

PURPOSE   Specifies the position of an element in a three-dimensional
                           stack (back to front).

INHERITED   No

VALUES   auto (stacks elements back to front in the order they
                           appear in the document) or number (overrides default
                           stacking order).

DEFAULT   auto

USED IN   All elements

SUPPORT   MSIE 3.0/Win95: No

                           MSIE 4.0/Win95: Yes

                           NN4.0/Win95: No

                           MSIE 3.0/Mac OS: No

                           MSIE 4.0/Mac OS: Yes

                           NN4.0/Mac OS: No

EXAMPLE   `{ z-index: 2 }`

TIP   Not supported by Netscape Navigator 4.

Printing Properties (CSS Level 2)

page-break-after

PURPOSE	Inserts a page break after the element when the document is printed.
INHERITED	No
VALUES	auto, always, left (insert page breaks until next even-numbered page is reached), right (insert page breaks until next odd-numbered page is reached).
DEFAULT	auto
USED IN	All elements
SUPPORT	MSIE 3.0/Win95: No
	MSIE 4.0/Win95: Yes
	NN4.0/Win95: No
	MSIE 3.0/Mac OS: No
	MSIE 4.0/Mac OS: Yes
	NN4.0/Mac OS: No
EXAMPLE	`{ page-break-before: always }`
TIP	You can specify a page break before the element with the page-break-before property.

page-break-before

PURPOSE	Inserts a page break before the element when the document is printed.
INHERITED	No
VALUES	auto, always, left (insert page breaks until next even-numbered page is reached), right (insert page breaks until next odd-numbered page is reached).

DEFAULT	auto
USED IN	All elements
SUPPORT	MSIE 3.0/Win95: No
	MSIE 4.0/Win95: Yes
	NN4.0/Win95: No
	MSIE 3.0/Mac OS: No
	MSIE 4.0/Mac OS: Yes
	NN4.0/Mac OS: No
EXAMPLE	`{ page-break-before: always }`
TIP	You can specify a page break after the element with the page-break-after property.

Text Properties

line-height

PURPOSE	Specifies the height (the distance between the baselines) of each line of text in an element.
INHERITED	No
VALUES	Specify a number to multiply the current font height), a length, or a percentage of the current font size, or auto (same as font size).
DEFAULT	auto
USED IN	Replaced and block-level elements
SUPPORT	MSIE 3.0/Win95: Yes
	MSIE 4.0/Win95: Yes
	NN4.0/Win95: Yes

MSIE 3.0/Mac OS: Yes

MSIE 4.0/Mac OS: Yes

NN4.0/Mac OS: Yes

EXAMPLE   `{ line-height: 24pt }` or `{ line-height: 2 }`

TIP   If the height is set to auto, the height is determined by the intrinsic height of the element. If you specify a number, you're specifying the number of times to multiply the current line size set by the height of the font (for a 12pt font, "2" gives you 24pt line heights, or double-line spacing).

letter-spacing

PURPOSE   Adds to the default spacing between characters.

INHERITED   Yes

VALUES   Specify a length

DEFAULT   normal

USED IN   Block-level elements

SUPPORT   MSIE 3.0/Win95: No

MSIE 4.0/Win95: Yes

NN4.0/Win95: No

MSIE 3.0/Mac OS: No

MSIE 4.0/Mac OS: No

NN4.0/Mac OS: No

EXAMPLE   `{ letter-spacing: 1pt }`

TIP   This property is not well-supported.

text-align

PURPOSE	Controls horizontal alignment of text.
INHERITED	Yes
VALUES	left, center, right, or justify.
DEFAULT	0
USED IN	Block-level elements
SUPPORT	MSIE 3.0/Win95: Yes
	MSIE 4.0/Win95: Yes
	NN4.0/Win95: Yes
	MSIE 3.0/Mac OS: Yes
	MSIE 4.0/Mac OS: Yes
	NN4.0/Mac OS: Yes
EXAMPLE	`{ text-indent: 0.5in }`
TIP	This property is well-supported.

text-decoration

PURPOSE	Adds decorations (such as strikethrough) to text.
INHERITED	Yes
VALUES	none, underline, overline, line-through, or blink.
DEFAULT	0
USED IN	Block-level elements
SUPPORT	MSIE 3.0/Win95: Yes
	MSIE 4.0/Win95: Yes
	NN4.0/Win95: Yes

MSIE 3.0/Mac OS: Yes

MSIE 4.0/Mac OS: Yes

NN4.0/Mac OS: Yes

EXAMPLE   `{ text-decoration: underline }`

TIP   Only MSIE 4.0/Win95 supports the overline value.

text-indent

PURPOSE   Indents the first line of text.

INHERITED   Yes

VALUES   Any valid length or a percentage of the element's width.

DEFAULT   0

USED IN   Block-level elements

SUPPORT   MSIE 3.0/Win95: Yes

                   MSIE 4.0/Win95: Yes

                   NN4.0/Win95: Yes

                   MSIE 3.0/Mac OS: Yes

                   MSIE 4.0/Mac OS: Yes

                   NN4.0/Mac OS: Yes

EXAMPLE   `{ text-indent: 0.5in }`

TIP   This property is well-supported.

text-transform

PURPOSE   Changes case.

INHERITED   Yes

VALUES	capitalize, uppercase, lowercase, none.
DEFAULT	none
USED IN	All elements
SUPPORT	MSIE 3.0/Win95: No
	MSIE 4.0/Win95: Yes
	NN4.0/Win95: Yes
	MSIE 3.0/Mac OS: No
	MSIE 4.0/Mac OS: Yes
	NN4.0/Mac OS: Yes
EXAMPLE	`{ text-transform: capitalize }`
TIP	The capitalize value capitalizes only the first character of each word. Use uppercase to capitalize everything. Because this property is supported inconsistently, you'll be wise to type the characters with the capitalization pattern you prefer.

word-spacing

PURPOSE	Adds to the default spacing between words.
INHERITED	Yes
VALUES	Specify a length.
DEFAULT	normal
USED IN	Block-level elements
SUPPORT	MSIE 3.0/Win95: No
	MSIE 4.0/Win95: Yes
	NN4.0/Win95: No
	MSIE 3.0/Mac OS: No

MSIE 4.0/Mac OS: No

NN4.0/Mac OS: No

EXAMPLE   { word-spacing: 1pt }

TIP   This property is not currently supported.

white-space (CSS Level 2)

PURPOSE   Controls handling of whitespace.

INHERITED   Yes

VALUES   normal (white space ignored by browser), pre (text spacing retained by browser), nowrap (lines broken only by BR element).

DEFAULT   none

USED IN   All elements

SUPPORT   MSIE 3.0/Win95: No

                       MSIE 4.0/Win95: No

                       NN4.0/Win95: No

                       MSIE 3.0/Mac OS: No

                       MSIE 4.0/Mac OS: No

                       NN4.0/Mac OS: No

EXAMPLE   { white-space: pre }

TIP   This property is not currently supported.

vertical-align

PURPOSE   Specifies the vertical position of an element relative to the current text baseline.

INHERITED   No

VALUES	baseline, sub (subscript), super (superscript), top (top of the line), text-top (top of the text), middle, bottom, text-bottom. You can also type a percentage of the line height or a length.
DEFAULT	baseline
USED IN	Replaced and block-level elements
SUPPORT	MSIE 3.0/Win95: Yes
	MSIE 4.0/Win95: Yes
	NN4.0/Win95: Yes
	MSIE 3.0/Mac OS: Yes
	MSIE 4.0/Mac OS: Yes
	NN4.0/Mac OS: Yes
EXAMPLE	{ width: 50%}
TIP	This property is most commonly used for superscript and subscript characters in technical documents.

List Properties

These properties affect the appearance of lists in your document.

list-style

PURPOSE	Provides a shorthand method for indicating several list format options.
INHERITED	Yes
VALUES	You can include any of the values from list-style-type, list-style-position, or list-style-image.
DEFAULT	Not defined
USED IN	Elements with the display property set to list-item

SUPPORT	MSIE 3.0/Win95: No
	MSIE 4.0/Win95: Yes
	NN4.0/Win95: Yes
	MSIE 3.0/Mac OS: No
	MSIE 4.0/Mac OS: Yes
	NN4.0/Mac OS: Yes
EXAMPLE	`{ list-style: upper-roman inside }`
TIP	Use the display property to set list elements to the list-item value.

list-style-image

PURPOSE	Specifies a graphic to be used in place of a bullet in an unordered list.
INHERITED	Yes
VALUES	capitalize, uppercase, lowercase, none.
DEFAULT	none
USED IN	Elements with the display property set to list-item
SUPPORT	MSIE 3.0/Win95: No
	MSIE 4.0/Win95: Yes
	NN4.0/Win95: Yes
	MSIE 3.0/Mac OS: No
	MSIE 4.0/Mac OS: Yes
	NN4.0/Mac OS: Yes
EXAMPLE	`{ list-style-image: url(picture.gif) }`
TIP	Use the display property to set list elements to the list-item value.

list-style-position

PURPOSE	Specifies how the list-item marker (bullet or number) should be positioned relative to the list-item's content.
INHERITED	Yes
VALUES	inside (the marker is placed at the beginning of the element's box) or outside (the marker is placed outside the element's box).
DEFAULT	outside
USED IN	Elements with the display property set to list-item
SUPPORT	MSIE 3.0/Win95: No
	MSIE 4.0/Win95: Yes
	NN4.0/Win95: Yes
	MSIE 3.0/Mac OS: No
	MSIE 4.0/Mac OS: Yes
	NN4.0/Mac OS: Yes
EXAMPLE	`{ list-style-position: inside }`
TIP	Use the display property to set list elements to the list-item value.

list-style-position

PURPOSE	Specifies how the list-item marker (bullet or number) should be positioned relative to the list-item's content.
INHERITED	Yes
VALUES	inside (the marker is placed at the beginning of the element's box) or outside (the marker is placed outside the element's box).
DEFAULT	outside

USED IN	Elements with the display property set to list-item
SUPPORT	MSIE 3.0/Win95: No
	MSIE 4.0/Win95: Yes
	NN4.0/Win95: Yes
	MSIE 3.0/Mac OS: No
	MSIE 4.0/Mac OS: Yes
	NN4.0/Mac OS: Yes
EXAMPLE	`{ list-style-position: inside }`
TIP	Use the display property to set list elements to the list-item value.

list-style-type

PURPOSE	Specifies the bullet or number style used in a list.
INHERITED	Yes
VALUES	disc, circle, square, decimal (decimal numbers), lower-roman (lower-case Roman numerals), lower-alpha (lowercase ASCII letters), upper-roman (uppercase Roman numerals), upper-alpha (uppercase ASCII letters), none (no marker).
DEFAULT	none
USED IN	List elements in which the display property has been set to list-item
SUPPORT	MSIE 3.0/Win95: No
	MSIE 4.0/Win95: Yes
	NN4.0/Win95: Yes
	MSIE 3.0/Mac OS: No
	MSIE 4.0/Mac OS: Yes

NN4.0/Mac OS: Yes

EXAMPLE

`{ list-style-type: disc }`

TIP

Use the display property to set list elements to the list-item value.

✦   ✦   ✦

About the CD-ROM

The CD-ROM in the back of the book contains trial versions of applications, your choice of browsers, and a selection of images and style sheets — all designed to help you get a Web site developed quickly.

Trial Software

Note, trial versions expire 15–30 days after you install them, depending on the software. Trial versions included on the CD are:

+ Fusion 3.0 by NetObjects
+ HomeSite 3.0 by Allaire
+ iWrite by Xanthus
+ PageMill by Adobe
+ Claris Home Page 3.0 by FileMaker
+ TextPad by Helios Software Solutions
+ Web Position by FirstPlace Software
+ GIF Movie Gear 2.51 by Gamani
+ ScriptBuilder by NetObjects
+ Microsoft Internet Explorer 4.0
+ Netscape Navigator 4.0

These products fall into one of three categories of software: Web development tools, Web position evaluator, or Web accessory development tools.

Most of the tools listed are the Web development tools discussed in Chapter 14.

Web Position by FirstPlace software can help you identify how your site ranks in searches on the various search engines.

GIF Movie Gear by Gamani and ScriptBuilder by NetObjects help you create accessories for your Web page: animated GIFs and JavaScript, respectively.

Browsers

Internet Explorer and Netscape Communicator are full-featured Web browsers. They are mentioned hundreds of times in this book. While you can download them from their respective Web sites, the file sizes are rather large. Installing from a CD is much faster.

Installing Programs from the CD-ROM

With all these software products, all you must do is double-click the filename associated with the application, as listed in Table H-1. A series of dialog boxes walk you through the installation. Be sure you don't have any other software applications open when you perform the installation.

Table H-1 Applications on CD-ROM and their file names		
Application	*PC*	*MAC*
Fusion 3.0	nof3.0.exe	NetObjects Fusion Trial
HomeSite	HomeSite301Eval.exe	
IWrite	iwrite_PR7.exe	
PageMill	Tryout5.exe	
HomePage	Setup.exe	Claris Home Page Installer
TextPad	tpe323322.exe	
Web Position	wpsetup.exe	
GIF Movie Gear	gmvgr251.exe	
ScriptBuilder	nosb2.exe	
Internet Explorer 4	iesetup.exe	IE4 folder
Communicator	CC32E404.EXE	Com4.05_PPC

Images and Style Sheets

We have also included nine images in a folder called Chap35, as well as an "HTML4 Way" image. Finally, we included four style sheets, which you can find in the Chap5 folder. You can copy all of these directly to your hard drive from the CD-ROM.

✦ ✦ ✦

Index

(continued)

(continued)

(continued)

(continued)

Q

Q (quote) element, 288, 290, 316, 762–763
  adding quotes with, 323
.QRY filename extension, 274
.QT file format, 529
.QTVR filename extension, 338
Quick Res utility, 204
QuickTimeVR movies, 32, 33, 529
  plug-in for, 540–541
Quilt Gallery Web site, 24
quotations
  adding to documents, 323
  indented, 310
  pull quotes, 481–483
quote marks (" ")
  enclosing attribute values in, 63, 67
  typographical, 199

R

RAD. *See* rapid application development
radio buttons, 570–571
radio value, TYPE attribute, 570–571
Rafael Garrido's Web site, 66, 67
rapid application development (RAD), 273, 276
  definition of, 274
readability, of HTML documents, 70–71
READONLY attribute, 789
RealAudio, 520, 522
RealPlayer plug-in, 540
recipes, hypertext, 119–120, 126
recording sound files, 521
  equipment for, 518
  sound editing software, 521–522
Recreational Software Advisory Council (RSAC), 698
REL attribute, 91, 298, 789
relationships
  database, 594
  referencing objects by, 627
relative positioning
  absolute positioning combined with, 461
  explained, 460
  for graphics, 465–466
  for text, 470–471
relative units of length, 409
relative values, 441
  for POSITION property, 459
  for table and cell widths, 422–423

repairing links, 248
reserved target names, 443
reserved word, *this*, 645–647
reset button, 573
reset event, 640
reset value, TYPE attribute, 573
retro.css file, 91
REV attribute, 298, 789
RGB color system, 64, 399
Rich Text Format (RTF), 331
RIGHT property, 849–850
right value, FLOAT property, 453
rows
  creating, 348–349
  in database tables, 593
  in framed documents, 439–441
  grouping, 353–356, 421
  horizontal cell alignment, 419, 421
  relative vs. absolute measurements for, 441
  spanning, 358–359
  vertical cell alignment, 421
ROWS attribute, 789
ROWSPAN attribute, 349, 358–359, 789
.RTF (Rich Text Format), 331
rules
  defining for tables, 426
  style sheet, 377–378
RULES attribute, 347, 426, 789
rules-checking software, 363
run-in value, DISPLAY property, 452

S

S (strikethrough) element, 763
SafeSurf rating system, 698
sales Web sites, 25–26
Sam the Toy Train Man Web site, 138
SAMP element, 316, 763–764
sample rate, 518
sans serif fonts, 429
SCHEDULE element, 589–590
scheduling precaching of channels, 589–590
SCHEME attribute, 789
SCOPE attribute, 789
scrambling, 214
SCRIPT element, 764
  event-driven scripts and, 297
  inserting JavaScript with, 647–648, 669

(continued)

(continued)

IDG BOOKS WORLDWIDE, INC.
END-USER LICENSE AGREEMENT

4. **<u>Restrictions On Use of Individual Programs.</u>** You must follow the individual requirements and restrictions detailed for each individual program in Appendix H of this Book. These limitations are also contained in the individual license agreements recorded on the Software Media. These limitations may include a requirement that after using the program for a specified period of time, the user must pay a registration fee or discontinue use. By opening the Software packet(s), you will be agreeing to abide by the licenses and restrictions for these individual programs that are detailed in Appendix H and on the Software Media. None of the material on this Software Media or listed in this Book may ever be redistributed, in original or modified form, for commercial purposes.

5. **<u>Limited Warranty.</u>**

    (a) IDGB warrants that the Software and Software Media are free from defects in materials and workmanship under normal use for a period of sixty (60) days from the date of purchase of this Book. If IDGB receives notification within the warranty period of defects in materials or workmanship, IDGB will replace the defective Software Media.

    (b) IDGB AND THE AUTHORS OF THE BOOK DISCLAIM ALL OTHER WARRANTIES, EXPRESS OR IMPLIED, INCLUDING WITHOUT LIMITATION IMPLIED WARRANTIES OF MERCHANTABILITY AND FITNESS FOR A PARTICULAR PURPOSE, WITH RESPECT TO THE SOFTWARE, THE PROGRAMS, THE SOURCE CODE CONTAINED THEREIN, AND/OR THE TECHNIQUES DESCRIBED IN THIS BOOK. IDGB DOES NOT WARRANT THAT THE FUNCTIONS CONTAINED IN THE SOFTWARE WILL MEET YOUR REQUIREMENTS OR THAT THE OPERATION OF THE SOFTWARE WILL BE ERROR FREE.

    (c) This limited warranty gives you specific legal rights, and you may have other rights that vary from jurisdiction to jurisdiction.

6. **<u>Remedies.</u>**

    (a) IDGB's entire liability and your exclusive remedy for defects in materials and workmanship shall be limited to replacement of the Software Media, which may be returned to IDGB with a copy of your receipt at the following address: Software Media Fulfillment Department, Attn.: *HTML 4 Bible*, IDG Books Worldwide, Inc., 7260 Shadeland Station, Ste. 100, Indianapolis, IN 46256, or call 1-800-762-2974. Please allow three to four weeks for delivery. This Limited Warranty is void if failure of the Software Media has resulted from accident, abuse, or misapplication. Any replacement Software Media will be warranted for the remainder of the original warranty period or thirty (30) days, whichever is longer.

(b) In no event shall IDGB or the authors be liable for any damages whatsoever (including without limitation damages for loss of business profits, business interruption, loss of business information, or any other pecuniary loss) arising from the use of or inability to use the Book or the Software, even if IDGB has been advised of the possibility of such damages.

(c) Because some jurisdictions do not allow the exclusion or limitation of liability for consequential or incidental damages, the above limitation or exclusion may not apply to you.

7. **U.S. Government Restricted Rights.** Use, duplication, or disclosure of the Software by the U.S. Government is subject to restrictions stated in paragraph (c)(1)(ii) of the Rights in Technical Data and Computer Software clause of DFARS 252.227-7013, and in subparagraphs (a) through (d) of the Commercial Computer — Restricted Rights clause at FAR 52.227-19, and in similar clauses in the NASA FAR supplement, when applicable.

8. **General.** This Agreement constitutes the entire understanding of the parties and revokes and supersedes all prior agreements, oral or written, between them and may not be modified or amended except in a writing signed by both parties hereto that specifically refers to this Agreement. This Agreement shall take precedence over any other documents that may be in conflict herewith. If any one or more provisions contained in this Agreement are held by any court or tribunal to be invalid, illegal, or otherwise unenforceable, each and every other provision shall remain in full force and effect.

my2cents.idgbooks.com

Register This Book — And Win!

Visit **http://my2cents.idgbooks.com** to register this book and we'll automatically enter you in our fantastic monthly prize giveaway. It's also your opportunity to give us feedback: let us know what you thought of this book and how you would like to see other topics covered.

Discover IDG Books Online!

The IDG Books Online Web site is your online resource for tackling technology — at home and at the office. Frequently updated, the IDG Books Online Web site features exclusive software, insider information, online books, and live events!

10 Productive & Career-Enhancing Things You Can Do at www.idgbooks.com

- Nab source code for your own programming projects.

- Download software.

- Read Web exclusives: special articles and book excerpts by IDG Books Worldwide authors.

- Take advantage of resources to help you advance your career as a Novell or Microsoft professional.

- Buy IDG Books Worldwide titles or find a convenient bookstore that carries them.

- Register your book and win a prize.

- Chat live online with authors.

- Sign up for regular e-mail updates about our latest books.

- Suggest a book you'd like to read or write.

- Give us your 2¢ about our books and about our Web site.

You say you're not on the Web yet? It's easy to get started with IDG Books' *Discover the Internet,* available at local retailers everywhere.

CD-ROM Installation Instructions

The CD-ROM that accompanies this book contains trial versions of commercial software discussed in the book and two browsers, as well as sample style sheets and sample image files that enable you to complete the exercises in two of the chapters. The CD will work on either a PC or a Mac.

To install any of these programs, place the disc in your CD-ROM drive and run the .exe file. To use the sample style sheets and image files, open the Chap5 or Chap35 folders and copy these files onto your hard drive.